C000082696

To Sue

Best regards

Ed P.——

7 MARCH '08

Credit Derivatives

Documenting and Understanding
Credit Derivative Products

Edmund Parker

Author
Edmund Parker

Publisher
Sian O'Neill

Editor
Carolyn Boyle

Marketing manager
Alan Mowat

Production
John Meikle, Russell Anderson

Publishing directors
Guy Davis, Tony Harriss, Mark Lamb

Credit Derivatives: Documenting and Understanding Credit Derivative Products
is published by
Globe Law and Business
Globe Business Publishing Ltd
New Hibernia House
Winchester Walk
London Bridge
London SE1 9AG
United Kingdom
Tel +44 20 7234 0606
Fax +44 20 7234 0808
Web www.gbplawbooks.com

Printed by Antony Rowe Ltd

ISBN 1-905783-03-5/978-1-905783-03-8

Credit Derivatives: Documenting and Understanding Credit Derivative Products
© 2007 Globe Business Publishing Ltd

DISCLAIMER
This publication is intended as a general guide only. The information and opinions which it contains are not intended to be a comprehensive study, nor to provide legal advice, and should not be treated as a substitute for legal advice concerning particular situations. Legal advice should always be sought before taking any action based on the information provided. The publishers bear no responsibility for any errors or omissions contained herein.

Table of contents

Foreword

To date, books focused on credit derivatives either have been written with only the trader or treasurer in mind and have included limited coverage of documentation, or, where written for the legal practitioner, have focused only on the 2003 International Swaps and Derivatives Association (ISDA) Credit Derivatives Definitions.

This book bridges the gap. It is divided into four parts. Part I gives an overview of what credit derivatives are, who buys them, why, and what the market looks like today. It covers the main types of 'unfunded' credit derivative product currently popular in the market, together with how these products are documented. It covers the role and history of ISDA in shaping the credit derivatives market, as well as each of its current templates. It also covers the main types of 'funded' credit derivative product currently popular in the market, together with how these products are documented, including the 'new generation' of credit derivative products such as constant proportion debt obligations (CPDOs) and synthetic constant proportion portfolio insurance (CPPI).

Part II covers the 2003 ISDA Credit Derivatives Definitions in depth. It is the most comprehensive analysis of the 2003 Definitions ever written. It dissects each of the 229 definitions and 10 articles, as well as the six exhibits, introduction and preamble.

Part III covers four key credit derivative products in depth: single name credit default swaps, synthetic collateralised debt obligations, credit index trading and credit default swaps on asset-backed securities (CDS on ADS). These products are given an overview in Part I, but Part III allows the more advanced user and/or those seeking clarification on specific points to examine these products in greater detail.

Part IV covers how an institution can manage a major credit event impacting on a variety of instruments held in its portfolio and provides many suggestions as to how risk can be minimised.

My thanks go to Alia Nimry for encouraging me and putting up with the demands on me while writing this book. Thanks also to my father Geoffrey for inspiring me with his 32 book. My thanks also go to Marcin Perzanowski for his invaluable assistance with many of the most complex areas of the book; to Jamila Piracci in relation to her insights on CDS on ABS; and to Sarah McBurney for her knowledge of listings. Any coincidences between the names of friends, Cadiz football players and streets, and Scottish villages, streets and schools, and those used in the hypothetical case studies, are entirely intentional.

Introducing credit derivatives

1. Introduction

On Friday June 8 2007 I typed the words 'credit derivatives' and 'opaque' into the Google search engine: 14,700 results. A random selection of the pages I looked at had phrases such as: "The market is so opaque that regulators and participants alike are unsure which party actually ends up holding the bag in the event of default on loans by commercial banks and on big lease contracts";[1] "The market remains maddeningly opaque, even to insiders";[2] and "The Federal Reserve Bank of New York has called a meeting of top Wall Street firms to discuss practices in the booming, if opaque, credit derivatives market".[3]

But is the market really opaque? Or, due to its late arrival and subsequent breathtaking development, is it just poorly understood? If the well-established equity and insurance markets had developed in similar circumstances, would they too have been treated with equal, or even greater, suspicion?

Although playing up the risks of credit derivatives and derivatives in general makes good journalistic copy, it is not backed up by evidence. A 2004 academic survey conducted by the International Swaps and Derivatives Association (ISDA) of 84 professors from the top 50 business schools found that 99% thought that the impact of derivatives on the global financial system was beneficial and 81% agreed that the risks of using derivatives had been overstated.[4]

This book aims to dispel the myth of credit derivatives opacity. It explains credit derivative products comprehensively, both with a clear focus on their documentation and in an understandable and concise manner.

2. What is a credit derivative?

2.1 Credit derivatives isolate credit risk from other risks present in an asset

SG Warburg arranged the first eurobond: a $15 million, 5% 10 to 15-year bond issued by Italian Autostrada on July 1 1963. The bondholders in that issue of securities accepted the bundle of risks set out in the next table.

The bondholders took on the currency risk that the exchange rate of the dollar

---

1   "The Real Risks of Credit Derivatives", McKinsey & Company.
2   "Credit Derivatives Play a Dangerous Game", Frank Partnoy and David Skeel, *Financial Times*, July 17 2006.
3   "Fed Officials Summon Wall St Firms to Discuss Derivatives", Riva D Atlas, *New York Times*, August 25 2005.
4   "A Survey of Financial Professors' Views On Derivatives", Survey conducted by the International Swaps and Derivatives Association, March 2004.

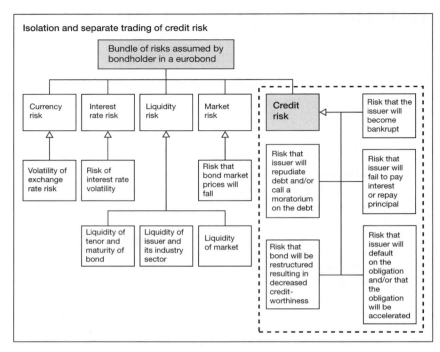

would collapse against the domestic currencies of their own jurisdictions. The bonds were fixed rate bonds so they also assumed interest rate risk – if USD-LIBOR interest rates rose above the fixed interest rate of the Autostrada bonds, then a bond holder would suffer this exposure (ie, the yield of the bonds would be low in comparison to other investments). Investors were also taking the risk that both the tenor of the securities and their maturity could prove to be illiquid.

Finally, investors were taking a risk on Autostrada's creditworthiness: the risk that Autostrada could become bankrupt; that it could default on the payment of interest or repayment of principal; that the bond could default for other reasons or be accelerated; that the company could repudiate the debt or declare a moratorium; or that the company could restructure the bond leading to a material decline in the company's creditworthiness.[5]

Those investors that wished only to assume and invest in the credit risk of Autostrada were forced to assume all of the other risks related to its obligations as well: currency risk, liquidity risk, interest rate risk, maturity risk and all other risks making up the bundle of risks inherent in any capital markets security. And this was the way it was for all bond and loan market investors until the invention of credit derivatives in the 1990s.

All derivatives derive their value from an underlying asset. In the case of credit derivatives, the underlying asset is the credit risk of an underlying reference entity, be

---

5   In fact, none of these events happened. The bonds were repaid in full and Autostrada returned to the eurobond markets in 2006.

it corporate, sovereign or a similar organisation. Credit derivatives aim to isolate the credit risk of a reference entity (eg, the issuer of a bond) from the other risks inherent in its obligations (ie, those described above). Credit risk can then be separately traded.

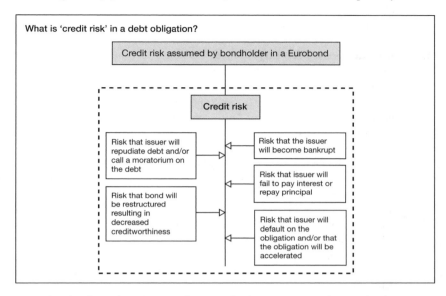

Let's take the Italian Autostrada example above. Imagine that credit derivatives had been invented in 1963: 30 years earlier than they actually were. An investor entering into a credit derivative transaction referencing Italian Autostrada could have sold credit protection to gain exposure to Autostrada's credit risk instead of buying eurobonds containing the rest of the bundle of risks. Instead of the investor assuming a portion of the eurobond's interest rate corresponding to credit risk, that investor's derivatives counterparty would be paying it a premium in return for it assuming the same credit risk.

Bilateral derivatives contracts require counterparties to take opposite views. That investor's counterparty might have chosen to purchase a corresponding amount of eurobonds to gain exposure to the other risks comprising the bundle of risks, while buying protection against Italian Autostrada's credit risk. This investor would have assumed currency risk, interest rate risk, liquidity risk and market risk, but would have been protected against the credit risk in return for it paying a premium.

The Italian Autostrada eurobond also preceded the interest rate and currency rate derivatives markets which developed in the 1960s and 1970s, but had these markets existed, an Italian Autostrada bondholder could have hedged itself against currency movements with a currency swap or against interest rate movements with an interest rate swap.

Credit derivatives, like their sister products currency derivatives and interest rate derivatives, allow particular risks to be isolated and separately traded. As we shall see below, credit risk can never be entirely isolated from other risks, but the credit derivative product allows other risks to be minimised.

The above example reflects that a credit derivative in its simplest form could replicate the credit risk of an individual cash asset. More complex credit derivatives repackage and redistribute the credit risk of a portfolio of different assets among different investors in accordance with their appetite for risk. The products which do this, and which are analysed in this book, are many and varied.

3. How do credit derivatives work?

Taking credit derivatives in their simplest form, and taking as the central premise of a credit derivative the isolation, transfer and separate trading of credit risk, a party entering a credit derivative will seek to buy or sell the credit risk of a reference entity - perhaps a FTSE 100 company. This reference entity will not be a party to the credit derivatives contract; indeed, most reference entities will probably be unaware of its existence.

The credit derivatives contract will be most commonly documented as a swap. The reference entity may be any corporate, a sovereign or any other form of legal entity which has incurred debt. A credit derivatives contract will (unless it is a structured 'funded' transaction) be made between two parties. One party, the buyer, will purchase protection against the credit risk of the relevant reference entity. To do this, it will pay a premium to the other party, the seller.

The credit derivatives market is very standardised and, in the majority of contracts, it views the credit risk of a reference entity as having six potential categories.

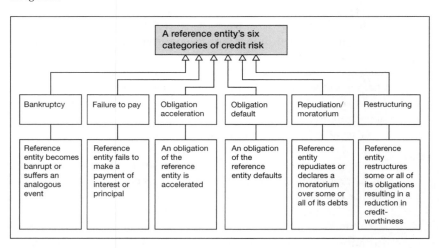

These six categories are as follows:
- bankruptcy – where the reference entity becomes bankrupt or suffers an analogous event;
- failure to pay – where the reference entity fails to make a payment of interest or principal;
- obligation acceleration – where one of the reference entity's obligations is accelerated;

- obligation default – where the reference entity defaults on one of its obligations;
- repudiation/moratorium – where the reference entity repudiates or declares a moratorium over some or all of its debts; and
- restructuring – where the reference entity arranges for some or all of its debts to be restructured causing a material change in their creditworthiness.

These categories of credit risk are known as 'credit events' and in each contract, usually on the basis of market practice, the parties choose which credit events will apply to the transaction. As important as which credit events apply is the identity of the obligations on which credit protection is bought and sold. The parties will decide minimum threshold amounts of obligations that must be affected by a credit event in order for credit protection to apply. They must also choose which of the reference entity's obligations are subject to credit protection and in this regard, whether credit protection should apply to:

- a single obligation only;
- a category of obligations; or
- a category of obligations fulfilling pre-determined characteristics.

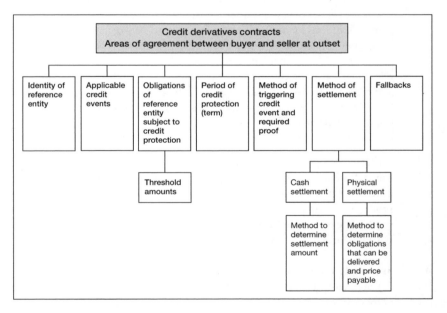

The parties agree:
- which of them may trigger a credit event;
- how this is done;
- what proof of the credit event must be shown; and
- whether a transaction will be settled by a payment of cash (and how this amount is determined) or the delivery of actual physical obligations in return for a full cash payment.

Finally the parties will agree the term of a transaction and a list of fallback positions for when 'unforeseen foreseeables' occur.

Fortunately, the credit derivatives market has very standardised norms and documentation. Definitions are crystallised in market standard documentation provided by ISDA, in particular in the 2003 ISDA Credit Derivatives Definitions.

International Swaps and Derivatives Association, Inc

ISDA is the dominant trade association for derivatives. It has a worldwide membership including banks, corporates, and other derivatives participants. ISDA was formed in 1985 and has over 797 institutions based in 54 countries among its members. Members include almost all of the major market players, together with law firms and other interested parties.

ISDA aims to reduce derivatives' risk and costs, to streamline documentation and to encourage the development of markets in different derivative products.

Its major achievements include the development of a documentation platform, which includes the ISDA Master Agreement, schedule, template confirmations and definitions for a wide range of transactions. The organisation has secured legal opinions from top-ranking law firms in many jurisdictions in relation to both the taking of collateral and netting. The organisation, through its system of members' working committees, is regularly drafting best practice statements and also producing user guides, supplements to definitions and promoting the understanding of derivatives through conferences. ISDA also fulfils a lobbying function on behalf of the industry.

ISDA also provides a standard form master agreement for documenting swap transactions, together with a variety of confirmations and ancillaries for documenting different type of credit derivative transactions. There are many credit derivative products in existence, from single name, basket and portfolio credit default swaps to synthetic collateralised debt obligations (CDO), credit linked constant proportion portfolio insurance and CDO squared transactions.

4. Size and history of the credit derivatives market

The credit derivatives market is a success story. The market is booming, outperforming all expectations.[6] From a near standing start in 1995, it was worth approximately $180 billion by 1996; by 2001 it had surged to over $1.1 trillion; by the end of 2006 it stood at $20 trillion. Current projections are for the market to reach $33 trillion during 2008.[7] Don't be surprised if this is also exceeded. Survey respondents to

---

6   The British Bankers' Association Credit Derivatives Report 2004, for example, had predicted that the credit derivatives market size would be $8.2 million by the end of 2006, $12 trillion short of its actual size.
7   Credit Derivatives Report 2006, British Bankers' Association.

Fitch Ratings' 2006 Global Credit Derivatives Survey[8] reported a market increase of 122% in 2005. This follows 86% gains in 2004 and 71% gains in 2003. The 2005 figure included a 900% increase in index-related products.

The London credit derivatives market continues to be the dominant world market. It grew from $2.23 trillion in 2004 to $7.18 trillion by the end of 2006.[9] The British Bankers' Association Credit Derivatives Report 2006 states that "the London market has grown by over 100 times in less than 10 years from $70 billion to over $7 trillion", and proclaims that although overall market share in the credit derivatives is declining as other financial centres develop their own markets, London "is still considered the main market centre".

The credit derivatives market began in the early 1990s when some US banks began using simple credit derivatives to hedge against the credit risk of loans they had made. These prototype credit derivatives were structured as basic credit default swaps and allowed the banks using these products to free up credit lines against certain sectors and borrowers by selling on the credit risk of certain customers to third parties in return for a premium. Credit derivatives gradually became more complex and began to be embedded into structured finance transactions such as synthetic CDOs; or adapted into new products such as basket credit default swaps (where the credit risk of a basket of reference entities was sold on).

The market went through a tough period in 2000 and 2001, when a widening of credit spreads combined with a series of large corporate defaults such as Enron and Worldcom, and sovereign defaults such as the Republic of Argentina. The market survived, although it was severely tested by these events. The benefits of financial dis-intermediation were clearly proven. Since then the market has grown relentlessly – with new and more complex products added regularly.

5.   Who are the market participants?

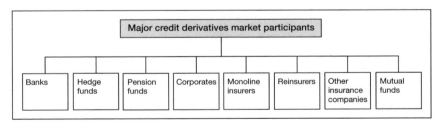

Credit derivatives market makers are financial institutions that quote a price for buying credit protection on a reference entity at the same time that they quote a price for selling credit protection. In doing so, they hope to make a profit on the bid/offer spread and create a credit derivatives market by allowing end buyers and end sellers to find each other.

---

8   Fitch Ratings, "Global Credit Derivatives Survey: Indices Dominate Growth as Banks' Risk Position Shifts", September 21 2006.
9   British Bankers' Association, Credit Derivatives Report 2006.

Market-making in credit derivative transactions is concentrated in relatively few institutions. In 2005, the 10 largest institutions (categorised by number of transactions) were Morgan Stanley, Deutsche Bank, Goldman Sachs, JP Morgan Chase, UBS, Lehman Brothers, Barclays, Citigroup, Credit Suisse First Boston and BNP Paribas. Together they accounted for 66% of market-making activity.[10]

The end buyers and the end sellers of credit protection generally fall into the same categories of institution, although the percentage make-up of each group is quite different. The buyer and seller groups both consist of banks, hedge funds, pension funds, general corporates, monoline insurers, reinsurers and other insurance companies, mutual funds and a limited group of other investors.

In terms of the breakdown of these various groups, banks make up the largest constituent user group in the credit derivatives market. However, their dominance has declined from 81% in 2000 to 59% of the buyer market and from 63% to 43% of the seller market. This means that although the amount of outstanding credit derivatives contracts is expanding exponentially, new and significant market participants continue to enter the market and expand their market share.

The British Banker's Association Credit Derivatives Report 2006, from where these and the following figures are sourced, breaks bank activity in the credit derivatives market into two separate areas: trading activity and loan portfolio hedging activity. Trading activity forms the dominant sector of activity on both the buy and the sell side.

Hedge funds make up 28% of the market on the buy side and 32% of the market on the sell side. Of the remainder, pension funds, corporates, monoline insurers, reinsurers, other insurance companies and mutual funds make up 12% of the market on the buy side and 23% on the sell side.

6. Reasons for investing in credit derivative products

This book's main focus is documenting and understanding individual credit derivative products. It is important for practitioners to understand the reasons that market participants enter into credit derivative transactions. Different categories of market participant have different reasons for entering into credit derivative transactions.

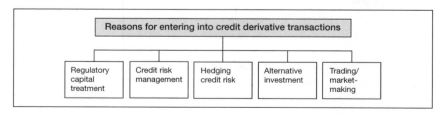

The principal reasons for entering into credit derivatives contracts usually consist of one or several of the following:

---

10   Fitch Ratings, "Global Credit Derivatives Survey: Indices Dominate Growth as Banks' Risk Position Shifts", September 21 2006

- regulatory capital treatment;
- portfolio management;
- hedging credit risk;
- alternative investments; and
- trading and market making.

Some of these overlap and, depending on the type of institution, the importance of each motivation is likely to have different significance. There are also many other ancillary reasons for entering into credit derivative transactions that may influence any decision to buy or sell credit protection.

6.1 Regulatory capital treatment

(a) Bank regulatory capital

Banks and insurance companies are major users of credit derivatives. Both these categories of institution are subject to regulatory capital requirements - requirements imposed by governments and regulators to protect the financial system against systemic collapse and market shocks. These requirements force a regulated institution to hold minimum levels of capital against its risk exposure. Determining the level of risk inherent in a specific amount of an obligation can be complex. Additionally, because the legally imposed requirements are minimum requirements, a financial institution will also have its own internal capital requirements to manage risk. These may oblige it to hold potentially greater amounts of capital against its credit risk.

Because credit derivatives allow financial institutions to isolate and separately trade credit risk, credit derivatives can allow regulated banks to continue to hold assets, while vastly reducing the amount of capital they must hold against these assets for regulatory capital purposes.

The regulatory capital framework for banks is in a state of flux at the moment during the transition between the Basel I and Basel II systems. At the same time, discussions have even started on the Basel III framework[11].

At the time of publication, Basel II has achieved various degrees of implementation and indeed various regulators, banks and politicians are still demanding changes to the scheme. The website of the Bank for International Settlements (www.bis.org) is a useful site to monitor the progress of the transition.

This section of the book does not discuss regulatory capital in depth. There are plenty of other books and articles that do that. Set out below is a brief summary of the current regulatory capital regime as it currently stands.

(i) Basel I

Basel I was set out in the in the July 1988 Basel Capital Accord, published by the Basel Committee on Banking Supervision. The accord did not have force of law, but was adopted by governments and regulatory authorities from the G10 countries. In the

---

11   Work on Basel III is at its preliminary stage. The future accord is likely to refine the definition of 'bank capital' and improve the sensitivity of the risk measures.

European Union, Basel I was implemented through the Consolidated Banking Directive and the Capital Adequacy Directive. The accord established minimum credit capital requirements and provided market risk capital guidelines. 1988 pre-dated the credit derivatives market by some years, but regulators in individual jurisdictions have interpreted credit derivatives as being analogous to guarantees, which were covered by the accord.

Basel I's capital requirements for credit risk were quite inflexible. This is due to the regime's 'one size fits all' approach. The framework requires a regulated bank to hold capital representing at least 8% of any relevant deemed risk exposure. The capital making up this 'risk based capital ratio' could include the bank's equity and reserves.

Although a bank must hold 8% capital against each exposure covered by the accord (eg, loans extended and bonds held), each liability is weighted. This means that an exposure will be allocated a weighting and the amount of the exposure will then be multiplied by that weighting. It is only against the resulting figure that the risk based capital ratio is applied. To take several examples, if a bank extends a €100 million fully funded loan to a corporate client, it is required to hold €8 million (ie, 8%) eligible capital against the credit risk. Under Basel I, term loans to corporate counterparties are weighted at 100%, a significant element of the cost of funding.

Where a bank has unfunded commitment to make a term loan of €100 million with a maturity of over one year, the accord applies a 50% risk weighting to the liability, meaning that the regulated bank must hold 8% of 50% of €100 million (ie, €4 million).

Credit derivative contracts can allow an institution to continue to hold an asset while reducing the amount of capital that the bank is required to hold against that obligation. Under Basel I, if, for example, a bank had extended a loan to a 100 % risk weighted corporate, the bank could reduce its 8% capital allocation on the loan through entering into a single name credit default swap with an Organisation for Economic Cooperation and Development (OECD) bank. The bank would then only be required to hold capital against its exposure to the OECD bank. Under Basel I, OECD banks have a 20% risk weighting. This would replace an 8% capital allocation against the loan with a 1.6 % capital allocation, freeing up funds for use elsewhere. To the extent that this results in more efficient and profitable use of capital, credit derivatives can be very beneficial.

Credit derivatives contracts can also give a regulated bank the ability to move an asset off its balance sheet for a limited period of time and without harming customer relationships. Both of these reasons allow enhanced balance sheet management. A bank may also be able to leverage its balance sheet (ie, by continuing to be able to bring in new business without exhausting its capital reserves).

However, at the time Basel I was drafted, credit derivatives were not as commonly used as they are today and that is why they were not included in the original framework. In order for credit derivatives to reduce capital requirements in a Basel I environment, they need to meet the criteria designed for guarantees. Credit derivatives had to wait for their formal recognition until the implementation of the Basel II framework.

(ii)   *Basel II*

Basel II is the replacement regulatory framework for Basel I. Work began on the project in 1999 and is still ongoing. It modifies Basel I and aims to improve both transparency and bank supervision. It also imports a more subjective regulatory capital framework, replacing Basel I's broad-brush approach. It does this by trying to match the requirement to hold capital against risk exposure by more accurately calculating the actual risk exposure.

On June 30 2006 the Consolidated Banking Directive and the Capital Adequacy Directive which established Basel I were both amended by the Capital Requirements Directive. The Capital Requirements Directive aims to implement the Basel II framework in the European Union in two phases. Most of the provisions came into force on January 1 2007 (or at least the directive required the EU member states to enforce them through relevant domestic laws by that date). However, the more sophisticated risk measurement approaches will only apply from January 1 2008. In the United Kingdom, the task of implementing the Capital Requirements Directive is split between the Financial Services Authority, which has transplanted most of the Capital Requirements Directive into domestic law using its powers under the Financial Services and Markets Act 2000, and Her Majesty's Treasury.

In the United States, however, it has been decided that only a handful of the biggest international banks will be obliged to comply with the entire Basel II framework. For all other banks, the old Basel I regime has been revised and relabelled as Basel IA. However, this has not yet been implemented.

Basel II has three distinct areas, called 'pillars'. The first pillar relates to minimum risk-based capital requirements. The second pillar gives regulators the power to impose stricter requirements than those set out in the first area, where specific exposures are not adequately covered. The third pillar imposes market discipline through greater transparency and disclosure requirements on regulated banks.

The first pillar, which relates to minimum capital requirements, provides three alternative regulatory capital approaches for credit risk. The first approach (the Standardised Approach) is quite similar to Basel I and was designed with the majority of small to medium banks in mind. The other two approaches constitute the most innovative aspect of Basel II, in that they allow bigger financial institutions to assess any credit risk internally (the Internal Ratings-Based (IRB) Approaches).

The Standardised Approach is designed to be used by all but the most sophisticated institutions. This is similar to the system in Basel I, with credit risk being assessed by a standard system using a fixed external methodology. Under this approach, the risk weightings of different types of obligor are determined by a combination of the obligor's characterisation (eg, a sovereign, bank or corporate) and its rating (eg, AAA or BB), with riskier assets and obligors attracting higher risk weightings. The introduction of ratings assessment and more detailed characterisation makes this framework more detailed than under Basel I.

The second and third methods are called the Foundation Internal Ratings-Based (F-IRB) Approach and Advanced Internal Ratings-based (A-IRB) Approach. A bank's regulator must give explicit approval for an institution to adopt either approach and they will only be used by the most sophisticated institutions. Such institutions are also likely to be among the heaviest users of credit derivative products, so advantages conferred by the IRB approaches are likely to provide strong motivation for regulated institutions to use credit derivative products.

Banks given permission by their regulator to use the IRB approaches will use their own internal systems to calculate their risk and determine their capital requirements. The difference between F-IRB and A-IRB is the level of discretion given to an institution to determine its risks.

Most importantly, from this book's point of view, Basel II expressly names credit derivatives as valid methods of risk mitigation. Basel II lists criteria which a credit derivative transaction should meet in order to qualify for the capital requirements purposes. This has already had a considerable impact on the market and standard documentation is being redrafted in order to comply with the relevant criteria.

Further, Basel II sets out a detailed regulatory framework for determining the amount of regulatory capital that must be held against an exposure to a traditional or synthetic securitisation. Under the securitisation framework, Basel II looks to the economic substance of a transaction rather than its legal form.

Although Basel II is more complex than Basel I, the motivation of using credit derivatives to improve usage of regulatory capital by banks will continue to be a key driver in the credit derivatives market.

(b) Insurance regulatory capital

Whereas Basel I and Basel II relate to banks, each jurisdiction is likely to have its own regulatory capital requirements for insurance companies. Insurance companies are already among the biggest users of credit derivative products and their importance in the market is likely to increase. Where credit derivatives are viewed favourably by a particular insurance regulatory capital regime, this will enhance the product's attractiveness. There are significant differences between jurisdictions. The regulatory frameworks, though, will generally be similar to Basel I and Basel II; and hence the motivations for entering into credit derivative products will be similar. Specific advice must be sought to understand the differences between each regime.

In the European Union, the minimum capital requirements for insurance companies are based on directives that go back to 1973. However, the initial standards were set quite low and were not risk sensitive. Subsequent improvements, notably the Solvency I Directive[12] published in 2002, brought only very modest changes. It is for this reason that regulators in Europe have adopted alternative approaches and, for example, in the United Kingdom, insurance companies need to hold twice the EU minimum requirements. Some local regulators were, or still are, very restrictive in the use of derivative products and there are considerable differences in the regulatory regimes of each EU member state.

The situation is likely to improve with the Solvency II Directive, which is expected to be published in 2007 and which should come into force in 2010. The proposed directive will establish a comprehensive regulatory regime for insurance companies based on three pillars. The first one will cover capital requirements; the second

---

12   Directive 2002/13/EC.

will determine the supervisory activities; and the third will cover disclosure of information. The first pillar, in turn, will contain two capital requirements approaches, the Minimum Capital Requirements and the Solvency Capital Requirements. This methodology, which is quite similar to that of the Financial Services Authority in the United Kingdom, will be risk-based and will require insurers to produce financial models. One of the aims of the new system will be to promote efficient risk management. This mean that the Solvency II Directive will create an environment very favourable towards derivatives, and insurance companies throughout the European Union may be forced to make even greater use of various derivatives products.

In the United States, capital requirements for insurance companies are regulated at the state, as opposed to federal, level and it is unlikely that this will change in the foreseeable future. However, regulators from a growing number of countries, for example South Africa, Australia and some Asian countries, are adopting solutions which are similar to those proposed by the Solvency II Directive. All of this should positively influence the demand for credit derivatives.

6.2 Credit risk management

A financial institution's desire to limit and/or diversify credit risk concentrations in its debt portfolios can make credit derivatives an attractive proposition and useful tool. Let's take an example. A bank with a successful business extending loans to French car part manufacturers might find that its loan portfolio becomes overly exposed to the French auto manufacturer sector, breaching its internal risk concentration limits and stopping it from expanding an otherwise lucrative area of business.

This bank could offset credit risk concentrations by entering into credit derivative products as a credit protection buyer referencing relevant entities from the sector. Another institution looking to diversify its own portfolio by including exposure to the French auto manufacturer sector, but without the business capability to do so through the traditional lending route, might choose to enter into similar credit derivative products as a credit protection seller.

For credit protection sellers, credit derivative products allow these market participants to gain exposure to particular and diverse sectors. This can be done more easily through the cash bond market where the number of available obligations may be limited.

6.3 Hedging credit risk

A financial institution's desire to hedge its actual credit exposure to particular obligations can often be satisfied by using credit derivatives. Imagine that a British bank has a key client, a multi-national drinks distributor. That bank has entered into a debt facility with its client and, although pleased with its fee and excited at the prospect of further work, it is worried about the amount of exposure it has. Selling the loan would cause offence to the client, but if the overall bank business were to grow, keeping the client (and the loan) would fit in well with the bank's business model. Entering into a credit default swap referencing the drinks distributor would hedge the bank's credit risk.

6.4 Alternative investment

A hedge fund, fund manager, insurance company or any other entity with a portfolio of investments will usually try to diversify those investments. Diversification is important not only among the assets of a particular class – for example, the manager of a portfolio will not wish to be overly exposed to a particular obligor, sector or geographical location. It also may wish to diversify among the classes of assets themselves.

If the equity market crashes, the bond market may not; likewise the credit derivatives market may also be protected. Credit derivatives provide an alternative class of investment. This in itself makes the product appealing.

6.5 Trading/market making

Prior to the advent of credit derivatives, the inability to separate credit risk from the other bundle of obligations making up a security made credit risk illiquid. Trading credit risk separately attracts more participants to the market, allowing trading to take place. Financial institutions are able to make a market standing as a central counterparty, taking as profit the difference between buy and sell prices. Other innovations, such as tranching (allowing investors to take particular slices of credit exposure depending on their risk appetite), also help to attract new participants to the market.

7. Additional and inherent risks of credit derivatives

"The isolation and separate trading of a reference entity's credit risk." If only this were the sole risk that the buyer or seller was trading in a credit derivatives transaction!

Unfortunately, although credit derivative products go a long way towards achieving this goal, other residual risks remain. Credit protection buyers and sellers assume many other risks in addition to the credit risk of the reference entity.

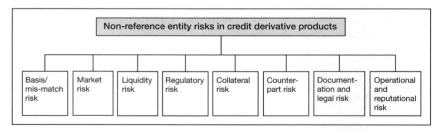

These residual risks fall into eight categories:
- basis/mis-match risk;
- market risk;
- liquidity risk;
- regulatory risk;
- collateral risk;
- counterparty risk;
- documentation and legal risk; and
- operation and reputational risk.

7.1   **Basis/mis-match risk**

Often credit derivatives are used to hedge against specific obligations held by the credit protection buyer. Problems may arise:

- where a reference entity, following a corporate reorganisation, is succeeded by multiple reference entities;
- where standardised credit derivatives documentation does not match a bespoke transaction; or
- where a corporate reorganisation or refinancing, perhaps pursuant to leveraged buy-out or private equity financing, leads to a shortage of deliverable obligations.

Examples include where a reference entity is succeeded by multiple successors and, under the rules applied by the 2003 Definitions, several new credit derivative transactions are created, forcing the buyer to purchase protection on entities that it does not want and leaving it with insufficient credit protection to hedge those assets which it actually holds.

Further examples of basis/mis-match risk can occur where the currency of a reference obligation does not match the currency of the derivatives transaction or where the maturity of an obligation does not match that of the relevant credit derivatives contract.

7.2   **Market risk**

Connected to liquidity risk is market risk. This can impact on the price of credit protection. Spread movements and the availability of bi-polar positions regarding the purchase and sale of credit protection can impact on the price of a credit derivative.

A further issue arises when a market participant tries to value its credit derivatives portfolio for accounting purposes. Some transactions, particularly those such as nth to default transactions, may be very difficult to value on a mark to market basis. An alternative valuation method called 'mark to model' is reliant on the accuracy of the model used. A failure to use the correct modelling or to value a credit derivatives portfolio correctly can expose a market participant to considerable market risk. Whether a model gives a true picture of market risk is also known as model risk.

7.3   **Liquidity risk**

Credit derivatives markets are not as liquid as the bond and other debt markets. This may mean that if a credit derivative is not as liquid as the obligations that underlie the derivatives contract, then the price of the credit derivatives against the relevant obligations may become distorted and prone to wider fluctuations in price.

7.4   **Regulatory risk**

Credit derivatives regularly catch the attention of regulatory bodies. Basel II, in particular, covers the capital weighting which must be made to cover credit derivatives' positions. A change in capital weightings which must be allocated to credit derivatives, or a requirement for certain credit events or provisions to be included in a credit derivatives contract, can potentially have an adverse effect on price.

7.5   Collateral risk

In any funded credit derivatives, the proceeds of the issue of debt securities are usually invested in highly rated low-risk securities. This is done to isolate the proceeds of the notes from other risks. 'Low risk' does not mean 'no risk' and this means that the noteholder in any credit-linked note or synthetic CDO is exposed to the risk that these underlying securities may themselves default, or decline in value, such that there are insufficient funds to repay the outstanding principal amount at the notes' maturity.

7.6   Counterparty risk

In unfunded credit derivative transactions, both the credit protection buyer and the credit protection seller are exposed to each other's credit risk. The buyer is exposed to the risk that, on settlement, the seller will not be in a position to pay the cash settlement amount or the physical settlement amount, leaving it without the credit protection that it had purchased.

The seller will be left with the lesser risk that, at any point during the transaction's term, it will not receive the fixed payments it is due.

To a certain extent, counterparty risk is inherent in all derivatives transactions. The parties are able to deal with this risk using existing ISDA documentation architecture (ie, the credit support annex and/or other collateral and credit support-related documentation).

A further risk is that a counterparty does not have the correct legal authority to enter into a credit derivative transaction. The early landmark cases relating to derivatives and capacity occurred in the 1980s and apply to derivatives in general. Proper diligence on any counterparty is essential and will depend to a large extent on the type and jurisdiction of the relevant reference entity. Otherwise, the risk remains that any credit derivatives contract could be unenforceable and/or that any fixed payments made were recoverable.

Funded credit derivatives also involve a swap counterparty (usually the transaction's arranger), which re-profiles the interest and principal payments from the highly rated securities and the credit protection payments under the credit default swap received by the issuer and converts them into the payments necessary to meet the issuer's obligations under the debt securities. This means that a noteholder in a funded derivatives transaction is also exposed to the risk that the swap counterparty will itself default under the transaction. Although arrangements are usually put in place for a replacement counterparty to be found, this may not be either possible or cost effective. This also exposes the funded derivative holder to structured swap counterparty risk.

Additionally, in funded credit derivative transactions which utilise a special purpose vehicle structure, noteholders and counterparties are exposed to the risk that the vehicle's bankruptcy remote structure could be struck down by a court, potentially leaving the vehicle without funds either to repay the noteholder's principal or to make credit protection payments under the credit default swap.

7.7   Documentation and legal risk

Regulators remain concerned about the documentation risks existing in the credit derivatives market.[13] The first major question is whether the credit derivatives documentation will work. Does it do what is intended and is it legal, valid, binding and enforceable? The credit derivatives market is now well established, and the standardisation efforts of ISDA have now reduced these risks as much as possible (eg, ISDA has obtained legal opinions in over 40 jurisdictions around the world on various enforceability issues). However, there is still a risk, particularly in the case of more bespoke products and/or where English or New York law is not used as the governing law, that documentation will not perform as intended and will not be legal, valid, binding and enforceable.

7.8   Operational/reputational risk

Market participants in the credit derivatives market are often large financial institutions. Legitimately, those institutions may try to hedge their loan or bond book through the use of credit derivatives. Problems may arise where a borrower under a loan or bond provides non-public price sensitive information to a lender or arranger, which then hedges its position through credit derivatives. Such information may have a material impact on the pricing of credit derivative transactions and particular care must be taken to ensure not only that the use of such information does not breach any law or regulation, but also that it causes no reputational damage to the market participant concerned.

Operational risk arises where, due to the sheer volume of transactions entered into by a market participant, either transactions are entered into without proper authorisation or diligence being carried out or delays arise in the documenting transactions after they have been agreed. The first area is most apparent where two institutions enter into a relationship trading credit derivatives (and perhaps other derivatives contracts as well), but the documentation process of agreeing and negotiating an ISDA Master Agreement and carrying out the requisite due diligence as to creditworthiness and legal risk does not proceed at the same pace.

The second area of confirmation backlogs has been an area of concern. In 2005 both the Federal Reserve in the United States, the Financial Services Authority in the United Kingdom and other key regulators pressured key dealers to resolve the issue.[14] Without a confirmation in place, the process of ascertaining what was actually agreed between the parties can become open to dispute and very difficult to determine.

Much progress has now been made on this front. In September 2005 more than 150,000 credit derivatives transactions did not have confirmations, including 98,000 that had been executed more than 30 days previously. By March 2006 this figure had been reduced to 74,000, with only 29,000 transactions remaining unconfirmed more than 30 days after they were agreed.[15] Progress continues to be made, but with the

---

13   "Credit Derivatives: Boon to Mankind or Accident Waiting to Happen?" Speech by Thomas Huertas, director, Wholesale Firms Division and Banking Sector Leader, Financial Services Authority Rhombus Research Annual Conference, London, April 26 2006.

14   "Showdown looming over credit derivatives backlog", *Financial Times*, September 29 2005, Richard Beales; "FSA targets derivatives delays", *Financial Times*, September 7 2005, Gillian Tett and Richard Beales.

15   "Credit Derivatives: Boon to Mankind or Accident Waiting to Happen?" Speech by Thomas Huertas, director, Wholesale Firms Division and Banking Sector Leader, Financial Services Authority Rhombus Research Annual Conference, London, April 26 2006.

relentless growth of the credit derivatives market operational risk remains an area of concern.

Part IV describes settlement risk: this is the risk that credit event notices or notices of physical settlement will not be sent when required, that valuation dates will be missed or that valuations of reference obligations will be incorrectly carried out.

8.   Restrictions on further development of the credit derivatives market

The main restrictions which are preventing further development of the credit derivatives market can be summarised as follows:

- lack of knowledge;
- inadequacy of trading systems and trade infrastructure;
- lack of liquidity in the market in general;
- pricing issues;
- regulatory issues;
- documentation inadequacies, particularly in relation to new products; and
- difficulty in the accounting treatment of derivatives

Credit derivative products and their documentation: unfunded credit derivatives

1. Introduction

The range of credit derivative products, their associated jargon and many acronyms dazzle:

- single name, basket, constant maturity, constant proportion and portfolio credit defaults swaps;
- full and tranched index trades;
- collateralised debt obligation (CDO) squared;
- CDO cubed;
- constant proportion portfolio insurance (CPPI); and
- constant proportion debt obligation (CPDO) transactions.

And these are just a few of the products in the credit derivatives arena.

New innovations regularly arrive to market, with trade press each year heralding a 'hot' new thing. *Credit* magazine's "The 2006 ABC of CDOs" stated that: "The growing popularity of certain types of asset backed securitisation…has given rise to a thriving market in CDOs of ABS". On the arrival of CPPI products, it pronounced that it was "[n]o surprise that [they are] being talked about as 2006's hot ticket". And *Credit* magazine is right: these are exciting times. Keeping up to date with the product universe is difficult, even for the most dedicated practitioner.

This chapter provides an overview of each of the most commonly traded 'unfunded' credit derivatives products in today's market. It also discusses the popularity breakdown of these and their sister 'funded' products. It is followed by a chapter that analyses ISDA's template documentation for unfunded credit derivatives and a further chapter discussing funded credit derivative products, such as credit linked notes, CDOs, CPPI and CPDOs.

2. The credit derivative product range

The British Bankers' Association periodically produces a report on credit derivatives market activity, based on survey returns of major market participants. Its most recent release, *The British Bankers' Association Credit Derivatives Report 2006*, lists the key credit derivative products making up the market as of the end of 2006. At the time of publication, these are the most up-to-date figures available.

The report discloses that 10 traded credit derivatives products make up 96.3% of the market. These products are:

[handwritten: Ch look at 7 most traded]

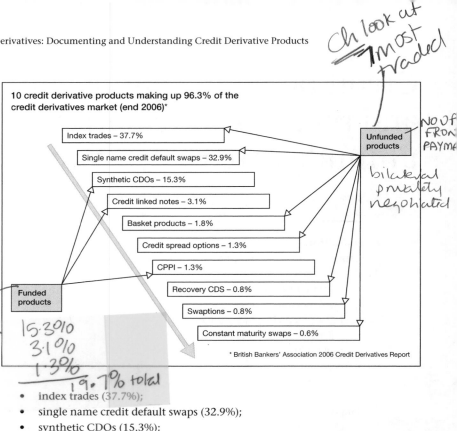

[handwritten annotations around figure: "No of FROM PAYME", "bilateral privately negotiated", "Involves issued a debt obligation — purchase by the effective seller (noteholder)", "15.3% / 3.1% / 1.3% = 19.7% total"]

- index trades (37.7%);
- single name credit default swaps (32.9%);
- synthetic CDOs (15.3%);
- credit linked notes (3.1%);
- basket products (1.8%);
- credit spread options (1.3%);
- CPPI (1.3%);
- recovery swaps (0.8%);
- swaptions (0.8%); and
- constant maturity swaps (0.6%).

Within these product types are certain sub-categories of products that are becoming increasingly popular, such as credit default swaps on asset-backed securities (CDS on ABS).

This chapter looks at the *seven* most traded types of unfunded credit derivative product: single name credit default swaps; index trades; basket products; credit spread options; swaptions; recovery swaps; constant maturity swaps; together with the 'hot new product' of CDS on ABS. Where ISDA has produced template documentation for these products, this is discussed further in the following chapter, alongside several bespoke (but significant) other products which ISDA has documented.

At the end of 2006, 87 % of the universe of credit derivative products, by volume, could be divided into three products: single name credit default swaps, index trades and synthetic CDOs. In recognition of this, these products, along with CDS on ABS, are covered in greater detail in Part III.

3. Types of credit derivatives: unfunded and funded products

Unfunded credit derivatives are bilateral, privately negotiated credit derivatives contracts. A simple single name credit default swap between two corporates is the most common example. These products are described as 'unfunded' because the seller (or those standing behind it) makes no upfront payment to cover its potential future liabilities.[1]

The seller will make a payment in an unfunded credit derivative only if the conditions to settlement are met. Consequently, the buyer takes a credit risk on whether the seller will be able to pay any cash settlement amount or physical settlement amount. Unfunded credit derivatives include: single name credit default swaps; index trades; basket products; credit spread options; swaptions; constant maturity swaps; recovery credit default swaps; and CDS on ABS. An overlap exists with funded credit derivative products, in that these products are usually embedded into a note structure when creating a funded credit derivative.

A funded credit derivative involves the issue of a debt obligation either by a special purpose vehicle (SPV) or a financial institution, which is purchased by the effective seller – the noteholder. The proceeds of the notes are 'collateralised' by investing their proceeds in highly rated securities, such as Organisation for Economic Cooperation and Development country government bonds; or in a guaranteed investment contract account.

The note proceeds are used to fund the payment of any cash settlement amount or physical settlement amount. This must be either paid pursuant to a credit default swap entered into by an SPV issuer or absorbed by the issuer pursuant to the conditions of the notes.

The structure of funded credit derivatives involves embedding a credit derivative product into the structure of the transaction. The type of credit derivatives embedded may include many of the unfunded derivatives products mentioned above. Funded credit derivatives are generally credit-linked notes; synthetic CDOs; synthetic CPPI transactions and CPDOs.

3.1 Single name credit default swaps   *32.9%*

The single name credit default swap is the cornerstone credit derivative product. Most other credit derivative products have been adapted from it and it still makes up 32.9% of the credit derivatives market.

A solid understanding of single name credit default swaps is essential for an understanding of the more complex credit derivative products, such as constant maturity credit default swaps, portfolio credit default swaps and synthetic CDOs. Part III contains a chapter dedicated to single name credit default swaps, which covers the product in more detail.

In a nutshell, the product can be defined as a privately negotiated bilateral contract between a 'buyer' and a 'seller', referencing the third-party credit risk of a single reference entity. In 2004, for example, the most commonly traded reference

---

1   Excluding any payments under a credit support annex.

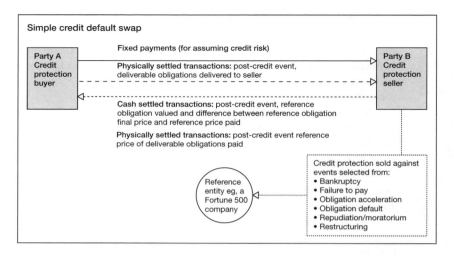

entities included General Motors, Ford, DaimlerChrysler, France Telecom, Italy, France and Japan.[2]

In a standard transaction, the parties agree that the buyer will purchase a pre-agreed notional amount of protection against the credit risk of the reference entity's obligations. The specific obligations against which the seller sells credit protection are decided at the outset. They may be specific named securities of the reference entity such as a €200 million floating rate note, or they may be a category of obligation, such as borrowed money, displaying certain characteristics (eg, listed bonds with a maximum maturity date of less than 30 years).

The credit risk against which the seller sells credit protection covers only the risk of certain pre-agreed credit events occurring in relation to a minimum amount of the obligations (or, in the case of the bankruptcy credit event, the reference entity itself). Credit events are likely to match a significant deterioration in the reference entity's credit quality: they will be any agreed combination of bankruptcy, failure to pay, the acceleration of an obligation, an obligation default, a repudiation or moratorium of debts, or a debt restructuring. In return for the seller assuming this credit risk, the buyer will periodically pay a premium. This will usually be a percentage of the credit default swap's notional amount, expressed in basis points. The amount of the premium will reflect the credit risk of the particular reference entity, with greater risks reflected in higher premiums.

The parties document their transaction by entering into an ISDA master agreement and schedule, and setting out the transaction's terms in a confirmation incorporating the 2003 ISDA Credit Derivatives Definitions. All of the market standard variables are set out in the 2003 Definitions. The parties select the applicable credit events, business days, conditions to settlement and other variables in accordance with market practice, which in turn may rely on the reference entity's jurisdiction of incorporation and/or its characterisation.

---

2   Fitch Ratings, "Global Credit Derivatives Survey: Risk Dispersion Accelerates", November 17 2005.

When a credit event occurs the seller (and often the buyer) has the right, but not the obligation, to trigger a credit event. The party triggering the credit event is called the notifying party and the date on which it does so is the event determination date. To trigger the credit event, the notifying party must satisfy the conditions to settlement (usually the delivery of a credit event notice) and (depending on what is specified in the relevant confirmation) a notice of publicly available information, plus a notice of physical settlement, if appropriate.

The credit event notice is addressed to the counterparty, specifies that a credit event has occurred and gives the facts relevant to that determination. A notice of publicly available information is usually incorporated into the credit event notice. It cites publicly available information from public sources (usually two), such as Bloomberg and the *Financial Times,* confirming facts relevant to the credit event's determination.

Credit default swaps can be either cash settled or physically settled. In cash settled transactions, the calculation agent (usually the seller) selects and values a reference entity obligation. Either the reference obligation is specified in the confirmation or the confirmation will provide a selection mechanism similar to that for establishing the reference entity's obligations, in which case the calculation agent will notify the counterparties of the reference obligation in a reference obligation notification notice.

The transaction will detail when the reference obligation will be valued. Usually, this valuation date is sufficiently far from the event determination date to allow a reference obligation's trading price to settle.

On the valuation date (which may be on one date or several dates), the calculation agent will go into the market and ask for quotations from dealers for a pre-agreed amount of the reference obligation. The calculation agent will then calculate the reference obligation's final price. The 2003 Definitions provide numerous options and fallbacks for the number of valuation dates, the amount of quotations that must be sought (and from whom), and how the final price is to be calculated.

The final price is expressed as a percentage (ie, the percentage value of the current value of the reference obligation compared to its nominal amount or a reference price), and is calculated using a pre-selected valuation method. The calculation agent notifies the parties of the final price in a final price notification notice. The transaction is then settled an agreed number of days later. The cash settlement amount paid by the seller will usually be the transaction's notional amount multiplied by the reference price (usually 100%) minus the final price (eg 50%). The transaction will then terminate.

Cash settlement as described above is the applicable settlement method in 23% of single name credit default swap transactions, with fixed amount settlements (ie, a fixed recovery rate) being the applicable settlement method in a further 3% of transactions.[3]

Where the parties have specified that physical settlement applies and the conditions to settlement are satisfied, the buyer has 30 calendar days to serve a notice

---

3   British Bankers' Association, Credit Derivatives Report 2006, p7.

of physical settlement. The transaction confirmation will set out either a specific obligation or the deliverable obligation category and the deliverable obligation characteristics which a reference entity obligation must satisfy for it to be a deliverable obligation. The notice of physical settlement sets out the actual deliverable obligations that the buyer will deliver on the physical settlement date. These deliverable obligations will usually be equal in face value to the transaction's notional amount.

The physical settlement date will be either as agreed by the parties or within the longest period customary in the market. On the physical settlement date, the buyer will deliver the deliverable obligations and the seller pays an amount equal to their face value. Physical settlement still remains the dominant form of settlement in the credit derivatives market. It is the applicable settlement method in 73% of transactions.[4]

Hypothetical case study: a single name credit default swap

Baularte Limited holds €800,000 of floating rate notes issued by a Portuguese drinks distributor, Donnel plc. The company is one of Baularte's largest clients and the debt holding has helped enhance the client relationship. Baularte is reluctant to sell its holdings but has become worried about the size of its exposure and the credit quality of Donnel. Baularte decides to protect itself by entering into a single name credit default swap with Castle Bank, with Donnel as the reference entity. Castle wishes to increase its exposure to the Portuguese beverage market, having had problems attracting clients from this sector to its corporate loan business. Donnel is unaware of the transaction's existence.

Although Baularte was initially looking only to protect itself against the risk of default on the €800,000 bond issue, it has decided that by buying credit protection in relation to a wider range of Donnel obligations it will help to insulate itself against any business disruption should Donnel collapse. The obligations that are the subject of credit protection are defined as being any bond or loan of Donnel.

Baularte purchases €1 million of credit protection on Donnel for a three-year period, so the swap has a notional amount of €1 million and a maturity date three years ahead. The parties select as credit events Donnel's bankruptcy, a failure to pay principal or interest on any of its bonds or loans above €1 million or any debt restructuring.

Donnel and Baularte use an ISDA standard credit default swap confirmation incorporating the 2003 Definitions. The confirmation incorporates a 1992 ISDA Master Agreement (as amended by a schedule), which the parties have also entered into.

To compensate Castle for taking on the Donnel risk, Baularte pays annual credit protection premiums of 2% of the notional amount of the swap. This is

---

4 British Bankers' Association, Credit Derivatives Report 2006, p7.

similar to the margin over its lending costs that Castle would have expected to make if it had entered into a loan transaction directly with Donnel.

Unfortunately for Castle, one year later Donnel defaults on an interest payment for an issue of $100 million 5% bonds due 2012 (the '2012 debt'). Donnel moves into restructuring talks with the creditors of the 2012 bonds. The value of Baularte's bonds plummets from 95% of their face value to 45%.

Several things could now happen. Donnel could restructure its 2012 debt, which could further devalue the value of Baularte's bonds; it could declare bankruptcy; or it could fail to make the interest payment on Baularte's bonds in a few months' time. Baularte is also likely to suffer business disruption in relation to its key client.

Baularte decides to trigger a credit event on its credit default swap and delivers a credit event notice to Castle. The credit event notice refers to their transaction and states that a 'failure to pay' credit event occurred when Donnel failed to pay an interest coupon in relation to the 2012 debt. The credit event notice incorporates a notice of publicly available information and attaches two pieces of publicly available information confirming that a credit event has taken place. One is a report from Bloomberg and the other is an article from the *Financial Times*.

In certain circumstances, Castle might have decided to trigger the credit event itself. This might have occurred if a restructuring had taken place resulting in a relatively small decrease in the value of Donnel securities, but the fear of a bankruptcy still remained.

The settlement process begins: the parties entered into a cash settled credit default swap and decided at the transaction's outset that an obligation of Donnel would be selected by Baularte, five business days after the delivery of the credit event notice. The five business day period had been chosen at the outset to allow the market to settle down following the delivery of any Donnel bad news. Baularte selects the worst performing obligation of Donnel which, by coincidence, happens to be the floating rate note issue that it holds. Baularte using a valuation process set out in the credit default swap confirmation values the obligations at 50% of their face value (a slight recovery in price). The final price of the obligations is 50% and Castle is then required to pay the difference between the notional amount of the credit default swap (ie, 100%) and the final price. Castle pays Baularte €500,000.

Baularte then decides to sell the €800,000 of Donnel bonds that it holds and realises €400,000 for them. It has made €100,000 over and above the extent of its loss and this helps to compensate Baularte for future business disruption.

If the parties had entered into a physically settled credit default swap, then within 30 calendar days following the delivery of the credit event notice[5], Baularte would have delivered a notice to Castle stating that it intended to physically settle the transaction. It would deliver eligible Donnel securities with a face value equal to the notional amount of the credit default swap to Castle.

---

5   See discussions of time periods.

[handwritten: Which is better scenario?]

Castle would be required to pay the notional amount of the credit default swap to Baularte. Baularte could then have delivered its €800,000 of Donnel notes and received their face value. It would also have needed to purchase €200,000 of Donnel notes at whichever price they were trading at, and would have received back their full face amount.

3.2   Basket credit default swaps   *[handwritten: 1·8%]*

[handwritten: more reference entities]

Basket credit default swaps are a step up in complexity from credit default swaps. In basket credit derivative products, there are a number of reference entities instead of just one. Basket products consist of two separate products: nth to default swaps and portfolio credit default swaps.

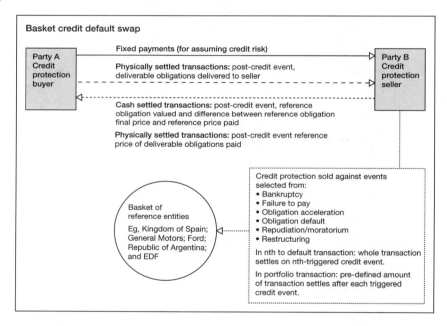

In a basket credit default swap, there are a number of reference entities (eg, Kingdom of Spain; General Motors; Ford; Republic of Argentina; and EDF). In an nth to default transaction, the transaction is structured so that when there have been an agreed number of credit events, a notifying party may meet the conditions to settlement and the transaction will cash settle or physically settle, depending on which settlement method the parties have elected. In a portfolio credit default swap, an agreed portion of the notional amount of the credit default swap will settle after each event determination date.

[handwritten: first to default or second to default]

(a)   Nth to default credit default swaps

The 'nth' in 'nth to default' refers to the number of defaults required before the conditions to settlement can be met (eg, a first to default credit default swap or a second to default credit default swap). A basket credit default swap may be a first to default product, which, using the example in the diagram above, would mean that if any of the five named reference entities suffered a credit event and the conditions to settlement were met, then the transaction would settle.

If the basket credit default swap were a third to default product, then if the Kingdom of Spain and the Republic of Argentina suffered credit events (and both event determination dates had occurred), the conditions to settlement could be met if, and only if, one of General Motors, Ford or EDF suffered a credit event. The transaction would then settle based on the transaction's full notional amount.

The seller in an nth to default credit default swap receives a flow of fixed payments until either the 'nth' default occurs or the termination date. First to default credit default swaps allow the seller to leverage the credit risk it is selling and so earn a higher overall yield than that which it would be able to obtain on any of the constituent reference entities forming the basket for a credit default swap with the same overall notional amount.

This leverage, though, is accompanied by greater risk for the seller. If a first to default credit default swap has a notional amount of $1 million and a term of three years, and the basket is composed of five reference entities, the likelihood of a credit event affecting one of these five reference entities is much greater than the corresponding risk in a single name credit default swap for the same notional amount referencing just one of these reference entities.

One way to view a first to default credit default swap is as a bundle of single name credit default swaps between the buyer and seller – that is, one credit default swap for the full notional amount for each reference entity. If the conditions to settlement for any of these credit default swaps are met, then the date on which this occurs will be the termination date for all of the other credit default swaps and the parties' obligations to each other will cease.

A seller wishing to leverage its credit risk to a lesser extent, but still wanting to receive a higher yield than that available under a single name credit default swap, might choose to enter into a second or third to default credit default swap. This will mean that the seller is less likely to suffer a loss event, but also that because the leverage is less, the premium will also be lower.

The amount of the fixed payments received by the seller in an nth to default credit default swap will be determined by several factors. These include:

- the number of defaults which must occur before the conditions to settlement can be met;
- the number of reference entities which are in the basket (the more reference entities in the basket, the greater the risk of a credit event occurring);
- the credit spread of each of the reference entities in the basket;
- the correlation between the reference entities (eg, if all of the reference entities are in the automobile sector and that industry encounters tough times, the likelihood of one of the reference entities defaulting increases);
- the likely recovery rate of the reference entity which defaults; and
- the term of the transaction (the longer the term, the more likely that the nth level of default will be reached).

Buyers and sellers may be attracted to nth default credit default swaps because they can take a view on the likely correlation of defaults by the reference entities comprising the basket. If a seller believes that there is a high implied correlation between the reference entities, selling first to default credit protection may be attractive because of the likelihood that a business environment may indeed cause all of the reference entities to default. If the seller believes that there is a low implied correlation between the reference entities, selling second to default credit protection may be attractive because of the likelihood that different sectors would have to suffer poor business conditions for more than one reference entity to default.

Credit protection buyers are most likely to utilise nth to default credit default swaps to hedge portfolio credit derivative products that they hold. In these circumstances an nth to default credit default swap may be cheaper than entering into several single name credit default swaps.

**Hypothetical case study: first to default credit default swap –
Alia Investments and Nimry Partners**

In September 2006 Alia Investments and Nimry Partners entered into a $1 million second to default physically settled credit default swap, under which Alia Investments was the buyer and Nimry Partners was the seller. The swap had a five-year term and selected bankruptcy, failure to pay and restructuring as the applicable credit events. Alia and Nimry documented the transaction using a 1992 ISDA Master Agreement and standard credit derivatives confirmation, which incorporated the 2003 Definitions.

The transaction referenced five reference entities: Bezares plc, Lima Corporation, Moran plc, Enrique SA and Fleurquin SA. There was a high correlation between the reference entities as each was a financial services company.

In 2007 the financial services industry went into recession and thousands of jobs were lost. Each of the reference entities suffered significant ratings downgrades on its debt securities. In August 2007 Bezares plc filed for bankruptcy. As permitted by the documentation, Alia delivered a credit event notice and notice of publicly available information causing an event determination date, though the conditions to settlement were not met as this was a second to default transaction. In September 2007 the global financial environment proved so tough that Lima Corporation also filed for bankruptcy.

Once again, Alia delivered a credit event notice and notice of publicly available information to Nimry. This time, the conditions to settlement were met. After serving a notice of physical settlement, Alia delivered a $1 million face value portfolio of Lima corporation debt securities which met the deliverable obligation category and characteristics specified in the documentation in return for payment of the $1 million physical settlement amount. The transaction then terminated.

(b)   Portfolio credit default swaps

Portfolio credit default swaps form the second category of credit derivative basket products. As with an nth to default credit default swap, the buyer purchases credit protection on a basket of reference entities. The number of reference entities in the basket tends to be greater than in nth to default credit default swaps. Instead of the relevant reference entities being referred to as a basket of reference entities, they are referred to as a portfolio of reference entities.

Portfolio credit default swaps operate very similarly to single name credit default swaps. The easiest way to conceptualise the product is to view it as consisting of a bundle of credit default swaps, with one credit default swap being in place (between the buyer and the seller) for each reference entity in the portfolio. This then provides documentation, pricing, administrative and diversification advantages to the parties.

Each time that a credit event occurs in relation to a reference entity and the conditions to settlement are met, the settlement procedure is the same as for a single-name credit default swap, except that instead of the transaction terminating on the settlement date, the reference entity will be removed from the basket or portfolio and the transaction will continue.

In portfolio credit default swaps, the transaction will have an overall notional amount (eg, $10 million) and consists of a notional amount for each reference entity. This is usually an equally weighted amount, with credit protection sold for each reference entity's reference entity notional amount only.

The attractions of entering into a portfolio credit default swap for both buyer and seller include both the diversity and/or low correlation of the reference portfolio. Portfolio credit default swaps are often used as the embedded credit derivative in synthetic CDO transactions.

**Hypothetical case study: portfolio credit default swap –
Alia Investments and Nimry Parters**

On January 1 2007, Alia Investments and Nimry Partners also decided to enter into a $20 million three-year cash settled portfolio credit default swap. In this transaction, Alia Investments was the buyer and Nimry Partners was the seller. The swap had a five-year term and selected bankruptcy, failure to pay and restructuring as the applicable credit events.

The transaction referenced 100 reference entities. These were spread across a variety of jurisdictions, ratings and industrial sectors. Each of the reference entities had a 1% weighting, which meant that each had a reference entity notional amount of $200,000 (ie, Alia and Nimry had effectively entered into 100 credit default swaps, each with a notional amount of $200,000).

In 2007 the portfolio suffered four defaults. Each time that it did, Alia delivered a credit event notice and notice of publicly available information to Nimry. An obligation of the affected reference entity was then valued and a cash

---

settlement amount paid by Nimry to Alia, as would have happened under a single name credit default swap. Following the payment of each cash settlement amount, the relevant reference entity was then stripped out of the portfolio and no further credit protection payments were made. In 2008 the portfolio suffered three defaults, with none in 2009. Each default was treated in the same manner.

By the scheduled termination date, the portfolio of 100 reference entities had suffered seven credit events. This meant that $1.4 million of the $20 million portfolio had been affected. Average recoveries were 50%, which meant that Nimry paid $700,000 in cash settlement amounts.

3.3 Index trades

(a) Overview

Credit index trading is discussed more fully in Part II, with a dedicated chapter. This section provides an overview. A credit derivatives index (or credit index) is an index comprised of a managed portfolio of commonly traded reference entities.

A credit derivative index usually consists of a portfolio of equally weighted reference entities that are rebased on a periodic basis. The rebalancing takes place under pre-agreed rules using the input of credit derivatives market makers. Inclusion of a reference entity in an index is generally by merited by a combination of some or all of the following:

- trading volume;
- geographical location;
- industry category; and
- creditworthiness over the previous six-month period.

A credit derivative index is generally a licensed product, which may have many uses. A market participant can use the index on payment of a fee to create its own product, perhaps a synthetic CDO referencing a credit index as it is periodically updated, or by entering into a bilateral over-the-counter (OTC) transaction with another market participant; or it may even create a market itself, standing as a central counterparty buying and selling credit protection on the index and taking the credit risk of each counterparty.

Credit indices increase market liquidity by increasing transaction volumes and lowering market entry barriers. Market makers create markets for trading linked credit derivative products based on standardised documentation. Participants can rely on the reference entity names and related obligations being correct and so reduce their transaction costs. This standardisation also allows automated matching and trading of products.

Credit indices can also allow funded products to have a quasi-form of management. For example, if a single tranche synthetic CDO references the most recent version of a credit index, this will mean that every six months the transaction will reference the most liquid names in a particular sector, possibly saving on management fees.

The credit derivatives index market began with several banks setting up their own credit derivatives indices. They then launched indices in partnerships with other banks. Rival ventures sprang up and this was then followed by a period of mergers which has resulted in two dominant families of indices, each administered by the same administrator and owned by substantially the same parties: iTraxx and CDX. Further consolidation between these two behemoths seems inevitable.

Index families publish rebased indices on a bi-annual basis in March and September. The process for updating the names in each series works generally as follows. In accordance with set rules, participating market makers submit the CDS volumes that they have dealt with over the previous period. A provisional list of reference entities selected in accordance with these rules is then published. The reference entities are then agreed and a finalised list is published. The coupon levels for each reference entity are then agreed and trading of the new issue begins.

(b) *iTraxx*

The iTraxx indices are owned by the International Index Company. There are two principal sub-families of iTraxx indices: those that relate to Europe and those that relate to Asia.

(i) *iTraxx Europe*

In relation to Europe, iTraxx provides three benchmark indices – iTraxx Europe, iTraxx Europe Crossover and iTraxx Europe HiVol.

iTraxx Europe focuses on European credit exposure and is grouped by industrial sector. On the finance side, these are senior financial institutions and subordinated financial institutions. On the non-financial side these sectors are for autos, consumers, energy, industrial, non-financials and TMT.

iTraxx Europe consists of 125 reference entities selected by market sector on the basis of credit default swap trading volume. iTraxx Europe HiVol has the top 30 highest spread names from iTraxx Europe. iTraxx Europe Crossover consists of the 50 most traded European sub-investment grade reference entities.

Each of these benchmark indices has three sector indices. These consist of a 100-reference entity sector index for non-financial reference entities, a 25-reference entity sector index for senior financials and a 25-reference entity sector index for subordinated financial reference entities.

iTraxx provides standard contracts of differing terms for each benchmark index and sector index. The standard maturities for iTraxx Europe and iTraxx HiVol are for three, five, seven and 10 years. For iTraxx CrossOver they are five and 10 years. For each iTraxx sector index they are five and 10 years.

iTraxx Europe also provides first to default baskets for autos, consumer, energy, senior and subordinated financials, industrials, TMT, HiVol, Crossover and Diversified. iTraxx has well over 30 licensed market makers, including nearly all of the major credit derivatives market participants.

(ii) *iTraxx Asia: iTraxxAsia (ex-Japan), iTraxx Japan and iTraxx Australia*

iTraxx Asia (ex-Japan) is an index of 50 equally weighted credit default swaps of Asian (non-Japanese) reference entities. iTraxx Australia is an index of 25 equally weighted credit default swaps on Australian reference entities. iTraxx Japan is an index of 50 equally weighted credit default swaps on Japanese reference entities. iTraxx Japan 80 is an index of 80 equally weighted credit default swaps on Japanese reference entities.

iTraxx Asia (ex-Japan) has three regional sub-indices: one for Korea, one for Greater China and one for Asia excluding Korea, Greater China and Japan. iTraxx Japan also has a sub-index: iTraxx Japan HiVol, which consists of 25 equally weighted credit default swaps on Japanese entities.

(iii)   *iTraxx standard credit default swap contracts*
iTraxx provides standard credit default swap contracts of differing terms for each benchmark index and sector index.

iTraxx provides standard annexes containing the relevant reference portfolio, with the full legal name of each reference entity and reference obligation, together with the relevant CLIP code (a code which unites together a relevant reference entity and reference obligation).

The standard form credit default swap contracts described above and related indices are made available on the websites of Markit (www.markit.com) and International Index Company (www.itraxx.com). iTraxx, for example, also provides certain other credit derivative products such as tranched iTraxx (exposure to five standardised tranches of iTraxx Europe) and iTraxx options (options related to movements in iTraxx indices spreads).

(c)   **CDX**
The CDX indices are owned by CDS IndexCo. The North American indices of CDX are also operated by Markit. This was not always the case – until recently the administrator was Dow Jones. For these historical reasons, indices relating to North America were referred to as CDX indices - for example, CDX.NA.IG.8-V1 - rather than using the iTraxx format. However, the principal indices have been renamed and are now known as the CDX family of credit derivative indices. They are comprised of North American investment grade and high yield reference entities, and emerging market corporate and sovereign reference entities.

The current credit indices consist of the following.

The CDX.NA.IG index, which is a North American investment grade index, is composed of 125 investment grade reference entities domiciled in North America. These are distributed among five sub-sectors.

The CDX.NA.IG.HVOL, a sub-index of the CDX.NA.IG, is comprised of the 30 highest volatility reference entities from that index.

The CDX.NA.HY, which is a North American high yield index, is composed of 100 non-investment grade entities domiciled in North America. It has three sub-indices.

CDX.NA.XO is a North American crossover index composed of 35 reference entities that either are domiciled in North America or have a majority of their outstanding bonds and loans denominated in dollars. Their ratings are split and 'cross over' between investment grade and high yield.

CDX.EM is an emerging markets index, composed of sovereign issuers.

CDX.EM Diversified is a diversified emerging market index is composed of sovereign and corporate issuers.

There are a variety of standard form credit default swap contracts with varying maturities available for use with each of the various CDX indices and sub-indices, covering both tranched and untranched products and dealer and non-dealer forms. They are also available on the website of Markit (www.markit.com).

(d) **Other significant credit indices**

In addition to iTraxx and CDX, International Index Company and CDS Index Co have recently released several other index families. These include ABX, TABX, CMBX and LevX.

The ABX family of indices relates to asset backed securities. The ABX.HE group (created in early 2006) is linked to sub-prime residential mortgage backed securities: the letters 'HE' stand for 'home equity'.

TABX, also known as the ABX tranche indices, was launched in early 2007. There are two sets of TABX indices - the first relates to the BBB ABX.HE index and the second to the BBB- ABX.HE index. Each TABX index references all of the reference obligations from the two previous rolls of the relevant index, and has four separate tranches for each of the BBB and BBB- sections.

The CMBX family is linked to commercial mortgage backed securities. There are five sub-indices, each of which references 25 similarly rated tranches from different transactions.

The LevX indices are indices of the most liquid lien credit agreements traded in the European leveraged loan credit default swap market. The LevX senior index consists of the 35 most liquid European first lien credit agreements and the LevX subordinated index consists of the 35 most liquid European second and third lien credit agreements.

(e) **Standard annexes and confirmations**

In addition to producing the indices, iTraxx and CDX provide two key types of products: tranched products and untranched products. Untranched products give an investor exposure to the whole relevant iTraxx index or sub-index, whereas untranched products give exposure to only a slice of that index. Untranched products allow investors to take a liquid exposure to a slice of credit risk on an unfunded basis.

The two principal index products are standard annexes, which set out each relevant index or sub-indices, and standard credit default swap confirmations for tranched and untranched transactions.

A standard annex can be referenced in any transaction or credit default swap.

Template credit default swap confirmations for tranched and untranched products are always physically settled. They operate very similarly to standard portfolio credit default swaps.

The iTraxx and CDX standard credit default swap contracts generally work in a similar way to many ISDA templates.

The most common structure is for the parties to enter into a short-form confirmation. This sets out:

- the identity of the relevant index or sub-index;
- the trade date;
- the scheduled termination date;
- the original notional amount; and
- the identity of the buyer and seller.

This short-form confirmation will incorporate the standard terms supplement by reference, and the standard terms supplement will incorporate the 2003 Definitions and the May 2003 supplement by reference.

3.4   Credit spread options

Credit spread products compare a reference entity obligation's creditworthiness with a risk-free benchmark. In North America, US Treasury bonds are used as the 'risk-free benchmark'. In Europe and other markets it is LIBOR itself; this is known as the asset swap spread.

Credit spread is calculated by subtracting the risk-free benchmark's yield or the asset swap spread from the reference entity bond's yield (to leave a percentage figure which reflects the credit risk of the reference entity). For, example, in a European transaction, if the asset swap spread is 3% and the yield of a bond is 5%, then the credit spread equals 2%. Credit spread products assume that movement in the risk-free benchmark's yield or asset swap spread will be due to external market risk factors, such as interest rate fluctuations, which will equally affect the reference entity's obligation (eg, a bond). As the 'risk-free' benchmark or asset swap spread will, by definition, be free of credit risk, any divergence between the two yields is assumed to be due to credit risk. For example, if the asset swap spread rises to 3.5% and the reference entity bond's yield stays at 5%, then the credit spread has decreased. However, if both the asset swap spread and the yield rise by 0.5%, then the credit spread has not changed.

Credit spread products are structured mainly as put and call options. A credit spread put option gives the put option buyer the right, but not the obligation, to sell its counterparty a specified reference bond (ie, a bond issued by the reference entity) at a future date. The option may be exercised when the reference bond's credit spread over the 'risk-free' benchmark or asset swap spread, exceeds a pre-determined level (the 'strike spread'). The price payable by the put option seller is referenced to this strike spread, and will be a price greater than the market price of the reference bond at the time which the option is exercised – generally speaking, a price which excludes the decline the reference bond's creditworthiness.

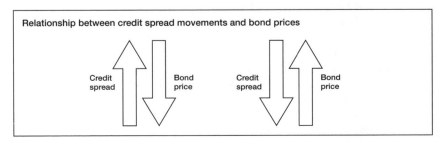

Relationship between credit spread movements and bond prices

A credit spread call option gives the call option buyer the right, but not the obligation, to buy from its counterparty a reference bond specified in the confirmation at a future date at a price linked to the strike spread. The option may be exercised when the reference bond's credit spread over the 'risk-free' benchmark or asset swap spread goes below the strike spread. The price payable by the call option buyer is referenced to this strike spread, and will be a price lower than the market price of the reference bond at the time which the option is exercised – generally speaking, a price which excludes the improvement in the reference bond's creditworthiness.

3.5   Swaptions

At the end of 2006, swaptions made up roughly 0.8% of the credit derivatives market. A swaption is a combination of a swap and an option. The option part of the agreement gives one party, the swaption buyer, the right, but not the obligation, to compel the swaption seller to enter into a credit default swap with it. Under this credit default swap part of the agreement, the swaption seller will either buy or sell credit protection at a price agreed at the outset of the swaption.

It is standard for credit derivatives swaptions to have a 'knock-out' option. 'Knock-out' options are option contracts where the option terminates if a specified event occurs. In credit derivatives swaptions, the knock-out event is where a credit event occurs in relation to the underlying reference entity prior to the swaption seller exercising its option to enter into the credit default swap. The knock-out event is triggered by one party delivering to the other a credit event notice and notice of publicly available information, just as in a standard credit default swap.

Credit derivatives swaptions usually use European-style options (ie, the option can be exercised only on a fixed date). The swaption buyer will pay the swaption seller a premium for assuming the risk that the underlying reference entity's credit spread will increase between the swaption's trade date and the option's exercise date. If the projected fixed rate under the credit default swap is less than the market rate at the date on which the swaption buyer is to exercise its option, it will let the option expire. If the market rate is above the transaction's projected fixed rate, then the swaption seller will gain the benefit of the difference between the two prices.

Credit derivative swaptions allow market participants to take a leveraged view of the future direction of a reference entity's credit spread. The motivation to enter into a swaption also depends on the buyer and seller having divergent views on the future direction of the reference entity's credit spread. The buyer must take the view that over time the reference entity's credit spread will widen (ie, meaning the purchase price of credit protection will increase) and the seller must take the view that this credit spread will narrow (ie, meaning that the sale price of credit protections will reduce).

Hypothetical case study: swaptions – Palencia Holdings

Valladolid Partners and Simancas Limited entered into a European-style credit derivatives knock-out swaption transaction. The parties entered into the contract

---

on April 23 2007. The swaption transaction gave Valladolid the option to enter into a physically settled credit default swap as buyer on April 23 2009. The credit default swap referenced Palencia Holdings as the reference entity

All of the potential credit default swap's terms were set out as a schedule to the swaption. In particular, the fixed payments that Valladolid would pay to Simancas were set at 0.25% per annum, roughly the existing level for credit defaults swaps trading Palencia as a reference credit.

Simancas was the swaption seller and received a premium for granting the option. If a credit event affecting Palencia occurred prior to April 23 2009, then either party could knock out the transaction by delivering a credit event notice and notice of publicly available information to the other party. Simancas might wish to do so (perhaps as close as possible to the option's exercise date), so that Valladolid did not exercise the option and then trigger a credit event under the credit default swap. Valladolid might wish to do so, so that it did not pay a premium when Simancas would almost certainly later knock out the transaction.

By the time April 23 2009 had arrived, Palencia's creditworthiness had declined and the price of obtaining credit protection was 1.25% per annum.

Valladolid exercised its option to enter into a credit default swap with Simancas and was able to obtain credit protection at a rate below the current market rate.

3.6 Recovery swaps

Recovery swaps (also known as recovery locks) are a relatively new product in the credit derivatives markets, first making an appearance in 2003. Today they make up 0.8% of the credit derivatives market. A recovery credit default swap allows each party to express different views of what the recovery rate will be for the obligations of a reference entity if a credit event occurs and the conditions to settlement are met.

Recovery swaps are usually physically settled transactions. They work as follows: following a credit event and the satisfaction of the conditions to settlement, the buyer purchases deliverable obligations from the seller in an amount equal to the credit default swap's notional amount. The price that the buyer pays to the seller for the deliverable obligations is agreed at the transaction's outset and set out in the confirmation. This is the strike price. The buyer can then sell the deliverable obligations into the market or use them itself as seller in a back-to-back credit derivative transaction.

Hypothetical case study: recovery swaps – Salmantino Corporation

Salmantino had been in deep trouble financially and had already defaulted on an interest payment under one of its eurobonds. As a widely traded reference entity in the credit derivatives market, market participants began triggering credit derivatives transactions referencing Salamantino.

Zamora Partners had previously entered into a physically settled credit default swap referencing Salamantino. This credit default swap had been triggered and Zamora was awaiting the delivery of a notice of physical settlement. The cheapest Salamantino obligation was trading at about 40% of face value. Zamora was concerned that the price of Salamantino obligations could deteriorate further and wished to cap its losses.

Zamora entered into a recovery credit default swap with Segovia corporation. The transaction referenced Salamantino Corporation as the reference entity. Under the recovery default swap, following delivery of a credit event notice and notice of physical settlement, Segovia was obliged to pay the reference price to Zamora. The reference price was set at 40%. This meant that Zamora would lose no more than 60% of the original credit default swap's notional amount on physical settlement. Segovia, on the other hand, was able to trade a positive view of the final value of Salamantino obligations (ie, if the trading price of Salamantino obligations was in fact above 40%). Segovia would be in the money.

3.7 Constant maturity credit default swaps

Constant maturity credit default swaps (also known as CMCDS transactions) make up 0.6% of the credit derivatives market. They are standard credit default swaps with one exception. Instead of the fixed payments from buyer to seller being for a fixed percentage amount of the transaction's notional amount throughout the life of the transaction, each fixed payment is reset at the outset of each fixed rate payer calculation period.

This is done at each reset date by referring to the existing credit spread of the relevant reference entity or reference entities (ie, the percentage rate figure for buying credit protection on the reference entity).

Constant maturity credit default swaps can perhaps be viewed as a series of credit default swaps referencing the same reference entities, with each credit default swap being for the length of the fixed rate calculation period. There are, of course, differences: a credit event which occurred during a previous calculation period could be triggered in a future one; however, the parties effectively take a new view of the reference entity's credit risk at the start of each fixed rate calculation period.

Therefore, the idea behind constant maturity credit default swaps is that the price of credit protection should vary in accordance with the market risk at any given point in time. The fixed leg of the credit default swap effectively becomes an additional floating leg.

Mechanically, the method for setting the quantum of fixed rate payments in any fixed rate payer calculation period usually takes the following form.

The parties may take the relevant reference entity's credit default swap spread for a given period (eg, three years). Alternatively, where the relevant reference entity is traded in an index (eg, iTraxx), the parties may use the corresponding published rate for that reference entity. The rate taken is called the reference rate.

At each reset date the reset date is multiplied by a 'participation rate' or 'gearing factor' to provide the percentage amount of the credit protection premium. The participation rate is a percentage proportion of the reference rate.

Constant maturity credit default swaps require the buyer and seller to take divergent views of whether the cost of purchasing credit protection against a particular reference entity will increase or decrease. Sometimes constant maturity credit default swaps also have caps and floors; although reaching a cap or floor will cause a constant maturity credit default swap to behave more like a standard credit default swap.

Hypothetical case study: constant maturity credit default swaps – Heriots plc

Watsonian Partners and Morrisons plc entered into a three-year constant maturity credit default swap which referenced Heriots plc as a reference entity. Watsonian was the buyer and Morrisons the seller.

The 'fixed' leg of the swap was to be reset annually by multiplying Heriots' three-year credit default swap credit spread as the reference rate, by a participation rate of 80%.

At the transaction's outset the reference rate was 2%. This meant that the 'fixed' leg for the transaction's first year was set at 1.6 %. At the first reset date Heriots' financial condition had deteriorated. Default looked likely and the reference rate had increased to 10%. This meant that the 'fixed' leg for the transaction's second year was set at 8%. In the transaction's final year, Heriots' financial condition had made a limited improvement and the reference rate had decreased to 5%. This meant that the 'fixed' leg for the transaction's final year was set at 4%.

This meant that the average price of credit protection over the swap's term was 4.53%. Watsonians would have been better off entering into a standard credit default swap, but Morrisons was in a better position.

---

4.   Credit default swaps referencing asset-backed securities[6]

4.1   Overview

Most credit default swaps reference a corporate or sovereign reference entity's credit risk. Recently a new category of credit default swap has developed, which instead references the credit risk of asset-backed securities. This was a hot product in 2005 and 2006 in both the funded and unfunded credit derivatives market. The product is dealt with in greater depth in Part III.

Credit default swaps referencing asset-backed securities have several monikers. Sometimes they are known as CDS on ABS; other times, asset-backed credit default swaps, ABCDS or synthetic ABS. In addition, CDS on ABS most commonly cover three types of asset-backed product: pure asset-backed securities, mortgage-backed securities

---

6   Extracts of this section expand upon "Documenting credit default swaps on asset backed securities", an article written by the author with Jamila Piracci and first published by Euromoney Handbooks, April 2007.

and collateralised debt obligations. This means that the acronyms 'CDS on MBS' and 'CDS on CDOs' are also in common parlance.

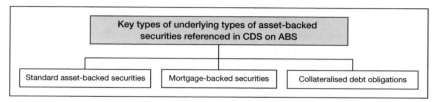

The principal reasons for buying and selling protection on the credit risk of asset-backed securities are similar to the reasons that market participants are active in the sovereign and corporate credit default swap market: regulatory capital treatment, portfolio management, hedging credit risk, alternative investments and trading and market making. Additionally, CDS on ABS can allow investors to access the credit risk of securities that they may not otherwise be able to purchase.

4.2   Key characteristics

The reasons for having specific CDS on ABS template documentation arise from the inherent characteristics of asset-backed-securities. Comparing any of the current CDS on ABS templates to the original single-name CDS confirmation set out in Exhibit A to the 2003 Definitions, the family resemblance is evident, with certain 'genetic' differences in the nature of ABS accounting for the substantial differences from standard CDS.

(a)   Asset-backed securities versus corporate bonds

Generally speaking, an issue of ABS is structured so that a bankruptcy-remote SPV will issue securities: these securities are usually tranched in priority of payment (meaning that each tranche has a different credit profile). The proceeds of the securities are used to purchase a portfolio of cash and/or synthetic assets. The cash flow that these assets generate is then used to service the payment of interest and principal and/or make distributions under the securities.

If the portfolio of assets performs badly, then the principal amount of ABS must be written down and/or the scheduled payments of interest under the notes will be postponed or cancelled. Most ABS will be structured so that in such circumstances this reduction of principal or interest will not constitute a default. Indeed, the amount of principal and/or interest owed may later be adjusted back up again. This is notwithstanding that the investor suffers a loss: the issuing vehicle will be a bankruptcy-remote SPV and any losses impacting on the underlying assets will result in a structured reduction of cash flows and principal due. This must be reflected in the types and number of credit events of a CDS on ABS template.

Corporate bonds are usually structured so that there is one repayment of principal, which is made on the maturity date. If this payment or any interest payment is missed, then a failure to pay credit event will occur in a standard credit default swap. ABS, however, are often structured to amortise over time, with the final maturity date being only an estimated one and interest payments being made only as and when available.

(b)   CDS on ABS versus single name CDS

In a standard credit default swap, a reference entity will have many relevant debt obligations outstanding and credit protection will generally be sold on a wide selection of obligations. Not so with a CDS on ABS. Either an issuer of ABS will be used once to issue a specific transaction or, in a multi-issuance structure, investors will have limited recourse to only the assets of their issue, making general credit protection meaningless. This means that CDS on ABS are designed to reference a specific tranche of a particular issue of asset-backed securities rather than the credit quality of a particular reference entity.

Asset-backed securities are not usually very liquid securities, particularly in a distressed situation; individual tranches may be issued in relatively small sizes. This means that a CDS on ABS post-credit event settlement needs to be more flexible than in a standard credit default swap.

4.3   Standard ISDA templates

The first CDS on ABS transactions were traded in 2003, but the market was initially hampered by a lack of buyers and standard documentation. It took off in 2005 and 2006, when ISDA published several template CDS on ABS confirmations which boosted liquidity in the market. ISDA has updated these templates on a number of occasions, and is likely to go on doing so.

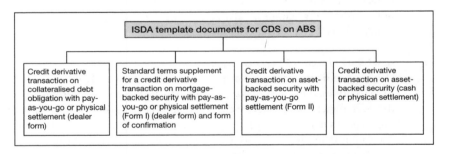

These standard form confirmations were:

- credit derivative transaction on asset-backed security (cash or physical settlement);
- standard terms supplement for a credit derivative transaction on a mortgage-backed security with pay-as-you-go or physical settlement (Form I) (Dealer Form) and form of confirmation;
- credit derivative transaction on asset-backed security with pay-as-you-go settlement (Form II); and
- credit derivative transaction on collateralised debt obligation with pay-as-you-go or physical settlement (Dealer Form).

These templates are discussed in further detail in Part III.

The ISDA suite of credit derivative documentation for unfunded credit derivatives

1. ISDA

Formed in 1985, the International Swaps and Derivatives Association Inc (ISDA) has taken the driving seat in creating a structure for documenting derivatives transactions. The organisation is the dominant derivatives trade association. It numbers 750 institutions spread across 54 countries among its worldwide membership of banks, corporates and other derivatives participants. All major credit derivatives market participants are ISDA members.

As it reaches its 22nd anniversary, ISDA can reflect well on its achievements. Its early production of the ISDA Master Agreement has since been followed by documentation to reduce credit exposure between counterparties, together with template documentation for a wide range of derivatives products including those relating to commodities, interest rates, equity, currency, inflation and funds.

The organisation has also obtained legal opinions from leading law firms and counsel on the enforceability of netting, collateral arrangements and credit derivatives themselves. It has obtained recognition from many regulatory authorities on the risk reduction benefits of netting and the use of credit derivatives in offsetting regulatory capital requirements. ISDA has promoted the understanding of derivatives from a public policy perspective. The organisation has also encouraged better risk management practices and has made huge strides in achieving its principal aims of reducing the risk and costs of derivatives, streamlining documentation and continually encouraging the development of markets in different derivatives products.

2. ISDA's suite of credit derivative documentation

ISDA's credit derivatives suite of documentation for unfunded credit derivatives consists of three inter-linking platforms: a primary platform, a secondary platform and a tertiary platform. The primary platform is the same for all ISDA's suites of derivatives documentation (eg, equity derivatives, interest rate derivatives and inflation derivatives). The other two platforms, though, are distinct.

2.1 The primary platform

ISDA's suite of credit derivatives documentation for unfunded credit derivatives utilises a primary platform of an ISDA Master Agreement (as amended by a schedule) and also an optional credit support annex to that Master Agreement (or in certain circumstances a credit support deed).

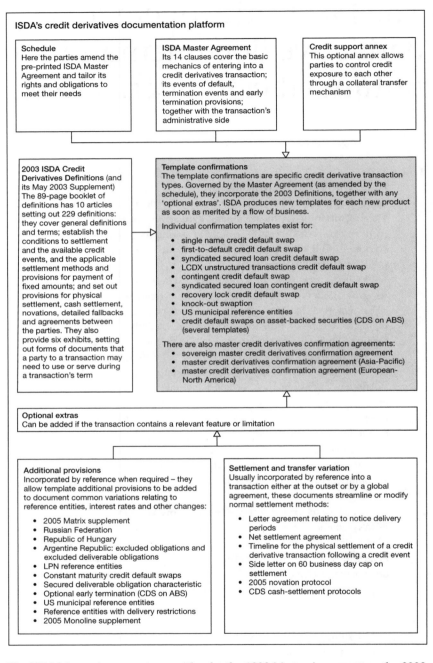

ISDA's credit derivatives documentation platform

Schedule
Here the parties amend the pre-printed ISDA Master Agreement and tailor its rights and obligations to meet their needs

ISDA Master Agreement
Its 14 clauses cover the basic mechanics of entering into a credit derivatives transaction; its events of default, termination events and early termination provisions; together with the transaction's administrative side

Credit support annex
This optional annex allows parties to control credit exposure to each other through a collateral transfer mechanism

2003 ISDA Credit Derivatives Definitions (and its May 2003 Supplement)
The 89-page booklet of definitions has 10 articles setting out 229 definitions: they cover general definitions and terms; establish the conditions to settlement and the available credit events, and the applicable settlement methods and provisions for payment of fixed amounts; and set out provisions for physical settlement, cash settlement, novations, detailed fallbacks and agreements between the parties. They also provide six exhibits, setting out forms of documents that a party to a transaction may need to use or serve during a transaction's term

Template confirmations
The template confirmations are specific credit derivative transaction types. Governed by the Master Agreement (as amended by the schedule), they incorporate the 2003 Definitions, together with any 'optional extras'. ISDA produces new templates for each new product as soon as merited by a flow of business.

Individual confirmation templates exist for:

- single name credit default swap
- first-to-default credit default swap
- syndicated secured loan credit default swap
- LCDX unstructured transactions credit default swap
- contingent credit default swap
- syndicated secured loan contingent credit default swap
- recovery lock credit default swap
- knock-out swaption
- US municipal reference entities
- credit default swaps on asset-backed securities (CDS on ABS) (several templates)

There are also master credit derivatives confirmation agreements:

- sovereign master credit derivatives confirmation agreement
- master credit derivatives confirmation agreement (Asia-Pacific)
- master credit derivatives confirmation agreement (European-North America)

Optional extras
Can be added if the transaction contains a relevant feature or limitation

Additional provisions
Incorporated by reference when required – they allow template additional provisions to be added to document common variations relating to reference entities, interest rates and other changes:

- 2005 Matrix supplement
- Russian Federation
- Republic of Hungary
- Argentine Republic: excluded obligations and excluded deliverable obligations
- LPN reference entities
- Constant maturity credit default swaps
- Secured deliverable obligation characteristic
- Optional early termination (CDS on ABS)
- US municipal reference entities
- Reference entities with delivery restrictions
- 2005 Monoline supplement

Settlement and transfer variation
Usually incorporated by reference into a transaction either at the outset or by a global agreement, these documents streamline or modify normal settlement methods:

- Letter agreement relating to notice delivery periods
- Net settlement agreement
- Timeline for the physical settlement of a credit derivative transaction following a credit event
- Side letter on 60 business day cap on settlement
- 2005 novation protocol
- CDS cash-settlement protocols

The ISDA Master Agreement may either be the 1992 Master Agreement or the 2002 Master Agreement (the former being the more popular). The 1992 Master Agreement has 14 clauses. These cover the basic mechanics of entering into the transaction, its

---

ISDA's primary documentation platform

| **Schedule** Here the parties amend the pre-printed ISDA Master Agreement and tailor its rights and obligations to meet their needs | **ISDA Master Agreement 1992 or 2002** Its 14 clauses cover the basic mechanics of entering into a credit derivatives transaction, its events of default, termination events and early termination provisions, together with the transaction's administrative side | **Credit support annex** This optional annex allows parties to control credit exposure to each other through a collateral transfer mechanism |

---

events of default, termination events and early termination provisions, as well as the administrative side of things. This pre-printed form is amended by the parties in a pre-printed schedule, where they make certain elections and tailor the Master Agreement to their requirements. The 2002 Master Agreement, an updated form, is less popular in the market, but contains certain refinements, variations and additions – in particular, in relation to close-out payments, set-off and *force majeure*.

The parties may also optionally enter into a credit support annex (or sometimes a credit support deed) which will form part of the Master Agreement and under which they will make transfers of collateral (either unilaterally or bilaterally) to control their risk exposure to each other. The primary platform will be used by the two parties for all of their derivatives transactions (eg, interest rate swaps, currency swaps, equity derivatives transactions and credit derivatives transactions).

2.2 The secondary platform

ISDA's secondary documentation platform

2003 ISDA Credit Derivatives Definitions (and its May 2003 Supplement) The 89-page booklet of definitions has 10 articles setting out 229 definitions: they cover general definitions and terms; establish the conditions to settlement and the available credit events, and the applicable settlement methods and provisions for payment of fixed amounts; and set out provisions for physical settlement, cash settlement, novations, detailed fallbacks and agreements between the parties. They also provide six exhibits, setting out forms of documents that a party to a transaction may need to use or serve during a transaction's term

Template confirmations
The template confirmations are specific credit derivative transaction types. Governed by the Master Agreement (as amended by the schedule), they incorporate the 2003 Definitions, together with any 'optional extras'. ISDA produces new templates for each new product as soon as merited by a flow of business.

Individual confirmation templates exist for:

- single name credit default swap
- first-to-default credit default swap
- syndicated secured loan credit default swap
- LCDX unstructured transactions credit default swap
- contingent credit default swap
- syndicated secured loan contingent credit default swap
- recovery lock credit default swap
- knock-out swaption
- US municipal reference entities
- credit default swaps on asset-backed securities (CDS on ABS) (several templates)

There are also master credit derivatives confirmation agreements:
- sovereign master credit derivatives confirmation agreement
- master credit derivatives confirmation agreement (Asia-Pacific)
- master credit derivatives confirmation agreement (European-North America)

Standing on the shoulders of the primary platform is a secondary platform. This consists of the 2003 ISDA Credit Derivatives Definitions and a series of template confirmations. Each template confirmation incorporates the parties' ISDA Master Agreement (as amended by the schedule) and, if applicable, a credit support annex.

A confirmation also incorporates the 2003 ISDA Credit Derivatives Definitions: an 89-page booklet of definitions divided into 10 articles providing 229 (often cross-referring) definitions. The 10 articles cover general definitions and terms; establish the conditions to settlement and the available credit events, the applicable settlement methods and provisions for payment of fixed amounts; and set out provisions for physical settlement, cash settlement, novations, detailed fallbacks and agreements between the parties. The 2003 Definitions also provide six exhibits. These set out forms of documents that a transaction party may need to use or serve during the transaction's term.

The most basic form of confirmation template – one for single name credit default swaps – is provided in Exhibit A to the 2003 Definitions. Additionally, ISDA has produced templates for various specific types of credit derivatives transaction, each new template being produced for a new product as soon as is merited by business flow. In addition to the single name credit default swap template, ISDA has produced template confirmations for:

- first-to-default credit default swap transactions;
- contingent credit default swaps;
- recovery lock transactions;
- syndicated secured credit default swap transactions;
- knock-out swaptions;
- transactions referencing US municipal reference entities; and
- credit default swaps on asset-backed securities (CDS on ABS).

In pursuit of its objective to streamline documentation, ISDA has produced a series of master credit derivatives confirmation agreements, which can be used by parties regularly trading the same type of credit derivatives transaction. Master credit derivatives confirmation agreements set out all of the standard terms that apply to each transaction of that type between the parties. The parties then enter into a transaction supplement for each individual transaction, which will set out the pricing details together with certain elections and agreed deviations from the master credit derivatives confirmation agreement. So far, ISDA has produced three master credit derivatives confirmation agreements:

- one for sovereigns;
- one for Asia and Pacific reference entities; and
- one for European and North American reference entities.

2.3 The tertiary platform

Completing this overall structure is a tertiary platform.

The tertiary platform has two distinct areas: additional provisions and settlement and transfer variations. Credit derivatives transactions may fall into certain categories. For example, a transaction might be a single name credit default swap, a first to default

---

ISDA's tertiary documentation platform

Additional provisions
Incorporated by reference when required – they allow template additional provisions to be added to document common variations relating to reference entities, interest rates and other changes:

- 2005 Matrix supplement
- Russian Federation
- Republic of Hungary
- Argentine Republic: excluded obligations and excluded deliverable obligations
- LPN reference entities
- Constant maturity credit default swaps
- Secured deliverable obligation characteristic
- Optional early termination (CDS on ABS)
- US municipal reference entities
- Reference entities with delivery restrictions
- 2005 Monoline supplement

Settlement and transfer variation
Usually incorporated by reference into a transaction either at the outset or by a global agreement, these documents streamline or modify normal settlement methods:

- Letter agreement relating to notice delivery periods
- Net settlement agreement
- Timeline for the physical settlement of a credit derivative transaction following a credit event
- Side letter on 60 business day cap on settlement
- 2005 novation protocol
- CDS cash-settlement protocols

---

credit default swap or a recovery lock transaction. The secondary platform's confirmation templates generally relate to the broadest categories of reference entities. Some reference entities or reference obligations may have specific features (eg, securities guaranteed by monoline insurers or issued by US municipal reference entities), which mean that specific amendments must be made to the 2003 Definitions and template confirmations.

Because the transactions occur only sporadically, ISDA has produced various 'additional provisions' documents which can be incorporated by reference into a confirmation and which amend the terms of the template confirmation or modify the 2003 Definitions. So far, ISDA has produced the following sets of additional provisions documents to cover the more widely traded variations:

- Additional provisions for the Russian Federation (August 13 2004);
- Additional provisions for the Republic of Hungary (February 14 2005);
- Additional provisions for the Argentine Republic: excluded obligations and excluded deliverable obligations (December 21 2005);
- Additional provisions for LPN reference entities (December 21 2005);
- Additional provisions for constant maturity credit default swaps (November 21 2005);
- Additional provisions for a secured deliverable obligation characteristic (June 16 2006);
- Additional provisions for optional early termination (CDS on ABS) (December 8 2006);
- Additional provisions for uses with US municipal reference entities; and
- Additional provisions for physically settled credit default swaps (monoline insurer as reference entity) (the 2005 Monoline Supplement).

A second leg to the tertiary platform consists of the several documents that ISDA has produced to modify the standard settlement and transfer provisions provided in the 2003 Definitions. The side letter on 60 business day cap on settlement, if incorporated by reference into a transaction, overrides various fallbacks set out in the 2003 Definitions and sets a 'hard-stop' date on physical settlement. The letter agreement relating to notice delivery periods "if parties choose to enter into it, allows parties to elect delivery methods, in addition to those in the 2003 ISDA Credit Derivatives Definitions, such as email or electronic messaging systems, for notices in relation to the occurrence of a Credit Event and the settlement of a Transaction after a Credit Event".[1] The net settlement agreement, which is intended for use in physically settled transactions "is an optional agreement allowing parties to bilaterally agree to settle Credit Derivative Transactions between them on a net basis".[2]

The CDS index protocols can be adhered to by transaction parties in relation to particular credit events to provide a sophisticated form of cash settlement in place of any previously agreed physical settlement. This is done where there is a shortage of deliverable obligations and will apply to all affected transactions between the parties. The 2005 novation protocol offers transaction parties "an efficient means to agree to a uniform process by which consents to transfer of interests in Credit Derivative Transactions…may be obtained".[3]

3.   How ISDA produces its credit derivative documentation

ISDA's credit derivative template documentation is the responsibility of its Credit Derivatives Market Practice Committee. The committee's general remit is to "address issues affecting the business and practice of credit derivatives trading. Taking in the views of dealers, end-user/hedgers and portfolio managers, the committee aims to find consensus on the most efficient, effective and appropriate means of conducting OTC credit derivatives transactions."[4] Issues that the committee has addressed include:

- the handling of material non-public information in credit portfolio management;
- capital treatment of credit derivatives; and
- US withholding tax issues.

As of March 2007, the committee was governed by two staff members of ISDA, together with representatives from Goldman Sachs, UBS, JP Morgan Securities Asia Pte Ltd, Mitsubishi Securities Co, Ltd and Sompo Japan Financial Guarantee. After joining ISDA, interested participants can join the committee as ordinary members, via the members' portal on the ISDA website.

From time to time, the committee's governing board will establish documentation working groups, which ordinary members of the committee are free to join. The governing board will then draft template documentation, which is then commented on by the working group. In this way ISDA is able to take on board the view of market participants and produce documentation, in conjunction with its outside counsel, which quickly becomes the market standard.

---

1   ISDA website, "Bookstore/Publications" section.
2   ISDA website, "Bookstore/Publications" section.
3   ISDA website.
4   ISDA website.

4. Primary documentation platform: the ISDA Master Agreement schedule and collateral annex

4.1 Master Agreement

From the beginnings of the derivatives market, market practitioners sought to streamline and commoditise their products as much as possible. Although there were different alternatives available, ISDA promoted the 'Master Agreement' concept. The Master Agreement allows the counterparties (through use of a schedule) to negotiate standard terms between them at the outset of their relationship. The parties enter into a confirmation for each transaction that incorporates these standard terms, with only the specific financial terms of the transaction then set out. Not only has this approach reduced both professional and administrative costs, but it has also reduced the amount of credit exposure between counterparties.

Today most over-the-counter (OTC) derivatives transactions are documented through the Master Agreement, which is published as a pre-printed form by ISDA. Market practice is not to amend the pre-printed form; instead, modifications to the standard form made through negotiation are set out in a further pre-printed form, the ISDA Schedule. Most transactions are documented using the 1992 ISDA Master Agreement. This form was updated by ISDA as the 2002 ISDA Master Agreement, but for several reasons – not least the burden of using two separate templates – this form has failed to catch on. This section discusses the 1992 ISDA Master Agreement only.

The Master Agreement sets out the important boilerplate contractual terms and is divided into 14 sections. These sections fall into three distinct areas.

The first area, clauses 1 to 4 (interpretation; obligations; representations; and agreements) covers the basic mechanics of entering into the transaction.

The second area, clauses 5 to 7, covers events of default, termination events and early termination of the transaction. These provisions set out when and by whom transactions can be terminated prior to their stated date of maturity, and related quantum and method of calculation of any payments between the parties.

The third area, clauses 8 to 14, covers:

- the administrative side of the transaction;
- transfer of derivatives contract;
- the contractual currency; and
- miscellaneous provisions such as the survival obligations on the termination of a transaction, offices, expenses, notices, governing law and jurisdiction.

4.2 Schedule to the Master Agreement

The schedule is also a pre-printed form and allows the parties to tailor their Master Agreement. It contains a number of choices that the parties may make in relation to the Master Agreement (including whether certain provisions should apply to both parties, to one party or to neither). The schedule may also modify provisions in the Master Agreement and set out additional provisions.

The ISDA schedule is divided into three parts. Part 1 deals with termination provisions. Part 2 covers agreements to deliver documents. Part 3 deals with miscellaneous matters such as addresses for notices, calculation agents, credit support, governing law and netting. In Part 4, the parties amend and delete various provisions of the ISDA Master Agreement as well as adding additional provisions.

Additional provisions that may be added can include that all agreements between the parties will terminate if:

- a change of control of a counterparty occurs;
- a counterparty disposes of a substantial portion of its assets; or
- its credit rating is downgraded.

4.3 Credit support annex

Each party to a derivative transaction will face some amount of credit exposure to the other party. Naturally, counterparties want to reduce this exposure as much as possible. One method of doing this is for the parties to agree at the outset that if certain events occur, such as a counterparty being downgraded by a rating agency or overall exposure exceeding a certain amount, it must deliver a certain amount of collateral to the other party based on its exposure to the other party pursuant to their outstanding transactions under the Master Agreement.

These provisions are usually annexed to the schedule in another ISDA pre-printed form called the ISDA credit support annex. By forming part of the Master Agreement, the annex avoids repeating its terms.

The credit support annex contains basic contractual terms, which are then customised by the counterparties. The English law annex works through allowing a transfer of title to the collateral. This differs from the New York law version, the credit support deed, which instead creates a security interest over the collateral.

5. Secondary documentation platform: the 2003 ISDA Credit Derivatives Definitions and template confirmations

5.1 2003 ISDA Credit Derivatives Definitions

Generally speaking, the ISDA Master Agreement (as amended by the related schedule) applies to all derivatives transactions between the two counterparties, with each individual transaction documented in a confirmation. The confirmation will state that the relevant ISDA Master Agreement and schedule apply to the transaction and will incorporate certain ISDA definitions by reference:

- An interest rate swap would incorporate the 2006 ISDA Definitions;
- A credit derivative transaction would incorporate the 2003 ISDA Credit Derivatives Definitions;
- An equity derivative transaction would incorporate the 2002 ISDA Equity Derivatives Definitions; and
- A commodity option transaction would incorporate the 2004 ISDA Commodity Derivatives Definitions.

The parties amend or disapply any of the provisions that they see fit in the relevant confirmation, perhaps taking advantage of the tertiary platform.

ISDA's cornerstone credit derivatives document is its 2003 ISDA Credit Derivatives Definitions, which updates the predecessor 1999 ISDA Credit Derivatives Definitions.

The 2003 Definitions are covered in great detail in Part II of this book. They are designed for use with the 1992 ISDA Master Agreement and the 2002 ISDA Master Agreement. Exhibit A to the 2003 Definitions provides a template single name credit default swap template.

Introduction	
Preamble	
Article I – Certain general definitions	
1.1	Credit derivative transaction
1.2	Confirmation
1.3	Term
1.4	Effective date
1.5	Trade date
1.6	Scheduled termination date
1.7	Transaction date
1.8	Event determination date
1.9	Notice delivery period
1.10	Requirements regarding notices
1.11	Grace period extension date
1.12	Grace period; grace period business day
1.13	Potential failure to pay
1.14	Calculation agent
1.15	Calculation agent city
1.16	Business day
1.17	Calculation agent city business day
1.18	2002 ISDA Master Agreement
1.19	Buyer
1.20	Seller
1.21	TARGET settlement day
Article II – General terms relating to credit derivative transactions	
2.1	Reference entity
2.2	Provisions for determining a successor
2.3	Reference obligation
2.4	Reference price
2.5	Fixed amount
2.6	Fixed-rate payer
2.7	Fixed-rate payer calculation amount
2.8	Fixed-rate payer period end date
2.9	Fixed-rate payer calculation period
2.10	Fixed-rate payer payment date
2.11	Business day convention
2.12	Floating-rate payer
2.13	Floating-rate payer calculation amount
2.14	Obligation
2.15	Deliverable obligation
2.16	Sovereign restructured deliverable obligation
2.17	Excluded obligation
2.18	Excluded deliverable obligation
2.19	Method for determining obligations
2.20	Method for determining deliverable obligations
2.21	Interpretation of provisions
2.22	Qualifying participation seller
2.23	Qualifying guarantee
2.24	Qualifying affiliate guarantee
2.25	Downstream affiliate and voting shares
2.26	Sovereign
2.27	Sovereign agency
2.28	Supranational organisation
2.29	Domestic currency
2.30	Substitute reference obligation
2.31	Merger of reference entity and seller
2.32	Restructuring maturity limitation and fully transferable obligation
2.33	Modified restructuring maturity limitation and conditionally transferable obligation
Article III – Conditions to settlement	
3.1	Settlement
3.2	Conditions to settlement
3.3	Credit event notice
3.4	Notice of physical settlement
3.5	Publicly available information

Here is a very brief primer: the 2003 Definitions are 89 pages long and divided into a table of contents, an introduction and preamble, and 10 articles, which are each then sub-divided. These 10 articles contain 229 definitions, many of which cross-refer to each other. Sometimes they are modified by other definitions when certain circumstances apply. The 10 articles provide general definitions and terms; establish the conditions to settlement and the available credit events, the applicable settlement methods and provisions for payment of fixed amounts; and set out provisions for physical settlement, cash settlement, novations, detailed fallbacks and agreements between the parties.

In addition, the 2003 Definitions provide six exhibits, setting out forms of documents that a party to a transaction may need to use or serve during the term of a transaction.

The definitions are designed with single name credit default swaps in mind. The more complex a credit derivatives product, the greater the amendments to the 2003 Definitions must be.

A thorough understanding of the 2003 Definitions is necessary for all credit derivatives practitioners and it is recommended that Part II of this book is read closely.

5.2   The template confirmations

ISDA has prepared many template confirmations relating to different equity, commodity, interest rate, currency and credit derivatives. A template confirmation sets out the term of the transaction, its key dates and various amounts and mechanics.

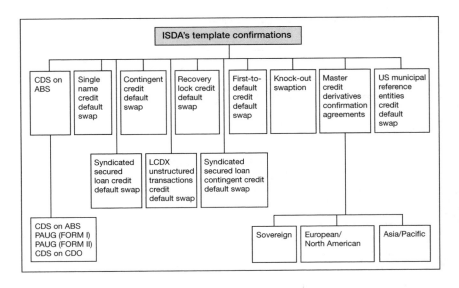

In credit derivatives transactions it will also incorporate the 2003 Definitions and its May 2003 supplement by reference, and apply the relevant ISDA Master Agreement and related schedule. Additionally, the confirmation will also set out administrative details such as bank accounts and the office from which each party is acting.

ISDA has produced a broad suite of credit derivatives documentation. Work is still ongoing and new standard form templates and documents are prepared by the working groups of ISDA's credit derivatives market practice committee on a regular basis, usually with several documents being released and/or updated each year. All of ISDA's credit derivatives documentation is designed for use in the unfunded OTC derivatives market, although any document may be adapted and used in funded transactions.

The ISDA template documentation is set out on its website www.isda.org under the 'Bookstore/Publications' section, and the 'ISDA credit derivatives definitions, supplements and commentaries' sub-section. All of the template publications are free to download as long as they are to be utilised in a transaction. Certain other documents, such as the 2003 Definitions themselves, can be downloaded only upon payment of a fee.

The template confirmations are for:
- single name credit default swaps;
- first-to-default credit default swaps;
- contingent credit default swaps;
- recovery lock credit default swaps;
- US municipal reference entities related credit default swaps;
- knock-out swaptions;
- master credit derivatives confirmation agreements for sovereigns, European/North American entities and Asia-Pacific entities; and
- credit default swaps on asset-backed securities (CDS on ABS, the pay-as-you-go form I, the pay-as-you-go form II and CDS on collateralised debt obligations).

(a)   *The template single name credit default swap: Exhibit A*

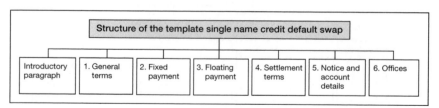

Due to their simplicity, single name credit default swaps dominate the credit derivatives market. The 2003 Definitions set out in Exhibit A a template single name credit default swap confirmation. This forms the foundation of all other ISDA template confirmations and, due to its overriding importance, is discussed in greater detail in Part III.

As with all ISDA confirmations, this document is structured as a letter which is addressed from one counterparty to the other. The confirmation incorporates the 2003 Definitions and is subject to the applicable ISDA Master Agreement that the parties have entered into. It is a nine-page document and is divided into six paragraphs. These are:

- general terms;
- fixed payments;
- floating payments;
- settlement terms;
- notice and account details; and
- offices.

The letter is executed by the party proposing the transaction and then confirmed by the signature of the counterparty. The confirmation relies heavily on the 2003 Definitions, using over 100 of its definitions and terms.

(i)   *Paragraph 1: General terms*
The 'General terms' section set out in paragraph 1 of the confirmation provides an area for the parties to insert the transaction's key general information. Paragraph 1 utilises 13 of the 2003 Definitions. In particular, it sets out:

- the trade date (ie, the date on which the parties agree to enter into the transaction);
- the effective date (ie, the date on which credit protection commences);
- the scheduled termination date (ie, the date on which credit protection is scheduled to end);
- which party is the floating-rate payer (ie, the credit protection seller);
- which party is the fixed-rate payer (ie, the credit protection buyer);
- which party performs the calculation agency function and from which city it performs those duties; and
- the applicable business day and business day convention that apply to the transaction.

Paragraph 1 sets out the identity of the reference entity on which credit protection is bought, and sold and for cash settled transactions (and some physically settled transactions) the identity of the reference obligation. It also provides whether 'all guarantees' is applicable and the reference price of any transaction.

(ii)   *Paragraph 2: Fixed payments*
Fixed payments are the payments made from the buyer to the seller for assuming the credit risk of the reference entity. The mechanics for making these payments are set out in paragraph 2. The paragraph sets out the fixed-rate payer calculation amount (the base amount upon which any fixed amounts to compensate the seller for providing credit protection on the reference entity are paid).

The term of the credit default swap is divided into calculation periods, with the buyer making a payment to the seller for providing it with credit protection during each period. The date on which each fixed-rate period ends is set out under 'fixed-rate payer period end date'; the date which these payments are made under 'fixed-rate payer payment dates'; the percentage amount of this rate under 'fixed-rate'; or alternatively an actual amount can be set out under 'fixed amount'. Where part of an annualised percentage amount is paid on more that one payment date during the year, the amount to be paid is calculated using a day count fraction, with the specified day count fraction being set out under 'fixed-rate day count fraction'.

(iii)   *Paragraph 3: Floating payments*
Floating payments are the payments made from the seller to the buyer if the conditions to settlement in relation to the reference entity are met. Paragraph 3 sets out the amount of credit protection sold, the conditions to settlement, the credit events specified by the parties and the 'obligations' of the reference entity that a credit event may affect.

'Floating-rate payer calculation amount' sets out the notional amount of credit protection sold. 'Conditions to settlement' then allows the parties to specify what these will usually be. The parties will usually insert 'credit event notice', 'notice of publicly available information' and, for physically settled transactions, a 'notice of physical settlement' here, together with whom the 'notifying party' will be and the number of 'public sources' of publicly available information required.

The parties will also specify in paragraph 3 which credit events are applicable to the transaction, choosing between bankruptcy, failure to pay, obligation default, obligation acceleration, repudiation/moratorium and restructuring. They will also specify here whether the grace period provisions are applicable to the failure to pay credit event and what the applicable payment requirement will be. For a restructuring credit event they will specify whether the modified restructuring or modified modified restructuring provisions will apply.

The parties will set out which obligation(s) of the reference entity may be affected by a credit event. Paragraph 3 provides a table, requesting that market participants select one obligation category from among 'payment', 'borrowed money', 'reference obligations only', 'bond', 'loan' and 'bond or loan'. It then requests the parties to select all (if any) of the 'obligation characteristics' which it wishes to apply from among: 'not subordinated', 'specified currency', 'not sovereign lender', 'not domestic currency', 'not domestic law', 'listed' and 'not domestic issuance'. Space is also provided for the parties to add any specific obligations of the reference entity or, under 'excluded obligations', to exclude any specific obligation(s).

(iv)   *Paragraph 4: Settlement terms*
The template confirmation can be used for both cash settled and physically settled transactions. Whether cash settlement or physical settlement is applicable is specified under 'settlement method'.

If cash settlement is selected, then the terms provided in the template for physical settlement are deleted. For cash settlement, the template provides, under 'valuation date' and 'valuation time', when the calculation agent must value the reference obligation, together with the amount of times which it must do so.

The parties specify the 'quotation method' which the calculation agent will use to obtain quotations for the reference obligation. Under 'quotation amount' and 'minimum quotation amount' they will specify the amount of the reference obligation for which the calculation agent will request a quotation. Under 'dealer' the parties will specify which dealers expected to be making markets in the reference obligation the calculation agent will approach to request quotation for the reference obligation. Under 'quotations' the parties will set out whether the quotations should include or exclude accrued interest.

The parties specify under 'valuation method' the method that the calculation agent will use to interpret the quotations it has received for the reference obligations. Various methods are provided by the 2003 Definitions, such as 'market', 'highest', 'average market' and 'average highest'.

The template provides, under 'settlement currency', an option for the parties to specify a settlement currency different to the currency of the floating-rate payer calculation amount. Under 'cash settlement date', the parties will specify the number of business days after the final price has been determined that the seller will pay the cash settlement amount to the buyer.

In fixed recovery transactions, the parties may specify a 'cash settlement amount'; otherwise the cash-settlement amount payable will be the greater of zero and the floating-rate payer calculation amount multiplied by the reference price, less the final price.

If physical settlement is the applicable settlement method, the 'terms relating to cash settlement' are deleted from the template and the 'terms relating to physical settlement' are used instead.

Here the parties specify the 'physical settlement period': the period of time after the conditions to settlement have been met during which physical settlement must take place. They specify the category of obligations of the reference entity that the buyer may deliver to the seller to effect physical settlement. This is done under 'deliverable obligations'.

The template provides a table, requesting that market participants select one 'deliverable obligation category' from among 'payment', 'borrowed money', 'reference obligations only', 'bond', 'loan' and 'bond or loan'. It then requests the parties to select all (if any) of the 'deliverable obligation characteristics' which it wishes to apply from among 'not subordinated', 'specified currency', 'not sovereign lender', 'not domestic currency', 'not domestic law', 'listed', 'not contingent', 'not domestic issuance', 'assignable loan', 'consent required loan', 'direct loan participation', 'transferable', 'maximum maturity', 'accelerated or matured' and 'not bearer'. Space is also provided for the parties to add any specific obligations of the reference entity; or, under 'excluded deliverable obligations', to exclude any specific obligation(s) which may otherwise be deliverable obligations.

Under paragraph 4, the parties also specify whether certain optional fallbacks provided under Article IX (Additional Representations and Agreements of the Parties) of the 2003 Definitions, should apply to the transaction. They do this by specifying whether any or all of 'partial cash settlement of consent required loans', 'partial cash settlement of assignable loans' and/or 'partial cash settlement of participations' are applicable.

Finally, under 'escrow', the parties may select whether deliverable obligations may be held in escrow.

(v)   *Paragraph 5 (notice and account details); paragraph 6 (offices) and execution*
In paragraph 5, the parties specify the accounts to which fixed and floating payments under the transaction must be made. They also specify their contact details for the delivery of notices, including telephone numbers to facilitate telephone notices.

In paragraph 6, each party specifies the office through which it is acting for the purposes of the credit derivatives transaction.

Finally, the closing section of the template requests that the confirming party, by executing and returning the document, agrees to be bound by the terms of it.

(b)   Template first-to-default confirmation

(i)   *What does the template do?*
Substantially similar to the template single name credit default swap, the template first-to-default confirmation was published by ISDA on July 15 2004. It is intended to be used to document credit derivative transactions which reference a basket or portfolio of reference entities (rather than a single reference entity) where settlement takes place after the conditions to settlement have been met for one of the reference entities in the basket. Its other key feature was disclosed on publication as "creating a documentation solution for the eventuality of a succession or unwinding once a merger has occurred to one or more reference credits within a basket of credits".[5] The template confirmation does this by modifying the standard provisions of the 2003 Definitions to provide mechanics to facilitate substitution of a reference entity following a succession event or where there is a merger of a reference entity and the transaction's seller.

In addition, ISDA has produced a note to the first-to-default confirmation template, which provides eight examples demonstrating how paragraph 6 (additional provisions where substitution is not applicable) and paragraph 7 (additional provisions where substitution is applicable) of the template function.

(ii)   *Main differences from the single name template*
The introductory paragraph to the confirmation states:

> *The Settlement Terms shall apply solely to one Reference Entity, which shall be the first Reference Entity with respect to which an Event Determination Date occurs or, if an Event Determination Date occurs in respect of more than one Reference Entity on the same day, the Reference Entity in respect of which the Credit Event Notice and the Notice of Publicly Available Information was first delivered on such day (such entity, the 'Affected Reference Entity').*

As with the single name credit default swap template, the confirmation contains general terms, fixed payments, floating payment and settlement paragraphs. Additionally, the first-to-default confirmation template has three additional paragraphs relating to successor provisions, additional provisions where substitution is not applicable and additional provisions where substitution is applicable.

---

5   Robert Pickel, executive director and chief executive officer of ISDA, ISDA Press Release, July 14 2004.

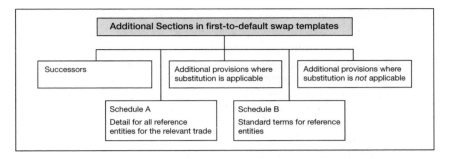

The second major difference from the template confirmation for single name credit default swaps relates to succession events. The provisions of Section 2.2 (successor) of the 2003 Definitions are very complicated (see the in-depth discussion in Part III). Having multiple reference entities makes them even more so.

Section 2.2(e)(i) of the 2003 Definitions provides that if the calculation agent determines that following a succession event there is more than one successor (eg, if following a demerger or spin-off of part of the reference entity there is more than one successor), then pursuant to clause 2.2(e), it must divide the transaction into as many new credit derivatives transactions as there are successors (where the original reference entity continues to be a reference entity it is also deemed to be a successor for these purposes).

Each entity that the calculation agent determines to be a 'successor' will be a reference entity for one of the new credit derivatives transactions. The amounts specified in the original confirmation for the fixed-rate payer calculation amount and the floating-rate payer calculation amount will be deemed to be divided by the number of successors and the resulting figures applied as the fixed-rate payer calculation amount and the floating-rate payer calculation amount respectively in each new credit derivatives transaction.

This language needs to be amended for first-to-default transactions and this is done in paragraph 5 of the template confirmation, which provides that "each successor will be a reference entity for the purposes of one of the new credit derivative transactions and each of the reference entities that is not a subject of the applicable succession event shall be a reference entity for the purposes of each and every one of the new credit derivative transactions".

Section 2.2(d) of the successor provisions in the 2003 Definitions, which deals with successor reference obligations following a successor event, is also modified by paragraph 5 of the first-to-default template so that where one or more successors has not assumed an original reference obligation, a substitute reference obligation is determined according to Section 2.30 of the 2003 Definitions instead.

The template introduces the concept of substitution of reference entities. Whether this 'substitution' is applicable is specified by the parties in paragraph 1 of the template confirmation. If the parties specify that substitution is not applicable, then paragraph 6 applies. If they specify that it does apply, then paragraph 7 instead applies.

Sections 2.2(a) to (g) of the 2003 Definitions set out comprehensive objective rules for a calculation agent to determine a successor or successors to a non-sovereign reference entity. These rules may determine a single successor or multiple successors. Paragraph 6 of the template provides that where one of the reference entities in the basket succeeds (through amalgamation, merger or other corporate event) to one of the other reference entities in the basket, and 'substitution' is not specified as applicable under the template confirmation, then that entity will be deemed to be the successor reference entity and there will be one less reference entity in the basket.

Where 'substitution' is applicable, paragraph 7 provides several additional provisions:

- treatment of certain succession events;
- selection of replacement reference entity;
- delivery of reference entity list;
- fallback successor process;
- eligible reference entity;
- effective date for substitution of reference entity following a succession event or seller merger event; and
- seller merger.

Paragraph 7 of the template provides that where one of the reference entities in the basket succeeds (through amalgamation, merger or other corporate event) to one of the other reference entities in the basket, and 'substitution' is specified as applicable under the template confirmation, then that entity will not be deemed to be a successor reference entity, and a successor will instead be determined under paragraph 7's 'selection of replacement reference entity' provisions.

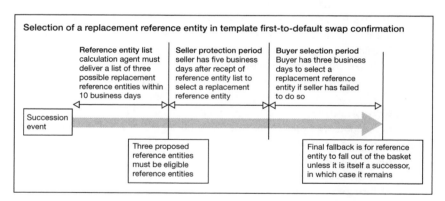

These provisions provide that for each replacement reference entity the calculation agent must, no later than 10 business days after the occurrence of a succession event or seller merger event, deliver a list of reference entities proposing at least three possible reference entities to replace the reference entity which has been succeeded. The seller then has five business days after it has received the reference entity list to select one of the proposed reference entities and notify its choice to the parties.

If the seller does not make an election during this seller selection period, then the buyer must make a selection from the reference entity list within three business days. The selected reference entity shall then be the replacement reference entity and the relevant standard terms set out in Schedule B for a reference entity of that type will apply.

Paragraph 7 also provides a fallback provision for where both parties fail to select a replacement reference entity in accordance with the 'selection of replacement reference entity' provisions. If this occurs then the original reference entity will cease to be a reference entity unless it itself is a successor; but each of the surviving reference entities in the basket shall remain there and continue to be a successor. The other terms of the transaction, including the fixed rate, will remain unaltered.

The three reference entities, which the calculation agent provides on the proposed reference entity list must all be 'eligible reference entities'. Paragraph 7 provides the criteria for a reference entity to be an eligible reference entity.

First, the proposed reference entity must be in the same industry group as Moody's, Standard & Poor's or any other specified reference entity. Second, it must have a bid-side credit spread, at the time that the list is provided to the seller, which is no greater than an agreed amount of the bid-side credit spread of the surviving reference entity. This 'credit spread requirement' is based on a credit default swap with market standard terms; a floating-rate payer calculation amount equal to at least 50% but not more than 100% of the first-to-default swap's floating-rate payer calculation amount; and with a term equal to the first-to-default swap's remaining term. The bid-side credit spreads are the unweighted arithmetic means of spread quotations obtained by the buyer from at least three dealers.

Second, credit derivatives contracts referencing the proposed reference entity must be traded in the same geographical region as the surviving reference entity. Third, the proposed reference entity must not be an affiliate of any of the reference entities, the buyer or the seller.

The substitution of a reference entity in accordance with paragraph 7 is deemed effective on the succession event or seller merger event's legally effective date.

Paragraph 7 also modifies the provisions of the 2003 Definitions relating to a merger of a reference entity and the seller, which are set out in Section 2.31. A reference entity can merge with the seller either directly or indirectly where, through application of Section 2.2, the seller is the successor reference entity. Paragraph 7 provides that in these circumstances the seller shall be deemed to be the surviving reference entity. Section 2.31 will then be deemed not to apply to the transaction and instead the 'substitution' provisions detailed in paragraph 7 shall apply.

(iii)   *Schedule A*

The template includes a Schedule A, where the parties provide 'details for all reference entities for the relevant trade'. Here they set out the name of each reference entity, the details of the reference obligation and each reference entity's entity type. The parties set out in 'entity type' which standard terms section set out in Schedule B is relevant to the particular reference entity.

(iv)   *Schedule B*

Due to the existence of multiple reference entities, Schedule B of the first-to-default template confirmation sets out separate standard terms for different types of reference entity. A footnote to Schedule B in the confirmation states that "the Standard Terms in Schedule B represent market conventions at the date of publication of the First-to-Default Confirmation". The footnote goes on to say:

> *Market conventions may change and ISDA anticipates that it may publish revised versions of Schedule B over time (including electronic publication on its website: www.isda.org). Unless otherwise agreed, where parties incorporate Schedule B into their First-to-Default Confirmation, they will automatically incorporate the version of Schedule B most recently published at the date on which they enter into the relevant Transaction, as Schedule B has been amended and supplemented through that date.*

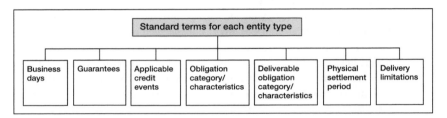

These standard terms set out:
- the applicable business days;
- whether 'all guarantees' is applicable;
- the applicable credit events;
- the obligation category and obligation characteristics;
- the deliverable obligation category and deliverable obligation characteristics;
- the physical settlement period; and
- whether any delivery limitation is applicable.

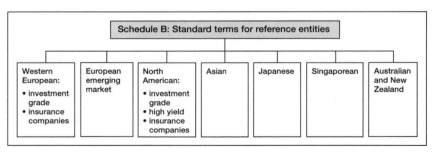

The standard terms supply *pro forma* elections for the following types of reference entity:
- Western European entities (including for investment grade companies and insurance companies);
- European emerging market entities;
- North American entities (including investment grade, high yield and insurance companies);
- Asian entities;

- Japanese entities;
- Singaporean entities; and
- Australian and New Zealand entities.

Each standard terms section is provided as an annex on a single page in schedule B – for example: 'Annex A: Standard terms for Western European entities'.

The standard terms annex works as follows. In paragraph 1, the parties specify the reference entities, which are stated to be "each entity identified as such in Schedule A and, in each case, any successor".

The reference entity section goes on to state that: "Each Reference Entity has been designated as a particular 'Entity Type' in Schedule A. References in this Confirmation to 'Standard Terms' means in respect of a Reference Entity the corresponding standard terms specified for its Entity Type in the Annexes to Schedule B."

As mentioned above, Schedule A provides a table. This table has three columns: a column for specifying the reference entity, a column for specifying the reference obligation and a column for specifying the entity type. The entity type specified in that column will apply the standard terms specified in the relevant annex set out in Schedule B to that reference entity.

Various provisions in the main body of paragraph 2 then cross-refer to the standard terms set out in Schedule B (eg, 'Credit event: In respect of a reference entity, the credit events specified in the applicable standard terms'; or for 'obligations: in respect of a reference entity, in accordance with Section 2.14 of the credit derivatives definitions on the basis of the obligation category and the obligation characteristic(s) specified in the applicable standard terms').

Physical settlement is the applicable settlement method; and the template confirmation introduces the concept of 'delivery limitation', which applies a 60 business day cap on settlement in the manner contemplated by the side letter on 60 business day cap on settlement discussed below.

(c)   ***Recovery lock transaction template***
ISDA's May 2 2006 press release announced "publication of a template for use with recovery lock credit derivative transactions. Recovery lock credit derivatives give the credit protection buyer the security of a fixed rate of recovery in case of a credit event." The press release quoted Robert Pickel, ISDA's chief executive officer: "Standard

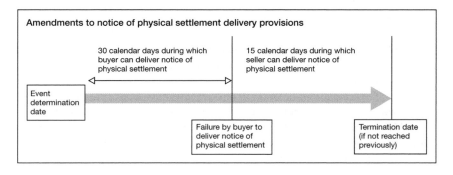

documentation for recovery lock credit derivative transactions will be helpful for the smooth and efficient functioning of the product sector."

And so the recovery lock transaction template does not provide a radically different structure from the single name credit default swap template, but instead is the same document with some additional provisions which, above all, reflect that recovery lock transactions are hedging transactions.

Paragraph 3 (floating payments) contains an additional section titled 'failure by buyer to deliver a notice of physical settlement'. This states that: "if buyer fails to deliver an effective notice of physical settlement on or before the 30th calendar day after the event determination date, such failure will not constitute an event of default or a termination event." This is the first difference from the single name credit default swap template, which provides for such a failure to be a termination event.

The provision continues: "Following such failure, buyer will have no right to deliver a notice of physical settlement. If buyer has not delivered an effective notice of physical settlement, seller will have the right, from and including the 30th calendar day after the event determination date to and including the 45th calendar day after the event determination date, to deliver a notice to buyer."

So, for the period covering 30 to 45 calendar days after the event determination date, the seller can deliver a notice of physical settlement, compelling the buyer to deliver it applicable deliverable obligations. If the seller does not deliver a notice of physical settlement during this additional period, then the 45th calendar day will be the transaction's termination date.

Recovery lock transactions are entered into to allow the seller to guarantee a source of deliverable obligations for another transaction under which it is the buyer, or for the buyer to offload deliverable obligations it has received under another transaction. The additional 15 calendar day period means that the seller in the recovery lock transaction can submit a notice of physical settlement under the transaction it is hedging and not lose credit protection under that transaction. It can then compel the buyer in the recovery lock transaction to source specific securities for it to deliver under the hedged transaction.

Other key differences in the recovery lock template include amending the words 'physical settlement amount' in the last line of the second paragraph of Section 8.1 (physical settlement) of the 2003 Definitions with the words 'floating-rate payer calculation amount'. This means that, as intended, the seller pays the full face value for the deliverable obligations. It will then receive the 'credit protection amount' under the hedged transaction.

The template also makes various changes to the 2003 Definitions' fallback procedures. In particular, the template provides that where cash settlement is applicable and the final price obtained is greater than 100%, then the final price will be deemed to be 100%.

The template's other most significant amendments are to Section 9.8 (partial cash-settlement terms) and Section 9.9 (buy-in of bonds not delivered) of the 2003 Definitions. Section 9.8 is amended so that where partial cash settlement is applicable, the cash-settlement amount will be the aggregate of the outstanding principal balance, the due and payable amount or the currency amount (as applicable) of each relevant obligation multiplied by its reference price, less the final price. This is instead of it being the greater of:

- zero; and
- the outstanding principal balance, the due and payable amount or the currency amount (as applicable) of each relevant obligation multiplied by its reference price, less the final price.

Where the cash-settlement amount is a positive amount, this amount is payable from the seller to the buyer, as one would expect. However, because this is a hedging transaction, if the cash-settlement amount is a negative amount, the buyer must pay the seller the absolute value of the cash-settlement amount.

Only the penultimate paragraph of Section 9.9 (buy-in of bonds not delivered) is amended. The original paragraph provides that on the third business day following delivery of a buy-in price notice, the buyer will be deemed to have delivered the relevant bought-in bonds. The seller then pays the buyer. The amount paid will be equal to the portion of the physical settlement amount corresponding to the bought-in bonds reduced (but not below zero) by the relevant bonds' buy-in price (which is expressed as a percentage), and multiplied by the outstanding principal balance of the relevant bonds for which a buy-in price was determined. Any reasonable brokerage costs in relation to purchasing the relevant bonds are subtracted from this amount.

This is modified in the recovery lock transaction template so that the cash-settlement amount can be payable either from seller to buyer if the amount is positive, or buyer to seller if it is negative. This reflects the transaction's back-to-back nature.

(d) Contingent credit default swap template

(i) Intended usage of the template

The contingent credit default swap transactions template was published by ISDA on February 6 2007. The commentary on the bookstore/publications page of ISDA's website provides:

> The Confirmation for a Contingent Credit Default Swap Transaction is designed for transactions where the parties desire to hedge the credit risk associated with counterparty default in derivative transactions. The principal distinction between this Confirmation and the standard single name credit default swap as documented under the 2003 ISDA Credit Derivatives Definitions relates to how the Floating-rate Payer Calculation Amount is determined upon a Credit Event.

The template's intended usage is summarised further in its first footnote: "This Confirmation template may be used for confirming Credit Derivative Transactions in respect of which the Floating-rate Payer Calculation Amount is determined as the amount that would be payable at mid-market on the early termination of a hypothetical derivative transaction."

The template is intended to be used with the credit derivatives physical settlement matrix. The 'floating-rate calculation amount' is, of course, the amount of credit protection bought and sold.

It is important to remember that the principal reason that a buyer in the contingent credit default swap will enter into the transaction is to buy protection against exposures which it has to the reference entity under outstanding derivatives transactions.

(ii)   *What is the 'hypothetical derivatives transaction'?*
Calculation of the contingent credit default swap template's floating-rate calculation amount is based on a 'reference derivative'. This is a hypothetical interest rate swap and is described in paragraph 3 (floating payments) of the template with its terms set out in the template's Exhibit A: 'Form of reference derivative terms for an interest rate swap'.

The reference derivative

The hypothetical interest rate swap or 'reference derivative' is deemed to be subject to a 'reference agreement': a hypothetical 1992 ISDA Master Agreement, without a schedule, except for the election of a 'reference derivative law'; a 'reference derivative currency' as the termination currency; and 'second method' and 'market quotation' for the purposes of close-out netting.
    The reference derivative law is the hypothetical transaction's governing law as set out by the parties in Annex A, failing which the fallback is New York law. The reference derivative currency is also set out in Annex A, failing which the fallback is US dollars.
    The hypothetical interest rate swap incorporates the 2006 ISDA Definitions by reference. When using the template, the parties will make elections in Exhibit A as to the transaction currency; governing law; notional amount; trade date; effective date and termination date, as well as, under 'fixed amounts' and 'floating amounts', elections for the standard provisions for an interest rate swap. They may also choose to utilise certain other standard interest rate swap provisions such as initial and final exchange and discounting. These elections will most probably reflect the underlying exposure.

(iii)   *Determining the amount of credit protection sold*
As alluded to above and as with many of the ISDA confirmation templates, this template takes the single name credit default swap template as its foundation and amends and builds on its provisions to create a template for use with contingent credit default swaps.
    Paragraph 1 (general terms) and paragraph 2 (fixed payments) are the same as in the single name credit default swap template. Paragraph 3 (floating payments), though, is significantly different.
    In the single name credit default swap template, the 'floating-rate payer calculation amount' (ie, the amount of credit protection sold) is usually specified as a notional amount. In the credit contingent credit default swap template, this amount

is calculated based on the 'close-out amount' of the reference derivative (the reference agreement of which is deemed to have had a termination event occur where the reference derivative is the sole affected transaction).

Close-out netting: a brief refresher

Close-out netting is the process, under an ISDA Master Agreement, where following the occurrence of an event of default or a termination event, the parties terminate their outstanding transactions under the Master Agreement; value the amounts owed under each outstanding transaction (including any unpaid amounts) and then lump these together to calculate a single net amount owed from one party to the other.

Central to calculating this close-out amount are the concepts of an 'exposed party' and the 'other party'.

The 'exposed party' and the 'other party'

The 'exposed party' and the 'other party' will generally be specified to be either the 'floating-rate payer' or 'fixed-rate payer' under the reference derivative. Which of the buyer or seller under the contingent credit default swap is specified here for each role will depend upon the underlying position which the buyer is trying to hedge.

The quantum of the 'floating-rate payer calculation amount' is defined as "an amount equal to the greater of (a) the sum of the mark-to-market value and the net interim payment and (b) zero".

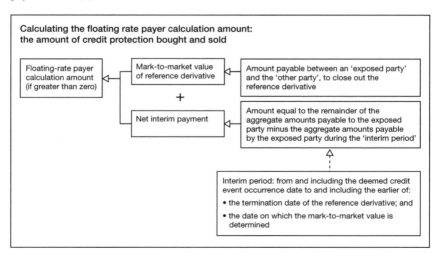

If the floating-rate payer calculation amount is deemed to be zero, then the parties' obligations to each other in respect of the contingent credit default swap cease. Unless any fallbacks apply, the floating-rate calculation amount is calculated on the 'initial derivative valuation date', which is the fifth business day following the relevant event determination date.

Mark-to market value, net interim payment and interim period

Mark-to-market value: The 'mark-to-market value' is defined as the amount payable between an 'exposed party' and the 'other party', to close out the hypothetical interest rate swap agreement. The template provides that the buyer and seller will attempt to agree on the mark-to-market value, the template then provides various fallbacks for where the parties are unable to do so under a 'determination valuation' section. The fallbacks involve the calculation agent approaching dealers for a quotation for the mark-to-market value of the hypothetical interest rate swap transaction, together with various progressive fallbacks where the relevant number of quotations cannot be obtained.

The net interim payment: The 'net interim payment' is the amount (if any) equal to the remainder of the aggregate of all amounts payable to the exposed party minus the aggregate of all amounts payable by the exposed party on any payment dates occurring in the 'interim period', assuming that the reference derivative was in effect.

The net interim payment should be agreed by the buyer and seller on the date that the mark-to-market value is determined, failing which the calculation agent will determine the quantum of the mark-to-market value.

The interim period: The 'interim period' is defined as the period "from and including the deemed credit event occurrence date to and including the earlier of (i) the termination date of the reference derivative; and (ii) the day on which the mark-to-market value is determined".

'Deemed credit event occurrence date' is the earliest of:

- the event determination date;
- the earliest date (if any) specified in the publicly available information as the date of occurrence of the relevant credit event; and
- the date on which publicly available information was first made available.

(iv)   *The look-back option*

The template also includes an election to apply a 'look-back option'. The template's relevant footnote provides that:

> *The look-back option should only be included in circumstances where the parties wish to assume that any payments due on the termination date of the reference derivative are*

not made if the event determination date occurs within [five] calendar days following the termination date of the reference derivative. In order for the look-back option to be effective, parties should ensure that the scheduled termination date of the contingent credit default swap transaction extends [five] calendar days beyond the termination date of the reference derivative to permit the delivery of a credit event notice during this period.

If the look-back option is elected to apply, then the net interim payment will be modified so that it will be equal to the amount payable *to* the exposed party, minus the amount payable *by* the exposed party, on the reference derivative's termination date.

(v)   *Settlement*
The template provides for physical settlement and the settlement process (ie, applicable credit events and conditions to settlement are applied as in any normal single name credit default swap which incorporates the physical settlement matrix).

(e)   **Knock-out swaption template**
The commentary on the 'Bookstore/publications' page of ISDA's website provides: "The knock-out swaption template is designed for credit default swaptions. It can be used for corporates and sovereigns, although attention should be given to the credit events elected. An optional transaction supplement may replace Part B of the template for those parties that have master credit derivatives confirmation agreements in place between them."

The knock-out swaption template, like the other templates, is in letter format. It consists of a Part A, which sets out the swaption transaction terms, and a Part B, which sets out the underlying swap transaction terms. The 2000 ISDA Definitions are additionally incorporated by reference into the swaption transaction, to cover the option aspects of the transaction. With the subsequent release of the 2006 Definitions, market participants may wish to update this reference accordingly in any future transaction executed.

(i)   *Part A (swaption transaction terms)*
Part A, which covers the swaption part of the transaction, is split into six paragraphs:
- general terms;
- procedures for exercise;
- settlement terms;
- additional provisions;
- notice and account details; and
- offices.

In paragraph 1 (general terms), the 'option style' is specified to be 'European', which means that it can be exercised only at the end of its term. This section also sets out:
- the identities of the swaption seller and the swaption buyer;
- the premium and the date on which the premium will be paid;

- the exercise business days;
- the business days for determining the premium payment date; and
- the identity of the calculation agent (which will usually be the calculation agent under the underlying swap transaction).

In paragraph 2 (procedures for exercise), the parties set out the date on which the option will expire (subject to the occurrence of a 'knock-out credit event determination date') under 'expiration date'. They also specify what will happen what happens if a 'knock-out credit event' occurs under 'occurrence of a knock-out credit event'.

Knock-out credit event

A 'knock-out credit event' is a credit event that occurs in relation to the underlying reference entity, at any time between one calendar day after the swaption's trade date and the swaption's exercise time on its specified exercise date.

The template provides that if a knock-out credit event occurs, then irrespective of whether the swaption buyer has exercised its rights under the underlying swap transaction, the underlying swap transaction will be deemed to have terminated with a zero value if either party delivers a corresponding credit event notice and notice of publicly available information.

Partial exercise of the option is not permitted unless a succession event occurs in relation to the reference entity, in which case the underlying swap transaction will be divided into 'new credit derivatives transactions', as provided under Section 2.2(e) of the 2003 Definitions (see further below).

Paragraph 2 (procedures for exercise) also provides for the parties to elect the swaption's exercise date and the earliest exercise time, as well as the swaption's exercise time.

In Paragraph 3 (settlement terms), physical settlement is applied and the template provides: "The particular terms of the underlying swap transaction to which the swaption transaction relates are as specified in Part B hereto. In the event of exercise or deemed exercise of the swaption transaction, the underlying swap transaction shall become effective on the terms specified in Part B hereto."

Paragraph 4 (additional provisions) modifies the 2003 Definitions' successor provisions to cover the situation where:

- a succession event occurs with respect to the underlying swap transaction's reference entity during the option's term; and
- this would result in the underlying swap transaction, if effective, being divided into two or more new credit derivative transactions as contemplated by Section 2.2(e) of the 2003 Definitions.

It provides that if a 'knock-out credit event determination date' occurs with respect to one of the new credit derivatives transaction's reference entities, then the portion of the original swaption transaction which corresponds to that new credit derivative transaction will terminate without any amounts being owed by either party. This will happen whether or not the swaption buyer has exercised its rights under the swaption transaction.

(ii)   *Part B (underlying swap transaction terms)*
Part B sets out the underlying swap transaction's terms. If the parties have a master credit derivatives confirmation agreement in place, they will instead use a transaction supplement annex, which is provided on the ISDA website.

Part B follows the single name credit default swap template very closely. However, amendments have been made to tie the document into the swaption. For example, the 'trade date' is defined as "The exercise date of the swaption transaction", and the 'effective date' as "The calendar day immediately following the exercise date of the swaption transaction".

(f)   **The syndicated secured loan credit default swap standard terms supplement and related confirmation**
ISDA published the syndicated secured loan credit default swap standard terms supplement on June 8 2006 and then updated it on May 22 2007. It is accompanied by the "Confirmation for use with the syndicated secured loan credit default swap standard terms supplement" and the Loan-Only Credit Default Swaps (LCDS) LCDS Auction Rules, to which are annexed the LCDS Auction Settlement Terms. The LCDS Auction Rules are shared between this template and the North American Loan Credit Default Swap Index (LCDX) standard form, which is discussed further below, since the rules are incorporated by reference into the standard terms of both forms.

As its title suggests, the template is intended for use in relation to credit derivatives referencing syndicated secured loans (and not any other asset class). Not so apparent is that the template is intended primarily for use in the US market. At the date of publication, ISDA has yet to produce corresponding documentation for the European market although draft documentation has been circulated and a template has been in the pipeline for some time.

The standard terms supplement works by the parties incorporating it by reference into the "Confirmation for use with the syndicated secured loan credit default swap standard terms supplement". This is done in the standard ISDA method for incorporation by reference (eg, "the syndicated secured loan credit default swap standard terms supplement as published by ISDA as of May 22 2007 (the 'syndicated secured loan CDS standard terms'), are incorporated into this confirmation").

The parties can then make any applicable amendments to the standard terms in the confirmation itself. The standard terms contain all of the boilerplate and market standard provisions that one would require for a US-syndicated secured loan credit default swap.

The standard terms are split into five sections:
- general terms;
- fixed payments;
- floating payments;

- settlement terms; and
- other provisions.

Paragraph 1 (general terms) follows the standard for the template single name credit default swap, except that the provision for reference obligation allows the parties to specify in the confirmation that 'secured list' is applicable. If this is the case, then the reference obligation will be "the loan of the designated priority specified as such on the relevant secured list from time to time".

'Relevant secured list' is also defined in paragraph 1 as: "With respect to any day, the list of Syndicated Secured Obligations of the Designated Priority of the Reference Entity published by Markit Group Limited or any successor thereto appointed by the Specified Dealers (the 'Secured List Publisher') on or most recently before such day, which list can be accessed currently at www.markit.com."

The template modifies the standard structure for physical settlement in a credit derivatives transaction. Instead of physical settlement taking place according to the terms of the 2003 Definitions, paragraph 4 (settlement terms) of the standard terms provides that it takes place "according to the terms of the version of the Syndicated Secured Loan Credit Default Swap Physical Settlement Rider published by the Loan Syndications and Trading Association, Inc (the most recently prior to the most recent effective date for an LCDX index sponsored by CDS IndexCo LLC (or its successor) (the 'Sponsor Agent') occurring on or prior to the trade date (the 'LCDS Physical Settlement Terms') (which can be accessed currently at http://www.lsta.org)".

What is the Loan Syndications and Trading Association?

The Loan Syndications and Trading Association is a US banking trade association, similar to the British Loan Market Association. Its website reveals that:

> In an effort to develop standard settlement & operational procedures, market practices, and other mechanisms to more efficiently trade the increasing volume of par & distressed bank debt, a small group of debt traders from major international financial institutions pooled their resources to form the Association in late 1995. In the ensuing years, the LSTA has become the principal advocate for the commercial loan asset class with the goal of promoting greater confidence for all market participants.

The organisation has over 192 industry participants "and LSTA membership provides member firms with the opportunity to participate in the decision-making process that ultimately establishes market practices, develops standard documentation and strengthens and influences the direction of industry infrastructure".

> **Syndicated secured loan credit default swap physical settlement rider published by the Loan Syndications and Trading Association, Inc: the physical settlement rider**
>
> The physical settlement rider is published on the website of the Loan Syndications and Trading Association (www.lsta.org). It can be accessed by clicking on 'Standard Documentation' on the home page, then scrolling down to 'Loan-Only Credit Default Swaps', where there is a hyperlink.
>
> The current version of the physical settlement rider was published in June 2006. A 14-page document, its introductory paragraph states that it is intended to be used "in conjunction with ISDA's syndicated secured loan credit default swap standard terms supplement". It may also be incorporated into other documents by reference. The rider is divided into three paragraphs and an annex. These are:
> - terms relating to physical settlement;
> - form of transfer documentation; and
> - deliverable obligation protocols.
>
> The annex applies where, post-settlement, a deliverable obligation is to be delivered using a participation which utilises LSTA standard terms.

Paragraph 4 (settlement terms) of the standard terms provides that a transaction will normally be physically settled. However, if certain conditions are met, cash settlement is also possible.

If the transaction is physically settled, the deliverable obligation category will be 'loan' and the form provides for two additional deliverable obligation characteristics: 'syndicated secured' and 'participation loan'.

'Syndicated secured' covers obligations to repay borrowed money arising from the funding of an unfunded commitment under a syndicated loan agreement; which trade as loans of at least the 'designated priority'. This will be specified in the confirmation and can be specified as a first lien loan, second lien loan or third lien loan.

'Participation loan', which is deemed to replace references in the 2003 Definitions to 'direct loan participation', covers loans in respect of which, pursuant to a participation or similar instrument, the buyer can create on behalf of the seller a contractual right of payment.

Paragraph 4 also refers to the LCDS Auction Rules which provide for cash settlement and are designed to facilitate the settlements of LCDS transactions. If certain conditions are satisfied, then the transaction will be cash settled and the final price will be determined by an auction. However, if the auction fails, for whatever reason, the transaction will be physically settled in accordance with the Physical Settlement Rider. The auction method is similar to the recently issued unsecured CDS protocols discussed later in Section 6.2(e).

Paragraph 5 (other provisions) of the standard terms provides sub-sections on:

- limitation on certain deliverable obligations;
- optional early termination; and
- relevant obligations.

The document also provides detailed provisions for dealing with any dispute as to whether a deliverable obligation meets the syndicated secured deliverable obligation characteristic.

ISDA has also provided a four-page standard form confirmation to be used with the standard terms supplement, which was also published on May 22 2007. All of the standard terms are contained in the supplement, so the parties are required only to insert specific trade terms. In addition to the specific terms that would be required in a master credit derivatives confirmation agreement, additional information with regard to the reference obligation is required. Under 'reference obligation', if a relevant secured list exists on the trade date, the parties will specify 'secured list: applicable' or if it does not, specify a single reference obligation. The parties will also specify the designated priority of the loan (ie, whether it is a first, second or third lien loan).

(g)   ***LCDX untranched transactions standard terms supplement and related confirmation***
On May 22 2007 ISDA published the trading documentation and auction rules relating to the North American Loan Credit Default Swap Index (LCDX).

What is LCDX?

LCDX is an index which includes 100 equally weighted underlying single-name loan-only credit default swaps (LCDS). The LCDX references entities whose loans trade in the secondary leveraged loan market and LCDS market.

LCDX has been created by CDS IndexCo, a consortium of 16 investment banks which are all licensed market makers in the CDX, CMBX and ABX Indexes. It is administered by Markit, which acts the licensing, marketing and calculation agent.

Following its current practice, ISDA published a long standard terms supplement, which is similar to the LCDS template. It makes the necessary changes to cover the LCDX transaction referencing only syndicated secured debt obligations.

The introductory paragraph to the standard terms states:

The parties agree that, by entering into a transaction governed by these LCDX Untranched Terms (a 'Master Transaction'), they have entered into a separate Credit Derivative Transaction (a 'Component Transaction') in respect of each Reference Entity listed in the Relevant Annex. Upon entering into a confirmation or other document (including in electronic form) (a 'Confirmation') incorporating these LCDX Untranched Terms, the parties thereto shall be deemed to have entered into a Confirmation in

*respect of each such Component Transaction with respect to the related Reference Entity
listed in the Relevant Annex.*

Consequently, the standard terms supplement is accompanied by a four-page long confirmation, where the parties specify the details applicable to their transaction. At the end of the confirmation there is the Relevant Annex, where, if applicable, the parties can list the entities by reference to which protection is being sold, their weighting in the overall portfolio and designated priority.

The settlement method under the LCDX form is very similar to the one in the LCDS template described above. In both forms physical settlement is the standard one, but they allow for cash settlements in certain circumstances. The LCDX form also incorporates by reference the LSTA's Physical Settlement Rider and the LCDS Auction Rules.

It is expected that the new LCDX form will ensure strong liquidity and will act as an efficient means of hedging credit exposure. However, ISDA has not said its last word and it is currently working on LCDX tranche documentation. For a further (and in-depth) discussion of credit index trading see Part III.

(h)   *Standard terms supplement and confirmation for syndicated secured loan
contingent credit default swap transaction and related confirmation*
This is one of the most recent templates; it was issued only on June 6 2007 and is in the format of a standard terms supplement accompanied by a short confirmation. As the other two forms in respect of syndicated secured loans described above, this one also incorporates by reference the LSTA's Physical Settlement Rider and the LCDS Auction Rules. Using the form, the parties can hedge the credit risk in respect of counterparty default in a syndicated secured loan credit default swap.

The template is based on the contingent credit default swap form described in-depth in section (d) above. In summary, it incorporates the mechanics as introduced in the contingent CDS documentation making necessary changes to cover North American standard syndicated secured loans. The main difference between this contingent LCDS template and the standard contingent CDS version is in the way the floating rate payer calculation amount is calculated.

(i)   *US municipal reference entity as reference entity credit default swap template*
ISDA's 'Form of confirmation for credit derivative transactions – US municipal entity as reference entity' template is very similar to the single name credit default swap template. This template is also designed for use with a sole reference entity which is a US state, a political sub-division of a US state or any US government agency, department or similar.

There are, however, several key differences. The US municipal template incorporates the 'Additional provisions for credit derivative transaction – US municipal entity as reference entity' by reference (see further description of this document below). The document is divided up into six paragraphs:
- general terms;
- fixed payments;

- floating payments;
- settlement terms;
- other provisions; and
- notice and account details.

Paragraph 1 (general terms) and paragraph 2 (fixed payments) are the same as for the single name credit default swap template. The key differences in paragraph 3 (floating payments) and paragraph 4 (settlement terms) are that three new obligation characteristics and deliverable obligation characteristics are added:

- 'full faith and credit obligation liability';
- 'general fund obligation liability'; and
- 'revenue obligation liability'.

The parties should select only one of these as applicable. Each of these new characteristics is defined in the 'Additional provisions for credit derivative transaction – US municipal entity as reference entity'.

A 'full faith and credit obligation liability' is a liability of the reference entity the payment of which is backed by the full faith and credit of the reference entity; or that is payable from taxes levied on taxable property within the reference entity's taxing jurisdiction.

A 'general fund obligation liability' is a liability of the reference entity (including a full faith and credit obligation liability), which is payable from the reference entity's general fund. Excluded from this definition, though, is any 'moral obligation liability': a reference entity liability that is contingent upon "an appropriation being made by the governing body or other official of the reference entity".

A 'revenue obligation liability' is a liability of the reference entity (excluding a moral obligation liability), which is payable from the same source of revenues as the reference obligation.

Paragraph 5 (other provisions) provides for a 60 business day cap on settlement.

(j)   The credit default swap on asset-backed security templates[6]

An ISDA Press Release on June 13 2005 announced that: "The International Swaps and Derivatives Association (ISDA) has announced publication of a template for documenting trades of credit default swaps (CDS) on asset-backed securities (ABS) intended for cash or physical settlement. A second template for use with CDS on ABS with a pay-as-you-go (PAUG) settlement approach will be published later this month". A lack of standardised documentation had hindered the nascent CDS on ABS market's advancement and the new forms ISDA announced in the June 2005 press release helped provide the necessary kick-start. Further market development has resulted in four templates:

- a CDS on ABS template with cash or physical settlement (since updated once) designed for CDS referencing asset-backed securities generally; and

---

6   This section partly sources an article written by the author with Jamila Piracci: "Documenting Credit Default Swaps on Asset Based Securities", first published by Euromoney Handbooks, April 19 2007.

- three templates incorporating a PAUG mechanism. One PAUG template (Form I) is designed for trades referencing US mortgage-backed securities and includes physical settlement as an option; another (Form II) is intended for ABS generally and does not include a physical settlement option; and a third is for CDS referencing underlying collateralised debt obligation (CDO) issuances.

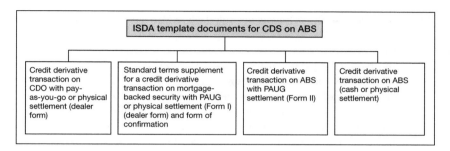

(i) *Credit derivative transaction on ABS (cash or physical settlement) template: the 'non-PAUG form'*

Also known as the 'non-PAUG' form, this is the European market's preferred template. It was published by ISDA on June 13 2005 and later updated on June 7 2006. It was developed with all ABS in mind.

Whereas the credit events for a standard CDS are bankruptcy, failure to pay and sometimes restructuring,[7] the non-PAUG template provides three principal credit events: failure to pay, loss event and restructuring. Bankruptcy and ratings downgrade are included in the form as optional credit events as well. Although bankruptcy and restructuring do not seem to be particularly relevant to bankruptcy remote vehicles and ABS, regulatory capital requirements may compel a seller to insist on their inclusion.

The 'failure to pay' credit event in the non-PAUG template modifies the 2003 Definitions' standard by defining the event as a non-payment on a scheduled distribution date of an amount due pursuant to the reference obligation's terms. A loss event occurs when the principal amount of the underlying ABS is irrevocably reduced, without resulting in the issuer breaching its obligations. A ratings downgrade credit event occurs when the reference obligation is downgraded below a level pre-agreed at the transaction's outset.

The non-PAUG form provides a hybrid cash and physical settlement method. Cash settlement is the default option unless the seller receives a notice of physical settlement prior to an agreed cut-off date after the conditions to settlement have been met. If the buyer opts for physical settlement, the mechanics closely resemble those used in the standard CDS template.

The parties can also at the transaction's outset elect for an additional settlement method called the 'synthetic delivery option'. If cash settlement applies and the

---

7   Obligation acceleration, obligation default and repudiation or moratorium are also available in the 2003 Definitions; however, they are not specified for CDS on corporate reference entities.

synthetic delivery option is applicable, at the valuation date either party may elect to provide the other with a total return swap quotation. This is a quotation to enter into a fully funded total return swap on the reference obligation and, if supplied, will be deemed to be the transaction's final price. The parties will then be deemed to have entered into the swap and will execute a confirmation and make the relevant ongoing payments.

(ii)   *Standard terms supplement for use with credit derivative transactions on mortgage-backed security with PAUG or physical settlement and credit derivative transaction on ABS with PAUG settlement (Form II): The Form I and Form II PAUG templates*
Shortly after it published the non-PAUG Form, ISDA produced a further template which, in its updated form, is now called the 'standard terms supplement for a credit derivative transaction on mortgaged-backed security with pay-as-you-go or physical settlement'. In the event that an interest shortfall, a writedown or a principal shortfall occurs with respect to the relevant underlying instrument and the buyer of protection notifies the seller within a set timeframe, the seller pays the buyer. As the name suggests, these protections may be multiple and can occur throughout the term of the CDS on ABS. PAUG Form I is intended primarily for US residential mortgage-backed securities and commercial mortgage-backed securities.

	CDS on ABS	Form I	Form II	CDS on CDO
Credit event	Failure to pay Loss event Restructuring Rating downgrade* Bankruptcy*	Failure to pay principal Writedown Distressed ratings downgrade Bankruptcy* Restructuring*	No credit events	Failure to pay principal Writedown Failure to pay interest Distressed ratings downgrade
Floating amount event	n/a	Writedown Failure to pay principal Interest shortfall	Writedown Principal shortfall Interest shortfall	Writedown Failure to pay principal Interest shortfall
Additional fixed payment event	n/a	Writedown reimbursement Principal shortfall reimbursement Interest shortfall reimbursement	Writedown reimbursement Principal shortfall reimbursement Interest shortfall reimbursement Amendment payment Make-whole premium payment	Writedown reimbursement Principal shortfall reimbursement Interest shortfall reimbursement

Events are additional options

Form II is a variation of Form I, but is designed for use in CDS on all types of ABS. Form II was released on December 19 2005. The forms differ in several key respects. Only Form I has credit events. In Form II, the seller makes payments only:

- if a floating amount event (writedown – a reduction in the principal or interest due), principal shortfall (non-payment or lesser payment of expected principal) or interest shortfall (non-payment or lesser payment of the expected interest amount) occurs; and
- the calculation agent or the buyer of protection notifies the seller that a floating payment is due.

These events allow ongoing settlement through the term of a CDS on ABS and compensate the buyer for below expected cash flows being generated from the underlying asset.

Form I specifies writedown, failure to pay principal and interest shortfall as floating amount events, and also allows for physical settlement in the event of a failure to pay principal or a writedown. Parties may also elect to include a distressed ratings downgrade as a credit event.

Form I alone includes implied writedown provisions requiring payments compensating for losses on the ABS resulting in a reduction of the outstanding principal when such losses are not provided for in the underlying instruments of the mortgage-backed securities. There are further differences between the two forms in relation to the definition of interest shortfall amounts.

Additional fixed amounts provide for the buyer to reimburse the seller if later adjustments to the underlying ABS mean that the buyer has been paid too much following a floating amount event. Additional fixed payment events may occur under both forms, triggering a writedown reimbursement, a principal shortfall reimbursement or an interest shortfall reimbursement. In addition, Form II implements any amendments to the underlying ABS, whereas Form I does not. Form II also treats make-whole premium payments (payments to the obligation holders of a make-whole premium in relation to events such as prepayments under the terms of the obligation) as additional fixed amount events.

Step-up provisions differentiate Form I from the other forms. A 'step-up' is an increase in the coupon of the reference obligation due to the failure of the issuer or a third party to redeem, cancel or terminate an obligation in accordance with the underlying instruments. The step-up provisions give the buyer the option to terminate the transaction or to continue at the higher rate. Under Form II, changes in the coupon of a fixed-rate obligation or the spread of a floating-rate obligation are implemented and the transaction continues at the new coupon.

(iii) *Credit derivative transaction on collateralised debt obligation with pay-as-you-go or physical settlement (dealer form)*

On June 7 2006, ISDA published the 'Credit derivative transaction on collateralised debt obligation with pay-as-you-go or physical settlement (dealer form)', which was later updated on June 6 2007. This form provides a PAUG template for CDOs. Like the PAUG forms, the buyer of protection may choose to have physical settlement of a

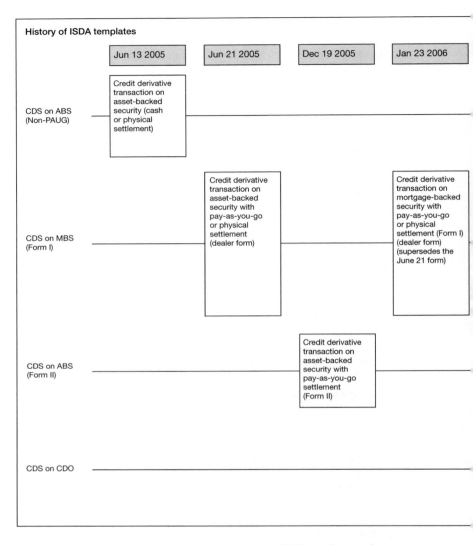

failure to pay principal or a writedown or use the PAUG mechanism by triggering payment by the seller of a floating amount. The key differences between the PAUG templates and the CDS on CDO template are the inclusion of a failure to pay interest as an additional credit event, the hard-wiring of distressed ratings downgrade as a credit event and an option for implied writedown.

(k)   *Master confirmations*

ISDA has also produced a series of template master confirmations for popular types of transaction. These are:

- the '2003 Master Credit Derivatives Confirmation Agreement (European-North American)';

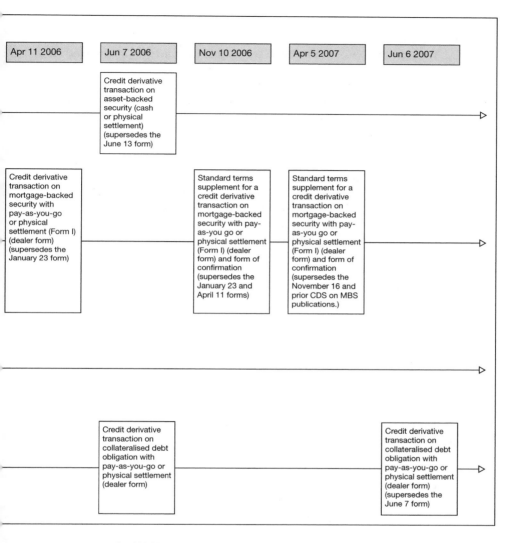

- the '2003 Master Credit Derivatives Confirmation Agreement (Asia-Pacific)'; and
- the '2004 Sovereign Master Credit Derivatives Confirmation Agreement'.

Master confirmations are intended for use where the parties have a course of dealing between them and are intending to enter into a series of similar transactions. Rather than state the terms in a confirmation for each transaction, all of the standard terms are put in a master credit derivatives confirmation agreement. This agreement is an intermediary document standing beside the ISDA Master Agreement.

Master credit derivatives confirmation agreements work as follows. The agreement consists of the master credit derivatives confirmation agreement itself, together with two exhibits: a general terms confirmation and a form of transaction supplement.

The agreement incorporates the 2003 Definitions and the May 2003 supplement. The parties confirm that they intend to enter into separate credit derivatives transactions, with respect to each reference entity, which is set out in a transaction supplement. They also confirm that for each applicable transaction a 'confirmation' will constitute the master confirmation agreement and the general terms confirmation, as supplemented by the applicable trade details, which are set out in the transaction supplement.

The parties are not required to use the master confirmation agreement for all transactions going forward between them. It is the responsibility of the seller to prepare the transaction supplement for each transaction entered into between the parties.

The general terms confirmation set out in Exhibit A then sets out the standard terms for a particular type of transaction (ie, North American and European reference entities or sovereigns). It takes the same form as the ISDA template for single name credit default swaps, except that, as far as possible, the details are completed. Among other things, it selects:

- the identity of the calculation agent;
- the location of the calculation agent city;
- the applicable business days and business day convention;
- the conditions to settlement;
- the applicable credit events;
- obligations; and
- settlement method.

The parties also enter their account details into the general terms confirmation.

The transaction supplement is a one-page document and generally requires the parties only to enter the following information:

- the identity of the reference entity and any reference obligation;
- the trade date;
- the effective date;
- the scheduled termination date;
- the identity of the floating-rate payer (ie, seller) and the fixed-rate payer (ie, buyer);
- the floating-rate payer calculation amount; and
- any additional bespoke terms which are not set out in the general terms confirmation.

The parties are also free to make whatever amendments to the template they wish to reflect the course of dealing between them.

(i)   *2003 Master credit derivatives confirmation agreement (European-North American)*
The 2003 Master Credit Derivatives Confirmation Agreement (European-North American) was published on June 6 2003 and is intended to be used where the relevant reference entities are from Europe and North America. As with the other master credit

derivatives confirmation agreements, the document inserts market standard provisions for these types of reference entity. For example, bankruptcy, failure to pay and restructuring (modified restructuring for North American reference entities and modified modified restructuring for European reference entities) are the applicable credit events. Physical settlement is the applicable settlement method.

(ii)   *2003 Master Credit Derivatives Confirmation Agreement (Asia-Pacific)*
ISDA published the 2003 Master Credit Derivatives Confirmation Agreement (Asia-Pacific) in July 2003. It is intended to be used where parties have a course of dealing relating to reference entities from any of Japan, Singapore, Australia, New Zealand or other Asian countries. As with the other master credit derivatives confirmation agreements, the general terms confirmation sets out the standard market provisions for reference entities from these geographical locations.

(iii)   *2004 Sovereign Master Credit Derivatives Confirmation Agreement*
ISDA published the 2004 Sovereign Master Credit Derivatives Confirmation on August 13 2004. It is intended to be used where market participants have a course of dealing between each other for sovereign reference entities from Asia, emerging European countries and/or Middle Eastern, Japanese, Latin American and Western European countries.
     The template elects the same credit events for all sovereigns: failure to pay and obligation acceleration and restructuring, but then there are three separate standard elections for obligation category and obligation characteristics depending on the jurisdiction of the reference entity: Europe and Japan; Asia (excluding Japan); or Latin America, the Middle East or emerging Europe.
     All of these have 'bond or loan' as the obligation category. There are no obligation characteristics for Europe and Japan, just as with non-sovereign reference entities. Asia and Latin America/Middle East/emerging Europe all have 'not subordinated', 'not sovereign lender', 'not domestic currency', 'not domestic law' and 'not domestic issuance' specified as obligation characteristics. The difference between the two sets of elections is that Asia additionally selects 'not sovereign lender' as an obligation characteristic.
     Deliverable obligations also have different characteristics depending on the jurisdiction of the sovereign. This time there are four separate standard selections: European, Japanese and Latin American, Middle Eastern and emerging European. All specify 'specified currency: standard specified currencies', 'not contingent', 'assignable loan', 'transferable', 'maximum maturity: 30 years' and 'not bearer' as deliverable obligation characteristics.
     Asia and Middle Eastern/Latin American/emerging European all additionally specify 'not subordinated', 'not domestic law' and 'not domestic issuance'. Asia also specifies 'not sovereign lender'. Japan additionally specifies 'not sovereign lender' and 'not domestic issuance'.

6.   ISDA's tertiary platform
As mentioned in the overview above, the tertiary platform has two distinct areas:

ISDA's tertiary platform	
Additional provisions: Incorporated by reference when required, they allow template additional provisions to be added, to document common variations, relating to reference entities, interest rates and other changes 2005 Matrix supplement • Russian Federation • Republic of Hungary • Argentine Republic: excluded obligations and excluded deliverable obligations • LPN reference entities • Constant maturity credit default swaps • Secured deliverable obligation characteristic • Optional early termination (CDS on ABS) • US municipal reference entities • Reference entities with delivery restrictions • 2005 Monoline supplement	**Settlement and transfer variation:** Usually incorporated by reference into a transaction either at the outset or by a global agreement, these documents streamline or modify normal settlement methods • Letter agreement relating to notice delivery periods • Net settlement agreement • Timeline for the physical settlement of a credit derivative transaction following a credit event • Side letter on 60 business day cap on settlement • 2005 novation protocol • CDS cash-settlement protocols

additional provisions and settlement and transfer variations. Credit derivatives transactions may fall into certain categories.

For example, a transaction might be a single name credit default swap, a first-to-default credit default swap or a recovery lock transaction. The secondary platform's confirmation templates generally relate to the broadest categories of reference entities. Some reference entities or reference obligations, though, may have specific features (eg, securities guaranteed by monoline insurers, or issued by US municipal reference entities), which mean that specific amendments must be made to the 2003 Definitions and template confirmations.

Because the transactions occur only sporadically, ISDA has produced various 'additional provisions' documents, which can be incorporated by reference into a confirmation and which amend the terms of the template confirmation or modify the 2003 Definitions, such as the additional provisions for the Russian Federation (August 13 2004) or the additional provisions for physically settled credit default swaps (monoline insurer as reference entity).

A second leg to the tertiary platform consists of the several documents which ISDA has produced to modify the standard settlement and transfer provisions provided in the 2003 Definitions, such as:

- the side letter on 60 business day cap on settlement;
- the letter agreement relating to notice delivery periods;
- the net settlement agreement;
- the CDS index protocols; and
- the 2005 novation protocol.

6.1   Additional provisions

ISDA has provided 11 separate sets of additional provisions that can be incorporated by reference into a credit derivatives confirmation.

These provisions are:

- the 2005 Matrix supplement;
- Additional provisions for the Russian Federation (August 13 2004);

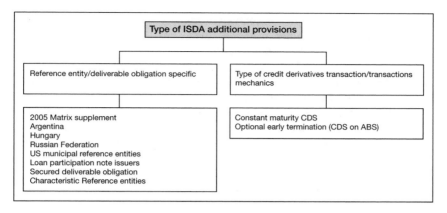

- Additional provisions for the Republic of Hungary (February 14 2005);
- Additional provisions for the Argentine Republic: Excluded obligations and excluded deliverable obligations (December 21 2005);
- Additional provisions for LPN reference entities (December 21 2005);
- Additional provisions for constant maturity credit default swaps (November 21 2005);
- Additional provisions for a secured deliverable obligation characteristic (June 16 2006);
- Additional provisions for optional early termination (CDS on ABS) (December 8 2006);
- Additional provisions for uses with US municipal reference entities;
- Additional provisions for physically settled credit default swaps (monoline insurer as reference entity); and
- Additional provisions for reference entities with delivery restrictions (February 1 2007).

Transaction parties will incorporate these additional provisions by reference only when a reference entity or type of credit derivatives transaction has certain characteristics which mean that standard amendments must be made to ISDA template credit default swaps.

Generally speaking, each set of additional provisions can be incorporated into a confirmation by adding into the introductory paragraph: "The Additional Provisions for [insert], published on [insert date] ('Additional Provisions') are incorporated by reference into this Confirmation."

The ISDA Credit Derivatives Working Group produces sets of additional provisions when there is appropriate trading volume of a particular sub-set of product to make the provisions useful.

The additional provisions fall into two categories. First, there are additional provisions that relate to various elections for reference entities from particular jurisdictions and for particular types of deliverable obligation (in relation to either the type of deliverable obligation or the characteristics of its obligor). Second, there are additional provisions for specific types of credit default product (currently there are additional provisions for constant maturity credit default swaps) and for specific transaction mechanics (currently there are additional provisions for optional termination of CDS on ABS credit default swaps).

(a)   ***2005 matrix supplement: Article XI (credit derivatives physical settlement matrix) and the credit derivatives physical settlement matrix***
In March 2005 ISDA released the 2005 matrix supplement to the 2003 Definitions. This works in conjunction with the credit derivatives physical settlement matrix.

The accompanying announcement published on the ISDA website stated: "The 2005 Matrix Supplement amends the 2003 ISDA Credit Derivatives Definitions by incorporating a new Article XI – the Credit Derivatives Physical Settlement Matrix."

It went on to describe the credit derivatives physical settlement matrix:

> *The Credit Derivatives Physical Settlement Matrix sets out certain elections that apply to certain Reference Entities under Credit Derivatives Transactions for which Physical Settlement applies as the relevant Settlement Method. Parties may express the elections set out in the Credit Derivatives Physical Settlement Matrix to apply to a Credit Derivative Transaction by referencing the 2005 Matrix Supplement in their Confirmation and including and identifying a Transaction Type in the Confirmation for that Credit Derivative Transaction.*

(b)   ***2005 Matrix supplement: Article XI***
The new Article XI consists of three sections:
- Section 11.1 (application of credit derivatives physical settlement matrix);
- Section 11.2 (credit derivatives physical settlement matrix); and
- Section 11.3 (60 business day cap on settlement).

Section 11.1 (application of credit derivatives physical settlement matrix) provides that where a credit derivatives confirmation identifies a 'transaction type' which is included in the credit derivatives physical settlement matrix, the terms set out in the physical settlement matrix for that transaction type are deemed to apply to the transaction.

Section 11.2 (credit derivatives physical settlement matrix) provides that: "'Credit Derivatives Physical Settlement Matrix' means 'Credit Derivatives Physical Settlement Matrix' as most recently amended and supplemented as at the Trade Date of the relevant Credit Derivatives Transaction (unless otherwise agreed by the parties) and as published by ISDA on its website at www.isda.org."

Section 11.3 (60 business day cap on settlement) provides, subject to various exceptions, that if the transaction's termination date has not occurred on or prior to the 60th business day following the physical settlement date, that 60th business day will be the transaction's termination date other than for any affected portion where a 'buy-in price has been obtained' or the buyer has purchased but not delivered deliverable obligations, in which case the termination date will be slightly later.[8]

---

8   See 'Article IX – Additional Representations and Agreements of the Parties' for a full discussion of buy-in price and fallbacks for delivery.

(c) ***Credit derivatives physical settlement matrix***

Since March 2005 the credit derivatives physical settlement matrix has been amended and adapted several times. There are two current physical settlement matrices at the date of publication, both of which are published on the ISDA website; the latest matrix for non-sovereigns was published on September 19 2005 and for sovereigns, the latest matrix was published on February 1 2007.

The matrix for non-sovereigns provides nine 'transaction types' for corporates:

- North America (investment grade and high yield);
- Europe;
- Australia;
- New Zealand;
- Japan;
- Singapore;
- Asia;
- subordinated European insurance; and
- Latin America.

For each transaction type a standard set of variables is provided for:

- business days;
- guarantees;
- conditions to settlement;
- credit events;
- settlement method;
- physical settlement period;
- deliverable obligation category;
- deliverable obligation characteristics;
- escrow; and
- the 60 business day cap on settlement.

The non-sovereign matrix also incorporates into the matrix three sets of additional provisions previously published by ISDA:

- Additional provisions for physically settled default swaps – monoline insurer as reference entity (January 21 2005);
- Additional provisions for the Russian Federation (August 13 2004); and
- Additional provisions for the Republic of Hungary (February 14 2005).

These additional provisions apply if, and only if, those transaction types are present in the relevant credit derivatives transaction. They are discussed further below. The particular elections made by the matrix are discussed in greater detail in Part II.

The matrix for sovereigns provides 10 sovereign 'transaction types':

- Asia;
- emerging Europe and Middle East;
- Japan;
- Australia;

- New Zealand;
- Singapore;
- Latin America; and
- Western Europe.

The sovereign matrix also incorporate into the matrix three sets of additional provisions previously published by ISDA:
- Additional provisions for the Russian Federation (August 13 2004);
- Additional provisions for the Republic of Hungary (February 14 2005); and
- Additional provisions for the Argentine Republic: Excluded obligations and excluded deliverable obligations (December 21 2005).

As with the other matrices, these additional provisions apply if, and only if, those transaction types are present in the relevant credit derivatives transaction and are discussed further below.

The objective of the physical settlement matrix is to shorten a confirmation's terms and allow transactions to be agreed more quickly.

ISDA has also published a template confirmation for use with each physical settlement matrix. The confirmations contain the following wording to incorporate the 2005 matrix supplement and the physical settlement matrix:

The definitions and provisions contained in the 2003 ISDA Credit Derivatives Definitions as supplemented by the May 2003 Supplement and the 2005 Matrix Supplement to the 2003 ISDA Credit Derivatives Definitions (as so supplemented, the '2003 Definitions'), as published by the International Swaps and Derivatives Association, Inc. ('ISDA®'), are incorporated into this Confirmation.

The confirmations are very short. The confirmation for use with non-sovereign confirmations is barely a page long, with only the following information being inserted:
- in paragraph 1 (general terms) – transaction type, trade date, effective date, scheduled termination date, floating-rate payer, fixed-rate payer, calculation agent, calculation agent city, reference entity and reference obligation;
- in paragraph 2 (fixed payments) – fixed-rate payer payments and fixed rate;
- in paragraph 3 (floating payment) – the floating-rate payer calculation amount; and
- in paragraph 5 (credit events) – only whether the restructuring credit event is applicable and whether the 60 business day cap on settlement applies.

(d) *Additional provisions for the Russian Federation: obligation characteristics and deliverable obligation characteristics (August 13 2004)*

ISDA published the 'Additional provisions for the Russian Federation: Obligation characteristics and deliverable obligation characteristics' on August 13 2004. These provisions are incorporated automatically into paragraph 5 of the sovereign general terms confirmation of the 2004 Sovereign Master Credit Derivatives Confirmation

Agreement (see further discussion of this document below) and also into the credit derivatives physical settlement matrix for sovereigns.

These additional provisions provide that certain types of Russian obligations that are restructured debt will not be considered to be 'obligations' or 'deliverable obligations' for the purposes of a credit derivatives transaction.

(e)   **Additional provisions for the Republic of Hungary: Obligation characteristics and deliverable obligation characteristics (February 15 2005)**
ISDA published the 'Additional provisions for the Republic of Hungary: Obligation characteristics and deliverable obligation characteristics' on February 14 2005. These provisions can either be used on a standalone basis or be incorporated into paragraph 5 of the sovereign general terms confirmation of the 2004 Sovereign Master Credit Derivatives Confirmation (see further discussion of this document below).

These additional provisions provide that 'obligations' and 'deliverable obligations' include National Bank of Hungary obligations and deliverable obligations which are either direct or indirect obligations of the National Bank of Hungary, depending upon whether 'all guarantees' or 'qualified affiliate guarantees' has been selected as applicable in the relevant confirmation.

To be 'obligations' or 'deliverable obligations', these National Bank of Hungary obligations must also fulfil four criteria. The obligation must be 'not subordinated' and meet the relevant obligation category and obligation characteristics; it (or any other National Bank of Hungary obligation) must also, if a default of the obligation occurs following any grace period, become immediately due and payable. The National Bank of Hungary will also be deemed to be a reference entity for the purposes of transactions where these additional provisions are incorporated.

(f)   **Additional provisions for the Argentine Republic: Excluded obligations and excluded deliverable obligations (December 21 2005)**
ISDA published the 'Additional provisions for the Argentine Republic: Excluded obligations and excluded deliverable obligations' on December 21 2005. These provisions are used on a standalone basis and must be incorporated directly into the relevant confirmation. The additional provisions seek to make Argentine sovereign debt issued on or prior to June 1 2005 excluded obligations and/or excluded deliverable obligations under any credit derivatives transaction. This means that credit protection sold on the Argentine Republic does not extend to obligations issued on or before this date, where these additional provisions are incorporated by reference into a relevant confirmation.

(g)   **Additional provisions for US municipal reference entities**
ISDA published the 'Additional provisions for US municipal reference entity as reference entity' on September 17 2004. These provisions are intended to be incorporated directly into the ISDA template confirmation for US municipal reference entities, when used (see commentary above).

They are intended to be used where the reference entity is a US state, a political sub-division of a US state or any US government agency, department or similar. The additional provisions make minor amendments to six parts of the 2003 Definitions:

- method for determining obligations;
- method for determining deliverable obligations;
- provisions for determining a successor;
- substitute reference;
- publicly available information; and
- public source.

In particular; these additional provisions add three new obligation characteristics and deliverable obligation characteristics:

- 'Full faith and credit obligation liability' is a liability of the reference entity, the payment of which is backed by the full faith and credit of the reference entity or that is payable from taxes levied on taxable property within the reference entity's taxing jurisdiction.
- 'General fund obligation liability' is a liability of the reference entity (including a full faith and credit obligation liability), which is payable from the reference entity's general fund. Excluded from this definition, though, is any 'moral obligation liability': a reference entity liability that is contingent upon 'an appropriation being made by the governing body or other official of the reference entity'.
- 'Revenue obligation liability' is a liability of the reference entity (excluding a moral obligation liability.

These amendments are designed to make each relevant confirmation fit more easily with the specifics of the US market.

(h) *Additional provisions for LPN reference entities*

ISDA published the 'Additional provisions for LPN reference entities' on October 3 2006. These provisions may be incorporated by reference into a confirmation where the parties wish to specify certain reference obligations relating to reference entities which issue debt through a loan participation note programme (LPN).

What is a loan participation note?

Under a loan participation note an issuer (usually a commercial bank) issues a note to investors. The resulting proceeds are used to fund a participation in a loan to an underlying company. The investors are looking to take credit risk on the underlying company and not on the issuer of the note. The issuer does not guarantee the notes in any way and investors cannot look to the issuer for repayment of the notes if the underlying borrower fails to repay the loan.

Where counterparties in a credit derivatives transaction are looking to trade credit risk on an underlying reference entity which has utilised a loan participation note programme, the 2003 Definitions, unless amended, will not achieve the desired result. The additional provisions for LPN reference entities make adjustments to the 2003 Definitions to ensure that loan participation notes and their underlying loans are correctly characterised.

These additional provisions disapply 'multiple holder obligation' for any reference obligation and underlying loan. They make any reference obligation specified in the confirmation an 'obligation', and also (if applicable) a 'deliverable obligation'. This is the case even if that obligation is not an obligation of the reference entity. They also provide that any reference obligation of the reference entity listed in a list of LPN reference obligations published by Markit Group Limited on the transaction's trade date or other relevant loan participation notes (fulfilling certain conditions) will also be reference obligations.

(i) *Additional provisions for secured deliverable obligation characteristic*

ISDA published the 'Additional provisions for a secured deliverable obligation characteristic' on June 16 2006. These provisions are intended for use where the applicable reference entity is a high yield entity and they may be optionally incorporated by reference into a confirmation where the parties wish to add an extra deliverable obligation characteristic because the reference obligation is a secured bond.

The additional provisions are intended to help to avoid the "moral hazard of the cheapest to deliver option", where a high yield entity restructures some, but not all, of its debt leading to its unsecured debt trading at a lower price to its restructured secured debt.

These additional provisions should not be used in transactions where the relevant reference obligation has been wrapped by a monoline insurance company.

The provisions provide a definition for a new deliverable obligation characteristic: 'secured'. This is deemed to be applicable as a deliverable obligation characteristic, where these additional provisions are incorporated. 'Secured' is then defined as meaning that the deliverable obligation is secured by a security interest as of the delivery date, with the relevant obligation having the right to receipt of proceeds from any enforcement of the security interest.

The additional provisions also provide additional provisions for determining a substitute reference obligation. The calculation agent is required only to identify a substitute reference obligation once requested (with a credit event notice also being deemed to be such a request). The calculation agent must then select a substitute reference obligation that has the benefit of a security interest. Finally, these additional provisions provide certain fallbacks for where the calculation agent is unable to determine a substitute reference obligation for meeting these criteria and also clarifying interpretation provisions.

(j) *Additional provisions for reference entities with delivery restrictions*

ISDA published the 'Additional provisions for reference entities with delivery restrictions' on February 1 2007. The accompanying statement on the ISDA website states that these additional provisions are:

offered as an additional optional field in the Credit Derivatives Physical Settlement Matrix, as published on February 1, 2007. These provisions may also be incorporated into a Confirmation if parties wish to specify its application in relation to certain Reference Entities to whom these restrictions would apply.

In general, these Additional Provisions are designed to address situations where a Reference Entity's issuance of bonds is subject to certain requirements of the Investment Company Act of 1940, such as particular transfer restrictions and the requirement that the bonds trade through certain 'gatekeeper' dealers, among other items.

In these additional provisions, the parties, in relation to any 'restricted reference entity', also represent that each is an 'eligible person'. This means that each is both a 'qualified institutional buyer' for the purposes of Rule 144A of the US Securities Act of 1933 and a 'qualified purchaser' for the purposes of the US Investment Company Act of 1940. They further represent that they will transfer the relevant credit derivatives transaction only to other eligible persons. Any breach of this representation is a termination event under the relevant transaction.

A list of 'restricted reference entities' is set out in Annex A to these additional provisions and will be updated from time to time.

(k) *2005 Monoline supplement*

ISDA published the 'Additional provisions for physically settled default swaps – monoline insurer as reference entity' on January 21 2005. These provisions are known as the 2005 Monoline supplement.

They are intended to be incorporated only into physically settled credit default swaps where the relevant reference entity is a monoline insurer which issues financial guaranty insurance policies or similar types of financial guarantees.

In addition, the parties should select:

- borrowed money or a sub-set of borrowed money (as modified by these additional provisions) as the transaction's obligation category;
- bond or loan, or a sub-set of bond or loan (as modified by these additional provisions) as the transaction's deliverable obligation category; and
- failure to pay and bankruptcy as the applicable credit events.

The parties may also, at their discretion, select restructuring as a credit event.

Monoline insurers: a primer

'Monoline insurers' can be defined as insurance companies that have only one line of business: providing financial guarantees. The market is dominated by four companies: MBIA, AMBAC, FSA and FGIC. Each company has AAA ratings from Standard & Poor's and Fitch, and an Aaa rating from Moody's. In return for a fee, these institutions provide irrevocable unconditional guarantees to lower rated

---

issuers of securities, which are then able to obtain a rating equal to the monoline insurers for their debt securities. This ensures that the lower rated issuer can obtain funding at a lower cost. This is known as 'wrapping' the security.

Any investor purchasing an underlying bond that has been wrapped by a monoline insurer will also be exposed to the credit risk of that monoline insurer and may wish to enter into a credit derivative transaction referencing that monoline insurer. The concept of the monoline insurance, though, does not fit easily with the 2003 Definitions and certain amendments must be made. These are dealt with in the 2005 Monoline supplement.

The 2005 Monoline supplement adds the concept of 'qualifying policy'. This is defined as "a financial guaranty insurance policy or similar financial guarantee pursuant to which a Reference Entity irrevocably guarantees or insures all Instrument Payments...of an instrument that constitutes Borrowed Money...for which another party is the obligor". The reference to 'instrument payments' is to the payments under the insured obligation.

Qualifying policies are then deemed to be treated the same as qualifying affiliate guarantees in the definition of 'obligation' and 'deliverable obligation', meaning that when a credit event occurs under a qualifying policy, the conditions to settlement can be met; and a qualifying policy can then be delivered together with a relevant underlying obligation as a deliverable obligation.

The 2005 Monoline supplement also makes various other minor amendments to the 2003 Definitions to ensure that certain definitions such as 'obligation category', 'borrowed money', 'deliverable obligation category', 'assignable loan', 'consent required loan', 'not contingent', 'deliver', 'restructuring credit event', 'modified restructuring provisions', 'successor' and other provisions are all interpreted or adjusted to ensure that the credit risk of the monoline insurer is effectively transferred.

(l) *Additional provisions for constant maturity credit default swaps*
The second category of additional provisions provided by ISDA is for particular types of credit derivatives transaction and transaction mechanics. To date, additional provisions for this category have been produced only for constant maturity swaps and for optional early termination of CDS on ABS. It is likely that more additional provisions of this type will be produced in the future.

Constant maturity credit default swaps are discussed in detail in Chapter 2. ISDA published the 'Additional provisions for constant maturity credit default swaps' on November 21 2005. These provisions are not incorporated by reference into the confirmation, but instead are used to replace the existing Section 2 of ISDA's template single name credit default swap.

The provisions are intended to be used primarily in inter-dealer transactions. The provisions allow inclusion of constant maturity swap specifics such as participation rate, rate reset notices, reference credit default swaps, seller's bid and related fallbacks.

(m) *Additional provisions for optional early termination (CDS on ABS)*

ISDA published the 'Additional provisions for optional early termination: credit derivatives transactions on asset-backed securities' on December 8 2006. These provisions also form part of the suite of CDS on ABS documentation that has been produced by ISDA since 2005.

The provisions are intended only to be used in credit default swaps referencing asset-backed securities. They may be optionally incorporated by reference into a confirmation where the parties wish to add an early termination option.

Because of the inherent characteristics of credit default swaps (ie, they reference a specific security only and have a long term) a party may wish optionally to terminate a CDS on ABS transaction because it wishes to dispose of the reference obligation.

However, because CDS on ABS transactions can involve continuous payments during the term of the transaction (ie, in relation to pay-as-you-go settlement), special provisions are needed to value the termination payment.

The 'Additional provisions for optional early termination: credit derivatives transactions on asset-backed securities' provide both the mechanics for termination of a CDS on ABS transaction and the methodology for calculating a termination payment.

6.2 Settlement and transfer variation

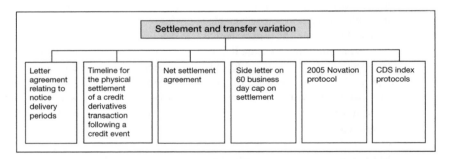

ISDA has released several publications aimed at streamlining settlement. These are:
- 'Letter agreement relating to notice delivery methods';
- 'Timeline for physical settlement of a credit derivative transaction following a credit event';
- 'Net settlement agreement'; and
- 'Side letter on 60 business day cap on settlement'.

Additionally, ISDA has produced a series of protocols for the last five major credit events (Dana Corporation, Delphi Corporation, Dura Corporation, Calpine Corporation, Delta and North West Airlines and CKC) which allow adhering parties to streamline the settlement process in relation to a particular credit event, notwithstanding what the provisions of the original documentation provide. Finally, ISDA has also produced the 'Novation Protocol II', to help parties streamline the transfer or interests in credit derivatives transactions and interest rate derivative transactions.

(a)   *Letter agreement relating to notice delivery methods*

ISDA published the 'Letter agreement relating to notice delivery methods' on February 7 2006. The letter agreement can be entered into in relation to single or multiple credit derivatives transactions by two counterparties with outstanding transactions. It has the effect of deeming to incorporate the language set out in Appendix 1 to the letter agreement into each specified transaction.

Appendix 1 then states that "notwithstanding any thing to the contrary in Section 1.10 (requirements regarding notices); Section 3.3 (credit event notice), Section 3.6 (notice of publication), Section 4.6(e) (repudiation/moratorium) and, in the case of physically settled transactions, Section 3.4 (notice of physical settlement), the parties agree to the additional provisions of the letter agreement".

They can then select that notices delivered pursuant to the above provisions can be delivered by using any of the methods specified in the letter agreement. The parties can select from using a specified electronic messaging system: email, fax, web-hosting services or any alternative method that they choose to specify. The parties must also set out the relevant address(es) where notice must be sent.

(b)   *Net settlement agreement*

ISDA published the 'Net settlement agreement' on May 8 2006. It provides an option to counterparties with a lot of outstanding credit derivatives transactions between them to settle their transactions on a net basis if a credit event occurs which affects multiple transactions.

The net settlement agreement is intended to be used only in physically settled transactions. It is a three-page document and is signed by the parties once a credit event has occurred and the conditions to settlement have been met. The parties list these transactions in an annex to the agreement, providing to the extent applicable the following information:

- dealer reference number;
- counterparty reference number;
- the relevant reference entity or index;
- the date of the credit event notice;
- the date of the notice of publicly available information;
- the identity of the buyer and seller; and
- the floating-rate payer calculation amount.

These credit derivatives transactions are called the 'net settlement transactions'.

The parties agree that, notwithstanding anything prior and to the contrary, in respect of the net settled transactions, their rights and obligations to each other under the net settlement transactions are terminated as of the 'effective settlement date'. This is a future date selected by the parties on which they will settle all of the net settlement transactions.

These rights and obligations under the net settlement transactions are replaced by a 'net settlement CDS', which is deemed to be in place from the effective settlement date. This is a hypothetical credit derivatives transaction under which the 2003 Definitions (as supplemented) are incorporated. There is a global floating-rate payer calculation amount, which is the sum of all of the net settlement transactions' floating-rate payer calculation amounts, and the buyer, seller and affected reference entity are deemed to be the same as the net settlement transactions.

The parties select an event determination date for the net settlement CDS and a global notice of physical settlement is served at a later date. If applicable and/or desirable, a specified credit derivatives physical settlement matrix is also deemed to be in place.

The parties further agree that up to and including the net settlement date, the net settlement transactions are terminated and no further payment or delivery obligations are due. An exception to this is for any accrued, but unpaid, fixed amounts, as of the event determination date.

So in summary, the net settlement agreement allows counterparties to settle physically settled credit derivatives transactions for which the conditions to settlement have been met on a net basis by the buyer delivering one global amount of deliverable obligations in return for payment by the seller of a global physical settlement amount, rather than by settling multiple transactions.

(c)   *Timeline for the physical settlement of a credit derivative transaction following a credit event*

ISDA published the 'Timeline for the physical settlement of a credit derivative transaction following a credit event' on February 7 2006. This document provides a useful timeline diagram. This was produced for information purposes only and set out a useful diagram to assist market participants in understanding the physical settlement process set out in the 2003 Definitions.

The accompanying ISDA press release stated:

> *The Timeline for the Physical Settlement of a Credit Derivative Transaction Following a Credit Event gives a summary of the sequence of certain settlement activities after a Credit Event. The Timeline is based on the basic provisions of the ISDA Credit Derivatives Definitions. It does not incorporate all provisions set forth in the Definitions, nor does it alter individual contracts, rather is designed to assist market participants by providing a short guide to basic settlement mechanics in those Definitions.*

(d)   *Letter agreement relating to 60 business day cap on settlement*

There is a risk that with the various fallbacks set out in the 2003 Definitions, the physical settlement process could continue for an indefinite period of time if sourcing applicable deliverable obligations becomes problematic. The 'Letter agreement relating to 60 business day cap on settlement', which ISDA published on August 5 2003, gives market participants the ability, subject to various exceptions, to provide that if the transaction's termination date has not occurred on or prior to the 60th business day following the physical settlement date, that 60th business day will be the transaction's termination date other than for any affected portion where a 'buy-in price has been obtained' or the buyer has purchased, but not delivered, deliverable obligations, in which case the termination date will be slightly later.

The letter agreement then functions by providing that certain language having the effect set out in the paragraph above, which is contained in Appendix I to the letter agreement, is deemed to be incorporated into the relevant confirmation.

(e)   ***Novation Protocol II***

Novating a contract (ie, substituting a new party for an existing one by substituting a new contract for an existing one) is ISDA's preferred method for trading derivatives contracts. A novation of a credit default swap involves the buyer and seller agreeing to replace an existing credit default swap between them with a new credit default swap between one of them and a new counterparty. The concept is valid under both English law and New York law transactions.[9]

The Novation Protocol II, which is also known as NPII, replaced the earlier Novation Protocol 2005. It was published on February 1 2006. The protocol aims to help tackle the industry-wide problem of the backlog of outstanding confirmations. It does this by providing a process to parties that adhere to the protocol to transfer credit derivative and interest rate derivative transactions from a transferor to a transferee with the consent of the transaction's remaining party.

The protocol itself is six pages long and attaches three exhibits relating to a form of adherence letter, a form of revocation notice and a standard email/Bloomberg message from the transferor to the remaining party. The protocol also attaches an annex that sets out the deemed amendments that will be made to the covered transactions.

The terms of the protocol state that the parties have entered into or anticipate entering into an ISDA Master Agreement. They agree that by entering into the protocol, amendments are deemed to be made to that Master Agreement, and that adhering parties will follow certain procedures when transferring by novation any transaction covered by the protocol. These amendments are set out in Annex 1 to the protocol.

For the protocol to apply to an individual credit derivatives transaction, both parties that have entered into a Master Agreement must adhere to the protocol and the relevant transaction must be covered by the protocol.

The protocol provides that to adhere to it, each adhering party must complete an adherence letter in the form set out in Exhibit 1 to the protocol. In the adherence letter, an adhering party agrees to be bound by the protocol and to appoint ISDA as its agent. It sets out its contact details and ISDA then publishes the letter, together with a list of adherents on its website.

The parties also make standard representations to each other under the protocol such as in relation to status, powers and credit support as well as agreeing certain boundaries permitting revocation.

The protocol is not intended to be negotiated. It covers all interest rate transactions and credit derivatives transactions which incorporate the 1999 and the 2003 Definitions.

---

9   ISDA has obtained legal opinions under both English and New York law to this effect, which are published on the ISDA website.

The deemed amendments to each covered transaction are set out in Annex I. Under this annex each party confirms that it is familiar with several ISDA documents which relate to novations, such as the 'ISDA statement on consent requirements for transfer of transactions', published on April 3 2003.

Novations involve three parties: a transferor, a transferee and a remaining party. The process set out in Annex 1 to the protocol assumes that all three parties have adhered to the protocol. In the event that only two of the three are adhering parties, the adhering parties are obliged to follow the Annex 1 process to the extent practicable.

Annex 1 obliges the transferor to seek the remaining party's consent to the proposed novation and to send sufficient information for the remaining party to identify the transaction being transferred. The minimum information which it must provide is set out in Exhibit A to the protocol.

Exhibit A provides that in a request to consent to a novation, the transferor must at least provide the following information to the remaining party (copied to the transferee):

- the transaction references;
- the identity of the transferor and transferee;
- the trade date, novation date and novated amount;
- the identity of the reference entity (together with relevant identifiers);
- the identity of the reference obligation; and
- a summary of any non-standard terms.

Once the transferor receives consent to the novation from the remaining party, it must provide evidence of this to the transferee.

Annex 1 obliges the remaining party to respond promptly to any request for novation on the day it receives the request. This response must state whether the remaining party consents and must also be communicated to the transferee.

Annex 1 obliges the transferee promptly to confirm with the remaining party after it receives evidence of consent to the novations all of the relevant trade details of the transaction transferred.

Each of the communications referred to above can be made by electronic messaging and communications systems.

The transferor and transferee are legally bound by the terms of a transfer by novation as soon as they agree the terms. This is subject only to the consent of the remaining party by not later than 6:00pm in the location of the transferee on the day that the transfer is agreed.

The protocol provides fallback provisions for when this consent is not received on time. The transferor and transferee are deemed not to have entered into a transfer by novation of the covered transaction, but instead have entered into an identical transaction in which the transferor takes the position of the remaining party and the transferee the position of the transferor. In effect, this means that the transferor enters into a back-to-back transaction with the transferee.

The parties also agree to enter into novation documentation as soon as reasonably practicable after the consent to transfer is received. The novation documentation contemplated for use in credit derivatives transactions is the ISDA 2002 Novation Agreement and the related novation confirmation. Novations are dealt with in Article X (novation provisions) of the 2003 Definitions. The novation agreement and novation confirmation are set out as Exhibit E and Exhibit F.

Failing to comply with the protocol does not result in an event of default under the ISDA Master Agreement.

(f)   CDS cash-settlement protocols

(i)   Introduction

A reference entity files for bankruptcy, but the amount of bonds and loans it has outstanding is dwarfed by the size of the position taken by the credit derivatives market on that reference entity's credit risk. Market participants may encounter technical difficulties when physically settling a credit derivatives transaction when a reference entity's deliverable obligations become scarce. This is often due to the sheer number of outstanding physically settled credit derivatives transactions chasing a limited number of deliverable obligations.

This can have the effect of artificially driving up the price of defaulted deliverable obligations. It can mean that where a seller must purchase a deliverable obligation in a physically settled transaction in order to settle, the inflated price can mean that its overall recovery amount is below the level that it could reasonably have been expected. This increases the risk of a credit derivatives contract taking market risk as well as credit risk.

Problems were encountered in particular following the Delphi credit event,[10] where the volume and price of Delphi deliverable obligations traded at a higher price after it filed for bankruptcy before then declining. These high bond prices occurred even though rating agency recovery models showed that Delphi's bonds should have been trading at significantly lower prices.

ISDA has been proactive in dealing with this problem. To combat it, it has produced a cash-settlement protocol for each of the last five major credit events: Dana Corporation, Delphi Corporation, Dura Corporation, Calpine Corporation, Delta and North West Airlines and CKC.

This protocol allows parties adhering to it to amend the terms of their physically settled credit default swaps on a multi-transactional basis. The protocol amends each covered transaction in relation only to the affected credit event to allow cash settlement instead of physical settlement, with a final price for a reference obligation determined through a complex auction process: "The protocol adapts covered transactions to allow cash settlement instead of physical settlement, with a final price for a reference obligation determined through a complex auction process."

ISDA prepares a new and specific cash-settlement protocol for each major credit event, adapting and fine-tuning the terms of the protocol to the particular situation. Once adhered to, the protocol will not amend relevant documentation for any future

---

10   "Delphi, Credit Derivatives and Bond Trading Behavior After a Bankruptcy Filing", November 28 2005, Fitch Ratings.

credit event (in the case of multi-reference entity credit default swaps), and although ISDA may prepare future protocols, market participants are not obliged to adhere to them.

Market participants are likely to opt to enter into a cash-settlement protocol only when there is a scarcity of deliverable obligations for a particular defaulted reference entity – meaning that some cash-settlement protocols will be more popular than others. If there is not a scarcity of deliverable obligations, then market participants which have entered into physically settled credit derivatives transactions to avoid the uncertainties of the cash-settlement process are likely to want to stay with the physical-settlement process originally envisaged. Likewise, the ISDA will not produce a cash-settlement protocol.

ISDA's cash-settlement protocols are not to be confused with the novation protocols described above. To analyse how the protocol works, we shall take as an example the ISDA protocol for the last major credit event: Dura Corporation, a US auto-parts manufacturer which filed for bankruptcy on October 30 2006. Future cash-settlement protocols may vary from this example, but the mechanics are likely to be substantially similar.

(ii)   *2006 Dura CDS protocol*
ISDA published the 2006 Dura CDS Protocol on November 8 2006. The protocol was applicable to transactions between adhering parties only if:

- the transaction had Dura Corporation as a reference entity;
- the transaction's effective date was on or before October 30 2006 (the date on which Dura filed for bankruptcy) and its scheduled termination date was on or after that date; and
- the transaction fell into one of the transaction types covered by the protocol.

The types of credit derivatives transactions covered by the protocol were:

- tranched and untranched transactions referencing either a bespoke portfolio or one of the major credit derivatives indices;
- single name credit default swaps;
- single name and portfolio constant maturity swaps;
- single name and portfolio swaptions;
- nth to default transactions;
- recovery lock transactions; and
- principal-only and interest-only transactions.

The cash-settlement protocol was optional. Market participants with outstanding Dura transactions were able to adhere to the protocol up until November 17 2006.

In addition to agreeing to adhere to the protocol, the parties made standard representations to each other in relation to status, powers and credit support, as well as agreeing certain boundaries such as the right to revoke.

Adhering parties also agreed that the documentation of the covered transactions was deemed to be amended. The amendments made were set out in Schedule 1 to the protocol.

Amendments to covered transactions made by the Dura protocol

The amendments generally covered the same points for each type of covered transaction (although there was some variation for particular product types).

They covered the effect of actual notices (eg, credit event notices), which had already been delivered. They provided that except for deemed notices, no further notices were required. They deemed a credit event notice with respect to the Dura portion of any transaction to have been served, and that this notice was also deemed to have specified bankruptcy and incorporated a notice of publicly available information meeting the requirements of the documentation. They removed the requirement to deliver a notice of physical settlement – this meant that the conditions to settlement were satisfied as of the cut-off date.

They specified that any fixed-rate of payment relating to Dura would accrue only until October 30 2006 (the date on which Dura filed for bankruptcy). The final amendment related to the settlement terms was to deem that each transaction would settle as if the applicable settlement method specified in the documentation were cash settlement.

In untranched transactions, recovery lock transactions and tranched transactions that were not based on credit derivatives index documentation, the amendment specified that the final price would be determined as per the auction methodology set out in Exhibit 3 to the protocol.

For tranched transactions based on credit derivatives index documentation, covered index tranched transactions, interest-only transactions, portfolio constant maturity swap transactions and principal-only transactions, the buyer was deemed to have delivered the selected obligation (under the terms of the transaction) with an outstanding obligation equal to the reference entity notional amount on the auction date.

The seller was not obligated to pay any amount for the selected obligation deemed to have been delivered, but instead was obliged to pay the final price determined pursuant to the auction methodology.

Where a tranched transaction based on index documentation was already specified to be cash settled, the protocol cash-settlement process over-rode the documentation's existing provisions.

The protocol had four exhibits:
- a form of adherence letter;
- a form of revocation notice;
- the auction methodology; and
- a form of bidding letter agreement (which allowed a market maker to participate in the auction).

Exhibit 1 – The adherence letter

Market participants were able to make the protocol binding by signing an adherence letter and delivering it to ISDA. Adhering parties agreed for the protocol to apply to all covered transactions, both at the date of the adherence and in the future: the protocol would therefore apply to any future novated transactions in which adherents ended up being counterparties. Adhering parties also agreed that the protocol was not to be negotiated or amended.

The adherence letter itself was a two-page document under which an adhering party appointed ISDA as its agent for the protocol's contemplated purposes and provided its DTC account number and contact details. Each executed adherence letter was placed on the ISDA website, along with a list of adherents, so that adhering parties could tell which of their transactions were covered by the protocol.

Exhibit 2 to the protocol was a form of revocation notice. This allowed an adhering party to designate an earlier cut-off date as the last date on which any counterparty could enter into the protocol, meaning that the protocol would not apply to any transactions which that party had with an adhering party joining after the earlier cut-off date.

Should a market participant use a protocol?

If a market participant is considering signing up to an ISDA cash-settlement protocol, apart from considering the commercial and efficiency merits of doing so, it should consider several points.

First, the prospective adherent should consider whether any of its outstanding affected transactions fall within the transaction types covered by the protocol. Any transaction that does not must be settled in the normal way. Additionally, some transactions not originally contemplated may also be caught within the ambit of covered transactions.

Second, it should check whether any of its counterparties in these affected transactions are intending to adhere to the protocol. All outstanding transactions where both counterparties do not adhere to the protocol must be settled as contemplated by the original documentation.

Third, it should check the deemed amendments made to each transaction by Schedule 1 to the protocol, in particular in relation to settlement.

Fourth, the prospective adherent should decide whether it wishes to participate in the auction itself and if so, closely study the auction methodology and the bidding agreement letter.

Once a prospective adherent had signed and submitted the adherence letter, and (if applicable) a bidding agreement letter, it awaited (or participated in) the determination of a final price for a reference obligation and then settled all relevant transactions in accordance with the cash-settlement process imposed by the protocol set out in Schedule 1.

The auction

Exhibit 3 of the protocol set out the methodology for the cash settlement process: the auction. It was under this complex process that the final price was determined for each of the covered transactions.

For the Dura cash settlement process the auction process consisted of six stages:

- auctioning selected deliverable obligations;
- the administrators calculating the 'open interest', 'inside market mid-point' and 'adjustment amounts';
- the administrators publishing the open interest and the inside market mid-point, together with the details of any adjustment amount;
- the participating bidders submitting limit bids and limit offers;
- the administrators determining the final price for the deliverable obligations; and
- the participating bidders entering into a reference Dura single name credit default swap and delivered or accepted auctioned Dura deliverable obligations, in return for payment of the final price.

Credit derivative products and their documentation: funded credit derivatives

1. What are funded credit derivatives?

So far we have discussed 'unfunded' credit derivatives: bilateral credit derivatives contracts, usually between counterparties of a similar standing (eg, a bank and an insurance company, or a hedge fund and a pension company).

In contrast, 'funded' credit derivatives are structured transactions where the credit derivatives contract is embedded in a debt obligation.

This underlying and embedded credit derivatives contract will often be based on a corresponding ISDA contract. The funded credit derivative structure will usually involve either:

- a thinly capitalised SPV issuing securities and entering into a credit derivatives contract with a financial institution; or
- a financial institution issuing securities with the credit derivatives terms set out in the conditions of the notes.

In a funded credit derivatives structure the special purpose vehicle (SPV) or bank issues a debt obligation which will fund (at least some of) the potential losses on the credit derivatives contract and pay an interest rate on the principal amount of the debt obligation, together with an amount corresponding to the premium for providing credit protection under the credit derivatives contract: the debt obligation 'funds' any credit protection payments which must be made under the embedded credit derivative following an event determination date relating to a reference entity.

Of course, it's more complicated than that. The proceeds of the notes must be invested to generate a return and the debt obligations themselves will often be tranched (and rated) according to priority of payment. They may also be listed on a stock exchange. The credit derivatives contracts themselves are often more complex too: the portfolio of reference entities referenced by a credit default swap may be managed by a manager who will decide on a periodic basis which reference entities may be included in the pool; this selection may be made following the application of complex tests. The notes themselves may be subordinated to an 'unfunded' 'super senior' credit default swap, meaning that the credit derivatives contract is only partly funded.

Some structures may try to guarantee repayment of principal, but put interest payments at risk (eg, synthetic constant proportion portfolio insurance (CPPI)); other even newer structures may try to chase an earlier return of principal with a higher than usual coupon (eg, the new constant proportion debt obligation (CPDO) transactions).

Unfunded credit derivatives have had all ISDA's attention. Although this will change soon, at the time of publication, not a single template or document which ISDA had published related to funded credit derivatives such as synthetic collateralised debt obligations (CDOs) and synthetic CPPI. Due to this, documentation for funded credit derivatives tends to be more bespoke. While recognising that there are many different ways to skin a cat, the commentary below also reflects this and, rather than go into every possible variation, takes a more general approach.

In this chapter we discuss synthetic CDOs, credit-linked notes and two new funded credit derivatives structures: synthetic CPPI and CPDO transactions. Because synthetic CDOs make up 15.3% of the credit derivatives market and are the third most widely traded credit derivatives product behind single name credit default swaps and index transactions, they have their own dedicated chapter in Part III. Coverage of CDOs in this chapter is intended to provide an overview. Unless otherwise stated, references to synthetic CDOs are to full capital structure synthetic CDOs.

2. Synthetic CDOs

2.1 Overview
In 2006, synthetic CDOs represented 15.3 % of the credit derivatives market.

What is a synthetic CDO (full capital structure[1])?

In a standard synthetic CDO, a thinly capitalised SPV enters into a portfolio credit default swap with a counterparty, usually the transaction's arranger. This portfolio credit default swap is usually cash settled.

Under the portfolio credit default swap, the SPV sells an amount of credit protection to the counterparty for each reference entity (eg, in a $200 million CDO, it might sell $2 million of credit protection for each of 100 reference entities in a portfolio).

This generates an agreed return in the form of fixed payments in relation to the notional amount of each of the reference entities in the portfolio, perhaps 0.75% per annum. The reference entities themselves will be selected from diverse industries and geographical locations to try to minimise the level of correlation between potential credit events: this will be particularly so in the case of rated transactions.

As already mentioned, the SPV is thinly capitalised, perhaps having only $2 capitalisation. It has no funds to make any credit protection payment should a credit event occur and the conditions to settlement must be met on a reference entity in the portfolio: it must therefore be funded.

To fund its potential obligations under the credit default swap, the SPV first

---

1   See further discussion below, or partial capital structure/single tranche CDO.

issues debt obligations in the form of notes to investors. These notes are often tranched, with progressively deeper levels of subordination. For example, the SPV could issue three classes of notes: a senior, a mezzanine and a junior tranche. Losses incurred under the credit default swap would attach first to the junior notes, then to the mezzanine notes and finally, if the principal amount of that tranche were exhausted, to the senior notes.

Second, the SPV enters into an unfunded 'super senior' credit default swap on the whole of the reference portfolio with a highly rated bank or other financial institution. Under this swap the SPV will be the buyer and the financial institution the seller. The super senior credit default swap will make up most of the capitalisation of the structure; losses will impact upon it only once the principal amounts of all of the tranches of notes have been exhausted. The 'super senior' swap is unfunded from the perspective of the financial institution, but because it is a back-to-back swap, it funds the SPV in the main credit derivatives transaction. In a rated transaction the 'super senior' swap is sometimes perceived to be above AAA by certain investors. The size of each tranche of notes will usually be driven (in rated transactions) by rating criteria designed to achieve a AAA rating for the senior tranche of notes and target ratings for the other tranches.

The proceeds of the debt obligations are invested, directly or indirectly (perhaps through a repo agreement), in high-quality securities or a guaranteed investment contract (GIC) account or a deposit account: along with the SPV's rights under the super senior credit default swap and other transaction documents, this is the 'collateral' of the collateralised debt obligation. The noteholders receive a blended return based on the credit protection payments received from the SPV and the return on the collateral, with the quantum of return also being referenced to the amount of risk assumed by a noteholder. The super senior credit default swap counterparty will receive only its share of the credit protection payments on the credit default swap received by the SPV.

Following any credit event under the credit default swap, any credit protection payment in the form of a cash settlement amount will be funded by selling an appropriate amount of highly rated securities[2] and delivering the proceeds to the SPV's swap counterparty. The principal amount of the notes will then be reduced accordingly. If the notes are tranched with differing levels of subordination, then the most deeply subordinated notes are always reduced in principal amount first. If the principal amounts of each class of notes become exhausted, the super senior credit default swap counterparty will be required to make payments under the super senior credit default swap to fund the SPV's payments under the credit default swap.

At the transaction's maturity the proceeds of the collateral are used to repay the remaining principal amount of the notes.

---

2   The sale of any collateral may take place through the repo agreement or alternatively by a withdrawal from a GIC account or deposit account.

The objective of a synthetic CDO is for the noteholders (and the super senior swap counterparty) to take synthetic exposure to a portfolio of static or actively managed reference entities or reference obligations, through a credit derivative. The underlying credit derivatives transaction can be documented in one of two ways. Either (and less commonly) the credit derivatives terms can be set out in the conditions of the notes (adapting the 2003 Definitions) and the arranger will book the transaction as a swap internally, or the SPV and the arranger will enter into a credit default swap utilising ISDA and/or iTraxx standard documentation, including the 2003 Definitions.

Portfolio credit default swaps

In a portfolio credit default swap, the buyer purchases credit protection on a basket of reference entities, perhaps as many as 200.

Portfolio credit default swaps operate very similarly to single name credit default swaps. The easiest way to conceptualise the product is to view it as consisting of a bundle of credit default swaps, with one credit default swap being in place (between the buyer and the seller) for each reference entity in the portfolio

Each time that a credit event occurs in relation to a reference entity and the conditions to settlement are met, the settlement procedure is the same as for a single name credit default swap, except that instead of the transaction terminating on the settlement date, the reference entity will be removed from the basket or portfolio and the transaction will continue.

In portfolio credit default swaps, the transaction will have an overall notional amount (eg, $300 million) and consist of a notional amount for each reference entity. This is usually an equally weighted amount, with credit protection sold for each reference entity's reference entity notional amount only.

A further type of synthetic CDO is a synthetic collateralised loan obligation; here, credit protection is provided by the SPV against loans which are held on the books of an originating bank. The originating bank is able to achieve regulatory capital relief on its loan assets, without transferring them (or notifying its customers). The originating bank will either structure the transaction itself or enter into a back-to-back swap with an arranging bank, which will then enter into the portfolio credit default swap with the SPV. The structuring of the transaction will be substantially similar, although credit protection will usually be limited to the particular loan assets held by the originating bank.

SPVs: why are they used in CDOs and issues of credit-linked notes?

In a synthetic CDO, an SPV is established with the objective of the transaction parties utilising it in a structured finance transaction to issue debt instruments, acquire underlying assets and/or enter into derivatives contracts with a view to providing a return to investors.

The transaction's arranger will establish the SPV in a low tax or no tax jurisdiction, such as the Cayman Islands or Jersey; or a country that has introduced a specific low tax regime for SPVs, such as Ireland, the Netherlands or Luxembourg.

The SPV will generally be an orphan company, run by directors from the relevant jurisdiction with its shares held in trust for the noteholders and/or a charity (so the SPV will not be categorised as a subsidiary of the arranger).

The assets held by the SPV will be secured so that they are available only to the holders of the related series of notes and/or any other secured parties under the transaction; in no circumstances are they available to any other creditor of the SPV.

Securities issued by the SPV will be 'limited recourse' securities. This means that the claims of the noteholders and other secured parties under a CDO will be limited only to the proceeds of the secured obligations. To the extent that secured obligations do not yield sufficient funds to satisfy the claims of the noteholders and the other secured parties, their claims will be extinguished.

Synthetic CDOs generally fall into two types: full capital structure or multi-tranche CDOs and partial capital or single-tranche CDOs. They are both described below.

2.2   Full capital structure synthetic CDOs

Full capital structure synthetic CDOs (see diagram, page 114) are usually multi-tranched, with an SPV issuing several classes of notes, each called a tranche.

Tranching

Tranching allows investors to take different slices of risk exposure in accordance with their risk/return appetite. It also acts as a form of credit enhancement.

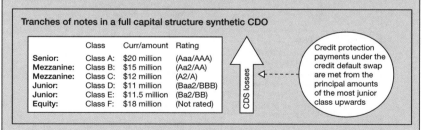

Tranches of notes in a full capital structure synthetic CDO

	Class	Curr/amount	Rating
Senior:	Class A:	$20 million	(Aaa/AAA)
Mezzanine:	Class B:	$15 million	(Aa2/AA)
Mezzanine:	Class C:	$12 million	(A2/A)
Junior:	Class D:	$11 million	(Baa2/BBB)
Junior:	Class E:	$11.5 million	(Ba2/BB)
Equity:	Class F:	$18 million	(Not rated)

CDS losses

Credit protection payments under the credit default swap are met from the principal amounts of the most junior class upwards

In a full capital structure synthetic CDO, the SPV will issue different classes (or tranches) of notes. The tranches will fall into four separate categories (in descending order of priority): senior debt, mezzanine debt, subordinated debt and equity. There may be multiple tranches within those categories.

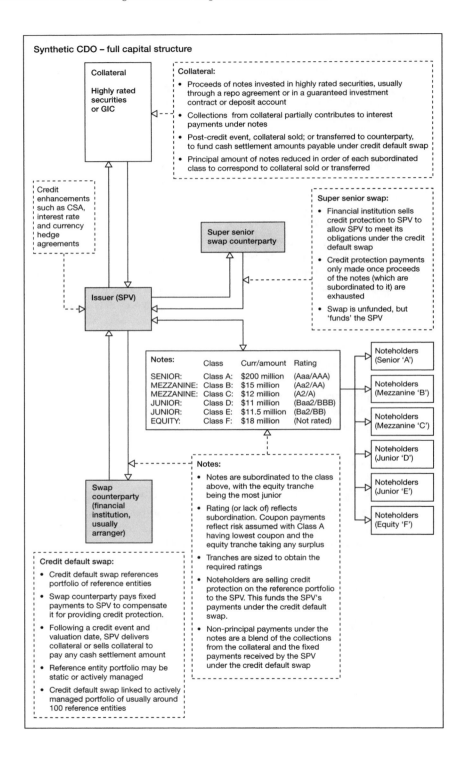

If there is a credit event under the credit default swap and the conditions to settlement are met, then following the valuation date(s), the issuer will be required to pay a cash settlement amount.

Payment of the cash settlement amount will be funded by the issuer either delivering an amount of collateral equal to the cash settlement amount or selling a corresponding amount of collateral, the proceeds of which are then paid to the counterparty. The collateral is usually held in the form of a deposit in a guaranteed investment account or in the form of highly rated securities invested pursuant to a repo agreement

The corresponding amount of the principal amount of the lowest available tranche of notes is then reduced. Each tranche of notes is protected by the tranche below it. This means that the more senior the tranche of notes, the less likely it is to suffer losses.

Usually, the notes are rated and the level of ratings will correspond to the seniority of any tranche of notes. Likewise, the higher level of risk attached to a tranche of notes, the higher its coupon and the lower its rating will be. As credit events impact on the portfolio, though, the level of return will diminish.

Above the tranches of notes often sits a more senior obligation: an unfunded credit default swap with a highly rated entity. This is called a super senior credit default swap, and sometimes it makes up over 80% of the synthetic CDO's notional amount.

Super senior credit default swaps

The super senior credit default swap usually makes up over 80% of a synthetic CDO's capitalisation. Unlike most of the tranches of notes below it, it will not be rated.

In a super senior credit default swap the seller will usually be an insurance company or a financial institution and, due to the subordinated tranches of notes below it, will regard its investments as representing a low risk. The buyer will be the SPV. The SPV therefore enters into a back-to-back credit default swap transaction.

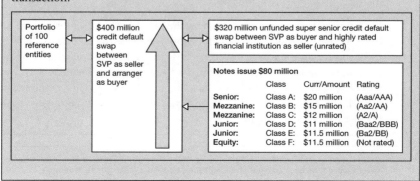

> A super senior credit default swap will involve the seller selling credit protection on the entire reference portfolio, but losses will attach to the super senior credit default swap only once the principal amount of the tranches below it has been exhausted.

If the portfolio of reference entities is fixed at the issue date, this is known as a static synthetic CDO. Alternatively, a manager may be appointed who will switch reference entities in and out of the portfolio with a view to maximising returns in return for a fee: this is known as a managed synthetic CDO.

Hypothetical case study: full capital structure synthetic CDO – Armageddon CDO

Hercules Bank launched a full capital synthetic CDO. It was structured so that an SPV would issue four classes of notes: a senior tranche, a mezzanine tranche, a junior tranche and an equity tranche.[3]

Hercules established the SPV in Jersey and named it Armageddon Limited. Hercules selected Jersey as a jurisdiction of incorporation due to its favourable tax regime. The notes were listed on the Irish Stock Exchange.

Armageddon issued four tranches of notes, with each class of notes being subordinated to the class of notes below it. The four classes of notes were:

- Class A notes – the senior tranche;
- Class B notes – the mezzanine tranche;
- Class C notes – the junior tranche; and
- Class D Notes – the equity (or first loss) tranche.

The Class A, B and C notes were rated by Standard & Poor's. The senior notes were rated AAA, the mezzanine notes AA and the junior notes A. The equity tranche was not rated and was retained by Hercules. The principal amounts of each tranche were as follows:

- Class A – $100 million;
- Class B – $50 million;
- Class C – $50 million; and
- Class D – $50 million.

Coupons payable reflected the risk involved, with the senior tranche attracting the lowest coupon and the junior tranche the highest (the equity tranche received the excess available after payment of the obligations above it).

In addition, Armageddon entered into a super senior credit default swap with Suez SA, a monoline insurer, where it bought $1.25 billion of credit protection on the reference portfolio. The four classes of notes were subordinated to the super senior credit default swap.

---

3   Terminology regarding names of tranches is not set in stone; transactions may refer to the most subordinated tranche as an equity tranche, junior tranche , first loss tranche or other.

Hercules structured the transaction so that the $250 million proceeds from the notes issue would be invested in UK government gilts, transferred pursuant to a repo agreement. It did this to reduce the credit exposure of the notes to factors other than the credit default swap by as much as possible. The gilts paid an annual interest rate of 4% and this amount was reprofiled to contribute towards the interest payments under the notes.

On the issue date Armageddon entered into a credit default swap for $1.5 billion with Hercules under which Armageddon sold credit protection on a portfolio of 100 reference entities. The potential credit protection payments that Armageddon could be required to make were funded by the $250 million of notes and the $1.25 billion of the monoline insurer's obligation under the senior swap.

The reference entities were selected from diverse industrial sectors and jurisdictions. This was designed to ensure that there was as low a correlation as possible between the reference entities, and was driven by rating agency criteria. Under the credit default swap Armageddon sold $15 million of credit protection in relation to each of the 100 reference entities. This added up to total credit protection of $1.5 billion – the total issue size of the synthetic CDO.

During the term of the transaction, on each occasion that a credit event occurred in relation to any of the reference entities, Hercules would deliver a credit event notice and notice of publicly available information to Armageddon confirming the credit event. Following valuation of the relevant reference obligation on the valuation date and the determination of the cash settlement amount payable, Armageddon would deliver under the repo agreement an amount of the highly rated securities forming the collateral, equal to the cash settlement amount to Hercules.

The principal amount of the notes was then reduced by the amount of the cash settlement amount. The notes had been tranched with losses always being absorbed by the lowest class of securities. This meant that until the Class D notes had been exhausted, no losses would be absorbed by the Class C notes; until the Class C notes had been exhausted, no losses would be absorbed by the Class B notes and so on.

At the transaction's maturity date, the CDO structure had suffered 10 credit events. The average final price obtained per reference entity had been 20%, meaning that $12 million had been paid under the credit default swap between Armageddon and Hercules as credit protection payments to Hercules. This had significantly depleted the Class D junior tranche, but left the other tranches and the super senior swap untouched. The other tranches of notes were repaid in full.

2.3 Single tranche CDOs/partial capital structure CDOs

A single tranche or partial capital structure CDO is a structured securities transaction where the transaction's arranger sells only a single tranche of a full capital structure synthetic CDO to an investor. Taking the above hypothetical case study for the Armageddon CDO, if Hercules were to sell only the Class B notes, which was the $50

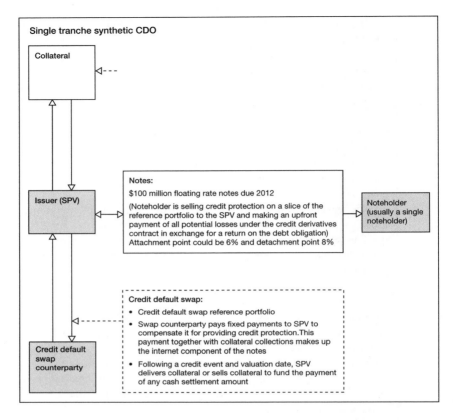

million mezzanine tranche, it would be selling a tranche of notes to which losses would be absorbed only once the $100 million of the Class C notes and Class D notes had been exhausted.

The 'attachment level' of the credit protection provided by the Class D notes would be 0% (of the total principal amount of the CDO transaction), and their 'detachment level' would be 3.33% once the $50 million principal amount of the Class D notes had been exhausted. The attachment level of the Class C notes would be 3.33% and their detachment level 6.66 %, once their $50 million principal amount had been exhausted. The Class B notes attachment level would be 6.66% and their detachment level 9.99%. The Class A notes attachment level would be 9.99% and the detachment level would be 15.65%. Finally, the super senior attachment level would be 15.65% and the detachment level would be 100%.

If Hercules sold the Class B notes only as a single tranche, the noteholder would be taking the credit risk on losses in the reference entity portfolio that exceeded 6.66% up to and including losses of 9.99%.

Hercules could try to make a return on the single tranche CDO through arbitrage techniques, by entering into credit derivatives transactions where it would buy credit protection on reference entities in the reference portfolio to take advantage of price differentials.

2.4   Documenting synthetic CDOs

(a)   Introduction

Generally speaking, the documentation for a synthetic CDO will include the following:

- a prospectus;
- an agency agreement;
- a trust deed and deed of charge;
- a note purchase agreement;
- a placement agreement;
- an account bank agreement;
- global notes; and
- one of a repo agreement, a custody agreement, a GIC account agreement or a deposit agreement.

There may also potentially be a liquidity agreement to assist with any temporary shortfalls in interest payments.

Documentation will be produced to establish and run the SPV. The SPV will enter into swap documentation with an ISDA Master Agreement (as amended by a schedule). Pursuant to this it will enter into a credit default swap confirmation, an interest rate confirmation and, if the notes are multi-currency or if the underlying collateral is denominated in a different currency, a foreign currency swap confirmation (potentially one for each currency). Where the transaction is rated and the SPV's counterparty (usually the arranging bank) does not have a credit rating as high as the highest class of notes issued under the structure, the counterparty may be obliged to enter into collateral support arrangements.

If the structure is managed, then a portfolio management agreement will be entered into and where various tests have to be performed, a portfolio administration agreement may also be entered into. Often, all of the definitions used in the various documents will be set out in a master schedule of definitions, which will then be

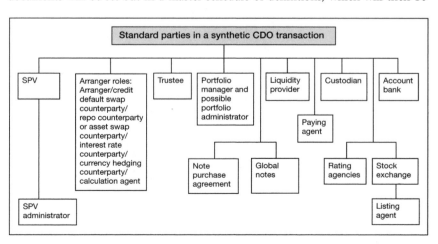

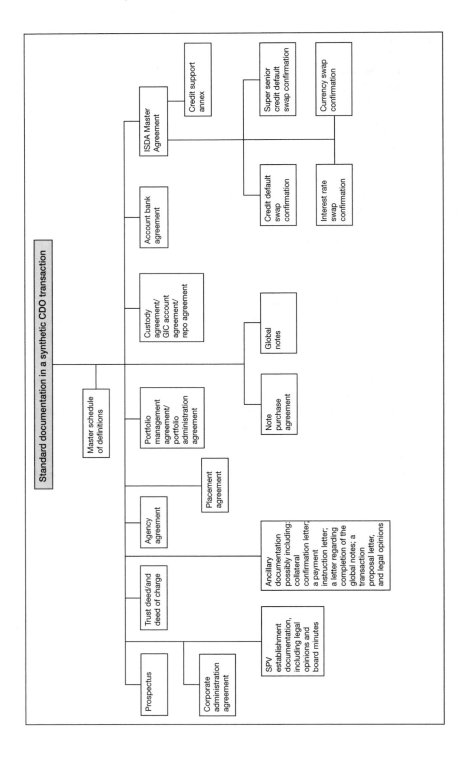

incorporated by reference into appropriate documents. There will also be various ancillary documents.

The parties to synthetic CDOs vary from transaction to transaction, depending on the structure. Usually, they will include:

- the SPV;
- an SPV administrator, to administrate the special purpose vehicle;
- the arranger, who will also perform the following roles:
  - credit default swap counterparty;
  - repo counterparty or asset swap counterparty (depending on how the highly rated securities held as collateral are held);
  - interest rate swap counterparty; and
  - possibly, currency hedging swap counterparty;
- in a managed transaction, a portfolio manager to manage the reference entity portfolio and possibly a portfolio administrator to perform any tests on the portfolio;
- the noteholders and super senior swap counterparty;
- a liquidity provider, to hedge any short-term liquidity issues;
- a trustee to represent the noteholders;
- a principal paying agent and a local paying agent in the jurisdiction of any listing;
- an account bank, to manage the issuer's accounts;
- a custodian to hold the collateral;
- if the transaction is to be listed, a listing agent (the relevant stock exchange will also review the offering document); and
- if the transaction is rated, the relevant rating agency which will be involved in negotiating the transaction.

(b) **Prospectus**

The prospectus sets out all of the necessary disclosure for investors to make a decision as to whether to purchase the notes issued under the synthetic CDO structure. It will set out investment considerations, risk factors, the conditions of the notes themselves and summary information on the main transaction documents.

The investment considerations provide disclosure information on whom the notes are most suitable for, with a particular emphasis that they should be purchased only by sophisticated investors. The risk factors set out various risks involved in purchasing the securities, of which investors should be aware.

The prospectus will also set out information on the issuer itself. The issuer is normally a newly incorporated SPV which has not yet produced accounts, so normally there is only a page or so of disclosure such as outlining the issuer's address, the names of its directors and registration and incorporation information.

In addition to the issuer, the prospectus provides disclosure on the key parties involved in the transaction: the arranger, the swap counterparty, the agents and any custodian. The prospectus will provide information on the underlying assets in which the proceeds of the notes are invested (eg, highly rated securities, a repo agreement or a deposit account).

The prospectus will also set out:

- any restrictions on the sale of the securities in a selling restrictions section;
- any general tax issues relating to the securities on a general relevant country-by-country basis; and
- certain other general information such as the form in which the notes are issued (eg, bearer instruments held in the clearing systems).

Where securities are listed on a stock exchange, this information is the most detailed and must comply with the rules of the relevant stock exchange. Even where synthetic CDO transactions are not listed, the general format of a prospectus will follow the structure set out above, but the level of detail of disclosure will be less.

(c) *Trust deed/deed of charge*

Each synthetic CDO transaction will have a trust deed. Sometimes the function of the trustee is divided into two roles: a security trustee and a note trustee. This happens where the arranger feels that, following any enforcement of the transaction, there may be a conflict between the trustee acting for the noteholders as secured parties and certain other of the secured parties, such as the arranger and the agents. When the trustee role is split between a note trustee and a security trustee, a transaction will often have a note trust deed and a security trust deed, with the provisions relating to taking security and its enforcement being set out in the security trust deed. Sometimes the security provisions are instead set out in a deed of charge.

The rest of the provisions will be set out in the note trust deed. The description below assumes that all of the provisions are set out in a single trust deed.

The trust deed constitutes the issue of securities. It sets out the powers and duties of the trustee. Under the trust deed the issuer grants security in favour of the trustee (on behalf of the noteholders) and other secured parties over the underlying assets (ie, the highly rated securities, deposit accounts and/or other transactions agreements).

The issuer makes various negative covenants, which are designed to restrict the commercial freedom and discretion of the issuer as far as possible, as well as positive covenants, which impose duties on the issuer such as the duty to produce annual accounts and to comply with the instructions of the trustee.

The enforcement provisions cover what happens if the issuer fails to make a payment of interest and principal when due (not if it is required to make a credit protection payment under the credit default swap); or commits another default such as a breach of covenant or other event of default. These rights include the right to appoint a receiver.

(d) *Custody agreement; deposit agreement; repo agreement*

Where the proceeds of the securities are invested in highly rated securities, these must be held as collateral by a custodian. The custody agreement will:

- appoint the custodian and set out its rights and duties;
- provide details of the accounts in which the securities are held and how the custodian should deal with certain issues that may arise relating to the securities, such as how to deal with voting rights; and

- outline the circumstances in which the custodian must act in accordance with the issuer's instructions and the circumstances in which it must act in accordance with the trustee's instructions (usually in an enforcement situation).

The custodian will normally have two accounts over which security is taken: the cash account and the securities account. The location of these accounts will depend upon where the highly rated securities are held. If they are held in either of Euroclear or Clearstream, then the custodian will hold the securities in an account with one of those institutions. These securities will then be charged in favour of the trustee on behalf of the secured parties. The custodian will also hold a cash account with the same institution, under which any cash payments of interest, amortisation amounts and later principal will be held. These payments will then be re-profiled under the asset swap agreement or a liquidity agreement. Sometimes the provisions relating to the custodian are set out instead in the agency agreement.

As an alternative to investing the proceeds of the notes in highly rated securities, the proceeds of the notes may be placed in a bank account held with the arranger or another financial institution. The rights of the issuer to the sums held in the account and how the financial institution segregates these proceeds, whom it allows to deal with the proceeds (eg, the trustee and/or the paying agent) and from whom and when it will take instructions will all be set out in a deposit agreement. The deposit agreement sometimes forms part of the account bank agreement.

Some transactions are structured so that the proceeds of the notes are invested in a repo agreement where the arranger will lend highly rated securities to the SPV, or a GIC agreement or deposit agreement where the proceeds of the notes will be placed in a secured high interest bearing account.

(e) *Agency agreement*

Once a CDO transaction has launched, the issuer's role is very limited, with all of the functions being carried out by agents. There will usually be a principal paying agent who arranges for the issuer's payments under the swaps to be made. If the transaction is listed, the relevant stock exchange will usually require a paying agent to be appointed in the jurisdiction of that stock exchange. If the securities carry a floating rate of interest or are a constant maturity or constant maturity credit default swap linked rate of interest, then there will also be a calculation agent (not to be confused with the calculation agent under the swap agreements). The agency agreement is used to appoint the agents and set out their rights and duties, the circumstances under which their appointment may be terminated and the circumstances under which they must act in accordance with the trustee's instructions.

(f) *The swap agreements*

Each synthetic CDO transaction will have a credit default swap transaction and, in the case of a fully structured transaction, a super senior credit default swap. Where the notes are of a different currency to the underlying assets or the credit default swaps, there may also be a currency swap in place. If the notes are multi-currency notes, there will be several currency swaps in place. The currency swaps and interest rate swaps are usually combined into a single transaction.

Where the rate and timing of interest under the securities and super senior credit default swap do not match the repo agreement/deposit agreement or GIC and the credit default swap, the transaction may be structured to isolate or iron out any interest rate/payment timing exposure. This is done by entering into an interest rate hedging agreement under which the issuer will pay on the various payment flows it receives in relation to the credit default swap, repo agreement, GIC or deposit agreement. In return, it will receive an amount equal to the interest payments that it must make under the notes, plus any fees payable to the transaction parties.

The issuer will enter into an ISDA Master Agreement (usually the 1992 ISDA Master Agreement) with the counterparty under the credit default swap and the other swaps. This is usually the same party – the arranger. Additionally, for a super senior credit default swap, the issuer will enter into an ISDA Master Agreement with the super senior credit default swap counterparty.

The ISDA Master Agreement will be amended in the schedule so that it reflects a structured securities transaction.

Each asset swap and interest/currency rate swap will contain special provisions (which will be set out in either the schedule or the confirmation) to reduce the notional amount of any transaction in line with the reduction in principal amount of the overall transaction, where there is a principal amount reduction following a settlement date.

These special provisions in the asset swap must also cover certain events that may impact on the underlying collateral. For example, the underlying collateral itself may default, or the underlying collateral or account agreements may become subject to withholding taxes.

(g) Portfolio management agreement

Where a synthetic CDO transaction is managed, there will also be a portfolio management agreement (sometimes called a portfolio advisory agreement). This involves the portfolio manager, the trustee and the issuer. Under this agreement the issuer will appoint the portfolio manager to perform advisory and administrative functions with respect to the portfolio of reference entities set out in the credit default swap.

The portfolio management agreement sets out the parameters of when the portfolio manager must substitute reference entities in the portfolio (perhaps on the basis of credit spread and other tests). It will also define the discretion that the portfolio manager has to make substitutions. As with the other agreements appointing transaction parties, the agreement will set out the remuneration of the portfolio manager, when its appointment can be terminated, when it must act in accordance with the instructions of the trustee and other boilerplate provisions. In more highly managed transactions, such as credit-linked CPPI, the agreement will set out highly detailed provisions providing the trading strategy which the portfolio manager must adopt and the various tests which will be performed on the portfolio. In some transactions, the functions may be set out in a trading agency agreement.

(h) Portfolio administration agreement

Where the management of a synthetic CDO involves a large administrative burden, especially in relation to the performance of certain tests on the portfolio to make sure that certain key thresholds are maintained, then a portfolio administrator may also be appointed to perform these tests. The portfolio administrator, the trustee and the issuer will enter into the portfolio administration agreement. This defines the scope of administrative tasks that the portfolio administrator must carry out. As with the other agreements appointing transaction parties, the agreement sets out the remuneration of the portfolio administrator, when its appointment can be terminated, when it must act in accordance with the instructions of the trustee and other boilerplate provisions.

(i)   Account bank agreement
At closing, the issuer will have had various accounts, into which funds will be paid (as described further above). Management of these accounts will be documented in the custody agreement or agency agreement, provided that there are no particularly complex issues involved. However, if the transaction structure requires more complex usage of accounts such as a reserve account or a liquidity account, this part of the transaction may be documented in a separate account bank agreement.

(j)   Placement agency agreement
In the placement agency agreement, one or more placement agents (usually the transaction's arranger and occasionally other financial institutions) agree to procure subscribers for the notes at a specified price. If they fail to do so, the placement agents must subscribe for the notes themselves.

The issuer and placement agents will agree to abide by certain selling restrictions. These are usually set out in the prospectus, which will usually contain certain representations in relation to the issuer such as obtaining a listing of the securities, as well as certain other representations as to the veracity of the prospectus, the status of the issuer, taxes and other areas of concern.

The issuer will also covenant on various matters, such as the efforts it will make to procure registration of the security. The placement agency agreement sets out the conditions precedent to the placing agents placing the notes and the fee that the placement agents will receive for their services.

(k)   Global notes
In the European market, synthetic CDO securities will usually be issued in bearer form. Rather than having an individual bearer note certificate representing each note, a global note is usually issued. To comply with certain US legal restrictions (usually Regulation S, which allows sales of notes which are structured to avoid sales being made into the United States and TEFRA D) these notes are issued in temporary form as a temporary global note. The note remains in this temporary global form during a distribution compliance period (usually around 40 days), during which there are restrictions on transfer. The temporary global note is then replaced by a permanent global note and these transfer restrictions are restricted.

Alternatively, the CDO securities may be issued in registered form. This means that there will be an additional party involved in the transaction – the registrar. In this case the permanent global note will be in registered form and the registrar will record transfers in the books of the common depository.

In the case of both bearer global notes and registered global notes, the global notes are authenticated by the issuer and agent on closing, whereupon the proceeds of the notes are released to the issuer and the global notes are held by an agent for a common depository. The common depository will, in the case of Regulation S notes, hold the notes on behalf of Euroclear and Clearstream (the two major clearing systems). Rule 144A notes, the global note, will be registered in the name of a nominee of DTC, with book-entry interests.

CDO securities may be issued in reliance upon both Regulation S and Rule 144A (which allows sales of notes which are structured to allow sales of notes into the United States, but only to certain sophisticated investors). In these CDO structures, all of the notes are usually issued in registered form.

Most investors will retain their holding of CDO securities through an account (held either directly or through a nominee) with either Euroclear or Clearstream. Transfers of securities between investors are then made through book entries in the clearing systems. Definitive bearer notes will usually be issued to noteholders only in certain limited circumstances (eg, where the clearing systems are closed for a period of 14 days or there is an event of default under the CDO securities).

The above description sets out the general market practice for the form in which CDO securities are held. For tax or other reasons, there are several other structures that may be used, although these will be for only a limited number of issues.

(l) **Note purchase agreement**

A note purchase agreement is an agreement signed by investors in the CDO transaction under which they make certain representations about their capacity to hold the notes and their understanding of the risks involved.

(m) **Master schedule of definitions**

Due to the number of transaction documents in any synthetic CDO transaction, many of which will use the same base definitions, it often makes sense to collate all of the definitions used in the transaction into a master schedule of definitions document. This is then incorporated by reference into each transaction document (with the exception of the offering document, as the only transaction document which investors will usually receive is the offering document, so this must be able to stand alone. Standard ISDA definitions will not normally be included in the master schedule of definitions.

(n) **Ancillary documentation**

A synthetic CDO transaction will also have several ancillary documents. Some of these may also be incorporated into the trust deed. The ancillary documents may consist of:

- a payment instruction letter;
- a letter regarding completion of the global notes;
- a transaction proposal letter;
- the issuer's board minutes;
- the legal opinion of the arranger's counsel; and
- the legal opinion of the issuer's counsel.

In the payment instruction letter, the issuer instructs the agent to pay the net proceeds of the notes to the asset swap counterparty as an initial exchange amount.

In the letter regarding completion of the global notes, the issuer gives written confirmation that now that the transaction's principal documents have been executed, the agent should prepare and authenticate the global notes.

Transaction proposal letters are prepared to demonstrate the independence of the SPV. The proposal letter is executed prior to the transaction's closing or pre-closing. The arranger proposes to the issuer that it issues securities under the CDO transaction in return for a fee. This fee is usually a few hundred dollars or euros.

The issuer will hold a board meeting using board minutes prepared by its counsel. These board minutes will set out a summary of the terms of the securities and the proposal to enter into the CDO transaction and issue the securities. The issuer will then agree to execute the transaction documents and enter into the transaction.

The arranger's counsel will provide a legal opinion, which can be relied upon by the arranger, the trustee and, if the transaction is rated, the relevant rating agencies. The arranger's counsel will opine, among other things, that both the transaction documents and the notes are legal, valid, binding and enforceable under English law and the choice of English law is valid. It will also opine that any security has been validly created and (if applicable) registered, and that financial regulations have been complied with. The arranger may also opine on any applicable taxes (or the lack thereof).

The issuer's counsel will also provide a legal opinion, which can be relied upon by the arranger, the trustee and, if the transaction is rated, the relevant rating agencies. The issuer's counsel will opine, among other things, that the issuer has the capacity to enter into the transaction. It will also opine on any taxes (or lack thereof) in the SPV's jurisdiction, and that in the SPV's jurisdiction the choice of law under the transaction documents is enforceable. Additionally, it will opine on the effectiveness of the transaction's limited recourse provisions and that, as far as local law is concerned, the security created under the documents is valid and enforceable.

2.5 Credit-linked notes: an overlap with synthetic CDO structures

(a) Credit-linked notes issued by an SPV

Credit-linked notes may be issued either by an SPV or by a financial institution. Where an SPV issues a credit-linked note it may be either as part of a CDO transaction with issues of multiple tranches or a single tranche issue. The cost of establishing an SPV and related documentation means that most financial institutions will arrange to issue single tranche CDOs only through a repackaging programme.

Most financial institutions that arrange large numbers of single tranche, credit-linked notes now establish structured note programmes utilising an SPV structure based on a modular system. Originally financial institutions set up programmes that mirrored the structure of vanilla debt securities medium-term note (MTN) programmes (see the discussion of credit-linked notes issued directly by financial institutions below). Under these MTN-style programmes, an SPV and the various other transaction parties would enter into programme documentation consisting of a principal trust deed, a programme dealer agreement, an agency agreement and a custody agreement. The conditions, disclosure and risk factors would be set out in a programme-offering document. For each issue, a separate supplemental offering document, a supplemental trust deed, purchase agreement and swap documentation would be documented.

This structure had the disadvantage that as an arranging bank's credit derivative/ repackaging business expanded and it established a number of special purposes and programmes, the same documentation would have to be produced (and updated) for each issuer. In addition, each issue of credit-linked notes produced a large amount of documentation, which tended to be identical, or virtually identical, for each issue.

Initially, the banks tackled the problem by establishing multi-issuer programmes, where a standard documentation platform was put in place and each new SPV issuer would then accede to this documentation. However, any non-standard amendments for an issue of notes greatly increased the amount of documentation required and each individual issue of notes was 'document heavy'. To avoid this, most banks began to adopt a more streamlined approach by using the modular structure.

Modules are prepared for every possible aspect of trades issued under the bank's SPV structured note programmes. These modules set out standard terms. Separate modules are also prepared which contain:

- the trust provisions and conditions of the notes (normally set out in the trust deed);
- the agency provisions (normally set out in the agency module);
- the swap provisions (normally set out in an ISDA Master Agreement) and schedule; and
- the custody provisions (normally set out in the custody agreement).

Some issues of notes may be bearer securities and other may be registered security. Some SPV issuers may be Irish incorporated or Netherlands incorporated – these are subject to different insolvency regimes. The modular system is very versatile, so separate modules can be prepared for different types of notes: a module can be prepared for bearer securities, with a separate module for registered securities. A module containing conditions of notes for Irish issuers, which incorporate the vagaries of the Irish insolvency regime, can be prepared, along with another one for Dutch issuers which reflects the specific provisions of Dutch insolvency law.

These relevant modules are then incorporated by reference and amended as necessary into a trust instrument, which is prepared for each issue of notes (see further description below). This trust instrument will constitute the issue of notes and will provide that each module relevant to the particular issue of notes is incorporated by reference. The trust instrument will then set out in a separate section any relevant amendments that must be made to each module to reflect the structure of the issue of notes.

The most significant amendments must be made to the terms and conditions module to reflect the terms of the transaction (eg, denomination, principal amount, currency, maturity date, specific collateral). The trust instrument will also often incorporate some of the ancillary documentation present in a synthetic CDO transaction, such as the letter regarding completion of the global notes and the common depositary instruction letter.

In addition to the trust instrument, each transaction will have an offering document. It is standard practice for each issuer to have a base prospectus which has been approved by a listing authority (eg, the Irish Stock Exchange). The base prospectus will set out similar information to the offering document in a synthetic CDO transaction (eg, investment considerations, risk factors, the conditions of the notes themselves, disclosure regarding the issuer, the arranger bank, selling restrictions).

The programme will have a large issue size – usually around €10 billion or equivalent. When an issue of notes is made under the programme, a prospectus will be issued which will then incorporate the base prospectus into it by reference. The prospectus will set out:

- more specific investment considerations;
- risk factors and selling restrictions;
- the terms of the notes (which are set out in the trust instrument);
- summaries of the swap agreements (sometimes the credit default swap is included as an exhibit);
- disclosure information on the highly rated securities in which the proceeds of the notes are invested; and
- the reference entities relevant to the credit derivatives transaction.

Where the issue of notes is listed, this disclosure will be more detailed as it must comply with the more exacting requirements of the Prospectus Directive and the particular stock exchange.

For each issue, the issuer will enter into two swap agreements with the arranging bank: an asset swap confirmation and a credit default swap confirmation. The terms of the swap agreement which are normally set out in an ISDA Master Agreement and schedule will be set out in the swap module. However, the swap confirmations will take the form of standard confirmations as used in synthetic CDO transactions.

As with a synthetic CDO transaction, there will be a transaction proposal letter and also legal opinions from the issuer and arranger's counsel.

The MTN approach in structured note programmes is still applicable where an arranging bank intends to issue only a limited number of structured securities. Where an arranging bank intends to establish a number of SPVs or to issue a wide variety of transactions, the modular approach provides more streamlined and cost-effective documentation.

Additionally, credit linked notes may be structured as nth to default transactions, single name credit default transactions, CMCDS transactions or in many other forms, with the credit derivative element of the transaction performing as described in the unfunded credit derivatives chapter; and the funded element as described above.

(b)   *Credit-linked notes issued by a financial institution*
Where a credit-linked note structure does not utilise an SPV, a financial institution may issue the credit-linked note. Every financial institution has an active euro MTN

programme. Financial institutions and large corporations used euro MTN programmes as a streamlined documentation platform for issuing bonds to meet their general funding requirements. When a financial institution issues a credit-linked note, it is issued by utilising the existing euro MTN programme.

This means that the documentation for a credit-linked note issued by a financial institution will be substantially the same as for any euro MTN issue. A base prospectus will already be in place. This is substantially similar to a base prospectus for a repackaging programme; however, the disclosure in relation to the issuer will be far greater. Unless the programme has been prepared with the objective of issuing credit-linked securities, the conditions of the notes will have to be substantially amended.

It appears to have become market standard for the terms of an issue to be set out in a final terms document, rather than a prospectus as is done for issues under a repackaging programme. This may perhaps comply with the letter of the Prospectus Directive, but it does not comply with the spirit and it is likely that this practice will change in the near future.

The final terms document sets out the various risk factors and investment considerations relevant to the issue of credit-linked notes and will set out the terms and conditions of the notes. As is often the case, if the euro MTN programme has not been prepared with the issue of credit-linked notes in mind, then a full set of terms and conditions, or terms and heavily amended conditions, must be set out in the final terms. Where the euro MTN programme has contemplated issues of credit-linked notes, the final terms may just contain the specific terms of the issue (eg, denomination, currency). The final terms will also set out any selling restrictions particular to the issue of notes, as well as disclosure on the reference entities and any party not contemplated in the base prospectus, such as a portfolio manager.

The remaining documentation for a financial institution issue of credit-linked notes is simpler than for an SPV issue. The issue of credit-linked notes is a direct obligation of the financial institution, so the proceeds of the notes are not invested in securities to be held as collateral. An arranger's legal opinion is not normally necessary either. This removes the need for a custody agreement and an asset swap agreement. The securities will usually be placed by the financial institution itself, removing the need for a placement agreement. It is also unusual for there to be a trustee, as much of the trustee's function is usually performed by a fiscal agent in a standard euro MTN programme. Any enforcement action would be against the assets of the bank itself rather than any collateral.

Additionally, although the issuing financial institution may itself hedge its liabilities in relation to the credit derivatives element of the transaction, it is unusual for any credit default swap to form part of the transaction documentation.

On occasion, where the credit derivative element of the transaction is particularly complicated, the final terms may set out the credit derivative in a form or hypothetical reference swap, which is not actually entered into, but reductions in principal amount of the notes are made on the basis of those which would have been made if the hypothetical swap had indeed been entered into.

2.6   Synthetic CDO^N and CDO squared and cubed transactions

Synthetic CDO^N transactions are a generic name for synthetic CDO squared and cubed transactions: these products make up 1.3% of the credit derivatives market.

CDO squared transactions are also known as CDO^2 transactions and CDO2 transactions.

They are synthetic CDO transactions with one key difference: instead of having a reference portfolio of reference entities against which credit protection is sold, the reference portfolio lists other credit derivatives.

These credit derivative transactions may reference other synthetic CDO or asset-backed transactions (in which case an ISDA credit default swap on asset-backed securities template will be utilised, or alternatively reference credit default swaps referencing other reference portfolios or corporate and sovereign reference entities.

A CDO squared transaction may even involve a combination of the two structures with credit default swap on ABS (cash CDOs and synthetic CDOs) and CDS on corporate and sovereign reference entities.

An arranger will most likely structure a synthetic CDO squared transaction for one of three principal reasons:

- to repackage existing CDO holdings;
- to take advantage of a ratings arbitrage; or
- to make use of arbitrage and capital relief opportunities.

In any year, an active CDO arranger will arrange many transactions, and for some of these it may be forced to retain residual holdings corresponding to parts of deals that it cannot sell. Such an arranger may choose to group these holdings together into a reference portfolio and structure this as a CDO squared transaction. For the arranger, this will have the effect of getting these holdings off its books and the investor will have the benefit of investing in a liquid product, which will in turn provide a higher return than would be generated by holding the individual holdings separately.

As discussed above, one of the attractions of the CDO squared transaction's two-tier structure is that it takes more credit events to impact on the reference portfolio for losses to impact on the CDO squared transaction. However, once losses do start to impact – particularly where certain reference entity names appear in several of the CDOs which make up the reference portfolio, or where recovery rates are particularly low or the pattern of losses does not conform to the modelling on which the transaction was based – the increased leverage may cause a CDO squared transaction to deteriorate more rapidly than a standard CDO tranche.

CDO cubed transactions are the second product forming the CDO^N category of credit derivatives. These are essentially synthetic CDOs which have other CDO squared transactions as the relevant names comprising the reference portfolio. CDO cubed transactions have, by their nature, greater leverage than CDO squared transactions.

2.7   Credit-linked CPPI

Generally speaking, a synthetic CPPI transaction is a synthetic CDO transaction structured to protect the principal amount of the noteholder's investment, while placing the potential future coupon payments at risk. The structure protects principal through a defensive strategy, while at the same utilising aggressive leveraged trading techniques potentially to generate enhanced returns, payable as coupons. If successful, the investor 'has its cake and eats it': its principal amount is protected and investment return is similar to more risky investments.

(a) *Overview*

Synthetic CPPI can utilise either a CDO structure or a credit-linked note structure. It also utilises constant proportion portfolio insurance techniques that were developed in the 1980s for use with equity products and funds.

Synthetic CPPI works as follows. An investor purchases a note, issued by either a special purpose vehicle or a financial institution. The transaction manager adjusts the

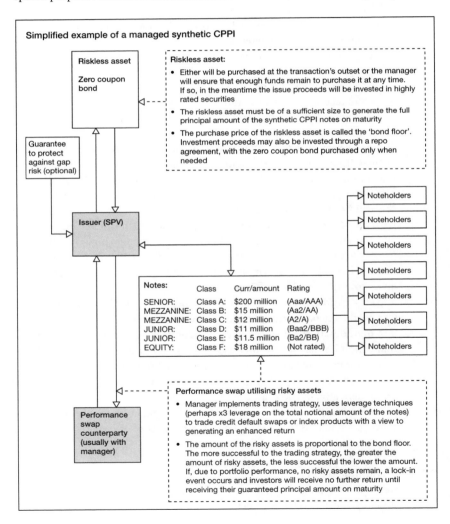

structure's exposure so that one part is to a risk-free asset and another is to a risky asset. Throughout the life of the transaction, the arranger continuously re-adjusts the exposure to the risky and risk-free assets with a view to always having enough funds to guarantee the repayment of the principal at the maturity date.

Generally, if the net asset value of the portfolio increases, then more funds are invested in the risky asset, thus boosting potential returns. However, if the value of the portfolio decreases, then the balance is shifted towards the risk-free asset (eg, a zero coupon bond or a repo agreement) in order to provide principal protection.

What is a zero coupon bond?

An example of the type of 'risk-free asset' that the arranger would be seeking would be a zero coupon bond issued with an issue price of, for example, 75% of its principal amount. This zero coupon bond would be repayable at 100% of its principal amount at maturity. The low issue price of the zero coupon bond would mean that the higher payment at maturity compensates for the lack of interest payments during the CPPI note's term. Therefore, the zero coupon bond's trading price will increase over time, because there will be fewer absent interest payments for which the bondholder must be compensated. This also means that the amount of cash required to purchase the riskless asset will also increase over time, meaning that unless the initial investment strategy in the risky asset is successful, the manager will have less money over time to invest in the risky asset.

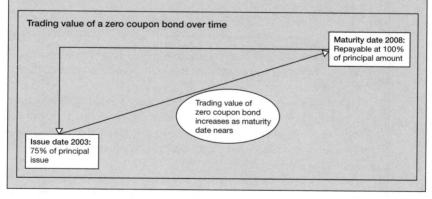

The manager of a synthetic CPPI transaction can invest a part of the portfolio in the risk-free asset at the outset of the transaction, or it can control the value of the portfolio to make sure that at any time it has enough money to be able to buy a zero-coupon bond which will allow the repayment of the principal of the synthetic CPPI note at its maturity date. However, it must bear in mind that the later it decides to buy such a bond, the more expensive it may be. The value necessary to buy the required amount of the risk-free asset is called the 'bond floor' and the net asset value of a CPPI product cannot fall below that level.

The 'risky asset' will usually be a portfolio of credit derivatives transactions. The portfolio (the risky asset) is then traded (often through a performance swap) in a leveraged format with the objective of maximising returns so that the investment will provide a target return over a LIBOR rate.

What is leverage?

In this context, leverage is a mechanism that allows a manager to allocate greater exposure to the risky asset than it has actual funds available (excluding the riskless asset) for meeting those obligations in a worst-case scenario.

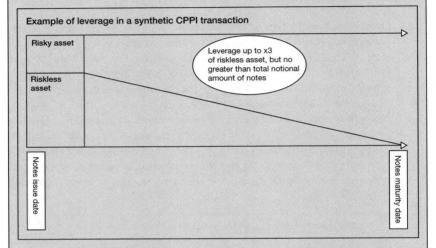

Example of leverage in a synthetic CPPI transaction

Risky asset

Riskless asset

Leverage up to x3 of riskless asset, but no greater than total notional amount of notes

Notes issue date

Notes maturity date

The maximum degree of leverage is also known as the level of exposure or the 'gearing factor'. The gearing factor remains constant throughout the life of a CPPI: hence 'constant proportion'.

Let's assume that a synthetic CPPI CDO transaction has $100 million of notes and the bond floor is $80 million. This means that a manager will need $80 million in order to buy a zero coupon bond at the transaction's outset which will generate $100 million at the maturity date, an amount equal to the principal amount of the synthetic CPPI notes.

This also means that the manager must have a surplus of $20 million. (This amount is often referred to as the 'reserve' or 'cushion'.) If the manager does not purchase the zero coupon bond at the outset of the transaction, its price will rise over time until maturity, when its price will reach the full principal amount of the synthetic CPPI notes.

If the manager purchases the zero coupon bond on the transaction's issue date and the gearing factor is three, then the manager can allocate $60 million to the risky asset ($20 million x 3 = $60) (ie, enter into credit derivatives where its potential exposure as seller is $60 million).

> However, the manager must monitor the value of the portfolio very closely and be ready to readjust the balance if the value of the risky asset changes. For example, if the risky strategy did not perform well and the portfolio lost $15 million as a result, then the value of the CPPI structure would be $85 million. If the bond floor was still $80 million, there would be only a $5 million excess to invest in the risky assets. The manager would need to adjust its risky exposure to $15 million ($5 million x 3 = $15 million) and invest $70 million ($85 million – $15 million = $70 million) in the risk-free asset.

The more money there is above the bond floor, the more can be invested in the risky assets. Conversely, if the net asset value of the strategy has fallen to just above the bond floor level, the exposure to the risky asset must be reduced accordingly. If the risky asset performs badly and the value of the portfolio hits the bond floor, the portfolio will be 'locked in' and all funds will be invested in a zero-coupon bond. In this way the principal amount of the note is guaranteed.

However, in a very unstable market, it is plausible that the net asset value of the strategy may fall below the floor level. This is called a 'gap risk'. To combat gap risk, the arranger may extend a guarantee to the transaction.

> **Hypothetical example of a credit-linked CPPI transaction: Featherstone CPPI transaction**
>
> Featherstone Investments arranged a credit-linked CPPI transaction in June 2006. It also managed the investments made under the transaction.
>
> Featherstone established a Jersey SPV, Fusion Limited, which issued €100 million of notes to investors, due in 2011. To protect this principal amount, Featherstone calculated a bond floor. This was the amount required to purchase a 'risk free' zero coupon bond maturing in 2011, which would generate a €100 million repayable amount to guarantee repayment of the CPPI note. A zero-coupon bond issued by Great Eastern Travel, a highly rated issuer, was available. Its trading price at the CPPI note's issue date was 75% of its principal amount.
>
> Featherstone therefore calculated the bond floor as €75 million, leaving €25 million. Featherstone did not arrange for Fusion to purchase the Great Eastern bond at this point. The deal was structured to allow a leveraged return on the risky asset and Featherstone allocated a leverage multiple of three. This meant that Featherstone could use three times the value of the risky asset – €75 million (€25 million multiplied by x3 leverage) to enter into a credit derivatives portfolio consisting of credit default swaps on 100 reference entities, where it sold credit protection. The remaining €25 million was invested in the Great Eastern Travel zero coupon bond.
>
> At the end of the first year the credit derivatives portfolio had made a 20% return (ie, €15 million on the €75 million invested). This meant that its value

now stood at €90 million and the value of the overall portfolio was €110 million. However, the bond floor had also increased – a zero coupon bond's market price increases over time; €80 million would now be required to purchase enough of the Great Eastern bond to generate the full €100 million principal amount of the CPPI note payable on maturity.

Consequently, the bond floor was €80 million. The cushion was $30 million (€110 million – €80 million), which meant that with x3 leverage the value of the risky asset was €90 million; €20 million (€110 million – €90 million) was left invested in the Great Eastern bond.

At the end of the second year, the credit derivatives portfolio had once again made a 20% return (ie, €18 million on the €90 million invested). This meant that the risky asset's value now stood at €108 million and the overall portfolio was worth €128 million. However, the bond floor had also once again increased. This time, €85 million would now be required to purchase enough of the Great Eastern bond to generate the full €100 million principal amount of the CPPI notes payable on maturity.

The cushion was €33 million (€128 million – €85 million), which meant that with x3 leverage the value of the risky asset was €99 million; €29 million (€128 million – €99 million) was left invested in the Great Eastern bond.

During the third year, the credit derivatives market suffered several major credit events and the portfolio had made a loss of €47 million on the €108 million invested. At the same time, the bond floor increased to €90 million. The value of the risky asset fell to €61 million (€108 million – €47 million) and the overall value of the portfolio was €90 million (€61 million + €29 million).

Featherstone closed out of its portfolio (a 'lock-in' event), and was forced to invest the €90 million remaining proceeds in the Great Eastern bond.

For the outstanding two years of the transaction, the portfolio was no longer managed and the CPPI bondholders received back the €100 million principal amount, which they had invested at the transaction's outset.

	Floor level (€million)	Risky portfolio (€million)	Risk-free portfolio (€million)	Profit/(loss) (€million)	Overall portfolio (€million)
Year 0	75	75	25	—	100
Year 1	80	90	20	15	110
Year 2	85	99	29	18	128
Year 3	90	0	90	(47)	90
Year 4	—	0	90	—	90
Year 5	—	0	90	—	90

(For reasons of simplification, in the example I have assumed that the risk-free asset and the proceeds of the notes that have been invested do not generate a return. Naturally, this is not the case and the value of the risk-free asset increases over time.)

(b)   Structure and documentation

A synthetic CPPI structure will utilise most of the standard documentation in a synthetic CDO or a credit-linked note issued by a financial institution or a repackaging vehicle. It is important to note that a synthetic CPPI structure will not utilise a super senior credit default swap. It will also not usually directly utilise a credit default swap. Instead, it will utilise a performance swap, under which the proceeds of the notes will be invested in highly rated securities through a repo agreement. The level of management will vary between transactions, from only controlling the levels of exposure to actively trading the riskless and risk-free assets. The mechanics of the synthetic CPPI element of the transaction will be set out in the performance swap, the portfolio management agreement, with disclosure provided in the prospectus.

It is also important to note that this is still a new product area; there are many variations on this structure, with bespoke transactions becoming progressively more complex.

3.   CPDO

Although CPDO is a brand-new product that only entered the market in October 2006, the total amount of CPDO issuance at the end of 2006 was above $2 billion. It is the latest development in the credit derivatives market and is a step on from CPPI. Whereas a credit-linked CPPI offers protection of the principal amount, a CPDO only specifies the coupon that an investor should be receiving throughout the term of the transaction.

3.1   What is a CPDO and how does it work?

Generally speaking, a CPDO can be summarised as a managed synthetic CDO which adopts a highly leveraged trading strategy, aimed at generating a specific and high coupon return. As any other synthetic CDO, a CPDO sells notes to investors and uses the proceeds to purchase highly rated securities.

It also sells credit protection for an agreed amount in relation to each entity in a portfolio of reference entities. The key difference from a standard synthetic CDO is that a CPDO transaction's exposure to the credit derivative element of the transaction is highly leveraged (ie, the SPV will sell credit protection to the value of many times its actual assets).

So far, all of the issued CPDOs have been referenced to credit indices (eg, CDX or iTraxx). One of the main characteristics of a CPDO trading strategy is that the constitution of its reference portfolio changes every six months. All transactions are then unwound and new transactions entered into. With the indices rolling every six months, the theory is that the weakest credits in the portfolio will disappear, thereby reducing the chance that a reference entity will incur a credit event. Usually, following each roll, all reference entities are investment grade (often triple A), which means less risk for the investors and ensures a high credit rating of the CPDO itself: the high rating of CPDO transactions is also a key selling point. The chances of multiple defaults of reference entities during any roll period are also deemed to be less.

The trading strategy of a CPDO is almost the exact opposite of a CPPI.

The net asset value of a CPDO is also divided between the 'risky' and 'risk-free' assets, though the exposure at which a lock-in event will occur will be much lower, perhaps when the portfolio value is at about 10% to 15% of its initial value: a 'cash out event'. However, the manager does not shift asset allocation between the risky and risk-free asset with a view to always having enough money to buy a risk-free zero coupon bond. Instead, the aim of shifting the asset allocation in a CPDO structure is to have enough money to pay a specified coupon. The coupon is not guaranteed.

This structure means that if the risky assets are incurring losses, then the leverage and therefore the exposure to the risky asset must be higher to make up for the shortfall.

CPDOs are highly leveraged, with the gearing ratio being often up to 15 to 20 times the value of the collateral. For example, if the CPDO structure had issued notes to the value of $100 million, then the SPV may sell protection for up to $1.5 billion on the notional portfolio (if leverage is up to 15 times).

However, if there are no or almost no defaults in the portfolio and there is a steady income, then the leverage is reduced (to, perhaps, seven to eight times). Conversely, if the strategy is unsuccessful and funds shrink to only $90 million, a manager will need to adopt an even higher leverage (perhaps 15 to 18 times) in order to obtain the same target amount. Although it may sound quite risky, all reference entities are highly rated, which means that the risk of them incurring a credit event is reduced.

CPDO and roulette

This CPDO structure can result in a management strategy comparable to a gambler chasing his losses. Let's assume that a gambler has $100 in his wallet and he wants to leave the casino when it closes with $110. He places a $5 bet on the roulette table on 'red or black' and hopes to double this amount. However, he loses and his funds shrink to $95. Now, instead of betting another $10 to achieve his target, he has to increase the amount of his bet to $7.50. If he wins, he will win $15 and he will have his desired $110.

However, he loses again and his funds are now at $92.50. To make up for the shortfall and win $110 before the casino closes, on the last bet of the night he now must place an even higher bet of $8.75. If he wins, he will win $17.50 and his 'portfolio' will be worth $110; if he loses, he will only have $84 left.

Fortunately, highly rated securities are far less risky than roulette, but a structural risk still remains.

The aim of the CPDO trading strategy is to have sufficient income to pay all future coupons and the principal at the maturity date. As soon as this happens, a 'cash-in' event is triggered and all funds are invested in riskless assets (eg, a zero coupon bond).

Most CPDOs also have a 'cash-out' event (as described above). Following a 'cash-out' event, the structure is usually unwound and any remaining proceeds are distributed to the noteholders. Alternatively, this remaining amount can be invested in a risk-free asset.

3.2 The economics behind a CPDO

In order to get a better insight into the nature of a CPDO, it is important to understand the economics behind it. Naturally, as in any other synthetic CDO, the profitability of a CPDO depends on whether, and to what extent, the reference entities are defaulting on their obligations. However, the fact that the portfolio of the reference entities changes every half a year also has a huge impact on the economics of this instrument.

A CPDO gains exposure to a portfolio of reference entities at the beginning of each six-month period. Throughout that period the CPDO makes a profit by getting premiums for its exposure and at the end of it all, transactions are unwound. Depending on the change in the credit quality of the reference entities during this six-month period, the CPDO either makes some additional profit or suffers a loss.

If the spread of a reference entity is wide at the beginning and then it tightens, this means that the credit quality of this entity has improved. This is good news for noteholders holding the CPDO notes, since by unwinding its position at the end of the period the strategy makes a profit. However, if the credit quality of a reference entity deteriorates and the spreads tighten, then by unwinding the transaction the noteholder will suffer a loss.

This means that the rolling of the indices can have a negative impact on the net asset value of the instrument. However, when it happens, this can theoretically be recouped by increasing the leverage.

3.3 Structure and documentation

The structure and documentation of a CPDO are very similar to a synthetic CPPI. The key difference is the amount of leverage involved and the actual trading strategy

3.4 Comparison with CPPI

A credit-linked CPPI and a CPDO are quite similar to each other in that they both operate by way of a synthetic CDO, with each having a pre-defined strategy. The main difference is that a CPPI offers principal protection and its leverage is related to the bond floor. This means that if a CPPI suffers a loss at the beginning of its lifetime, it will be very difficult to recoup it.

For example, if the value of the note is $100 million, the bond floor is $80 million and the gearing ration is three, then $60 million ($20 million x 3) can be invested in the risky asset. If in one year the strategy suffers losses of, say, $15 million, the value of the cushion will fall to $5 million ($20 million – $5 million) and the risky asset will have to be reduced from $60 million to a mere $15 million ($5 million x 3). Quite clearly, this will have a considerable impact on the profitability of the instrument.

Conversely, the leveraged mechanism of a CPDO means that the instrument can recoup any losses very easily, but at the price of greater risk to the principal. When the net asset value of a CPDO decreases, the instrument is structured to 'chase' its losses until it either has a profit or loses all (or most) of its money.

Overview of the 2003 ISDA Credit Derivatives Definitions

The 2003 ISDA Credit Derivatives Definitions are the market standard definitions for credit derivative transactions. Part II of this book covers them in depth.

If you check the ISDA website, you will see that ISDA has opted not to produce a user's guide for the 2003 Definitions. The only thing to help you through them are the document's index, its table of contents and a limited number of publications. Now there is also this book, with Part II acting as a user's guide. It is the most comprehensive analysis of the 2003 Definitions ever written. It dissects each of the 229 definitions and 10 articles, as well as the six exhibits, introduction and preamble. Part II has 11 chapters. The first[1] provides an overview of how the 2003 Definitions work and a summary aimed at giving the reader a quick understanding of their mechanics.

The remaining chapters sequentially cover each of the 2003 Definitions' 10 articles in greater depth, dealing with each section in turn, as well as (where applicable) the six exhibits annexed to the 2003 Definitions. The purpose of this two-tier approach is to allow the reader to gain a general understanding of the 2003 Definitions prior to covering them in greater depth. At the risk of there being some repetition, Part II also aims to provide both a reference resource for specific points that arise in credit derivatives transactions and a comprehensive text which can be read in its entirety, with a view to gaining a solid understanding of the 2003 Definitions.

Part II analyses the structure of the 2003 Definitions, how the various definitions work, how they inter-relate with each other and what they say. This is all done in a straightforward, easily understandable and interesting way, providing diagrams and using hypothetical and actual case studies wherever possible. To get the most out of Part II, the reader must understand how credit default swaps work, either by reading the first two chapters in Part I and the chapter on single name credit default swaps in Part III or through other experience.

1. Structure

Perhaps you are an in-house lawyer or a treasurer, or you work in sales or trading in a bank. Perhaps you practise in a law firm; or maybe you are studying. If you are involved in credit derivatives, you must understand the 2003 Definitions well enough to be able to review them, advise on them or maybe even structure or price credit derivatives transactions.

---

[1] Much of this chapter is sourced from a chapter previously written by the author and published in *Practical Derivatives: A Transactional Approach*, edited by Denton J (Globe Law and Business, June 2006).

The 2003 Definitions contain the building blocks for all credit derivatives transactions. You cannot understand credit derivatives without knowing the 2003 Definitions like the back of your hand. This is not easy.

Taking a look at the credit derivative transaction in its simplest form, the nine-page footnoted single-name credit default swap set out in Exhibit A to the 2003 Definitions, it is clear that even this 'no-frills' credit derivative contains over 100 defined terms from the 2003 Definitions. (The document also requires users to understand the ISDA Master Agreement incorporated into it by reference.) It is also apparent to the user that if this is a no-frills credit derivative, the interaction between the 2003 Definitions and more sophisticated credit derivatives, such as portfolio credit default swaps, collateralised debt obligation squared transactions and credit linked notes, will be even more complex.

The 2003 Definitions are not an easy read. They are 89 pages long and divided into a table of contents; an introduction and preamble; and 10 articles, which are each then sub-divided as follows.

Introduction	
Preamble	
Article I – Certain general definitions	
1.1	Credit derivative transaction
1.2	Confirmation
1.3	Term
1.4	Effective date
1.5	Trade date
1.6	Scheduled termination date
1.7	Transaction date
1.8	Event determination date
1.9	Notice delivery period
1.10	Requirements regarding notices
1.11	Grace period extension date
1.12	Grace period; grace period business day
1.13	Potential failure to pay
1.14	Calculation agent
1.15	Calculation agent city
1.16	Business day
1.17	Calculation agent city business day
1.18	2002 ISDA Master Agreement
1.19	Buyer
1.20	Seller
1.21	TARGET settlement day
Article II – General terms relating to credit derivatives transactions	
2.1	Reference entity
2.2	Provisions for determining a successor
2.3	Reference obligation
2.4	Reference price
2.5	Fixed amount
2.6	Fixed-rate payer
2.7	Fixed-rate payer calculation amount
2.8	Fixed-rate payer period end date
2.9	Fixed-rate payer calculation period
2.10	Fixed-rate payer payment date
2.11	Business day convention
2.12	Floating-rate payer
2.13	Floating-rate payer calculation amount
2.14	Obligation
2.15	Deliverable obligation
2.16	Sovereign restructured deliverable obligation
2.17	Excluded obligation
2.18	Excluded deliverable obligation
2.19	Method for determining obligations
2.20	Method for determining deliverable obligations

Article IX – Additional representations and agreements of the parties	
9.1	Additional representations and agreements of the parties
9.2	Additional representations and agreements for physical settlement
9.3	Partial cash settlement due to impossibility or illegality
9.4	Partial cash settlement of consent required loans
9.5	Partial cash settlement of assignable loans
9.6	Partial cash settlement of participations
9.7	Latest permissible physical settlement date
9.8	Partial cash settlement terms
9.9	Buy-in of bonds not delivered
9.10	Alternative procedures relating to loans not delivered
Article X – Novation provisions	
10.1	Novation
10.2	Novation transaction
10.3	Transferor
10.4	Transferee
10.5	Remaining party
10.6	Old transaction
10.7	New transaction
10.8	Old agreement
10.9	New agreement
10.10	ISDA Master Agreement
10.11	Old confirmation
10.12	Novated amount
10.13	Novation agreement

There are 229 definitions in the 2003 Definitions, many of which cross-reference each other, though sometimes they are modified by other definitions in certain circumstances. There are also six exhibits, setting out forms of documents which a party to a transaction may need to use or serve during the term of the transaction.

Exhibits
Exhibit A – Form of confirmation
Exhibit B – Form of credit event notice and form or notice of publicly available information
Exhibit C – Form of notice of physical settlement
Exhibit D – Form of repudiation/moratorium extension notice and notice of publicly available information
Exhibit E – Novation agreement
Exhibit F – Form of novation agreement

2. Introduction and preamble

The 10 articles are preceded by both an introduction and a preamble. The introduction states that the 2003 Definitions are intended for use in "confirmations of individual credit derivatives transactions" which are governed by either the 1992 Master Agreement or the 2002 Master Agreement. It goes on to say that:

- the 2003 Definitions can provide the basic framework for documenting privately negotiated credit derivatives transactions;
- the 2003 Definitions have fallback provisions which will apply where the parties do not provide otherwise in a transaction; and
- market participants may adapt or supplement the 2003 Definitions as they wish.

Apart from a lengthy liability disclaimer, the introduction also says that the 2003 Definitions are free-standing and so therefore, "for most transactions, there is no need to incorporate any other ISDA definitions booklets (such as the ISDA 2000 Definitions) into the Confirmation of a Credit Derivatives Transaction" – a point often forgotten.

3. Article I – Certain general definitions

Article I's definitions cover four distinct areas. First, they cover a transaction's identity and its documentary structure, with the definitions of 'credit derivative transaction', 'confirmation' and '2002 ISDA Master Agreement'.

Second, they cover a transaction's landmark dates:

- the date when the parties agree to enter into a transaction;
- the trade date;
- how long the parties want the period of credit protection to last (the term);
- the date when the term will begin (the effective date);
- when the term is scheduled to end (the scheduled termination date); and
- definitions of a transaction's relevant business days – business day, grace period business day, calculation city business day and TARGET settlement day.

Third, the Article I definitions cover the time periods set running and key dates fixed when a potential or actual credit event occurs – these are:

- the definitions of 'event determination date' and 'grace period extension date';
- the definitions of periods in the credit event settlement process in which the parties may deliver notices – 'notice delivery period', 'grace period extension date', 'grace period' and 'potential failure to pay'; and
- the date when the transaction will end before or after its scheduled termination date (the termination date).

Fourth, the Article I definitions cover the identity and location of the parties, with definitions of 'buyer', 'seller', 'calculation agent' and 'calculation agent city'.

4. Article II – General terms relating to credit derivative transactions

The key provisions of Article II relate to:

- reference entities and their successor(s);
- the mechanics of payment;
- determination of obligations, reference obligations, substitute obligations and deliverable obligations (including special provisions in relation to the restructuring credit event); and
- merger of a reference entity with the seller.

4.1 Reference entities and their successors

Reference entities are specified in the confirmation.[2] From time to time, however, reference entities which are corporates merge, demerge and spin off, and reference entities which are sovereigns are partitioned or annexed. The successor's identity is important because the new entity or entities may have a different level of credit-worthiness from the predecessor.

The 2003 Definitions address shortcomings in the 1999 Definitions that were exposed by market events[3] (in particular, ambiguities relating to multiple successors).

---

2   Section 2.1.

3   For example, the demerger of National Power into Innogy plc and International Power plc – two differently rated corporates – led to disputes in the market as to which entity was the successor reference entity. As a result, ISDA published the 2001 Successor and Credit Events Supplement which, subject to some minor amendments, is incorporated directly into the 2003 Definitions.

For non-sovereign reference entities, 'succession events' include mergers and demergers, consolidations and amalgamations, asset and liability transfers, spin-offs or other similar events where one entity succeeds to another's obligations.[4] Other non-related obligation exchanges are excluded from the definition.

Once the calculation agent becomes aware of a succession event, it must establish the successor(s).[5] However, it must do so no earlier than 14 calendar days after the succession event's legally effective date.

The calculation agent must first determine which of the reference entity's obligations are relevant obligations.[6] These are bonds or loan obligations outstanding immediately prior to the succession event. The calculation agent uses best available information.[7] This includes information which a reference entity provides to its primary stock exchange/securities regulator[8] or, if it does not file this sort of information, the best publicly available information that the calculation agent can obtain. Best available information cannot include information made available more than 14 calendar days after the legally effective date of the succession event.

The calculation agent will determine the successor(s) as follows:

- If an entity succeeds to at least 75% of the relevant obligations, it will be the sole successor.
- If only one entity succeeds to over 25% of the relevant obligations and the original reference entity retains no more than 25%, then the succeeding entity will be the sole successor.
- If more than one entity succeeds to over 25% of the relevant obligations, but the original reference entity retains 25% or less, then each succeeding entity will be a successor. If one or more of these successors has not assumed a reference obligation, then the calculation agent must determine a successor reference obligation.[9]
- If one or more entities succeed to 25% or more of the relevant obligations, but the original reference entity retains more than 25%, then each succeeding reference entity as well as the original reference entity will be a successor.[10]
- If one or more entities succeed to part only of the relevant bonds or loans, and no entity succeeds to more than 25% but the reference entity continues to exist, then there will be no change of reference entity.
- If one or more entities succeed to part of the bonds and loans, but no entity succeeds to more than 25% of the relevant obligations and the reference entity ceases to exist, then the entity which succeeds to the greatest percentage of the bonds and loans will be the only successor.

Sovereign succession events are far less common. Consequently, they receive less coverage in the 2003 Definitions. The rules applicable to them are not as detailed and

---

4   Section 2.2 (b).
5   Section 2.2 (a)(vi).
6   Section 2.2(f).
7   Section 2.2(g).
8   Such as the Financial Services Authority in the case of a UK reference entity.
9   'Successor reference obligations' are determined in accordance with Section 2.30.
10   A successor obligation will be determined as in the above footnote.

remain subjective. 'Sovereign' successors are defined only as direct or indirect successor(s), irrespective of whether they assume the predecessor's obligations.[11]

4.2   Obligations

The reference entity's obligations are at the heart of the credit default swap, triggering five of the six possible credit events, being valued in cash settlement and delivered in physical settlement. Article II defines the relevant terms and sets out how each obligation type is determined.

The reference entity's obligations are its direct and indirect (ie, guaranteed) obligations.[12] They do not include any excluded obligations[13] set out in the transaction.

The parties do not want every reference entity obligation to enjoy credit protection. If they do not select a specific obligation in the confirmation, they will use the mechanism set out in Section 2.19(a) (obligation category) and Section 2.20(b) (obligation characteristics) to define which of the reference entity's obligations are credit protected. An obligation category and all of the obligation characteristics must be present to qualify as an obligation.

There are six obligation categories. Only one obligation category can be selected for each reference entity. The obligation categories are:

- payment (ie, any present, future or contingent obligations to repay money, including borrowed money), a broad category that includes payments under guarantees, trading debts and derivative transactions;
- borrowed money (ie, any obligation to pay or repay borrowed money), a narrower category than the previous one;
- reference obligation only (ie, any obligation that is a reference obligation);
- bond (ie, borrowed money in the form of a bond, note (other than a note delivered under a loan) or debt security);
- loan (ie, borrowed money documented by a term loan agreement, revolving loan agreement or other similar credit agreement); and
- bond or loan (ie, any obligation that is either a bond or a loan).

There are seven obligation characteristics. Provided that they are not contradictory, any number may be chosen. Some relate only to bonds and others to loans. Obligation characteristics are not usually selected for Western European or North American reference entities. They are selected when it is necessary to isolate a reference entity's more liquid and internationally traded obligations. The obligation characteristics are as follows:

- 'Not subordinated' means that obligations are not subordinated in payment priority to the most senior reference obligation. If no reference obligation is specified in the confirmation, the obligation must not be subordinated to any borrowed money obligation.
- 'Specified currency' aims, along with 'not domestic currency' and 'not

---

11   Section 2.2(h).
12   Section 2.14.
13   Section 2.17.

domestic law', to exclude the reference entity's domestic obligations from credit protection. Obligations will include only those payable in a currency specified in the confirmation. If 'specified currency' is selected as a characteristic but no currency is selected, then the relevant obligation must be denominated in one of the currencies of Canada, Japan, Switzerland, the United Kingdom and the United States, or in euros (these being standard specified currencies).

- 'Not sovereign lender' excludes any obligation owed primarily to a sovereign or supranational organisation (including Paris Club debt).
- 'Not domestic currency' excludes obligations payable in the reference entity's home currency.
- 'Not domestic law' excludes obligations governed by the law of the reference entity's home jurisdiction.
- 'Listed' means that the obligation must be quoted, listed or ordinarily purchased and sold on an exchange. By its nature, it relates only to bonds.
- 'Not domestic issuance' permits only obligations issued and offered for sale outside of the reference entity's domestic market.

4.3 Deliverable obligations

Deliverable obligations are the reference entity's obligations which can be delivered by way of physical settlement. They include:

- any of the reference entity's direct or indirect (ie, guaranteed) obligations satisfying the deliverable obligation category and deliverable obligation characteristics;
- any reference obligation (unless an excluded deliverable obligation);
- in the case of a restructuring credit event for a sovereign reference entity, any restructured deliverable obligation fulfilling certain criteria (unless it is an excluded reference obligation); and
- any other specified obligation of the reference entity.

Although the deliverable obligations provisions are meant to relate only to physically settled transactions, it is common for market participants to adapt them as a method for selecting a reference obligation in a cash-settled transaction, when none is specified in the confirmation. The 2003 Definitions assume that a reference obligation will be selected in the confirmation. Some buyers wish to have discretion when selecting the reference obligation and so will, in the confirmation, deem the provisions relating to deliverable obligation category and deliverable obligation characteristics to apply to the reference obligation selection.

There are six deliverable obligation categories. These replicate the obligation categories, with reference obligation having only the effect of fixing the deliverable obligation. There are 15 deliverable obligation characteristics: the seven obligation characteristics replicated and eight new characteristics added. These eight new characteristics are outlined below:

- 'Not contingent' refers to an obligation with unconditional principal payments. An example of a contingent obligation would be a credit linked note issued by a financial institution. This characteristic prevents reference entity obligations whose value is affected by factors other than the reference entity's creditworthiness from being valued or delivered following a credit event. This definition specifically carves out certain convertible, exchangeable[14] and accreting obligations from being contingent obligations.

- 'Convertible' is an obligation of the reference entity convertible wholly or partly into its equity securities at the holder's option.[15] An exchangeable obligation is a reference entity obligation which may be exchanged into another issuer's equity securities at the holder's option.[16] An accreting obligation is any obligation (including a convertible or exchangeable obligation) which, if accelerated, will pay the original issue price plus additional amounts (on account of original issue discount or other interest accruals) – for example, a deeply discounted or zero coupon bond.

- 'Assignable loan' is a loan that can be assigned or novated without the consent of a reference entity or any guarantor, to at least a commercial bank or financial institution which is not already one of the loan lenders or syndicate members.

- 'Consent required loan' is a loan that can be assigned or novated to another party – not only a commercial bank or institution, but also, with the consent of the reference entity, any relevant guarantor or syndicate agent. If both assignable loan and consent required loan are specified, it will be necessary only for an obligation to have one characteristic.

- 'Direct loan participation' relates to non-transferable loans and loans where a necessary party will not consent to transfer. The provision permits a participation agreement between buyer and seller transferring a specified share of the loan payments to the seller to be a deliverable obligation.

- 'Transferable' is a provision that does not apply to loans. The obligation must be transferable to institutional investors 'without any contractual, statutory or regulatory restriction'. The definition carves out US resale restrictions under Regulation S and Rule 144A safe harbours. All eurobonds are subject to one or other of these safe harbours. Failure to carve these out would exclude eurobonds from being obligations. Restrictions on permitted investments such as statutory or regulatory investment restrictions on insurance companies and pension funds are also carved out.

- 'Maximum maturity' means that on the physical settlement date, the deliverable obligation must not have a maturity date later than the period specified in the confirmation. It is market practice for this to be 30 years.

- 'Accelerated or matured' refers to obligations that are fully due and payable before the delivery date because they have matured (but have not been redeemed), have been accelerated (ie, an event of default has been declared), or would have been due and payable but for insolvency laws (eg, the

---

14   In the case of contingent obligations and exchangeable obligations, the relevant option must not have been exercised.
15   Or a trustee or agent acting for the holder.
16   Or a trustee or agent acting for the holder.

application of Chapter 11 of the US Bankruptcy Code).

The characteristic 'not bearer' applies to bonds only. The bonds must be either registered bonds or, if they are bearer bonds, cleared via Euroclear, Clearstream or any other internationally recognised clearing system.

4.4 Guarantees

The 2003 Definitions address perceived ambiguities in the 1999 Definitions relating to credit events and guarantees given on underlying obligations. Article II covers which obligation categories and obligation characteristics relate to guarantees and which to underlying obligations, as well as which guarantees are relevant as obligations. Article II differentiates between two categories of guarantee: qualifying guarantees and qualifying affiliate guarantees.

A qualifying guarantee is one in which the reference entity agrees in writing to pay all amounts due under an underlying obligation (ie, an obligation for which another party is the obligor). The guarantee must not be subordinated to any of the underlying obligor's borrowed money when the credit event occurs. Qualifying guarantees exclude surety bonds, financial guarantee insurance policies, letters of credit and arrangements which can be modified otherwise than because of a non-payment event. The qualifying guarantee's benefit must be capable of being delivered together with the underlying obligation (eg, a guaranteed eurobond).

A qualifying affiliate guarantee is a qualifying guarantee provided by the reference entity to one of its downstream affiliates.[17] It is a narrower category than the qualifying guarantee. It is selected for jurisdictions where market participants believe that upstream and cross-stream guarantees have a greater legal risk than downstream guarantees.

Unless the parties select 'all guarantees' as applicable, the fallback is that only qualifying affiliate guarantees apply.

ISDA issued the May 2003 Supplement to the 2003 Definitions to address, among other things, concerns raised about guarantees. Incorporating the supplement into a confirmation is optional. Article II sets the date on which share ownership should be assessed for establishing whether an underlying obligor is a downstream affiliate as the date of the credit event or delivery date. In practice, this may be difficult to establish. The May 2003 Supplement makes the determination date that on which the qualifying guarantee is issued.

The May 2003 Supplement provides that for the purposes of applying obligation characteristics and deliverable obligation characteristics, both the qualifying guarantee and the underlying obligation must satisfy any of the following:

- not subordinated;
- specified currency;
- not sovereign lender;
- not domestic currency; and
- not domestic law.

---

17   Section 2.25 defines this as a 50% directly or indirectly owned subsidiary of the reference entity. The ownership must be of shares which have the power to elect the board of directors.

If the parties incorporate the May 2003 Supplement, but do not select 'not subordinated' as an obligation characteristic or a deliverable obligation characteristic, a guarantee which is subordinated to the underlying obligor's borrowed money obligations will be an obligation or deliverable obligation. This will not be the case if the May 2003 Supplement is not incorporated.

4.5 Merger of reference entity and seller

Article II[18] provides that if the reference entity merges, amalgamates or transfers all or substantially all of its assets to the seller (or if the reference entity and seller become affiliates), an additional termination event under the 2002 ISDA Master Agreement is deemed to have occurred with the seller as the sole affected party.[19,20] This is because if a post-merger credit event were to occur, the buyer would be left looking to the reference entity to pay its settlement amount.

5. Article III – Conditions to settlement

A credit event is triggered only once a credit event has occurred (as set out in Article IV) and the conditions to settlement (as set out in Article III) have been satisfied.[21]

In a cash-settled transaction, the date on which the conditions to settlement are satisfied is the event determination date,[22] which is the date of delivery of a credit event notice[23] and, if required in the confirmation, a notice of publicly available information.[24] In a physically settled transaction, a notice of physical settlement[25] must also be delivered following the event determination date.

5.1 Credit event notice

A credit event notice describes a credit event that has occurred between the transaction's effective date and the latest of the transaction's scheduled termination date or, if applicable, a grace period extension date or repudiation/moratorium evaluation date.

It describes the facts relevant to the determination in reasonable detail. The credit event need not be continuing when the credit event notice is delivered: for example, a missed interest payment could potentially trigger a failure to pay credit event even if the payment is made before the credit event notice is delivered.

A credit event notice cannot be revoked.[26] It can be delivered only by a notifying party. The buyer will always be a notifying party; however, the confirmation may specify that the buyer is also. A seller might wish to trigger a credit event if:

---

18   Section 2.31.
19   This provision will be varied where a credit derivative transaction forms part of a credit linked note issued by a special purpose vehicle or is a self-referenced credit linked note.
20   Article II also contains provisions which, if applied to a transaction, will create a variation of the restructuring credit event. These provisions are discussed in the section on Article IV – Credit events.
21   The 2003 Definitions have been drafted in view of the counterparties entering only in a single-name credit derivatives transaction.
22   Section 1.8.
23   Section 3.2(a)(i).
24   Section 3.4.
25   Section 3.6.
26   Section 3.3.

- it had hedged its position by entering into another credit default swap as a buyer and it wishes to trigger that transaction; or
- it suspects that the reference entity's creditworthiness could decline further and it would be cheaper to trigger a credit event now.

5.2 Notice of publicly available information

A notice of publicly available information is normally a condition to settlement. It can be incorporated into the credit event notice with the publicly available information[27] acting as an independent verification that a credit event has occurred.[28] This information must:

- have been published in a specified number[29] of public sources;[30,31]
- be received from (or published by) the reference entity[32] or a trustee or agent in one of its obligations;
- constitute information contained in the reference entity's bankruptcy, insolvency or related proceedings; or
- constitute information contained in any court, tribunal or similar administrative or regulatory body's document.

If the buyer, acting in a trustee or agency capacity under an obligation, is the sole information source and is also a holder of the obligation which has suffered the credit event, it must deliver a certificate signed by one of its officials of managing director rank, certifying the occurrence of the credit event.

Publicly available information is not usually released for the purposes of triggering a credit event and so does not always give the details necessary to verify the occurrence of a credit event. Publicly available information that is difficult to obtain may include:

- the voting shares percentage necessary to determine whether an obligation is a qualifying affiliate guarantee;
- whether the payment requirement or default requirement levels have been met;
- the necessary grace period; and
- information or details of certain credit events' subjective criteria.

These requirements have therefore been disapplied.[33]

---

27 Section 3.5.
28 A counterparty may bring the relevant information into the public domain. In *Australia & New Zealand Banking Group v Deutsche Bank AG* (1999), Justice Langley ruled that the publicly available information requirements had been met in a hedging swap between Deutsche Bank and Daiwa (Europe) Limited, notwithstanding that Daiwa was relying on a news story reporting the credit event that it had placed in the *International Financing Review*.
29 It is market practice, and also the ISDA fallback, to require two public sources.
30 Section 3.7.
31 Public sources can be defined either in the confirmation or (as is market practice), if none are specified, then from the list given in the 2003 Definitions. The sources listed include Bloomberg, the *Financial Times*, the *Wall Street Journal* and other leading financial newspapers, publications and subscription services.
32 Or where the reference entity is a sovereign, a sovereign agency.
33 Section 3.5(d).

5.3   Notice of physical settlement

In a physically settled transaction, the credit protection buyer must deliver a notice of physical settlement within 30 calendar days of the event determination date. The notice is irrevocable, but can be amended as many times as the buyer wishes prior to the end of the 30-day period.

The notice states that the buyer will physically settle the transaction and contains a detailed description[34] of the deliverable obligations that it intends to deliver.

5.4   Credit event notice after restructuring

Except for restructuring credit events, the conditions to settlement can be satisfied only once per reference entity. Restructuring[35] can have a relatively minor effect on creditworthiness;[36] and so the notifying party is permitted to deliver multiple restructuring credit event notices each time triggering a credit event for only part (the exercise amount)[37] of the reference entity notional amount.

If this happens, there are deemed to be two transactions. The new transaction's notional amount is deemed to be the exercise amount and the old transaction's notional amount is deemed to be its existing notional amount less the exercise amount. The calculation agent will then make any necessary modifications to preserve the economic effects of the two transactions.

6.   Article IV – Credit events

Article IV sets out the six credit events:

- bankruptcy;
- failure to pay;
- obligation acceleration;
- obligation default;
- repudiation/moratorium; and
- restructuring.

The credit events selected will depend on relevant market standards for the reference entity's jurisdiction and characterisation.[38] Article III makes the determination of credit events objective and removes various common law defences such as a reference entity not having capacity to enter into an obligation or an obligation being unenforceable or invalid.[39]

---

34   This includes the outstanding principal balance or due and payable amount of each deliverable obligation it intends to deliver as well as any available Committee on Uniform Securities Identification Procedures or International Securities Identification Number numbers (or, if not available, the rate and tenor of the deliverable obligation).
35   Section 3.9.
36   Following a restructuring event in relation to Xerox, the final price achieved in relation Xerox's obligations was approximately 95%.
37   Each exercise amount.
38   For example, the market standard for North American insurance reference entities includes only bankruptcy and failure to pay as credit events; whereas the market standard for European emerging market reference entities includes bankruptcy, failure to pay, obligation acceleration, repudiation/ moratorium and modified modified restructuring as credit events.
39   Section 4.1.

6.1 Bankruptcy

Bankruptcy[40] is the only credit event which relates to the reference entity itself rather than its obligations. The definition gives a detailed list of events which constitute bankruptcy. Subject to some minor changes, it tracks Section 5(a)(vii) of the 1992 ISDA Master Agreement.

6.2 Obligation acceleration

Obligation acceleration[41] requires the obligation's lenders or bondholders to accelerate a greater amount of the obligation than the default requirement[42] following a default, event of default or similar provision.

6.3 Obligation default

Obligation default[43] mirrors obligation acceleration except there is no requirement for the obligation to be accelerated following a default. Only one of obligation acceleration or obligation default can be selected per reference entity.

6.4 Failure to pay

Failure to pay[44] occurs if the reference entity fails to pay any amounts equal to or greater than the payment requirement[45] under any of its obligations. The failure to pay must take place after the expiration of an obligation's grace period[46] (this period is set out in the obligation itself) or after the satisfaction of any conditions precedent to that grace period commencing. If an obligation does not have a grace period, or if it has a grace period of less than three business days, then the grace period is deemed to be three business days.

6.5 Repudiation/moratorium

Repudiation/moratorium[47] relates to where a reference entity's authorised officer repudiates or declares a moratorium on any of its obligations in an aggregate amount of at least the default requirement. It can also relate to an authorised officer of a governmental authority,[48] such as a minister of finance, repudiating or declaring a moratorium over a reference entity's obligations. This is a potential repudiation/moratorium.

The potential repudiation/moratorium must be followed by an actual failure to pay or restructuring on or prior to the repudiation/moratorium evaluation date.[49] A failure to pay is determined without regard to the payment requirement and a restructuring is determined without regard to the default requirement.

---

40   Section 4.2.
41   Section 4.3.
42   If the default requirement is not defined in the confirmation, the ISDA fallback is $10 million.
43   Section 4.4.
44   Section 4.5.
45   Section 4.8(d). If the payment requirement is not defined in the confirmation, the ISDA fallback is $1 million.
46   Section 1.12.
47   Section 4.6.
48   Section 4.8(b).
49   Section 4.6(b).

If the relevant obligations include bonds, the repudiation/moratorium evaluation date is the later of 60 calendar days following the potential repudiation/moratorium date and the bond's first post-potential repudiation/moratorium payment date (taking into account any grace period). If the relevant obligations do not include bonds, the repudiation/moratorium evaluation date is 60 calendar days after the potential repudiation/moratorium.

If a potential repudiation/moratorium has occurred, but the repudiation/moratorium evaluation date cannot occur before the scheduled termination date, then unless the parties elect in the confirmation that the repudiation/moratorium extension condition[50] applies, the transaction will terminate before a credit event can occur.

If the parties select that the repudiation/moratorium extension condition applies, then where a potential repudiation/moratorium occurs on or before the scheduled termination date but the repudiation/moratorium evaluation date cannot occur until afterwards, the notifying party can deliver a repudiation/moratorium extension notice.[51]

This is an irrevocable notice describing a potential repudiation/moratorium that has occurred prior to the scheduled termination date. It contains a description in reasonable detail of the facts relevant to determining the potential repudiation/moratorium and indicates the date when it occurred. The confirmation may also require it to be accompanied by a notice of publicly available information. The notifying party can then deliver a credit event notice and (if applicable) a notice of publicly available information up to 14 calendar days after the repudiation/moratorium evaluation date.

6.6   Restructuring

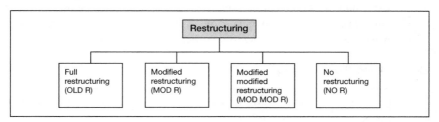

Restructuring[52] is the most controversial credit event. There are four variations:

- full restructuring;
- modified restructuring;
- modified modified restructuring; and
- no restructuring.

Selection depends on the reference entity's jurisdiction and characterisation (eg, North American insurance entity).

---

50   Section 4.6(d).
51   Section 4.6(e).
52   Section 4.7.

Restructuring applies when any one of a list of specified events binding all of the holders occurs to an aggregate amount of the reference entity's obligations at least equal to the default requirement. These events must not be contemplated under the obligation's terms in effect at the later of the trade date or the obligation's issue date. The specified events are:

- an interest payment or accrual reduction;
- a principal or premium reduction;
- a postponement of payment of accruals or interest, or principal or premium;
- a change of an obligation's priority of payment, causing that obligation's subordination; and
- any change in currency of interest or principal other than to a permitted currency.[53]

Exceptions apply where:

- the event does not directly or indirectly result in the reference entity's creditworthiness or financial condition deteriorating;
- an EU member state converts its currency to the euro; or
- the restructuring events occur because of an administrative, accounting, tax or technical adjustment in the ordinary course of business.

(a) Full restructuring

Market events exposed certain weaknesses in the 1999 'restructuring' definition. Although the 2003 Definitions do not vary the definition itself, they do provide options to limit the obligations which may be 'deliverable'. When these options are not selected, this is full restructuring chosen by selecting restructuring as a credit event alone. Full restructuring is no longer market standard for most types of reference entity in physically settled transactions. It is selected only for cash-settled transactions where the reference obligation is not specified at the transaction's outset.

(b) Modified restructuring

> Credit events: The following credit event[s] shall apply to this transaction:
> Restructuring
> Restructuring maturity limitation and fully transferable
> obligation: applicable

Modified restructuring aims to reduce the moral hazard of what is known as the 'cheapest to deliver option'. It is used mainly for North American reference entities. The option has been fully incorporated into the 2003 Definitions. When selected, a deliverable obligation must fulfil two characteristics following a restructuring credit event. First, the final maturity date must be no later than 30 months after the

---

53　This is defined in Section 4.7 as any G7 member or Organisation for Economic Cooperation and Development country currency of an AAA-rated country.

restructuring date or the latest final maturity date of any restructured bond or loan, whichever is earliest. The deliverable obligation's maturity date must not be earlier than the transaction's scheduled maturity date or later than 30 months after the scheduled maturity date.[54] The second characteristic relates to a fully transferable obligation.[55] The deliverable obligation must be either a transferable[56] bond or a loan capable of being assigned or novated without consent. It must also be possible to transfer the deliverable obligation to eligible transferees.[57] These include various finance and corporate entities or their affiliates with total assets of at least $500 million, as well as individual and groups of investment vehicles with total assets of at least $100 million.

(c) *Modified modified restructuring*

Modified restructuring was unpopular with European dealers and was not adopted. They felt that it did not take account of European loan market practice. In particular, it excluded consent-required loans from being deliverable obligations, preventing loans documented according to Loan Market Association standards from being deliverable obligations. To deal with these concerns, the 2003 Definitions include a further option for the European market known as 'modified modified restructuring'.

If modified modified restructuring is selected, an obligation must fulfil the following characteristics to qualify as a deliverable obligation following a restructuring credit event:

- Regarding the modified restructuring maturity limitation date,[58] the deliverable obligation's final maturity date must be no later than the earlier of the transaction's scheduled termination date and 30 months after the restructuring (although this is extended from 30 to 60 months where the deliverable obligation is a restructured bond or loan); and
- Regarding the conditionally transferable obligation,[59] the deliverable obligation must be either a transferable[60] bond or a loan capable of being assigned or novated without consent. It must be possible to transfer the deliverable obligation to a modified eligible transferee.[61]

This definition is based on the broader Loan Market Association standard form and includes any bank, financial institution or other entity regularly involved in making, purchasing or investing in loans, securities and other assets.

(d) *Restructuring credit event not selected*

It is market standard not to select the restructuring credit event for certain types of reference entity, for example North American corporate high yield and North American insurance reference entities.

---

54   Section 2.32(c).
55   Section 2.32(b).
56   Section 2.20(b)(v).
57   Section 2.32(f).
58   Section 2.33(c).
59   Section 2.33(b).
60   Section 2.20(b)(v).
61   Section 2.32(f).

(e)   *Multiple holder obligation*

Unless disapplied in the confirmation, a restructuring credit event can occur only in relation to a multiple holder obligation.[62] This is an obligation held at the time of the restructuring credit event:

- by at least four non-affiliated holders; and
- whose terms require that 66.66% of the holders consent to the restructuring.

A shortcoming was identified soon after the 2003 Definitions were published. It is market practice for eurobonds to require 75% of bondholders voting to approve a restructuring and fix a meeting's quorum at 75% of bondholders. This means that any market standard eurobond which restructures could be approved by only 56% of bondholders and fail the multiple holder obligation test. ISDA addressed the problem in the May 2003 Supplement, which provides that a bond will automatically be construed to be a multiple holder obligation.

(f)   *Sovereign restructured deliverable obligation*

Unless excluded in the confirmation, where a restructuring credit event occurs in relation to a sovereign, the class of deliverable obligation will be widened to include obligations which satisfied the deliverable obligation category and deliverable obligation characteristics immediately before the restructuring was legally effective, even if they do not meet them afterwards. This varies from the standard provisions, which assess whether an obligation is a deliverable obligation as of the delivery date.

7.   Article V – Fixed amounts

Fixed amounts are those paid by the buyer to the seller to compensate it for assuming the credit risk. This technical article covers the mechanics of the payment in conjunction with the definitions set out in Article II. It details that the calculation of fixed amount[63] will be arrived at by multiplying the fixed-rate payer calculation amount[64] (which is usually the notional amount of the credit default swap) by the fixed rate[65] (which is agreed between the parties and expressed as a per annum percentage) by the day count fraction.[66]

8.   Article VI – General terms relating to settlement

Article VI is a short article. It is an enabling provision which defines 'settlement method',[67] 'settlement date'[68] and 'settlement currency'.[69] The two settlement methods contemplated by the 2003 Definitions are cash settlement[70] and physical settlement. Each is chosen by being specified in a relevant confirmation. If cash

---

62   Section 4.9.
63   Section 5.1.
64   Section 2.7.
65   Section 5.2.
66   Section 5.3.
67   Section 6.1.
68   Section 6.2.
69   Section 6.3.
70   Section 7.1.

settlement is selected (or if it is deemed to apply because physical settlement is impossible or impractical),[71] the provisions of Article VII will apply.[72] If physical settlement is selected, the provisions of Article VIII will apply.

The settlement date will be either the cash settlement date[73] or the physical settlement date[74] (as applicable). The settlement currency will be as stated in the relevant confirmation, with the ISDA fallback being the currency of the floating-rate payer calculation amount.[75]

9. Article VII – Terms relating to cash settlement

9.1 Cash settlement date

The cash settlement date[76] is the date, following the satisfaction of the conditions to settlement and the valuation date,[77] on which the cash settlement amount[78] is paid. It can be stated in the relevant confirmation and it will usually be a selected number (or range) of business days following the calculation of the final price (the ISDA fallback is three business days).

9.2 Valuation of the reference obligation and calculating the final price

Once the conditions to settlement have been satisfied, the calculation agent must arrange for the reference obligation to be valued to ascertain its current market value (ie, its final price).

On the valuation date[79] at the valuation time,[80] the calculation agent will contact five or more dealers[81] (all as specified in the confirmation) and ask them to provide firm quotations (defined as 'full quotations')[82] for an amount of the reference obligation specified in the confirmation (the quotation amount).[83]

Depending on what is specified in the confirmation as the quotation method,[84] the calculation agent may request bid quotations, offer quotations or mid-market quotations (ie, a bid and an offer quotation which is then averaged by the calculation agent).

The calculation agent must obtain at least two full quotations on the valuation date. The very nature of a credit event will mean that the reference obligation will be a distressed asset and, as such, quotations may be hard to come by.

---

71 Sections 9.3, 9.4 and 9.5.
72 As adjusted by Article IX.
73 Section 7.2.
74 Section 8.4.
75 Section 2.13.
76 Section 7.2.
77 Section 7.8.
78 Section 7.3.
79 If there are multiple valuation dates, it will do so on each valuation date.
80 Section 7.14.
81 Section 7.15. Dealers are those in the type of obligation for which the quotation is being obtained.
82 Section 7.10.
83 Section 7.12. Where no amount is specified in the confirmation, the ISDA fallback is for the quotation amount to be the floating-rate payer calculation amount.
84 Section 7.9. Where no quotation method is detailed in the confirmation, the ISDA fallback is 'bid'.

9.3 The fallbacks

The 2003 Definitions provide extensive fallbacks to deal with problems in obtaining the required number of full quotations.[85] If the necessary quotations cannot be obtained during a so-called 'fallback' stage, the next fallback stage applies.

Fallback 1: Calculation agent tries to obtain at least two full quotations from five dealers daily for the next three business days.

Fallback 2: Calculation agent attempts to obtain the same full quotations until the tenth post-valuation date business day. On each day that it is unsuccessful, it attempts to obtain a weighted average quotation.

Calculation agent is a transaction party	Calculation agent is not a transaction party
Fallback 3A: The calculation agent's counterparty may attempt to obtain the quotations. If the counterparty can obtain at least two full quotations or a weighted average quotation within the next five business days, then the calculation agent must use these quotations.	**Fallback 3B:** Each of the buyer and seller may attempt to obtain five or more full quotations and, if two or more full quotations are not available, a weighted average quotation.
Fallback 4A: The final price will be calculated using any full quotation the counterparty has obtained from a dealer at the valuation time on the fifth business day.	**Fallback 4B:** If either or both parties can obtain two or more full quotations or a weighted average quotation on the same business day within an additional five business days, then the calculation agent must use these quotations.
Fallback 5A: On the same day as Fallback 4A, the weighted average of: • any firm quotations for the reference obligation obtained on the fifth business day for the aggregate portion of the quotation amount for which quotations were obtained; and • a quotation deemed to be zero for the balance of the quotation amount for which quotations were not obtained on that day.	**Fallback 5B:** The parties attempt to obtain between them two or more full quotations or a weighted average quotation on the same business day within the next five business days.

---

85   Section 7.7.

A weighted average quotation can be obtained when dealers are prepared only to give quotations for less than the quotation amount. The calculation agent then takes a weighted average of the firm quotations obtained. The quotation amounts must be at least equal to the minimum quotation amount specified in the confirmation. If no amount is specified, this will be the lower of $1 million and the quotation amount. These quotations, when added together in aggregate, must approximately equal the quotation amount.

Fallback 6B: The quotations are deemed to be *any* full quotation obtained from a dealer at the valuation time on such business day.

Fallback 7B: On the same day as Fallback 6B, the weighted average of:
- any firm quotations for the reference obligation obtained from dealers on the fifth business day for the aggregate portion of the quotation amount for which quotations were obtained; and
- a quotation deemed to be zero for the balance of the quotation amount for which quotations were not obtained on that day.

9.4 Final price and valuation method

The calculation agent uses the quotations to calculate the final price according to the valuation method[86] selected in the confirmation. The final price represents the decline in the value of the reference obligation.

There are eight different valuation methods. The one selected in the confirmation is based on the number of reference obligations to be valued and the number of valuation dates. Each of the valuation methods is based either on the highest quotation given or on the market value. While the concept of choosing the highest quotation given is straightforward, market value depends as follows on the number of full quotations and weighted average quotations received.

Quotations received	Calculation agent action for market value
More than three full quotations	Disregard the highest and lowest full quotations and calculate the arithmetic mean. If two full quotations have the same highest or lowest value, only one is discarded.
Exactly three full quotations	Disregard the highest and lowest full quotations and calculate the arithmetic mean. If two full quotations have the same highest or lowest value, only one is discarded.

---

86   Section 7.5

Quotations received	Calculation agent action for market value
Exactly two full quotations	Calculate the arithmetic mean of the full quotations.
One full quotation and a weighted average quotation	Weighted average quotation used.
One full quotation only or no full quotations	Five business-day period commences, operating until two or more full quotations or a weighted average quotation is obtained. If two full quotations or a weighted average quotation is not obtained by the end of the period, market value is calculated as per Fallbacks 3A/B to 5A/7B above.

The valuation method will be specified in the confirmation as one of the following:

Valuation method	Number of reference obligations	Number of valuation dates	Definition
Market	One	One	The reference obligation's market value.
Highest	One	One or multiple	The highest quotation obtained (the ISDA fallback).
Average market	One	Multiple	The unweighted arithmetic mean of the market values.
Average highest	One	Multiple	The unweighted arithmetic mean of the highest quotations.
Blended market	Multiple	Single	The unweighted arithmetic mean of the market values of each reference obligation.
Blended highest	Multiple	Single	The unweighted arithmetic mean of the highest quotations.
Average blended market	Multiple	Multiple	On each valuation date the blended market value is calculated. The arithmetic mean of those values is then calculated.
Average blended highest	Multiple	Multiple	On each valuation date the blended highest is calculated. The arithmetic mean of those values is then calculated.

Whether the quotation for the reference obligation will include or exclude any accrued but unpaid interest will be specified in the confirmation[87] as either 'include accrued interest' or 'exclude accrued interest'. If neither is stated in the confirmation, then the calculation agent will consult the parties and, based on the current market practice for the reference obligation, will decide whether the quotation should include or exclude accrued interest.

The calculation agent will then calculate the reference obligation's final price in accordance with the applicable valuation method. The final price is expressed as a percentage. As soon as practicable after obtaining all of the quotations, the calculation agent will notify each of the parties in writing of each quotation that it receives and provide a written computation showing its calculation of the final price. In practice, this is known as the final price notification.

9.5 Settlement amount

Unless otherwise specified, the cash settlement amount[88] is calculated by multiplying the floating-rate payer calculation amount by the reference price (usually 100%) to give a percentage figure, and subtracting the final price. The cash settlement amount will then be paid on the cash settlement date. The cash settlement date is the transaction's termination date.

9.6 Variations of the valuation procedure

In some transactions the parties may decide that satisfaction of the conditions to settlement will cause the fixed amounts to be reduced only. In other transactions the parties may agree that a fixed credit protection payment will be made once the conditions have been satisfied.

10. Article VIII – Terms relating to physical settlement

10.1 Delivery

Physical settlement is the most popular settlement method. If it is selected and the conditions to settlement are met, then the seller is obliged to accept delivery[89] from the buyer of the deliverable obligations detailed in the notice of physical settlement[90] on or before the physical settlement date. In return, the seller pays a physical settlement amount[91] to the buyer on the physical settlement date.[92] The physical settlement amount is the notional amount of the transaction multiplied by its reference price (usually 100%). This will usually result in the seller paying the face value of each deliverable obligation even though its actual value is far less.

The latest permissible physical settlement date is the last day of the longest

---

87   Section 7.7(c).
88   Section 7.3.
89   Section 8.2.
90   Section 8.1.
91   Section 8.5.
92   Section 8.4.
93   Section 8.6.

possible physical settlement period.[93] Either the physical settlement period can be defined in the confirmation or the calculation agent will, in consultation with the parties, determine the longest number of business days for settlement for the deliverable obligation in accordance with market practice.

The delivery[94] of the deliverable obligation may be not only by physical delivery, but also by novation, transfer (including, for qualifying guarantees, transfer of the benefit of the qualifying guarantee), assignment or sale. The delivery must convey all rights, title and interests in the deliverable obligation free of liens, charges, claims and encumbrances. Any of the non-permitted defences set out in Section 4.1 (credit event) which relate to credit events or any set-off right of the reference entity or any underlying obligor is forbidden.

In the case of direct loan participations, 'delivery' means to create or procure the creation of a participation the seller's favour.

10.2   Accrued interest

A deliverable obligation will often have some accrued but unpaid interest. In the case of borrowed money, if 'include accrued interest' is specified in the confirmation, then the calculation agent (in consultation with the parties) will take account of any accrued interest when calculating the amount of deliverable obligations to be delivered. Where 'exclude accrued interest' is specified, any accrued interest will be excluded from this amount. If neither term is mentioned in the confirmation, then 'exclude accrued interest' is the ISDA fallback.

In the case of deliverable obligations which are not borrowed money, the buyer must deliver deliverable obligations with a 'due and payable amount'[95] (ie, the amount due and payable on the delivery date due to acceleration, maturity, termination or otherwise, but excluding default interest, indemnities and tax gross-ups) (or an equivalent 'currency amount'),[96] equal to the settlement amount.

If the deliverable obligations contain provisions which contemplate an obligation to pay an amount greater than the obligation's outstanding principal balance as of the delivery date, that additional amount is ignored.

10.3   Provisions applicable to convertible, exchangeable and accreting obligations

Special provisions[97] apply when calculating the outstanding principal balance of convertible obligations,[98] exchangeable obligations[99] and accreting obligations.[100] The outstanding principal balance for an accreting obligation is its accreted amount.[101] This is the deliverable obligation's original issue price plus any amount payable at maturity which has already accreted less any cash payments that the

---

94   Section 8.2.
95   Section 8.8.
96   Section 8.9. The currency amount is an amount denominated in a currency other than the settlement currency (Section 6.3).
97   Section 8.7.
98   Section 8.7(b)(iii).
99   Section 8.7(b)(iv).
100   Section 8.7(b)(v).
101   Section 8.7(b)(i).

reference entity has made to reduce the obligation's redemption amount. The accreted amount will include accrued and unpaid periodic cash interest payments only if 'include accrued interest' is stated in the confirmation.

An exception to the above is if the accreting obligation is expressed to accrete pursuant to a straight-line method or if its yield to maturity cannot be ascertained from its offering document. For the purposes of calculating the portion of the amount payable at maturity that has already accreted, the accreted amount is calculated using a rate equal to the accreting obligation's yield to maturity. For exchangeable obligations, the accreted amount does not include any amount payable relating to the value of the equity securities for which the reference obligation can be exchanged.

11. Article IX – Additional representations and agreements of the parties

Article IX covers the parties' additional representations and agreements, as well as delivery fallbacks for physically settled transactions.

The parties represent and agree that:

- neither has made any representation to the other about the reference obligation or any of the reference entity's or underlying obligor's related obligations;[102]
- they will perform the transaction irrespective of credit exposure to the reference entity;
- they need not suffer any loss or prove loss if a credit event occurs;[103]
- the transaction will create no rights or obligations for any parties other than the transaction parties;[104]
- the parties, their affiliates and the calculation agent may deal in the reference entity's or underlying obligor's obligations, and may also conduct banking and investment business with these parties which might actually cause a credit event to happen;[105]
- there is no obligation to disclose any material information;[106] and
- unless information is otherwise subject to confidentiality requirements, it will not trigger any confidentiality obligation and related losses will be indemnified.[107]

11.1 Additional representations and agreements for physical settlement

When the buyer makes a delivery, it is deemed to represent that, except in the case of direct loan participations, it is transferring full title, and that it will indemnify the buyer should this prove not to be the case.[108]

Unless it provides an indemnity to the seller, the buyer is deemed to represent, when it makes a delivery, that (except for some minor exclusions) accepting the deliverable obligations will not lead to any commitment to lend additional funds

---

102   Section 9.1(a).
103   Section 9.1(b)(i).
104   Section 9.1(b)(ii).
105   Section 9.1(b)(iii).
106   Section 9.1(b)(iv).
107   Section 9.1(b)(v).
108   Section 9.2(a).
109   Section 9.2(b).

(including outstanding commitments).[109]

The parties also agree to carry out the necessary steps in relation to documentation and obtaining consents for delivery to take place.[110]

11.2 Delivery fallbacks for physical settlement

The 2003 Definitions set out alternative procedures for when the buyer is unable to deliver the securities detailed in the notice of physical settlement. The primary fallback is for either party to designate an affiliate to deliver or take delivery of the deliverable obligations.[111] There are different fallback provisions for bonds and for loans, which begin when a seller is unable to deliver the deliverable obligation within five business days of the physical settlement date.

11.3 Buy-in of bonds not delivered

Where a buyer cannot deliver all of the bonds in the notice of physical settlement, then unless this is due to impossibility or illegality, the seller has the right to buy them in.[112] It must first give the buyer at least two business days' notice, in the form of a buy-in notice, of which bonds it intends to buy in. This notice must specify the anticipated buy-in date, the relevant bonds and the outstanding principal balance to be bought in.

On the buy-in date, the seller will conduct a dealer poll asking for firm quotations for the bonds (the buy-in offers). If the seller can obtain only one buy-in offer, then that will be the buy-in price; otherwise, the lowest buy-in offer will be the buy-in price.

If the seller cannot obtain a buy-in offer for the bond's full outstanding principal balance on the buy-in date, it will attempt to obtain buy-in offers for all or a portion of the bonds on each business day following the buy-in date until the fourth business day after the buy-in date or the date the buy-in price is determined, whichever is earlier.

The buyer's right to deliver the bonds is suspended during the buy-in period. It recommences at the end of this period if settlement has still not taken place, but only to the extent that the seller has not determined the buy-in price for any relevant bonds. The buyer will continue to try to obtain the outstanding deliverable obligations.

On the sixth business day after the end of the buy-in period, the seller has the right to recommence the buy-in process in accordance with the previous procedures. This process can then be repeated until final settlement of the transaction.

On the date that the buy-in price is determined or as soon as practicable thereafter, the seller delivers a buy-in price notice to the buyer of the outstanding principal balance of the bonds for which it obtained buy-in prices.

On the third business day following this notice, the buyer will be deemed to have delivered the bought-in bonds. The seller then pays the buyer. The amount paid will be equal to the portion of the physical settlement amount corresponding to the

---

110   Section 9.2(c)(i).
111   Section 9.2(c)(iv).
112   Section 9.9.

bought-in bonds reduced (but not below zero) by the relevant bonds' buying price (which is expressed as a percentage), and multiplied by the outstanding principal balance of the relevant bonds for which a buy-in price was determined. Any reasonable brokerage costs in relation to purchasing the relevant bonds are subtracted from this amount.

11.4 Alternative procedures relating to loans not delivered

If the buyer has not delivered any loans specified in the notice of physical settlement by the fifth business day after the physical settlement date, then 'alternative procedures' apply unless one of the following has been specified in the confirmation:

- 'reference obligation only';
- in the case of a consent-required loan, 'partial cash settlement of consent-required loan'; or
- in the case of an assignable loan, 'partial cash settlement of assignable loans applicable'.

In addition, the alternative procedures will not apply if the loans are affected by illegality or impossibility, in which case partial cash settlement due to impossibility or illegality[113] provisions will apply.

Where the buyer cannot obtain the necessary consents to deliver a loan specified in the notice, it must provide a certificate signed by one of its officers of managing director or equivalent rank certifying that it used reasonable efforts to attempt to obtain the consents. The seller may then require the buyer to deliver a bond (instead of a loan) that has transferable and not bearer-deliverable obligation characteristics. The buyer may also deliver an assignable loan instead. In both cases the new deliverable obligation must meet the other deliverable obligation category and characteristics (other than consent-required loan and direct loan participation). If the relevant credit event is restructuring and either modified restructuring or modified modified restructuring applies, then the buyer must also comply with these deliverable obligation restrictions.

The bond or loan will then be deemed to have been specified in the notice of physical settlement. This is subject to the seller identifying a holder (other than the seller itself or one of its affiliates) of the bond or loan willing and able to deliver the bond or loan to the buyer, free of any consents, at a price less than the reference price.

11.5 Partial cash settlement due to impossibility or illegality

If, due to an event beyond the parties' control, it is impossible or illegal for the buyer to deliver or for the seller to accept any of the deliverable obligations listed in the notice of physical settlement, then on or before the physical settlement date the buyer must deliver any deliverable obligations for which it is possible to accept delivery. The seller must then pay the portion of the physical settlement amount corresponding to the amount of deliverable obligations that are delivered in accordance with the current market practice for that deliverable obligation. The relevant party must give

---

113   Section 9.3.

the reasons for the impossibility or legality to the other in writing.

If, following the occurrence of any impossibility or illegality, the amount of deliverable obligations specified in the notice of physical settlement cannot be delivered before the latest permissible physical settlement date (defined in Section 9.7 as 30 calendar days), then the partial cash settlement terms apply to these undeliverable obligations.

11.6 The partial cash settlement terms

The 2003 Definitions provide for three partial cash settlement provisions. These relate to 'partial cash settlement of consent required loans',[114] 'partial cash settlement of assignable loans'[115] and 'partial cash settlement of participations'.[116] Each provision is applicable only if selected in the relevant confirmation (eg, by stating 'partial cash settlement of consent required loans applicable').

The partial cash settlement terms[117] will be deemed to apply if transfer is not possible due to a lack of consent in the case of consent-required loans and assignable loans; and, in the case of a participation, if a participation is not effected (in each case, prior to the latest permissible physical settlement date).

The cash settlement amount will be the greater of:

- zero; and
- the outstanding principal balance, the due and payable amount or the currency amount (as applicable) of each relevant obligation multiplied by its reference price, less the final price.

The cash settlement date will occur three business days after the calculation of the final price on the relevant valuation date (which is two business days after the latest permissible physical settlement date).

For the purposes of partial cash settlement, when calculating the final price, the following are deemed to apply:

- highest valuation method (with certain fallbacks);
- bid quotation method; and
- a quotation amount equal to the outstanding principal balance or due and payable amount or currency amount (as applicable).

12. Article X – Novation provisions

Novation is the method used to transfer all derivatives transactions based on ISDA documentation from one party to another. The 2003 ISDA Credit Derivatives Definitions attach the standard form 2002 Novation Agreement and Novation Confirmation as exhibits[118] and incorporate certain enabling language in Article X to ensure that novations occur in accordance with the 2002 Novation Agreement.

---

114   Section 9.4.
115   Section 9.5.
116   Section 9.6.
117   Section 9.8.
118   Exhibit E and Exhibit F respectively.

Introduction, preamble and Article I – Certain general definitions

1.   Introduction

> The 2003 ISDA Credit Derivatives Definitions (the 'Definitions') are intended for use in confirmations of individual credit derivatives transactions (**'Confirmations'**) governed by agreements such as the 1992 ISDA Master Agreements or the 2002 ISDA Master Agreement published by the International Swaps and Derivatives Association, Inc ('ISDA').

The 10 articles of the 2003 Definitions are preceded by both an introduction and a preamble. The introduction provides that the 2003 Definitions are intended for use in confirmations of individual credit derivatives transactions, which are governed either by the 1992 Master Agreement or the 2002 Master Agreement. It goes on to say that:

- the 2003 Definitions can provide the basic framework for documenting privately negotiated credit derivatives transactions;
- the 2003 Definitions have fallback provisions that will apply where the parties do not provide otherwise in a transaction; and
- market participants may adapt or supplement the 2003 Definitions as they wish.

Apart from a lengthy liability disclaimer absolving ISDA from any guilt should market participants misuse the definitions and reminding users that the 2003 Definitions will not automatically apply to transactions which incorporated the preceding 1999 Definitions, the introduction also sets out that the 2003 Definitions are free standing and so "for most transactions, there is no need to incorporate any other ISDA definitions booklets (such as the ISDA 2000 Definitions) into the Confirmation of a Credit Derivatives Transaction".

It is not uncommon to come across a credit derivatives transaction which incorporates the ISDA 2000 Definitions. However, unless there are floating rate interest payments to be made, this is usually unnecessary as the 2003 Definitions set out all of the relevant interest rate and business day provisions such as:

- the day count fractions (30/360, 30E/360, A/360, Act/360, Actual/360, Actual/365, Actual/365 (fixed), and Actual/Actual);
- business day and the business day conventions (followed, modified following, preceding and other variations);
- target settlement days;

- floating rate and fixed rate payment dates; and
- their payers and other applicable payment infrastructure provisions.

2. Preamble

The introduction does not form part of the 2003 Definitions. The preamble does.

> **2003 ISDA Credit Derivatives Definitions**
> Any or all of the following definitions and provisions may be incorporated into a document by wording in the document indicating that to, or to the extent to which, the document is subject to the 2003 Definitions.

It states that the definitions and provisions in the 2003 Definitions may be incorporated into a document by inserting wording that "the document is subject to the 2003 ISDA Credit Derivatives Definitions (as published by the International Swaps and Derivatives Associations, Inc. ('ISDA')) (the '**Definitions**')". It is universal in credit default swap transactions to include the following wording in the first paragraph of the confirmation:

> The definitions and provisions contained in the 2003 ISDA Credit Derivatives Definitions (the 'Credit Derivatives Definitions'), as published by the International Swaps and Derivatives Association, Inc, are incorporated into this Confirmation. In the event of any inconsistency between the Credit Derivatives Definitions and this Confirmation, this Confirmation will govern.

The preamble goes on to provide that all terms, definitions and provisions incorporated into a document will be applicable unless otherwise modified. It also states that any definitions of currencies in a document incorporating the 2003 Definitions will have the same meaning as the 2000 ISDA Definitions. This reinforces the point that it is not necessary to incorporate the 2000 ISDA Definitions into a credit derivatives transaction which incorporates the 2003 Definitions.

3. Article I – Certain general definitions

Article I – Certain general definitions			
1.1	Credit derivative transaction	1.12	Grace period; grace period business day
1.2	Confirmation	1.13	Potential failure to pay
1.3	Term	1.14	Calculation agent
1.4	Effective date	1.15	Calculation agent city
1.5	Trade date	1.16	Business day
1.6	Scheduled termination date	1.17	Calculation agent city business day
1.7	Transaction date	1.18	2002 ISDA Master Agreement
1.8	Event determination date	1.19	Buyer
1.9	Notice delivery period	1.20	Seller
1.10	Requirements regarding notices	1.21	TARGET settlement day
1.11	Grace period extension date		

At first sight, Article I's 21 general definitions appear to be a hotchpotch of mechanical and boilerplate definitions to be utilised or adapted in all credit derivatives transactions. They appear to be in no particular order, with definitions for 'trade date', 'effective date', 'scheduled termination date', 'buyer', 'seller' and 'event determination date' mixed with definitions for grace periods, notice requirements, and the role and duties of the calculations agent.

But look closer: instead of a hotchpotch, the Article I definitions cover four distinct areas. First, they cover a transaction's identity and its documentary structure, with the definitions of 'credit derivative transaction', 'confirmation' and '2002 ISDA Master Agreement'. Second, they cover a transaction's landmark dates:

- the date when the parties agree to enter into a transaction ('trade date');
- how long the parties want the period of credit protection to last ('term');
- the date when the term will begin ('effective date'); and
- when the term is scheduled to end ('scheduled termination date').

In addition, they include definitions of a transaction's relevant business days: 'business day', 'grace period business day', "calculation city business day' and 'TARGET settlement day'.

Third, the Article I definitions cover the time periods set running and key dates fixed when a potential or actual credit event occurs. These are:

- the definitions of 'event determination date' and 'grace period extension date';
- the definitions of periods in the credit event settlement process in which the parties may deliver notices ('notice delivery period', 'grace period extension date', 'grace period' and 'potential failure to pay'); and
- the date when the transaction will end before or after its scheduled termination date ('termination date').

Fourth, the Article I definitions cover the identity and location of the parties, with definitions of 'buyer', 'seller', 'calculation agent' and 'calculation agent city'.

Four areas of Article 1

AREA I: Article I definitions relating to transaction identity
1.1   Credit derivative transaction
1.2   Confirmation
1.18   2002 ISDA Master Agreement

AREA II: Article I definitions relating to the transaction's fixed time parameters
1.3   Term
1.4.   Effective date
1.5.   Trade date
1.6.   Scheduled termination date
1.12   Grace period business day
1.16   Business day
1.17   Calculation agent city business day
1.21   TARGET settlement day

AREA III: Article I definitions relating to fixing the termination date

1.7   Termination date

1.8   Event determination date

1.9   Notice delivery period

1.10   Requirements regarding notices

1.11   Grace period extension date

1.12. Grace period

1.13   Potential failure to pay

AREA IV: Article I definitions relating to the identity and location of the transaction parties

1.14   Calculations

1.15   Calculation agent city

1.19   Buyer

1.20   Seller

3.1   Area I: transaction identity and documentary structure

The purpose of this letter (this 'Confirmation') is to confirm the terms and conditions of the Credit Derivative Transaction entered into between us on the Trade Date specified below (the 'Transaction'). This Confirmation constitutes a 'Confirmation' as referred to in the ISDA Master Agreement specified below.

The definitions and provisions contained in the 2003 ISDA Credit Derivatives Definitions (the 'Credit Derivatives Definitions'), as published by the International Swaps and Derivatives Association, Inc., are incorporated into this Confirmation.

extract from a standard confirmation

Article I provides definitions for confirming the transaction's identity as a credit derivatives transaction and its documentary structure. First, Section 1.1 (credit derivative transaction) specifies that any transaction will be a credit derivatives transaction if it identifies itself as such or it incorporates the 2003 Definitions. In practice, this is done in the way set out in the figure above.

Second, Section 1.2 (confirmation) provides that a credit derivative transaction is confirmed or its terms evidenced by taking together 'one or more documents and other confirming evidence exchanged between the parties or otherwise effective'.

Section 1.18 (2002 ISDA Master Agreement) provides that various definitions used but not defined in the 2003 Definitions – 'additional termination event', 'affected party', 'affected transaction', 'affiliate', 'close-out amount', 'stamp tax' and 'tax' – have the same meaning as in the 2002 ISDA Master Agreement.

This is important because the derivatives market has not, over the five years since it was released, adopted the 2002 ISDA Master Agreement as its standard. This was not expected when the 2003 Definitions were released, and so parties which have a 1992 ISDA Master Agreement in place covering all of their derivatives transactions will, by incorporating the 2003 Definitions into a credit derivatives transaction, be 'upgrading' certain key provisions of their 1992 Master Agreement to 2002 Master Agreement norms.

Eight sections of the 2003 Definitions use defined terms from the 2002 Master Agreement. The affected provisions are:

- Section 2.30(f) (substitute reference obligation), in the definition of 'relevant obligations', which uses 'additional termination event', 'affected transaction' and 'close-out amount';
- Section 2.31 (merger of reference entity and seller), which uses 'additional termination event', 'affiliates', 'affected party' and 'close-out amount';
- Section 2.32 (restructuring maturity limitation and fully transferable obligation), in the definition of 'eligible transferee', which uses 'affiliates';
- Section 2.33 (modified restructuring maturity limitation and conditionally transferable obligation), Section 3.5 (publicly available information), Section 4.8 (certain definitions relating to credit events), Section 7.15 (dealer) and Section 9.1 (additional representations and agreements of the parties), which all use 'affiliates'; and
- Section 9.2 (additional representations and agreements for physical settlement), which uses 'affiliates', 'stamp tax' and 'tax'.

3.2 Area II: definitions relating to the transaction's fixed time parameters

1. General terms:	
Trade date:	January 10 2007
Effective date:	January 18 2007
Scheduled termination date:	January 2010

(a) *Trade date, effective date, scheduled termination date and term*

Just as in the extract above from a standard credit default swap, each transaction will set out as specific terms, in its general terms section, the date when the parties agree to enter into a transaction as the 'trade date'. This is usually a few days before the

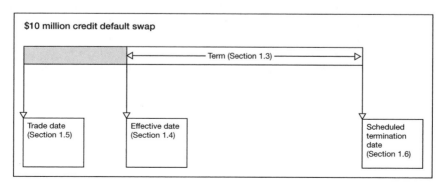

'effective date', which is when any confirmation will actually be signed and the date when the parties want the credit protection period to commence.

A transaction's term runs from the effective date until the scheduled termination date, which is the agreed date for credit protection to end, unless a credit event or a potential credit event causes the transaction to terminate either before or after the scheduled termination date.

(b)   Business days

Business days: London, New York and TARGET settlement day

Article I provides definitions for four types of business day: 'grace period business day' (Section 1.12); 'business day' (Section 1.16); 'calculation agent city business day' (Section 1.17) and 'TARGET settlement day' (Section 1.21).

Various activities in credit derivatives transactions can be carried out only on business days (eg, valuation dates and effective delivery of notices). Section 1.16 provides that a business day in a transaction will be any day on which commercial banks and foreign exchange markets are generally open to settle payments in the places listed in the confirmation. In the confirmation extract above these are London and New York. A business day may also be a target settlement day, which is separately defined in Section 1.21. Section 1.21 adopts the standard 2000 ISDA Definitions wording, providing that a TARGET settlement day will be "any day on which TARGET (the Trans-European Automated Real-time Gross settlement Express Transfer system) is open".

The business days that the parties select will usually depend on the currency of the credit derivatives transaction and the location of the parties (in particular, the calculation agent). If no business days are set out in the confirmation, the business day definition provides a fallback. This is for the business day to be a day on which commercial and foreign exchange markets are generally open to settle payments in the currency of the 'floating rate payer calculation amount' (ie, the currency of the seller's leg of the swap). This fallback is fragile. If the jurisdiction of the dollar, for example, is the United States, it could be confusing, owing to the varied public holidays in different states, to establish which days are US business days. Likewise, it would also be difficult to establish the jurisdiction of the euro, although common sense would dictate that TARGET settlement days should apply for euros and New York business days for dollars. Best practice is therefore to list the business day jurisdictions in the confirmation and not to rely on the fallback.

The definitions of 'grace period business day' and 'calculation agent city business day' are discussed below, in connection with the grace period and calculation agent city definitions.

3.3   Area III: Time parameters fixed once an actual or potential credit event occurs

Credit events

The following credit events shall apply to this transaction:

Failure to pay
Grace period extension applicable
Grace period: 30 days

Repudiation/moratorium
Repudiation/moratorium extension condition: applicable

Article I has eight definitions which:
- cover the time periods around and key dates fixed when an actual or potential credit event occurs;
- fix the transaction's termination date (either earlier or later than scheduled); and
- allow the settlement process to continue after the scheduled termination date.

(a)   Event determination date

The event determination date (Section 1.8) is the date when a credit event is deemed to have occurred, and according to the definition, this is "the first date on which both the credit event notice and, if applicable, the notice of publicly available information are effective" (ie, 'delivered within the notice delivery period' and 'meeting the requirements regarding notices'). It is the event determination date that sets the credit event settlement process rolling.

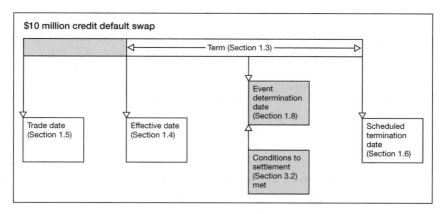

(b)   Fixing the termination date

Section 1.7 (termination date) provides that if no credit event or potential credit event occurs during the transaction's term, then the transaction will terminate on its scheduled termination date (ie, the agreed fixed date set out under 'scheduled termination date' in the confirmation). A transaction's termination date, though, is not necessarily the scheduled termination date. Section 1.7 further provides that if certain actual or potential credit event linked circumstances occur, this may cause a transaction to terminate either before or after its scheduled termination date.

Where a grace period extension applies and, following a potential failure to pay, an actual failure to pay credit event occurs after the scheduled termination date, the termination date may instead be determined through the grace period extension date definition set out in Section 1.11 (grace period extension date). Where the applicable credit event is repudiation/moratorium, the termination date may in some circumstances be determined through Section 4.6(b) (repudiation/moratorium evaluation date).

In physically settled transactions, if the conditions to settlement have been met, the termination date may be the date crystallised pursuant to the notice of physical settlement definition set out in Section 3.4 (notice of physical settlement) and pursuant to the definition of 'physical settlement date' set out in Section 8.4 (notice of physical settlement). Alternatively, the termination date may be determined by applying the provisions set out in Article IX (additional representations and agreements of the parties), in particular:

- Section 9.2(c)(ii) (additional representations and agreements for physical settlement);
- Section 9.3 (partial cash settlement due to impossibility or illegality); and
- Section 9.8 (partial cash settlement terms).

Where, following a credit event, the transaction is cash settled, the termination date may be determined through the cash settlement date definition set out in Section 9.8 (cash settlement date).

In summary, where the termination date is not the scheduled termination date, the termination date may fall before the scheduled termination date if, post-event determination date, the transaction physical settles, cash settles or partially cash settles prior to the scheduled termination date. On the other hand, the 'unscheduled' termination date may fall after the scheduled termination date, if the credit event settlement process cannot be completed until after the scheduled termination date (eg, because although the conditions to settlement are satisfied prior to the scheduled termination date, the related cash settlement date or physical settlement date cannot happen until afterwards).

Additionally, the transaction may terminate after the scheduled termination date because:

- a potential credit event has occurred, perhaps in relation to a repudiation/ moratorium or a failure to pay (where the grace period provisions apply) and whether or not the credit event has actually occurred cannot be determined until after the scheduled termination date; or
- the notice delivery period has not yet expired.

(c) *Notice delivery period*

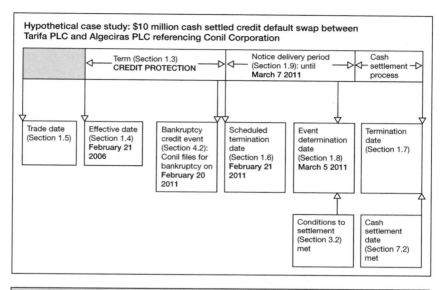

Hypothetical case study: $10 million cash settled credit default swap between Tarifa PLC and Algeciras PLC referencing Conil Corporation

Hypothetical case study: notice delivery period I – Conil Corporation

Tarifa PLC entered into a $10 million cash settled credit default swap with Algeciras PLC. Under this swap Tarifa sold credit protection to Algeciras on Conil Corporation, a US travel company. The credit protection period ran from February 21 2006 to February 21 2011. One day before the scheduled termination date, on February 20 2011, Conil Corporation filed for bankruptcy. Algeciras, the buyer, had until March 7 2011 (14 calendar days later) to deliver a credit event notice and notice of publicly available information to crystallise an event determination date. It did so on March 5 2011 and the process of cash settling the transaction then commenced.

The notice delivery period definition set out in Section 1.9 (notice delivery period) contemplates that although credit protection on a reference entity only lasts during the transaction's term, a notifying party should be allowed an additional period of time to trigger a credit event which occurred during the credit protection period, once credit protection has ceased.

This is because:

- if a credit event occurs close to the termination date (eg, the day before), the party intending to trigger its affected transactions may need time to organise the credit event process and analyse the relevant documentation; or
- certain potential credit events have occurred prior to the scheduled termination date, which are, with the progress of time, likely to become actual credit events.

The notice delivery period relates only to delivering credit event notices and notices of publicly available information (ie, crystallising the event determination date). If neither the grace period extension date nor the repudiation/moratorium evaluation date applies to a transaction, then the notice delivery period will run from the effective date until 14 calendar days after the scheduled termination date. If the final calendar day is not a business day, it will be adjusted in accordance with the relevant business day convention.

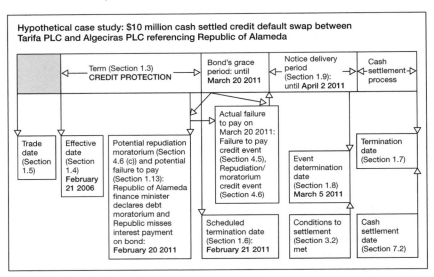

Hypothetical case study: $10 million cash settled credit default swap between Tarifa PLC and Algeciras PLC referencing Republic of Alameda

Hypothetical case study: notice delivery period II – Republic of Alameda

Tarifa PLC and Algeciras PLC entered into another $10 million cash settled credit default swap. This time Tarifa sold credit protection on a sovereign reference entity – the Republic of Alameda. The transaction had the same term as the Conil swap: February 21 2006 to February 21 2011. Tarifa and Algeciras selected both failure to pay (with grace period extension as applicable) and repudiation/moratorium as the applicable credit events.

On February 20 2011, one day before the credit default swap's scheduled termination date, the finance minister of the Republic of Alameda declared a repudiation of the country's international debts. This was a potential repudiation/moratorium according to Section 4.6, as well as a potential failure to pay according to Section 1.13. February 20 2011 was also an interest payment date for a €100 million of floating rate eurobonds issue, issued by the republic.

Although the republic had missed the payment, because the bond documentation contained a 30-day grace period (which would not end until March 20 2011), the bonds would not default (and the potential failure to pay could not crystallise as an actual failure to pay) until 29 days after the credit default swap's scheduled termination date.

As expected, the republic did not make the interest payment on the eurobond issue on March 20 2011 and a failure to pay credit event occurred. As far as triggering a failure to pay credit event was concerned, Algeciras then had 14 calendar days (ie, until April 3 2011) to deliver a credit event notice and notice of publicly available information.

The potential repudiation/moratorium had now also been accompanied by an actual failure to pay. This meant that a repudiation/moratorium credit event had also occurred. As was the case with the failure to pay credit event, Algeciras was alternatively able to deliver a credit event notice and notice of publicly available information relating to the repudiation/moratorium credit event up to and including April 3 2011. Algeciras met the conditions to settlement on April 2 2011 and the cash settlement process began.

If a transaction has both failure to pay and grace period extension selected in its credit event section and a potential failure to pay occurs prior to the scheduled termination date (eg, the reference entity misses an interest payment date), but the grace period for the relevant obligation does not end until after the scheduled termination date, then as described above, the transaction's termination date will not be until the grace period extension date and the notice delivery period will not expire until 14 calendar days after the grace period extension date.

If the relevant credit event is a repudiation/moratorium credit event and the potential repudiation/moratorium provisions and repudiation/moratorium extension condition are applicable, then it is not until 14 calendar days after a repudiation/moratorium evaluation date falling after the scheduled termination date that the notice delivery period will expire.

(d) Requirements regarding notices and calculation agent city

Section 1.9 (notice delivery period), discussed above, determines the parameters of the period in which a party can meet the conditions to settlement. Section 1.10 (requirements regarding notices) determines when any notice (not just a credit event notice and notice of publicly available information) is deemed to be delivered, regardless of its actual delivery date. The definition also links in two other definitions: 'calculation agent city' (Section 1.15) and 'calculation agent city business day' (Section 1.17).

Deemed delivery date is important, because if a notice is actually delivered on one day but is deemed to be delivered on another, it could theoretically affect not only whether an event determination date occurs within the notice delivery period, but also the date on which any valuation date will fall, in turn affecting an obligation's final price.

If a notice is not delivered before 4:00pm (calculation agent city time) on a calculation agent city business day, it is deemed to be delivered on the following calculation agent city business day. The calculation agent city will usually be set out in the transaction documentation.

Calculation agent city: London.

If it is not, the fallback under Section 1.15 (calculation agent city) is for it to be the "the city in which the office through which the Calculation Agent is acting for the purposes of the credit derivative transaction is located". As discussed in more detail below, 'calculation agent city business day' is defined in Section 1.17 as "a day on which commercial banks and foreign exchange markets are generally open to settle payments in the calculation agent city".

Section 1.10 does not require a notice to be in writing. It can be given by telephone; in such case delivery is deemed to occur when the call takes place. Telephone notices can be useful when a party is triggering a credit event in relation to multiple transactions and is facing a tight deadline to deliver a notice prior to the cut-off time. A telephone notice must be followed up within one business day (*not* one calculation agent city business day), with a written confirmation "confirming the substance" of the notice.

If the party delivering the notice fails to follow up with a written confirmation, there is no sanction or consequence and the definition states that "failure to provide that written confirmation will not affect the effectiveness of that telephonic notice".

Where a third party is the calculation agent, the definition requires that calculation agent is also delivered a copy the notice. However, if the calculation does not receive a copy, the notice will still be valid and effective, and the 2003 Definitions provide no sanction or consequence for the failure.

(e) *Potential failure to pay; grace period; grace period business day and grace period extension*

(i) *What is a grace period?*

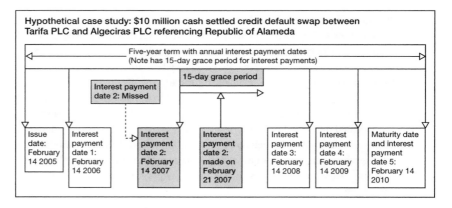

Hypothetical case study: $10 million cash settled credit default swap between Tarifa PLC and Algeciras PLC referencing Republic of Alameda

As far as payments are concerned, a grace period is a provision in a company or sovereign's debt documentation giving it an additional penalty-free period to make a payment, when it is unable to do so on a scheduled payment date. A grace period provision is intended to prevent a missed payment due to administrative reasons triggering an actual default.

Example of a grace period in a eurobond's failure to pay event of default
It shall be an event of default if:
(c) the issuer fails to pay an amount of interest on the notes for 15 days after such interest has become due.

In international capital markets loans and bonds, grace periods are almost universal and the length of these periods is often heavily negotiated. They may vary from a few days to a month or longer, depending on the jurisdiction and the relevant market standard for the type of borrower or issuer.

(ii)   *Why are a reference entity's obligation's grace periods important in credit derivative transactions?*

Loan and bond grace periods are not drafted with credit derivative transactions in mind. Conceptually, grace periods do not fit easily with credit derivative transactions when:

- a reference entity misses a payment under one of its obligations before a credit derivative transaction's scheduled termination date; and
- that obligation's relevant grace period will not expire until after the scheduled termination date.

This is problematic because credit derivatives relate to concrete 'credit risk' events impacting on a reference entity's credit quality during the credit derivative transaction's term (ie, a bankruptcy, a bond or loan restructuring, an actual failure to pay, a repudiation or moratorium or an obligation acceleration or default). However, when a corporate or sovereign misses a payment under one of its obligations this missed payment may be due to administrative reasons. It may in fact meet the payment shortly afterwards and before the grace period ends: no harm done, especially when the terms of the obligation impose no sanction for the omission nor view it as a default. In such circumstances, one can argue that this should certainly not be grounds for triggering a credit event.

One can argue the toss, though: often when a reference entity misses a payment under a bond or loan, it is a precursor to an actual event of default, and whenever there is a failure to pay event of default in a bond issue or loan containing a payment grace period, by definition this follows the issuer or borrower previously missing the scheduled payment date and the grace period ending. So in such cases, with the benefit of hindsight (ie, after the actual failure to pay has occurred), one can argue that a counterparty should be able to trigger a failure to pay credit event, for which the initial missed payment occurred before the scheduled termination date, notwithstanding that the actual failure to pay occurred after the credit derivative transaction's scheduled termination date.

(iii)   *How do the 2003 Definitions deal with the grace period problem?*
The 2003 Definitions deal with the grace period dilemma by:

- allowing counterparties to decide at the transaction's outset which side of this argument they wish to follow; and
- imposing a minimum period of at least three grace period business days before any missed payment under a reference entity obligation can be deemed to be a failure to pay (regardless of what is actually stated in the underlying documentation).

The 2003 Definitions give the transaction parties the option to decide whether to apply grace period extension provisions. If they are applied, credit protection (in relation to a failure to pay credit event) may extend beyond the scheduled termination date, in certain circumstances where the reference entity first misses the relevant payment before the scheduled termination date but the grace period does not expire until afterwards. If the grace period extension provisions are not applied (and the fallback is not for them to apply automatically), then if the reference entity has missed the relevant payment before the scheduled termination date, but the grace period has yet to expire at the scheduled termination date, credit protection will not be extended beyond the scheduled termination date to 'wait and see' whether the potential failure to pay becomes an actual failure to pay.

The 2003 Definitions imply a minimum payment grace period of three grace period business days into all of a reference entity's obligations, notwithstanding that the relevant documentation may not have a grace period. This is to prevent a credit event being triggered for an administrative error, which has no bearing on the reference entity's credit quality.

(iv)   *When are the grace period extension provisions applied?*
In practice, generally the parties do not negotiate the non-pricing terms of a transaction in relation to each individual reference entity, but instead apply the general market practice for a particular type of reference entity (eg, standard terms for Western European sovereign or Japanese entities). These standard terms will probably dictate whether the transaction parties decide to select the grace period extension provisions as applicable for any individual reference entity. If you take a look at the ISDA template first to default confirmation (which relates only to non-sovereign reference entities), there are 10 separate standard terms sections for different types of reference entity. These are categorised by jurisdiction and reference entity type, and include Western European entities, European emerging market entities and Australian and New Zealand entities. Of these 10 categories it is only in the standard terms for European emerging market entities that the grace period extension provisions are applicable. In the standard terms set out in the ISDA 2004 Sovereign Master Credit Derivatives Confirmation Agreement, it is only for sovereigns in emerging European countries, Latin American countries and Middle Eastern countries which the grace period extension provisions are applied. So for the majority of reference entities, the

grace period extension provisions will not be applicable; but for a significant minority, they will be.

(v) *How do the 2003 grace period provisions work?*

Eight definitions linked to grace periods	
1.7 Termination date	1.9 Notice delivery period
1.11 Grace period extension date	1.12 Grace period; grace period
1.13 Potential failure to pay	business day
4.5 Failure to pay	4.8(b) Payment requirement

The 2003 Definitions have eight principal definitions covering payment grace periods in a reference entity's obligations and how to deal with them, if they become relevant in a credit derivative transaction. These provisions are not easy to follow.

Whether a potential failure to pay occurs in relation to any of a reference entity's obligations is determined by applying the criteria set out in the definitions of potential failure to pay, failure to pay and payment requirement. If these criteria are satisfied, the 2003 Definitions' operative grace period provisions, grace period and grace period business day, and grace period extension date, are applied to determine how the potential failure to pay is treated in any credit derivative transaction.

Collectively, these grace period provisions can be summed up as 'wait and see' provisions. They allow a seller to receive the benefit of credit protection when a reference entity fails to pay under one of its obligations prior to the credit derivative transaction's scheduled termination date, but due to the reference entity having the benefit of its own grace period under its contractual documentation, the actual credit event does not occur until after the scheduled termination date. Just as the reference entity benefits from the grace period, the seller benefits from it too. Also, by imposing a deemed grace period on obligations with no or a limited payment grace period, the provisions help to ensure that credit protection is sold against concrete credit risk events.

Hypothetical case study: the grace period provisions in action

Kilrymont Bank PLC is a Hungarian bank with financial problems. It has over €3 billion of bonds outstanding; it is losing money; it has few cash reserves left and its situation is dire. The bank's legal department negotiated the same failure to pay event of default and grace period in all of the bank's bonds: "It shall be an event of default…if Kilrymont Bank PLC fails to pay an amount of interest or principal on the Notes for five days after such interest or principal has become due."

Kilrymont was also a widely traded reference entity in the credit default swap market and on August 7 2007 it missed a quarterly interest payment on a €100 million, 6% note issue. It was now evident that the bank had real difficulties and five days later, on August 12 2007, at the end of the grace period, Kilrymont defaulted and failed to make the payment.

Madras Holdings had entered into two credit default swaps where it had bought credit protection on Kilrymont. Both were cash settled credit default swaps and had a notional amount of €10 million. In one credit default swap, New Park Inc sold credit protection to Madras and, in the other, St Leonards sold credit protection to New Park. In both transactions the scheduled termination date was August 10 2007 and failure to pay was an applicable credit event. However only in the New Park transaction was a 'grace period extension' selected to apply, and this led to differing outcomes in the two transactions.

Madras Holding/New Park Inc credit default swap

Credit events: *Bankruptcy*
Failure to pay
Grace period extension: applicable
Grace period: 10 days
Obligation acceleration
Restructuring

Payment requirement: $1 million

When Kilrymont missed its €1.5 million interest payment on August 7 2007, this was a potential failure to pay in accordance with Section 1.13 of the 2003 Definitions, as it was a failure to pay notwithstanding any grace period in the notes documentation and (at the current euro/dollar exchange rate) for an amount above the €1 million payment requirement (Section 4.8(b)). Once Kilrymont had missed its scheduled payment, no actual payment default could occur until August 12 2007.

Although the scheduled termination date fell on August 8 2007, four days before any actual failure to pay could take place, because the transaction had selected 'grace period extension' to apply, credit protection was extended beyond the scheduled termination date. In accordance with the 2003 Definitions, the grace period extension date was to be for the lesser of the grace period specified in Kilrymont's potentially defaulting bond (ie, four days), and the 'grace period', specified in the confirmation (ie, 10 days). The transaction's termination date was extended to August 12 2007, the grace period extension date.

When the actual default under the Kilrymont bond occurred on August 12 2007, Madras then had 14 calendar days to deliver a credit event notice and notice of publicly available information to New Park to crystallise an event determination date and start the credit event settlement process moving. It did so on August 15 2007, the defaulting Kilrymont bond was the reference obligation and the final price obtained was 10%. New Park duly paid Kilrymont a cash settlement amount of €9 million.

Madras Holdings/St Leonards PLC credit default swap

Credit events: *Bankruptcy*
Failure to pay
Obligation acceleration
Restructuring

When Kilrymont missed its interest payment on August 7 2007, although this was a potential failure to pay, the actual failure pay could not occur until after the scheduled termination date. Without the grace period extension provisions from the 2003 Definitions being incorporated into the transaction, the transaction's termination date, in accordance with Section 1.7, was the scheduled termination date, August 8 2007. As no credit event had occurred during the transaction's term, Madras could not trigger a credit event and received no cash settlement amount from St Leonards.

The grace period provisions in each of the credit derivative transactions ended up being worth €10 million to one or other of the parties.

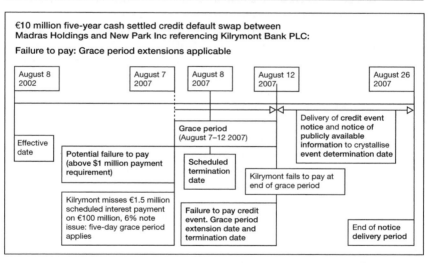

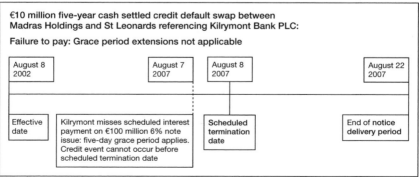

The grace period provisions do not apply automatically to a credit derivative transaction.[1] As the Kilrymont hypothetical case study shows, the parties must state 'grace period extension: applicable' below 'Failure to pay' in the credit event section of a confirmation.[2] If this is not done and a potential failure to pay occurs on or before the scheduled termination date, but the actual failure to pay does not occur until after the scheduled termination date, then the buyer will not have any credit protection for the later default, because the transaction's termination date will be the scheduled termination date.

If 'grace period extension: applicable' is inserted in the confirmation, and a potential failure to pay occurs on or prior to the scheduled termination date, the termination date will be extended out until the grace period extension date. A 'potential failure to pay' covers when a reference entity fails to make "when and where due, any payments in an aggregate amount of not less than the payment requirement under one or more obligations". The definition requires this failure to be determined without taking into account any grace period in the relevant obligation's documentation or any conditions precedent to the grace period beginning. The 'payment requirement' is a minimum amount calculated in accordance with Section 4.8(d); unless the confirmation states otherwise, this will be the fallback amount of $1 million or its equivalent. Therefore, if a reference entity's potential default is for less than the payment requirement, there will be no potential failure to pay. This may be more likely in capital markets transactions than may first seem. Take a $100 million floating rate bond issue paying quarterly interest at USD-LIBOR-BBA plus 1%. USD-LIBOR-BBA fell as low as 2% during the first half of the decade. When this was the case, the bond issuer would be required to pay only $3 million of interest per annum or $750,000 per quarter. So a missed interest payment under this bond would not exceed the default payment requirement.

The 'grace period extension date' will be the date which is the number of days in the grace period after the potential failure to pay.[3] 'Grace period' itself, however, can have several meanings. It can mean the grace period set out in the obligation under which there has been a potential failure to pay (subject to a maximum of 30 calendar days). If 'grace period' has been defined in the confirmation as being a set number of days, though – for example:

Credit events: Failure to pay
                Grace period extension: applicable
                Grace period: 10 days

– and this period is shorter than the grace period in the obligation documentation, then the number of days in the grace period set out in the confirmation will be the grace period. Alternatively, if the relevant obligation does not have the benefit of a

---

[1]   Section 1.11 states : "If grace period extension is not specified as applicable in the related confirmation, grace period extension shall not apply to the credit derivative transaction."

[2]   This is usually done by inserting 'grace period extension: applicable', below 'failure to pay' in the confirmation's credit event section.

[3]   Section 1.12(a)(b).

grace period in its documentation or if it does have a grace period but it is for less than three grace period business days, then the grace period will be three grace period business days. A 'grace period business day' is effectively defined as being a business day in the obligation documentation, failing which a business day in the jurisdiction of the obligation currency.

If a failure to pay credit does occur during the grace period, then the notifying party has 14 calendar days from the grace period extension date[4] to deliver a credit event notice (and, if applicable, a notice of publicly available information). If the conditions are not satisfied before then, the grace period extension date will be the transaction's termination date. If a grace period extension does not apply, then a transaction's termination date will be the scheduled maturity date, even if a potential failure to pay occurs before then.

The third alternative described above can have an interesting consequence. Section 1.12 (grace period; grace period business day) states that: "(a) 'Grace period' means: ...if ...no grace period with respect to payments or a grace period with respect to payments of less than three grace period business days is applicable under the terms of such obligation, a grace period of three grace period business days shall be deemed to apply to such obligation." This means that where a reference entity fails to pay under one of its obligations, even if there is no grace period in the underlying documentation (and so an actual failure to pay has occurred), the 2003 Definitions will deem a grace period of three business days to apply. This provision applies both where a grace period extension is selected as applicable and where it is not. If a grace period extension is not selected as applicable, this synthetic grace period will be deemed to end on the scheduled termination date.

The practical effect of this is that a failure to pay credit event may occur later than the actual default and failure to pay under the underlying documentation. If time is of the essence, the party triggering the credit event may be able to do so sooner under the 'obligation default' or 'obligation acceleration' credit events if they are applicable to the transaction.

**Actual case study: why there are deemed grace periods –
ANZ Banking Group Limited[5] Deutsche Bank v ANZ**

Deutsche Bank had entered into a credit default swap with Daiwa (Europe) Limited under which it had bought credit protection on the City of Moscow. Deutsche Bank had also entered into a back-to-back credit default swap with ANZ Banking Group Limited. Both credit default swaps contained failure to pay credit events.

In September 1997, during a period of high market risk, the City of Moscow defaulted on a $50 million loan on its maturity date, failing to repay around one-

---

4   Section 1.9.
5   2000 WL 1151384 (QBC (Comm Ct).

quarter of the principal amount. It made up this shortfall the following business day, together with default interest. The City of Moscow's loan did not have a grace period and so although the loan was repaid in full, Daiwa (Europe) Limited delivered a credit event notice to Deutsche Bank, notwithstanding that the loan had now been repaid. Deutsche Bank paid the resulting cash settlement amount (which took account of the low trading price of City of Moscow 'obligations') to Daiwa (Europe), but when it triggered the back-to-back swap with ANZ Banking Group, ANZ refused to pay. The case went to court and Justice Langley, taking a strict interpretation of the terms of the contract, ruled that it must be honoured.

Under the 2003 Definitions, the deemed grace period of three business days would mean that a credit event would not have occurred in this case.

3.4   Area IV – identity and location of the parties

Identity of the parties		
Buyer	Seller	Calculation agent

Buyer:	Lawhead PLC
Seller:	Hallowhill Investments
Calculation agent:	Seller

(a)   *Calculation agent*
Section 1.14 sets out the role, duties and responsibilities of the calculation agent.

(i)   *Who is the calculation agent?*

Calculation agent duties hypothetical case study – Hallowhill Investments

Hallowhill Investments entered into four credit default swaps with Lawhead PLC. Two of the swaps were cash settled transactions and the other two were physically settled transactions. Under each transaction Hallowhill sold €100 million of credit protection on the transaction's reference entity: Canongate Corporation, a Scottish utility company. Hallowhill and Lawhead did not specify the identity of the calculation agent in any of the confirmations, so by virtue of the fallback in Section 1.14 of the 2003 Definitions, Hallowhill was appointed calculation agent.

The calculation agent may be the credit protection buyer, the credit protection seller or a third party. When the parties do not specify a calculation agent, the seller is the calculation agent by default. In fact, in most cases, other than in structured transactions, the seller is the calculation agent anyway.

Fulfilling the role of calculation agent requires considerable expertise, and because of the determinations the calculation agent must make, any counterparty or third party taking on the role must have a solid understanding of the duties (and the risks) involved. Understanding the role is not easy considering that the calculation agent definition is 458 words long, including one 391-word sentence!

Owing to the calculation agent's central and active role in all credit derivative transactions, this section of this chapter is very detailed and focuses on clarifying and analysing the calculation agent's roles and responsibilities.

(ii)   *The inherent conflict of interest*
Where the calculation agent is either the buyer or the seller, there is an inherent conflict of interest: the calculation agent may be required to make determinations that are not in its interests. Even if the calculation agent is a third party, because both the buyer and seller have the same agent, there will still be a conflict of interest. For this reason, the definition of 'calculation agent' provides that each party agrees that the calculation agent is not acting as a fiduciary or adviser to either party.

(iii)   *The calculation agent's 12 core duties*
The calculation agent has 12 duties: these are all set out in the definition, although sometimes restated in other definitions. The definition also obliges the calculation agent to notify the parties 'as soon as reasonably practicable' of any determinations that it makes when carrying out these 12 duties.

The calculation agent's 12 core duties: a summary table
(Most roles are carried out in consultation with the parties; calculation agent must notify the parties 'as soon as reasonably practicable' of any determinations that it makes)

1.	Determining a reference entity's successor	*Summary:* The calculation agent must determine which new entity or entities replaces an existing reference entity and assumes its obligations, if the existing reference entity merges, de-merges, reorganises, is taken over or spun off
2.	General reference obligation determinations: • whether aggregate amounts due under a reference obligation have been materially reduced	*Summary:* In cash settled transactions, the calculation agent must determine whether reference obligation nominal amounts are reduced, whether reference obligations remain valid and make determinations on qualified guarantees

- whether any reference obligation is an underlying obligation with a reference entity's qualifying guarantee
- except following a credit event, whether that qualifying guarantee has become unenforceable
- except following a credit event, or as above, whether a reference obligation is still an obligation of a reference entity

3.	Identifying and determining substitute reference obligations	*Summary:* In cash settled transactions, determining whether a reference obligation ceases to be a reference obligation (eg, because it has matured) and deciding upon a new reference obligation.
4.	Making adjustments for multiple credit event notices	*Summary:* If a transaction is only partially triggered following a restructuring credit event, then the calculation agent must make certain adjustments to the transaction
5.	Obtaining quotations	*Summary:* In cash settled transactions, during the credit event settlement process, the calculation agent must obtain quotations for the reference obligation
6.	Converting quotation amounts into the relevant obligation currency	*Summary:* In cash settled transactions, during the credit event settlement process, if the calculation agent is getting quotations for reference obligations denominated in currencies other than the currency stated for the quotation amount, it must do a foreign exchange conversion of the quotation amount (eg converting €25,000 into dollars)
7.	Determining dealers and substituting dealers	*Summary:* In cash settled transactions, the calculation agent must decide which dealers to approach for a quotation, and pick new dealers where existing ones are unavailable

8.	Determining the currency rate	*Summary:* In physically settled transactions where the seller is delivering deliverable obligations in a currency other than the settlement currency, the calculation agent must decide the currency rate to use
9.	Determining the representative amount	*Summary:* In cash settled transactions, if the parties have not pre-agreed a figure for quotation amounts, they may choose to decide 'representative amounts' on a case-by-case basis
10.	Determining the number of business days in each physical settlement period	*Summary:* In physically settled transactions, determining the number of days in a physical settlement period, where a subjective decision must be made
11.	If 'accrued interest' is specified with respect to deliverable obligations, determining accrued but unpaid interest	*Summary:* In physically settled transactions, determining the amount of accrued but unpaid interest which relates to a deliverable obligation
12.	Determining the accreted amount of any obligation	*Summary:* In physically settled transactions, for accreted obligations such as convertible and exchangeable bonds, determining the accreting amount (ie, the obligation's original issue price plus any amount payable at maturity which has already accreted less any cash payments that the reference entity has made to reduce the obligation's redemption amount)

Six of the calculation agent's 12 duties relate only to cash settled transactions, four relate only to physically settled transactions and two relate to both cash and physical transactions. Three of the duties are carried out before a credit event occurs and nine of them are carried out afterwards.

Duty 1 – determining a successor reference entity: A daily look through the financial pages of any newspaper will throw up stories of companies merging with other companies, companies de-merging and splitting into different companies or perhaps spinning off part of a business. Likewise, sovereign states may partition (as did Yugoslavia in the 1990s), or assume another country, perhaps by invasion (as did Iraq with Kuwait).

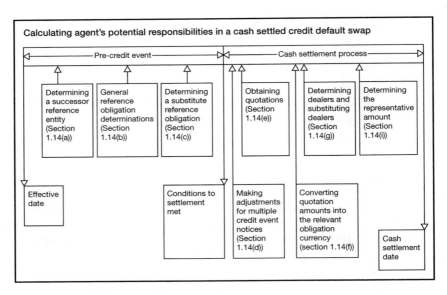

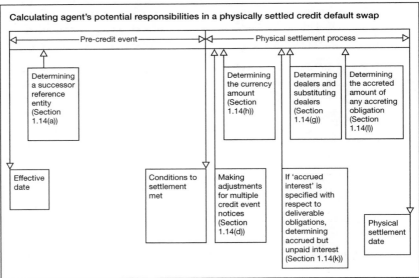

When changes like these occur, and the affected company or state is a reference entity in a credit derivative transaction, the calculation agent must determine the new entity or entities, if any, which succeed the original reference entity. There may be no new reference entity, one new reference entity or several reference entities. It all depends on whether the old reference entity's obligations have been assumed and, if so, how they have been divided. In making its determination, the calculation agent must apply the detailed rules set out in Section 2.2 (provisions for determining a successor).

Hallowhill Investments hypothetical case study:
calculation agent duty 1

A year after the trade date, Canongate, the reference entity in each of the four credit default swaps, merged with a rival utility company, Eden Electricity. The new entity changed its name to Eden PLC. Hallowhill, as calculation agent, analysed the takeover and determined, following Section 2.2 (provisions for determining a successor), that Eden PLC was the successor to all of Canongate's obligations and that therefore Eden now replaced Canongate as the reference entity in each of the four transactions.

Duty 2 – in cash settled transactions, making general determinations on reference obligation validity: reduction of reference obligation amounts; qualifying guarantee enforceability; and reference obligation validity: The determinations that the calculation agent must make under Section 1.14(b) relate solely to cash settled transactions. These determinations are made during the term of a transaction and prior to the conditions to settlement being met.[6] During this period, the calculation agent may end up making three potential types of determination on reference obligation status and validity:

- A reference obligation's principal amount may be reduced – for example, a floating rate note issued with a principal amount of $100 million may later have a $50 million principal amount. If this is not due to a scheduled amortisation, prepayment or redemption of the reference obligation, then the calculation agent must determine what the new principal amount is.
- The 2003 Definitions provisions on whether a guarantee given by a reference entity can, together with an underlying obligation, be a reference obligation are quite complex. If doubts arise as to a guarantee's enforceability, the calculation must determine whether the guarantee is valid and enforceable in accordance with its terms.
- From time to time, reference obligations may be redeemed, or they may be exchanged for equity or perhaps, as part of an internal group restructuring, an issuer changed for another group entity. In each case, the calculation agent must determine whether the reference obligation is still an obligation of the reference entity.

Hallowhill Investments hypothetical case study:
calculation agent duty 2

When Hallowhill and Lawhead entered into the two cash settled credit default swaps in March 2006, they agreed that each swap would have three Canongate reference obligations:

---

6   Except in relation to multiple credit events relating to a restructuring credit event.

- a €80 million 7% syndicated loan due 2021, where Canongate was the borrower;
- a €150 million floating rate notes issue due 2015 issued by Jubilee PLC, a Canongate subsidiary, and guaranteed by Canongate; and
- a $100 million exchangeable notes issue due 2012 issued by Canongate.

In the following two years, three events occurred affecting these reference obligations, which required Hallowhill, as calculation agent, to make determinations following Section 1.14:

- The first determination – Canongate had entered into the 7% fixed rate syndicated loan in 1998. From the early part of the new century, interest rates were significantly lower than this. The loan had an optional prepayment provision, allowing Canongate (ie, Eden) to prepay the loan from March 2008 onwards. At its first opportunity Eden prepaid as much as it could afford: €25 million. Following Section 1.14(b)(i), Hallowhill determined that the aggregate amount due under this reference obligation had been materially reduced, and that this prepayment was not scheduled. Hallowhill notified Lawhead accordingly.
- The second determination – prior to the Eden merger, Canongate had guaranteed a debt issue of one of its unprofitable subsidiaries, Jubilee PLC. Under the 2003 Definitions, the guarantee was a qualifying guarantee; the Jubilee bond was its underlying obligation; and together, this qualifying guarantee and underlying obligation formed the second reference obligation. Following the Canongate/Eden merger, Eden decided to sell off Jubilee to a competitor, Balgove Energy PLC. The Jubilee bondholders voted to allow the Eden guarantee to be replaced by a guarantee from Balgove Energy. The Jubilee bond was listed on the London Stock Exchange. Hallowhill reviewed the prospectus covering the amended structure and analysed the new guarantee and the amended Jubilee bond. Hallowhill determined that, pursuant to Section 1.14(b)(ii), the original 'qualifying guarantee' was "no longer a valid and binding obligation of [Eden] enforceable in accordance with its terms".
- The third determination – at the start of the decade Canongate had tried to branch out into online electricity trading, and started up a subsidiary called Craigtoun Online. To finance Craigtoun Online's start-up costs, Canongate issued $1 million of notes mandatorily exchangeable into Craigtoun shares, once the value of those shares reached a strike price. The shares hit that strike price in 2008 and the exchangeable notes were converted into Craigtoun shares. This meant that Hallowhill was obliged to determine that although the exchangeable bonds were originally a reference obligation, pursuant to Section 1.14(b)(iii), this was no longer the case.

Duty 3 – in cash settled transactions, identifying and determining a substitute reference obligation: If the calculation agent does determine that a reference obligation has ceased to exist, it must, in consultation with the other parties, determine a substitute reference obligation. The calculation agent must determine the substitute reference obligation using the rules set out in Section 2.30 (substitute reference obligation).

Hallowhill Investments hypothetical case study: calculation agent duty 3

Hallowhill had determined that both the Jubilee bond together with its qualifying guarantee and the notes mandatorily convertible into Craigtoun Online shares were no longer reference obligations under the cash settled credit default swaps. This meant that in each case, Hallowhill was obliged, under Section 1.14(c), to determine substitute reference obligations.

Hallowhill identified four other Eden obligations that could potentially be reference obligations and consulted Lawhead. Taking into account Lawhead's views, Hallowhill selected a $50 million floating rate note due 2015 and a €150 million convertible note due 2017, both issued under Eden's EMTN programme as substitute reference obligations.

Duty 4 – if multiple credit event notices have been issued following a restructuring credit event, making the required modifications to the transaction: For all credit events other than restructuring credit events, if a credit event occurs and the conditions to settlement are met, any settlement will relate to the full notional amount for that reference entity (ie, either the transaction's full notional amount in the case of a single name credit default swap or a lesser, pre-agreed amount per reference entity where there is a portfolio of reference entities).

When a restructuring credit event occurs, the notifying party can state in its credit event notice that it is meeting the conditions to settlement in relation either to the full reference entity notional amount or to just a part of it.

If the notifying party decides to deliver a credit event notice specifying only a part of the reference entity notional amount and a further credit event occurs in relation to that reference entity, then a notifying party (which potentially can be either party) can meet the conditions to settlement either partially, in the same manner as before in the case of a further restructuring credit event, or fully for the remaining reference entity notional amount for any other credit event.

Therefore, if a restructuring credit event notice is delivered specifying that it applies to less than the full reference entity notional amount, the calculation agent must make various adjustments to the transaction, such as to reduce the transaction's notional amount. It must do this in consultation with the parties.

> **Hallowhill Investments hypothetical case study:**
> **calculation agent duty 4**
>
> A cash crunch and a loss of investor confidence in the electricity market forced Eden to restructure its bank debt. Following (and because of) the restructuring, Eden was still fundamentally a healthy company: indeed, its debt was trading at 90% of its face value.
>
> As was its right, Lawhead decided that it wanted to trigger a restructuring credit event for only part of each of the four credit default swap's notional amount. Lawhead did this so that it could wait and see whether Eden's credit quality would decline further or the company would make a full recovery, before deciding whether to trigger further restructuring credit event(s) on the rest of the notional amount or, should a different credit event occur, the full notional amount.
>
> Lawhead delivered a credit event notice and notice of publicly available information to Hallowhill for €10 million of each credit default swap's notional amount. After the conditions to settlement had been met and the credit event settlement process followed through, Hallowhill consulted with Lawhead and determined that the notional amount of each credit default swap had been reduced by €10 million to €40 million. This meant that the amount of credit protection under each transaction was reduced and that Hallowhill would receive lower credit protection payments on each fixed rate payment date in the future.

Duty 5 – in cash settled transactions, obtaining quotations and determining a reference obligation's final price: In a cash settled credit derivatives transaction, if the transaction's conditions to settlement are met, when each valuation date arrives the calculation agent must go out into the market and ask each dealer (selected in accordance with the terms of the transaction documentation) for either a bid or offer quotation for an agreed amount of the reference obligation. This agreed amount will be set out in transaction documentation under 'quotation amount'. The quotation amount will be either an exact monetary figure or a reference to a 'representative amount'.

The calculation agent must consult with the parties to determine whether these quotations for the reference obligation shall include in their price interest which the reference obligation has accrued, but has not been paid.

Once the calculation agent has obtained the quotations for a valuation date, it is obliged to notify the parties of its determinations as soon as reasonably practicable. Therefore, when there are multiple valuation dates the calculation agent must send a quotation notice to the parties, setting out the quotations that it has obtained, after each valuation date, rather than waiting until it has determined a final price after the final valuation date.

> **Hallowhill Investments hypothetical case study:**
> **calculation agent duty 5**
>
> Following the restructuring credit event, the valuation date for each of the two cash settled credit default swaps fell 10 business days after the conditions to settlements had been met. Under the transaction documentation for each swap, Hallowhill had to approach five dealers to attempt to obtain a bid quotation from each one for any of the four reference obligations.
>
> Hallowhill contacted Bruges Bank, Salamanca Bank, Swaffham International, First Gorleston and Bulbeck & Co and asked for bid quotations for $20 million of the $50 million floating rate note due 2015 (ie, one of the substitute reference obligations). Hallowhill and Lawhead agreed that these quotations should be exclusive of accrued but unpaid interest.
>
> Following the transaction's valuation method, Hallowhill took the lowest of the five valuations provided by the dealers to determine the final price. The lowest quotation came from First Gorleston and was 88% of the reference obligation's face value. The final price was therefore 88%.

Duty 6 – converting the quotation amount into the relevant obligation currency: Section 1.14(f) of the calculation agent definition obliges the calculation agent to convert 'the quotation amount into the relevant obligation currency'. The currency of a credit default swap's quotation amount provision is usually only one currency, be it euros, dollars or any other currency. The currency of the credit default swap's reference obligations, though, can be in any number of currencies. For example, a $100 million credit default swap could have one reference obligation denominated in dollars and another in euros. However, because the credit default swap is itself denominated in dollars, the quotation amount provided in the confirmation will also be in dollars. This means that the calculation agent must convert the dollar quotation amount to a euro quotation amount before it approaches dealers for quotations on the euro denominated reference obligation.

The calculation agent is obliged by virtue of the 'quotation amount'[7] definition to carry out this conversion "in a commercially reasonable manner by reference to exchange rates in effect at the time that the relevant quotation is being obtained". Once a quotation amount is converted into the obligation currency, the resulting amount may not be one that the calculation agent can realistically ask for quotations to be provided. For example, a dollar amount of $30 million converted to euros might give a euro amount of €21,333,221.06. In such circumstances, the calculation agent would need to exercise its commercial judgement and round the amount up or down to the nearest acceptable trading amount. This weakness should perhaps be addressed in a successor edition to the 2003 Definitions.

---

7   Section 7.12.

> **Hallowhill Investments hypothetical case study:**
> **calculation agent duty 6**
>
> Each of the four credit default swaps was denominated in euros. In the two cash settled transactions, when Hallowhill contacted the dealers to ask for bid quotations for the dollar denominated reference obligation (ie, the $50 million floating rate note due 2015), it had to convert the quotation amount of €25 million set out in the confirmation:
>
> > "Quotation amount: €25 million"
>
> into an equivalent amount in dollars. At the current spot rate, this was $20 million. Hallowhill then approached the dealers to ask for bid quotations for $20 million of the $50 million floating rate note due 2015.

Duty 7 – determining (after consultation with the parties) the dealers where none have been specified in the confirmation) and substituting dealers: The parties will usually agree the identity of the dealers that the calculations agent must approach to ask for a quotation when valuing a reference obligation in the documentation. Where no dealers are listed in the transaction documentation, the calculation agent will liaise with the parties and agree upon dealers.

Where the parties have agreed upon dealers in the documentation and later on a dealer ceases to be in existence and there are no successors, the calculation agent will select a substitute dealer in consultation with the parties. This will also be the case where the dealer ceases to be a dealer in the reference obligation.

> **Hallowhill Investments hypothetical case study:**
> **calculation agent duty 7**
>
> Under each cash settled credit default swap, Hallowhill was obliged to approach five dealers to obtain quotations for a reference obligation. In one of the cash settled credit default swaps the confirmation listed five dealers which were to be approached:
>
> > "Dealers: Bruges Bank, Salamanca Bank, Swaffham International, First Gorleston, and Toledo Securities Inc."
>
> Toledo Securities had gone out of business the previous year and so Hallowhill consulted with Lawhead and they agreed to substitute Bulbeck & Co as a dealer.
>
> In the second cash settled credit default swap, the documentation did not list which dealers Hallowhill should approach, so Hallowhill contacted Lawhead and they agreed that quotations should obtained from the same five dealers as in the first cash settled credit default swap.

Duty 8 – determining the currency rate: In a physically settled transaction, when the buyer wishes to deliver deliverable obligations of the reference entity which are denominated in a currency other than the transaction's settlement currency, the calculation agent must calculate just how much of these deliverable obligations must be delivered to equal the physical settlement amount. The calculation agent must determine the exchange rate or the 'currency rate' in accordance with Section 8.10 (currency rate). The seller will then use this rate to determine the 'currency amount' (ie, the amount of deliverable obligations that it must deliver to get the physical settlement amount).

Hallowhill Investments hypothetical case study: calculation agent duty 8

Lawhead delivered a notice of physical settlement for the Eden restructuring credit event under the physically settled credit default swap. Lawhead wished to trigger €50 million of the transaction's €500 million notional amount. This meant that it was obliged to deliver €50 million of Eden's obligations selected in accordance with the applicable deliverable obligation category and deliverable obligation characteristics. The €50 million of deliverable obligations could either be fully or partially denominated in the settlement currency (ie, euros), or fully or partially denominated in other currencies.

Lawhead opted to settle the transaction by delivering dollar denominated floating rate notes. This meant that Hallowhill, as calculation agent, had to convert the settlement currency €50 million into dollars. Hallowhill made this determination by converting 'currency rate', following Section 8.10. Because the settlement currency was in euros, Hallowhill was obliged to take "the MEAN price as displayed on Reuters Page EUROFX/1 as of 12:00pm (London time) on the date the notice of physical settlement is effective" and communicate this to Lawhead. Lawhead then used this rate to calculate that it must deliver $72.55 million of the dollar denominated Eden floating rate notes.

Duty 9 – determining (after consultation with the parties) the representative amount): When the calculation agent obtains quotations from the dealers for an amount of the reference obligation, that amount can be either for the quotation amount (as described above) or for the representative amount. The representative amount, which is defined in Section 7.16 as being "an amount that is representative for a single transaction in the relevant market and at the relevant time, such amount to be determined by the calculation agent in consultation with the parties", is agreed between the parties at the time which quotations are sought. The concept of the representative amount gives the parties additional flexibility, but at the same time removes some objective certainty from a transaction.

Hallowhill Investments hypothetical case study: calculation agent duty 9

One of the cash settled transactions stated that the quotation amount was the 'representative amount'. This meant that instead of the quotation amount being a fixed euro amount, which Hallowhill would then use to get bid quotations for the reference obligation, Hallowhill had to consult with Lawhead to determine what the size of quotation amount would be. The parties agreed that the quotation amount should be $20 million.

Duty 10 – determining (after consultation with the parties) the number of business days in each physical settlement period: Where the transaction documentation does not set out a specific physical settlement period (eg, five business days), the calculation agent is responsible for determining how long the buyer has to deliver the deliverable obligations to the seller. The calculation agent must consult with both parties to make this determination, with the presumption being that this should be the longest number of business days for settlement in accordance with the market practice for that deliverable obligation.

Hallowhill Investments hypothetical case study: calculation agent duty 10

Once Lawhead had triggered the physically settled credit default swap for the Eden restructuring credit event, it had 30 calendar days in which to deliver its notice of physical settlement. It was allowed to amend the notice as many times as it wished, but once those 30 calendar days were up, the period in which Lawhead had to settle the transaction by actually delivering the Eden deliverable obligations began.

The confirmation did not define how many business days the physical settlement period should last, and the 2003 Definitions fallback provides that the physical settlement period will be "the longest number of business days for settlement in accordance with then current market practice of such deliverable obligation, as determined by the calculation agent after consultation with the parties". Hallowhill consulted with Lawhead and together they determined that the Lawhead should have 30 business days to settle the transaction.

Duty 11 – if 'include accrued interest' is specified in the related confirmation with respect to deliverable obligations, determining (after consultation with the parties) accrued but unpaid interest: A transaction's documentation will usually state whether the calculation agent when asking for quotations for a reference obligation should request that those quotations should be on the basis that the relevant obligation has accrued interest, which is owed but unpaid. This is done by either stating 'include accrued interest' or 'exclude accrued interest' in the section relating to quotations. If 'include accrued interest' is selected then the calculation agent must determine, following consultation with the parties, just how much interest has accrued but not been paid and request quotations from dealers accordingly.

Hallowhill Investments hypothetical case study: calculation agent duty 11

"Quotations: include accrued interest"

'Include accrued interest' had been specified in both of the cash settled credit default swap transactions. This meant that when Hallowhill went to the dealers to get quotations for the quotation amount of the reference obligation, it was obliged to ask the dealers to quote on the basis that the Eden obligations owed accrued but unpaid interest. Hallowhill was responsible for calculating just how much interest was deemed to have been accrued and it did this in consultation with Lawhead.

Because this was a 'soft' credit event and payment of these interest amounts was likely to occur on the deliverable obligation's next interest payment date, the accrued interest made a significant difference to the final price.

Duty 12 – determining the accreted amount of any accreting obligation: Accreting obligations[8] are obligations such as convertible or exchangeable bonds which, if accelerated, pay out their original issue price plus additional amounts. Because the face value of an accreting obligation will differ from the amount owed, accreting obligations add a layer of complexity in physically settled transactions.

If the buyer selects an accreting obligation as the deliverable obligation that it wishes to deliver in a physically settled transaction then the calculation agent must calculate the accreted amount.[9] This is the deliverable obligation's original issue price plus any amount payable at maturity which has already accreted, less any cash payments that the reference entity has made to reduce the obligation's redemption amount.

Hallowhill Investments hypothetical case study: calculation agent duty 12

One of the new Eden reference obligations that Hallowhill selected as a substitute reference obligation was a €150 million convertible note due 2010, issued under Eden's EMTN programme. Lawhead decided to use the convertible

---

8   Section 8.7(b)(ii).
9   Section 8.7(b)(i).

bond to physically settle €25 million of the physically settled credit default swap for the restructuring credit event.

Under the 2003 Definitions, the convertible bond was an accreting obligation and so subject to special rules when calculating how much of the convertible bond's face value amount was required to be delivered so as to be equal to the €25 million outstanding principal balance which Lawhead was obliged to deliver towards the physical settlement amount.

Hallowhill calculated that the exchangeable bond's original issue price was 80% of its principal amount (ie, an €20 million purchase price would have bought an €25 million principal amount of securities on the obligation's issue date), but that its accreted amount was 90%. Hallowhill determined that a face value amount of €27.5 million of the 2017 notes was the amount equal to the required €25 million outstanding principal balance equalling the physical settlement amount.

(iv)   *The ICMA and ISDA explanatory note on calculation agent role for certain derivative linked securities*

On Tuesday October 10 2006, the International Capital Market Associations (ICMA) and ISDA released an explanatory note on the role of the calculation agent. The note focused on three issues:

- identifying a calculation agent at least seven working days prior to the calculation agent assuming its role;
- documenting the calculation agent's duties correctly and appropriately; and
- considering certain issues where derivative securities have been hedged through another transaction and one party is acting as calculation agent in both transactions.

The note does not alter any of the provisions in Section 1.14 (calculation agent); however, market participants should be aware of both its existence and its recommendations. The note is published on the ISDA website.

(b)   *Buyer and seller*

The buyer, which buys credit protection on a reference entity, and the seller, which sells that credit protection, are the two counterparties in any transaction. In the 2003 Definitions the 'buyer' is defined in Section 1.19 as "the fixed rate payer" and the 'seller' in Section 1.20 as "the floating rate payer". These terms are in turn defined in Section 2.6 and Section 2.7 respectively, where the fixed rate payer is defined as "the party obligated to make one or more payments of a fixed amount as specified in the related confirmation"; and the floating rate payer is defined as "the party specified as such in the related confirmation"; and the 'fixed amount' is then further defined in Section 2.5.

The buyer and seller are defined in this manner because credit default swaps involve bilateral payment flows. The buyer receives a premium in return for selling credit protection on the reference entity. In standard transactions these premium payments are a percentage amount of the notional amount of the credit default swap. The premium payments are therefore referred to as 'fixed amounts', payable by the 'fixed rate payer' on periodic 'fixed rate payment dates'. It is for this reason that the buyer is known as the 'fixed rate payer'.

The seller, on the other hand, will be required to make a payment only if a credit event occurs and a physical settlement or cash settlement amount is payable; and in these circumstances the actual amount payable will depend on the deliverable obligations delivered or the final price of an obligation; for this reason the seller in the floating rate payer and the payments (if any) which it makes are floating rate amounts.

Article II – General terms relating to credit derivative transactions

2.23	Qualifying guarantee:
	Underlying obligation
	Underlying obligor
2.24	Qualifying affiliate guarantee
2.25	Downstream affiliate voting shares
2.26	Sovereign
2.27	Sovereign agency
2.28	Supranational organisation
2.29	Domestic currency
2.30	Substitute reference obligation.
2.31	Merger of reference entity and seller
2.32	Restructuring maturity limitation and fully transferable obligation:
2.32(a)	Restructuring maturity limitation and fully transferable obligation applicable
2.32(b)	Fully transferable obligation
2.32(c)	Restructuring maturity limitation date
2.32(d)	Restructuring date
2.32(e)	Restructured bond or loan
2.32(f)	Eligible transferee
2.33	Modified restructuring maturity limitation and conditionally transferable obligation:
2.33(a)	Modified restructuring maturity limitation and conditionally transferable obligation applicable
2.33(b)	Conditionally transferable obligation
2.33(c)	Modified restructuring maturity limitation date
2.33(d)	Restructuring date
2.33(e)	Restructured bond or loan
2.33(f)	Modified eligible transferee

1. Overview

Article II contains 33 sections. It is the longest and most detailed article in the 2003 Definitions. Whereas Article I is supposed to contain 'certain general definitions' and Article II 'general terms relating to credit derivative transactions', the two in fact overlap. Article II contains many general definitions such as those for 'reference obligation', 'reference price' and 'fixed amount'; and Article I contains several general terms such as those definitions relating to grace period extensions and calculation agent.

Article II consists of 79 terms and definitions, spread through its 33 sections. As with Article I, these definitions can be grouped into distinct areas.

Article II's definitions cover seven areas. These are:

- the identity of the reference entity and its successors;
- the buyer's fixed rate premium payments to the seller in return for selling credit protection on the reference entity;
- the seller's credit protection payments to the buyer following a credit event;
- determining the reference entity's obligations against which the seller sells credit protection to the buyer;
- determining the obligations which may be valued and the deliverable obligations which may be delivered following a credit event;
- limiting the deliverable obligations which may be delivered by the buyer to the seller following a restructuring credit event (modified restructuring and modified modified restructuring); and
- the provisions relating to business day conventions.

1.1 Area I: the reference entity and its successors

Article II has 10 definitions that relate to the reference entity and its successors. These are the definitions and terms for:

- 'reference entity' (Section 2.1);

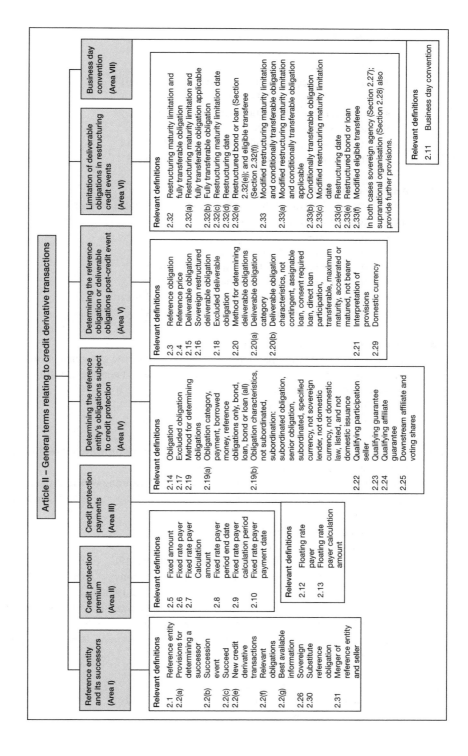

- 'provisions for determining a successor' (Section 2.2(a));
- 'succession event' (Section 2.2(b));
- 'succeed' (Section 2.2(c));
- 'new credit derivative transactions' (Section 2.2(e));
- 'relevant obligations' (Section 2.2(f));
- 'best available information' (Section 2.2(g));
- 'sovereign' (Section 2.26);
- 'substitute reference obligation' (Section 2.30); and
- 'merger of reference entity and seller' (Section 2.31).

1.2 Area II: credit protection premium

Article II has six definitions that cover the buyer's fixed rate premium payments to the seller in return for selling credit protection on the reference entity. These are:

- 'fixed amount' (Section 2.5);
- 'fixed rate payer' (Section 2.6);
- 'fixed rate payer calculation amount' (Section 2.7);
- 'fixed rate payer period end date' (Section 2.8);
- 'fixed rate payer calculation period' (Section 2.9); and
- 'fixed rate payer payment date' (Section 2.10).

1.3 Area III: credit protection payments

Article II has two definitions that cover the identity of the party making the credit protection payments to the buyer following a credit event and the quantum of credit protection that it sells to the buyer. These are:

- 'floating rate payer' (Section 2.12); and
- 'floating rate payer calculation amount' (Section 2.13).

1.4 Area IV: determining the reference entity's obligations on which it sells credit protection to the buyer

Article II has 27 terms and definitions that cover determining which of the reference entity's obligations are subject to the credit protection that the seller has sold to the buyer. These are:

- 'obligation' (Section 2.14);
- 'excluded obligation' (Section 2.17);
- 'method for determining obligations' (Section 2.19);
- 'obligation category', 'payment', 'borrowed money', 'reference obligations only', 'bond', 'loan', 'bond or loan' (all Section 2.19(a));
- 'obligation characteristics', 'not subordinated', 'subordination', 'subordinated obligation', 'senior obligation', 'subordinated', 'specified currency', 'not sovereign lender', 'not domestic currency', 'not domestic law', 'listed' and 'not domestic issuance' (all Section 2.19(b));
- 'qualifying participation seller' (Section 2.22);
- 'qualifying guarantee' (Section 2.23);
- 'qualifying affiliate guarantee' (Section 2.24); and
- 'downstream affiliate' and 'voting shares' (Section 2.25).

1.5   Area V: post-credit event – determining the reference obligation to be valued or the deliverable obligations to be delivered by the buyer to the seller

Article II has 20 terms and definitions which relate to determining the reference entity's obligations which may, following a credit event, be valued in cash settled transactions to calculate the cash settlement amount or delivered by the buyer to the seller in physically settled transactions. These are:

- 'reference obligation' (Section 2.3);
- 'reference price' (Section 2.4);
- 'deliverable obligation' (Section 2.15);
- 'sovereign restructured deliverable obligation' (Section 2.16);
- 'excluded deliverable obligation' (Section 2.18);
- 'method for determining deliverable obligations' (Section 2.20);
- 'deliverable obligation category' (Section 2.20(a));
- 'deliverable obligation characteristics', 'not contingent', 'assignable loan', 'consent required loan', 'direct loan participation', 'transferable', 'maximum maturity', 'accelerated or matured', 'not bearer' (Section 2.20(b));
- 'interpretation of provisions' (Section 2.21); and
- 'domestic currency' (Section 2.29).

1.6   Area VI: limiting the deliverable obligations that may be delivered by the buyer to the seller following a restructuring credit event – modified restructuring and modified modified restructuring

Article II has 14 definitions, which can be applied in distinct combinations to allow the restructuring credit event to mutate into two of the alternative types of restructuring credit event: modified restructuring and modified modified restructuring. The purpose of this is to limit the deliverable obligations that may be delivered by the buyer to the seller following a restructuring credit event.

This is done in the case of modified restructuring through applying Section 2.32 (restructuring maturity limitation and fully transferable obligation), which contains the following six further definitions:

- 'restructuring maturity limitation and fully transferable obligation applicable' (Section 2.32(a));
- 'fully transferable obligation' (Section 2.32(b));
- 'restructuring maturity limitation date' (Section 2.32(c));
- 'restructuring date' (Section 2.32(d));
- 'restructured bond or loan' (Section 2.32(e)); and
- 'eligible transferee' (Section 2.32(f)).

In the case of modified modified restructuring this is done through applying Section 2.33 (modified restructuring maturity limitation and conditionally transferable obligation), which contains the following six further definitions:

- 'modified restructuring maturity limitation and conditionally transferable obligation applicable' (Section 2.33(a));
- 'conditionally transferable obligation' (Section 2.33(b));
- 'modified restructuring maturity limitation date' (Section 2.33(c));

- 'restructuring date' (Section 2.33(d));
- 'restructured bond or loan' (Section 2.33(e)); and
- 'modified eligible transferee' (Section 2.33(f)).

In both cases 'sovereign agency' (Section 2.27) and 'supranational organisation' (Section 2.28) contain further provisions.

1.7 Area VII: business day convention

Finally, Article II also contains provisions to modify any business day referred to anywhere in the 2003 Definitions with the definition of 'business day convention' (Section 2.11), which contains further definitions of 'following', 'modified/modified following' and 'preceding business day conventions'.

2. Area I: the reference entity and its successors

2.1 Reference entity

Reference entity: Pitemween plc

Credit derivative transactions have as their underlying asset the credit quality of a third party which is not party to the transaction[1] – the reference entity. Section 2.1 provides that these reference entities are those specified in the confirmation, together with any successor determined pursuant to the successor provisions in Section 2.2 (provisions for determining a successor).

The way the reference entity is categorised will be important in a transaction. First, whether the reference entity is a sovereign (as defined in Section 2.26 (sovereign)) affects whether several other provisions of the 2003 Definitions apply. In Section 2.2, Section 2.2(a) applies for determining non-sovereign successor reference entities, Section 2.2(b) applies for determining sovereign successor reference entities and Section 2.16 (sovereign restructured deliverable obligation) applies in relation to modified restructuring and modified modified restructuring credit events. Different rules apply to determining the deliverable obligations that can be delivered depending on whether a reference entity is a sovereign.[2]

Further, market standards have developed in the credit derivative market outside of the 2003 Definitions. These apply different elections depending on the jurisdiction and business area of any reference entity. To take an example, the ISDA template first to default confirmation, which relates to non-sovereign reference entities, has 10 separate standard terms sections for different types of reference entity. The template provides standard terms for:

- Western European entities (including for investment grade companies and insurance companies);

---

1   Except in the case of self-referenced credit linked notes.
2   See further discussion of the treatment of sovereigns below.

- European emerging market entities;
- North American entities (including investment grade, high yield and insurance companies);
- Asian entities;
- Japanese entities;
- Singapore entities; and
- Australia and New Zealand entities.

In addition, ISDA's Sovereign Master Credit Derivatives Agreement contains market standard terms for Asian, emerging European, Middle Eastern, Japanese, Latin American and Western European sovereigns. These varying market standards are referred to throughout Part II.

In credit derivative contracts it is essential that the parties are certain which entity they are buying and selling protection on. This is not always straightforward and problems have arisen previously in the market.

Actual case study: the importance of certainty of reference entity – Armstrong World Industries Ltd

Armstrong World Industries, Inc was a subsidiary of Armstrong Holdings. On December 6 2000 Armstrong World Industries filed for bankruptcy under Chapter 11 of the US Bankruptcy Code.

Outstanding between Deutsche Bank and UBS was a $10 million credit default swap under which Deutsche Bank had bought credit protection from UBS on 'Armstrong'. UBS had intended to buy credit protection on Armstrong World Industries, but the confirmation stated that the reference entity was Armstrong Holdings. However, Armstrong Holdings had no debt outstanding and did not file for bankruptcy or default on its obligations.

UBS delivered a credit event notice to Deutsche Bank, and later a notice of intended physical settlement (the forerunner to the 2003 Definitions' notice of physical settlement). Deutsche Bank refused to accept the deliverable obligations: there had been no credit event on Armstrong Holdings. UBS filed a claim in the High Court in London. Whether the court would have taken the more literal interpretation of the 2003 Definitions taken in *Deutsche Bank v ANZ Banking Group Limited*,[3] or looked further into the intention of the parties as in *International Plc v Credit Suisse First Boston International*[4] is not certain – the case was settled out of court.[5]

The litigation exposed the execution risk involved in selecting the right reference entity and reference obligation and resulted in Goldman Sachs, JP

---

3   2000 WL 1151384 (QBC (Comm Ct)).
4   [2003] EWHC 160.
5   A similar case also arose in relation to Armstrong between Swiss Re Financial Products and XL Insurance Ltd. This was also settled out of court.

Morgan Chase and Deutsche Bank launching Project RED, a reference entity database which pooled information on the current legal existence of traded reference entities, their correct names, existing reference obligations, as well as the contractual relationship between reference entities and their reference obligations.[6] The widely subscribed system was sold to Mark-It Partners (the owner of iTraxx) in 2003,[7] which later developed a numbering system for reference entities and reference obligations with Cusip Services Bureau[8] as part of Project RED. This was later enhanced through a partnership with Standard & Poor's which integrated Reference Entity Link, a product linking reference entities in the Mark-It RED database with Standard & Poor's information on credit quality.[9]

2.2 Provisions for determining a successor

(a) Background

The years 2005 and 2006 saw a boom in M&A activity. Stories of high-level mergers – such as that between Bank of America and MBNA Corporation in 2005 and the £7 billion Alliance UniChem merger with Boots in 2006 – dominated the front pages of the *Financial Times* on a daily basis. When (as they often are) these corporations are also traded reference entities in credit derivatives transactions, each merger, demerger, spin-off or other corporate event requires the calculation agent to assess the status of the reference entity and make determinations on whether a new entity (or entities) succeeds the original reference entity. Carrying out these assessments is not just limited to corporations. Historically, sovereigns have always partitioned and merged with, or been taken over by, other countries. The former Yugoslavia partitioned in the early 1990s; West Germany and East Germany merged in 1990; and France invaded Algeria as far back as the 1800s.

Credit derivative transactions deal with the isolation and separate trading of a reference entity's credit risk. So when a corporate reference entity merges, is spun off or undergoes another corporate event, or when a sovereign reference entity partitions or is invaded, this is likely to impact on the reference entity's overall credit quality. While making this determination is often straightforward (eg, a reference entity is fully merged with a larger company), sometimes it isn't (eg, when a conglomerate is broken up or a country disintegrates and there is no clear choice of successor reference entity). The 2003 Definitions contain detailed provisions for determining successors, in particular where there may be multiple corporate successors or a choice of successor. They try to make the calculation agent's decision as objective as possible.[10]

---

6   *Risk* Magazine, April 2002, Vol 15, No 4.
7   "Deutsche Bank, Goldman Sachs and JP Morgan Finalise Agreement to Sell Credit Derivatives Reference Entity Database to Mark-it Partners", Mark-It Partners Press Release, August 28 2003.
8   "Mark-it Partners Joins with CUSIP to Develop Numbering System for Project RED", Mark-It Partners Press Release, September 22 2003.
9   "Standard & Poor's launches Reference Entity Link in conjunction with Mark-It RED" Mark-it Partners, Press Release, October 13 2005.
10 See the wider discussion of the calculation agent's duties in Chapter 5.

Objectivity is especially important, because where there is a choice of a successor reference entity or entities and these have different level of creditworthiness from the original reference entity, there will be different probabilities of default and differences in the true value of any credit protection. If the 2003 Definitions did not have objective rules, the buyer and seller could have opposing views on the identity of a successor; and if the calculation agent were one of the parties, there could be a particularly strong conflict of interest.

Background to Section 2.2: provisions for determining a successor

The predecessor to the 2003 Definitions, the 1999 ISDA Credit Derivatives Definitions, had a short subjective provision dealing with successors for corporate reference entities. This provision stated:

> *'Successor' means…a direct or indirect successor to a Reference Entity that assumes all or substantially all of the obligations thereof by way of merger, consolidation, amalgamation, transfer or otherwise, whether by operation of law or pursuant to any agreement, as determined by the Calculation Agent (after consultation with the parties).*[11]

Its weakness was exposed when National Power plc, a widely traded English reference entity, demerged into two successor companies – International Power plc and Innogy Holdings plc – on September 30 2000.[12] The division of National Power's liabilities between the two entities was broadly similar, with International Power assuming most of National Power's loans and Innogy assuming most of National Power's bonds. Crucially, though, the ratings of the two new entities differed. Standard & Poor's and Moody's rated Innogy's senior debt obligations as investment grade with BBB+ and Baa1 ratings respectively; while they assigned long-term credit ratings of BB and Ba3 respectively to International Power's senior debt obligations, making International Power's ratings high yield.

The 1999 Definitions contemplated only a single successor to a reference entity. This meant that if it were decided that Innogy was the successor to National Power, then this would favour the seller because it would be selling protection against a higher rated entity (ie, one less likely to default on its obligations). If it were decided that International Power were the successor to National Power, then that would be less favourable to the seller, because it would be selling protection on a lower rated entity (ie, one more likely to default on its

---

11   Section 2.2, ISDA 1999 Credit Derivatives Definitions.
12   "Commentary on Supplement Relating to Successor and Credit Events to the 1999 ISDA Credit Derivatives Definitions", ISDA 2001; "The Credit Derivatives Market: its development and possible implications for financial stability"; D Rule, Financial Stability Review: June 2001; International Power Annual Report 2000; "Proposed Demerger to Create Innogy Holdings plc and International Power plc and Recent Transactions", National Power Press Release, August 21 2000.

obligations). The position of the buyer might be more complex if the seller were hedging against particular securities that were transferred to the party which was not selected as the successor and that entity then defaulted, leaving the buyer without protection.

Anecdotal evidence suggests that most market participants selected International Power, the lower rated entity, as the reference entity. This may have been because it assumed slightly more of the overall debt. However, the weakness of the existing Definitions was clearly exposed.

ISDA's Credit Derivatives Market Practice Committee decided, following the recommendation of its 'G6' sub-committee, that "instead of the 'all or substantially all' language in Section 2.2, a revised definition of successor should set forth clear numerical thresholds".[13] The result was the Supplement Relating to Successor and Credit Events to the 1999 ISDA Credit Derivatives Definitions, which was published on November 28 2001. Parties to credit derivative transactions were able to apply this Successor Supplement to a particular transaction by incorporating it by reference into a confirmation along with the 1999 Definitions. The Successor Supplement's provisions were incorporated in full into the 2003 Definitions and function as detailed below.

(b) **How the successor provisions work**

The 2003 Definitions addressed the shortcomings of the original 1999 Definitions that had been exposed by the National Power demerger by incorporating the Successor Supplement in full.

The new rules, set out in Section 2.2, have two definitions for 'successor': one for non-sovereign reference entities, which is a rules based test, and another for sovereign reference entities, which is a more subjective test.

(c) **Non-sovereign successor provisions**

The successor provisions for non-sovereign reference entities are rules based provisions which attempt to make the calculation agent's decision on successor reference entities, following a succession event, as objective as possible. The 2003 Definitions contain seven principal definitions which inter-relate to become the successor provisions for non-sovereigns:

- 'successor' (Section 2(a));
- 'succession event' (Section 2(b));
- 'succeed' (Section 2(c));
- 'substitute reference obligation' (Section 2.30);
- 'new credit derivative transactions' (Section 2(e);
- 'relevant obligations' (Section 2(f)); and
- 'best available information' (Section 2(g)).

---

13   Commentary to Supplement Relating to Successor and Credit Events to the 1999 ISDA Credit Derivatives Definitions.

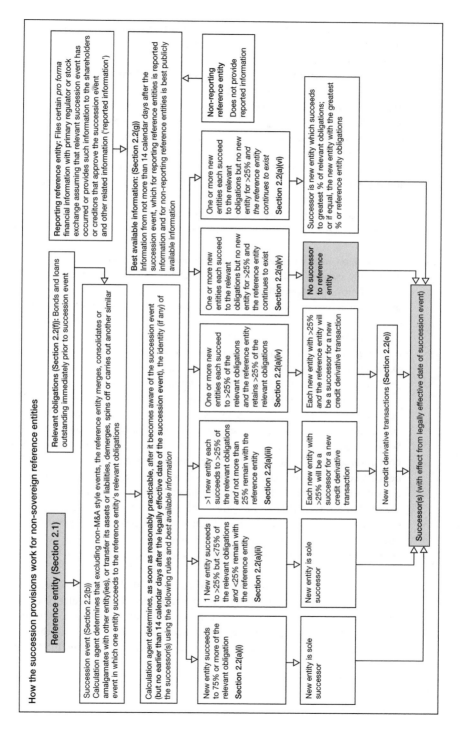

How the succession provisions work for non-sovereign reference entities

2.3 Successor, succession event , succeed, substitute reference obligations, new credit derivative transaction, relevant obligations and best available information

Due to the sophistication required to perform the role, any party that acts as a calculation agent is unlikely to do so only in relation to a single transaction. Therefore, any calculation agent should actively monitor the market to see whether any of the reference entities selected in its transactions become involved in corporate events such as a mergers, consolidations, amalgamations or one of the other events detailed in the 'succession event' definition. In particular, the calculation agent should have access to the Mark-it RED Database and Reference Entity Link, a product linking reference entities in the Mark-it RED Database with Standard & Poor's information on credit quality.

If, on a *prima facie* basis, it seems likely that a corporate may have occurred, the calculation agent should follow the following procedure.

(a) Stage 1: determine whether a succession event has occurred

'Succession events', as defined in the 2003 Definitions, are events such as "a merger, consolidation, amalgamation, transfer of assets or liabilities, demerger, spin-off or other similar event in which one entity *succeeds*[14] to the obligations of another entity".[15] A succession event can occur either by operation of law (eg, a court order or statute) or by agreement. The definition is designed to cover M&A-style events and so it excludes standard capital markets transactions such as convertible and exchangeable bonds and other similar transactions which are not M&A related.

Central to the 'succession event' definition is the definition of what 'succeeds' means. This is set out in Section 2.2(b). It is where another party assumes or becomes liable for the reference entity's relevant obligations or issues bonds which are then exchanged for relevant obligations. 'Relevant obligations' in turn are defined in Section 2.2(f) as obligations which are debt or loan securities of the reference entity, outstanding immediately prior to the succession event's effective date. Intra-group debt is excluded from the definition. Also excluded are any of the reference entity's obligations which would fall within the wider category of 'payment'.[16] 'Obligations' (defined in Section 2.19) are obligations of the reference entity that are either direct obligations or those where the reference entity provides a qualifying affiliate guarantee (Section 2.24) or qualifying guarantee (Section 2.23) (as selected in the confirmation) determined in accordance with Section 2.19 (method for determining obligations).

The calculation agent should pay particular attention when determining whether a succession event has occurred (and later for the purposes of calculating the relevant thresholds), which of the reference entity's obligations are relevant obligations. For example, in a transaction where 'qualifying affiliate guarantees' (rather than 'all guarantees') had been selected as applicable, then a guarantee given by the reference

---

14   Emphasis added.
15   Section 2.2(b)
16   As defined in Section 2.19(a)(i)

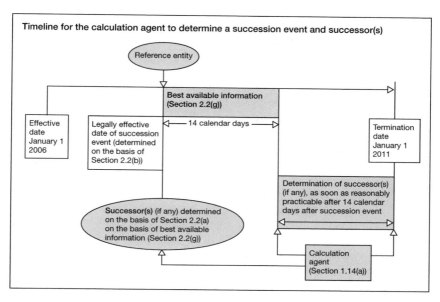

Timeline for the calculation agent to determine a succession event and successor(s)

Reference entity

Best available information
(Section 2.2(g))

Effective
date
January 1
2006

Legally effective
date of succession
event (determined
on the basis of
Section 2.2(b))

← 14 calendar days →

Termination
date
January 1
2011

Determination of successor(s)
(if any), as soon as reasonably
practicable after 14 calendar
days after succession event

Successor(s) (if any) determined
on the basis of Section 2.2(a)
on the basis of best available
information (Section 2.2(g))

Calculation
agent
(Section 1.14(a))

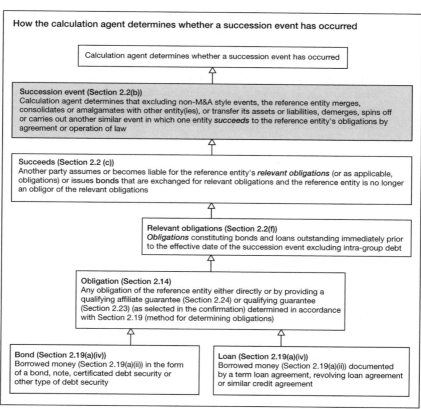

How the calculation agent determines whether a succession event has occurred

Calculation agent determines whether a succession event has occurred

Succession event (Section 2.2(b))
Calculation agent determines that excluding non-M&A style events, the reference entity merges, consolidates or amalgamates with other entity(ies), or transfer its assets or liabilities, demerges, spins off or carries out another similar event in which one entity *succeeds* to the reference entity's obligations by agreement or operation of law

Succeeds (Section 2.2 (c))
Another party assumes or becomes liable for the reference entity's *relevant obligations* (or as applicable, obligations) or issues **bonds** that are exchanged for relevant obligations and the reference entity is no longer an obligor of the relevant obligations

Relevant obligations (Section 2.2(f))
Obligations constituting bonds and loans outstanding immediately prior to the effective date of the succession event excluding intra-group debt

Obligation (Section 2.14)
Any obligation of the reference entity either directly or by providing a qualifying affiliate guarantee (Section 2.24) or qualifying guarantee (Section 2.23) (as selected in the confirmation) determined in accordance with Section 2.19 (method for determining obligations)

Bond (Section 2.19(a)(iv))
Borrowed money (Section 2.19(a)(ii)) in the form of a bond, note, certificated debt security or other type of debt security

Loan (Section 2.19(a)(iv))
Borrowed money (Section 2.19(a)(ii)) documented by a term loan agreement, revolving loan agreement or similar credit agreement

entity for the intra-group debt of a sister company (which was not a downstream affiliate) would not be a relevant obligation.

(b)   *Stage 2: the waiting period*
Once the calculation agent has determined that a succession event has occurred, it must take no further action for a minimum of 14 calendar days from the legally effective date of the succession event.

(c)   *Stage 3: collate best available information*
As soon as reasonably practicable after the waiting period has expired, the calculation agent must determine the original reference entity's successor (if any), by applying the tests set out in Section 2.2(a).

To make its determination, the calculation agent uses the best available information available to it.[17] The definition of 'best available information' is set out in Section 2.2(g), which applies different meanings to the term depending on the type of reference entity. For a reference entity that files information with its primary stock exchange/securities regulator,[18] best available information includes unconsolidated *pro forma* financial information that "assumes that the relevant succession event has occurred". Similarly, if the reference entity has creditors or shareholders or other persons who must approve the succession event, and they are provided with unconsolidated *pro forma* financial information assuming that the relevant succession event has occurred, this will likewise be best available information.

After providing the unconsolidated *pro forma* financial information, the reference entity may provide further information by written communication to its primary stock exchange/securities regulator or its shareholders, creditors and others who must approve the succession event. Any such information released before the end of the 14 calendar-day period can also be used by calculation agent as best available information.

If the reference entity does not file any of the above information with its primary stock exchange/securities regulator or provide it to its shareholders, creditors and others required to approve the succession event, then the definition of 'best available information' provides a different meaning to the term. In these circumstances, best available information means the best publicly available information that the calculation agent can obtain. In all cases best available information cannot include information made available more than 14 calendar days after the legally effective date of the succession event. This will be the case even if the later information is contradictory and/or more accurate.

(d)   *Stage 4: determine successor(s) (if any) by applying Section 2.2(a) tests using 'best available information'*
Once the waiting period has expired, the calculation agent will, as soon as reasonably practicable, apply the six tests set out in Section 2.2(a). It will do this using the best

---

17   Section 2.2(g).
18   Such as the Financial Services Authority in the case of a UK reference entity.

available information which it has sourced, to determine whether there is a successor to the original reference entity and, if so, how many. The calculation agent should apply each of the following tests to determine a successor or decide that the original reference entity should remain as the sole reference entity. Only one test can be satisfied and in each case the succession must be by way of a 'succession event'.

(i)   Test I – Section 2.2(a)(i)
If another entity has succeeded to at least 75% of the reference entity's relevant obligations, the new entity will be the sole successor. This first test will be satisfied where the reference entity is taken over by and merged with another company.

(ii)   Test II – Section 2.2(a)(ii)
If one entity only has succeeded to over 25% (but less than 75%) of the reference entity's relevant obligations and the original reference entity retains not more than 25% of its relevant obligations, then the new entity will be the sole successor for the whole credit derivative transaction.

This second test may be satisfied where the reference entity was a group holding company which guaranteed all of the group's debt and its largest subsidiary was sold, meaning that the guarantees were transferred to the purchaser.

(iii)   Test III – Section 2.2(a)(iii)
The third test is satisfied if more than one entity succeeds to over 25% of the reference entity's relevant obligations, but the original reference entity retains 25% or less of its relevant obligations. If this test is satisfied, each of the new succeeding entities will be successor reference entities and the original reference entity will cease to be a reference entity. If one or more of these successors has not assumed a reference obligation specified in the confirmation, then the calculation agent must determine a successor reference obligation.[19] The third test might be satisfied where the same example scenario applied as in the second test, but instead the holding company spun off two subsidiaries to different purchasers.

(iv)   Test IV – Section 2.2(a)(iv)
The fourth test is satisfied if one or more entities each succeed to 25% or more of the reference entity's relevant obligations, but the original reference entity itself also retains more than 25% of its relevant obligations. If this test is satisfied then each of the succeeding reference entities will be a successor reference entity and the original reference entity will also remain a reference entity.[20] This test could also be satisfied in the spin-off scenario described in the second test.

(v)   Test V – Section 2.2(a)(v)
The fifth test is satisfied if one or more entities succeed to only part of the reference entity's relevant obligations, but none of them succeeds to more than 25% of them

---

19   Successor reference obligations are determined in accordance with Section 2.30.
20   A successor obligation will be determined as in the above footnote.

and the reference entity continues to exist. In this case there will be no successor reference entity and the original reference entity will remain the same. The fifth test is most likely to be satisfied where a group holding company is a reference entity and it disposes of one or more subsidiaries which have debt (guaranteed by the reference entity) accounting for less than 25% of the total group debt.

(vi)   *Test VI – Section 2.2(a)(vi)*
The sixth test is satisfied if one or more entities succeed to part of the reference entity's relevant obligations, but no entity succeeds to more than 25% of them and the reference entity ceases to exist.

If this test is satisfied, the entity that succeeds to the greatest percentage of the original reference entity's bonds and loans will be the only successor. However, if two new entities succeed to the same percentage of the reference entity's relevant obligations, the new entity which succeeds to the greatest percentage of obligations (ie, obligations including trade debt, letters of credit and other liabilities which would fall under the 'payment' obligation category) will be the only new reference entity and the sole successor to the original reference entity.

The sixth test could be satisfied if a conglomerate were broken up and its constituent parts spun off, perhaps in response to the sort of US antitrust legislation which saw the break-up of AT&T in the early 1980s.

(e)   **Stage 5: notify the parties of any successor and (if applicable) create 'new credit derivative transactions'**
If the calculation agent does determine that there is a successor reference entity or entities, it is obliged, pursuant to Section 1.14 (calculation agent), to notify the parties of its determination as soon as reasonably practicable thereafter.

Additionally, if the calculation agent determines that either the second test or third test is satisfied (ie, there is more than one successor), then pursuant to Section 2.2(e) it must divide the transaction into as many 'new credit derivative transactions' as there are successors (where the original reference entity continues to be a reference entity it is also deemed to be a successor for these purposes).

Each entity that the calculation agent determines to be a successor will be a reference entity for one of the new credit derivative transactions. The amounts specified in the original confirmation for the fixed rate payer calculation amount and the floating rate payer calculation amount will be deemed to be divided by the number of successors, and the resulting figures applied as the fixed rate payer calculation amount and the floating rate payer calculation amount respectively in each new credit derivative transaction. If no floating rate calculation amount was specified in the original confirmation, then the cash settlement amount will be deemed to be the floating rate payer calculation amount.

All of the terms in the original confirmation will be deemed to be replicated in each new transaction. However, the calculation agent is obliged to modify these terms in each new credit derivative transaction as it deems necessary (after consulting with the parties) to preserve the original transaction's economic effects across all of the new credit derivative transactions. A new confirmation should be executed for each new credit derivative transaction. In basket and portfolio transactions, this language must be specifically adjusted.

Hypothetical case study: succession event resulting in multiple successors – break-up of Grazalema Telecommunications

Grazalema Telecommunications was the monopoly telecommunications operator in an Eastern European state. It was also a widely traded reference entity. The government decided to enhance competition in the telecommunications market by breaking up Grazalema into three separate companies: Chipiona, Arcos and Ronda.

Paloma Bank, an active credit derivative market participant, was acting as a calculation agent in over 300 transactions, including 43 where Grazalema was a reference entity. As soon as Paloma became aware that the Grazalema spin-off had taken place, the bank's credit derivative desk set about establishing whether a succession event had occurred. By consulting public sources, it determined that a succession event had indeed occurred, because Grazalema had transferred its assets and liabilities to Chipiona, Arcos and Ronda by operation of law and the three new entities had succeeded to Grazalema's obligations. Paloma determined that the succession event took place on November 14 2007.

Paloma then had to wait until November 28 2007 before determining which entities (if any) would succeed Grazalema as the reference entity in transactions where Paloma was the calculation agent.

During this two-week period, Paloma sourced best available information. Grazalema was listed on the London Stock Exchange. On the date of the spin-off it filed unconsolidated *pro forma* financial information with the London Stock Exchange. Paloma analysed this information to determine which of Grazalema's relevant obligations (ie, bonds and loans) had been transferred to Chipiona, Arcos and Ronda.

Paloma established that Grazalema had €1 billion of outstanding bonds and loans. As a result of the spin-off it retained €160 million of bonds and loans, and each of Chipiona, Arcos and Ronda then each directly succeeded to €280 million of bonds and loans.

Applying the six tests set out in Section 2.2(a) of the 2003 Definitions, Paloma determined that the Grazalema succession event satisfied the test set out in Section 2.2(a)(iii):

If more than one entity each directly or indirectly succeeds to more than 25% of the Relevant Obligations of the Reference Entity by way of a Succession Event, and not more 25% of the Relevant Obligations of the Reference Entity remain with the Reference Entity, the entities which succeed to more than 25% of the Relevant Obligations will each be a Successor for a New Credit Derivative Transaction determined in accordance with Section 2.2(e).

Paloma calculated that Grazalema had retained 16% of its relevant obligations (ie, €160 million), and that each of Chipiona, Arcos and Ronda had succeeded to 28% of Grazalema's relevant obligations (ie, €280 million each). Therefore, Paloma determined that Chipiona, Arcos and Ronda were each successor reference entities, and that Grazalema was no longer a reference entity in any of the relevant transactions. Paloma immediately informed the parties in each of the 16 affected transactions that referenced Grazalema, of its determination.

Pursuant to Section 2.2(e), each of the affected transactions was a single name credit default swap.

Paloma arranged for three further confirmations (ie, new credit derivative transactions) to be executed for each of the 16 affected transactions. Each new confirmation had identical terms to the original transaction, except that both the fixed rate payer calculation amount and the floating rate payer calculation amount were for one-third of the amount specified in the original transaction. The original credit derivative transactions then ceased to exist.

It is just as important for the calculation agent to be able to conclude that no succession event has occurred as to conclude that one has. Set out below is an analysis of Rentokil's 2005 corporate reorganisation. Rentokil is a widely traded reference entity and its corporate reorganisation in 2005 was closely analysed by market participants.

Actual case study: analysing a potential succession event – the Rentokil 'succession event'

On June 20 2005 the English High Court agreed to allow Rentokil, the world's largest pest control group, to carry out a corporate reorganisation and introduce a new listed holding company into its group structure. The group wanted to do to this to ensure that it had enough distributable reserves remaining both for accounting purposes and to support future dividend payments to shareholders.

Rentokil Group's original holding company had been incorporated as Rentokil Initial plc. As part of the reorganisation process, it changed its name to Rentokil Initial 1927 plc. After the change of name, the new listed holding company was then incorporated as Rentokil Initial plc (ie, taking the original holding company's previous name), and took its place as the group holding company.

Before the new holding company was incorporated, the original holding company had previously issued bonds. As part of the reorganisation, the new holding company became the issuer of these bonds and the original holding company became the guarantor of their interest and principal.

The original Rentokil Initial plc was a widely traded reference entity and calculation agents across the market had to decide whether a succession event had occurred. This required a close analysis of Section 2.2 (provisions for determining a successor) of the 2003 Definitions, which states that if, by way of a succession event,[21] an entity directly or indirectly succeeds to any of a reference entity's relevant obligations, the calculation agent must determine the successor in accordance with the relevant thresholds set out in Section 2.2(a) on the basis of best available information.

The 2003 Definitions provide that relevant obligations[22] are obligations which are the reference entity's bonds and loans outstanding immediately prior to the succession event's effective date and that a succession event includes a transfer of liabilities where one reference entity succeeds to another's obligations.[23]

To 'succeed' to a reference entity's relevant obligations, though, an entity must:

- assume or become liable for the relevant obligations, whether by operation of law or pursuant to any agreement; or
- issue bonds that are exchanged for relevant obligations.

However, in both cases, it will not succeed if the original reference entity is a guarantor of the relevant obligations. [24]

Because the original Rentokil holding company remained as primary guarantor of 100% of the relevant obligations, the new holding company did not succeed to them. This meant that:

- no succession event occurred, so no thresholds needed to be calculated in accordance with Section 2.2(a) of the 2003 Definitions; and
- the original Rentokil holding company continued as the reference entity in outstanding credit derivative transactions where it had been referenced.

If the original Rentokil holding company had not guaranteed the relevant obligations, then the calculation agent in any transaction would have been obliged to determine that the new holding company was the successor reference entity and notify the parties accordingly.

(f)   Weaknesses of the successor provisions

The 2003 Definitions successor provisions have several weaknesses.[25] First, a buyer may be entering into a credit derivative transaction to buy protection on particular assets that it holds. Following a succession event and the determination of multiple successors, the buyer may be left with several new credit derivative transactions. It

---

21   Section 2.2(a)(i).
22   Section 2.2 (f).
23   Section 2.2 (b).
24   Section 2.2 (c).
25   On Monday November 13 2006, ISDA's Credit Derivatives Market Practice Committee set up a conference call attended by leading credit derivative practitioners, which discussed several of the weaknesses discussed in this section. The outcome of the conference call was that these weaknesses would be addressed either by means of a supplement or in a future version of the Definitions.

may find that it is buying protection on entities that it does not wish to and is left with insufficient credit protection to hedge those assets that it actually holds.

Second, a reference entity's group may undergo a corporate reorganisation. Where the reference entity has provided a qualifying guarantee in relation to an underlying obligor's underlying obligations, problems may occur in certain circumstances. If the reference entity's guarantee remains in place and the relevant obligations are transferred to a new underlying obligor, the guarantee will still remain a qualifying guarantee, so pursuant to Section 2.2(c) the new entity will not 'succeed' to the obligations. A problem arises where further issues by the new underlying obligor are not guaranteed by the reference entity, meaning that once the 'old' obligations mature, the credit derivative transaction no longer has any potential deliverable obligations. This is indeed a possibility in the Rentokil example described above. This issue will be difficult to address, as it is virtually impossibility to second-guess a group's future funding strategy.

Third, once the calculation agent has determined that a succession event has occurred, it must take no further action for a minimum of 14 calendar days from the legally effective date of the succession event. During this period it collates the best available information and will then use this to make its determination event regarding the succession event. A problem may occur where insufficient information can be obtained during the 14-day period, or where better information obtained after this period clarifies or contradicts the earlier information. An analogous problem is where the calculation agent is in possession of confidential information which contradicts or clarifies the public information available. In each case the calculation agent will be bound to ignore the better information.

Fourth, it is possible that a corporate event such as a spin-off could lead to the reference entity being able to retire all, or substantially all, of its debt through the proceeds of a sale, while the entity spun off succeeds to none of the reference entity's relevant obligations, or the structure of the spin-off leads to an effective transferral of debt from the original reference entity to the new entity without a succession event occurring (due to there being no transfer of relevant obligations). In these circumstances the buyer would remain liable to make credit protection payments even though there were no relevant obligations left with the original reference entity and hence no deliverable obligations. A similar situation, which could potentially be more complex than was the case with Six Continents (see the case study opposite) would be where the repayment of the original debt and the new drawdown do not occur simultaneously, or if different banks are involved in each financing. The market consensus appears to be that although this issue must be addressed, a definitive solution is most desirable for covering situations where, following the corporate restructuring, the original reference entity no longer has any deliverable obligations.

Fitch Ratings[26] has recently raised a concern that "that there has been a substantial increase in corporate event risk" due to corporate restructurings and spin-offs of underperforming business units, much of it driven by activist shareholders and

---

[26]   CDOs/Global Special Report: "CDS Update: Corporate Restructurings and LBOs Refocus Market on CDS 'Successor' Language", April 21 2006.

emboldened private equity investors flush with cash. "Viacom Inc, Tyco International Ltd and Cendant Corp are just some examples of companies engaging in spin-offs." This has "brought to the forefront the issue of whether bond investors and CDS protection sellers are affected in a symmetrical fashion when a corporate restructuring or spin-off (called a 'succession event' for CDS) occurs." Fitch's concern is not a new one, but stems from an issue that arose when the 2003 Definitions were first published and Six Continents PLC, a widely traded reference entity, demerged.

Actual case study: Six Continents plc

On October 1 2002 Six Continents plc's board announced a proposal to separate the group's hotel and soft drinks businesses from its retail business to create a listed hotel company (InterContinental Hotels Group plc) and a listed retail company (Mitchells & Butler plc), and return £700 million of capital to shareholders.[27] The separation became effective on April 15 2003.[28]

Six Continents used a bridging loan to fund the demerger and also to buy back around £525 million of its debenture and medium-term notes. Following the separation, InterContinental Hotels Group and Mitchells & Butler each entered into a syndicated loan of their own, which they then used to repay Six Continents' bridging loan. As part of the separation, Six Continents had become a subsidiary of InterContinental Hotels Group, but it now had only approximately £18 million of debt outstanding.[29]

The 2003 Definitions had been published in February 2003 and the Six Continents corporate event was proving to be their first big test. The problem was that the new syndicated loans were not relevant obligations under the 2003 Definitions because they were not bonds or loans of Six Continents "outstanding immediately prior to the effective date of the Succession Event". The definition of 'succeed' set out in Section 2.2(c) does include as relevant obligations "Bonds that are exchanged for Relevant Obligations". In this case, though, bonds were not exchangeable for the relevant obligations. So applying the tests set out in Section 2.2(a), Six Continents had no successors and remained the reference entity in credit derivative transactions that incorporated the 2003 Definitions.

Market participants that had bought credit protection on Six Continents found their transactions to be virtually worthless as Six Continents had almost no debt, yet they were still obliged to pay their counterparty the full amount of credit protection payments.

In the end, the problem resolved itself in June 2003 when Six Continents and InterContinental Hotels Group gave cross-guarantees to the lending banks

---

27 Six Continents Plc Press Release, October 1 2002: "Proposed Separation and Return of Capital"; Shareholder Circular and Listing Particulars for InterContinental Hotel Group plc and Mitchells & Butlers plc, February 17 2003; Intercontinental Hotels Group Annual Report and Financial Statements 2003.

28 Six Continents plc Press Release, April 15 2003- Demerger effective and trading to commence in IHG and MAB.

29 "Six Continents demerger drives uncertainty (Credit derivatives)" *Euromoney*, July 2003.

under the new facility agreement. This meant that where 'all guarantees'[30] had been selected as applicable (as is the market standard) in a credit derivative transaction, credit protection buyers once again had meaningful credit protection against the credit risk that now resided with InterContinental Hotels Group.

Although the situation in Six Continents resolved itself, the events exposed a weakness in the 2003 Definitions' successor provisions, which is still present today.

Fifth, the provisions for new credit derivative transactions work well for transactions where there is only one reference entity, but are unwieldy where there is a portfolio or basket of reference entities. Section 2.2(e)(ii) allows the "calculation agent (in consultation with the parties) to preserve the economic effects of the original Credit Derivative Transaction in the New Credit Derivative Transaction". However, this wording must be adapted in any portfolio or basket transaction to take account that creating a new credit derivative transaction is not an appropriate method for dealing with succession events that produce multiple successors.

2.4   Determining a sovereign successor

Sovereign successors are far less common than non-sovereign successors. Consequently, they receive less coverage in the 2003 Definitions. These state in Section 2.2(h) only that, in relation to a sovereign reference entity, 'successor' means "any direct or indirect successor(s) of that Reference Entity irrespective of whether such successor(s) assumes any of the obligations of such Reference Entity".

So in many ways the sovereign successor definition in the 2003 Definitions contains the same weaknesses of the old non-sovereign successor definition prior to the 2001 Successor Supplement. In particular, the definition does not contemplate multiple successors. To take but one example, if the Basque province and Catalonia were to break away from Spain, and each assumed a share of the national debt, the consequences for transactions referencing the Kingdom of Spain as a reference entity would be unclear.

Sovereign successor events from the past, which would have unclear consequences were they to occur today, include the break-up of Yugoslavia into Slovenia, Croatia, Macedonia, Bosnia, Serbia, Montenegro and Kosovo in the early 1990s, and the 1971 split of Bangladesh from Pakistan. Although there was not perhaps a sufficient amount of credit derivative trading in sovereign reference entities likely to be affected by some form of successor event when the 2003 Definitions were prepared, addressing sovereign successor(s) more fully in any successor edition to the 2003 Definitions must surely be a good idea.

---

30   If 'qualifying affiliate guarantee' had been selected (note, however, that this is not the market standard for Western European investment grade reference entities), the problem would have remained, because the Six Continents guarantee would have been an upstream guarantee.

2.5 Merger of reference entity and seller

If, in any standard transaction,[31] a reference entity merges with the seller, then the buyer will lose its credit protection. After all, if the seller and reference entity were the same company and the company went bankrupt, the seller would be in no position to pay a cash settlement amount or physical settlement amount after the conditions to settlement for a bankruptcy credit event had been met. The buyer would be left as an unsecured creditor. This issue is more likely to arise than one might think.

International Index Company compiles and manages the iTraxx series of credit indices of widely traded reference entities. On September 15 2006, when it released "Europe Series 6", a portfolio of the 125 most actively traded reference entities, 25 of these were financial institutions such as ABN Amro, Barclays Bank and Deutsche Bank. The British Bankers' Association Credit Derivatives Report 2006 discloses that financial institutions make up over 95% of market participants in the credit derivatives market. In the future, some of the largest market participants by market share will inevitably merge with other large market participants, just as Chase Manhattan Bank and JP Morgan did in January 2002. Both banks had originally been in the iTraxx index and they were also among the most active market participants in the credit default swap market. Section 2.31 (merger of reference entity and seller) of the 2003 Definitions covers such a situation, and as other reference entities merge with sellers in the future its provisions will be applied as follows.

Section 2.31 provides that if the reference entity in a credit derivative transaction merges, amalgamates or transfers all or substantially all of its assets to the seller (or if the reference entity and the seller become affiliates), an additional termination event under the 2002 ISDA Master Agreement is deemed to have occurred with the seller as the sole affected party.[32] Each credit derivative transaction that involves the relevant reference entity will be an affected transaction. The 2002 Master Agreement 'close-out amount' provision will apply, irrespective of whether the parties have a 1992 Master Agreement or 2002 Master Agreement in place. Each affected transaction will then terminate in accordance with the 2002 Master Agreement.

3. Area II: credit protection premium

3.1 Article II's credit protection payment definitions and their interaction with Article V

Article II has six definitions that cover the payments of the credit protection premium that the buyer must make to the seller during the transaction's term. These are:

- 'fixed amount' (Section 2.5);
- 'fixed rate payer' (Section 2.6);
- 'fixed rate payer calculation amount' (Section 2.7);
- 'fixed rate payer period end date' (Section 2.8);
- 'fixed rate payer calculation period' (Section 2.9); and
- 'fixed rate payer payment date' (Section 2.10).

---

31   That is, other than in a specifically structured self-referenced credit-linked note.
32   This provision will be varied where a credit derivative transaction forms part of a credit-linked note issued by an SPV or is a self-referenced credit linked note.

These six sections interact with four further definitions in Article V, relating to fixed amounts. These are:

- 'calculation of fixed amount' (Section 5.1);
- 'fixed rate' (Section 5.2);
- 'fixed rate day count fraction' (Section 5.3); and
- 'relating fixed rate payer payments to fixed rate payer calculation period' (Section 5.4).

---

2. Fixed payments:

Fixed rate payer calculation amount: €30 million

Fixed rate payer period end date: Each fixed rate payer payment date

Fixed rate payer payment date: March 31, June 30, September 30 and December 31 in each year

---

Fixed rate payments are the payments made by the buyer to the seller to compensate it for providing credit protection on the reference entity. The payments are made periodically during the transaction's term, with Article II (in conjunction with Article V) providing the necessary terms and definitions. 'Fixed rate payer' is defined in Section 2.6 as "the party obligated to make one or more payments of a fixed amount", which is, of course, the buyer.

'Fixed amount' either can be a numerical figure stated in the confirmation or, if a figure is not stated, can be determined using the formula set out in Section 5.1(b) (calculation of fixed amounts). If this formula is used, then the fixed amount will be calculated by multiplying the fixed rate payer calculation amount by the fixed rate and the fixed rate day count fraction. Both 'fixed rate' and 'fixed rate day count fraction' are defined in Article V.

The fixed amounts are paid by the fixed rate payer on each fixed rate payer payment date. These payment dates will be specified in the confirmation. The 'fixed rate payer payment date' definition further provides that if an event determination date occurs before the transaction's termination date, the earlier of the settlement date (ie, the cash settlement date or physical settlement date) and the termination date will be the final fixed rate payer payment date.

Where fixed amounts are calculated on the basis of Article V, it will be necessary to establish the fixed rate payer calculation amount. This is either the amount stated in the confirmation or the floating rate payer calculation amount (ie, the notional amount of credit protection sold). The fixed rate payer calculation amount will then be multiplied by the fixed rate. 'Fixed rate' is defined in Section 5.2 as "a rate, expressed as a decimal, equal to the per annum rate specified in the related confirmation". This rate will be multiplied by the fixed rate day count fraction. A day count fraction is a method, used generally in capital markets transactions when there is more than one interest payment in any year, to calculate the fraction of a year falling between two set dates, for determining the amount of interest payable on any interest payment date. 'Fixed rate payer day count fraction' is defined in Section 5.3 (fixed rate payer day count fraction). The section provides a number of alternatives that may be selected and used in the confirmation.

Each fixed amount payable is calculated on the basis of the fixed rate payer calculation period. The 'fixed rate payer calculation period' is defined in Section 2.9 as being each period from and including a fixed rate payer period end date to (but excluding) the next one. The first fixed rate payer calculation period commences on the transaction's effective date and the last finishes on the earlier of the event determination date, should one occur, or if not, the scheduled termination date. This means that credit protection payments are not payable once an event determination date has occurred or if the transaction's termination date falls after the scheduled termination date, due to the grace period provisions or repudiation/moratorium extension provisions.

The actual fixed rate payer period end date (defined in Section 2.8) is normally specified in the confirmation; if it is not, the fallback is for the fixed rate payer period end date to be the fixed rate payer payment date.

**Hypothetical case study: fixed rate payments –
Loretto's fixed payments**

Loretto plc entered into a €10 million credit default swap with Glenalmond Corporation under which Loretto bought credit protection on Fettes plc, a leisure company.

1. *General Terms*

    Fixed Rate Payer: Loretto PLC (the 'Buyer')

2. *Fixed Payments:*

    Fixed rate payer calculation amount: €10 million

    Fixed rate payer period end date: Each fixed rate payer payment date

    Fixed rate payer payment date: March 31, June 30, September 30 and
                                                  December 31 in each year.

    Fixed rate: 1%

    Fixed rate payer day count fraction   Actual/365

Loretto as buyer was the fixed rate payer. It bought €10 million of credit protection and so this amount was inserted in the confirmation as the fixed rate calculation amount (ie, the basis amount on which the credit protection payments were to be calculated). Loretto and Glenalmond agreed that Loretto's

---

credit protection payments would be made quarterly, so the parties selected March 31, June 30, September 30 and December 31 in each year as the fixed rate payer payment dates. The quantum of each fixed rate payment was to be calculated on the basis of the fixed rate payer calculation period, which was to run from (and include) each fixed rate payer period end date to (but excluding) the next one. The parties decided to specify that each fixed rate payer period end date would be the same as each fixed rate payer payment date.

The parties also decided that the fixed amount should be calculated on the basis of Section 5.1(b) rather than by inserting a specific figure for the fixed amount in the confirmation. They agreed that the fixed rate would be 1%. On each fixed rate payer payment date, the calculation agent was obliged to multiply the fixed rate payer calculation amount (ie, €10 million) by the fixed rate (ie, 1%). This gave a figure of €100,000, which was then multiplied by the day count fraction, which resulted in the €100,000 being multiplied by the actual number of days in the relevant floating rate calculation period and then divided by 365.

This meant in the case of the first fixed rate payer payment date that the €100,000 figure was multiplied by 90 divided by 365 (ie, 0.2465), and that the first fixed amount payable by Loretto to Glenalmond was €24,650.

The definitions of 'fixed rate payer calculation amount', 'fixed rate payer period end date' and 'fixed rate payer calculation period' are relevant only where the fixed amount falls to be determined under Section 5.1(b). Usually a numerical fixed amount is not stated in the confirmation.

4.   **Area III: credit protection payments – the floating payments**
The credit protection payments made by the buyer to the seller make up the fixed rate leg of the swap. The floating rate payments under the floating rate leg to the credit default swap will be made only if an event determination date occurs. If this happens, the seller will be required to pay either a cash settlement amount or a physical settlement amount to the buyer. This payment is called the floating payment. Article II contains two definitions relating to the floating payment:

- 'floating rate payer' (Section 2.12); and
- 'floating rate payer calculation amount' (Section 2.13).

1. General terms	
Fixed rate payer:	Loretto PLC (the 'buyer')
Floating rate payer:	Glenalmond Corporation (the 'seller')
3. Floating payment	
Floating rate payer calculation amount: €30 million	

'Floating rate payer' is defined in Section 2.12 as "the party specified as such in the related confirmation". This will invariably be the seller. 'Floating rate calculation amount' is defined in Section 2.13 as "the amount specified as such in the related confirmation". This amount will be the amount of credit protection that the seller sells to the buyer. The floating payment itself will, in a cash settled transaction, be the cash settlement amount and in a physically settled transaction the physical settlement amount (as defined in Articles VIII and IX respectively).

5. Area IV: determining the reference entity's obligations subject to credit protection

5.1 Introduction

The objective of a credit derivative transaction is to isolate and separately trade a reference entity's credit risk. To do this, credit derivatives focus not only on a reference entity's bankruptcy risk, but also specifically on providing and quantifying compensation for events which materially impact on the credit quality of the reference entity's obligations, such as a failure to pay.

Any reference entity, though, will have a universe of obligations covering everything from letters of credit, loans, bonds and derivative transactions to payment of its paper bill. The 2003 Definitions provide a framework, which is set out in Article II, to allow the parties to determine which of a reference entity's obligations are the subject of the credit protection provided under a relevant credit derivative transaction.

The parties may decide that the scope of credit protection under the credit derivative transaction should cover only the reference entity's obligations which are unsubordinated borrowed money; or perhaps, more specifically, they may decide that only those obligations which are listed bonds and loans should be covered.

It is the reference entity's obligations that are at the heart of the credit default swap, triggering five of the six possible credit events, being valued in cash settlement and delivered in physical settlement. Which of a reference entity's obligations are covered by a particular transaction, which will be valued to determine a cash settlement amount and which will be delivered in return for a physical settlement amount must be agreed between the parties and set out in the confirmation.

Article II provides the relevant terms infrastructure for making these choices, by providing 27 definitions:

- 'obligation' (Section 2.14);
- 'excluded obligation' (Section 2.17);
- 'method for determining obligations' (Section 2.19);
- 'obligation category', 'payment', 'borrowed money', 'reference obligations only', 'bond', 'loan', 'bond or loan' (all Section 2.19(a));
- 'obligation characteristics', 'not subordinated', 'subordination: subordinated obligation', 'senior obligation', 'subordinated', 'specified currency', 'not sovereign lender', 'not domestic currency', 'not domestic law', 'listed' and 'not domestic issuance' (all Section 2.19(b));
- 'qualifying participation seller' (Section 2.22);

- 'qualifying guarantee' (Section 2.23);
- 'qualifying affiliate guarantee' (Section 2.24); and
- 'downstream affiliate' and 'voting shares' (Section 2.25).

This infrastructure is discussed in detail below.

5.2 How do the various 'obligations' definitions inter-relate?

All of the credit events, except bankruptcy, occur in relation to obligations of the reference entity that fall within the definition of 'obligation' in Section 2.14, rather than in relation to the reference entity itself. Not all of a reference entity's legal obligations, though, will qualify as 'obligations' for the purposes of any credit derivative transaction. This means that if any of a failure to pay, an obligation acceleration, an obligation default, a restructuring or a repudiation/moratorium credit event occurs in relation to an obligation of a reference entity, which does not fall within the parameters of 'obligation' as crafted by the parties, this will not be a credit event for the purposes of a transaction. Defining in any credit derivative transaction which of the reference entity's obligations fall within the definition of 'obligations' is crucial.

The parties tailor the definition of 'obligation' in each transaction by selecting whether different variables set out in Section 2.19 (method for determining obligations) are applicable, together with specifying which of Section 2.23 (qualifying guarantee) and Section 2.24 (qualifying affiliate guarantee) applies. In addition, the transaction's reference obligation will be an 'obligation', as will any other obligations specifically selected. The parties may exclude certain of the reference entity's obligations by selecting them as 'excluded obligations' (Section 2.17).

5.3 Excluded obligation

'Excluded obligation' is defined in Section 2.17, as "any obligation of a reference entity specified as such or of a type described in the related obligation". Excluded obligations will be selected only on a bespoke basis, and may include individual securities or categories of securities – for example, tier one debt.

5.4 Determining which obligations are 'obligations'

Section 2.19 (method for determining obligations) states that "for the purposes of Section 2.14(a) the term 'Obligation' may be defined as each obligation of each Reference Entity described by the Obligation Category specified in the related Confirmation and having each of the Obligation Characteristics (if any) specified in the related Confirmation". The definition carves out excluded obligations.

So this means that if the parties decide not to limit the 'obligation' definition to specific named securities, the seller will sell credit protection to the buyer in relation to all of the reference entity's obligations which:

- fall within a selected one of the six categories listed in Section 2.19(a); and
- have any of the selected characteristics from Section 2.19(b).

Set out in the following table is the table from the ISDA standard short form confirmation which the parties use to make these selections.

Obligation(s)

Obligation category
(select only one)

Obligation characteristics
(select all that apply)

☐ Payment
☐ Borrowed money
☐ Reference obligations only
☐ Bond
☐ Loan
☐ Bond or loan

☐ Not subordinated
☐ Specified currency
☐ Not sovereign lender
☐ Not domestic currency
☐ Not domestic law
☐ Listed
☐ Not contingent
☐ Not domestic issuance

Excluded obligations: None

Source: Exhibit A to the 2003 Definitions which sets out a standard form single name credit default swap.

In reality, and as discussed above, the parties will select the obligation category and obligations characteristics according to the market standard terms for a particular reference entity, decided by the reference entity's type and location, rather than on a case-by-case basis.

5.5 Obligation categories

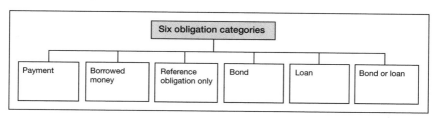

Section 2.19(a) (obligation category) lists six obligation categories. Only one obligation category can be selected for each reference entity. The obligation categories are:

- payment (ie, any present, future or contingent obligations to repay money (including borrowed money) – a broad category that includes contingent payments such as guarantees, trade debts and derivative transactions, such as swaps and repos;
- borrowed money (ie, any obligation to pay or repay borrowed money) – a narrower category than payment because the obligation must be borrowed rather than just owed. It excludes trading debts and many derivative transactions, such as swaps and repos, but specifically includes deposits (which would catch payments owed by a bank to its account holders) and reimbursement obligations under letters of credit;

- reference obligations only (ie, any obligation that is specified as a reference obligation in the confirmation);
- bond (ie, borrowed money in the form of a bond, note (other than a note delivered under a loan) or debt security);
- loan (ie, borrowed money documented by a term loan agreement, revolving loan agreement or other similar credit agreement); and
- bond or loan (ie, any obligation that is either a bond or loan).

Some categories are wider than others, and selecting one category as opposed to another will affect the number of the reference entity's obligations that will be 'obligations'. Payment is the broadest obligation category and reference obligations only the narrowest.

Obligation category by reference entity type according to market standard terms					
Payment	Borrowed money	Reference obligation only	Bond	Loan loan	Bond or loan
N/A	Western European Western European insurance Australian and New Zealand Japanese North American investment grade North American high yield	N/A	N/A	N/A	European emerging markets Singapore Asia North American insurance

As far as the standard terms for reference entity types are concerned, borrowed money is the obligation category for:
- Western European reference entities;
- Western European insurance entities;
- Australian and New Zealand entities;
- Japanese entities;
- North American investment grade entities; and
- North American high yield entities.

Bond or loan is the obligation category for:
- European emerging markets entities;
- Singaporean entities;
- Asian entities; and
- North American insurance entities.

Payment, bond and loan are not widely used as obligation categories, and reference obligation only, bond and loan tend to be used only where a buyer is hedging a specific obligation that it physically holds or where the transaction is more bespoke.

5.6 Obligation characteristics

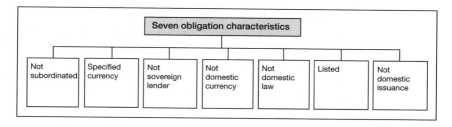

Section 2.19(b) (obligation characteristics) sets out seven obligation characteristics:

- not subordinated;
- specified currency;
- not sovereign lender;
- not domestic currency;
- not domestic law;
- listed; and
- not domestic issuance.

Provided that they are not contradictory, any number may be chosen in the confirmation to apply. Obligation characteristics are the second method by which the parties limit the amount or number of reference entity obligations that are the subject of credit protection. Obligation characteristics are not specified in all transactions and they tend to be selected to apply in transactions when it is necessary to isolate a reference entity's more liquid and internationally traded obligations from those which may be less so.

The seven obligation characteristics have the following meanings:

- Not subordinated – to be included as an 'obligation', the relevant reference entity's obligations must not be subordinated in payment priority to the reference entity's most senior reference obligation. However, if no reference obligation is specified in the confirmation, the relevant obligation must not be subordinated to any borrowed money obligation.
- Specified currency – this aims, along with 'not domestic currency' and 'not domestic law', to exclude an emerging market reference entity's domestic obligations from credit protection. 'Obligations' will include only those obligations payable in a currency specified in the confirmation. If 'specified currency' is selected as an obligation characteristic, but no currency is selected, then the relevant obligation must be denominated in one of the currencies of Canada, Japan, Switzerland, the United Kingdom and the United States, or in euros (these being 'standard specified currencies').

- Not sovereign lender – this excludes any obligation owed primarily to a sovereign or supranational organisation (including Paris Club debt).
- Not domestic currency – this excludes obligations payable in the reference entity's home currency (where in general the reference entity is incorporated in an emerging market jurisdiction). 'Domestic currency' itself is defined in Section 2.29 as being the currency specified as such in the confirmation and its successor currencies. Where no currency is mentioned in the confirmation, the domestic currency is defined to be the lawful or successor currency of the reference entity for sovereign reference entities; and for non-sovereign reference entities, the jurisdiction where the reference entity is organised. In view of the new countries that have recently entered, or are about to enter, the European Union and the possibility that these countries may, in the future join the euro, it is worth noting that the domestic currency definition specifically carves out the specified currencies.
- Not domestic law – this excludes obligations governed by the law of the reference entity's home jurisdiction.
- Listed – this means that the obligation must be quoted, listed or ordinarily purchased and sold on an exchange. By its nature, this characteristic relates only to bonds and this is specifically set out in Section 2.21 (interpretation of provisions), in relation to both obligation characteristics and deliverable obligation characteristics.
- Not domestic issuance – this limits obligations to those issued and offered for sale outside of the reference entity's domestic market.

Of the seven obligation characteristics, two require more detailed discussion: not subordinated and not sovereign lender. The definition of 'not subordinated' is the most complex. It ties in four other definitions, which are set out in Section 2.19(b)(i)(B):

- 'subordination';
- 'subordinated obligation';
- 'senior obligation'; and
- 'subordinated'.

These definitions interact to create the definition of 'not subordinated' as follows.

'Subordinated' is construed by reference to the definition of 'subordination', with 'subordination' covering the situation where a reference entity has obligations that rank differently in priority of payment. The definition compares two of the reference entity's obligations: a senior obligation and a subordinated obligation. For a subordination to occur, there must in the relevant documentation be some form of contractual, trust or similar arrangement which provides that on "the liquidation, dissolution, reorganisation or winding-up of the reference entity, the claims of the senior obligation will be satisfied prior to the claims of the holders of the subordinated obligations". Alternatively, the definition provides that 'subordination' will occur if the holders of the subordinated obligation are not entitled to receive or keep payments made under the subordinated obligation, while the senior obligation has arrears or is in default

When determining whether 'subordination' exists, preferred creditors arising by operation of law (eg, the tax authorities), collateral, credit support and credit enhancement arrangements are excluded. An exception to this is that priorities arising by operation of law are taken into account in the case of sovereign reference entities.

'Subordinated' is determined by establishing whether a 'subordination' exists. The 'not subordinated' obligation characteristic is defined as meaning that the relevant reference entity obligation is not subordinated to the reference entity's most senior reference obligation in priority of payment. If the confirmation does not refer to a reference obligation, then the relevant obligation is compared to any 'unsubordinated borrowed money' obligation. The definition also crystallises at what point this comparison is made, providing that this must be the later of the transaction's trade date and the reference obligation's issue date.

Second, the definition of 'not sovereign lender' is also more complex than first appears. It mentions that Paris Club debt is specifically included as sovereign debt and therefore falls within the exclusion. This carve-out is included because what is Paris Club debt is not, at first sight, altogether clear. The Paris Club is an informal group of 19 permanent members which are both official creditors and wealthy industrialised nations; plus other nations invited on a case-by-case basis. Paris Club debt is therefore debt owed to the 19 sovereign nation Paris Club official creditors, on an individual basis. The Paris Club is mentioned specifically in the 'not sovereign lender' definition, because the club's informal nature could lead to it not being considered a supranational, while at the same time if the relevant debt were to be construed as 'primarily owed' to the Paris Club as a whole rather than to its 19 member industrialised nations, not sovereign debt. For this reason, the 'not sovereign lender' definition seeks to clarify this.

Obligation characteristics by reference entity type according to market standard terms						
Not subordinated	Specified currency	Not sovereign lender	Not domestic currency	Not domestic law	Listed	Not domestic issuance
European emerging markets	Singaporean	Singaporean	European emerging markets	European emerging markets	N/A	European emerging markets
Japanese Singapore Asia	(Standard plus SGD)	Asian	Asian	Asian		Asian

As far as the various market standard terms are concerned, obligations characteristics are selected only as applicable for reference entities that are not domiciled in Western Europe or North America. In the market standard terms for reference entities for other jurisdictions, there is some variation on which obligation characteristics are selected as applicable. For European emerging markets entities, not subordinated, not domestic currency, not domestic law and not domestic issuance are selected. For Japanese entities, not subordinated is the only obligation characteristic selected. For Singaporean entities not subordinated, specified currency – standard specified currencies, plus Singapore dollars and not sovereign lender are selected. For Asian entities, not subordinated, not sovereign lender, not domestic currency, not domestic issuance and not domestic law are selected. Listed tends to be selected only in more bespoke transactions.

6. **Area V: determining the reference obligation or deliverable obligations post-credit event**

Article II has 18 definitions relating to the obligations which may, following a credit event, be valued in cash settled transactions or delivered in physically settled transactions. These are the definitions for:

- 'reference obligation' (Section 2.3);
- 'reference price' (Section 2.4);
- 'deliverable obligation' (Section 2.15);
- 'sovereign restructured deliverable obligation' (Section 2.16);
- 'excluded deliverable obligation' (Section 2.18);
- 'method for determining deliverable obligations' (Section 2.20);
- 'deliverable obligation category' (Section 2.20(a));
- 'deliverable obligation characteristics', 'not contingent', 'assignable loan', 'consent required loan', 'direct loan participation', 'transferable', 'maximum maturity', 'accelerated or matured', 'not bearer' (Section 2.20(b));
- 'interpretation of provisions' (Section 2.21); and
- 'domestic currency' (Section 2.29).

6.1 Deliverable obligations

(a) *Deliverable obligation*

The definition of 'obligations' in Section 2.14, together with the provisions for determining them in Section 2.19, deals with determining which of the reference entity's obligations are the subject of credit protection. The definition of 'deliverable obligations' in Section 2.15, together with the provisions for determining them in Section 2.20, deal with two different situation – both follow an event determination date, with one relating to physically settled transactions and the other to cash settled transactions.

In physically settled transactions, the obligations of the reference entity which fall within the definition of 'deliverable obligations' are those which may be delivered by the buyer to the seller in return for payment of the physical settlement amount. In the case of cash settled transactions, although the deliverable obligations provisions are meant to relate only to physically settled transactions, it is common to adapt them in cash settled transactions as a method for selecting a reference obligation to be valued, when none is chosen in the confirmation.

Section 2.15 defines 'deliverable obligations' as:

- any of the reference entity's direct or indirect (ie, guaranteed[33]) obligations satisfying the deliverable obligation category and deliverable obligation characteristics;
- any reference obligation (unless it is defined to be an excluded deliverable obligation);
- in the case of a restructuring credit event for a sovereign reference entity, any restructured deliverable obligation fulfilling certain criteria (unless it is an excluded reference obligation); and
- any other specified obligation of the reference entity.

For both obligations satisfying the deliverable obligation category and the deliverable obligation characteristics and those satisfying the restructured deliverable obligation criteria, there are a series of second leg tests that must be satisfied for a reference entity obligation to be a deliverable obligation.

First, the obligation must be payable in an amount equal to its outstanding principal balance or due and payable amount. 'Due and payable amount' is a concept defined in Section 8.8. It means an amount due and payable in accordance with the terms of the obligation on the 'delivery date' (ie, on the date which the deliverable obligation is actually delivered in a physically settled transaction). This refers to the actual amount due and payable due to acceleration, maturity, termination or otherwise, but excludes amounts which relate to default interest, indemnities, tax gross-ups and similar.

Second, the obligation must not be subject to any counterclaim or defence. An exception to this is if the counterclaim or defence is based on:

- any lack of authority or capacity for the reference entity to enter into the obligation;
- any unenforceability, illegality or impossibility with respect to the obligation or, if it is a guarantee, the underlying obligation;
- any law or judicial ruling; or
- any exchange control or similar.

Third, where there is a qualifying guarantee instead of a qualifying affiliate guarantee, the guarantee must, at the delivery date, be capable of immediate assertion or demand for an amount equal to the outstanding principal amount or the 'due and payable amount'. It is not necessary for the underlying obligation to actually be accelerated. (see table overleaf).

(b) *Excluded deliverable obligation*

'Excluded deliverable obligation' is defined in Section 2.18; the provision mirrors the definition of 'excluded obligation' in Section 2.17. As with excluded obligations, excluded deliverable obligations will be specified only on a bespoke basis.

---

33 Which guaranteed obligations are applicable will depend on whether 'qualifying affiliate guarantees' or 'all guarantees' is selected in the confirmation.

Deliverable obligation(s	Deliverable obligation category (select one)	Deliverable obligation characteristics (select all that apply)
☐ Payment ☐ Borrowed money ☐ Reference obligations only ☐ Bond ☐ Loan ☐ Bond or loan	☐ Not subordinated ☐ Specified currency ☐ Not sovereign lender ☐ Not domestic currency ☐ Not domestic law ☐ Listed ☐ Not contingent ☐ Not domestic issuance	☐ Assignable loan ☐ Consent required loan ☐ Direct loan participation ☐ Indirect loan Participation qualifying Participation seller: ☐ ☐ Transferable ☐ Maximum maturity ☐ Accelerated or matured ☐ Not bearer and: *[Specify any other obligations of a reference entity]*

Excluded obligation(s): None

(c)   *Deliverable obligation category*

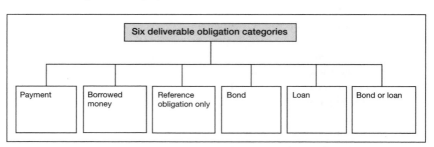

There are six deliverable obligation categories. These replicate the obligation categories (described above). In the case of deliverable obligations, 'reference obligation only' has the effect of fixing the deliverable obligation at the transaction's outset. Whether an obligation is a deliverable obligation is assessed at the date of the event constituting the credit event, as opposed to the transaction's effective date or the event determination date. 'Bond or loan' is the applicable market standard in each of the market standard terms for different reference entity types.

(d) *Deliverable obligation characteristics*

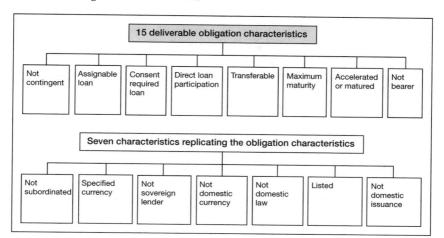

There are 15 deliverable obligation characteristics. Seven of these are replicated from the obligation characteristics. These are: not subordinated, specified currency, not sovereign lender, not domestic law, listed and not domestic issuance. The deliverable obligation characteristics perform the same function as the obligation characteristics (ie, to isolate a reference entity's more tradable obligations).

Additionally, eight new characteristics are added. These are: not contingent, assignable loan, consent required loan, direct loan participation, transferable, maximum maturity, accelerated or matured and not bearer.

These eight new characteristics are outlined below:

- Not contingent – this refers to an obligation with unconditional principal payments. An example of a contingent obligation would be a credit-linked note issued by a financial institution. This characteristic prevents reference entity obligations whose value is affected by factors other than the reference entity's creditworthiness from being valued or delivered following a credit event. This definition specifically carves out certain convertible, exchangeable[34] and accreting obligations from being contingent obligations.

- Assignable loan – this is a loan that can be assigned or novated, without the consent of a reference entity or any guarantor, to at least a commercial bank or financial institution which is not already one of the loan lenders or syndicate members. This characteristic can apply only to loans and is relevant only if loans are included as a deliverable obligation category. This is specifically set out in Section 2.21.

- Consent required loan – this is a loan that can be assigned or novated to another party (not only a commercial bank or institution), but only with the consent of the reference entity, any relevant guarantor or a syndicate agent. If

---

34   In the case of contingent obligations and exchangeable obligations, the relevant option must not have been exercised.

both assignable loan and consent required loan are specified, then it will be necessary for an obligation to have only one of these deliverable obligation characteristics. This characteristic can apply only to loans and is relevant only if loans are included as a deliverable obligation category. This is specifically provided for in Section 2.21.

- Direct loan participation – this refers to loans where the buyer can transfer a specified share of the loan's principal and interest payments to the seller. Direct loan participations are a method to facilitate a quasi form of transfer for loans which are not transferable either through contractual prohibition or because a borrower or guarantor will not consent to the transfer. The direct loan participation characteristic applies only to loans and is relevant only if loans are included as a deliverable obligation category. This is specifically set out in Section 2.21. For a loan to meet the direct loan participation deliverable obligation characteristic, it must be capable of being entered into between either the seller and the buyer (to the extent that the buyer is a lender under the loan or one of the banks in the lending syndicate), or a 'qualifying participation seller', to the extent that one is then a member of the lending syndicate. 'Qualifying participation seller' is defined in Section 2.22 as being any participation seller that meets the requirements specified in the related confirmation; but if no requirements are specified, there will be no qualifying participation seller.
- Transferable – this does not apply to loans. It is specifically set out in Section 2.21. The obligation must be transferable to institutional investors "without any contractual, statutory or regulatory restriction". The definition carves out US resale restrictions under the Regulation S and Rule 144A safe harbours. All eurobonds are subject to one or other of these safe harbours. If the 2003 Definitions had failed to carve these provisions out, eurobonds, for example, would be excluded from being deliverable obligations. Restrictions on

Deliverable obligation characteristics by reference entity type according to Market Standard Terms

Not subordinated	Specified currency	Not sovereign lender	Not domestic currency	Not domestic law	Listed	Not contingent	Not domestic issuance
W European	W European	Singapore	N/A	Eur emerg market	N/A	W European	Eur emerg market
W Eur Insurance	W Eur Insurance	Asian		Asian		W Eur insurance	Asia
Eur emerg market	Eur Emerg Market					Eur emerg market	
Aus/New Zealand	Aus/ New Zealand					Aus/ New Zealand	
Singapore	Singapore					Singapore	
Asian	Asian					Asian	
Japanese	Japanese					Japanese	
N Am inv. grade	N Am inv. grade					N Am inv grade	
N Am insurance	N Am insurance					N Am insurance	
N Am high yield	N Am high yield					N Am high yield	

permitted investments such as statutory or regulatory investment restrictions on insurance companies and pension funds are also carved out.

- Maximum maturity – this means that on the physical settlement date, the deliverable obligation must not have a maturity date later than the period specified in the confirmation. It is market practice for this to be 30 years.
- Accelerated or matured – this refers to obligations that are fully due and payable before the delivery date because they have matured (but have not been redeemed), have been accelerated (ie, an event of default has been declared) or would have been due and payable but for insolvency laws (eg, the application of Chapter 11 of the US Bankruptcy Code).
- Not bearer – by its nature, this relates only to bonds. It is specifically set out in Section 2.21. To meet the requirements of this deliverable obligation characteristic, the bonds must be either registered bonds or, if they are bearer bonds, cleared via Euroclear, Clearstream or any other internationally recognised clearing system.

Section 2.21 provides that if any of the 'payment', 'borrowed money', 'loan' or 'bond or loan' deliverable obligation categories are selected in a confirmation and more than one of 'assignable loan', 'consent required loan' or 'direct loan participation' are also selected, then it is not necessary for a loan to satisfy all of these characteristics to be a deliverable obligation: one is enough.

(e)   *How are the deliverable obligation characteristics used in practice?*
Looking at the market standard terms for each different type of reference entity, the deliverable obligation characteristics are very similar (see table overleaf). Standard terms for Western European entities, Western European insurance entities, European emerging market entities, Australian and New Zealand entities, Singaporean entities,

Assignable loan	Consent Required Loan	Direct Loan Participation	Transferable	Maximum Maturity	Accelerated or Matured	Not Bearer
W European	W European	N/A	W European	W European	N/A	W European
W Eur insurance	W Eur insurance		W Eur insurance	W Eur insurance		W Eur insurance
Eur emerg market	Eur emerg market		Eur emerg market	Aus/New Zealand		Eur Emerg market
Aus/New Zealand	Aus/New Zealand		Aus/New Zealand	Singaporean		Aus/New Zealand
Singapore	Japanese		Singapore	Asian		Singaporean
Asian	N Am inv grade		Asian	Japanese		Asian
Japanese	N Am insurance		Japanese	N Am inv grade		Japanese
N Am inv grad	N Am high yield		N Am inv grade	N Am insurance		N Am inv grade
N Am insurance			N Am insurance	N Am high yield		N Am insurance
N Am high yield			N Am high yield			N Am high yield

243

Asian entities, Japanese entities, American investment grade entities, North American insurance entities and North American high yield entities all select not subordinated, specified currency (standard specified currencies), not contingent, assignable loan, transferable and not bearer as applicable. The only wrinkles to this are that Australian and New Zealand entities add Australian and New Zealand dollars to the definition of 'standard specified currencies' and Singaporean entities add Singapore dollars to the definition.

All of the emerging market reference entity types other than European emerging markets add 'maximum maturity: 30 years' as a deliverable obligation characteristic. Singaporean and Asian reference entities include 'not sovereign lender' as a deliverable obligation characteristic, but do not include 'consent required loan', which is selected for all of the other standard reference entity types. European emerging market reference entities have 'not domestic law' as a deliverable obligation characteristic. These reference entities, in common with Asian reference entities, also select 'not domestic issuance' as a deliverable obligation characteristic. None of the reference entity types, though, selects 'not domestic currency', 'listed', 'direct loan participation' or 'accelerated or matured' as deliverable obligation characteristics, leaving these to be applied in more bespoke transactions.

(f)   *Not contingent: convertible, exchangeable and accreting obligations*
The 'not contingent' deliverable obligation characteristic is the most complex of the 15 deliverable obligation characteristics. It is defined as meaning any of the reference entity's obligations which, on the delivery date and after, have an outstanding principal balance, or for obligations which are not 'borrowed money' a 'due and payable amount', which cannot be reduced otherwise than due to non-payment.

> **Actual case study: the not contingent deliverable obligation characteristic – Nomura International Plc v Credit Suisse First Boston International**
>
> *Railtrack, the company that controls Britain's rail infrastructure, has been put into administration. The government asked the High Court to take the action after it refused to put any more money into the struggling company. The order means Railtrack is now under the control of government-appointed administrators, who will continue to run the railways.* BBC News, October 8 2001.
>
> This bankruptcy credit event exposed a weakness in the 'not contingent' deliverable obligation characteristic of the 1999 Definitions.
> A $10 million physically settled credit default swap referencing Railtrack plc was outstanding between Nomura International Plc and Credit Suisse First Boston International (CSFB) on the date Railtrack was put into administration. Under the swap, Nomura had purchased credit protection from CSFB; and following the administration, Nomura served a credit event notice specifying that Railtrack's administration amounted to a bankruptcy credit event. There was no doubt that

a credit event had occurred, but as this was a physically settled transaction, Nomura had to select the Railtrack obligations that it intended to deliver to CSFB. These obligations had to satisfy, among other things, the deliverable obligation characteristics specified in the swap, one of which was 'not contingent'. The definition of 'not contingent' under the 1999 Definitions was ambiguous.

Railtrack had several obligations outstanding at the time of the credit event. One of these was a $10 million 3.5% exchangeable bond due 2009, which could be exchanged for shares in Railtrack Group. The exchangeable bond was trading at a lower price than Railtrack's other obligations making it the 'cheapest to deliver' obligation.

Nomura served a notice of intended physical settlement (the forerunner to the notice of physical settlement) on CSFB specifying that it intended to deliver $10 million of these exchangeable bonds on the physical settlement date. CSFB refused to accept delivery of the exchangeable bonds.

It claimed that they were contingent obligations because, notwithstanding that Railtrack was in administration and could not insist that the bonds be exchanged for underlying shares, the bondholder did have a right to exchange the bonds for Railtrack group shares. In certain circumstances the bond trustee could, acting in its absolute discretion, make an automatic exchange on behalf of the bondholders when a very favourable share price was available in the days immediately preceding the exchangeable bond's maturity date. If CSFB were right, then Nomura would have to purchase more expensive obligations and would therefore receive a lesser net credit protection payment. The parties went to court.

In the resulting case, *Nomura International Plc v Credit Suisse First Boston International*,[35] Justice Langley ruled that the Railtrack exchangeable bonds were 'not contingent' obligations within the definition of 'not contingent' in Section 2.18(B) of the 1999 Definitions. Justice Langley first looked at whether the bondholders' option to exchange the bonds for Railtrack shares made the bonds deliverable obligations. Ruling that it did not, he stated that:

> In all probability the 'Credit Event' itself will reflect and crystallise the lack of benefit to be derived from the exchange right and the fact that the holder chooses to deliver the bonds will reflect the commercial reality that they are worth less than the obligation of the seller of protection. That, after all, is what the buyer has bought: protection against the credit risk of the issuer.

In his analysis of the automatic exchange clause, he also ruled that this was not enough to make the bonds contingent, as the contingency, following the bankruptcy credit event, was highly unlikely to happen.

Prior to the court proceedings, ISDA has released an opinion from Robin

---

35   [2003] EWHC 160.

Potts QC (who also acted for Nomura) on October 28 2001, reaching a similar conclusion. It had previously released a memorandum to members on October 18 2001 stating that "bonds that are convertible at the option of the bondholder or a trustee on behalf of the bondholders should be deliverable under standard credit derivatives contracts".[36]

The case was worth litigating by CSFB, especially if one considers *Deutsche Bank v ANZ Banking Group Limited*,[37] where the court took a very literal interpretation of the existing grace period definition. However, the weakness in the 1999 Definitions had been exposed. ISDA acted quickly and released the Supplement Relating to Convertible, Exchangeable or Accreting Obligations on November 9 2001. It was structured as a supplement or addendum to the 1999 Definitions and could be incorporated by reference into transactions. These provisions addressed not only the issues relating to the convertible and exchangeable obligations which had been raised in the Railtrack credit event, but also an outstanding issue relating to accreting obligations, "such as zero coupon bonds, low coupon bonds issued at a discount and non-discounted bonds that accrete during their term".[38] The supplement was later fully incorporated into the 2003 Definitions.

A 'convertible' obligation is an obligation of the reference entity convertible wholly or partly into its equity securities at the holder's option.[39] An exchangeable obligation is one which may be exchanged into another issuer's equity securities at the holder's option[40] and an accreting obligation is any obligation (including a convertible or exchangeable obligation) which, if accelerated, will pay the original issue price plus additional amounts (on account of original issue discount or other interest accruals) – for example, a deeply discounted or zero coupon bond. These terms are all defined in Article VIII (physical settlement).

The definition of 'not contingent' provides that a convertible obligation, exchangeable obligation or accreting obligation which satisfies the deliverable obligation category and deliverable obligation characteristics, as of the delivery date, will be a deliverable obligation.

Additionally, the 'not contingent' definition modifies the rule making any reference obligation a deliverable obligation by additionally providing that the conversion and exchange rights must not have been exercised on or before the delivery date.

In the case of convertible and exchangeable obligations, the 2003 Definitions provide further criteria for determining whether a convertible obligation or exchangeable obligation can meet the 'not contingent' deliverable obligation characteristic. The reference entity, or, if there is one, the underlying obligor must not

---

36   ISDA News, October 2001.
37   2000 WL 1151384 (QBC (Comm Ct)).
38   Commentary on Supplement relating to Convertible, Exchangeable or Accreting Obligations, ISDA November 2001.
39   Or a trustee or agent acting for the holder.
40   Or a trustee or agent acting for the holder.

have exercised any right that it has to convert or exchange the obligation for equity securities or pay the purchase or redemption price in equity securities on or before the delivery date. If it has exercised this right before the delivery date, but the right has been effectively rescinded before the delivery date, this will not affect an obligation becoming a deliverable obligation.

(g)　*Transferable obligations*

The 'transferable' definition states that obligations must be transferable to institutional investors without any contractual, statutory or regulatory restrictions (as discussed above). Carved out from this are the Rule 144A or Regulation S restrictions promulgated under the US Securities Act of 1933.

What are Regulation S and Rule 144A and why are they important?

In the aftermath of the US stock market collapse in 1929, tough laws were introduced to protect investors. One of these was the Securities Act of 1933, Section 5 of which prevented use of US inter-state mails to sell or deliver a security unless the issuer had filed a registration statement. This registration statement is a document containing extensive disclosure that is filed with the US Securities and Exchange Commission (SEC). They are expensive to prepare, and because Section 5 of the Securities Act is so widely drafted, there is a risk that securities which are issued outside of the United States by non-US issuers which have no intention of selling securities to US investors could fall foul of the act and be liable to US criminal sanctions.

To prevent this from happening, the SEC introduced Regulation S.[41] It is a safe harbour provision. If foreign issuers and financial institutions meet the regulation's criteria for reselling unregistered securities outside of the United States, then the terms 'offer', 'offer to sell', 'sell', 'sale' and 'offer to buy' set out in Section 5 are deemed not to include offers and sales which take place outside the United States.

The provisions are quite complex, but in summary, an offer or sale by securities by an issuer or distributor that complies with the various restrictions is deemed to occur outside the United States if the offer or sale is made in an offshore transaction and no directed selling efforts are made in the United States. After two years have elapsed, the securities are deemed to have seasoned and may be sold without restriction. Due to the complexity of the rules, determining when this period has expired is difficult.

The tough securities laws in the United States are aimed at protecting the small investor from being defrauded or making dangerous investments; especially those proverbial 'widows and orphans'. Large institutions, though,

---

41　Regulation S is promulgated under Rule 903 – Offers or Sales of Securities by the Issuer, a Distributor, Any of Their Respective Affiliates, or Any Person Acting on Behalf of Any of the Foregoing; Conditions Relating to Specific Securities.

should be able to look after themselves and so the SEC introduced Rule 144A to allow foreign issuers to issue securities which could then be resold to US institutions deemed to have enough wealth and experience to make their own judgements.

Rule 144A operates in a similar way to Regulation S – it also acts as a safe harbour. Under Regulation S, after two years has elapsed, foreign issued securities can be sold into the United States without breaching Section 5 of the Securities Act. Under Rule 144A, offers and sales of securities can be made only to a class of institution called qualified institutional buyers: these are institutions managing at least $100 million of investments or, in the case of broker dealers, $10 million. Certain other restrictions and disclosure requirements apply – in particular, that the securities must not be publicly traded in the United States.

Regulation S and Rule 144A are important in credit derivative transactions because post credit-event in physically settled transactions, they impact upon what is and what is not a deliverable obligation; and this determination is more complex than the 2003 Definitions suggest. The credit derivatives practitioner must have a solid understanding of certain aspects of US securities law.

Although the definition of the transferable deliverable obligation characteristic includes as deliverable obligations Regulation S and Rule 144A securities, many counterparties may be legally prohibited from holding these securities.

In particular, for Rule 144A securities, this will usually be the case for credit linked notes issued by a special purpose vehicle from one of the tax havens such as the Cayman Islands or Jersey, as these companies are usually thinly capitalised and are unlikely to be managing the requisite amount of assets. What this means is that the universe of deliverable obligations in physically settled transactions might be smaller than first meets the eye. This may mean that a buyer cannot deliver the cheapest securities available and/or Section 9.3 (partial cash settlement due to impossibility or illegality) of the 2003 Definitions will apply. A buyer in a physically settled credit derivative transaction should pay particular attention to whether the seller is legally able to take delivery of Regulation S and Rule 144A securities. Where this ability is restricted, the transaction should be priced accordingly.

Where a reference entity has issued predominately Regulation S and Rule 144A securities, particular care and diligence should be undertaken by a buyer or its counterparty and, if appropriate, specific representations set out in the relevant confirmation.

When checking whether one of the reference entity's obligations is a deliverable obligation and whether a security issued by a non-US entity is a Regulation S security, a Rule 144A security or has a registration statement will usually be set out on the front page of the prospectus. Many issuances have a Regulation S tranche and a Rule 144A tranche and it is important for any buyer intending to deliver deliverable obligations to check the ISIN or CUSIP of the relevant security against the relevant tranche in the prospectus.

6.2   Guarantees

(a)   *Qualifying guarantee and qualifying affiliate guarantee, and their interaction with the interpretation of provisions section*

The 2003 Definitions provisions relating to guarantees, along with those relating to grace periods, the restructuring credit event, the repudiation/moratorium credit event and the various cash and physical settlement fallbacks, are among the most complex parts of the 2003 Definitions to master. This section deals with guarantees in considerable depth.

In any credit derivative transaction, it is of paramount importance to determine the extent of credit protection provided against the relevant reference entity. This is done (with the exception of the bankruptcy credit event) through determining the identity of the reference entity's obligations covered (ie, which of the reference entity's obligations are 'obligations' and, post-credit event, which of these obligations can be valued as reference obligations in cash settled transactions or delivered as deliverable obligations in physically settled transactions. Making these determinations is more complex when assessing whether an obligation which the reference entity has guaranteed (perhaps an obligation of a subsidiary, a sister company or a parent company) is one of that reference entity's 'obligations', a reference obligation or a deliverable obligation.

The 2003 Definitions provide extensive provisions on guarantees to allow the parties to make these determinations as simply, comprehensively and decisively as possible. They do this by providing two specific, but alternative, definitions for the types of guarantee which may be deemed to be 'obligations', reference obligations or deliverable obligations. These are:
* 'qualifying guarantee' (Section 2.23); and
* 'qualifying affiliate guarantee' (Section 2.24).

The transaction parties then select which of the two options shall apply, with their election depending on the treatment of guarantees in the jurisdiction where the reference entity is incorporated.

The 'qualifying guarantee' and 'qualifying affiliate guarantee' definitions are then used to shape the definitions of 'obligation' (Section 2.14), 'deliverable obligation' (Section 2.15), 'substitute reference obligation' (Section 2.30) and 'restructuring' (Section 4.7(c)). They also apply to 'interpretation of provisions' (Section 2.21(d)) and the definition of 'deliver' (Section 8.2).

The treatment of guarantees under the 2003 Definitions addresses perceived ambiguities in the 1999 Definitions. A 'qualifying guarantee', as defined in Section 2.23, is an arrangement where the reference entity irrevocably agrees by either guarantee of payment or an equivalent legal arrangement (eg, a keepwell agreement), to pay all amounts due under an 'underlying obligation', to which another party is the 'underlying obligor'.

At the time of the credit event the arrangement must not be subordinated to any of the underlying obligor's unsubordinated borrowed money. Whether the arrangement is subordinated or borrowed money is determined by applying the definition of 'subordination' in Section 2.19(b)(B) (method for determining obligations) and 'borrowed money' in Section 2.19(a)(ii) (method for determining obligations). However, the 'subordination' definition is modified in the 2003 Definitions for the purposes of qualifying guarantees so that references to subordination of the reference entity are deemed to be references to the subordination of the underlying obligor.

The definition of 'qualifying guarantee' excludes surety bonds, financial guarantee insurance policies, letters of credit and equivalent legal arrangements. It also excludes arrangements where the payment obligation of the reference entity can be "discharged, reduced, assigned or otherwise altered as a result of the occurrence or non-occurrence of an event or circumstance (other than payment)".

The final criterion for qualifying guarantees is that their benefit must be capable of being delivered together with the underlying obligation. This would be the case in a negotiable instrument such as a eurobond, but not in the case of a loan where the guarantee was given only to a named beneficiary.

The alternative option, 'qualifying affiliate guarantee', is defined in Section 2.24 as a qualifying guarantee provided by the reference entity only to one of its downstream affiliates.[42] It is a narrower category of guarantee than that provided for in the 'qualifying guarantee' definition and is selected for reference entities from jurisdictions where market participants believe that upstream and cross-stream guarantees have a greater legal risk than downstream guarantees.

Section 2.21(d) provides six sub-sections with detailed provisions giving further colour to the treatment of guarantees under the 2003 Definitions.

First, it provides that a qualifying guarantee is deemed to satisfy the same obligation category or deliverable obligation category as would an underlying obligation. Second, in the case of obligation and deliverable obligation characteristics, both the qualifying guarantee and the underlying obligation must satisfy the 'specified currency', 'not sovereign lender' and 'not domestic currency' deliverable obligation characteristics if these are specified. For these purposes, the G7 currencies and the euro are carved out of the 'not domestic currency' definition. Also, English law and New York law are carved out of the 'domestic law' definition.

Third, when applying the obligation and deliverable obligation characteristics, only the qualifying guarantee must satisfy the 'not subordinated' obligation and/or deliverable obligation characteristic on the relevant date.

Fourth, and also for the purposes of applying the obligation and deliverable obligation characteristics, only the underlying obligation must satisfy the 'listed', 'not contingent', 'not domestic issuance', 'assignable loan', 'consent required loan', 'direct loan participation', 'transferable', 'maximum maturity', 'accelerated or matured' and 'not bearer' obligation/deliverable obligation characteristics if they are selected in the transaction's confirmation.

Fifth, and also in relation to the obligation/deliverable obligation characteristics, references to the reference entity are deemed to be references to the underlying obligor.

---

42   Section 2.25 defines this as a 50% directly or indirectly owned subsidiary of the reference entity. The ownership must be of shares that have the power to elect the board of directors.

Sixth, and finally, 'outstanding principal balance' and 'due and payable amount' are used throughout the definitions. However, when they are used in connection with qualifying guarantees, they are deemed to refer to the 'outstanding principal balance' or 'due and payable amount' of the underlying obligation supported by the qualifying guarantee.

(b)   ***All guarantees***

All guarantees:	[Applicable][Not applicable]

Unless the parties select 'all guarantees' as applicable in the confirmation, the fallback is for qualifying affiliate guarantees to apply instead. This selection is made either in paragraph 1 of the confirmation or in each standard terms section, where there are multiple reference entities in different jurisdictions.

The concept of 'all guarantees' is referred to in all sections of the 2003 Definitions which cross-refer to qualifying guarantees and qualifying affiliate guarantees. These sections include the following language: "(either directly as provider of a Qualifying Affiliate Guarantee or, if All Guarantees is specified as applicable in the related Confirmation, as provider of any Qualifying Guarantee)."

The standard terms for all jurisdictions other than North American investment grade entities, North American insurance entities and North American high yield entities select 'all guarantees' as applicable. Due to concerns about the enforceability of cross-stream and down-stream guarantees in North America, the market convention is for qualifying affiliate guarantee only to be applicable.

(c)   ***The interaction of qualifying guarantees and qualifying affiliate guarantees with 'obligation' and 'deliverable obligation'***
Each of the definitions of 'obligation' in Section 2.14 and 'deliverable obligation' in Section 2.15 specifically includes obligations of the reference entity as a provider of a qualifying affiliate guarantee or, if 'all guarantees' is specified, a qualifying guarantee.

(d)   ***The interaction of qualifying guarantees and qualifying affiliate guarantees with the definition of obligation category and deliverable obligation category***
The interpretation of provisions section (Section 2.21(d)) provides further colour to the criterion for determining whether a qualifying guarantee or qualifying affiliate guarantee meets an obligation category or deliverable obligation category by providing that when making a determination, the qualifying guarantee is deemed to satisfy the same categories as the underlying obligation.

(e)   ***The interaction of qualifying guarantees and qualifying affiliate guarantees with the definition of 'obligation characteristic' and 'deliverable obligation characteristic'***
Section 2.21(d) goes on to provide that for the purposes of applying the obligation/ deliverable obligation characteristics to an underlying obligation, the references to

reference entity are deemed to be to the underlying obligor.

Section 2.21(d) also sets out which of the obligation/deliverable obligation characteristics are deemed to apply to the qualifying guarantee only; which are deemed to apply to the underlying obligation only; and which are deemed to apply to both the qualifying guarantee and the underlying obligation.

The qualifying guarantee only must satisfy the not subordinated obligation/ deliverable obligation characteristic on the relevant date.

The underlying obligation only must satisfy the following obligation/deliverable obligation characteristics: listed, not contingent, not domestic issuance, assignable loan, consent required loan, direct loan participation, transferable, maximum maturity, accelerated or matured and not bearer.

The qualifying guarantee and the underlying obligation must both satisfy four of the obligation/deliverable obligation characteristics: specified currency, not sovereign lender, not domestic currency and not domestic law. For these purposes, the currencies of Canada, Japan, Switzerland, the United Kingdom, the United States and the euro are not deemed to be domestic currencies. English law and New York law are not deemed to be domestic law.

(f) **The interaction of qualifying guarantees and qualifying affiliate guarantees with the definition of 'outstanding principal balance' and 'due and payable amount'**

The term 'due and payable amount' is defined in Section 8.8 and means the amount which is due and payable on the delivery date in accordance with a deliverable obligation's terms, whether through acceleration, maturity, termination or otherwise (excluding various sums such as default interest and gross-up). The term 'outstanding principal balance' is not defined as such, but is used in conjunction with 'due and payable amount' in various definitions as the self-explanatory alternative. Where these terms are used in conjunction with guarantees, they are deemed to refer to the due and payable amount or the outstanding principal balance of the underlying obligation.

(g) **The interaction of qualifying guarantees and qualifying affiliate guarantees with the definition of 'substitute reference obligation'**

The definition of 'substitute reference obligation' in Section 2.30 specifically includes obligations of the reference entity as provider of a qualified affiliate guarantee, or if 'all guarantees' is specified, as provider of a qualifying guarantee.

Qualifying guarantees and qualifying affiliate guarantees are also important for determining whether a reference obligation must be substituted. If a reference obligation is an underlying obligation with a qualifying guarantee and, other than due to a credit event, the qualifying guarantee ceases to be a valid and binding obligation of the reference entity, then the calculation agent must identify a substitute reference obligation.

According to Section 2.30(b), any substitute reference obligation becomes an 'obligation' of a reference entity if the reference entity is the provider of a qualifying guarantee or if 'all guarantees' is specified, additionally 'qualifying affiliate guarantees'.

(h)   ***The interaction of qualifying guarantees and qualifying affiliate guarantees with the restructuring credit event***

Section 4.7 (restructuring) provides that a credit event occurs where the reference entity restructures one or more of its 'obligations' and the restructuring does not fall within any of the carve-outs that Section 4.7 provides. For the purposes of clarification, Section 4.7(c) restates the provision of the Section 2.14 definition that 'obligation' is deemed to include underlying obligations where the reference entity provides a qualifying affiliate guarantee or, if applicable, a qualifying guarantee.

(i)   ***The interaction of qualifying guarantees and qualifying affiliate guarantees with the definition of 'deliver'***

The definition of 'deliver' (Section 8.2) forms part of Article VIII (terms relating to physical settlement) and refers to the actual delivery or a deliverable obligation in a physically settled transaction. 'Deliver' is defined as including the transfer "of the benefit of the qualifying guarantee". The definition further provides that to the extent that the deliverable obligations consist of qualifying guarantees, "Delivery means to deliver both the Qualifying Guarantee and the Underlying Obligation".

(j)   ***How the May 2003 supplement amends the treatment of guarantees in the 2003 Definitions***

Following the publication of the 2003 Definitions in April 2003, certain shortcomings soon became apparent. To combat these, ISDA issued the May 2003 Supplement to the 2003 Definitions to address concerns raised about guarantees, among other things. Incorporating the supplement into a confirmation is optional. Article II sets the date on which share ownership should be assessed for establishing whether an underlying obligor is a downstream affiliate as the date of the credit event or delivery date. In practice, this may be difficult to establish. The May 2003 Supplement makes the determination date that on which the qualifying guarantee is issued.

The May 2003 Supplement provides that for the purposes of applying obligation characteristics and deliverable obligation characteristics, both the qualifying guarantee and underlying obligation must satisfy any of the following:

- not subordinated;
- specified currency;
- not sovereign lender;
- not domestic currency; and
- not domestic law.

If the parties incorporate the May 2003 Supplement, but do not select 'not subordinated' as an obligation characteristic or a deliverable obligation characteristic, a guarantee which is subordinated to the underlying obligor's borrowed money obligations will be an obligation or deliverable obligation. This will not be the case if the May 2003 Supplement is not incorporated.

(k)   ***Reference price***

In cash settled transactions, once the calculation agent has determined the reference obligation, it must then value it in accordance with Article VII (terms relating to cash settlement) and determine the cash settlement amount that must be paid by the seller to the buyer. This either can be a fixed amount stated in the confirmation or can be ascertained by valuing the reference obligation in the market. This valuation will provide the calculation agent with a final price. Section 7.4 (final price) provides that this is expressed as a percentage amount. To determine the cash settlement amount, the calculation agent complies with Section 7.3 (cash settlement amount). This provides that the cash settlement amount will be the greater of:

- the floating rate payer calculation amount multiplied by the reference price less the final price; and
- zero.

The 'floating rate payer calculation amount' is defined in Section 2.13 as being the amount specified in the confirmation. It is normally the same as the fixed rate payer calculation amount (ie, the amount of credit protection sold). 'Reference price' is defined in Section 2.4 as the amount specified in the confirmation or, if none is specified in the confirmation, 100%. The reference price is intended to reflect the original price of the security at the outset of a transaction, before the decline in the reference entity's creditworthiness.

7. Area VI: variation of the restructuring credit event

Article II has 14 definitions which, when incorporated into a transaction, allow the restructuring credit event to mutate into either of the alternative types of restructuring credit events: modified restructuring or modified modified restructuring. Each of these provisions relates to physically settled transactions and covers what deliverable obligations can be delivered following a restructuring credit event. If 'physical settlement' and 'restructuring maturity limitation and fully transferable obligation' are specified as applicable in the transaction confirmation together with the restructuring credit event, then the parties will have selected 'modified restructuring' as the credit event. If physical settlement and 'modified restructuring maturity limitation and conditionally transferable obligation' are specified in a confirmation together with the restructuring credit event, then the parties will have selected 'modified modified restructuring' as the credit event. If they do not use either Section 2.32 or Section 2.33, but still select the restructuring credit event, then the restructuring credit event will apply without modification.

Where modified restructuring is selected, the following definitions set out in Section 2.32 will then apply:

- 'fully transferable obligation' (Section 2.32(b));
- 'restructuring maturity limitation date' (Section 2.32(c));
- 'restructuring date' (Section 2.32(d));
- 'restructured bond or loan' (Section 2.32(e)); and
- 'eligible transferee' (Section 2.32(f))

Where modified modified restructuring is selected, the following definitions set out in Section 2.33 will apply:

- 'modified restructuring maturity limitation and conditionally transferable obligation applicable' (Section 2.33(a));
- 'conditionally transferable obligation' (Section 2.33(b));
- 'modified restructuring maturity limitation date' (Section 2.33(c));
- 'restructuring date' (Section 2.33(d));
- 'restructured bond or loan' (Section 2.33(e)); and
- 'modified eligible transferee' (Section 2.33(f)).

8. Area VII: business day convention

Business day conventions are used to ensure that events which are required to take place on business days, such as fixed rate payer payment dates and fixed rate payer period end dates, occur on business days. When the relevant date occurs on a date that is not otherwise a business day, the 2003 Definitions provide various options that the parties can select to decide whether the relevant business day selected is a preceding or following one. However, the 2003 Definitions also state that the definitions of 'effective date' (Section 1.4) and 'scheduled termination date' (Section 1.6) are not to be adjusted by a business day convention.

The business day convention provisions are set out in Section 2.11. They provide three options that may be selected in any transaction:
- 'following';
- 'modified following' or 'modified'; and
- 'preceding'.

The 'following' business day convention means that if the date would otherwise fall on a day that is not a business day, the date will be deemed to fall on the following business day. The 'modified following' or 'modified' business day convention means that the relevant date will be the following business day unless it would fall into the next calendar month, in which case the date will be the immediately preceding business day. If 'preceding' is specified as the business day convention, then the relevant date will be deemed to be the immediately preceding business day.

The applicable business day convention for a transaction is specified in the confirmation. If no business day convention is specified, then the following business day convention applies.

Several time periods in the 2003 Definitions relate to calendar day periods rather than business day periods. Where, in a transaction, a calendar day period ends on a day that is not a business day, Section 2.11 provides that the last calendar day will be deemed to be adjusted in accordance with the applicable business day convention. The use of the business day convention to modify the end of these periods can have a crucial effect on determinations made under a transaction and it is important to be aware of these provisions.

This modification occurs in several different parts of the 2003 Definitions. In Section 1.9 (notice delivery period), the notice delivery period is a 14-calendar-day period. In Section 2.2(a) (provisions for determining a successor) the 'successor' definition has a 14-calendar-day period relating to determining a successor event and the 'best available information' definition limits best available information to information made available no more than 14 calendar days after the legally effective date.

In relation to determining credit events, Section 1.12(a)(ii) (grace period) for the purposes of a grace period extensions regulates the length of the grace period in certain circumstances to the lesser of 30 calendar days and the period set out in the underlying documentation. When determining a bankruptcy credit event, there is a 30-calendar-day time period for the reference entity to dismiss bankruptcy proceedings in Section 4.2(d)(ii) and to dismiss proceedings where a secured party takes control of the reference entity's assets in Section 4.2(e).

In particular, several calendar day periods relate to physical settlement. There is a 30-calendar-day period following an event determination date in which the notice of physical settlement condition to settlement can be satisfied under Section 3.2(d) (conditions to settlement). In Section 3.4 (notice of physical settlement), if the physical settlement condition to settlement has not been met within that 30-calendar-day period, then that date will be the termination date. Finally, the definition of 'latest permissible physical settlement date' in Section 9.7 defines the physical settlement date as 30 calendar days after the physical settlement date where there is a partial cash settlement due to impossibility or illegality.

9. Area VIII: substitute reference obligations

9.1 Substitute reference obligation

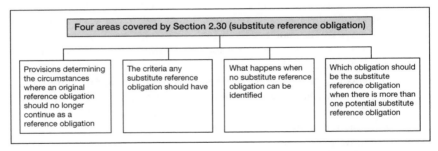

When a reference obligation is disclosed in a confirmation, circumstances can occur which mean that the reference obligation no longer exists. Section 2.30 (substitute reference obligation) covers four areas:

- the circumstances in which an original reference obligation should no longer continue as a reference obligation;
- which criteria any substitute reference obligation should have;
- what happens when no substitute reference obligation can be identified; and
- which obligation should be the substitute reference obligation when there is more than one potential substitute reference obligation.

Section 1.14 (calculation agent) gives the calculation agent responsibility for making these determinations in consultation with the other parties.

9.2　Should the calculation agent replace a reference obligation?

The calculation agent should determine, in consultation with the other parties, that it should replace a reference obligation in the following circumstances.

A reference obligation may be replaced if it is fully redeemed. It may also be replaced if the calculation agent determines that the reference obligation's aggregate amounts have been materially reduced by redemption or otherwise. This must be due to reasons other than scheduled redemption, amortisation or prepayments.

If a reference obligation is an underlying obligation with a qualifying guarantee and, other than due to a credit event, the qualifying guarantee ceases to be a valid and binding obligation of the reference entity, the calculation agent must identify a substitute reference obligation.

If, due to a credit event, a reference obligation ceases to be an 'obligation' of the reference entity, perhaps due to a restructuring, then there will not be a substitute reference obligation.

9.3　What criteria must the substitute reference obligation fulfil?

Section 2.30 provides that any substitute reference obligation must rank *pari passu* in payment with the original reference obligation. This is determined on the later of the confirmation's trade date and the date on which the original reference obligation was issued. No later changes in priorities of payment are taken into account. Where there is no substitute reference obligation ranking *pari passu* in payment with the original reference obligation, at the buyer's option the calculation agent may select a substitute reference obligation-ranking senior in payment to the original reference obligation.

The substitute reference obligation must also preserve the economic equivalent of the parties' delivery and payment obligations under the credit derivative transaction. It must also be either a direct obligation of the reference entity or an obligation where the reference entity provides a qualifying affiliate guarantee, or if selected, a qualifying guarantee.

Once the calculation agent has identified one or more substitute reference obligations it must, without further action, replace the original reference obligation(s). Section 1.14 obliges the calculation agent to make all determinations regarding substitute reference obligations as soon as reasonably practicable and then to notify the parties of its determination.

9.4　What happens when the calculation agent cannot identify a substitute reference obligation for some or all of the reference obligations?

Once the calculation agent has determined that it needs to identify a substitute reference obligation and has reviewed the reference entity's outstanding obligations to establish a substitute reference obligation, it may be unable to identify substitute reference obligations for some or all of the reference obligations. Sections 2.30(c), (d) and (e) provide different rules which are applied depending on whether the calculation is required under Section 2.30(a) to replace some or all of the transaction's original reference obligations, or it is unable to identify any substitute reference obligations.

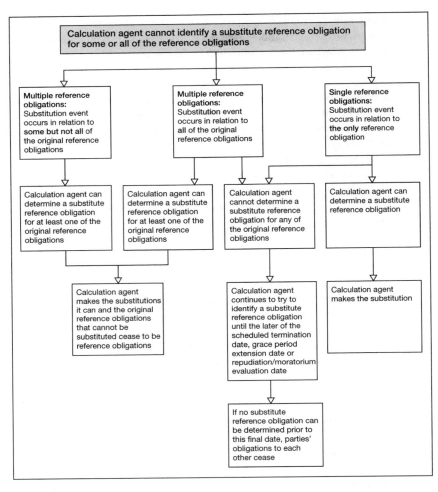

Sometimes a transaction will list several original reference obligations. If one of the substitution events disclosed in Section 2.30(a) occurs in relation to some but not all of the original reference obligations, and the calculation agent is able to identify a substitute reference obligation for at least one of these original reference obligations, then it will make the substitutions that it can. The original reference obligations for which it cannot identify a substitute reference obligation will then cease to be reference obligations.

If, on the other hand, any of the substitution events disclosed in Section 2.30(a) occurs in relation to all of the original reference obligations, a separate rule applies. The calculation agent must (if it can) determine at least one substitute reference obligation; it will then substitute all the original reference obligations that may be substituted for this substitute reference obligation. Those original reference obligations for which the calculation agent cannot identify a substitute reference obligation will then cease to be reference obligations.

It is more problematic if there is a single reference obligation and the calculation agent cannot identify a successor reference obligation, or there are multiple reference obligations and the calculation agent cannot identify reference obligations for any of them. If this is the case, then the calculation agent will go on trying to identify a substitute reference obligation until the later of the scheduled termination date or if there is one any grace period extension date or repudiation/moratorium evaluation date.

If the calculation agent cannot determine a substitute reference obligation before this final date, then in a cash settled transaction where the cash settlement amount is determined through a reference obligation or in a physically settled transaction where the reference obligation is the only deliverable obligation, the parties' obligations to each other will cease. This means that in such circumstances, if a credit event occurs in relation to the reference entity, the buyer will not receive a cash settlement amount or physical settlement amount. This is currently the case for any credit default swaps entered into before Parmalat's bankruptcy which have not yet been triggered.

9.5 Which obligation should be the substitute reference obligation when there is more than one potential substitute reference obligation?

If there is a choice of substitute reference obligations then, subject to consulting with the parties, the calculation agent has a general discretion in the choice it makes.

Where the calculation agent is one of the parties, there will be an inherent conflict: if the calculation agent is the buyer, it will wish to select the most expensive obligation; if it is the seller, it will wish to select the cheapest. These divergent positions are tempered though Section 2.30(a), which requires the calculation agent to make any choice "in consultation with the parties" and Section 1.14, which requires the calculation agent to exercise its judgement "in good faith and in a commercially reasonable manner".

9.6 Change of reference entity CUSIP or ISIN number

Section 2.30(f) clarifies that if a reference obligation's CUSIP, ISIN or other similar identifier is changed, this in itself changes that reference obligation into a different 'obligation'.

9.7 Weaknesses in the substitute reference obligations provisions

An identifiable weakness in Section 2.30 relates to what happens when the calculation agent cannot identify a substitute reference obligation. The 2003 Definitions assume that because there are no longer any 'obligations', the derivative no longer isolates credit risk and so if a credit event occurs, no credit protection payment can be made. As with the successor provisions, because the 2003 Definitions adopt a rules-based approach to remove subjectivity and make determinations as objective as possible, the reality may be different. Restructurings, for example, may not take account of the credit derivatives market and an equity for debt exchange may result in debt holders making considerable losses on any exchange, but with credit derivative protection buyers left unable to capture that loss in their transactions.

10. Treatment of sovereign reference entities

10.1 Which parts of the 2003 Definitions cover sovereigns?

The 2003 Definitions treat sovereign and non-sovereign reference entities differently, with non-sovereign entities being more comprehensively covered.

Sections 2.2(a) to (g) set out comprehensive objective rules for the calculation agent to determine a successor or successors to a non-sovereign reference entity, while Section 2.2(h) provides only that a successor sovereign reference entity is "any direct or indirect successor(s) to that Reference Entity irrespective of whether such successor(s) assumes any of the obligations of such Reference Entity".

Twelve sections in the 2003 Definitions specifically relate or refer to sovereigns:

- Section 2.2 (provisions for determining a successor);
- Section 2.15 (deliverable obligation);
- Section 2.16 (sovereign restructured deliverable obligation);
- Section 2.19 (method for determining obligations);
- Section 2.20 (method for determining deliverable obligations);
- Section 2.21 (interpretation of provisions);
- Section 2.26 (sovereign);
- Section 2.27 (sovereign agency);
- Section 2.28 (supranational organisation);
- Section 2.29 (domestic currency);
- Section 2.32 (restructuring maturity limitation and fully transferable obligation); and
- Section 3.5 (publicly available information).

These sections cover four areas:

- determining and defining sovereign and quasi sovereign;
- determining a successor;
- determining obligations and deliverable obligations; and
- defining publicly available information.

10.2 What is a sovereign?

Section 2.27 defines 'sovereign' as "any state, political subdivision or government, or any agency, instrumentality, ministry, department or other authority (including, without limiting the forgoing, the central bank) thereof".

This means that bonds issued by a municipal authority (eg, New York) will be sovereign obligations. It is also worth bearing in mind that where a seller is a municipal authority or central bank selling protection on its own country, this will be a self-referencing credit derivative.

The definition of 'sovereign' also refers to "any agency, instrumentality, ministry, department or other authority". These are each defined as a 'sovereign agency' in Section 2.27); a definition that is relevant in the definitions of 'supranational organisation', 'restructuring maturity limitation and fully transferable obligation' and 'publicly available information'.

The 2003 Definitions also deal with quasi sovereigns that are supranational organisations. Section 2.28 defines these as organisations established by two or more sovereigns or two or more sovereign agencies of two or more sovereigns. Sovereign agencies include institutions such as the International Monetary Fund, the European Bank for Reconstruction and Development and the International Bank for Reconstruction and Development. Supranational organisations are referred to in Section 2.19 (method for determining obligations), Section 2.20 (method for determining deliverable obligations) and Section 2.32 (restructuring maturity limitation and fully transferable obligation).

10.3 Sovereigns

Article II contains six sections that provide specific provisions for determining 'obligations' and deliverable obligations for sovereign reference entities. These are:
- Section 2.15 (deliverable obligation);
- Section 2.16 (sovereign restructured deliverable obligation);
- Section 2.19 (method for determining obligations);
- Section 2.20 (method for determining deliverable obligations);
- Section 2.29 (domestic currency); and
- Section 2.32 (restructuring maturity limitation and fully transferable obligation).

Section 2.19 contains 'not sovereign lender' as an obligations characteristic. Where selected, this obligation characteristic excludes any obligation that is "not primarily owed to a Sovereign or Supranational Organisation". Section 2.20 also includes 'not sovereign lender' as a deliverable obligation characteristic.

Section 2.29 (domestic currency), which is used in the 'not domestic currency' obligation characteristic and deliverable obligation characteristic, can have a slightly different meaning depending on whether the reference entity is a sovereign. If the domestic currency is defined in the confirmation, that will be the domestic currency. The ISDA fallback provides that where the domestic currency is not specified, in the case of non-sovereigns it will be the currency or successor currency of the jurisdiction in which the reference entity is organised. In the case of sovereigns, it will be the currency or successor currency of the sovereign. G7 currencies, including the euro, are carved out of the domestic currency definition.

Additionally, the definition of 'sovereign restructured deliverable obligation' sets further parameters for which of a sovereign reference entity's obligations can be delivered in physical settlement. 'Sovereign restructured deliverable obligation' is defined as a sovereign reference entity 'obligation' which:
- is the subject of a restructuring referred to in a credit event notice; and
- meets the deliverable obligation category and any deliverable obligation characteristics on the date immediately preceding the legally effective date of the restructuring.

Whether the obligation would meet the deliverable obligation category and any characteristics after the restructuring date is not taken into account.

Sovereign restructured deliverable obligations are referred to in Section 2.15(c), which provides that only where a restructuring credit event is applicable to a sovereign reference entity will sovereign restructured deliverable obligations be deliverable obligations. This excludes any 'excluded deliverable obligation'. Section 2.15(c) provides that to be a deliverable obligation, a sovereign restructured deliverable obligation must be payable in an amount equal to its outstanding principal balance or its due and payable amount. It must also not be subject to any counterclaim or defence. Counterclaims or defences based on the exceptions carved out in Section 4.1 (credit event) are not deemed to be counterclaims or defences. These are:

- lack of authority or capacity of the reference entity or underlying obligor to enter into the sovereign restructured deliverable obligations or underlying obligation;
- actual or alleged unenforceability, illegality, impossibility or invalidity of the sovereign restructured deliverable obligation or underlying obligation;
- a change in judicial interpretation of any law; and
- the imposition of exchange or capital restrictions.

A sovereign restructured deliverable obligation must also not be subject to any right of set-off by the sovereign reference entity or underlying obligor.

Section 2.32 is the 'modified restructuring' provision. Sovereigns, sovereign agencies and supranational organisations are included in the definition of 'eligible transferee'. In 'modified restructuring', if the deliverable obligation is a loan, it must be capable of being assigned or novated to all eligible transferees.

Notably, in Section 2.33, the 'modified modified restructuring' sister provision, the corresponding definition of 'modified eligible transferee' does not include sovereigns, sovereign agencies or supranational organisations. Thus, where a deliverable obligation is a loan, it does not have to be capable of being assigned or novated to all eligible transferees.

10.4 Defining publicly available information

It is standard market practice for a transaction to provide that, following a credit event, it is a condition to settlement for the notifying party to provide two sources of publicly available information confirming the credit event in a notice of publicly available information. This information must be received from a number of sources, one of which is received from, or published by, a reference entity that is not a party to the transaction. Section 3.5 (publicly available information) also provides that in the case of sovereign reference entities, the information may be received from, or published by, the sovereign reference entity itself.

10.5 How are the 2003 Definitions used in sovereign reference entity credit default swaps?

In August 2004, ISDA released its template Sovereign Master Credit Derivatives Agreement. This contained the market standard terms for Asian, emerging European, Middle Eastern, Japanese, Latin American and Western European sovereigns.

The template had as its credit events failure to pay, obligation acceleration and restructuring.

It has three separate standard elections for obligation category and obligation characteristics depending on the jurisdiction of the reference entity:

- Europe and Japan;
- Asia (ex-Japan); or
- Latin America, the Middle East and emerging Europe.

All of these have 'bond or loan' as the obligation category. There are no obligation characteristics for Europe and Japan, just as with non-sovereign reference entities. Both Asia and Latin America/Middle East/emerging Europe have 'not subordinated', 'not sovereign lender', 'not domestic currency', 'not domestic law' and 'not domestic issuance' specified as obligation characteristics. The difference between the two sets of elections is that Asia additionally selects 'not sovereign lender' as an obligation characteristic.

Deliverable obligations also have different characteristics depending on the jurisdiction of the sovereign. This time there are four separate standard selections: European, Japanese and Latin American, Middle Eastern and emerging European. All specify 'specified currency: standard specified currencies', 'not contingent', 'assignable loan', 'transferable', 'maximum maturity: 30 years' and 'not bearer' as deliverable obligation characteristics.

Asia and Middle Eastern/Latin American/Emerging European all additionally specify 'not subordinated', 'not domestic law' and 'not domestic issuance'. Asia also specifies 'not sovereign lender'. Japan additionally specifies 'not sovereign lender' and 'not domestic issuance'.

Other than this there are no further specific provisions for sovereigns set out in ISDA template documentation (although ISDA does from time to time produce additional provisions which deal with individuals sovereigns, such as the Additional Provisions for the Republic of Hungary: Obligation Characteristics and Deliverable Obligation Characteristics, which were released in August 2004).

Article III – Conditions to settlement

Conditions to settlement: credit event notice

Notifying party: buyer [or seller]

[Notice of physical settlement]

[Notice of publicly available information applicable]

[Public source(s): ☐]

[Specified number: ☐]

1. Overview

Article III (conditions to settlement) covers the conditions which must be satisfied in order for a transaction to be physically or cash settled following the occurrence of a credit event. The article is divided into nine sections:

- settlement (Section 3.1);
- conditions to settlement (Section 3.2);
- credit event notice (Section 3.3);
- notice of physical settlement (Section 3.4);
- publicly available information (Section 3.5);
- notice of publicly available information (Section 3.6);
- public source (Section 3.7);
- specified number (Section 3.8); and
- credit event notice after restructuring (Section 3.9).

These nine provisions cover five areas, as follows:
- the parties' performance of their settlement obligations, once the conditions to settlement are satisfied (Section 3.1);
- the conditions to settlement (Section 3.2);

- the content and timing of delivery of credit event notices and notices of publicly available information (Sections 3.3, 3.6 and 3.4);
- the definition of publicly available information and how much must be provided: 'publicly available information' (Section 3.5); 'public source' (Section 3.7); and 'specified number' (Section 3.8); and
- the occurrence of multiple credit events to the same reference entity for restructuring credit events: (Section 3.9).

In a cash settled transaction, the date on which the conditions to settlement are satisfied is the event determination date,[1] which is the date of delivery of a credit event notice[2] and, if required in the confirmation, a notice of publicly available information.[3] In a physically settled transaction, a notice of physical settlement[4] must also be delivered.

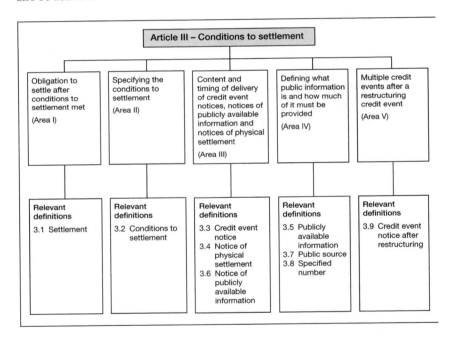

2. Area I – obligation to settle after conditions to settlement met

Section 3.1 provides that once a credit event has occurred and the conditions to settlement have been satisfied, the parties must perform their respective obligations in accordance with the transaction's settlement method: this means, for a cash settled transaction, in accordance with Article VII (terms relating to cash settlement); and for

1   Section 1.8.
2   Section 3.2 (a)(i).
3   Section 3.4.
4   Section 3.6

a physically settled transaction, in accordance with Article VIII (terms relating to physical settlement) and the physical settlement provisions (if applicable) of Article IX (additional representations and agreements of the parties).

3. Area II – specifying the conditions to settlement

Section 3.2 (a) (conditions to settlement) specifies that the conditions to settlement for cash settled transactions are the delivery of a credit event notice and (if specified in the confirmation) a notice of publicly available information. For physically settled transactions it specifies them to be the delivery of a credit event notice, notice of physical settlement and (if specified in the confirmation) a notice of publicly available information. The parties may also add further conditions to settlement in any individual transaction.

Section 3.2(b) sets out exactly how each of the requirements of the credit event notice, notice of publicly available information and notice of physical settlement conditions to settlement are satisfied.

The credit event notice condition to settlement set out in Section 3.2(b) utilises the definitions of:

- 'buyer' (Section 1.19);
- 'seller' (Section 1.20);
- 'notice delivery period' (Section 1.9); and
- 'notifying party' (Section 3.2)(e). 'Notifying party' is defined as each party specified in the confirmation or, if neither the buyer nor the seller is specified as a notifying party, then both of them.

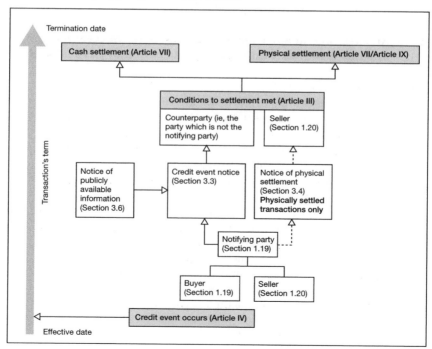

Section 3.2(b) provides that if the buyer is specified as the sole notifying party in the confirmation, then the credit event notice condition to settlement will be satisfied by the buyer delivering the credit event notice to the seller during the notice delivery period.

If both the buyer and seller are specified as notifying parties in the confirmation (or if neither of them is, in which case the fallback is that both parties are notifying parties), then the credit event notice condition to settlement can be satisfied by either party delivering a credit event notice to the other during the notice delivery period.

It may seem unusual for a seller to trigger a credit event which will result in it paying a cash or physical settlement amount to the buyer when it has the option not to; however, a seller may choose to do this to mitigate its losses if a credit event occurs and the seller expects the credit quality of the reference entity to deteriorate further with time. Alternatively, the buyer may have hedged its position by entering into another identical credit default swap as buyer and may wish to trigger the other transaction.

The notice of publicly available information condition to settlement is satisfied by the notifying party delivering a notice of publicly available information to the other party during the notice delivery period.

The notice of physical settlement condition to settlement is satisfied by the buyer delivering a notice of physical settlement to the seller. The notice must be effective no later than 30 calendar days after the event determination date. This means that in physically settled transactions, if the seller fails to meet the notice of physical settlement condition to settlement within 30 calendar days of the event determination date, it will lose credit protection.

4. Area III: content and timing of delivery of credit event notices, notices of publicly available information; and notices of physical settlement

4.1 Credit event notice

Section 3.3 defines 'credit event notice' as an irrevocable notice from a notifying party which describes a credit event. The credit event notice must describe the facts relevant to the credit event in reasonable detail. Importantly, the credit event need not be continuing at the time the credit event notice is delivered. This means, for example, that if a reference entity missed an interest payment on a loan, but subsequently made the interest payment after the applicable grace period had expired, a notifying party could still trigger a failure to pay credit event.

The credit event notice can be delivered by telephone. This is a useful option for market participants which are triggering multiple transactions, if timing is tight or if valuation dates falling on certain dates are desirable.

The credit event notice must be delivered before the end of the notice delivery period (Section 1.10) and must describe a credit event which has occurred between 12:01am, Greenwich Mean Time (GMT), on the effective date and at or prior to 11:59pm GMT on the latest of the scheduled termination date (Section 1.6), and (if applicable) the grace period extension date (Section 1.11) or the repudiation/moratorium evaluation date (Section 4.6(b)).

A credit event notice relating to a credit event which occurred after the scheduled termination date, but on or before the grace period extension date, must relate to a failure to pay credit event and the potential failure to pay must have occurred prior to 11:59pm Greenwich Mean Time on the scheduled termination date. A credit event notice relating to a credit event which occurred after the scheduled termination date, but on or before the repudiation/moratorium evaluation date, must relate to a repudiation/moratorium credit event and the potential repudiation/moratorium must have occurred prior to 11:59pm GMT on the scheduled termination date. Additionally, the repudiation/moratorium extension condition (Section 4.6(d)) must be satisfied. The parties are free, however, to specify an alternative cut-off time in the confirmation.

A form of credit event notice is set out in Exhibit B to the 2003 Definitions. A credit event notice is also subject to the requirements of Section 1.10.

4.2   Notice of publicly available information

Except in cases where it can be difficult to acquire publicly available information, such as credit default swaps referencing specific loans, it is standard practice for a notice of publicly available information to be a condition to settlement.

Section 3.6 defines a 'notice of publicly available information' as an irrevocable notice from the party delivering the credit event notice to the other party. The notice must cite 'publicly available information'; and this publicly available information must confirm that the credit event described in the credit event notice has actually occurred. The notice can confirm this by doing one of two things. It can actually attach the publicly available information (eg, the relevant news cuttings); or it can give 'a description in reasonable detail' of the publicly available information.

Section 3.6 (notice of publicly available information) also states that a notice of publicly available information can be either given on its own or incorporated into a credit event notice. A form of notice of publicly available information is set out in Exhibit B to the 2003 Definitions; however, it is market practice is for the notice of publicly available information to be incorporated into the credit event notice.

The notice of publicly available information is used not only with credit event notices but also with repudiation/moratorium extension notices.

5.   Area IV – defining what public information is and how much of it must be provided

Section 3.6 describes the notice's formalities and how it is delivered, but Sections 3.5, 3.7 and Section 3.8 define what publicly available information is, where it must come from and how much of it there must be for a notice of publicly available information to be valid.

5.1   Publicly available information

Section 3.5 defines what constitutes publicly available information. Publicly available information is information that confirms the facts relevant to determining the credit event described in the credit event notice. Publicly available information can come from five potential sources. First, it can be information that has been published in a

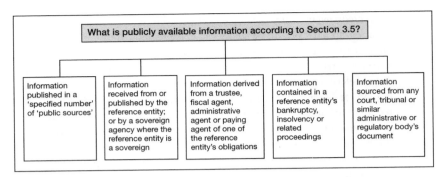

'specified number' of 'public sources'. These terms are defined in Section 3.7 and Section 3.8 respectively.

If either of the parties or their affiliates is the sole source of the information, then the information is not deemed to be publicly available information. A notifying party could be the sole source of publicly available information if it had itself placed a story in a newspaper, which was a public source. When structuring a credit derivative it may be important to consider what the potential sources of publicly available information may be when the reference entity has a limited number of obligations or is domiciled in an emerging market (where any defaults may not always be publicly disclosed). A buyer will try to avoid the situation where it has knowledge that a credit event has occurred in relation to the reference entity, but is unable to produce publicly available information and so cannot meet the conditions to settlement.

Section 3.5 provides five exceptions to this rule:

- One of the parties can be the sole source of publicly available information where it is acting in its capacity as trustee, fiscal agent, administrative agent, clearing agent or paying agent for one of the reference entity's obligations;
- The publicly available information can be information received from or published by reference entity; or by a sovereign agency where the reference entity is a sovereign;
- It can derive from a trustee, fiscal agent, administrative agent or paying agent of one of the reference entity's obligations;
- It can derive from information contained in the reference entity's bankruptcy, insolvency or related proceedings; and
- It can be sourced from information contained in any court, tribunal or similar administrative or regulatory body's document.

If the buyer, acting in a trustee or agency capacity under an obligation, is the sole information source and is also a holder of the obligation which has suffered the credit event, it must deliver a certificate signed by one of its officials of managing director rank (or equivalent), certifying the occurrence of the credit event.

Publicly available information is not usually released for the purposes of triggering a credit event and so does not always give the details necessary to verify the occurrence of a credit event. Publicly available information that is difficult to obtain may include:

- the voting shares percentage necessary to determine whether an obligation is a qualifying affiliate guarantee;
- whether the payment requirement or default requirement levels have been met;
- the necessary grace period; and
- information or details of certain credit events' subjective criteria.

These requirements have therefore been disapplied in Section 3.5(b).

A notice of publicly available information may also be required where the seller serves a repudiation/moratorium extension notice on the buyer, if this is specified in the confirmation.

5.2 Public source and specified number

The first option in the definition of 'publicly available information' in Section 3.5(a)(i) provides that publicly available information can be information that has been published in a specified number of public sources. The definition of a 'public source' is set out in Section 3.7. The relevant public source can be specified in the confirmation itself, for example the *Financial Times* and Dow Jones News Wire. Most commonly, though, the public sources are not set out in the confirmation and the parties rely on the fallback sources detailed in Section 3.7.

These are: Bloomberg Service, Dow Jones Telerate Service, Reuter Monitor Money Rates Services, Dow Jones News Wire, *Wall Street Journal*, *New York Times*, *Nihon Keizai Shinbun*, *Asahi Shinbun*, *Yomiuri Shinbun*, *Financial Times*, *La Tribune*, *Les Echos* and *The Australian Financial Review*. Successor publications are also included. Additionally, the main source(s) of business news in the country in which the reference entity is organised are also public sources, as are "any other internationally recognised published or electronically displayed news sources".

In summary, to give a notice of publicly available information which meets the conditions to settlement, the notice must meet all of the requirements of Section 3.6 and contain public available information which meets the criteria set out in Section 3.5 from the specified number of public sources (Sections 3.8 and 3.7 respectively).

Hypothetical case study: Finn Investments and Becca Holdings – meeting the credit event notice and notice of publicly available information conditions to settlement

Finn Investments bought credit protection on Polo Corporation, an Italian sportswear company, from Becca Holdings in a $10 million five-year cash settled credit default swap. The parties entered into the credit default swap on December 3 2005. The following year, Polo Corporation filed for bankruptcy on November 24 2006.

Both Finn Investments and Becca Holdings were specified as notifying parties in the confirmation and so were entitled to meet the conditions to

---

settlement. However, because of the severity of the credit event, it was only ever likely that Finn Investments would trigger a credit event.

The confirmation set out the following conditions to settlement:

3. Floating payment:

    Conditions to settlement: *Credit event notice*
                                 Notifying party: buyer or seller
                                 Notice of publicly available information:
                                 Applicable public source(s): 2

To meet the conditions to settlement, Finn Investments was required to deliver a credit event notice and a notice of publicly available information, with two sources of publicly available information, to Becca Holdings.

Finn Investments determined that Polo's bankruptcy was a bankruptcy credit event fulfilling the criteria set out in Section 4.2 (bankruptcy). It then sourced two pieces of publicly available information relating to the Polo Corporation bankruptcy, which met the requirements of Section 3.7. The first piece of publicly available information was an article from the *New York Times*, and the second an article from the *Financial Times*. Finn Investments checked the articles to confirm that they fulfilled the relevant criteria of Section 3.5. It determined that each public source confirmed the facts relevant to determine that the bankruptcy credit event had occurred.

Finn Investments drafted a combined credit event notice and notice of publicly available information.

The notice read:

To: Becca Holdings
Fax: +44 20 7826 9718
Date: November27 2006

CREDIT EVENT AND NOTICE OF PUBLICLY AVAILABLE INFORMATION
Credit Derivative Transaction Details: Reference: JT234324 Trade Date: November 27 2005. Effective Date: December 3 2005. Reference Entity: Polo Corporation.
    Reference is made to the Credit Derivative Transaction described above (the **'Transaction'**), *between us, as Buyer, and you, as Seller. Capitalised terms used and not otherwise defined in this letter shall have the meanings given them in the confirmation of the Transaction.*
    This letter is our Credit Event Notice to you that a Bankruptcy Credit Event occurred pursuant to Section 4.2(c) of the 2003 ISDA Credit Derivatives Definitions with respect to Polo Corporation when Parma Bankruptcy Court gave a judgment of bankruptcy against Polo Corporation. This letter also comprises our notice of publicly available information with respect to this credit event and we hereby provide you with two public sources of publicly available information attached hereto.

> *Nothing in this letter shall be construed as a waiver of any of the rights we may have with respect to the Transaction.*
>
> *Yours faithfully*
> **R Jimena**
> **Legal Counsel**
>
> The credit event notice attached the two sources of publicly available information:
>
> **New York Times:** *November 25 2006*
> **Polo Corporation declared bankruptcy**
> *Yesterday the Italian sportswear manufacturer Polo Corporation, one of the world's leading leisurewear companies employing over 30,000 people in 28 countries, was declared bankrupt by Parma Bankruptcy Court....*
>
> **Financial Times:** *November 25 2006*
> **Creditors finally throw in the towel on Polo**
> *As had been widely predicted by City analysts, Polo Corporation was declared bankrupt yesterday by Parma Bankruptcy Company, the ailing company had at its peak....*
>
> Finn Investments delivered the credit event notice and notice of publicly available information to Becca Holdings on November 27 2006 at 3:55pm, meeting the conditions to settlement and crystallising this date as the event determination date.

5.3   Notice of physical settlement

For physically settled transactions, Section 3.2 provides for an additional condition to settlement. A transaction's event determination date is crystallised when the credit event notice and notice of publicly available information are effective (Section 1.10), but in physically settled transactions, the credit protection buyer must deliver a notice of physical settlement within 30 calendar days of the event determination date. The notice is irrevocable, but can be amended as many times as the buyer wishes prior to the end of this 30-day period.

A notice of physical settlement must state that the buyer will physically settle the transaction and contains a detailed description of the deliverable obligations that it intends to deliver. This detailed description includes the outstanding principal balance or due and payable amount of each deliverable obligation it intends to deliver, as well as any available CUSIP or ISIN numbers (or, if not available, the rate and tenor of the deliverable obligation).

Section 3.4 details the requirements and formalities of a notice of physical settlement. A form of notice of publicly available information is set out in Exhibit C to the 2003 Definitions.

Section 3.4 provides that notice:
- must be from the buyer to the seller;
- can be by telephone; and
- must meet the requirements for notices set out in Section 1.10.

The notice must state that the buyer irrevocably intends to physically settle the transaction and contain a detailed description of the deliverable obligations that it intends to deliver to the seller, including the outstanding principal balance or the due and payable amount

The buyer can change its mind about the deliverable obligations that it intends to deliver to the seller as many times as it likes, provided that the notice is effective on or prior to the physical settlement date. Section 4.3 also provides that the buyer can correct any errors or inconsistencies in the detailed description of the deliverable obligations by means of an amended notice up until the delivery date.

Hypothetical case study: notice of physical settlement –
Finn Investments, Howe PLC and Polo Corporation

Finn Investments has also entered into a credit default swap on similar terms to those described above with Howe PLC, where it also bought credit protection on Polo Corporation. In contrast, this was a physically settled transaction, and so required Finn Investments to deliver a notice of physical settlement to Howe PLC on or before 30 calendar days after the event determination date.

Finn Investments delivered a credit event notice and notice of publicly available information to Howe PLC on November 27 2006, crystallising that date as the event determination date. Finn Investments then had until 4:00pm (GMT) on December 27 2006 (ie, 30 calendar days after the event determination date) to deliver a notice of physical settlement to Howe PLC.

Finn Investments knew that a $100 million floating rate note issued by Polo Corporation was trading at the cheapest price. The bond met the deliverable obligation category and characteristics and so Finn Investments selected it as the deliverable obligation that it intended to use to physically settle the transaction.

On December 12 2006, Finn Investments sent a notice of physical settlement to Howe PLC with the following text:

To: Howe PLC
Fax: +44 20 7556 9797
Date: December 12 2006

NOTICE OF PHYSICAL SETTLEMENT

Credit Derivative Transaction Details: Reference: PR83835 Trade Date: November 27 2005. Effective Date: December 3 2005. Reference Entity: Polo Corporation.

> *Reference is made to the Credit Derivative Transaction described above (the* **'Transaction'**)*, between us, as seller, and you, as Buyer. Capitalised terms used and not otherwise defined in this letter shall have the meanings given them in the confirmation of the Transaction.*
>
> *This letter constitutes a Notice of Physical Settlement. Any capitalised term not otherwise defined in this letter will have the meaning, if any, assigned to such term in the confirmation of the Transaction or, if no meaning is specified therein, in the 2003 ISDA Credit Derivatives Definitions.*
>
> *We hereby confirm that we will settle the Transaction and require performance by you in accordance with the Physical Settlement Method. Subject to the terms of the Transaction, we will deliver to you on or before the Physical Settlement Date, $10 million of the following Deliverable Obligation:*
>
> *$100 million Floating Rate Notes due 2015 issued by Polo Corporation (ISIN: XS01838535).*
>
> *Yours sincerely*
> **R Jimena**
> **Legal Counsel**

Finn Investments had now met the transaction's conditions to settlement. On November 23 2006, Finn Investments noticed that the deliverable obligation that it had selected was no longer the cheapest to deliver obligation and one of Polo Corporation's fixed rate notes was trading at a lower price. Finn Investments sent an amended and restated notice of physical settlement to Howe PLC selecting the fixed rate bond as the deliverable obligation that it intended to deliver. Physical settlement then took place in accordance with 2003 Definitions.

5.4   Area V – multiple credit events after a restructuring credit event

Except for restructuring credit events, the conditions to settlement can be satisfied only once per reference entity. A restructuring credit event can have a relatively minor effect on creditworthiness;[5] and so the notifying party is permitted to deliver multiple restructuring credit event notices each time triggering a credit event for only part (the exercise amount)[6] of the reference entity notional amount.

Section 3.9 (credit event notice after restructuring) provides a framework for allowing a notifying party to trigger a credit event in relation to only part of a transaction when a restructuring credit event occurs. In transactions where restructuring is specified as a credit event, this right applies unless otherwise stated.

When a restructuring credit event occurs, the notifying party can state in its credit event notice that it is meeting the conditions to settlement either in relation to the full reference entity notional amount or to just a part of it.

---

5   Following a restructuring event in relation to Xerox, the final price achieved in relation Xerox's obligations was approximately 95%.

6   Each exercise amount.

If the notifying party decides to deliver a credit event notice specifying only a part of the reference entity notional amount and a further credit event occurs in relation to that reference entity, then a notifying party (which potentially can be either party) can meet the conditions to settlement either partially, in the same manner as before in the case of a further restructuring credit event, or fully for the remaining reference entity notional amount for any other credit event.

Therefore, if a restructuring credit event notice is delivered specifying that it applies to less than the full reference entity notional amount, the calculation agent must make various adjustments to the transaction, such as to reduce the transaction's notional amount. It must do this in consultation with the parties.

If this happens, Section 3.9 provides that there are deemed to be two transactions. The new transaction's notional amount is deemed to be the exercise amount and the old transaction's notional amount is deemed to be its existing notional amount less the exercise amount. The calculation agent will then make any necessary modifications to preserve the economic effects of the two transactions. The new transaction will then be settled in accordance with the 2003 Definitions.

Section 3.9 specifies that the exercise amount for a credit event other than restructuring will automatically be for the whole of the floating rate payer calculation amount.

Section 3.9 also provides that the minimum exercise amount for a restructuring credit event is 1 billion units of the floating rate payer calculation amount currency. An exception to this is where the floating rate payer calculation amount currency is Japanese yen, in which case the minimum exercise amount is Y100 million. In each case any exercise amount can be exercised only in integral multiples of these amounts.

Hypothetical case study:
Credit event notice after restructuring

Thorburn PLC entered into a $10 million credit default swap with Pettigrew PLC, where Thorburn bought credit protection on Tally Corporation, a US technology company. Tally Corporation had a liquidity crisis and restructured its outstanding loans with its bankers, to lengthen their maturities.

Tally still had a strong business and after the restructuring of its bonds and loans were trading at 85% of their face amount. Thorburn was not convinced of Tally's long- term financial health, but at the same time wished to take the benefit of some of the credit protection that it had purchased in case Tally's obligations recovered to 100% of their face value and no credit event occurred during the credit default swap's term.

Thorburn determined that a restructuring credit event had occurred and, pursuant to Section 3.9 (credit event after restructuring) of the 2003 Definitions, decided to deliver a credit event after restructuring in relation to less than the full floating rate payer calculation amount. Thorburn delivered a credit event notice and notice of publicly available information to Pettigrew. The credit event

---

notice specified that it related to an 'exercise amount' of $3 million, (ie, 30% of the floating rate payer calculation amount), and an integral multiple of 1 million currency units.

This meant that there were now deemed to be two credit derivatives transactions: a transaction for $3 million for which Thorburn had met the conditions to settlement; and a transaction (ie, the old transaction) for $7 million for which the conditions to settlement had not been met.

Pettigrew was also the calculation agent and made the amendments to the transactions which were necessary to preserve its economic effect (in accordance with Sections 3.9 and 1.14(d) (calculation agent)).

The next year Tally's situation worsened further and it ended up filing for Chapter 11 bankruptcy protection. This meant that a bankruptcy credit event had occurred. Following Tally's bankruptcy its obligations were trading at 40% of their notional amount. Thorburn delivered a credit event notice and notice of publicly available information to Pettigrew specifying a bankruptcy credit event in relation to the full floating rate payer calculation amount of the remaining 'old' transaction.

Article IV – Credit events

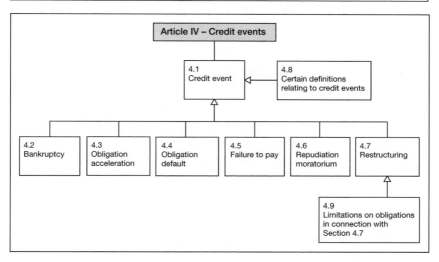

1. Overview

Article IV relates to the credit events themselves. There are six credit events and Section 4.1 (credit event) lists them. These are then defined in Sections 4.2 to 4.7:

- bankruptcy (Section 4.2);
- failure to pay (Section 4.3);
- obligation acceleration (Section 4.4);
- obligation default (Section 4.5);
- repudiation/moratorium (Section 4.6); and
- restructuring (Section 4.7).

Section 4.1 also sets out various circumstances which will not prevent an event that otherwise meets the criteria in any of the individual credit event definitions from being a credit event. Section 4.8 (certain definitions relating to credit events) sets out four further definitions: 'default requirement', 'governmental authority', 'obligation currency' and 'payment requirement'; these are used in different criteria for determining whether certain credit events have occurred. Section 4.9 (limitation on obligations in connection with Section 4.7) provides a further limitation on the restructuring credit event by providing that this can occur only in relation to a multiple holder obligation (ie, an obligation held at the time of the restructuring credit event by at least four non-affiliated holders and whose terms require that 66.66% of the holders consent to the restructuring).

Credit events: The following credit event[s] shall apply to this transaction:

      [Bankruptcy]
      [Failure to pay]
         [Grace period extension applicable]
         [Grace period:]
         Payment requirement: [   ]]
      [Obligation default]
      [Obligation acceleration]
      [Repudiation/moratorium]
      [Restructuring]
         [Restructuring maturity limitation and fully transferable
           obligation: [Applicable]]
         [Modified restructuring maturity limitation and conditionally
           transferable obligation: [Applicable]]
         [Multiple holder obligation: [Applicable]]
         [Default requirement:]

---

2. Credit event

Section 4.1 defines 'credit event' as meaning "one or more of bankruptcy, failure to pay, obligation acceleration, obligation default, repudiation/moratorium or restructuring". The definitions for each of these credit events are then provided in the immediately following sections. Only those credit events that are specified in a confirmation will be credit events for any relevant transaction. There are no fallbacks. The credit events that the parties select are likely to depend upon relevant market standards for the reference entity's jurisdiction and characterisation.

The market standards terms for reference entity/type jurisdiction vary as follows. Both bankruptcy and failure to pay are credit events for each of the reference entity-type standard terms (ie Western European entities; Western European insurance entities; European emerging market entities; Australian and New Zealand entities; Japanese entities; Singaporean entities; Asian entities; North American investment grade entities, insurance entities and high yield entities).

Restructuring is a credit event for all of the standard terms except for North

American insurance entities and high yield entities. Obligation acceleration is a credit event only for Western European insurance entities and European emerging market entities. Neither repudiation/moratorium nor obligation default is a credit event for any of the 10 standard terms relating to non-sovereigns. The standard terms for sovereign reference entities have failure to pay; repudiation/moratorium and restructuring as the applicable credit events (but not bankruptcy).

The greatest variations between the different sets of standard terms relate to how the different credit events are modified by the grace period options set out in Article I and the restructuring options predominately set out in Article II. This is discussed in more depth below.

In addition to providing the definition of 'credit event', Section 4.1 tries to enhance objectivity when determining a credit event. It does this by carving out four sets of common law defences and circumstances that a party could potentially use to argue that a particular credit event was not valid. These are where:

- the reference entity is alleged to or actually lacks the authority to enter into an obligation or guarantee an underlying obligation;
- any obligation or underlying obligation is alleged to be or actually is unenforceable, illegal, invalid or impossible;
- the relevant circumstance or defence arises from a law, a court or administrative decision or interpretation, or similar; or
- a monetary or other authority changes or imposes exchange controls or capital restrictions.

**Hypothetical case study:
determining a credit event for an uncertain obligation**

Montrose PLC entered into a $10 million physically settled credit default swap with Newport PLC, where it bought credit protection on the City of Arbol, an American municipal authority. Arbol had one large outstanding bond issue of $70 million, which represented 80% of its outstanding debt. Arbol was unable to balance its debts and defaulted on the $70 million obligation. A new local government was elected and, on reviewing the background to the bond issue, noticed that Arbol did not actually have the power to issue bonds. A court ruling agreed and the obligation was ruled invalid, leaving the bondholders without remedy against Arbol. Most bondholders lost all of their money, but Montrose was able to trigger the credit default swap. The $70 million bond was only an 'obligation' for the purposes of triggering the credit event. The carve-outs in Section 4.1, though, relate only to the definition of credit event; they do not extend to the definition of 'obligation' or 'deliverable obligation', meaning that the 8% bond was not a deliverable obligation. This meant that Montrose could not deliver the $70 million and instead had to purchase another Arbol 'obligation' – a loan – and deliver this instead.

---

3.   Bankruptcy

Bankruptcy is the only credit event which relates to the reference entity itself rather than its obligations. The definition gives a detailed list of events that constitute bankruptcy. Subject to some minor changes, Section 4.2 tracks Section 5(a)(vii) of the 1992 ISDA Master Agreement.

Section 4.2 provides a list of eight circumstances which will be deemed to constitute a bankruptcy event. The breadth of the circumstances is first, to ensure that any determination made will be as objective as possible; and second, and contrastingly, in recognition that because bankruptcy laws vary significantly between different jurisdictions, the definition must be sufficiently broad to capture any events analogous to the Anglo-American concept of bankruptcy, which may not necessarily constitute an actual bankruptcy in the relevant jurisdiction.

These circumstances can be summarised as follows. It will be a bankruptcy credit event if the reference entity is dissolved other than due to a consolidation, amalgamation or merger; and likewise if the reference entity becomes insolvent or unable to pay its debts, or fails to pay them when due. If the reference entity admits in writing "in a judicial, regulatory, or administrative proceeding or filing" that it is unable generally to pay it debts when they become due, this will also be a bankruptcy credit event; as will if the reference entity makes a "general assignment, arrangement, or composition with or for the benefit of its creditors"; or where the reference entity has instituted or has had instituted against it a proceeding seeking a bankruptcy or insolvency judgment or similar relief.

If a petition is presented or proceeding initiated requesting that the reference entity be wound up or liquidated, this will be a bankruptcy credit event only if:

- it results in an actual bankruptcy or insolvency judgment, or an order for relief, winding-up or liquidation; or
- the petition or proceeding is not "dismissed, discharged, stayed or retrained" within 30 calendar days of it being presented.

This is to prevent bankruptcy proceedings against a reference entity, which are without merit being used to trigger a credit event.

It is also a bankruptcy credit event if the reference entity itself passes a resolution for it to be wound up or go into an official management or liquidation, other than due to a consolidation, amalgamation or merger. Appointments made for certain of the roles (eg, liquidators, receivers and trustees) relating to bankruptcies which apply to all or substantially all of the reference entity's assets are bankruptcy credit events.

If a secured party takes possession of all or substantially all of the reference entity's assets, this will be a bankruptcy credit event. This will also be the case where a "distress, execution, attachment, sequestration, or other legal process" is applied to all or substantially all of the reference entity's assets and the secured party maintains possession. In each case, it will not constitute a bankruptcy credit event if the relevant process is "dismissed, discharged, stayed, or restrained" within 30 calendar days.

Finally, Section 4.2 provides a catch-all provision stating that any event under the applicable laws of any jurisdiction which has an "analogous effect" to any of the other circumstances listed in Section 4.2 will also be a bankruptcy credit event.

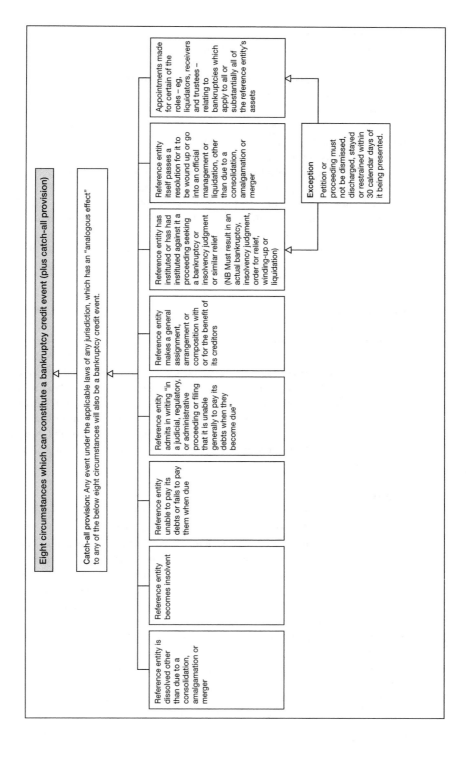

Eight circumstances which can constitute a bankruptcy credit event (plus catch-all provision)

Catch-all provision: Any event under the applicable laws of any jurisdiction, which has an "analogous effect" to any of the below eight circumstances will also be a bankruptcy credit event.

Reference entity is dissolved other than due to a consolidation, amalgamation or merger

Reference entity becomes insolvent

Reference entity unable to pay its debts or fails to pay them when due

Reference entity admits in writing "in a judicial, regulatory, or administrative proceeding or filing that it is unable generally to pay its debts when they become due"

Reference entity makes a general assignment, arrangement or composition with or for the benefit of its creditors

Reference entity has instituted or has had instituted against it a proceeding seeking a bankruptcy or insolvency judgment or similar relief

(NB Must result in an actual bankruptcy, insolvency judgment, order for relief, winding-up or liquidation)

Reference entity itself passes a resolution for it to be wound up or go into an official management or liquidation, other than due to a consolidation, amalgamation or merger

Appointments made for certain of the roles – eg, liquidators, receivers and trustees – relating to bankruptcies which apply to all or substantially all of the reference entity's assets

Exception

Petition or proceeding must not be dismissed, discharged, stayed or restrained within 30 calendar days of it being presented.

4. Obligation acceleration

When an obligation is accelerated, it means that following an event of default the noteholders, lenders or trustee declares that the obligation is immediately due and payable. Section 4.3 limits the obligation acceleration credit event to where the obligation's lenders or bondholders accelerate a greater amount of one or more obligations in aggregate totalling more than the default requirement (Section 4.8(a) (default requirement)). Carved out of the obligation acceleration credit event is where the event of default under the obligation is a failure to pay, which is instead covered by the provisions of the failure to pay credit event.

Section 4.8 (certain definitions relating to credit events) provides that the default requirement can be specified in the relevant confirmation. If so, it will be this specified amount or "its equivalent in the relevant obligation currency". If no default requirement amount is specified, the fallback default requirement amount is $10 million or "its equivalent in the relevant obligation currency". 'Obligation currency' itself is defined in Section 4.8(c) as "the currency or currencies in which an obligation is denominated". In each case, the equivalent of the obligation currency is calculated as of the occurrence of the relevant credit event.

5. Obligation default

Obligation default, which is set out in Section 4.4, mirrors the obligation acceleration credit event except that there is no requirement for the obligation to be accelerated following the event of default. Obligation acceleration and obligation default are alternative credit events and only one can be selected per reference entity. Obligation default, though, is not a popular choice and is not specified in any of ISDA's standard terms for reference entities. This is because a default which the relevant parties to an obligation decide to waive will most probably not have a significant impact on the overall credit quality of the relevant reference entity, and if it does the default will most probably result in a restructuring, which may in turn trigger a restructuring credit event.

6. Failure to pay

The failure to pay credit event is defined in Section 4.5. A failure to pay credit event will occur if the reference entity fails to pay any amounts equal to or greater than the payment requirement under any of its obligations. The failure to pay must take place after the expiration of an obligation's grace period (this period is set out in the obligation itself) or after the satisfaction of any conditions precedent to that grace period commencing. If an obligation does not have a grace period, or if it has a grace period of less than three business days, then the grace period is deemed to be three business days. The provisions relating to determining a grace period are set out in Section 1.12 (grace period, grace period business day).

Section 4.8 provides that the payment requirement can be specified in the relevant confirmation. If so it will be this specified amount or "its equivalent in the relevant obligation currency". If no payment requirement amount is specified, the fallback default requirement amount is $1 million or "its equivalent in the relevant obligation currency". 'Obligation currency' itself is defined in Section 4.8(c) as "the currency or currencies in which an obligation is denominated". In each case, the equivalent of the obligation currency is calculated as of the occurrence of the relevant credit event.

Although the failure to pay credit event applies for each of ISDA's standard terms for reference entities for both sovereigns and non-sovereigns, the credit event is modified in the case of European emerging market entities and for sovereigns in emerging European countries, Latin American countries and Middle Eastern countries, by applying the 2003 Definitions grace period extension provisions.

7. Repudiation/moratorium

7.1 General

Under English law, a party repudiates its debts or obligations if it states that it does not intend to honour them. A moratorium occurs if a party declares that it intends to delay honouring its obligations. Both a repudiation and a moratorium can occur prior to any actual default or failure to pay. Both are also most closely associated with the acts of sovereigns. It is market practice for the repudiation/moratorium credit event to apply only to sovereign reference entities; and this credit event is not included in any of ISDA's standard terms relating to non-sovereign reference entities. The ambit of this credit event was wider in the predecessor to the 2003 Definitions, but the circumstances in which a repudiation/moratorium credit event will apply where a failure to pay credit event will not are so limited that it is relatively rare that the repudiation/moratorium credit event will be used when meeting the conditions to settlement.

The repudiation/moratorium credit event is defined in Section 4.6. It has two limbs which must both be satisfied in order for a repudiation/moratorium credit event to occur.

First, a reference entity's authorised officer or, alternatively, a governmental authority (eg, a minister of finance) must repudiate or declare a moratorium on any of the reference entity's obligations. This must be in an aggregate amount of at least the default requirement (as defined in Section 4.8). This first test is defined in Section 4.7(c) as a 'potential repudiation/moratorium'.

Second, this potential repudiation/moratorium must be followed by an actual failure to pay or restructuring on or prior to the repudiation/moratorium evaluation date (Section 4.6(d)). This actual failure to pay is determined without regard to the payment requirement and a restructuring will be determined without regard to the default requirement.

7.2 Repudiation/moratorium evaluation date

A repudiation/moratorium credit event becomes significant in two circumstances. The first is where the repudiation/moratorium occurs before the scheduled termination date, but the actual failure to pay or restructuring credit event occurs after the scheduled termination date, but during the notice delivery period (as defined in Section 1.9 (notice delivery period)). The second is where the failure to pay is for an amount less than the payment requirement (ie, usually $1 million) or if the restructuring relates to an aggregate amount of obligations of less than the default requirement (ie, usually $10 million).

ISDA's standard terms for sovereign reference entities include both failure to pay and restructuring as credit events, which means that outside of the two circumstances detailed in the paragraph above, the repudiation/moratorium credit event replicates the protection provided by the failure to pay and restructuring credit events.

So the repudiation/moratorium credit event is intended to provide a similar option to parties as the grace period extension provisions – that is, the parties can look back during the notice delivery period at an event which occurred during the transaction's term to see whether it represented the moment when the reference entity's credit quality declined or whether the event was not in fact significant.

The repudiation/moratorium evaluation date is defined in Section 4.6(b). It is the end date by which the actual failure to pay or restructuring must have occurred in order for there to be a repudiation/moratorium credit event.

The potential repudiation/moratorium must occur before the scheduled termination date. The length of the evaluation period, between the potential repudiation/moratorium and the repudiation/moratorium evaluation date, will vary depending on whether the obligations to which the potential repudiation/ moratorium relates include bonds.

If the obligations do include bonds, the repudiation/moratorium evaluation date will be the later of 60 calendar days following the potential repudiation/moratorium date and the bond's first post-potential repudiation/moratorium payment date (taking into account any grace period, pursuant to Section 1.12).

If the obligations do not include bonds, the repudiation/moratorium evaluation date will be 60 calendar days after the potential repudiation/moratorium.

7.3 Repudiation/moratorium extension condition

The repudiation/moratorium extension condition, if satisfied, allows a repudiation/moratorium credit event to take place after the scheduled termination date during the notice delivery period (ie, in the 14 calendar days following the scheduled termination date). This works as follows: if a potential repudiation/ moratorium has occurred pre-scheduled termination date, but the repudiation/ moratorium evaluation date cannot occur until after the scheduled termination date, then if the repudiation/moratorium extension condition is satisfied, the parties can 'wait and see' during the post-scheduled termination date notice delivery period, to see whether the potential repudiation/moratorium turns into an actual repudiation moratorium. If it does, then the notifying party must deliver a credit event notice and, if applicable, a notice of publicly available information within the 14-calendar-day post-scheduled termination date notice delivery period.

The 'repudiation/moratorium extension condition' is defined in Section 4.6(d) as a condition which is satisfied by the notifying party delivering a repudiation/ moratorium extension notice.

'Repudiation/moratorium extension notice' is in turn defined in Section 4.6(e) as being an irrevocable notice describing a potential repudiation/moratorium that has occurred on or after the transaction's effective date, but on or prior to its scheduled termination date. The notice must contain a description in reasonable detail of the facts relevant to determining the potential repudiation/moratorium and indicate the date when it occurred. The notice may, if necessary, be given by telephone, and must comply with the other requirements of Section 1.10 (requirements regarding notices).

The confirmation may also require that the repudiation/moratorium extension notice be accompanied by a notice of publicly available information. The requirements for the notice of publicly available information are the same as for a notice of publicly available information for a credit event, and the notice of publicly available information can be incorporated into the repudiation/moratorium extension notice. A form of the repudiation/moratorium extension notice is set out in Exhibit D to the 2003 Definitions.

Hypothetical case study: the repudiation/moratorium credit event

Beat Partners entered into a $10 million credit default swap with Iglesias Corporation under which Beat bought credit protection on the Republic of Gades, a South American sovereign. The transaction's effective date was October 17 2005 and its scheduled termination date was October 17 2007. The credit events were failure to pay, repudiation/moratorium and restructuring. In accordance with ISDA's standard terms, a Latin American sovereign grace period extension was applicable to the failure to pay credit event.

On August 15 2007, following tense elections, a new Marxist government was elected. The new finance minister immediately declared that, going forward, the republic would not pay any of its international bond or loan obligations. This amounted to a potential repudiation/moratorium pursuant to Section 4.6(c) of the 2003 Definitions, as an authorised officer of the reference entity had "declared...a moratorium...with respect to one or more Obligations in an aggregate amount of not less than the Default Requirement". In the terms of the confirmation, the default requirement was the ISDA fallback of $10 million and the republic had approximately $1 billion of obligations outstanding, spread across three eurobonds and two international syndicated loans.

The first interest payment date under any of these obligations was October 20 2007, three calendar days after the credit default swap's scheduled termination date. In addition, the relevant obligation, a $50 million floating rate bond, had the benefit of a five-day grace period, meaning that no actual default could occur until October 25 2007. This meant that that the repudiation/moratorium evaluation date (as defined in Section 4.6(b)) could not occur until "the later of ...60 days after the potential repudiation/moratorium" – that is, October 14 2007 – and "the first payment date under any...Bond...after the...potential repudiation/moratorium", which, taking account of the bond's grace period, was October 25 2007. This was after the credit default swap's October 17 2007 scheduled termination date, but before the end of its 14-

---

calendar-day post-scheduled termination date notice delivery period (in accordance with Section 1.9 (notice delivery period)).

It seemed inevitable that there would indeed be a failure to pay. To gain the benefit of credit protection, Beat prepared a repudiation/moratorium extension notice, which it delivered to Iglesias on the day before the scheduled termination date: October 16 2007. This satisfied the repudiation/moratorium extension condition, defined in Section 4.6 (c).

The notice read:

To: Iglesias Corporation
Fax: +44 20 7458 3434
Date: October 16 2007

Repudiation/Moratorium Extension Notice
Credit Derivative Transaction Details: Reference: ERE838434 Trade Date: October 10 2005. Effective Date: October 17 2005. Reference Entity: Republic of Gades.

*Reference is made to the Credit Derivative Transaction described above (the '**Transaction**'), between us, as Seller, and you, as Buyer. Capitalised terms used and not otherwise defined in this letter shall have the meanings given them in the confirmation of the Transaction.*

This letter is our Repudiation/Moratorium Extension Notice to you that a Potential/Repudiation Moratorium occurred with respect to Republic of Gades on August 15 2007 when the Minister of Finance, Juan Rodriguez, issued a press release stating that the Republic of Gades would not honour any of its international bond and loan obligations going forward.

Nothing in this letter shall be construed as a waiver of any of the rights we may have with respect to the Transaction.

Yours faithfully
M Falla
Legal Counsel

As the minister of finance had promised, the Republic of Gades failed to make an interest payment on October 20 2007 on its $50 million floating rate bond. The bond's grace period expired on October 25 2007, without payment having been made. This constituted a failure to pay. The bond had quarterly interest payments and its current annual floating rate interest payment of USD LIBOR plus margin stood at 7%; the missed payment therefore amounted to $875,000. This would not have met the $1 million payment requirement for a failure to pay credit event, but was a failure to pay nonetheless, as the payment requirement is not taken into account for the purpose of a failure to pay relating to a repudiation/moratorium credit event.

> On October 25 2007 Beat delivered a credit event notice and notice of publicly available information to Iglesias meeting the transaction's conditions to settlement and crystallising an event determination date.

8. Restructuring

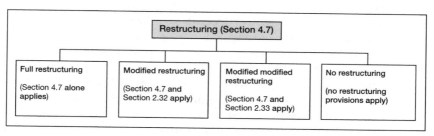

When a corporate or sovereign finds that it is unable to pay its debts when they fall due, this can be either because it simply does not have enough money to do so and is unlikely to have in the future, or because it has had a cash-flow crisis – that is, it is unable to pay its debts now, but with some adjustment of maturity dates, modification of interest rates or rolling over of loans, it will be able to meet its obligations in the future. Corporate and sovereign debt restructurings are regular occurrences in the capital markets: the Republic of Argentina, Marconi, Xerox and Conseco are all recent examples.

The restructuring credit event is defined in Section 4.7. In addition, several other provisions in the 2003 Definitions also relate directly to restructuring:

- sovereign restructured deliverable obligation (Section 2.16);
- restructuring maturity limitation and fully transferable obligation (Section 2.32);
- modified restructuring maturity limitation and conditionally transferable obligation (Section 2.33); and
- credit event notice after restructuring (Section 3.9).

Other provisions also treat events surrounding the restructuring credit event differently from other credit events:

- calculation agent (Section 1.14(d)); and
- repudiation/moratorium (Section 4.6).

Restructurings are rarely carried out with the credit derivatives market primarily in mind – not unless the creditor banks or bondholders involved in the restructuring have also hedged their positions with credit derivatives.

Restructuring is problematic as a credit event for two reasons. First, if credit derivatives are intended to isolate and separately trade credit risk, with payments made from seller to buyer intended to reflect a decline in the creditworthiness of the reference entity, then a restructuring which prevents a further decline in the creditworthiness of the reference entity (eg, perhaps through lengthening the maturities of its bonds and the reference entity granting security over its assets) is arguably a contradiction, especially if in the long term the reference entity's creditworthiness improves. Other than in the case of sovereigns, the fact that a reference entity does not file for bankruptcy demonstrates that its directors, shareholders and creditors believe in the reference entity's long-term financial health.

The second reason is what has become known as the 'moral hazard of the cheapest to deliver option'. Restructurings do not always relate to all of the reference entity's obligations. The creditors of restructured obligations are likely to seek greater protection for agreeing to any restructuring, such as the reference entity granting security over its assets. This can mean that a restructured obligation trades at a much higher price than those obligations of the reference entity which have not been restructured. Following a credit event, the reference obligation valued in cash settled transactions or the deliverable obligation delivered in physically settled transactions need not be the restructured obligation. Once again, this can lead to a contradiction: the event which has occurred to the restructured obligation which represents the decline in creditworthiness of the reference entity is measured against other obligations which may now be worth far less than the restructured obligation.

It is arguable that these fundamental problems should mean that restructuring should not be a credit event at all, but for regulatory capital reasons restructuring is a necessary, if flawed, credit event.

For the above reasons, restructuring is the most controversial of the six credit events. It has faced tough market tests over the past few years, which have resulted in four variations of it being used in ISDA's various standard terms for reference entities. These four variations are known as:

- full restructuring;
- modified restructuring;
- modified modified restructuring; and
- no restructuring.

Which is which is not apparent from looking at the 2003 Definitions themselves, where the only reference to modified restructuring relates in fact to the modified modified restructuring variation, and modified modified restructuring is not mentioned at all. Other than for no restructuring, the variations do not affect whether a restructuring credit event has occurred, but affect instead the deliverable obligations which can be delivered in physically settled transactions following the credit event.

The parties to any transaction will select which variation applies, depending on which category of ISDA's standard terms for reference entities applies. The ISDA standard terms apply full restructuring only for Japanese, Singaporean and Asian reference entities and sovereigns. They apply modified restructuring for the three types of North American reference entity – investment grade entities, insurance entities and high yield entities – as well as for Australian and New Zealand entities. They apply modified modified restructuring to the two types of Western European reference entity: Western European entities and insurance entities. They do not apply restructuring at all (ie, no restructuring) to the standard terms for European emerging market entities.

Section 4.7 provides that a restructuring credit event occurs when any one of a list of specified events binding all of the holders occurs to an aggregate amount of the reference entity's obligations at least equal to the default requirement (as determined by Section 4.8(a)). These events must not be contemplated under the obligation's terms in effect at the later of the trade date or the obligation's issue date. The specified events are:

- an interest payment or accrual reduction;
- a principal or premium reduction;
- a postponement of payment of accruals or interest, or principal or premium;
- a change of an obligation's priority of payment, causing that obligation's subordination; and
- any change in currency of interest or principal other than to a permitted currency.[1]

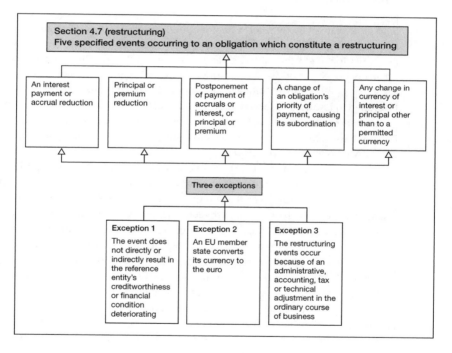

Exceptions apply where:

- the event does not directly or indirectly result in the reference entity's creditworthiness or financial condition deteriorating;
- an EU member state converts its currency to the euro; or
- the restructuring events occur because of an administrative, accounting, tax or technical adjustment in the ordinary course of business.

---

1   This is defined in Section 4.7 as any G7 member or Organisation for Economic Cooperation and Development country currency of an AAA-rated country.

8.1 Full restructuring

> Credit events: The following credit event[s] shall apply to this transaction:
> Restructuring

Market events exposed certain weaknesses in the 1999 'restructuring' definition. Although the 2003 Definitions do not vary the definition itself, they do provide options to limit the reference entity's obligations which may be deliverable obligations. When these options are not selected, this is full restructuring chosen by selecting restructuring as a credit event alone.

> **Actual case study: Conseco exposes weaknesses in the restructuring credit event**
>
> To understand why there are different options for restructuring, one must first look at the restructuring credit event's history. In the late 1990s Conseco, a US corporation, had a liquidity crisis and in September 2000 agreed to restructure its bank debt. As part of the restructuring, the loans' interest rates were increased by 250 basis points and additional collateral was provided to the lenders. This resulted in a structural subordination of Conseco's bonds, as the bonds were not restructured and so did not benefit from the restructuring provisions. This caused Conseco's loans to trade at 92% of their face value, while its bonds traded at only 68% of their face value.
>
> Certain banks involved in the loan restructuring had hedged their positions with physically settled credit default swaps and the restructuring allowed them to trigger a restructuring credit event thereunder. Although the restructured loans were the obligations which triggered the credit event, the banks were free to deliver any Conseco obligation meeting the deliverable obligation category and deliverable obligation characteristics detailed in the relevant transactions. Certain of these counterparties chose, as was their right, to exercise the 'cheapest to deliver' option. This meant that they selected as the deliverable obligation one of the bonds trading at 68%, although they had been hedging against a loan trading at around 92%. Some market participants viewed this as a windfall. A seller could sell its restructured loan into the market at 92% of face value, purchase a Conseco bond at 68% and deliver it to the seller in return for 100% of the face value: a 24% windfall. Not all sellers were happy with this.

8.2 Modified restructuring

> Credit events: The following credit event[s] shall apply to this transaction:
> Restructuring
> Restructuring maturity limitation and fully transferable
> obligation: applicable

In response to the Conseco credit event concerns raised by sellers, in November 2001 ISDA released the restructuring supplement. This introduced the modified restructuring variation, which aims to reduce the moral hazard of the 'cheapest to deliver' option.

It is used mainly for North American reference entities. The option has been fully incorporated into the 2003 Definitions, in Section 2.32 (restructuring maturity limitation and fully transferable obligation). Section 2.32 contains five definitions: 'fully transferable obligation', 'restructuring maturity limitation date', 'restructuring date', 'restructured bond or loan' and 'eligible transferee'.

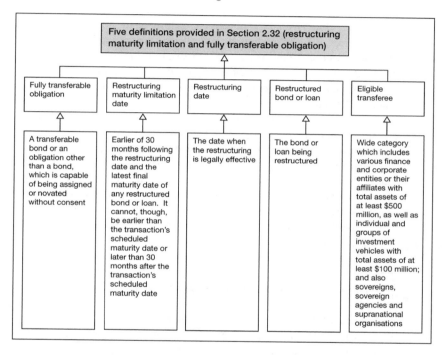

The section provides that if 'physical settlement' and 'restructuring maturity limitation and fully transferable obligation applicable' are specified in a confirmation and restructuring is the only credit event specified in a credit event notice delivered by the buyer, then any deliverable obligation must fulfil two characteristics. Limiting the modified restructuring provisions to where the buyer has delivered the credit event notice means that if the seller is the notifying party, it waives its protections relating to the 'cheapest to deliver' option if it decides to trigger a restructuring credit event.

The modified restructuring criteria require first that the deliverable obligation must be a 'fully transferable obligation'. This is defined in Section 2.32(b) as meaning that the deliverable obligation is a transferable bond (as defined in Section 2.20(v) (method for determining deliverable obligations)). Alternatively, it can be an obligation other than a bond which is capable of being assigned or novated without consent; this will most likely be a loan as the obligation category for each of ISDA's standard terms is 'bond or loan'.

It is also a criterion that these loans are transferable to eligible transferees. 'Eligible transferees' are defined in Section 2.32(f) and include various finance and corporate entities or their affiliates with total assets of at least $500 million, as well as individual and groups of investment vehicles with total assets of at least $100 million; and also sovereigns, sovereign agencies and supranational organisations.

The definition of 'fully transferable obligation' specifically states that "any requirement that notification of novation, assignment or transfer be provided to a trustee, fiscal agent, administrative agent, clearing agent" will not be considered to be a consent for these purposes.

Second, the deliverable obligation's maturity date must be no later than the restructuring maturity limitation date. 'Restructuring maturity limitation date' is defined in Section 2.32(c) as the earlier of 30 months following the restructuring date (defined in Section 2.32 (d) as the date when the restructuring is legally effective) and the latest final maturity date of any restructured bond or loan. The restructuring maturity limitation date cannot, though, be earlier than the transaction's scheduled maturity date or later than 30 months after the scheduled maturity date.

In summary, then, in physically settled transactions where the buyer triggers a restructuring credit event and the modified restructuring provisions are applicable, the buyer may deliver only deliverable obligations which are fully transferable obligations and have a final maturity date not later that the restructuring maturity limitation date – that is, the earlier of 30 months following any restructured bond or loans restructuring date and the latest final maturity date of any restructured bond or loan, subject to a total date range from the scheduled termination date to 30 months from the scheduled termination date.

Hypothetical case study: modified restructuring

On August 1 2006 Calderon SA entered into a $10 million, three-year physically settled credit default swap with Menacho SA, where it bought credit protection on Lopez Corporation, an American insurer. In accordance with ISDA's standard terms for North American insurers, the transaction applied restructuring as a credit event and stated: "Restructuring maturity limitation and fully transferable obligation: applicable" and "Modified restructuring maturity limitation and conditionally transferable obligation: not applicable". Therefore, modified restructuring applied to the transaction.

Following a hurricane which hit the west coast of America, Lopez discovered that it had more liabilities than it previously thought. This led to it being downgraded by the ratings agencies in August 2007 and unable to roll over its commercial paper, causing a liquidity crisis at what was fundamentally a financially health company.

Lopez had $2 billion of debt outstanding. In particular, it had a $500 million floating rate bond which was due to be repaid the following month, in September 2008. The liquidity crisis meant that Lopez would be unable to make

---

this payment on the bond's maturity date. A default could result in the company's bankruptcy and, as an insurer, Chapter 11 bankruptcy would be unlikely to save it in the longer term.

Lopez entered into restructuring negotiations with its bondholders on August 15 2008. Together they agreed that, in return for an enhanced coupon and Lopez granting security over certain of its assets, the maturity date of the bond would be extended from September 2008 until August 2011, 36 months later.

The restructuring constituted a restructuring credit event because first, pursuant to Section 4.7, in relation to Lopez's $500 million floating rate note there had been a postponement of the date for repayment of principal (in accordance with Section 4.7(a)(iii)); and this had been binding on all of the obligation holders. Second, this had occurred with respect to more than the $1 million default requirement provided in the confirmation.

Calderon delivered a credit event notice and notice of physical settlement to Menacho. This was followed 15 calendar days later by a notice of physical settlement. Calderon was obliged to select in the notice of physical settlement the Lopez obligation that it wished to deliver on the physical settlement date. Its choices were limited. The deliverable obligation had to comply with the deliverable obligation category and deliverable obligation characteristics: 'bond or loan'; 'not subordinated'; 'specified currency – standard specified currencies'; 'not contingent; assignable loan'; 'consent required loan'; 'transferable'; 'maximum maturity 30 years'; and 'not bearer', respectively.

The deliverable obligation also had to comply with the modified restructuring criteria set out in Section 2.32 – that is, it had to be a fully transferable obligation and have a final maturity date not later than the restructuring maturity limitation date, which could be delivered to an eligible transferee.

The 'fully transferable obligation' requirement was not an additional restriction in the case of Lopez bonds, because 'transferable' was already a deliverable obligation characteristic. In the case of loans, though, Calderon could select only loans that were capable of being "assigned or novated to all eligible transferees without the consent of any person being required". The 'eligible transferees' had to be transferees such as finance and corporate entities or their affiliates with total assets of at least $500 million, as well as individual and groups of investment vehicles with total assets of at least $100 million.

The restructuring maturity limitation date was February 15 2011, being the earlier of 30 months following the restructuring date (which, according to Section 2.32(d), was the date on which the restructuring was legally effective – August 15 2008), and September 15 2011 (the final maturity date of the restructured bond).

This meant that the restructured $100 million floating rate bond was not a deliverable obligation, as it matured after the restructuring maturity limitation date. Calderon instead was forced to select a different bond which was trading at a higher price, a fixed rate security not maturing in April 2008, and specify that as the deliverable obligation in the notice of physical settlement.

8.3   Modified modified restructuring

> Credit events: The following credit event[s] shall apply to this transaction:
> Restructuring
> Modified restructuring maturity limitation and conditionally
> transferable obligation: Applicable

Modified restructuring was unpopular with European dealers and was not applied for European reference entities. They felt that it did not take account of European loan market practice. In particular, it excluded consent-required loans from being deliverable obligations, preventing loans documented according to Loan Market Association standards from being deliverable obligations. To deal with these concerns, the 2003 Definitions include a further option for the European market known as 'modified modified restructuring'.

This option is used in ISDA's standard terms for Western European reference entities and for Western European insurance entities where the obligation is senior insurance debt (although not where the obligation is subordinated insurance debt).

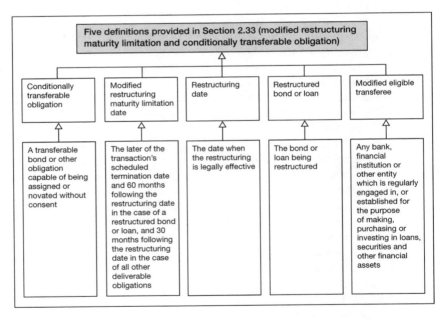

The modified modified restructuring option is incorporated into the 2003 Definitions in Section 2.33 (modified restructuring maturity limitation and conditionally transferable obligation). Section 2.33 contains five definitions:

- 'conditionally transferable obligation';
- 'modified restructuring maturity limitation date';
- 'restructuring date';

- 'restructured bond or loan'; and
- 'modified eligible transferee'.

Both 'restructuring date' and 'restructured bond or loan' have identical definitions in modified restructuring provisions.

Section 2.33 provides that if 'physical settlement' and 'modified restructuring maturity limitation and conditionally transferable obligation applicable' are specified in a confirmation and restructuring is the only credit event specified in a credit event notice delivered by the buyer, then any deliverable obligation must fulfil two characteristics. As with modified restructuring, limiting the modified modified restructuring provisions to where the buyer has delivered the credit event notice means that if the seller is the notifying party, it waives its protections relating to the cheapest to deliver option if it decides to trigger a restructuring credit event.

The modified modified restructuring criteria require first that the deliverable obligation must be a 'conditionally transferable obligation'. This is defined in Section 2.33(b) as meaning that the deliverable obligation is a transferable bond (as defined in Section 2.20(v) (method for determining deliverable obligations). Alternatively, it can be an obligation other than a bond which is capable of being assigned or novated without consent; this will most likely be a loan as the obligation category for each of ISDA's standard terms is 'bond or loan'.

It is also a criterion that these loans can be transferred to modified eligible transferees (in contrast with eligible transferees in modified restructuring). Modified eligible transferees are defined in Section 2.33(f) as "any bank, financial institution or other entity which is regularly engaged in or established for the purpose of making, purchasing or investing in loans, securities and other financial assets". 'Modified eligible transferees' is therefore a wider category of transferee than 'eligible transferees'. This definition is based on the broader loan market association standard form and includes any bank, financial institution or other entity regularly involved in making, purchasing or investing in loans, securities and other assets.

As with the definition of 'fully transferable obligation', the definition of 'conditionally transferable obligation' specifically states that "any requirement that notification of novation, assignment or transfer be provided to a trustee, fiscal agent, administrative agent, clearing agent" will not be considered to be a consent for these purposes.

In addition, the definition of 'conditionally transferable obligation' states that a loan will still be a deliverable obligation where the reference entity, agent or any guarantor's consent is required for a novation, assignment or transfer, as long as the terms of the obligation provide that "such consent may not be unreasonably withheld or delayed".

Second, the deliverable obligation's maturity date must be no later than the modified restructuring maturity limitation date. 'Modified restructuring maturity limitation date' is defined in Section 2.33(c) as the later of the transaction's scheduled termination date and 60 months following the restructuring date in the case of a restructured bond or loan and 30 months following the restructuring date in the case of all other deliverable obligations.

Modified modified restructuring can be summarised as follows. In physically settled transactions where the buyer triggers a restructuring credit event and the modified modified restructuring provisions are applicable, the buyer may deliver only deliverable obligations which are 'conditionally transferable obligations' (ie, effectively deliverable obligations that are either transferable,[2] in the case of bonds, or loans capable of being assigned or novated without consent to eligible transferees). These bonds or loans must also have a final maturity date not later than the modified restructuring maturity limitation date – that is, the deliverable obligation's final maturity date must be no later than the earlier of the transaction's scheduled termination date and 60 months, where the deliverable obligation is a restructured bond or loan, or 30 months for other deliverable obligations.

Hypothetical case study: modified modified restructuring

On September 1 2007 Sacramento SA entered into a €10 million three-year physically settled credit default swap with Vicente SA, where it bought credit protection on Alma SA, a French insurer. In accordance with ISDA's standard terms for Western European insurance entities, the transaction applied restructuring as a credit event and stated: "modified restructuring maturity limitation and conditionally transferable obligation: applicable" and "restructuring maturity limitation and fully transferable obligation: not applicable". Modified modified restructuring therefore applied to the transaction.

Following an oil tanker leak which hit the north coast of France, Alma discovered that it had more liabilities than it previously thought. This led to it being downgraded by the ratings agencies in October 2008, and unable to roll over its commercial paper, causing a liquidity crisis in what was fundamentally a financially health company.

Alma had $2 billion of debt outstanding. In particular, it had a €800 million syndicated loan which was due to be repaid the following month, in November 2008. The liquidity crisis meant that Alma would be unable to make this payment on the bond's maturity date. A default could result in the company's bankruptcy.

Alma entered into restructuring negotiations with its creditor banks and on October 15 2008 they agreed that in return for an enhanced interest payments and Alma granting security over certain of its assets, the maturity date of the bond would be extended from November 15 2008 until November 15 2011, 36 months later.

The restructuring constituted a restructuring credit event, because with respect to more than $1 million (or equivalent) one of Alma's obligations, (the €800 million syndicated loan) there had been a postponement of the date for repayment of principal (in accordance with Section 4.7(a)(iii)); and this had been binding on all of the obligation holders.

---

2   Section 2.20(b)(v).

Sacramento delivered a credit event notice and notice of physical settlement to Vicente. This was followed 15 calendar days later by a notice of physical settlement. Sacramento was obliged to select in the notice of physical settlement the Alma obligation that it wished to deliver on the physical settlement date. Its choices were limited. The deliverable obligation had to comply with the deliverable obligation category and deliverable obligation characteristics: 'bond or loan'; 'not subordinated'; 'specified currency – standard specified currencies'; 'not contingent; assignable loan'; 'consent required loan'; 'transferable'; 'maximum maturity 30 years'; and 'not bearer'.

The deliverable obligation also had to comply with the modified modified restructuring criteria set out in Section 2.33 – that is, it had to be a 'conditionally transferable obligation' and have a final maturity date not later than the 'modified restructuring maturity limitation date'.

The 'conditionally transferable obligation' requirement was not an additional restriction in the case of Alma's Bonds, because 'transferable' was already a deliverable obligation characteristic. In the case of loans, though, Calderon could select only loans that were capable of being "assigned or novated to all modified eligible transferees without the consent of any person being required".

The modified eligible transferees were a broad category based on the Loan Market Association standard form and included any bank, financial institution or other entity regularly involved in making, purchasing or investing in loans, securities and other assets.

The modified restructuring maturity limitation date was October 15 2013, being the later of 60 months following the restructuring date (which, according to Section 2.32(d), was the date on which the restructuring was legally effective – October 15 2008) and the credit default swap's scheduled maturity date, August 1 2010.

This meant that Sacramento could detail in the notice of physical settlement any deliverable obligation which met the deliverable obligation category and deliverable obligation characteristics and had a maturity date prior to October 15 2013. The restructured €800 million syndicated loan was a deliverable obligation as it matured on November 15 2011 and was capable of being transferred to modified eligible transferees. Calderon specified in its notice of physical settlement that it intended to deliver the restructured loan on the physical settlement date.

8.4 Restructuring credit event not selected

It is market standard not to select the restructuring credit event for certain types of reference entity, for example North American corporate high yield and insurance reference entities. This is known as 'no restructuring'.

8.5 Section 4.9: multiple holder obligation

Whereas Sections 2.32 and 2.33 limit the deliverable obligations which can be delivered in physically settled transactions following a credit event, Section 4.9

(limitation on obligations in connection with Section 4.7) limits the obligations that can actually trigger a restructuring credit event.

Unless 'multiple holder obligation' is specified as not being applicable in the relevant confirmation, a restructuring credit event can occur only in relation to a multiple holder obligation. 'Multiple holder obligation' is defined as an obligation held at the time of the restructuring credit event:

- by at least four non-affiliated holders; and
- whose terms require that 66.66% of the holders consent to the restructuring.

ISDA's standard terms for reference entities make 'multiple holder obligation' applicable for Western European entities, Western European insurance entities, Australian and New Zealand entities, Singaporean entities, Asian entities and North American investment grade entities. For European emerging market entities, 'multiple holder obligation' applies to loans, but not to bonds. It does not apply at all to the three standard terms where restructuring is not applicable: Japanese entities, North American high yield and insurance. In the case of sovereigns, 'multiple holder obligation' is applicable for emerging European, Middle Eastern and Latin American sovereigns, but not for all other types of sovereign.

The role of this provision is to prevent a creditor in a limited creditor group agreeing to a restructuring which is not advantageous, safe in the knowledge that it will not suffer the consequences of what it has agreed to because it has hedged its credit risk by entering into a credit derivative contract. If the future of banking increasingly places banks as financial intermediaries which then hedge credit risk through credit derivative contracts, this will weaken restructuring as a credit event further, as it is foreseeable that each creditor bank involved in a restructuring may have hedged some or all of its exposure through credit derivative contracts.

A shortcoming in Section 4.9 was identified soon after the publication of the 2003 Definitions. It is market practice for eurobonds to require that 75% of bondholders vote to approve a restructuring and to fix a meeting's quorum at 75% of bondholders. This means that any market standard eurobond which restructures could be approved by only 56% of bondholders and would then fail the multiple holder obligation test. ISDA addressed the problem in the May 2003 supplement, which provides that a bond will automatically be construed to be a multiple holder obligation. The May 2003 supplement must be specifically incorporated into a confirmation, in addition to the 2003 Definitions. It is market practice to do so:

The definitions and provisions contained in the 2003 ISDA Credit Derivatives Definitions as supplemented by the May 2003 Supplement to such Definitions (the 'Credit Derivatives Definitions'), as published by the International Swaps and Derivatives Association, Inc., are incorporated into this Confirmation.

Hypothetical case study: multiple holder obligation

Cervantes Bank entered into a $20 million credit default swap with Najera SA where it bought credit protection on Solano Corporation, a North American investment grade pharmaceutical company. Restructuring was one of the applicable credit events.

Cervantes Bank was active in the North American market and was one of four lenders in a $300 million syndicated loan to Solano. Concerned about the extent of its credit exposure to Solano, and also to the North American pharmaceuticals industry in general, Cervantes hedged its entire $100 million holding in the loan through the credit default swap with Najera.

A year later, Solano had a liquidity crisis and was forced to restructure its syndicated loan or face bankruptcy. One of the four creditor banks sold its holding to one of its co-creditor banks, leaving only three lenders. Solano agreed with its creditor banks to extend the maturity of the syndicated loan and provide an enhanced security package. Cervantes Bank took a stronger line in the negotiations than it would otherwise have done when it realised that it was not hedged against a restructuring of the syndicated loan, because it was not a 'multiple holder obligation'. This was because even though at the time of the restructuring event the loan's terms required that 66.66% of the holders consent to the restructuring, the syndicated loan was held by only three and not the minimum four non-affiliated holders.

Without the 'multiple holder obligation' requirement, Cervantes would have had no incentive to expend resources negotiating the restructuring.

8.6   Sovereign restructured deliverable obligation

A final additional variation relating to deliverable obligations following a restructuring credit event relates to the restructured deliverable obligations of sovereigns. The definition of 'sovereign restructured deliverable obligation' is set out in Section 2.16. Unless excluded in the confirmation, where a restructuring credit event occurs in relation to a sovereign, the class of deliverable obligation will be widened to include obligations which satisfied the deliverable obligation category and deliverable obligation characteristics immediately before the restructuring was legally effective, even if they do not meet them afterwards. This varies from the standard provisions, which assess whether an obligation is a deliverable obligation as of the delivery date.

Article V – Fixed amounts

Article V – Fixed amounts	
5.1	Calculation of fixed amount
5.2	Fixed-rate
5.3	Fixed-rate day count fraction
5.4	Relating fixed-rate payer payments to fixed-rate payer calculation periods

Fixed payments:

Fixed rate payer calculation amount:	$10 million
Fixed rate payer payment dates:	March 31, June 30, September 30 and December 31 each year
Fixed rate:	1%
Fixed rate day count fraction:	Actual/360

1. Calculation of the fixed amount; fixed rate

Fixed amounts are the payments that the buyer makes to the seller to compensate it for assuming the credit risk of the reference entity. Fixed amounts are dealt with in Article V of the 2003 Definitions. The provisions of this article interact with the following provisions in Article II:

- fixed amount (Section 2.5);
- fixed rate payer (Section 2.6);
- fixed rate payer calculation amount (Section 2.7);
- fixed rate payer period end date (Section 2.8);
- fixed rate payer calculation period (Section 2.9); and
- fixed rate payer payment date (Section 2.10).

Section 5.1 provides the methodology for determining what the fixed amount payable by a fixed rate payer on a fixed payer payment date will be. 'Fixed rate payer' is defined in Section 2.6 and 'fixed rate payer payment date' is defined in Section 2.10. In summary, though, the fixed rate payer will be the seller and the fixed rate payer payment dates will be each date on which the parties have agreed that a credit protection payment will be made.

If an actual amount is specified in the confirmation as a fixed amount, the buyer will pay that amount to the seller on each fixed rate payer payment date. Usually, though, a specific amount is not specified and the actual amount payable is calculated according to a formula set out in Section 5.1(b).

The formula requires the fixed rate payer calculation amount[1] (which is usually the notional amount of the credit default swap) to be multiplied by the fixed rate[2] (which is agreed between the parties and expressed as a per annum percentage) and by the day count fraction,[3] to give the fixed amount.

2. Fixed rate day count fraction

> 2. Fixed payments:
>
> Fixed rate day count fraction: Actual/360

In interest rate transactions, fixed rates of interest are expressed as percentage amounts payable on a principal or notional amount (eg, 5% of a notional amount of €100 million per annum). This is also the case for payments of fixed amounts in credit derivative transactions.

These payments, though, are often made more frequently than once a year, and in the credit default swap market the market convention is for fixed amounts to be paid quarterly, with the fixed rate payer payment dates being on March 31, June 30, September 30 and December 31 in each year. To work out how much is due on each fixed rate payer payment date, the parties apply day count fractions to determine how much of the annual fixed amount is payable on a fixed rate payer payment date. Day count fractions are used not only in credit derivatives, but also in fixed income securities and derivatives generally whenever there are payments of part of an annual amount more than once a year.

Section 5.3 provides five different day count fractions, of which the parties may select any one of to apply to a transaction. These are:
- Actual/365 or 'Actual/Actual';
- Actual/365 (fixed);
- Actual/360, Act/360, A/360;
- '30/360' or 'Bond Basis'; and
- '30E/360'or 'Eurobond Basis'.

The fixed rate day count fraction selected to apply to the transaction is set out in the fixed payments section of the confirmation. If the parties do not specify a fixed rate day count fraction, the fallback is for 'actual/360' to apply. Actual/360 is also the market standard fixed rate day count fraction.

2.1 Actual/365 or Actual/Actual

The Actual/365 or actual/actual convention works as follows. Where a fixed rate payer calculation period does not have any days falling in a leap year, the buyer takes the

---

1   Section 2.7.
2   Section 5.2.
3   Section 5.3.

actual number of days in the fixed rate payer calculation period and divides this number by 365.

Where a fixed rate payer calculation period does contain a leap year, the buyer takes the actual number of days in the portion of the fixed rate payer calculation period falling in the leap year and divides this figure by 366. The buyer then takes the actual number of days (if any) in the portion of the fixed rate payer calculation period which fall in the non-leap year and divides this figure by 365. The buyer then adds these two figures together to determine the day count fraction.

Hypothetical case study:
fixed rate payer day count fraction – Actual/365 or Actual/Actual

A credit default swap with a $10 million notional amount (ie, fixed rate payer calculation amount) has fixed amounts which are payable semi-annually on March 31 and September 30 each year. The transaction's effective date is March 31 2007. The fixed rate is 1% per annum. The first fixed rate payer calculation period runs from March 31 2007 to September 30 2007.

The buyer calculated the number of days in the first fixed rate payer period end date (which includes the effective date and September 30 2007, the first fixed rate payer period end date) as 183 days. The buyer then divided this by 365 to give a day count fraction of 0.501369. When calculating the fixed amount payable for the fixed rate payer calculation period ending on September 30 2007, the buyer multiplied the $10 million fixed rate payer calculation amount by the 1% fixed amount and the 0.501369 day count fraction to give an amount payable of $50,136.99.

The next fixed rate payer calculation period ran from October 1 2007 until (and including) March 31 2008. As 2008 was a leap year, the buyer added together the number of days in fixed rate payer calculation period falling in 2007. There were 92 days in the period and the buyer divided this by 365, to give a figure of 0.252054.

The buyer then counted the number of days in the fixed rate payer calculation period which fell in 2008, the part of the period falling in the leap year. There were 91 days in this portion of the period. The buyer divided 91 by 366 to produce a figure of 0.248633. The buyer then added 0.24863 and 0.252054 together to give a day count fraction of 0.500687. When calculating the fixed amount payable for fixed rate payer calculation period ending on March 31 2008, the buyer multiplied the $10 million fixed rate payer calculation amount by the 1% fixed amount and the 0.500687 day count fraction to determine an amount payable of $50,068.78.

2.2 Actual/365 (fixed)

If 'Actual/365' is selected as the day count fraction convention, the buyer will take the actual number of days in the fixed rate payer calculation period and divide this number by 365, irrespective of whether any of the fixed rate payer calculation period falls in a leap year, to determine the day count fraction. The calculation of the fixed amount will be made in the same manner as described in the hypothetical case study for actual/365 above, for the March 31 2007 to September 30 2007 interest period.

2.3 Actual/360, Act/360 or A/360

If any of 'Actual/360', 'Act 360' or 'A/360' is selected as the day count fraction convention, the buyer will take the actual number of days in the fixed rate payer calculation period and divide this number by 360 to determine the day count fraction. The calculation of the fixed amount will be made in the same manner as described in the hypothetical case study for actual/365 above, for the March 31 2007 to September 30 2007 interest period, except that 360 instead of 365 will be used as the denominator.

2.4 30/360 or Bond Basis

30/360 or bond basis differs from actual/360 in its treatment of the numerator. If either of '30/360' or 'Bond Basis' is selected as the day count fraction convention, the buyer will calculate the numerator by assuming that each month is made up of 30 days, regardless of the actual number of days in the relevant month, and divide this by a denominator of 360 to determine the day count fraction. The 30-day numerator represents a year of 360 days divided into 12 30-day months.

It may be modified if the last day of the fixed rate payer calculation period is the 31st day of the relevant month, but the fixed rate payer calculation period's first day is not the 30th or 31st day of a month. In this case the initial month is not deemed to be a 30-day month and the actual number of days in the month is taken instead.

The numerator is also modified if the last day of the fixed rate payer calculation period is February 28 or 29. In this case, February is not deemed to be lengthened to a 30-day month, but the actual number of days in a February is taken instead.

Hypothetical case study:
fixed rate payer day count fraction – 30/360 or Bond Basis

A credit default swap with a $10 million notional amount (ie, fixed rate payer calculation amount) has fixed amounts which are payable quarterly on March 31, June 30, September 30 and December 31 each year. The transaction's effective date is October 1 2009. The fixed rate is 1% per annum. The first fixed rate payer calculation period runs from September 30 2009 to December 31 2009.

The buyer calculated the number of days in the first fixed rate payer period end date (which includes the effective date of October 1 2009 and December 31, the first fixed rate payer period end date) as 90 days (ie, three 30-day months).

The buyer then divided 90 by 360 to give a day count fraction of 0.246575. When calculating the fixed amount payable for the fixed rate payer calculation period ending on December 31 2009, the buyer multiplied the $10 million fixed rate payer calculation amount by the 1% fixed amount and the 0.246575 day count fraction to give a figure of $24,657.53.

> The next fixed rate payer calculation period ran from January 1 2010 until (and including) March 31 2010. The buyer calculated that there were 90 days in the fixed rate payer calculation period (ie, two deemed 30-day months – January and March – and a 28-day month, February). The buyer divided 90 by 360 to give a day count fraction of 0.25.
>
> When calculating the fixed amount payable for the fixed rate payer calculation period ending on March 31 2009, the buyer multiplied the $10 million fixed rate payer calculation amount by the 1% fixed amount and the 0.25 day count fraction to give a figure of $25,000.

2.5   30E/360 or Eurobond Basis

If either of '30E/360' or 'Eurobond Basis' is selected as the day count fraction convention, then as with 30/360 or bond basis, the buyer will calculate the numerator by taking the number of months in the fixed rate payer calculation period and deeming each to have 30 days instead of the actual number of days in the month. The buyer will then calculate the day count fraction by dividing the numerator by a denominator of 360.

30E/360 or Eurobond Basis differs from 30/360 or bond basis because, although the 30-day periods used in calculating the numerator represent a year of 360 days divided into 12 30-day months, this is taken without regard to the first day or last day of the fixed rate payer calculation period. An exception to this is if the last day of the final fixed rate payer calculation period is the last day of February. In this case then, once again, the actual number of days in February will be taken.

3.   Relating fixed rate payer payments to fixed rate payer calculation periods

Section 5.4 covers how fixed rate payer payment dates interact with fixed rate payer calculation periods (ie, whether they are they included within a fixed rate payer calculation period). Section 5.4 appears to replicate the definition of 'fixed rate payer calculation period' in Section 2.9.

Section 5.4 provides that unless otherwise specified in the confirmation, where the fixed amount is calculated according to the formula set out in Section 5.1(b), the fixed rate payer calculation period will exclude the relevant fixer rate payer period end date (which is normally the fixed rate payer payment date). This section also provides that for the final fixed rate payer calculation period, which will end on the earlier to occur of an event determination date or the scheduled termination date, the event determination date or scheduled termination date is included in the fixed rate payer calculation period.

Article VI – General terms relating to settlement

Article VI – General terms relating to settlement	
6.1	Settlement method
6.2	Settlement date
6.3	Settlement currency

Article VI is very short, providing just three definitions. It is an enabling provision which defines 'settlement method' in Section 6.1, 'settlement date' in Section 6.2 and 'settlement currency' in Section 6.3. The two settlement methods contemplated by the 2003 definitions are set out in Section 6.1: cash settlement and physical settlement. Section 6.2 provides that either settlement method is chosen by being specified in a relevant confirmation. If cash settlement is selected (or if it is deemed to apply because physical settlement is impossible),[1] the provisions of Article VII (terms relating to cash settlement)[2] will apply. If physical settlement is selected, the provisions of Article VIII (terms relating to physical settlement) and Article IX (additional representations and agreements of parties) will apply.

Section 6.2 provides that the settlement date will be either the cash settlement date (as defined in Section 7.2) or the physical settlement date (as defined in Section 8.4 (each as applicable). Section 6.3 provides that the currency of settlement will be as stated in the relevant confirmation, with the ISDA fallback being the currency of the floating rate payer calculation amount.

---

1   Sections 9.3, 9.4 and 9.5.
2   As modified further by Article IX if any of Sections 9.3, 9.4 and 9.5 are applicable.

Article VII – Terms relating to cash settlement

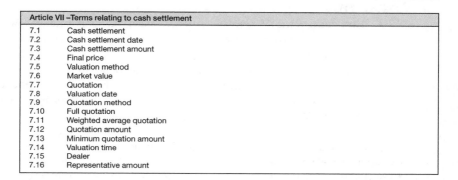

Article VII –Terms relating to cash settlement	
7.1	Cash settlement
7.2	Cash settlement date
7.3	Cash settlement amount
7.4	Final price
7.5	Valuation method
7.6	Market value
7.7	Quotation
7.8	Valuation date
7.9	Quotation method
7.10	Full quotation
7.11	Weighted average quotation
7.12	Quotation amount
7.13	Minimum quotation amount
7.14	Valuation time
7.15	Dealer
7.16	Representative amount

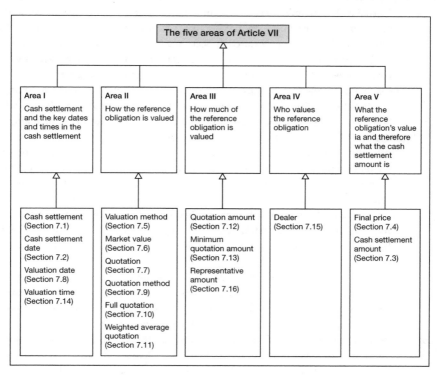

1.   Overview

Article VII is divided into 16 sections. The article covers five different areas of the cash settlement process, as follows:

- The definition of 'cash settlement' and the key dates and times in the cash settlement process – cash settlement (Section 7.1); cash settlement date (Section 7.2); valuation date (Section 7.8); and valuation time (Section 7.14).
- How the reference obligation is valued – valuation method (Section 7.5); market value (Section 7.6); quotation (Section 7.7); quotation method (Section 7.9); full quotation (Section 7.10); and weighted average quotation (Section 7.11).
- How much of the reference obligation is valued – quotation amount (Section 7.12); minimum quotation amount (Section 7.13); and representative amount (Section 7.16).
- Who values the reference obligation – dealer (Section 7.15).
- What the reference obligation's value is and therefore what the cash settlement amount is – final price (Section 7.4) and cash settlement amount (Section 7.3).

Article VII applies both to cash settled credit derivatives transactions and to physically settled transactions where physical settlement is not fully possible pursuant to Section 9.3 (partial cash settlement due to impossibility of illegality); Section 9.4 (partial cash settlement of consent required loans); Section 9.5 (partial cash settlement of assignable loans); and Section 9.6 (partial cash settlement of participations). Certain terms of Article VII may be varied by Section 9.8 (partial cash settlement terms).

The provisions of Article VII apply only if the conditions to settlement are met and cover the period of the transaction from this moment until the termination date. In cash settled transactions, these provisions work as follows. Once the notifying party satisfies the conditions to settlement, the calculation agent arranges for the reference obligation to be valued to ascertain its current market value. The calculation agent does this by contacting an agreed number of dealers on the valuation date(s) at the valuation time and asking them to provide quotations for an amount of each reference obligation specified in the confirmation. The quotation method – for example, bid or offer – and the amount of the reference obligation for which the calculation agent asks for quotations will be set out in the confirmation.

The calculation agent will apply a valuation method to the quotations to calculate the reference obligation's final price. Whether the calculation agent will take the highest or the lowest price, or perhaps an average of prices, will be specified in the confirmation.

The final price represents the decline in the value of the reference obligation and is expressed as a percentage. The calculation agent then multiplies the floating rate payer calculation amount by the reference price (usually 100%) to give a percentage figure, and then subtracts the final price (also a percentage figure) to determine the cash settlement amount (ie, a percentage of the floating rate payer calculation amount). The seller must then pay the cash settlement amount to the buyer on the cash settlement date, which will be the transaction's termination date. Alternatively, in a fixed recovery credit derivative transaction, the cash settlement amount will be set out in the confirmation, meaning that there will be no requirement to value a reference obligation. Article VII also makes provision for this.

Article VII not only provides for this to be the cash settlement procedure, but also provides the parties with a whole range of options and fallbacks for how cash settlement should take place: there are nine different options for 'valuation method'; three different options for 'quotation method'; two different options for 'valuation date'; plus detailed fallbacks for obtaining the requisite number of quotations to calculate a final price.

Cash settlement as set out in Article VII also operates in a similar way where there is partial cash settlement in a physically settled transaction, although Section 9.8 modifies and/or replaces 10 of Article VII's definitions – in some cases significantly, in others by deeming certain elections to apply. The definitions amended or modified are: 'cash settlement amount'; 'cash settlement date'; 'reference obligation'; 'valuation date'; 'valuation method'; 'quotation method'; 'quotation amount'; 'valuation time'; 'market value' and 'quotation'.

2. Area I: cash settlement and the key dates and times in the cash settlement process

2.1 Cash settlement

Section 7.1 provides that if 'cash settlement' is specified in a transaction or is deemed to apply pursuant to any of Section 9.3, Section 9.4, Section 9.5 and Section 9.6, then if the conditions to settlement are met, the seller must pay the buyer the cash settlement amount on the cash settlement date.

2.2 Cash settlement date

The seller must make its settlement payment to the buyer on the cash settlement date. Section 7.2 defines when this date is. Where the cash settlement amount is not specified in the confirmation, this takes place once the reference obligation has been valued and the cash settlement amount has been calculated. The cash settlement date can be specified in the confirmation to be a number of days after the calculation agent has calculated the final price; if not, it will be deemed to be three business days after the calculation agent had calculated the final price.

In fixed recovery transactions, the cash settlement date either will be specified in the transaction as being a certain number of business days after the notifying party has met the conditions to settlement, or if not, will be three business days thereafter.

2.3 Valuation date

The calculation agent must approach the dealers at a specified time or times to ask for quotations, in order for it to determine the reference obligation's final price. The times when the calculation agent does this are crystallised by two definitions: valuation date (Section 7.8) and valuation time (Section 7.14).

Article VII provides two different options in Section 7.8, which can be selected in the confirmation. The calculation agent can obtain the quotations either on a single date or on multiple valuation dates. In each case, Article VII provides the methodology for calculating the various averages.

The parties can specify in the confirmation that 'single valuation date' applies.

Valuation date:	Single valuation date:	Five business days

Where this is the case, the valuation date will be the number of business days specified in the confirmation after the notifying party has satisfied the conditions to settlement.

Valuation date:	Multiple valuation dates:	Five business days; and each fifth business day thereafter
	Number of valuation dates:	three

Alternatively, the parties can specify in the confirmation that multiple valuation dates apply. This is done by specifying 'multiple valuation dates', together with the number of valuation dates and the dates on which they fall. If 'multiple valuation dates' is specified in the confirmation, but the number of valuation dates is not, then there is a fallback of five valuation dates. If 'multiple valuation dates' is specified as applicable, but when those dates fall is not, the first valuation date is deemed to fall five business days after the notifying party meets the conditions to settlement and then each fifth business day thereafter.

'Multiple valuation dates' requires the calculation agent to do more work and is a more complex procedure, but it helps to remove some of the volatility risk involved in having only a single valuation date.

If neither 'single valuation date' nor 'multiple valuation dates' is specified in the confirmation, a five business-day single valuation date fallback applies.

2.4 Valuation time

The calculation agent is required not only to approach the dealers which provide quotations on each valuation date, but more specifically to do so at the same time: the valuation time. This is defined in Section 7.14 as the time specified in the confirmation or, where no time is specified, 11:00am in the principal trading market of the reference obligation.

3. Area II: how the reference obligation is valued

Quotation method:	[Bid][Offer][Mid-market]]
Quotation amount:	[ ][Representative amount]
Minimum quotation amount:	[ ]
Dealer(s):	[ ]
Quotations:	[Include accrued interest]
	[Exclude accrued interest]

On the valuation date at the valuation time, the calculation agent contacts the dealers (all as specified in the confirmation) and asks them to provide quotations. The calculation agent will use these quotations to calculate the final price.

Section 7.7 defines 'quotation' as each "full quotation and weighted average quotation obtained and expressed as a percentage with respect to a valuation date". Section 7.7 then sets out the manner and method which the calculation agent must use to obtain these quotations, including how many quotations it must obtain, together with a series of fallbacks which can be used in establishing the final price.

A 'full quotation' is defined in Section 7.10 as a firm quotation obtained from a dealer at the valuation time for an amount of the reference obligation "with an outstanding principal balance equal to the quotation amount". 'Quotation amount' itself is defined in Section 7.12 as the amount specified in the confirmation. This can be a defined amount, or the confirmation may state that it is to be determined by reference to a representative amount. 'Representative amount' in turn is defined in Section 7.16 as "an amount that is representative for a single transaction in the relevant market and at the relevant time", and is determined by the calculation agent in consultation with the parties.

Where no quotation amount is specified in the confirmation, the fallback is for the quotation amount to be deemed to be the floating rate calculation amount. Where the reference obligation is denominated in a different currency from the quotation amount, the calculation agent is obliged to convert the quotation amount to the 'obligation currency'. It must do this in a commercially reasonable manner using the relevant exchange rate at the time that it obtains the quotation.

A weighted average quotation relates to where the calculation agent is unable to obtain a quotation from a dealer for the full quotation amount. Weighted averages are calculated by taking a number of quantities and multiplying each quantity by its weight or proportional relevance. The amounts are then added together and the resulting figure is then divided by the sum of the weights.

Weighted averages are calculated by taking a number of quantities and multiplying each quantity by its weight or proportional relevance. The amounts are then added together and the resulting figure is then divided by the sum of the weights. How this works in a credit derivative transaction is best explained by means of an example (see the hypothetical case study overleaf).

A 'weighted average quotation' is defined in Section 7.11 as "the weighted average of firm quotations obtained from dealers at the valuation time". The quotations must, to the extent reasonably practicable, be for as large a size as available; and for as close to the minimum quotation amount as possible. All of these quotations must in aggregate be approximately equal to the quotation amount. The minimum quotation amount is defined in Section 7.13 (minimum quotation amount) as either the amount specified in the confirmation or its equivalent or the lower of $1 million and the quotation amount.

Hypothetical case study: weighted average quotations

Palencia SA entered into a €10 million cash settled credit default swap with Roche SA, where it bought credit protection on Pectri Corporation, a US electricity company. Pectri had filed for bankruptcy and Palencia had met the conditions to settlement for a bankruptcy credit event. The first valuation date was five business days later and Roche, the calculation agent, asked the five dealers listed in the confirmation for a 'full quotation' for the quotation amount ($100,000) of the reference obligation: a 6% bond due 2015 issued by Pectri Corporation. The five dealers were Torre Bank, Lubet Brothers, Rosalia Bank, Soledad Daponte and Naves Castillo.

Pectri Corporation's distressed assets were not very liquid. On the first business day only Torre Bank gave a quotation for the reference obligation for the full quotation amount: 14%. This was the same on each of the second and third business days. Section 7.7(a) allowed Roche to obtain a weighted average quotation instead of a full quotation on the third business day to establish a final price for the reference obligation.

The confirmation stated that the minimum quotation amount was $25,000. Roche requested quotations from the four dealers which had not given a quotation for at least $25,000 of the reference obligation; or, if that was not possible, as close to $25,000 as possible. Roche received quotations for the reference obligation from Lubet Brothers for $35,000 at 11%; Rosalia Bank for $25,000 at 13%; and Soledad Daponte for $40,000 at 14%.

Together these three quotations added up to the $100,000 quotation amount. To calculate the weighted average quotation, Roche took each quotation and multiplied each of these percentage figures by the respective weight of the quotation amount in the total $100,000 of quotations (ie, Lubet by 35%, Rosalia by 25% and Soledad Duponte by 40%).

This gave respective figures of 3.8%, 3.5% and 5.2%, which totalled 12.55%. The weighted average quotation was therefore 12.55%.

Section 7.7 sets out the method by which the calculation agent determines the final price. 'Quotations' are defined as full quotations and weighted average quotations. The type of full quotation or weighted average quotation that the calculation agent seeks is determined through two other definitions: quotation method (section 7.9) and valuation method (section 7.5).

Section 7.9 provides three options for quotation method; whichever of the three is specified in the confirmation will determine whether the calculation agent approaches the dealers for bid quotations, offer quotations or mid-market quotations (ie, a bid and an offer quotation which is then averaged by the calculation agent).

Quotation method: Bid

Section 7.7 provides that calculation agent must attempt to obtain at least two full quotations on each valuation date from five or more dealers. If the calculation agent is unable to do this, then it must use the detailed fallbacks set out in Section 7.7 to meet the quotation criteria and determine a final price.

Hypothetical case study: cash settlement I

On September 1 2007 Palma SA entered into a $10 million cash settled credit default swap with Vidal SA, where it bought credit protection on Alba SA, a Spanish construction company.

1. *General terms*
   Reference price: 100%.

3. *Floating payment*
   Floating rate payer calculation amount: $10 million

On October 1 2008 Alba filed for bankruptcy. As this constituted a bankruptcy credit event, Palma delivered a credit event notice and notice of publicly available information to Vidal on October 4 2008.

4. *Settlement terms*
   Settlement method: cash settlement
   Terms relating to cash settlement

Section 7.1 obliged Vidal to pay Palma the cash settlement amount on the cash settlement date.

Vidal was the calculation agent under the transaction. The reference obligation was disclosed in the transaction as:

Reference Obligation:	*$100 million Floating Rate Note due 2016 issued by Alba SA (XS923483249)*

The dealers were specified as:

Dealers:	*Milena Bank; Frontera Bank; Sirenas Brothers; Neptuno Parada; Oporto Bank*

Oporto Bank had itself become bankrupt and so was no longer in existence. Vidal, in its capacity as calculation agent, consulted with Palma, and they decided that Oporto Bank should be substituted as a dealer for Betis Bank.

For valuation dates and valuation time the confirmation stated:

Valuation dates:	*Multiple valuation dates* *Ten business days and each five business days thereafter*
Number of valuation dates:	*Three*
Valuation Time:	*11:00 am (London time)*

For obtaining quotations, the confirmation stated:

Quotation method:	*Bid*
Quotation account:	*€50,000*
Minimum quotation amount:	*€20,000*
Quotations:	*Exclude accrued interest*
Valuation method:	*Average highest*

This meant that Vidal was obliged to ask Milena Bank, Frontera Bank, Sirenas Brothers, Neptuno Parada and Betis Bank to provide a 'bid' quotation for €50,000 of an issue of $100 million floating rate note due 2006 issued by Alba SA. Vidal had to do this on each of the three valuation dates, which were Friday October 17 2008, Friday October 24 2008 and Friday October 31 2008.

Vidal had to ask that the quotations exclude the interest, which had accrued, but not been paid, on the reference obligation. Vidal received the following quotations on each valuation date:

Dealer	First valuation date	Second valuation date	Third valuation date
Milena Bank	*57%*	*56.75%*	*59%*
Frontera Bank	*56%*	*56.55%*	*60.25%*
Sirenas Brother	*56.5%*	*56.5%*	*60%*
Neptuno Parada	*56.75%*	*57%*	*60.5%*
Betis Bank	*57%*	*58%*	*59.5%*

After each valuation date Vidal communicated the prices that it had obtained to the parties in a quotation amount notice.

On the third valuation date, Vidal calculated the final price of the reference obligation using the 'average highest' valuation method, which meant that Vidal took an unweighted arithmetic mean of the highest quotations. The highest quotation on the first valuation date was 57%, on the second valuation date it was 58% and on the third valuation date it was 60.5%. This meant that the final price was 58.5%.

Vidal was obliged to pay Palma a cash settlement amount of $4.15 million on the cash settlement date, three business days after it had calculated the final price. Vidal calculated the cash settlement amount by subtracting the final price from the reference price, giving a percentage figure of 41.5% and multiplying it by the $10 million floating rate payer calculation amount.

Once the calculation agent has met the quotation criteria, it uses the quotations to determine a final price. The way it makes this determination depends upon what is specified in the confirmation as the valuation method. Section 7.5 provides eight different options that can be selected by the parties in a confirmation: market; highest; average market; average highest; blended market; blended highest; average blended market and average blended highest.

Valuation method:	Highest

Which valuation method the parties select will depend upon the number of reference obligations that the calculation has to value and the number of valuation dates. The table below sets out which valuation method can be applied depending on the number of reference obligations and valuation dates, as well as a summary of the valuation method's definition.

Valuation method	Number of reference obligations	Number of valuation dates	Definition
Market	One	One	The reference obligation's market value
Highest	One	One or multiple	The highest quotation obtained (the ISDA fallback)
Average market	One	Multiple	The unweighted arithmetic mean of the market values
Average highest	One	Multiple	The unweighted arithmetic mean of the highest quotations
Blended market	Multiple	Single	The unweighted arithmetic mean of the market values of each reference obligation
Blended highest	Multiple	Single	The unweighted arithmetic mean of the highest quotations
Average blended market	Multiple	Multiple	On each valuation date the blended market value is calculated. The arithmetic mean of those values is then calculated
Average blended highest	Multiple	Multiple	On each valuation date the blended highest is calculated. The arithmetic mean of those values is then calculated

Whether the quotation for the reference obligation will include or exclude any accrued but unpaid interest will be specified in the confirmation[1] as either 'include accrued interest' or 'exclude accrued interest'.

---

1   Section 7.7(c).

Quotations:	Exclude accrued interest

If neither is stated in the confirmation then the calculation agent will consult the parties and, based on the current market practice for the reference obligation, will decide whether the quotation should include or exclude accrued interest. In ISDA's standard terms for reference entities, 'exclude accrued interest' is the standard for each type of reference entity.

Each of the valuation methods is based either on the highest quotation given or on the market value. Highest, average highest, blended highest and average blended highest are based on the highest quotation given. Average market, blended market and average blended market are based on the market value of the reference obligation.

The concept of choosing the highest quotation given is straightforward. Market value, though, is more complex and is defined in Section 7.6. 'Market values' are based on the number of full quotations and weighted average quotations received. How the calculation agent determines market values for the average market blended market and average blended market valuation methods is set out in the table below.

Quotations received	Calculation agent action to determine market value
More than three full quotations	Disregard the highest and lowest full quotations and calculate the arithmetic mean. If two full quotations have the same highest or lowest value, only one is discarded
Exactly three full quotations	Disregard the highest and lowest full quotations and calculate the arithmetic mean. If two full quotations have the same highest or lowest value, only one is discarded
Exactly two full quotations	Calculate the arithmetic mean of the full quotations
One full quotation and/or a weighted average quotation	Weighted average quotation used
One full quotation only or no full quotations	Five business-day period commences, operating until two or more full quotations or a weighted average quotation is obtained. If two full quotations or a weighted average quotation is not obtained by the end of the period, market value is calculated as per fallbacks 3A/B to 5A/7B above

4. Area III: how much of the reference obligation is valued

Whereas Area II of Article III relates to how the reference obligation is valued, Area III relates to how much of the reference obligation must be valued on a valuation date.

The relevant definitions for determining the quantum of reference obligation to be valued are:

- quotation amount (Section 7.12);
- minimum quotation amount (Section 7.13); and
- representative amount (Section 7.16).

As discussed in relation to Area II, Section 7.12 provides that the quotation amount for any transaction is the amount specified in the confirmation. This can be a defined amount, or the confirmation may state that it is to be determined by reference to a representative amount. 'Representative amount' in turn is defined in Section 7.16 as "an amount that is representative for a single transaction in the relevant market and at the relevant time", and is determined by the calculation agent in consultation with the parties.

Where no quotation amount is specified in the confirmation, the fallback is for the quotation amount to be deemed to be the floating rate calculation amount. Where the reference obligation is denominated in a different currency from the quotation amount, the calculation agent is obliged to convert the quotation amount to the 'obligation currency'. It must do this in a commercially reasonable manner, using the relevant exchange rate at the time that it obtains the quotation.

As discussed in relation to Area II, the concept of minimum quotation amounts is relevant to weighted average quotations as defined in Section 7.11. When obtaining a weighted average quotation, the quotations must, to the extent reasonably practicable, be for as large a size as available and for as close to the 'minimum quotation amount' as possible. All of these quotations must in aggregate be approximately equal to the quotation amount. The minimum quotation amount is defined in Section 7.13 as either the amount specified in the confirmation or its equivalent, or the lower of $1 million and the quotation amount.

5. Area IV: who values the reference obligation

Where the cash settlement amount is not set out in the confirmation, once the notifying party has satisfied the conditions to settlement, the calculation agent must arrange for the reference obligation to be valued to ascertain its current market value (the final price). It does this by approaching dealers and asking them to make a bid or offer for the reference obligation.

'Dealer' is defined in Section 7.15. The definition excludes the parties or their affiliates from being dealers (although in practice this is sometimes modified in individual transactions). 'Dealers' are defined as dealers "in obligations of the type of obligation(s) for which quotations are to be obtained"; they include any dealers specified in any individual confirmation. If a dealer specified in the confirmation is no longer in existence and has no successors when the valuation is to take place, or is not an active dealer in the obligations, the calculation agent must consult with the parties and substitute the original dealer for one that does deal in the obligations. If the confirmation does not specify any dealers, the calculation agent must consult with the parties and select the dealers.

6. Area V: what the reference obligation's value is and therefore what its cash settlement amount is

6.1 Final price

The concept of the reference obligation's final price is defined in Section 7.4. The 'final price' represents the decline in value of the reference entity's obligations, and is central to calculating the payment that the seller must make to the buyer covering the difference in value of the reference entity's obligations at the transaction's outset and their current value post-credit event.

The calculation agent calculates the reference obligation's final price in accordance with the applicable valuation method. The final price is expressed as a percentage. As soon as practicable after obtaining all of the quotations for the reference obligation, the calculation agent must notify each of the parties in writing of each quotation that it receives and provide a written computation showing its calculation of the final price. In practice, this is known as the final price notification.

6.2 Cash settlement amount

The cash settlement amount is the amount paid by the buyer to the seller on the cash settlement date. The payment represents the compensation payment from buyer to seller, which isolates the buyer from the credit risk of the reference entity. 'Cash settlement amount' is defined in Section 7.3 as either, in the case of a fixed recovery swap, the amount specified in the confirmation, or otherwise the floating rate payer calculation amount multiplied by the percentage figure of the reference price (usually 100%), less the final price. The cash settlement amount is subject to a minimum of zero. It is payable on the cash settlement date, which will then be the transaction's termination date.

7. Problems getting quotations: the fallbacks

Reference obligations post-credit event are by their nature distressed assets. The secondary market for distressed securities is relatively small and illiquid compared to the normal securities market. Debt obligations rank above equity and will almost always have a value, because even when a company is liquidated it will still have some assets. This means that there will usually be a market in the reference entity's securities; however, in some circumstances or trading conditions, the calculation agent may be unable to get two full quotations for the reference obligations on the valuation date. Section 7.7 therefore provides extensive fallbacks to deal with these problems. These work as follows, with the calculation agent moving to the next fallback each time that it is unable to get the required quotations.

> **Fallback 1:** Calculation agent tries to obtain at least two full quotations from five dealers daily for the next three business days
>
> **Fallback 2:** Calculation agent attempts to obtain the same full quotations until the tenth post-valuation date business day. On each day that it is unsuccessful, it attempts to obtain a weighted average quotation

Calculation agent is a transaction party	Calculation agent is not a transaction party
Fallback 3A: The calculation agent's counterparty may attempt to obtain the quotations. If the counterparty can obtain at least two full quotations or a weighted average quotation within the next five business days, then the calculation agent must use these quotations	**Fallback 3B:** Each of the buyer and seller may attempt to obtain five or more full quotations and, if two or more full quotations are not available, a weighted average quotation
Fallback 4A: The final price will be calculated using any full quotation the counterparty has obtained from a dealer at the valuation time on the fifth business day	**Fallback 4B:** If either or both parties can obtain two or more full quotations or a weighted average quotation on the same business day within an additional five business days, then the calculation agent must use these quotations
Fallback 5A: On the same day as Fallback 4A, the weighted average of: • any firm quotations for the reference obligation obtained on the fifth business day for the aggregate portion of the quotation amount for which quotations were obtained; and • a quotation deemed to be zero for the balance of the quotation amount for which quotations were not obtained on that day	**Fallback 5B:** The parties attempt to obtain between them two or more full quotations or a weighted average quotation on the same business day within the next five business days
	Fallback 6B: The quotations are deemed to be *any* full quotation obtained from a dealer at the valuation time on such business day
A weighted average quotation can be obtained when dealers are prepared only to give quotations for less than the quotation amount. The calculation agent then takes a weighted average of the firm quotations obtained. The quotation amounts must be at least equal to the minimum quotation amount specified in the confirmation. If no amount is specified, this will be the lower of $1 million and the quotation amount. These quotations, when added together in aggregate, must approximately equal the quotation amount	**Fallback 7B:** On the same day as Fallback 6B, the weighted average of: • any firm quotations for the reference obligation obtained from dealers on the fifth business day for the aggregate portion of the quotation amount for which quotations were obtained; and • a quotation deemed to be zero for the balance of the quotation amount for which quotations were not obtained on that day

Hypothetical case study: cash settlement II

On September 1 2007 Rubia SA entered into a €10 million cash settled credit default swap with Zorilla SA, where it bought credit protection on Tinte SA, an Italian information technology company.

1. *General terms*
   Reference price: 100%

3. *Floating payment*
   Floating rate payer calculation amount: €10 million

On October 1 2008 Tinte filed for bankruptcy. As this constituted a bankruptcy credit event, Rubia delivered a credit event notice and notice of publicly available information to Zorilla on October 4 2008.

4. *Settlement terms*
   Settlement method: cash settlement
   Terms relating to cash settlement

Section 7.1 of the 2003 Definitions obliged Zorilla to pay Rubia the cash settlement amount on the cash settlement date. Zorilla was the calculation agent under the transaction. The reference obligation was disclosed in the transaction as:

Reference obligation:	*€300 million 6% notes due 2012 issued by Tinte SA(XS98349374)*

The dealers were specified as:

Dealers:	*Milena Bank; Frontera Bank; Sirenas Brothers; Neptuno Parada; Betis Bank*

For valuation dates and valuation time the confirmation stated:

Valuation dates:	*Single valuation date*
	Ten business days
Valuation time:	*11:00am (London time)*

For obtaining quotations, the confirmation stated:

Quotation method:	*Bid*
Quotation amount:	*€50,000*
Minimum quotation amount:	*€20,000*
Quotations:	*Exclude accrued interest*
Valuation method:	*Market*

This meant that Zorilla was obliged to ask each of Milena Bank, Frontera Bank, Sirenas Brothers, Neptuno Parada and Betis Bank to provide a 'bid' quotation for €50,000 of an issue of €300 million 6% notes due 2012 issued by Tinte SA. Zorilla had to do this on the valuation date, which was Friday October 17 2008.

Zorilla had to ask that the quotations exclude the interest, which had accrued but had not been paid, on the reference obligation. On the valuation date Zorilla asked each of the five banks for their quotations, but none provided a quotation.

Zorilla followed Section 7.7 of the 2003 Definitions to the letter; in accordance with the first fallback set out in Section 7.7(a) on the next business day, Monday October 21, and the two following days, Zorilla tried again,but was each time unsuccessful in getting any full quotations.

Zorilla then moved to the second fallback set out Section 7.7(a) and attempted to obtain the same full quotations from Thursday October 24 until the 10th post-valuation date business day: Monday November 4. On each day that it was unsuccessful, it also attempted to obtain a weighted average quotation, which was equally unsuccessful.

Zorilla was, of course, the seller as well as the calculation agent and so a different set of fallbacks applied from if a third party had been the calculation agent. The third fallback, which is provided for in Section 7.7(b), was for Rubia to attempt to obtain the quotations. Rubia attempted to obtain at least two full quotations or a weighted average quotation for the next five business days from Tuesday November 5 until and including Monday November 5. If it had been able to do so, the calculation agent would have used these full quotations or weighted average quotation to calculate the final price. Unfortunately, the reference obligation remained highly illiquid and it could not obtain any full quotations or a weighted average quotation.

However, Rubia had received two firm quotations for €20,000 each of the reference obligation on the fifth and final business day. The quotations were from Milena Bank and Frontera Bank and for 7% and 8%. The aggregate of the quotation amounts was €40,000. This was €10,000 short of the €50,000 quotation amount required to calculate a weighted average quotation.

The quotation process now moved to the final fallback. If Rubia had failed to get any quotations at all, then the final price of the reference obligation would have been deemed to be zero, but because it did, Zorilla took the weighted average of the two firm quotations and deemed there to be a third firm quotation of 0% for the remaining €10,000. Rubia then calculated a weighted average quotation by taking Milena Bank's 7% quotation, Frontera Bank's 8% quotation and the deemed 0% quotation. Rubia multiplied each of these percentage figures by the respective weight of the quotation amount in the total $50,000 quotation (ie, Milena Bank by 40%, Frontera Bank by 40% and the deemed 0% quotation by 10%).

This gave respective figures of 2.8%, 3.2% and 0%, which totalled 6%. The weighted average quotation was therefore 6%. Zorilla now had one weighted average quotation for the reference obligation, which it could use to calculate the final price.

The confirmation stated that the valuation method was market:

Valuation method: *Market*

This meant that Zorilla had to determine the reference obligation's market value in accordance with Section 7.6; because only a weighted average quotation had been obtained, the 6% figure was used as the final price.

Zorilla was obliged to pay Rubia a cash settlement amount of €9.4 million on the cash settlement date, three business days after it had calculated the final price on Thursday November 14. Zorilla calculated the cash settlement amount by subtracting the final price from the reference price, giving a percentage figure of 94% and multiplying it by the €10 million floating rate payer calculation amount.

Article VIII – Terms relating to physical settlement

Article VIII – Terms relating to physical settlement	
8.1	Physical settlement
8.2	Deliver
8.3	Delivery date
8.4	Physical settlement date
8.5	Physical settlement amount
8.6	Physical settlement period
8.7	Provisions applicable to convertible, exchangeable and accreting obligations
8.8	Due and payable amount
8.9	Currency amount
8.10	Currency rate
8.11	Escrow

1.   Overview

Traditionally, physical settlement has been more popular than cash settlement as a settlement method.

Article VIII relates solely to physically settled transactions. It provides the documentary infrastructure for physically settling credit derivative transactions. Its provisions come into play in transactions specifying the physical settlement method once the buyer has satisfied the conditions to settlement by delivering a notice of physical settlement following an event determination date. Article VIII provisions are supplemented by certain provisions from Article IX (additional representations and agreements of the parties), which provide detailed fallbacks for when the buyer is unable to deliver deliverable obligations to the seller or the situation where the seller is unable to accept a delivery of deliverable obligations from the buyer.

Article VIII is divided into 11 sections. These cover first the mechanics of how physical settlement takes place, including determining the deliverable obligations that the buyer must deliver and defining what constitutes a delivery. This is done through the article's main enabling definition set out in Section 8.1 (physical settlement) and in the definition of 'deliver' in Section 8.2. Article VIII also covers when a delivery takes place, the amount of deliverable obligations which must be delivered by the buyer and the period when delivery must take place. This is also facilitated through Section 8.1, in conjunction with the definitions of:

- 'delivery date' (Section 8.3);
- 'physical settlement date' (Section 8.4);
- 'physical settlement amount' (Section 8.5);
- 'physical settlement period' (Section 8.6);
- 'provisions applicable to convertible, exchangeable and accreting obligations' (Section 8.7);

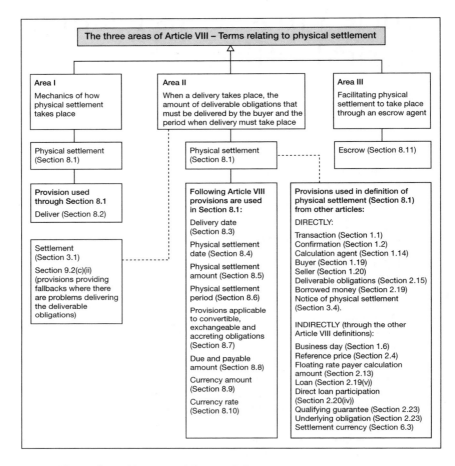

- 'due and payable amount' (Section 8.8);
- 'currency amount' (Section 8.9); and
- 'currency rate' (Section 8.10).

Article VIII also contains provisions facilitating physical settlement to take place through use of an escrow agent (Section 8.11), where one or both of the parties require this.

2. Mechanics of how physical settlement works: Section 8.1

2.1 Structure

Section 8.1 provides the documentation infrastructure and mechanics to facilitate physical settlement of credit derivative transactions, once the buyer has delivered a notice of physical settlement. At first sight, and considering the importance of physical settlement in credit derivative transactions, Section 8.1 is a relatively short provision (as is the four-page Article VIII in general).

However, the section relies heavily on other definitions, making it a complex section to work through. Section 8.1 directly or indirectly uses 11 of the 12 other definitions in Article VIII, and provides two other definitions itself: 'include accrued interest' and 'exclude accrued interest'. In addition, the section also directly and indirectly is subject to other sections and relies on 16 other definitions from the 2003 Definitions outside of Article VIII.

From Article VIII, Section 8.1 directly relies on the definitions of:

- 'include accrued interest';
- 'exclude accrued interest';
- 'deliver';
- 'delivery date;
- 'physical settlement date';
- 'physical settlement amount';
- 'due and payable amount';
- 'currency amount'; and
- 'provisions applicable to convertible, exchangeable and accreting obligations'.

It indirectly uses the remaining provisions (with the exception of escrow), because 'physical settlement date' relies on the definition of 'physical settlement period' and the definition of 'currency amount' relies on the definition of 'currency rate'.

Outside Article VIII, Section 8.1 is subject to Section 3.1 (settlement) (ie, the occurrence of a credit event and the satisfaction of all of the conditions to settlement); and Section 9.2(c)(ii) (the provisions providing fallbacks where there are problems delivering the deliverable obligations). Section 8.1 also uses the definitions of:

- 'credit derivative transaction' (Section 1.1);
- 'confirmation' (Section 1.2);
- 'calculation agent' (Section 1.14);
- 'buyer' (Section 1.19);
- 'seller' (Section 1.20);
- 'deliverable obligations' (Section 2.15);
- 'borrowed money (Section 2.19); and
- 'notice of physical settlement' (Section 3.4).

The other Article VIII definitions on which Section 8.1 indirectly relies through the other Article VIII definitions it uses are:

- 'business day' (Section 1.6);
- 'reference price' (Section 2.4);
- 'floating rate payer calculation amount' (Section 2.13);
- 'loan' (Section 2.19(v));
- 'direct loan participation' (Section 2.20(iv));
- 'qualifying guarantee' (Section 2.23);
- 'underlying obligation' (Section 2.23); and
- 'settlement currency' (Section 6.3).

2.2 How it works

Section 8.1 provides that if physical settlement is specified as the settlement method in a transaction and the conditions to settlement are met, then the seller is obliged to accept delivery of the deliverable obligations detailed in the notice of physical settlement on or before the physical settlement date. In return, the seller must pay the physical settlement amount to the buyer on the physical settlement date.

The physical settlement amount (ie, the seller's payment to the buyer) is defined in Section 8.5 as the floating rate payer calculation amount (ie, the notional amount of the transaction) multiplied by its reference price (usually 100% unless the reference entity's 'obligations' are trading at a discount on the transaction's effective date). The essence of physical settlement (ie, how the buyer isolates itself from the reference entity's credit risk) is that, post-satisfaction of the conditions to settlement, the seller is obliged to purchase deliverable obligations from the seller at their original price (ie, their price at the transaction's outset), leaving the seller to suffer the decline in value. How much of a loss the seller suffers will depend on the severity of the credit event.

Physical settlement must take place within an agreed period: the physical settlement period. This is defined in Section 8.6 as either the number of business days specified in the confirmation or the longest number of business days for settling the deliverable obligation according to market practice. Market practice is determined by the calculation agent in consultation with the parties. The ISDA standard terms for each type of reference entity specify that the physical settlement period is 30 business days. This would most likely mean that if a physical settlement period is not specified in the confirmation, the calculation agent will probably determine that the market practice for settling a deliverable obligation is 30 business days.

Subject to the various fallbacks set out in Article IX, the last day when physical settlement can take place is the physical settlement date. This is defined in Section 8.4 as the last day of the longest physical settlement period following the satisfaction of the conditions to settlement (ie, probably 30 business days after the date on which the buyer delivers the notice of physical settlement). The physical settlement date is also the transaction's termination date.

The date when the buyer delivers the deliverable obligation to the seller is the 'delivery date'. This is defined in Section 8.3 and the buyer must make the delivery in accordance with the market practice applicable to the deliverable obligation on the delivery date.

Section 8 also contains complex interpretation provisions for determining the amount of deliverable obligations that the buyer must deliver on the delivery date. These are discussed below.

2.3 Delivery

Section 8.2 provides the criteria for what does and what does not constitute a delivery of deliverable obligations. The section provides that the delivery of the deliverable obligation may be not only by physical delivery in the traditional sense, but also by novation, transfer (including, for qualifying guarantees, transfer of the benefit of the qualifying guarantee), assignment or sale. The delivery must be carried out using the customary settlement method for the deliverable obligation and the seller must convey all rights, title and interests in the deliverable obligation free of liens, charges, claims and encumbrances.

The deliverable obligations must also be free of any counterclaims or defences, or right of set-off by the reference entity or any underlying obligor. The non-permitted defences set out in Sections 4.1 (a) to (d) of the 2003 Definitions are not deemed to be counterclaims or defences for these purposes where:

- the reference entity is alleged to or actually lacks the authority to enter into an 'obligation' or guarantee an underlying obligation;
- any 'obligation' or underlying obligation is alleged to be or actually is unenforceable, illegal, invalid or impossible;
- the relevant circumstance or defence arises from a law, a court or administrative decision or interpretation, or similar; or
- a monetary or other authority changes or imposes exchange controls or capital restrictions.

In the case of direct loan participations, 'delivery' means to create or procure the creation of a participation in the seller's favour. In the case of deliverable obligations consisting of qualifying guarantees, 'delivery' means to deliver the qualifying guarantee together with the underlying obligation. In the case of loans, the parties must affect the delivery using market standard documentation.

Hypothetical case study: physical settlement 1

On June 7 2009 Teniente SA entered into a €10 million physically settled credit default swap with Goleta SA, where it bought credit protection on Servanda PLC, a British financial services company.

1. General terms
   Reference price: 100%

3. Floating payment
   Floating rate payer calculation: €10 million
   Amount

Conditions to settlement: Credit event notice
Notifying party: Buyer
    Notice of physical settlement
    Notice of publicly available information
      applicable
    Public sources: two

On June 1 2009 Servanda filed for bankruptcy. As this constituted a bankruptcy credit event, Teniente delivered a credit event notice and notice of publicly available information to Goleta on June 4 2009. This was the event determination date. Fourteen calendar days later, on June 15 2009, Teniente

---

delivered a notice of physical settlement to Goleta, irrevocably confirming that it would settle the transaction and require performance in accordance with the physical settlement method. This met the conditions to settlement.

The notice stated that Teniente would deliver $10 million of an issue of $200 million floating rate notes issued by Servanda PLC on the physical settlement date. These deliverable obligations met the bond or loan deliverable obligation category. They also met the deliverable obligation characteristics as they were not subordinated; were not contingent; were transferable; had a maturity of under 30 years; were denominated in a standard specified currency; and fulfilled the 'not bearer' criterion.

Teniente was now obliged to deliver the deliverable obligations detailed in the notice of physical settlement to Goleta on or before the physical settlement date.

4. *Terms relating to physical settlement:*
    Physical settlement period: 10 business days
    Deliverable obligations: exclude accrued interest.

The physical settlement date in accordance with Section 8.4 was the last day of the physical settlement period. This was 10 business days after the conditions to settlement were met: June 15 2009

Teniente delivered the deliverable obligations to Goleta on June 10 2009: the delivery date. Goleta in return paid the €10 million physical settlement amount (being the €10 million floating rate payer calculation amount multiplied by the 100% reference price).

2.4 The amount of deliverable obligations which must be delivered by the buyer and the period when delivery must take place

Determining the amount of deliverable obligations which the seller must deliver to the buyer in exchange for the physical settlement amount can be more complex where:

- the deliverable obligations are denominated in a different currency from the physical settlement amount;
- the terms of the deliverable obligation contemplate paying a greater amount than the deliverable obligation's outstanding principal balance if a specified event occurs or does not occur;
- the obligation has accrued interest, but this has not been paid; or
- the deliverable obligation is an accreting obligation.

(a) *Currency of deliverable obligation different from settlement currency*

The deliverable obligations may be denominated in a currency other than that of the physical settlement amount – for example, the deliverable obligations could be bonds from an issue of $100 million floating rate bonds due 2016, but the credit derivative floating rate payer calculation amount is €10 million. Where this is the case, Section 8.1 provides that the buyer must deliver the equivalent currency amount of deliverable obligations to the seller. 'Currency amount' is defined in Section 8.9 as any amount denominated in a currency "other than the settlement currency". Section 8.9 also provides that this amount will be converted to the "settlement currency using the currency rate". Settlement currency, which is defined in Section 6.3, will almost always be the currency of the floating rate payer calculation amount unless otherwise specified.

'Currency rate' is defined in Section 8.10 and specifies conventions for the calculation agent to convert the currency of the deliverable obligation into dollars, euros and more generally into other currencies. If the settlement currency of the credit derivatives transaction is dollars, the calculation agent will make the conversion using the Federal Reserve Bank of New York 10:00am (New York time) mid-point rate as displayed on Reuters' FEDSPOT Page. If the settlement currency of the credit derivative transaction is euros, then the calculation agent will use the MEAN Price displayed on Reuters' EURO FX/1 at 12:00pm (London time). In both cases the calculation agent will make the conversion on the date on which the notice of physical settlement is effective. If the buyer subsequently amends the notice of physical settlement prior to the expiry of the post-event determination date 30-calendar-day period, then the calculation agent must take the rate on the last date that the notice of physical settlement is effective.

Alternatively, Section 8.10 provides that the calculation agent can instead make the conversion to the settlement currency using a rate determined "in a commercially reasonable manner in consultation with the parties". This is also the approach that the calculation agent must take where the settlement currency is a currency other than dollars or euros.

(b) **The terms of the deliverable obligation contemplate paying a greater amount than the deliverable obligation's outstanding principal balance if a specified event occurs or does not occur**

Section 8.1 provides that if the terms of a deliverable obligation specify that due to a future event either occurring or not occurring it will pay a greater amount than its outstanding principal balance at the delivery date, then this additional amount will not be taken into account when calculating the amount of deliverable obligations that the buyer must deliver to the seller. What is and what is not considered to be the deliverable obligation's outstanding principal balance is defined further in Section 8.7 and is discussed further below.

(c) **The amount of deliverable obligations to be delivered: due and payable amount**

Section 8.1 provides for two different criteria to determine the amount of deliverable obligations to be delivered on the delivery date. In doing so it requires the calculation agent to treat deliverable obligations that are 'borrowed money' differently from those which are not.

Although the 2003 Definitions could make it clearer, this distinction relates not to whether 'borrowed money' is the deliverable obligation category for selecting the deliverable obligation, but instead to whether the particular deliverable obligation falls into the criteria set out in Section 2.19(a)(ii) (provisions for determining deliverable obligations) for borrowed money (ie, the deliverable obligation is an obligation to pay or repay borrowed money). Therefore, where the deliverable obligation category is bond or loan, as is the case for each of ISDA's standard terms for reference entities, deliverable obligations meeting this deliverable obligation category will fall within the borrowed money criteria of Section 8.1.

Obligations that do not constitute borrowed money are deliverable obligations that fall within the 'payment' deliverable obligation category only. These would include trade debts and payments under derivative transactions.

In the case of deliverable obligations that are not borrowed money, the buyer must deliver a due and payable amount of deliverable obligations equal to the settlement amount to the seller. 'Due and payable amount' is defined in Section 8.8. It is the amount due and payable on the delivery date due to acceleration, maturity, termination or otherwise, but excluding default interest, indemnities and tax gross-ups (or an equivalent 'currency amount'), equal to the settlement amount.

(d)   *Determining the value of a deliverable obligation's accrued but unpaid interest*
Except for restructuring credit events, when a credit event occurs it is quite likely that the reference entity will have accrued interest on its obligations which has not been paid. In the case of a failure to pay credit event, the failure to make an interest payment may be the event that caused the credit event to occur. The reference entity will remain obliged to pay these amounts to the holders of its obligations. The 2003 Definitions provide the parties with the option to decide whether credit protection will apply in physical settlement to a reference entity's interest payments as well as principal payments for borrowed money obligations.

In both physically settled and cash settled transactions, it is market practice, as set out in each of ISDA's standard terms for reference entities, not to take account of accrued interest when calculating the final price of a reference obligation or the amount of deliverable obligations that the seller must deliver.

Section 8.1 provides the option for the parties to make this choice and specify whether the calculation agent is to take account of accrued but unpaid interest on any deliverable obligation. It provides that if 'include accrued interest' is specified in the confirmation, then the calculation agent (in consultation with the parties) will take account of any accrued interest when calculating the amount of deliverable obligations to be delivered; and if 'exclude accrued interest' is specified, any accrued interest will be excluded from this amount. If neither term is mentioned in the confirmation, then 'exclude accrued interest' is the ISDA fallback.

---

4.   Terms relating to physical settlement:
     Deliverable obligations: exclude accrued interest.

Whether 'include accrued interest' or 'exclude accrued interest' applies will usually be set out in the confirmation under 'Terms relating to physical settlement'.

(e)   *The amount of deliverable obligations to be delivered*

As mentioned above, if the deliverable obligations which the buyer intends to deliver are 'borrowed money', which will usually be the case, then the buyer must deliver deliverable obligations with an outstanding principal balance equal to the physical settlement amount.

Section 2.20(b)(i) (method for determining deliverable obligations), which relates to what is and what is not a 'not contingent' deliverable obligation for the purpose of the deliverable obligations characteristic, defines which convertible and exchangeable obligations can constitute deliverable obligations. Section 8.7 provides definitions for 'convertible obligations', 'exchangeable obligations' and also for 'accreting obligations'.

Section 8.7 definitions

Convertible obligations: A convertible obligation is an obligation, usually a bond, which can be converted in whole or in part into the equity securities of the issuer of the obligation (ie, equity securities (including options and warrants) of the reference entity, together with any of the reference entity's other property which is distributed to or made available to the security holders from time to time). Depositary receipts, which represent the equity securities of the issuer of the reference obligation, are also deemed to be equity securities.

The conversion must be solely at the option of the security holders or a trustee or agent acting on their behalf. A convertible obligation which permits conversion into a cash equivalent of the equity securities is also deemed to be a convertible obligation, if this can be done only at the option of the issuer or the security holders or their representatives.

Exchangeable obligation: An exchangeable obligation is similar to a convertible obligation except that instead of converting the obligation issuer's debt into its equity securities, the debt is exchanged for the equity securities of another entity. As with convertible obligations, the exchange must be solely at the option of the security holders or a trustee or agent acting on their behalf; and an exchangeable obligation which permits an exchange for a cash equivalent of the equity securities if this is done at the option of the issuer or the security holders or their representatives.

Accreting obligation: An accreting obligation is an obligation which "provides for an amount payable upon acceleration equal to the obligation's original price plus additional amounts which may accrete". These additional amounts may be on account of an 'original issue discount' (ie, the security was issued at a discount to a face amount, but the full principal amount is repayable) or other accruals of interest or principal that have not been paid on a periodic basis. These amounts are deemed to be accreted amounts even if the payment is

---

subject to a contingency or is determined according to an index or formula. An accreting obligation may also be a convertible obligation or an exchangeable obligation.

Accreted amount: The outstanding principal balance for an accreting obligation is its accreted amount. This is the deliverable obligation's original issue price plus any amount payable at maturity which has already accreted, less any cash payments that the reference entity has made to reduce the obligation's redemption amount. The accreted amount will include accrued and unpaid periodic cash interest payments only if 'include accrued interest' is stated in the confirmation.

An exception to the above is if the accreting obligation is expressed to accrete pursuant to a straight-line method or if its yield to maturity cannot be ascertained from its offering document. For the purposes of calculating the portion of the amount payable at maturity that has already accreted, the accreted amount is calculated using a rate equal to the accreting obligation's yield to maturity.

For exchangeable obligations, the accreted amount does not include any amount payable relating to the value of the equity securities for which the reference obligation can be exchanged.

If the buyer wishes to deliver a convertible or accreting obligation to the seller, then it must apply the relevant tests set out in Section 8.7 (provisions applicable to convertible, exchangeable and accreting obligations), which determine the amounts owed (or potentially owed) under these obligations which will be included in calculating a deliverable obligation's 'outstanding principal balance'.

Section 8.7 provides that the outstanding principal balance of an accreting obligation is its accreted amount. It states that the 'outstanding principal balance' of an exchangeable obligation, which is not an accreting obligation, excludes "any amount that may be payable under the terms of such obligation in respect of the value of the equity securities for which such obligation is exchangeable". Section 8.7 does not provide any additional provisions relating to determining the outstanding principal balance of convertible obligations, which are not accreting obligations.

Hypothetical case study: physical settlement II

On February 21 2009 Galdas SA entered into a €10 million physically settled credit default swap with Carmen SA, where it bought credit protection on Gentil PLC, a British drinks distribution company.

On July 1 2010 Gentil failed to make a repayment of principal on a $200 million floating rate note. Galdas triggered a failure to pay credit event and met all of the conditions to settlement by July 8 2010, when it delivered a notice of physical settlement.

The Gentil obligations trading at the lowest price were a $100 million 2% exchangeable bond due 2013, exchangeable into the shares of Barrocal PLC, one of Gentil's subsidiaries; and a €100 million zero coupon bond due 2015. Both of these obligations were trading at 55% of their face value, compared to Gentil's other debt obligations, which were trading at 60%.

The credit default swap's deliverable obligation category was 'bond or loan' and its deliverable obligation characteristics were not subordinated; in a specified currency (standard specified currencies); not contingent; assignable loan, transferable and not bearer. Both the exchangeable bond and the convertible bond met both the deliverable obligation category and the deliverable obligation characteristics. In particular, the deliverable obligations met the 'not contingent' deliverable obligation characteristic, because the outstanding principal balance of each obligation could not be reduced by "the occurrence or non-occurrence of an event or circumstance (other than payment)"; and in addition, the right to exchange the exchangeable obligation had not been exercised.

The physical settlement amount of the swap was the floating rate payer calculation amount (ie, €10 million) multiplied by the reference price (100%). Galdas was obliged to deliver deliverable obligations with an 'outstanding principal balance' equal to the physical settlement amount. Galdas wanted the deliverable obligations to consist of 50% of the zero coupon bond and 50% of the exchangeable bond. This meant delivering a €5 million outstanding principal balance of each security and calculating the actual face amount of each security that it was obliged to deliver.

The zero coupon bond was an accreting obligation. Its issue price had been 70% of its face value. Its terms provided that if the bond were accelerated, an amount equal to the bond's issue price plus additional amounts which had accreted would be payable. To deliver €5 million, Galdas had to calculate how much of the face amount of the accreting obligation it was obliged to deliver, so that this would equal €5 million of the zero coupon bond's accreted amount.

To do this Galdas calculated the accreted amount by taking the zero coupon bond's original issue price. The bond had been issued with an original issue price of 70% of its principal amount, but 100% of the principal amount was repayable on maturity. Of the 30% difference between the original issue price and the principal amount, Galdas calculated the amount that had already accreted. The bond had been issued on July 30 2006 and Gentil had made no payments. The bond's maturity date was July 30 2011 and the delivery date of the deliverable obligations was due to be July 30 2008. This meant that exactly two-fifths of the 30% additional amount payable on maturity had accreted (ie, €12 million). For Galdas to deliver €5 million of the zero coupon bond to Carmen, it needed to deliver a face amount of €4.25 million.

The outstanding principal balance of the exchangeable bond excluded "any amount that may be payable...in respect of equity securities for which such obligation is exchangeable". Galdas had therefore to deliver the €5 million principal amount of the exchangeable bond to Carmen. The exchangeable bond was denominated in dollars, whereas the credit default swaps settlement currency was euros. This meant that Galdas was obliged to deliver the equivalent 'currency amount' of the zero coupon bonds to Carmen. As Carmen was the calculation agent, Galdas liaised with Carman to establish the exchange rate. The currency amount was converted by Carmen into the settlement currency using the currency rate, which in accordance with Section 8.10 was the Federal Reserve Bank of New York 10:00am (New York time) mid-point rate as displayed on Reuters' FEDSPOT Page on the date which the notice of physical settlement was effective (ie, July 8 2010).

Carmen calculated that €5 million equated to $6,100,534 dollars. This caused a slight problem for Galdas, as the minimum denomination of the exchangeable obligation available was $10,000. This meant that on the delivery date, Galdas was forced to deliver $6.11 million of Gentil exchangeable bonds, together with €4.25 million of the zero coupon bond, in return for the physical settlement amount or €10 million from Carmen. The additional $9,466 dollars of exchangeable bonds was a windfall for Carmen. Carmen also benefited because the parties had specified the exclude accrued interest applied to deliverable obligations, and the exchangeable bonds had some accrued but unpaid interest, which added to their overall value.

2.5 Escrow

In common law, escrow involves a third party holding property for two contractual parties while they perform their obligations. Once these obligations are completed, the third party releases the property to the designated party. This may be cash, documents or securities. Section 8.11 (escrow) of the 2003 Definitions provides for the parties to have the option to have physical settlement take place through escrow.

Escrow in credit derivative transactions involves a financial institution acting as an escrow agent. The buyer then delivers the deliverable obligations to the escrow agent and the seller pays the physical settlement amount to the escrow agent. Once the escrow agent is holding both the deliverable obligations and the physical settlement amount, it releases the physical settlement amount to the buyer and the deliverable obligations to the seller.

The parties elect in the confirmation whether the escrow provisions apply:

Escrow: Applicable

If they do make this election:
- they can specify the identity of the escrow agent in the confirmation; or
- the buyer can specify an independent third-party financial institution prior to the physical settlement date.

The circumstances in which the parties may choose to use an escrow agent include where:

- either of the parties has concerns as to the creditworthiness of the counterparty; or
- the parties are in different time zones, making settlement on the same day logistically difficult.

Section 8.11(c) provides that if physical settlement takes place through an escrow agent, no adjustment is made to the timings for physical settlement. Section 8.11(a) provides that the party requiring the escrow arrangement is responsible for bearing the escrow costs.

Article IX – Additional representations and agreements of the parties

1. Overview

Article IX covers the various additional representations and agreements that the parties make to and with each other, as well as various fallbacks if problems are encountered when physically settling a transaction.

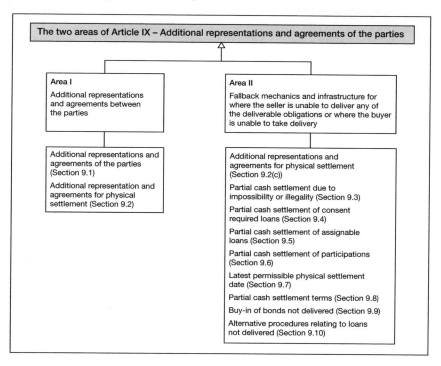

The two areas of Article IX – Additional representations and agreements of the parties

Area I

Additional representations and agreements between the parties

Area II

Fallback mechanics and infrastructure for where the seller is unable to deliver any of the deliverable obligations or where the buyer is unable to take delivery

Additional representations and agreements of the parties (Section 9.1)

Additional representation and agreements for physical settlement (Section 9.2)

Additional representations and agreements for physical settlement (Section 9.2(c))

Partial cash settlement due to impossibility or illegality (Section 9.3)

Partial cash settlement of consent required loans (Section 9.4)

Partial cash settlement of assignable loans (Section 9.5)

Partial cash settlement of participations (Section 9.6)

Latest permissible physical settlement date (Section 9.7)

Partial cash settlement terms (Section 9.8)

Buy-in of bonds not delivered (Section 9.9)

Alternative procedures relating to loans not delivered (Section 9.10)

The article is divided into 10 sections, which cover two areas. The first area consists of additional representations and agreements between the parties, both generally and also in respect of physical settlement:

- additional representations and agreements of the parties (Section 9.1); and
- additional representation and agreements for physical settlement (Section 9.2).

The second area consists of the fallback mechanics and infrastructure for where the seller is unable to deliver any of the deliverable obligations or where the buyer is unable to take delivery:

- additional representations and agreements for physical settlement (Section 9.2(c));
- partial cash settlement due to impossibility or illegality (Section 9.3);
- partial cash settlement of consent required loans (Section 9.4);
- partial cash settlement of assignable loans (Section 9.5);
- partial cash settlement of participations (Section 9.6);
- latest permissible physical settlement date (Section 9.7);
- partial cash settlement terms (Section 9.8);
- buy-in of bonds not delivered (Section 9.9); and
- alternative procedures relating to loans not delivered (Section 9.10).

2. Area I – additional representations and agreements of the parties; additional representations and agreements for physical settlement

In Section 9.1, the parties represent and agree that:

- neither they nor any of their affiliates have made any representation to the other party about the reference obligation or any of the reference entity's or underlying obligor's related obligations on which they can rely;
- they will perform the transaction as agreed irrespective of credit exposure to the reference entity;
- they need not suffer any loss or prove loss if a credit event occurs;
- the transaction will create no rights or obligations for any parties other than the transaction parties;
- the parties, their affiliates and the calculation agent may deal in the reference entity's or underlying obligor's obligations, and may also conduct banking and investment business with these parties which might actually cause a credit event to happen;
- there is no obligation to disclose any material information; and
- unless information is otherwise subject to confidentiality requirements, it will not trigger any confidentiality obligation and related losses will be indemnified.

Section 9.2(a) provides that the buyer agrees that when the buyer makes a delivery, it is deemed to represent that, except in the case of direct loan participations, it is transferring full title (including counterclaims or defences). The non-permitted defences set out in Sections 4.1(a) to (d) of the 2003 Definitions are not deemed to be counterclaims or defences for these purposes – that is, where:

- the reference entity is alleged to or actually lacks the authority to enter into an obligation or guarantee an underlying obligation;
- any obligation or underlying obligation is alleged to be or actually is unenforceable, illegal, invalid or impossible;
- the relevant circumstance or defence arises from a law, a court or administrative decision or interpretation, or similar; or
- a monetary or other authority changes or imposes exchange controls or capital restrictions.

If this turns out not to be the case, the buyer must indemnify the seller for any losses and expenses it incurs arising for the buyer breaching any of the representations described in the paragraph above. Any breach of representation under Section 9.2(a) is not deemed to constitute an event of default in the master agreement governing the credit derivative transaction.

Section 9.2(b) provides that unless the buyer provides an indemnity to the seller, the buyer is deemed to represent, when it makes a delivery, that (except for some minor exclusions) accepting the deliverable obligations will not lead to any commitment to lend additional funds (including outstanding commitments).

Section 9.2(c) sets out the agreements between the parties and the necessary steps that they must take to document the delivery of deliverable obligation and gain the consents required for an effective transfer to take place.

In Section 9.2(c)(i), the parties agree to "execute, deliver, file and record any specific assignment, novation or other document" and take any other action to facilitate the delivery of the deliverable obligations. This includes the buyer demonstrating to the seller's reasonable satisfaction that it has taken all reasonable steps to gain required consents. The buyer must also keep the seller informed of any circumstances of which it is aware (or should reasonably be aware) that may affect its ability to deliver the deliverable obligations. The buyer and seller also agree to cooperate reasonably in respect of these matters.

In Section 9.2(c)(ii), the buyer and seller agree that the buyer may deliver only the deliverable obligations and respective amounts set out in the notice of physical settlement. This happens only if none of the following sections of the 2003 Definitions applies:

- partial cash settlement due to impossibility or illegality;
- partial cash settlement of consent required loans;
- partial cash settlement of assignable loans;
- partial cash settlement of participations;
- buy-in of bonds not delivered; or
- alternative procedures relating to loans not delivered.

This provision then sets out the time period when the buyer may continue to attempt to deliver the deliverable obligations after the physical settlement date. The time period is not limited in the case of bonds and loans, but for other deliverable obligations the delivery must be made within five business days of the physical settlement date.

The provision clarifies that if a buyer fails to deliver the deliverable obligations specified in the notice of physical settlement, this will not constitute an event of default under any ISDA master agreement governing the credit derivative transaction.

This provision also provides further detail as to when the termination date of a physically settled transaction will be, subject to the following provisions not applying:

- partial cash settlement due to impossibility or illegality;
- partial cash settlement of consent required loans;
- partial cash settlement of assignable loans;
- partial cash settlement of participations;
- buy-in of bonds not delivered; or
- alternative procedures relating to loans not delivered.

This will be the latest of:

- the date that the buyer completes the delivery of the deliverable obligations;
- the date that the seller completes the buy-in (pursuant to Section 9.9) of all bonds that the buyer has failed to deliver; or
- the date that the buyer completes an alternative delivery (pursuant to Section 9.10), with respect to any undelivered loans.

In certain circumstances, two of these three 'latest dates' may be modified. Where the deliverable obligations include obligations which are not bonds or loans, the date when the buyer completes delivery of the deliverable obligations is deemed to be modified to the later of the date when the buyer completes delivery of the deliverable obligations and the date that is five business days after the physical settlement date. In the case of the latest date relating to when the seller completes a 'buy-in', if the relevant bonds cease to exist (perhaps because they have been redeemed pursuant to an insolvency), then this will be the deemed latest date.

Section 9.2(c)(iii) clarifies that if an event would constitute an 'impossibility or illegality' under Section 9.3 and it would also entitle a party to terminate the transaction pursuant to its ISDA master agreement, Section 9.3 will be deemed to apply and termination under the ISDA master agreement will not be permissible.

Section 9.2(c)(iv) permits either party to designate any of its affiliates to make or take delivery of the deliverable obligations and perform the related obligations. This designation, though, does not remove the relevant party's obligations. This designation is not permitted in two circumstances:

- If it was illegal for the affiliate to take or make the delivery; or
- If the delivery would give rise to the other party suffering a tax or any other loss or cost. In this circumstance the designation would be permitted if the other party were provided with an acceptable indemnity.

Section 9.2(c)(v) provides that in assignments of loans or regarding participations, where any fees or charges incurred by the buyer are payable to the agent under a loan, these shall be payable equally by the buyer and seller on the delivery date or the latest permissible physical settlement date.

Section 9.2(c)(vi) states that if a stamp tax is payable in connection with a delivery of the reference obligation or a deliverable obligation of the same type as the reference obligation, then the party that would ordinarily bear the stamp tax in a contract for purchase is liable for it. Where there is no reference obligation or the deliverable obligations are not of the same type as the reference obligation, the buyer is liable for the stamp tax.

3. Area II – delivery fallbacks for physical settlement

The 2003 Definitions set out alternative procedures for when the buyer is unable to deliver the securities detailed in the notice of physical settlement. The primary fallback is for either party to designate an affiliate to deliver or take delivery of the deliverable obligations. There are different fallback provisions for bonds and for loans, each of which begins when a seller is unable to deliver the deliverable obligation within five business days of the physical settlement date.

The first fallback applies where it impossible or illegal for physical settlement to partially or fully take place.

3.1 Partial cash settlement due to impossibility or illegality

Section 9.3 provides that if, due to an event beyond the parties' control, it is impossible or illegal for the buyer to deliver or for the seller to accept any of the deliverable obligations specified in the notice of physical settlement, then on or before the physical settlement date, the buyer must deliver any deliverable obligations for which it is possible to accept or make delivery. The seller must then pay the portion of the physical settlement amount corresponding to the amount of deliverable obligations that are delivered in accordance with the current market practice for that deliverable obligation. The relevant party must give the reasons for the impossibility or illegality to the other in writing.

If, following the occurrence of any impossibility or illegality, the amount of deliverable obligations specified in the notice of physical settlement cannot be delivered before the latest permissible physical settlement date (as defined in Section 9.7), then the partial cash settlement terms (as set out in Section 9.8) will apply to these undeliverable obligations.

'Impossibility or illegality' includes any clearing system failure or circumstances arising from any law, regulation or court order, but does not include market conditions or, in the case of loans, the failure to obtain any required consent.

3.2 Partial cash settlement of consent required loans; partial cash settlement of assignable loans; and partial cash settlement of participations

Sections 9.4, 9.5 and 9.6 each provide additional provisions to facilitate (as applicable) partial cash settlement of undeliverable loan obligations, unassignable obligations or undeliverable obligations, where specified in the confirmation.

These provisions will apply only where consent required loans, assignable loans and direct loan participations, as the case may be, are specified as deliverable obligations characteristics in the confirmation and as deliverable obligations in the notice of physical settlement.

4. Settlement Terms:	Partial cash settlement of consent required loans applicable
	Partial cash settlement of assignable loans applicable
	Partial cash settlement of participations applicable

Each of the three provisions then has certain other criteria which must be met for the partial cash settlement terms detailed in Section 9.3 to apply. In the case of consent required and assignable loans:

- due to 'non-receipt of any required consents', the consent required loans must not, on the physical settlement date, be capable of being assigned or novated to the seller or its designee; and
- the relevant consents must not have been obtained or deemed to be given by the latest permissible physical settlement date (as defined in Section 9.7).

In the case of participations, the relevant participation must not have been effected on or before the latest permissible physical settlement date (as defined in Section 9.7).

For consent required loans and assignable loans, there is a further proviso for the partial cash settlement terms to apply – either:

- 'direct loan participation' must not be specified as a deliverable obligation; or
- if it is, the relevant participation must not be effected on or before the latest permissible physical settlement date.

If the relevant criteria are met, then Section 9.8 will apply. The relevant consent required loans will be deemed to be 'undeliverable loan obligations'; any affected assignable loans will be deemed to be 'unassignable obligations'; and any direct loan participations will be deemed to be 'undeliverable participations'.

3.3 Latest permissible physical settlement date

Section 9.7 defines the final date when the seller can deliver deliverable obligations to the buyer, before the partial cash settlement terms apply as described in Sections 9.3, 9.4, 9.5, 9.6 and 9.8.

Which date is the 'latest permissible physical settlement date' will depend on the background to the delivery. It will be 30 calendar days after the physical settlement date where there is a partial cash settlement due to impossibility or illegality; but in respect of partial cash settlement of consent required loans, assignable loans and participations, it will be deemed to be 15 business days after the physical settlement date.

The definition also states that where "Section 2.33(b)(i)(C) applies" the latest permissible physical settlement date will be the "date deemed pursuant to that section". Section 2.33 (modified restructuring maturity limitation and conditionally transferable obligation) relates to the modified modified restructuring credit event option. Unfortunately, although sub-paragraph (b)(i) has an 'A' and a 'B', it does not have a 'C', and it remains uncertain as to how Section 2.33(b)(i)(C) applies.

3.4   Partial cash settlement terms

The partial cash settlement terms set out in Section 9.8 will be deemed to apply if transfer of deliverable obligations is not possible due to a lack of consent in the case of consent-required loans (Section 9.4) and assignable loans; and, in the case of a participation, if a participation is not effected (in each case, prior to the latest permissible physical settlement date) (Section 9.6 or 9.3). Section 9.8 does not apply in other circumstances.

Section 9.8 provides that if the partial cash settlement terms apply, physical settlement will not apply to the affected obligations; instead, the affected part of the credit derivative transaction will be cash settled in accordance with Section 9.8, instead of by the physical settlement method. The seller will be obliged to pay the buyer a cash settlement amount on the cash settlement date, which will be the greater of:

- zero; and
- the outstanding principal balance or the due and payable amount or the currency amount (as applicable) of each relevant obligation multiplied by its reference price, less the final price.

The cash settlement date will occur three business days after the calculation of the final price on the relevant valuation date (which is two business days after the latest permissible physical settlement date). The cash settlement date is also deemed to be the transaction's termination date.

For the purposes of partial cash settlement, when calculating the final price, the following are deemed to apply:

- The reference obligation is deemed to be each undeliverable obligation, undeliverable loan obligation, unassignable obligation or undeliverable participation;
- The valuation method is deemed to be the highest valuation method, unless fewer than two full quotations are obtained or a weighted average quotation applies, in which case it is deemed to be the market valuation method;
- The quotation method is deemed to be the bid quotation method;
- The quotation amount is deemed to be a quotation amount equal to the outstanding principal balance or due and payable amount or currency amount (as applicable), with no minimum quotation amount; and
- The valuation date is deemed to be two business days after the latest permissible physical settlement date, with the valuation time being that specified in the confirmation or, if none is specified, 11:00am in the obligation or participation's principal trading market.

The definitions of 'market value' and 'quotation' are subject to more vigorous amendment. The definition of 'market value' set out in Section 7.6 is restated and adapted in paragraph (j) of Section 9.8. Sections 9.8(j)(i) to (iv) set out the same procedures and fallbacks as Sections 7.6(a) to (d). However, the two provisions differ with:

- the addition at Section 9.8(v) of a fallback for 'indicative quotations' (which applies where the relevant part of a transaction is being cash settled due to impossibility or illegality); and

- the modification of the corresponding provisions in Sections 7.6(e) and (f).

Section 9.8(m) provides that these modifications apply only to obligations which are undeliverable due to illegality or impossibility.

Section 9.8(m) provides that indicative quotations become applicable under Section 9.8 when it is impossible or illegal for the buyer to make a delivery or the seller to take a delivery, pursuant to Section 9.3. These 'indicative quotations' are incorporated into the 2003 Definitions to provide for situations where, due to impossibility or illegality, dealers are not prepared to provide quotations for an obligation.

They are defined in Section 9.8(l) as a quotation obtained for an amount of the undeliverable obligation, to the extent reasonably practicable, equal to the quotation amount, which reflects the dealer's reasonable assessment of the undeliverable obligation's price. Section 9.8(l) specifically provides that the dealer's assessment may take into account any factors that it considers relevant, including historical prices and recovery.

The partial cash settlement terms work by the calculation agent going out into the market and attempting to obtain full quotations on the valuation date (ie, two business days after the latest permissible physical settlement date). As with the cash settlement process for cash settled transactions, the calculation agent must approach five dealers. The process then works as outlined below.

Quotations received	Calculation agent action to determine market value
More than three full quotations	Disregard the highest and lowest full quotations and calculate the arithmetic mean. If two full quotations have the same highest or lowest value, only one is discarded
Exactly three full quotations	Disregard the highest and lowest full quotations and calculate the arithmetic mean. If two full quotations have the same highest or lowest value, only one is discarded
Exactly two full quotations	Calculate the arithmetic mean of the full quotations
One full quotation and/or a weighted average quotation	Weighted average quotation used
Indicative quotations are applicable	Disregard the highest and lowest full quotations and calculate the arithmetic mean. If two full quotations have the same highest or lowest value, only one is discarded

One or no full quotations, no weighted average quotation, fewer than three indicative quotations (if applicable)	Subject to Section 9.8k(ii), the next business day which two or more full quotations, a weighted average quotation or, if applicable, three indicative quotations can be determined
One full quotation only or no full quotations	Five business-day period commences, operating until two or more full quotations, a weighted average quotation (or, if applicable, three indicative quotations are obtained). If two full quotations or a weighted average quotation is not obtained by the end of the period, market value is calculated as per Section 9.8(k)(ii)

The definition of 'quotation' set out in Section 7.7 is modified in Section 9.8(k). The amended definition also takes account of indicative quotations provided for obligations which are illegal or impossible to deliver, and recognises that undeliverable obligations, undeliverable obligations, undeliverable loan obligations, undeliverable participations and unassignable obligations are the most distressed of distressed assets. As with Section 7.7, the calculation agent must attempt to obtain full quotations on the valuation date from each five or more dealers[1] on the valuation date. If it is unable to do so, the fallbacks provided in Section 9.8(k) apply, with the calculation agent moving to the next fallback each time that it is unable to get the required quotations. The method by which the quotations for the relevant obligations are obtained works identically to the provisions for cash settled transactions set out in Section 7.7, except for the introduction of the concept of 'indicative quotations'.

The fallbacks under Section 9.8(k) work as outlined below.

Fallback 1: Calculation agent tries to obtain at least two full quotations from five dealers daily for the next three business days.

Fallback 2A (to run concurrently with Fallback 2B): Calculation agent attempts to obtain the same full quotations until the tenth post-valuation date business day. On each day that it is unsuccessful, it attempts to obtain a weighted average quotation.

Fallback 2B: If indicative quotations are applicable, obtain three indicative quotations from at least five or more dealers.

---

[1] Section 9.8(i) states that 'The Calculation Agent shall attempt to obtain Full Quotations with respect to each Valuation Date', even though there is deemed to be only one valuation date.

Calculation agent is either the buyer or seller	Calculation agent is not the buyer or seller
Fallback 3A: The calculation agent's counterparty may attempt to obtain the quotations. If the counterparty can obtain at least two full quotations, a weighted average quotation, or (if applicable) three indicative quotations, on any of the next five business days, then the calculation agent must use these quotations.	**Fallback 3B:** Each of the buyer and seller may attempt to obtain five or more full quotations or (if applicable) three indicative quotations and, if two or more full quotations are not available, a weighted average quotation or (if applicable) three indicative quotations.
Fallback 4A: The final price will be calculated using any full quotation the counterparty has obtained from a dealer at the valuation time on the fifth business day.	**Fallback 4B:** If either or both parties can obtain two or more full quotations or a weighted average quotation or (if applicable) three indicative quotations on the same business day within an additional five business days, then the calculation agent must use these quotations.
Fallback 5A: On the same day as Fallback 4A, the weighted average of: • any firm quotations (or, if applicable, indicative quotations) for the reference obligation obtained on the fifth business day for the aggregate portion of the quotation amount for which quotations were obtained; and • a quotation deemed to be zero for the balance of the quotation amount for which quotations or (if applicable) indicative quotations were not obtained on that day.	**Fallback 5B:** The parties attempt to obtain between them two or more full quotations or a weighted average quotation or (if applicable) three indicative quotations on the same business day within the next five business days.
	Fallback 6B: The quotations are deemed to be *any* full quotation obtained from a dealer at the valuation time on such business day.
A weighted average quotation can be obtained when dealers are prepared only to give quotations for less than the quotation amount. The calculation agent then takes a weighted average of the firm quotations obtained. The quotation amounts must be at least equal to the minimum quotation amount specified in the confirmation. If no amount is specified, this will be the lower of $1 million and the quotation amount. These quotations, when added together in aggregate, must approximately equal the quotation amount.	**Fallback 7B:** On the same day as Fallback 6B, the weighted average of: • any firm quotations or (if applicable) indicative quotations for the reference obligation obtained from dealers on the fifth business day for the aggregate portion of the quotation amount for which quotations were obtained; and • a quotation deemed to be zero for the balance of the quotation amount for which quotations were not obtained on that day.

Section 9.8(k)(iii) provides that the calculation agent will determine, after consulting with the parties, whether the quotation for the relevant obligation includes or excludes accrued or unpaid interest.

Finally, Section 9.8(k)(iv) provides that if the relevant obligation is an accreting obligation then any quotation which is expressed as a percentage of the amount payable at maturity will be expressed as a percentage of the security's outstanding principal balance, when determining the final price.

Hypothetical case study: partial cash settlement applies

On July 24 2005 Menacho SA entered into a $2 million physically settled credit default swap with Melkart SA, where it bought credit protection on Woodstock Corporation, a US travel company. On February 21 2008, Woodstock filed for bankruptcy. Menacho met the conditions to settlement by delivering a credit event notice and notice of publicly available information on February 23 2008 and later a notice of physical settlement on April 12 2008. The notice of physical settlement provided that on the physical settlement date Menacho would deliver $2 million of a $50 million floating rate bond due 2012 issued by Woodstock Corporation to Melkart.

Melkart SA, the credit protection seller, was a successful South American pension fund incorporated in Chile.

Unfortunately, following the collapse of a rival pension fund between the date of the notice of physical settlement and the physical settlement date (which was May 11 2008), new emergency regulations were introduced in Chile forbidding pension funds from purchasing sub-investment grade securities. This made it illegal for Melkart to pay Menacho the physical settlement amount for the Woodstock bonds (which now had a default rating). Pursuant to Section 9.3, the Woodstock bonds were 'undeliverable obligations'. Melkart was obliged to provide Menacho with a description in "reasonable detail of the facts giving rise to the impossibility or illegality":

The notice read:

To: Menacho SA
Fax: +34 956 343 9393
Date: March 21 2008

NOTIFICATION OF ILLEGALITY OF TAKING DELIVERY OF
DELIVERABLE OBLIGATIONS
Credit Derivative Transaction Details: Reference: HD838383 Trade Date: November 27 2005. Effective Date: July 24 2005. Reference Entity: Woodstock Corporation.

Reference is made to the Credit Derivative Transaction described above (the 'Transaction'), between us, as Seller, and you, as Buyer. Capitalised terms used and not otherwise defined in this letter shall have the meanings given them in the confirmation of the Transaction.

We inform you that on March 19 2008 new emergency regulations were promulgated in Chile (Ley de regulación de fondos 2008/35), prohibiting Chilean regulated pension companies from purchasing international securities, which do not have an investment grade rating. Menacho SA is a Chilean regulated pension company to which the new law is applicable and consequently it is illegal for us to take delivery of the Deliverable Obligations (which are not investment grade securities) specified in the Notice of Physical Settlement.

Nothing in this letter shall be construed as a waiver of any of the rights we may have with respect to the Transaction.

Yours faithfully
Bernado O'Higgins
Legal Counsel

The deliverable obligations specified in the notice of physical settlement remained undelivered at the latest physical settlement date (which was defined in the confirmation as 30 calendar days after the conditions to settlement had been met (ie, May 10 2009). This meant that pursuant to Section 9.3, the partial cash settlement terms were deemed to apply.

Melkart was the calculation agent under the transaction. In this capacity, it was obliged to cash settle the transaction in accordance with Section 9.8. First of all, Melkart had to go out into the market and attempt to obtain full quotations on the valuation date (ie, two business days after the latest permissible physical settlement date: May 12 2009, in accordance with Section 9.8(d)) at the valuation time (ie, 11:00am in the Woodstock bonds' principal trading market, New York)). As with the cash settlement process for cash settled transactions, Melkart was obliged to approach the five dealers. As none had been specified in the confirmation, the parties agreed the identity of the dealers between them.

The process then worked as follows. Melkart requested quotations for the quotation amount of the undeliverable obligations. This was deemed to be the outstanding principal balance of the Woodstock bonds (in accordance with Section 9.8(g)). Even though there was a market for the Woodstock bonds, and the illegality related specifically to Melkart being able to accept delivery of the deliverable obligations, Melkart was also obliged to seek 'indicative quotations', which are intended to be used when there is no market for undeliverable obligations, pursuant to Sections 9.8(k) and 9.8(l).

Melkart had to ask that the quotations exclude the interest which had accrued, but not been paid, on the undeliverable obligation. This was in accordance with Section 9.8(k)(iii), because after consulting with Menacho, the parties determined that it was not market practice for quotations for Woodstock bonds to include accrued interest.

The Woodstock bonds turned out to be very illiquid and Melkart was unable to get at least two full quotations on the same business day in any of the next three business days. During the following seven business days (until 10 business days following the valuation date) Melkart continued to attempt to obtain full quotations from five or more dealers. On each day Melkart tried to obtain at least two full quotations, failing which a weighted average quotation, without success. When neither of these options was available, Melkart tried to obtain three indicative quotations from five or more dealers. On each business day, Melkart was unsuccessful.

Melkart was the seller as well as the calculation agent, and so a different set of fallbacks applied from if a third party had been the calculation agent. The third fallback, which is provided for in Section 9.8(k)(ii), was for Menacho to attempt to obtain the quotations. Menacho attempted to obtain at least two full quotations, a weighted average quotation or three indicative quotations on the same business day for the next five business days. If it had been able to do so Melkart, in its capacity as calculation agent, would have used these full quotations, weighted average quotation or indicative quotations to calculate the final price. Unfortunately, the Woodstock bonds remained highly illiquid and Menacho could not obtain any full quotations, weighted average quotation or indicative quotations.

This meant that the parties proceeded to the next fallback to determine whether Menacho had received any full quotation on the fifth business day. It had not, so the parties moved to the next fallback: had Menacho received a weighted average quotation or three indicative quotations on the fifth business day? Menacho had received three indicative quotations for the Woodstock bonds on that fifth business day. These were from Liberatador Bank, Ambrose Bank and Riquelme Bank, which all provided quotations consistent with Section 9.8(l) reflecting their reasonable assessment of the price of the Woodstock bonds, based on factors that they considered relevant such as historical prices and recovery rates for defaulted US (formerly) investment grade corporate securities.

The indicative quotations obtained were as follows:

Liberatador Bank:	66%
Ambrose Bank:	65%
Riquelme Bank:	65.5%

This meant that Melkart was obliged to determine the final price of the Woodstock bond in accordance with the market quotation valuation method (because, in accordance with Section 9.8(e), less than two full quotations or a weighted average quotation was available). To do this, Melkart determined the 'market value' of the Woodstock bonds in accordance with Section 9.8(j)(v), and because exactly three indicative quotations had been obtained, Melkart disregarded the highest and lowest quotations: (ie, Libertador Bank's 66% quotation and Riquelme Bank's 65.5% quotation). Melkart took Ambrose Bank's 65% quotation as the final price for the Woodstock bond.

In accordance with Section 9.8(a), Melkart then determined that the cash settlement amount which it must pay to Menacho was the $2 million

> outstanding principal balance of the Woodstock bonds specified in the notice of physical settlement, multiplied by the transaction's reference price (which was 100%), less the final price. This was an amount of $700,000 (ie, $2 million x (100% – 65% = 35%) = $700,000).
>
> Melkart paid the $700,000 cash settlement amount to Menacho three business days after it calculated the final price, in accordance with Section 9.8(b).

3.5 Buy-in of bonds not delivered

Where a buyer cannot deliver all of the bonds in the notice of physical settlement, then unless this is due to impossibility or illegality, the seller has the right to buy them in.[2] It must first give the buyer at least two business days' notice, in the form of a buy-in notice, of which bonds it intends to buy in. This notice must specify the anticipated buy-in date, the relevant bonds and the outstanding principal balance to be bought in.

On the buy-in date, the seller will conduct a dealer poll asking for firm quotations for the bonds (the buy-in offers). If the seller can obtain only one buy-in offer, then that will be the buy-in price; otherwise, the lowest buy-in offer will be the buy-in price.

If the seller cannot obtain a buy-in offer for the bond's full outstanding principal balance on the buy-in date, it will attempt to obtain buy-in offers for all or a portion of the bonds on each business day following the buy-in date until the fourth business day after the buy-in date or the date the buy-in price is determined, whichever is earlier.

The buyer's right to deliver the bonds is suspended during the buy-in period. It recommences at the end of this period if settlement has still not taken place, but only to the extent that the seller has not determined the buy-in price for any relevant bonds. The buyer will continue to try to obtain the outstanding deliverable obligations.

On the sixth business day after the end of the buy-in period, the seller has the right to recommence the buy-in process in accordance with the previous procedures. This process can then be repeated until final settlement of the transaction.

On the date that the buy-in price is determined or as soon as practicable thereafter, the seller must deliver a buy-in price notice to the buyer of the outstanding principal balance of the bonds for which it obtained buy-in prices.

On the third business day following this notice, the buyer will be deemed to have delivered the bought-in bonds. The seller then pays the buyer. The amount paid will be equal to the portion of the physical settlement amount corresponding to the bought-in bonds reduced (but not below zero) by the relevant bonds' buy-in price (which is expressed as a percentage), and multiplied by the outstanding principal balance of the relevant bonds for which a buy-in price was determined. Any reasonable brokerage costs in relation to purchasing the relevant bonds are subtracted from this amount.

---

2   Section 9.9.

**Hypothetical case study: physical settlement III –
buy-in of bonds not delivered**

On March 15 2008 Genoves SA entered into a €20 million physically settled credit default swap with Osorio SA, where it bought credit protection on Magistral PLC, a British tobacco company.

On July 1 2010 Magistral filed for bankruptcy. Genoves triggered a bankruptcy credit event and met all of the conditions to settlement by July 8 2010, when it delivered a notice of physical settlement. Genoves did not own any of Magistral's securities and so was obliged to purchase the deliverable obligations that it intended to deliver to Osorio on the delivery date. Magistral's credit quality had been declining for a number of years and it had effectively been shut out of the capital markets. In order to pay off its debts, Magistral had spun off various subsidiaries, leaving it with only two outstanding debt obligations: a €80 million floating rate note due 2012 and a €250 million floating rate note due 2015. Prior to Magistral spinning off several of its reference entities, Magistral had been a widely traded reference entity. Even though the Magistral group had reduced in size considerably, there were no successor reference entities.

When the credit event occurred there were a large number of physically settled credit default swaps outstanding, but relatively few deliverable obligations. Genoves had stated in its notice of physical settlement that it intended to deliver €10 million of the Magistral 2012 bond and €10 million of the 2015 bond. Genoves was able to obtain €10 million of the 2012 bond, but only €6 million of the 2015 bond.

The physical settlement date, which was defined as 30 business days after the conditions to settlement had been met, came and went on Wednesday August 18 2010. Genoves had delivered the deliverable obligations that it was able to on the physical settlement date, but five business days later, on Wednesday August 15 2010, it was still unable to deliver the remaining €6 million of the 2015 bond.

This allowed Osario to invoke the 'buy-in of bonds not delivered' procedure set out in Section 9.9 of the 2003 Definitions. Osario was obliged to give Genoves two business days' notice that it intended to buy-in the outstanding €6 million of the 2015 bonds, in the form of a buy-in notice. On Thursday August 16 2010, Osario sent a buy-in notice in the following form to Genoves:

To: Genoves SA
Fax: +34 95 343 4343
Date: Friday August 16 2010

BUY-IN NOTICE FOR BONDS NOT DELIVERED
Credit Derivative Transaction Details: Reference: GF34343 Trade Date: March 10 2008. Effective Date: March 15 2008. Reference Entity: Magistral PLC.

*Reference is made to the Credit Derivative Transaction described above (the '**Transaction**'), between us, as Seller, and you, as Buyer. Capitalised terms used* *and not otherwise defined in this letter shall have the meanings given them in the confirmation of the Transaction.*

Pursuant to the Notice of Physical Settlement, which you delivered to us on July 8 2010, specifying that you intended to deliver to us the following Deliverable Obligations:

€10 million of an issue of €80 million Floating Rate Note due 2012 (XS192822928) issued by the Reference Entity; and

*€10 million of an issue of €250 million Floating Rate Note due 2015 issued by the Reference Entity (the '**2015 Notes**'),*

*you have been unable to deliver to us an outstanding principal balance of €4 million of the 2015 Notes (the '**Relevant Bonds**'). Pursuant to Section 9.9 of the 2003 ISDA Credit Derivatives Definitions, this letter is our Buy-In Notice to you that with respect to Magistral PLC, we intend to buy-in an outstanding principal balance of €4 million of the Relevant Bonds on Tuesday August 20 2010 (the '**Buy-in Date**').*

Nothing in this letter shall be construed as a waiver of any of the rights we may have with respect to the Transaction.

Yours faithfully
F Gonzalez
Legal Counsel
Osorio SA

This meant that Genoves's right to deliver the outstanding bonds was suspended during the buy-in procedure. On the buy-in date, Osorio attempted to obtain firm quotations from five dealers for the sale of the 'relevant bonds'. Osorio received quotations from four of the dealers it approached. The lowest firm quotation was for 60%. This meant that the buy-in price was established at 60%.

Osorio then delivered a buy-in price notice. This was done on the date that the buy-in price was determined (ie, on Monday August 19). The buy-in price notice took the following form:

To: Genoves SA
Fax: +34 95 343 4343
Date: August 20 2010

BUY-IN PRICE NOTICE FOR BONDS NOT DELIVERED
Credit Derivative Transaction Details: Reference: GF34343 Trade Date: March 10 2008. Effective Date: March 15 2008. Reference Entity: Magistral PLC.

*Reference is made to the Credit Derivative Transaction described above (the '**Transaction**'), between us, as Seller, and you, as Buyer. Capitalised terms used and not otherwise defined in this letter shall have the meanings given them in the confirmation of the Transaction.*

Pursuant to the Buy-in Notice, which we delivered to you specifying that we intended to exercise our right to buy-in the outstanding principal balance of €4 million of an issue or €250 million Floating Rate Note due 2015 issued by the Reference Entity (the 'Relevant Bonds'), pursuant to Section 9.9 of the 2003 ISDA Credit Derivatives Definitions, on Tuesday August 20 2010 (the 'Buy-in Date'), we inform you that we obtained the following bid quotations for the full outstanding principal balance of the Relevant Bonds:

Balenario Bank –	*72%*
San Roque Bank –	*74.5%*
Candelaria Bank –	*73.2%*
Castellar Bank –	*74.5%*
Bolivar Bank –	*72.5%*

The lowest price obtained was 72% from Balenario Bank, which shall be the Buy-in Price. We have committed to buy the Relevant Bonds from Balenario Bank and shall pay to you on August 23 2010, the sum of €1.12 million (less any relevant brokerage costs) (being an amount equal to the Physical Settlement Amount of €4 million less the Buy-in price of €2.88 million).

Nothing in this letter shall be construed as a waiver of any of the rights we may have with respect to the Transaction.

Yours faithfully
F Gonzalez
Legal Counsel
Osorio SA

On the third business day after the buy-in date, Friday August 20 2010, Osorio paid this amount to Genoves, as required by the 2003 Definitions, and Genoves was deemed to have delivered the outstanding principal balance of the relevant bonds.

In the hypothetical case study above, the buy-in of bonds was achieved by the seller at the first attempt. When the deliverable obligations are particularly illiquid assets, the parties may need to rely on the more extensive fallbacks in the 2003 Definitions (as described above and in the hypothetical case study below).

**Hypothetical case study: physical settlement IV –
Buy-in of bonds not delivered: fallbacks exhausted**

On June 30 2007 Pavoni SA entered into a €5 million physically settled credit default swap with Bezares SA, where it bought credit protection on Medina Corporation, an American brewer.

On May 8 2009 Medina filed for bankruptcy. Pavoni triggered a bankruptcy credit event and met all of the conditions to settlement by May 12 2009, when it delivered a notice of physical settlement. Pavoni did not own any of Medina's securities and so was obliged to purchase the deliverable obligations that it intended to deliver to Bezares on the delivery date. All of its debt, except for a single bond, was bank debt. Medina had negotiated into each loan that its consent was required for any transfer to be effective. Medina's trustee in bankruptcy stated that it did not intend to give consent for any loan obligation to be transferred. This meant that the only outstanding deliverable obligation that could be used to settle the transaction was a €30 million floating rate note due 2021 issued by Medina. Medina was a widely traded reference entity and there were far in excess of €30 million worth of credit default swaps referencing Medina.

Pavoni had stated in its notice of physical settlement that it intended to deliver €5 million of the Medina bond. The physical settlement date, which was defined as 30 calendar days after the conditions to settlement had been met, was June 11 2009. Pavoni was unable to deliver any of the Medina deliverable obligations on the physical settlement date or by June 18 2009 (five business days afterwards).

Realising that the scarcity of Medina bonds was likely to make their price artificially high, and that in the future prices would decrease as settlements took place, Bezares decided to invoke the 'buy-in of bonds not delivered' procedure set out in Section 9.9 of the 2003 Definitions. Bezares was obliged to give Pavoni two business days' notice that it intended to buy in the Medina deliverable obligations, in a buy-in notice. It sent the buy-in notice to Bezares on June 19 2009 specifying that it intended to buy-in the Medina bonds on June 23 2009 (the buy-in date).

The scarcity of Medina bonds meant that Bezares was unable to obtain a buy-in offer for any of the Medina bonds on the buy-in date. It then attempted to obtain buy-in offers on each of the four business days after the buy-in date until June 29 2009.

Pavoni's right, as seller, to deliver the Medina bonds was suspended during the buy-in period. On June 30 2009, after Bezares had failed to buy-in the Medina bonds, pursuant to the 2003 Definitions, Pavoni now had a right to try to obtain the Medina bonds and deliver these to Bezares during the next six business days, until July 5 2009.

Pavoni once again failed to obtain and deliver the Medina bonds, and on July 5 2009 Bezares once again had the right to recommence the buy in process. On July 6 2009 Bezares decided to commence another buy-in process and delivered a buy-in notice to Pavoni stating that it intended to buy in the bonds on July 8 2009.

The process operated as in the first buy-in process and Bezares attempted to obtain the Medina bonds for four business days until July 19 2009, following which, once again, the right to deliver the Medina bonds reverted to Pavoni. The transaction remained unsettled for a further six months until Medina Corporation was liquidated and the bonds were redeemed: the bondholders in fact received 50% of the principal amount of their obligations, once Medina's business had been broken up and sold.

At this point it became impossible for Pavoni to deliver the deliverable obligations to Bezares, and the transaction was settled pursuant to Section 9.2 of the 2003 Definitions.

3.6 Alternative procedures relating to loans not delivered

Whereas Section 9.9 deals with bonds which are not delivered, Section 9.10 sets out alternative procedures for where the buyer is unable to deliver a loan which it has specified as a deliverable obligation in the notice of physical settlement to the seller.

In these circumstances, if by the fifth business day after the physical settlement date the buyer has been unable to deliver the specified loans to the seller, then the 'alternative procedures' set out in Section 9.10 apply. This fifth business day after the physical settlement date is defined as the 'alternative procedures start date' and the alternative procedures detailed in Section 9.10 apply unless one of the following has been specified in the confirmation:

- 'reference obligation only';
- in the case of a consent-required loan, 'partial cash settlement of consent-required loan applicable';
- in the case of an assignable loan, 'partial cash settlement of assignable loans applicable'; or
- in the case of participations, 'partial cash settlement of participations applicable'.

In these cases, instead of Section 9.10, Section 9.4 will apply to consent required loans; Section 9.5 will apply to assignable loans; and Section 9.6 will apply to participations.

In addition, these alternative procedures will not apply if the loans are affected by illegality or impossibility pursuant to Section 9.3. If any of these other sections is applicable, then the part of a transaction relating to those obligations affected will be settled in accordance with Section 9.8.

So assuming that Section 9.10 is applicable, then where the buyer cannot obtain the necessary consents to deliver a loan specified in the notice of physical settlement, it can provide a certificate, at any time after the 'alternative procedure start date', signed by one of its officers of managing director or equivalent rank certifying that it used reasonable efforts to attempt to obtain the consents. This certificate can be delivered in relation to all or part of the deliverable obligations, as applicable.

Once this has been done, the buyer is then entitled to deliver a bond (instead of a loan) that has transferable and not bearer-deliverable obligation characteristics. The buyer may also deliver an assignable loan instead. In both cases the new deliverable obligation must meet the other deliverable obligation category and characteristics (other than consent-required loan and direct loan participation). If the relevant credit event is restructuring and either modified restructuring or modified modified restructuring applies, then the buyer must also comply with these deliverable obligation restrictions.

At any time after the 15th business day following the alternative procedure start date, if any of the loans referred to in the buyer's certificate is still undelivered and the buyer has not delivered bonds meeting the criteria set out above, then it is the seller's turn to direct proceedings.

At this point, the seller can instruct that the buyer deliver a bond to it that has transferable and not bearer-deliverable obligation characteristics; or instead, an assignable loan. In each case, the new deliverable obligation must meet the other deliverable obligation category and characteristics (other than consent-required loan and direct loan participation) on both the physical settlement date and the delivery date. If the relevant credit event is restructuring and either modified restructuring or modified modified restructuring applies, then the buyer must also comply with these deliverable obligation restrictions.

The bond or loan will then be deemed to have been specified in the notice of physical settlement. This is subject to the seller identifying a holder (other than the seller itself or one of its affiliates) of the bond or loan willing and able to deliver the bond or loan to the buyer, free of any consents, at a price less than the reference price. The relevant instrument must also be able to be delivered by the buyer to the seller, without any other person's consent.

**Hypothetical case study: physical settlement V –
alternative procedures relating to bonds not delivered**

On September 18 2006 Broussard Corporation entered into a €3 million physically settled credit default swap with Stephanie SA, where it bought credit protection on Nantes SA, a French insurance company.

On September 20 2010 Nantes SA failed to repay the principal amount of a €80 million floating rate note. Once the relevant grace periods had expired, Broussard Corporation triggered a failure to pay credit event and met all of the conditions to settlement by October 15 2010, when it delivered a notice of physical settlement.

Broussard did not own any of Nantes' securities and so was obliged to purchase the deliverable obligations that it intended to deliver to Stephanie on the delivery date. The universe of Nantes' deliverable obligations was very limited and, due to its widely traded nature as a reference entity, limited deliverable obligations were available at a realistic price.

Broussard had stated in its notice of physical settlement that it intended to deliver €2 million of a €30 million Nantes floating rate syndicated loan due 2014. Nantes sourced €2 million of the Nantes loan, but the bankruptcy administrator refused to consent to the transfer.

The physical settlement date passed and because it was unable to obtain the requisite consent, Broussard was unable to deliver any of the Nantes deliverable obligations on the physical settlement date or within five business days afterwards. This fifth business day was the 'alternative procedures start date'

---

according to Section 9.10 and, because the confirmation did not specify 'reference obligation only' in the deliverable obligation category or 'partial cash settlement of consent required loans applicable', and because there was no impossibility or illegality as contemplated in Section 9.3, this meant that the alternative procedures detailed in Section 9.10 were now applicable.

Broussard delivered a certificate to Stephanie in the following terms:

To: Stephanie SA
Fax: +33 93 88 83 81
Date: November 21 2010

Alternative Procedures Relating to Undelivered Loan
Credit Derivative Transaction Details: Reference: GR23838 Trade Date: September 10 2006. Effective Date: September 15 2006. Reference Entity: Nantes SA.

Reference is made to the Credit Derivative Transaction described above (the **'Transaction'***), between us, as Seller, and you, as Buyer. Capitalised terms used and not otherwise defined in this letter shall have the meanings given them in the confirmation of the Transaction.*

In the Notice of Physical Settlement, which we delivered to you on October 15 2010 we specified that we would deliver to you €2 million of a €30 million floating rate syndicated loan due 2015 lent to Nantes SA (the **'Deliverable Obligation'***) on the Physical Settlement Date. I certify that we have made reasonable efforts to obtain the necessary consents set out in the documentation relating to the Deliverable Obligation to allow a transfer of the Deliverable Obligation firstly to us and then to you, but have been unable to do so.*

Nothing in this letter shall be construed as a waiver of any of the rights we may have with respect to the Transaction.

Yours faithfully
F Deauville
Managing Director

Although Stephanie was the credit protection seller, it had noticed that the Nantes bond obligations were trading at a significantly higher price than its loan obligations. Stephanie was worried that eventually Broussard would be able to gain the necessary consents to facilitate transfer of the loan deliverable obligation.

Fifteen business days after the alternative procedures start date, Stephanie instructed Broussard to instead deliver a €2 million of a €30 million floating rate note due 2018 issued by Nantes SA.

This bond met the 'transferable' and 'not bearer' deliverable obligation characteristics, as well as the 'bond or loan' deliverable obligation category and all of the other deliverable obligation characteristics (other than consent-required loan and direct loan participation) on both the physical settlement date and the delivery date.

> This meant that the floating rate note was deemed to have been specified in the notice of physical settlement. Stephanie also sourced a dealer willing to sell the floating rate note to Stephanie at 70% of its face value. Broussard purchased €2 million of the floating rate note for €1.4 million and delivered it to Stephanie in return for payment of the €2 million physical settlement amount.

3.7 Settlement variation

Some market participants may be concerned that the physical settlement fallbacks may lead to a situation where settlement does not occur. The parties can therefore agree at the outset to vary these physical settlement fallbacks by entering into a 60-business-day cap on settlement letter agreement through the 2005 Matrix Supplement to the 2003 Definitions. The supplement is incorporated directly into a confirmation and adds a new Article 11 to the 2003 Definitions.

The effect of the letter agreement is to provide that if the transaction's termination date has not occurred by the 60th business day following the physical settlement date, then that date shall be the transaction's termination date. There are two exceptions. First, if a buy-in price notice, effective at least three business days before the 60th business day, has been delivered in relation to a portion of the transaction, then the termination date for that portion of the transaction shall be the third business day after the notice becomes effective. The second exception relates to the alternative procedures relating to loans not delivered. Where, on the 60th business day, the buyer still has not delivered the deliverable obligations which the seller has specified, then the relevant portion's termination date will be the tenth business day after the seller has informed the buyer of the identity of the deliverable obligations.

If incorporated, the 2005 Matrix Supplement also incorporates the most recent Credit Derivatives Physical Settlement Matrix published by ISDA. The matrix sets out the current market standards for reference entities from different jurisdictions and industry sectors (eg, New Zealand Corporate and Subordinated European Insurance Corporate).

Article X – Novation provisions

Article X – Novation provisions	
10.1	Novation
10.2	Novation transaction
10.3	Transferor
10.4	Transferee
10.5	Remaining party
10.6	Old transaction
10.7	New transaction
10.8	Old agreement
10.9	New agreement
10.10	ISDA Master Agreement
10.11	Old confirmation
10.12	Novated amount
10.13	Novation agreemen

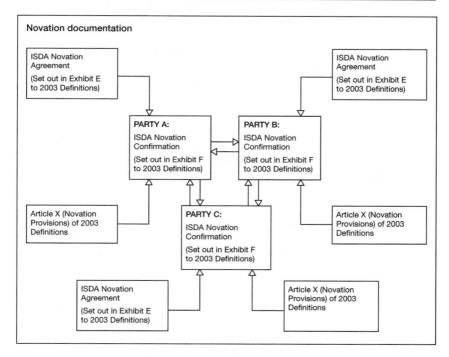

1. Trading credit derivatives contracts through novation

Novating a contract – substituting a new party for an existing one, by substituting a new contract for an existing one – is ISDA's preferred method for trading derivative contracts. In credit derivative transactions, Article X of the 2003 Definitions facilitates novation derivative trading with 13 enabling provisions. They work in conjunction with a specially tailored novation agreement and novation confirmation. The forms of these are set out in Exhibits E and F. The novation process for credit derivative transactions is relatively straightforward. It can be best explained through a worked example.

2. Hypothetical case study of a novation

Hyopthetical case study: Quintana Bank novates its credit default swap with Sesma Corporation to Armando PLC

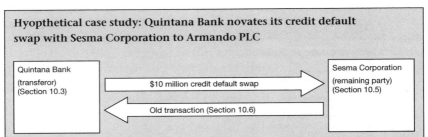

Quintana Bank had entered into a $10 million credit default swap with Sesma Corporation on November 14 2005, where Quintana had bought credit protection on Nano Securities. Later, Quintana suffered losses on its derivatives portfolio and decided to sell off a number of its derivatives. It arranged to sell its credit default swap to Armando PLC. The parties agreed that the transfer would take place by novation. The contract was to be novated by means of a novation agreement using the provisions set out in Article X of the 2003 Definitions (which in turn referred to the form of novation confirmation in Exhibit F and the novation agreement in Exhibit E); these had, of course, been incorporated by reference into the credit default swap.

Quintana Bank, Sesma and Armando entered into a novation confirmation in the form set out in Exhibit F to the 2003 Definitions. The confirmation stated that the provisions contained in Article X of the 2003 Definitions were incorporated into it. It also stated that the transferor (Section 10.3) was Quintana Bank, the transferee (Section 10.4) was Armando and the remaining party (Section 10.5) was Sesma.

The parties wanted the novation to take place on November 22 2007, the novation date. They also agreed the following terms, which were also set out in the confirmation.

Novation date:	*November 22 2007*
Novated amount:	*$10 million [Section 10.12]*
Transferor:	*Quintano Bank [Section 10.3]*
Transferee:	*Sesma Corporation [Section 10.4]*
Trade date of old transaction:	*November 14 2005*
Fixed rate payer and floating rate payer calculation amount of old transaction:	*$10 million*

The initial fixed rate payer calculation period with respect to the novated amount under the novated transaction shall commence on and include: November 22 2007

Drawing on the definitions set out in Article X, the novated amount (Section 10.12) was for the whole of the credit default swap (ie, $10 million). The trade date (Section 1.5) for the old transaction (Section 10.6) was two weeks before its effective date (ie, October 31 2005).

The fixed rate payer calculation amount (Section 2.7) and the floating rate payer calculation amount (Section 2.13) of the old transaction were $10 million. Finally, the period in which credit protection under the new transaction was due to commence was agreed to be November 22 2007.

The novation confirmation also stated that is was subject to the provisions of the novation agreement set out in Exhibit E to the 2003 Definitions. This meant that only the novation confirmation needed to be executed.

This novation agreement also incorporated the terms of Article X; furthermore, it incorporated by reference the terms defined in the 2002 ISDA Master Agreement. The novation agreement had several key provisions. Quintana Bank and Sesma Corporation were each released and discharged from further obligations in respect of the old transaction's novated amount. Sesma Corporation (the remaining party) and Armando PLC (the transferee) both undertook liabilities and obligations towards each other and acquired rights against each other identical to the economic terms of the old transaction. Importantly, these rights included the right to trigger a credit event occurring before the novation date.

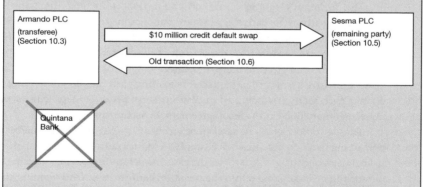

The novation meant that the ISDA Master Agreement (Section 10.10) between Quintana Bank and Sesma Corporation (ie, the old agreement (Section 10.8)) was replaced by an ISDA Master Agreement between Sesma Corporation and Armando (the new agreement (Section 10.9)).

One week after the novation, on November 29 2007, Armando discovered that Nano Securities had failed to pay an interest payment under one of its bonds on November 8 (two weeks before the novation date). Armando then duly delivered a credit event notice to Sesma Corporation.

3. How do credit derivatives novations work?

A novation of a credit default swap involves the buyer and seller agreeing to replace an existing credit default swap between them with a new credit default swap between one of them and a new counterparty. The concept is valid under both English law and New York law transactions.[1]

Article X provides the architecture for novations, first by defining 'novation' using Section 10.2 (novation transaction) and second through the definition of 'novation' in Section 10.1 (novation).

Section 10.2 defines a 'novation transaction' as one where a transferor (ie, either the buyer or the seller) transfers by novation to a transferee (a new party) all of its 'rights, liabilities, duties and obligations' with respect to the remaining party (ie, the party which is not transferring its obligations). Section 10.1 then provides that the parties may document a novation transaction by specifying in a novation confirmation that the novation transaction is subject to and governed by Article X and the novation agreement's novation provisions.

The novation takes place between three parties: a transferor, a transferee and a remaining party. 'Transferor' is defined in Section 10.3, 'transferee' in Section 10.4 and 'remaining party' in Section 10.5 'transferee'. The 'transferor' is "the party which transfers by novation to a transferee all of its rights, liabilities, duties and obligations with respect to a remaining party under and in respect of the novated amount of a credit derivative transaction"; with the 'transferee' being the party that accepts these rights, liabilities, duties and obligations; and the remaining party the party that consents to the transfer by novation of the novated amount and the acceptance by the transferee of the transferor's rights liabilities, duties and obligations.

The novation's subject is an old transaction (to which the transferor and remaining party were party) and a new transaction (to which the transferee and remaining party will be party). 'Old transaction' and 'new transaction' are defined in Section 10.6 and Section 10.7, respectively. The transferor and remaining party will also have been party to an ISDA Master Agreement, an 'old agreement'. This is defined in Section 10.8. The transferee and the remaining party should put in place an ISDA Master Agreement (itself defined in Section 10.10) between them. This ISDA Master Agreement is defined as the 'new agreement' in Section 10.9.

The definition of 'new agreement' recognises that if the transferee and the remaining party do not already have an ISDA Master Agreement in place, then it may take time to negotiate one. If this is the case, the definition provides wording which is deemed to be incorporated into the novation confirmation. This wording states that the transferee and the remaining party "agree to use all reasonable efforts promptly to negotiate, execute and deliver an agreement in the form of the ISDA Master Agreement". The wording goes on to say that until an ISDA Master Agreement is in place, a 1992 ISDA Master Agreement (if any of the novation documents refers to the 1992 ISDA Master Agreement) or otherwise, a 2002 ISDA Master Agreement shall be deemed to be in place. A schedule is not deemed to be put in place, except other than

---

1   ISDA has obtained legal opinions under both English and New York law to this effect, which are published on the ISDA website.

to elect the governing law set out in the novation confirmation and select euros as the termination currency for English law-governed transactions and dollars for New York law-governed transactions.

Section 10.13 (novation agreement) details that by exchanging a novation confirmation the transferor, transferee and remaining party are deemed to enter into a novation agreement in the form set out in Exhibit E (as supplemented in the novation confirmation and by Article X).

A novation does not have to be for the whole of the credit derivative transaction and Section 10.12 defines 'novated amount' as "the portion of the fixed rate calculation amount and the floating rate payer calculation amount of the old transaction that is the subject of the novation transaction". Where the novated amount is less than 100% of the old transaction, there are two transactions:

- between the transferor and the remaining party; and
- between the transferee and the remaining party.

The fixed rate payer calculation amount and the floating rate payer calculation amount are adjusted in each transaction to reflect respective size.

4.   Exhibit E – the novation agreement

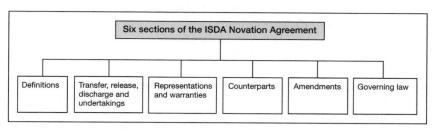

The novation agreement set out in Exhibit E is adapted from the 2002 ISDA Novation Agreement. It is divided into a preamble and six sections:

- definitions;
- transfer, release, discharge and undertakings;
- representations and warranties;
- counterparts;
- amendments; and
- governing law.

The preamble states that a novation agreement is subject to, and incorporates by reference, Article X of the 2003 Definitions. In clause 1, the definitions in the 2002 ISDA Master Agreement are incorporated by reference into the novation agreement. In clause 2, the novation agreement provides that from and including the novation date, the remaining party and the transferor are released from further obligations to each other in respect of the novated amount of the old transaction.

The clause further provides that in respect of the new transaction, the remaining party and the transferee each undertake liabilities and obligations with identical economic terms to the old transaction. Importantly, the clause specifically permits credit events which occurred before the novation to be triggered after the novation. Finally, the clause provides that the new transaction shall be governed by and form part of the new agreement.

5   Exhibit F – the novation confirmation

The form of novation confirmation is set out in Exhibit F. If the parties decide to attach the old confirmation to the novation agreement, the following wording is added to the confirmation: "A copy of the old confirmation relating to the old transaction is attached." It is submitted that this is best practice. The confirmation states that it is "subject to the provisions set forth as Exhibit E to the 2003 ISDA Credit Derivatives Definitions". This removes any need to execute the novation agreement.

The novation confirmation then provides for the parties to insert:

- the novation date and the novated amount;
- the identity of the three parties (ie, the transferor, the transferee and the remaining party);
- the trade date of the old transaction;
- the old transaction's fixed rate payer and floating rate payer calculation amounts;
- the date on which the initial fixed rate payer calculation period commences in the new transaction;
- the identity of the reference entity; and
- the scheduled termination date.

The confirmation also provides various square bracketed information, which the parties may choose to include. The parties may decide to insert the transferee, transferor and remaining party confirmation reference numbers, as well as the governing law of the ISDA agreement, in the new transaction and account information. Additionally, where a credit event has occurred prior to the novation date, options are provided for the parties to enter information setting out whether a credit event and/or a notice of publicly available information delivered under the old transaction is deemed to be delivered under the new transaction. In a physically settled transaction where an event determination date has already occurred, the parties may set out whether a notice of physical settlement has been delivered. If the buyer has delivered a notice of physical settlement, this should be attached to the confirmation. The parties may also choose to summarise any information contained in any notice in a 'notice information' section.

The novation confirmation is executed by the remaining party, the transferor and the transferee.

Introduction to Part III

In Part I, the first chapter gave an overview of the credit derivatives market. The second explained the key unfunded credit derivative products, from single name credit default swaps to first to default credit default swaps and portfolio credit default swaps.

In the third chapter, ISDA's full unfunded suite of documentation was analysed and the fourth chapter covered funded credit derivative products such as collateralised debt obligation (CDO), constant proportion portfolio insurance (CPPI) and constant proportion debt obligation (CPDO) transactions and credit-linked notes. With Part II of the book covering the 2003 ISDA Credit Derivatives Definitions, the role of Part III is to consolidate and expand upon some of the key areas.

Single name credit default swaps, for example, make up almost one-third of the credit derivatives market and warrant special attention. Conscious that for the new user, the traditional divide in credit derivatives materials between explaining how a credit default swap works and then how the 2003 Definitions function can lead to a disjointed approach, "Single name credit default swaps" focuses on drawing all of this information together, allowing a user to work through the single name credit default swap template with ease. There is some repetition from earlier sections, but a clear explanation of this cornerstone product is more readily achieved.

CDOs and index products come close to making up a further two-thirds of the market. They have already been mentioned in Part I, but "Synthetic collateralised debt obligations" and "Credit index trading" revisit these products in greater depth.

Credit default swaps on asset-backed securities (CDS on ABS) is today's hot product. Although the market is in its early stages, it should feature heavily in the next set of statistics for credit derivative usage. CDS on ABS template documentation is highly complex and difficult to follow. Part I provides an overview of this product, but "Credit default swaps on asset-backed securities" puts meat on the bones and includes an explanation of certain product intricacies such as the 'shortfall annex' and 'applicable percentage'.

Single name credit default swaps

1. Introduction

It's a common complaint. A credit derivatives book closely analyses the 2003 Definitions, but then when the reader looks at the most basic of confirmations, the single name credit default swap template, a frustrating process begins of flipping back and forth between each term in the confirmation and the explanation in the textbook covering the relevant section of the 2003 Definitions.

Vice versa, when a textbook (and there aren't that many) covers only that confirmation, the practitioner misses out on the intricacies of how the 2003 Definitions work. So why not cover both viewpoints? This will mean some repetition of earlier parts of this book, admittedly, but results in a text that gets closer to its goal of making credit derivatives more understandable and less opaque.

This is exactly what this chapter does. It is aimed at new users, as well as those wanting a refresher on the cornerstone credit derivatives document: the single name credit default swap template. Of course, Part II must still be consulted when needing to get into some of the finer detail of the 2003 Definitions. Without mixing too many metaphors, though, this chapter tries to provide an 'in the trenches' view rather than a 'helicopter' one.

Single name credit default swaps make up almost one-third of the credit derivatives market. This figure alone merits these transactions being given extra coverage; but on top of this, the single name credit default swap template is the foundation document from which so many of the other ISDA template confirmations are adapted (eg, the first to default credit default swap template and even the CDS on ABS templates).

This chapter collates the existing information in the book – the parts on how credit default swaps work; the breakdown of the single name credit default swap template – and then draws together (or repackages) the relevant definitions from the 2003 Definitions described in Part II of the book and summarises and applies these according to their order in the single name credit default swap template.

2. How do single name credit default swaps work?

Single name credit default swaps are privately negotiated bilateral contracts between a 'buyer' and a 'seller', referencing the third-party credit risk of a single reference entity

In a standard transaction, the parties agree that the buyer will purchase a pre-agreed notional amount of protection against the credit risk of the reference entity's obligations. The specific obligations against which the seller sells credit protection are

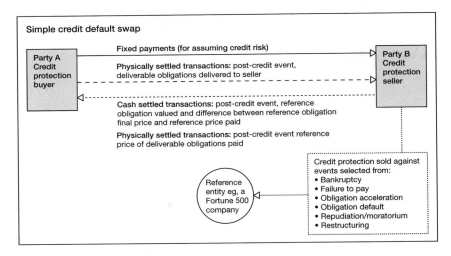

decided at the outset. They may be specific named securities of the reference entity, such as a €200 million floating rate note, or they may be a category of obligation, such as borrowed money, displaying certain characteristics (eg, listed bonds with a maximum maturity date of less than 30 years).

The credit risk, which the seller sells credit protection against, covers only the risk of certain pre-agreed credit events occurring in relation to a minimum amount of the obligations (or in the case of the bankruptcy credit event, the reference entity itself). Credit events are likely to match a significant deterioration in the reference entity's credit quality – they will be any agreed combination of:

- bankruptcy;
- failure to pay;
- the acceleration of an obligation;
- an obligation default;
- a repudiation or moratorium of debts; or
- a debt restructuring.

In return for the seller assuming this credit risk, the buyer will periodically pay a premium. This will usually be a percentage of the credit default swap's notional amount, expressed in basis points. The amount of the premium will reflect the credit risk of the particular reference entity, with greater risks reflected in higher premiums.

The parties document their transaction by entering into an ISDA Master Agreement and schedule, and setting out the transaction's terms in a confirmation incorporating the 2003 Definitions.

All of the market standard variables are set out in the 2003 Definitions. The parties select the applicable credit events, business days, conditions to settlement and other variables in accordance with market practice, which in turn may rely on the reference entity's jurisdiction of incorporation and/or its characterisation.

When a credit event occurs the seller (and often the buyer) has the right, but not the obligation, to trigger a credit event. The party triggering the credit event is called the notifying party and the date on which it does so is the event determination date. To trigger the credit event, the notifying party must satisfy the conditions to settlement (usually the delivery of a credit event notice) and (depending on what is specified in the relevant confirmation) a notice of publicly available information, plus a notice of physical settlement, if appropriate.

CZARNOCKI PLC
894 Ulica Grzybowska
Warsaw
Poland

Date: 20 December 2006

To: Alameda Corporation

Re: Linean Republic Failure to Pay Credit Event

Attention: The Directors

Email: creditevents@alameda.com

CREDIT EVENT NOTICE AND NOTICE OF PUBLICLY AVAILABLE INFORMATION

Credit Derivative Transaction Details

Our Reference: J15673473. Trade Date: 7 June 2005. Effective Date: 28 June 2005. Reference Entity: The Linean Republic. (the "**Affected Reference Entity**").

Reference is made to the Credit Derivative Transaction described above (the "**Transaction**") between you and us. Capitalised terms used and not otherwise defined in this letter shall have the meanings given them in the confirmation of the Transaction.

This letter is our Credit Event Notice to you that a Failure to Pay Credit Event occurred with respect to the Affected Reference Entity on 11 December 2006, when a Failure to Pay in relation to an outstanding issue of U.S.$300,000,000 Floating Rate Notes due 2010 issued by the Reference Entity occurred on 11 December 2006. This letter also comprises our Notice of Publicly Available Information with respect to the Credit Event, we provide the Publicly Available Information attached hereto.

Nothing in this letter shall be construed of a waiver of any rights we may have with respect to the Transaction.

Yours faithfully,
For and on behalf of

Czarnocki PLC

By: _____   By: _____
Name: Name:
Title: Authorised Signatory   Title: Authorised Signatory

The credit event notice is addressed to the counterparty, specifies that a credit event has occurred and gives the facts relevant to that determination. A notice of publicly available information is usually incorporated into the credit event notice. It cites publicly available information from public sources (usually two) such as Bloomberg and the *Financial Times,* confirming facts relevant to the credit event's determination.

Credit default swaps can be either cash settled or physically settled. In cash settled transactions, the calculation agent (usually the seller) selects and values a reference entity obligation. Either it is specified in the transaction or the transaction will provide a selection mechanism similar to that for establishing the reference entity's obligations.

The calculation agent will notify the counterparties of the reference obligation in a reference obligation notification notice.

CZARNOCKI PLC
894 Ulica Grzybowska
Warsaw
Poland

Date: 20 February 2007

To: Tavira PLC

Re: Linean Republic Repudiation/Moratorium Credit Event

Attention: The Directors

Email: creditevents@tavira.com

REFERENCE OBLIGATION NOTIFICATION

Credit Derivative Transaction Details
Our Reference: H98234739. Trade Date: 6 October 2004. Effective Date: 18 October 2004. Reference Entity: The Linean Republic. (the "**Affected Reference Entity**").

Reference is made to the Credit Derivative Transaction described above (the "**Transaction**") between you and us and to the Reference Obligations referred to therein. Capitalised terms used and not otherwise defined in this letter shall have the meanings given them in the confirmation of the Transaction. Reference is also made to the relevant Credit Event Notice and Notice of Publicly Available Information previously delivered to you.

This letter constitutes a Reference Obligation Notification for the purposes of the Transaction and the Reference Obligation identified below. Pursuant to the terms of the Transaction, we hereby notify you that the issue of U.S.$300,000,000 Floating Rate Notes due 2010 (ISIN: XS10439584) issued by the Affected Reference Entity has been selected as the Reference Obligation.

Nothing in this letter shall be construed of a waiver of any rights we may have with respect to the Transaction.

Yours faithfully,
For and on behalf of

CzarnockiPLC

By: _____   By: _____
Name: Name:
Title: Authorised Signatory   Title: Authorised Signatory

The transaction will detail when the reference obligation will be valued. Usually, this valuation date is sufficiently far from the event determination date to allow a reference obligation's trading price to settle.

On the valuation date (which may be on one date or several dates), the calculation agent will go into the market and ask for quotations from dealers for a pre-agreed amount of the reference obligation. The calculation agent will then calculate the reference obligation's final price. The 2003 Definitions provide numerous options and fallbacks for the number of valuation dates, the amount of quotations that must be sought (and from whom) and how the final price is to be calculated.

The final price is expressed as a percentage (ie, the percentage value of the current value of the reference obligation compared to its nominal amount or a reference price) and is calculated using a pre-selected valuation method. The calculation agent notifies the parties of the final price in a final price notification notice. Where there are multiple valuation dates, the calculation agent will notify the parties of the quotations obtained on each quotation date.

CZARNOCKI PLC
894 Ulica Grzybowska
Warsaw
Poland

Date: 20 February 2007

To: Mentidero S.A.

Re: Linean Republic Failure to Pay Credit Event

Attention: The Directors

Email: creditevents@mentidero.com

NOTICE OF QUOTATIONS OBTAINED ON A VALUATION DATE

Credit Derivative Transaction Details

Our Reference: K4309433. Trade Date: 6 July 2004. Effective Date: 18 July 2004. Reference Entity: The Linean Republic. (the "**Affected Reference Entity**").

Reference is made to the Credit Derivative Transaction described above (the "**Transaction**") between you and us and to the Reference Obligations referred to therein. Capitalised terms used and not otherwise defined in this letter shall have the meanings given them in the confirmation of the Transaction. Reference is also made to the relevant Credit Event Notice and Notice of Publicly Available Information previously delivered to you.

Pursuant to Section 7.4 of the 2003 ISDA Credit Derivatives Definitions, incorporated into the Default Swap, we hereby notify you in our capacity as Calculation Agent of the second Valuation Date on 20 February 2007 for the Reference Obligation (as stated in the Reference Obligation Notification delivered on 1 February 2007).

The Full Quotations obtained were as follows:

Pectri Bank – 74.25 per cent;

Conil Bank – 74.00 per cent; and

Chiclana Bank – 73.50 per cent.

Nothing in this letter shall be construed of a waiver of any rights we may have with respect to the Transaction.

Yours faithfully,
For and on behalf of

Czarnocki PLC

By: _____   By: _____
Name: Name:
Title: Authorised Signatory   Title: Authorised Signatory

The transaction is then settled an agreed number of days later. The cash settlement amount paid by the seller will usually be the transaction's notional amount multiplied by the reference price (usually 100%) minus the final price (eg, 50%). The transaction will then terminate.

Cash settlement as described above is the applicable settlement method in 23% of transactions, with fixed amount settlements (ie, a fixed recovery rate) being the applicable settlement method in a further 3% of transactions.[1]

Where the parties have specified that physical settlement applies, if the conditions to settlement are satisfied, the buyer has 30 calendar days to serve a notice of physical settlement. The transaction will set out either a specific obligation or the deliverable obligation category and the deliverable obligation characteristics, which a reference

---

1   British Bankers' Association, Credit Derivatives Report 2006, p 7.

CZARNOCKI PLC
894 Ulica Grzybowska
Warsaw
Poland

Date: 20 February 2007

To: Mentidero S.A.

Re: Linean Republic Failure to Pay Credit Event

Attention: The Directors

Email: creditevents@mentidero.com

FINAL PRICE NOTIFICATION

Credit Derivative Transaction Details
Our Reference: K4309433. Trade Date: 6 July 2004. Effective Date: 18 July 2004. Reference Entity: The Linean Republic. (the "**Affected Reference Entity**").

Reference is made to the Credit Derivative Transaction described above (the "**Transaction**") between you and us and to the Reference Obligations referred to therein. Capitalised terms used and not otherwise defined in this letter shall have the meanings given them in the confirmation of the Transaction. Reference is also made to the relevant Credit Event Notice and Notice of Publicly Available Information previously delivered to you.

Pursuant to Section 7.4 of the 2003 ISDA Credit Derivatives Definitions, incorporated into the Default Swap, we hereby notify you in our capacity as Calculation Agent of third Valuation Date on 3 March 2007 for the Reference Obligation (as stated in the Reference Obligation Notification delivered on 1 February 2007).

The Full Quotations obtained were as follows:
Pectri Bank – 78.25 per cent;
Conil Bank – 77.00 per cent; and
Chiclana Bank – 77.50 per cent.

The Final Price was calculated by using the Highest Full Quotation obtained on any of the three Valuation Dates which was 80.00 per cent obtained on the first Valuation Date.

The Loss Determination Amount as at the date of this notice is EUR 3,200,000

Nothing in this letter shall be construed of a waiver of any rights we may have with respect to the Transaction.

Yours faithfully,
For and on behalf of

CzarnockiPLC

By: _____   By: _____
Name: Name:
Title: Authorised Signatory   Title: Authorised Signatory

entity obligation must satisfy for it to be a deliverable obligation. The notice of physical settlement sets out the actual deliverable obligations that the buyer will deliver on the physical settlement date. These deliverable obligations will be equal in face value to the transaction's nominal amount.

The physical settlement date will be either as agreed by the parties or within the longest period customary in the market. On the physical settlement date, the buyer delivers the deliverable obligations and the seller pays an amount equal to their face value. Physical settlement still remains the dominant form of settlement in the credit derivatives market with it being the applicable settlement method in 73% of transactions.[2]

---

2   British Bankers' Association, Credit Derivatives Report 2006, p 7.

CZARNOCKI PLC
894 Ulica Grzybowska
Warsaw
Poland

Date: 3 January 2007

To: Alameda Corporation

Re: Linean Republic Failure to Pay Credit Event

Attention: The Directors

Email: creditevents@alameda.com

NOTICE OF PHYSICAL SETTLEMENT

Credit Derivative Transaction Details
Our Reference: J15673473. Trade Date: 7 June 2005. Effective Date: 28 June 2005. Reference Entity: The Linean Republic. (the "**Affected Reference Entity**").

Reference is made to the Credit Derivative Transaction described above (the "**Transaction**") between you and us and to the Credit Event Notice and Notice of Publicly Available Information dated 20 December 2006 previously delivered to you. Capitalised terms used and not otherwise defined in this letter shall have the meanings given them in the confirmation of the Transaction.

This letter constitutes a Notice of Physical Settlement. We hereby confirm that we will settle the Transaction and require performance by you in accordance with the Physical Settlement Method. Subject to the terms of the Transaction, we will deliver to you on or before the Physical Settlement Date, U.S.$10,00,000 of U.S.$300,000,000 Floating Rate Notes due 2010 (ISIN: XS10439584) issued by the Affected Reference Entity.

Nothing in this letter shall be construed of a waiver of any rights we may have with respect to the Transaction.

Yours faithfully,
For and on behalf of

CzarnockiPLC

By: _____   By: _____
Name: Name:
Title: Authorised Signatory   Title: Authorised Signatory

Hypothetical case study: single name credit default swap

Bank Pogrel PLC has cumulatively lent $100 million to a Las Vegas casino chain, Ricardo Corporation. Pogrel is Ricardo's banker and has sourced a large amount of business from Ricardo. Pogrel's success with Ricardo means that it is in a position to source further business from casino operations and the gaming sector generally. This, though, would lead to it having an excessive risk concentration in this sector.

Due to the importance of its client relationship, Pogrel is reluctant to sell its existing debt but would like to reduce its Ricardo exposure so that it can access new business. It would also like to benefit from the arbitrage between the credit protection payments it would have to pay under a credit default swap and the corresponding higher payments representing Ricardo's credit risk, which Pogrel receives as a component of the interest payments under the loans.

Unbeknown to Ricardo, Pogrel enters into a single name credit default swap, referencing Ricardo, with Ladjim Partners. Ladjim Partners is a hedge fund looking to gain exposure to the gaming market.

The obligations that are the subject of credit protection are defined as being any of Ricardo's bonds or loans. The swap has a term of three years and a notional amount of $100 million. The applicable credit events are Ricardo's bankruptcy, a failure to pay principal or interest on any of its bonds or loans above $1 million or any restructuring of Ricardo's debt. The transaction is documented using the ISDA single name credit default swap template.

To compensate Ladjim for taking on the Ricardo risk, Ricardo makes annual credit protection payments of 3% of the notional amount of the swap (ie, $3 million per annum and $9 million over the entire term of the swap).

Eighteen months later, a regulatory change banned gambling in Nevada, leaving Ricardo to file for Chapter 11 bankruptcy. Ricardo in fact had very little in the way of assets: it leased its buildings and the value of its business was mainly its goodwill. This left Ricardo obligations trading at only 10% of their face value.

A recovery seemed unlikely, so Pogrel decided to trigger a credit event on its credit default swap and deliver a credit event notice to Ladjim, rather than pursue a restructuring of the debt.

The credit event notice referred to their transaction and stated that a 'bankruptcy' credit event occurred when Ricardo filed for Chapter 11 bankruptcy. The credit event notice incorporated a notice of publicly available information and attached two pieces of publicly available information confirming that a credit event had taken place. One of these was a report from Bloomberg and the other was an article from the *New York Times*. An event determination date had occurred and the conditions to settlement had been met.

The settlement process began: a Ricardo senior loan was the reference obligation selected at the transaction's outset. Pogrel, using a valuation process set out in the credit default swap confirmation, valued the reference obligation at 10% of its face value: its final price.

Ladjim was then required to pay the cash settlement amount to Pogrel. This was the difference between the notional amount of the credit default swap and the reference obligation's final price (ie, 100% less the final price). Ladjim paid Pogrel $90 million. Pogrel then sold the Ricardo obligations that it held into the open market.

If the parties had entered into a physically settled credit default swap then following the delivery of the credit event notice and notice of publicly available information, Pogrel would (within 30 calendar days) have delivered a notice of physical settlement to Ladjim stating that it intended to physically settle the transaction: at this point the conditions to settlement would be met. Before the end of the physical settlement period Pogrel would be required to deliver to Ladjim eligible Ricardo securities (meeting the pre-defined deliverable obligation category and deliverable obligation characteristics) with a face value equal to the notional amount of the credit default swap.

Ladjim would be required to pay a physical settlement amount equal to the notional amount of the credit default swap (or other agreed amount of credit protection) to Pogrel.

3. The template single name credit default swap: Exhibit A to the 2003 Definitions

3.1 Introduction

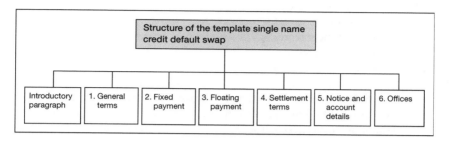

The 2003 Definitions sets out in Exhibit A a template single name credit default swap confirmation: the cornerstone document. References in this chapter to numbered articles and sections are to the corresponding articles and sections in the 2003 Definitions.

This document is structured, as with all ISDA confirmations, as a letter which is addressed from one counterparty to the other.

Date: January 16 2007

To: Amerique Investments
From: Mysteriuese Partners
Re: Credit Derivative Transaction: Reference Entity: Picaros PLC

Dear Sirs:
The purpose of this letter (this 'Confirmation') is to confirm the terms and conditions of the Credit Derivative Transaction entered into between us on the Trade Date specified below (the 'Transaction'). This Confirmation constitutes a 'Confirmation' as referred to in the ISDA Master Agreement specified below.

The definitions and provisions contained in the 2003 ISDA Credit Derivatives Definitions (the 'Credit Derivatives Definitions'), as published by the International Swaps and Derivatives Association, Inc, are incorporated into this Confirmation. In the event of any inconsistency between the Credit Derivatives Definitions and this Confirmation, this Confirmation will govern.

This Confirmation supplements, forms a part of and is subject to, the ISDA Master Agreement dated as of July 4 2005, as amended and supplemented from time to time (the 'Agreement'), between you and us. All provisions contained in the Agreement govern this Confirmation except as expressly modified below.

The terms of the Transaction to which this Confirmation relates are as follows:

The confirmation incorporates the 2003 Definitions and is subject to the applicable ISDA Master Agreement, which the parties have entered into. It is a nine-page document and is divided into six paragraphs. These are:

- general terms;
- fixed payments;
- floating payment;
- settlement terms;
- notices; and
- account details and offices.

The letter is executed by the party proposing the transaction and then confirmed by signature by the counterparty. The confirmation relies heavily on the 2003 Definitions, using over 100 definitions and terms from it.

3.2 Paragraph 1: General terms

1. General terms:	
Trade Date:	January 10 2007
Effective Date:	January 18 2007
Scheduled Termination Date:	January 18 2010

Each grey box in this chapter is an extract, in either template form or hypothetical transaction form, of the single name credit default swap template set out in the 2003 Definitions.

The general terms section set out in paragraph 1 of the confirmation provides an area for the parties to insert the transaction's key general information. Paragraph 1 utilises 13 definitions from the 2003 Definitions.

In particular, it sets out:

- the trade date (ie, the date on which the parties agree to enter into the transaction);
- the effective date (ie, the date on which credit protection commences);
- the scheduled termination date (ie, the date on which credit protection is scheduled to end);
- which party is the floating rate payer (ie, the credit protection seller);
- which party is the fixed rate payer (ie, the credit protection buyer);
- which party performs the calculation agency function and from which city it performs those duties; and
- the applicable business day and business day convention applying to the transaction.

Additionally, paragraph 1 sets out the identity of the reference entity on which credit protection is bought and sold and for cash settled transactions (and some physically settled transactions) the identity of the reference obligation. It also provides whether 'all guarantees' is applicable and the 'reference price' of any transaction.

The 'trade date' is usually a few days before the 'effective date', which is the date when any confirmation will actually be signed and when the parties want the credit protection period to commence. (References in text and diagrams in this chapter to 'sections' are always to the 2003 Definitions themselves.)

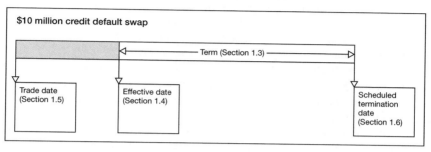

A transaction's 'term' runs from the effective date until the 'scheduled termination date', which is the agreed date for credit protection to end – that is, unless a credit event or a potential credit event causes the transaction to terminate either before or after the scheduled termination date.

Floating Rate Payer:	Amerique Investments (the **'Seller'**)
Fixed-Rate Payer:	Mysterieuse Partners (the **'Buyer'**)

The 'buyer', which buys credit protection on a reference entity, and the 'seller', which sells that credit protection, are the two counterparties in any transaction. In the 2003 Definitions the 'buyer' is defined in Section 1.19 (buyer) as 'the fixed rate payer' and the 'seller' in Section 1.20 (seller) as 'the floating rate payer'. These terms are in turn defined in Section 2.6 and Section 2.7 respectively, where the 'fixed rate payer' is defined as "the party obligated to make one or more payments of a fixed amount as specified in the related confirmation"; and the 'floating rate payer' is defined as "the party specified as such in the related confirmation"; 'fixed amount' is then further defined in Section 2.5 (fixed amount).

The buyer and seller are defined in this manner because credit default swaps involve bilateral payment flows. The buyer receives a premium in return for selling credit protection on the reference entity. In standard transactions these premium payments are a percentage amount of the notional amount of the credit default swap. The premium payments are therefore referred to as 'fixed amounts', payable by the 'fixed rate payer' on periodic 'fixed rate payment dates'. It is for this reason that the buyer is known as the 'fixed rate payer'.

The seller, on the other hand, will be required to make a payment only if a credit event occurs and a physical settlement or cash settlement amount is payable, and in these circumstances the actual amount payable will depend on the deliverable obligations delivered or the final price of an obligation. For this reason, the seller in the floating rate payer and the payments (if any), which it makes are floating rate amounts.

Calculation Agent:	Seller

The calculation agent may be the credit protection buyer, the credit protection seller or a third party. When the parties do not specify a calculation agent, the seller is the calculation agent by default. In fact, in most cases other than in structured transactions, the seller is the calculation agent anyway.

Fulfilling the role of calculation agent requires considerable expertise, and because of the determinations the calculation agent must make, any counterparty or third party taking on the role must have a solid understanding of the duties (and the risks) involved. Understanding the role is not easy considering that the calculation agent definition in the 2003 Definitions is 458 words long, including a 391-word sentence.

The calculation agent has 12 duties, which are mostly carried out in consultation with the parties: these are all set out in the 'calculation agent' definition, although they are sometimes restated in other definitions. This definition also obliges the calculation agent to notify the parties 'as soon as reasonably practicable' of any determinations that it makes when carrying out these 12 duties.

The calculation agent's 12 core duties: a summary table

1.	Determining a reference entity's successor	*Summary:* The calculation agent must determine which new entity or entities replaces an existing reference entity and assumes its obligations, if the existing reference entity merges, de-merges, reorganises, is taken over or spun off
2.	General reference obligation determinations: • whether aggregate amounts due under a reference obligation have been materially reduced • whether any reference obligation is an underlying obligation with a reference entity's qualifying guarantee • except following a credit event, whether that qualifying guarantee has become unenforceable	*Summary:* In cash settled transactions, the calculation agent must determine whether reference obligation nominal amounts are reduced, whether reference obligations remain valid and make determinations on qualified guarantees

- except following a credit event,
  or as above, whether a
  reference obligation is still an
  obligation of a reference entity

3. Identifying and determining
   substitute reference obligations

   Summary: In cash settled transactions,
   determining whether a reference
   obligation ceases to be a reference
   obligation (eg, because it has matured)
   and deciding upon a new reference
   obligation

4. Making adjustments for multiple
   credit event notices

   Summary: If a transaction is only
   partially triggered following a
   restructuring credit event, then the
   calculation agent must make certain
   adjustments to the transaction

5. Obtaining quotations

   Summary: In cash settled transactions,
   during the credit event settlement
   process, the calculation agent must
   obtain quotations for the reference
   obligation

6. Converting quotation amounts
   into the relevant obligation
   currency

   Summary: In cash settled transactions,
   during the credit event settlement
   process, if the calculation agent is
   getting quotations for reference
   obligations denominated in currencies
   other than the currency stated for the
   quotation amount, it must do a foreign
   exchange conversion of the quotation
   amount (eg, converting €25,000 into
   dollars)

7. Determining dealers and
   substituting dealers

   Summary: In cash settled transactions,
   the calculation agent must decide
   which dealers to approach for a
   quotation and pick new dealers where
   existing ones are unavailable

8. Determining the currency rate

   Summary: In physically settled
   transactions where the seller is
   delivering deliverable obligations in a
   currency other than the settlement
   currency, the calculation agent must
   decide the currency rate to use

9.	Determining the representative amount	*Summary*: In cash settled transactions, if the parties have not pre-agreed a figure for quotation amounts, they may choose to decide 'representative amounts' on a case-by-case basis
10.	Determining the number of business days in each physical settlement period	*Summary*: In physically settled transactions, determining the number of days in a physical settlement period, where a subjective decision must be made
11.	If 'accrued interest' is specified with respect to deliverable obligations, determining accrued but unpaid interest	*Summary*: In physically settled transactions, determining the amount of accrued but unpaid interest which relates to a deliverable obligation
12.	Determining the accreted amount of any obligation	*Summary*: In physically settled transactions, for accreted obligations such as convertible and exchangeable bonds determining the accreting amount (ie, the obligation's original issue price plus any amount payable at maturity which has already accreted less any cash payments that the reference entity has made to reduce the obligation's redemption amount)

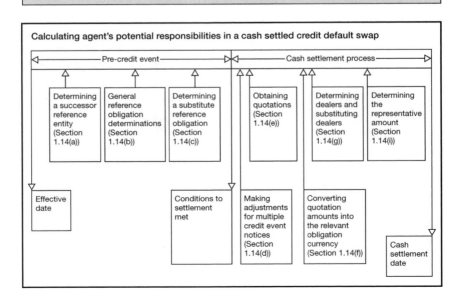

Calculating agent's potential responsibilities in a cash settled credit default swap

Six of the calculation agent's 12 duties relate only to cash settled transactions, four relate only to physically settled transactions and two relate to both cash and physical transactions. Three of the duties are carried out before a credit event occurs and nine of them are carried out afterwards.

Various tasks must be carried out by certain times: these are all provided for by the 2003 Definitions. For example, Section 1.9 (notice delivery period) determines the parameters of the period in which a party can meet the conditions to settlement. Section 1.10 (requirements regarding notices) determines when any notice (not just a credit event notice and notice of publicly available information) is deemed to be delivered, regardless of its actual delivery date. The definition also links to the definitions of 'calculation agent city' (Section 1.15) and 'calculation agent city business day' (Section 1.17).

Calculation Agent City:	London

'Calculation agent city' (here the parties specify in the confirmation the city which is the calculation agent's principal place of business) is important because of the date of deemed delivery of any notice. This is because notwithstanding that a notice is actually delivered on one day, it may be deemed to be delivered on another. This may theoretically affect not only whether an event determination date occurs within the notice delivery period, but also the date on which any valuation date will fall, in turn affecting an obligation's final price.

If a notice is not delivered before 4:00pm (calculation agent city time) on a calculation agent city business day, it is deemed to be delivered on the following calculation agent city business day.

If the calculation agent city is not specified in the confirmation, the fallback under Section 1.15 is for it to be the "the city in which the office through which the

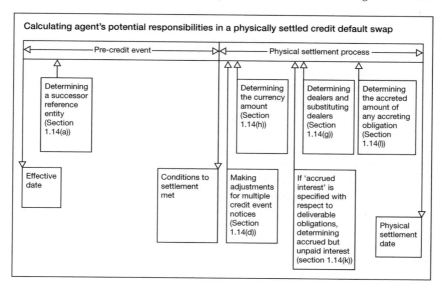

calculation agent is acting for the purposes of the credit derivative transaction is located".

Business Day:	London, New York
Business Day Convention:	Modified following

Various activities in credit derivative transactions can be carried out only on business days (eg, valuation dates and effective delivery of notices). Section 1.16 provides that a 'business day' in a transaction will be any day on which commercial banks and foreign exchange markets are generally open to settle payments in the places listed in the confirmation. In the confirmation extract above these are London and New York. A business day may also be a TARGET settlement day, which is separately defined in Section 1.21. Section 1.21 adopts the standard 2000 ISDA Definitions wording, providing that a TARGET settlement day will be "any day on which TARGET (the Trans-European Automated Real-time Gross settlement Express Transfer system) is open".

The business days that the parties select will usually depend on the currency of the credit derivative transaction and the location of the parties (in particular, the calculation agent). If no business days are set out in the confirmation, the 'business day' definition provides a fallback. This is for the business day to be a day on which commercial and foreign exchange markets are generally open to settle payments in the currency of the 'floating rate payer calculation amount' (ie, the currency of the seller's leg of the swap).

Reference Entity:	Picaros PLC

Credit derivative transactions have as their underlying asset the credit quality of a third party, which is not party to the transaction:[3] the reference entity. Section 2.1 provides that that these reference entities are those specified in the confirmation, together with any successor determined pursuant to the successor provisions in Section 2.2. Determination of a successor reference entity is one of the most complex areas of credit derivatives and particular difficulties can occur where there are multiple reference entities. A full and detailed discussion is set out in Part II; however, as a brief summary, the successor provisions for non-sovereign reference entities are 'rules-based' provisions that attempt to make the calculation agent's decision on successor reference entities. Determinations are made utilising Section 2.2 of the 2003 Definitions in accordance with the diagram opposite.

For sovereign successors the process is simpler: the 2003 Definitions state that 'successor' means "any direct or indirect successor(s) of that reference entity irrespective of whether such successor(s) assumes any of the obligations of such reference entity".

---

3   Except in the case of self-referenced credit linked notes.

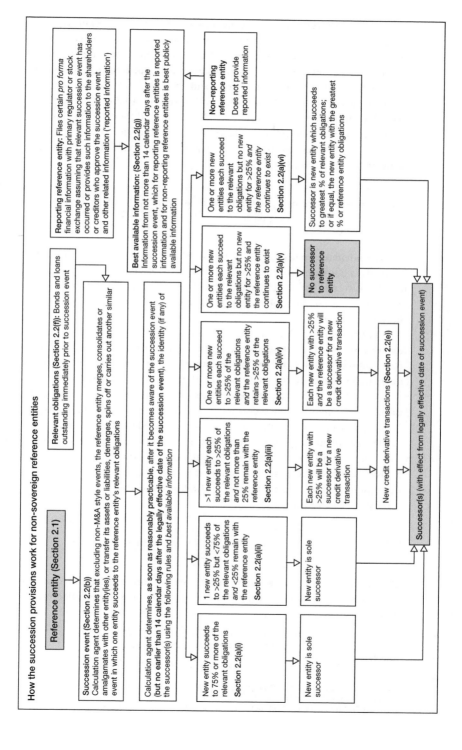

How the succession provisions work for non-sovereign reference entities

Single name credit default swaps

387

How any reference entity is categorised will also be important in a transaction. First, whether the reference entity is a sovereign (as defined in Section 2.26) affects whether several other provisions of the 2003 Definitions apply. In Section 2.2 (provisions for determining a successor), Section 2.2(a) applies for determining non-sovereign successor reference entities and Section 2.2(b) applies for determining sovereign successor reference entities; and in relation to modified restructuring and modified modified restructuring credit events, different rules apply to the determining the deliverable obligations which can be delivered depending on whether a reference entity is a sovereign: Section 2.16 (sovereign restructured deliverable obligation).[4]

Reference Obligation:	$250 million floating rate note (ISIN: 2398742389) due 2012, issued by Picaros PLC

The reference obligation is relevant and/or applicable only to cash-settled credit derivatives transactions, where the conditions to settlement have been met.

Once the conditions to settlement have been satisfied, the calculation agent must arrange for the reference obligation to be valued to ascertain its current market value (ie, its final price).

On the valuation date[5] at the valuation time,[6] the calculation agent will contact five or more dealers[7] (all as specified in the confirmation) and ask them to provide firm quotations (defined as 'full quotations')[8] for an amount of the reference obligation specified in the confirmation (the quotation amount).[9]

Depending on what is specified in the confirmation as the quotation method,[10] the calculation agent may request bid quotations, offer quotations or mid-market quotations (ie, a bid and an offer quotation which is then averaged by the calculation agent).

The calculation agent must obtain at least two full quotations on the valuation date. The very nature of a credit event will mean that the reference obligation will be a distressed asset, and as such quotations may be hard to come by. The 2003 Definitions provide a complex series of fallbacks to cover this. (These are covered extensively in Part II.)

All Guarantees:	[Applicable] [Not applicable]

The concept of 'all guarantees' relates to what is and what is not subject to credit protection in a credit default swap, and in particular which obligation categories and

---

4	See further discussion of the treatment of sovereigns below.
5	If there are multiple valuation dates, it will do so on each valuation date.
6	Section 7.14.
7	Section 7.15. Dealers are those in the type of obligation for which the quotation is being obtained.
8	Section 7.10.
9	Section 7.12. Where no amount is specified in the confirmation, the ISDA fallback is for the quotation amount to be the floating-rate payer calculation amount.
10	Section 7.9. Where no quotation method is detailed in the confirmation, the ISDA fallback is 'bid'.

obligation characteristics relate to guarantees and which to underlying obligations, as well as which guarantees are relevant as obligations. Article II differentiates between two categories of guarantee: qualifying guarantees and qualifying affiliate guarantees. 'All guarantees' is referred to in all of the sections of the 2003 Definitions which cross-refer to qualifying guarantees and qualifying affiliate guarantees. These sections include the following language: "(either directly as provider of a qualifying affiliate guarantee or, if all guarantees is specified as applicable in the related confirmation, as provider of any qualifying guarantee)."

A qualifying guarantee is one in which the reference entity agrees in writing to pay all amounts due under an underlying obligation (ie, an obligation for which another party is the obligor). The guarantee must not be subordinated to any of the underlying obligor's borrowed money when the credit event occurs. Qualifying guarantees exclude surety bonds, financial guarantee insurance policies, letters of credit and arrangements which can be modified otherwise than because of a non-payment event. The qualifying guarantee's benefit must be capable of being delivered together with the underlying obligation (eg, a guaranteed eurobond).

A qualifying affiliate guarantee is a qualifying guarantee provided by the reference entity to one of its downstream affiliates.[11] It is a narrower category than the qualifying guarantee. It is selected for jurisdictions where market participants believe that upstream and cross-stream guarantees have a greater legal risk than downstream guarantees.

Unless the parties select 'all guarantees' as applicable, the fallback is for qualifying affiliate guarantees only to apply.

The standard terms for all jurisdictions other than North American investment grade entities, North American insurance entities and North American high yield entities select 'all guarantees' as applicable. Due to concerns about the enforceability of cross-stream and down-stream guarantees in North America, the market convention is for qualifying affiliate guarantee only to be applicable.

ISDA issued the May 2003 Supplement to the 2003 Definitions to address concerns raised about guarantees, among other things. Incorporating the supplement into a confirmation is optional. Article II sets the date on which share ownership should be assessed for establishing whether an underlying obligor is a downstream affiliate as the date of the credit event or delivery date. In practice, this may be difficult to establish. The May 2003 Supplement makes the determination date that on which the qualifying guarantee is issued.

The May 2003 Supplement provides that for the purposes of applying obligation characteristics and deliverable obligation characteristics, both the qualifying guarantee and underlying obligation must satisfy any of the following:

- not subordinated;
- specified currency;
- not sovereign lender;
- not domestic currency; and
- not domestic law.

11　Section 2.25 defines this as a 50% directly, or indirectly owned subsidiary of the reference entity. The ownership must be of shares that have the power to elect the board of directors.

If the parties incorporate the May 2003 Supplement, but do not select 'not subordinated' as an obligation characteristic or a deliverable obligation characteristic, a guarantee which is subordinated to the underlying obligor's borrowed money obligations will be an obligation or deliverable obligation. This will not be the case if the May 2003 Supplement is not incorporated.

3.3   Paragraph 2: Fixed payments

> 2.   Fixed payments:
>
> Fixed Rate Payer Calculation Amount: $100 million
> Fixed Rate Payer Period End Date: January 10 in each year

Fixed payments are the payments made from the buyer to the seller for assuming the credit risk of the reference entity. The mechanics for making these payments are set out in paragraph 2. The fixed rate payer calculation amount is the base amount upon which any fixed amounts to compensate the seller for providing credit protection on the reference entity are paid. If the fixed rate payer calculation amount is not specified here, then the fallback is for it to be 100%.

> Fixed-Rate Payer Payment Dates: January 10 in each year
> Fixed Rate: 1.375%
> Fixed-Rate Day Count Fraction: Actual/360
> [Fixed Amount: $1,375,000]

The term of the credit default swap is divided into calculation periods, with the buyer making a payment to the seller for providing it with credit protection during each period. The date on which each fixed rate period ends is set out under 'fixed rate payer period end date'; the date which these payments are made under 'fixed rate payer payment dates'; the percentage amount of this rate under 'fixed rate'; or alternatively an actual amount can be set out under 'fixed amount'. Where part of an annualised percentage amount is paid on more than one payment date during the year, the amount to be paid is calculated using a day count fraction, with the specified day count fraction being set out under 'fixed rate day count fraction'.

The 'fixed rate payer calculation amount' is the base figure used to calculate the actual premium paid by the seller for assuming the risk of credit protection. It is normally the same as the 'floating rate payer calculation amount'.

3.4   Paragraph 3: Floating payments

> 3.   Floating payment
> Floating Rate Payer Calculation Amount: $100 million

Floating payments are the payments made from the seller to the buyer if the conditions to settlement in relation to the reference entity are met. Paragraph 3 sets out the amount of credit protection sold, the conditions to settlement, the credit events specified by the parties and the 'obligations' of the reference entity that a credit event might affect. 'Floating rate payer calculation amount' sets out the notional amount of credit protection sold.

Conditions to Settlement:	Credit Event Notice
	Notifying Party: Buyer or Seller
	[Notice of Physical Settlement]
	Notice of Publicly Available Information
	[Public Source(s):]
	Specified Number: 2

A credit event is triggered only once a credit event has occurred (as set out in Article IV) and the conditions to settlement (as set out in Article III) have been satisfied: the event determination date. This is the date when a credit event is deemed to have occurred and according to the definition, this is "the first date on which both the credit event notice and, if applicable, the notice of publicly available information are effective" – that is, 'delivered within the notice delivery period' and 'meeting the requirements regarding notices'. The event determination date sets the credit event settlement process rolling.

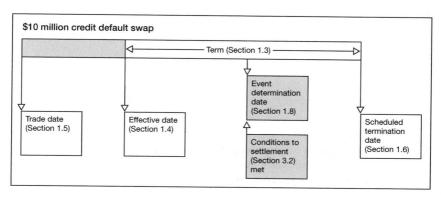

Under 'conditions to settlement', the parties specify what these will be usually be. The parties will usually insert 'credit event notice'; 'notice of publicly available information' and for, physically settled transactions a 'notice of physical settlement' here, together with who the notifying party will be and number of public sources of publicly available information required.

In a cash settled transaction, the date on which the conditions to settlement are satisfied is the event determination date,[12] which is the date of delivery of a credit

---

12   Section 1.8.

CZARNOCKI PLC
894 Ulica Grzybowska
Warsaw
Poland

Date: 20 December 2006

To: Alameda Corporation

Re: Linean Republic Failure to Pay Credit Event

Attention: The Directors

Email: creditevents@alameda.com

CREDIT EVENT NOTICE AND NOTICE OF PUBLICLY AVAILABLE INFORMATION

Credit Derivative Transaction Details

Our Reference: J15673473. Trade Date: 7 June 2005. Effective Date: 28 June 2005. Reference Entity: The Linean Republic. (the "**Affected Reference Entity**").

Reference is made to the Credit Derivative Transaction described above (the "**Transaction**") between you and us. Capitalised terms used and not otherwise defined in this letter shall have the meanings given them in the confirmation of the Transaction.

This letter is our Credit Event Notice to you that a Failure to Pay Credit Event occurred with respect to the Affected Reference Entity on 11 December 2006, when a Failure to Pay in relation to an outstanding issue of U.S.$300,000,000 Floating Rate Notes due 2010 issued by the Reference Entity occurred on 11 December 2006. This letter also comprises our Notice of Publicly Available Information with respect to the Credit Event, we provide the Publicly Available Information attached hereto.

Nothing in this letter shall be construed of a waiver of any rights we may have with respect to the Transaction.

Yours faithfully,
For and on behalf of

Czarnocki PLC

By: _____   By: _____
Name: Name:
Title: Authorised Signatory   Title: Authorised Signatory

---

event notice[13] and, if required in the confirmation, a notice of publicly available information.[14] In a physically settled transaction, a notice of physical settlement[15] must also be delivered following the event determination date.

A credit event notice describes a credit event that has occurred between the transaction's effective date and the latest of the transaction's scheduled termination date or, if applicable, a grace period extension date or repudiation/moratorium evaluation date.

It describes the facts relevant to the determination in reasonable detail. The credit event need not be continuing when the credit event notice is delivered: for example, a missed interest payment could potentially trigger a failure-to-pay credit event even if the payment is made before the credit event notice is delivered.

---

13   Section 3.2(a)(i).
14   Section 3.4.
15   Section 3.6.

A credit event notice cannot be revoked.[16] Only a notifying party can deliver it. The buyer will always be a notifying party; however, the confirmation may specify that the buyer is also. A seller might wish to trigger a credit event if:

- it had hedged its position by entering into another credit default swap as a buyer and it wishes to trigger that transaction; or
- it suspected that the reference entity's creditworthiness could decline further and it would be cheaper to trigger a credit event now.

A notice of publicly available information is normally a condition to settlement. It can be incorporated into the credit event notice with the publicly available information[17] acting as an independent verification that a credit event has occurred. This information must:

- have been published in a specified number[18] of public sources;[19, 20]
- be received from (or published by) the reference entity[21] or a trustee or agent in one of its obligations;
- constitute information contained in the reference entity's bankruptcy, insolvency or related proceedings; or
- constitute information contained in any court, tribunal or similar administrative or regulatory body's document.

If the buyer, acting in a trustee or agency capacity under an obligation, is the sole information source and is also a holder of the obligation which has suffered the credit event, it must deliver a certificate signed by one of its officials of managing director rank, certifying the occurrence of the credit event.

Publicly available information is not usually released for the purposes of triggering a credit event and so does not always give the details necessary to verify the occurrence of a credit event. Publicly available information that is difficult to obtain may include:

- the voting shares percentage necessary to determine whether an obligation is a qualifying affiliate guarantee;
- whether the payment requirement or default requirement levels have been met;
- the necessary grace period; and
- information or details of certain credit events' subjective criteria.

These requirements have therefore been disapplied.[22]

In a physically settled transaction, the credit protection buyer must deliver a notice of physical settlement within 30 calendar days of the event determination date.

---

16   Section 3.3.
17   Section 3.5.
18   It is market practice, and also the ISDA fallback, to require two public sources.
19   Section 3.7.
20   Public sources can be defined either in the confirmation or (as is market practice) if none are specified then from the list given in the 2003 Definitions. The sources listed include Bloomberg, the *Financial Times*, the *Wall Street Journal* and other leading financial newspapers, publications and subscription services.
21   Or where the reference entity is a sovereign, a sovereign agency.
22   Section 3.5(d).

CZARNOCKI PLC
894 Ulica Grzybowska
Warsaw
Poland

Date: 3 January 2007

To: Alameda Corporation

Re: Linean Republic Failure to Pay Credit Event

Attention: The Directors

Email: creditevents@alameda.com

NOTICE OF PHYSICAL SETTLEMENT

Credit Derivative Transaction Details
Our Reference: J15673473. Trade Date: 7 June 2005. Effective Date: 28 June 2005. Reference Entity:
The Linean Republic. (the "**Affected Reference Entity**").

Reference is made to the Credit Derivative Transaction described above (the "**Transaction**") between you
and us and to the Credit Event Notice and Notice of Publicly Available Information dated 20 December
2006 previously delivered to you. Capitalised terms used and not otherwise defined in this letter shall have
the meanings given them in the confirmation of the Transaction.

This letter constitutes a Notice of Physical Settlement. We hereby confirm that we will settle the
Transaction and require performance by you in accordance with the Physical Settlement Method. Subject
to the terms of the Transaction, we will deliver to you on or before the Physical Settlement Date,
U.S.$10,00,000 of U.S.$300,000,000 Floating Rate Notes due 2010 (ISIN: XS10439584) issued by the
Affected Reference Entity.

Nothing in this letter shall be construed of a waiver of any rights we may have with respect to the
Transaction.

Yours faithfully,
For and on behalf of

CzarnockiPLC

By: _____   By: _____
Name: Name:
Title: Authorised Signatory   Title: Authorised Signatory

The notice is irrevocable, but can be amended as many times as the buyer wishes prior to the end of the 30-day period.

The notice states that the buyer will physically settle the transaction and contains a detailed description[23] of the deliverable obligations that it intends to deliver.

Except for restructuring credit events, the conditions to settlement can be satisfied only once per reference entity. Restructuring[24] can have a relatively minor effect on creditworthiness;[25] and so the notifying party is permitted to deliver multiple restructuring credit event notices each time triggering a credit event for only part (the exercise amount)[26] of the reference entity notional amount.

---

23 This includes the outstanding principal balance or due and payable amount of each deliverable obligation
    it intends to deliver as well as any available Committee on Uniform Securities Identification Procedures or
    International Securities Identification Number numbers ('CUSIPs') (or if not available, the rate and tenor
    of the deliverable obligation).
24 Section 3.9.
25 Following a restructuring event in relation to Xerox, the final price achieved in relation to Xerox's
    obligations was approximately 95%.
26 Each exercise amount.

If this happens, there are deemed to be two transactions. The new transaction's notional amount is deemed to be the exercise amount and the old transaction's notional amount is deemed to be its existing notional amount less the exercise amount. The calculation agent will then make any necessary modifications to preserve the economic effects of the two transactions.

> Credit Events: The following Credit Event[s] shall apply to this Transaction:
> [Bankruptcy]
> [Failure to Pay]
> [Grace Period Extension Applicable]
> [Grace Period:]
> Payment Requirement: [   ]]
> [Obligation Default]
> [Obligation Acceleration]
> [Repudiation/Moratorium]
> [Restructuring]
>> [[Restructuring Maturity Limitation and Fully Transferable
>> Obligation: [Applicable]]
>> [[Modified Restructuring Maturity Limitation and
>> Conditionally Transferable Obligation: [Applicable]]
>> [[Multiple Holder Obligation: [Applicable]]
>> [Default Requirement: [   ]]

The parties will also specify in paragraph 3 which credit events are applicable to the transaction, choosing between:

- bankruptcy;
- failure to pay;
- obligation default;
- obligation acceleration;
- repudiation/moratorium; and
- restructuring.

They will also specify here whether the grace period provisions are applicable to the failure to pay credit event and what the applicable payment requirement will be. For a restructuring credit event, they will specify whether the modified restructuring or modified modified restructuring provisions will apply.

The credit events selected will depend upon relevant market standards for the reference entity's jurisdiction and characterisation.[27] Article III makes the determination of credit events objective and removes various common law defences

---

27 For example, the market standard for North American insurance reference entities includes only bankruptcy and failure to pay as credit events; whereas the market standard for European emerging market reference entities includes bankruptcy, failure to pay, obligation acceleration, repudiation/ moratorium and modified modified restructuring as credit events.

28 Section 4.1.

such as a reference entity not having capacity to enter into an obligation or an obligation being unenforceable or invalid.[28]

Bankruptcy[29] is the only credit event that relates to the reference entity itself rather than its obligations. The definition gives a detailed list of events that constitute bankruptcy. Subject to some minor changes, it tracks Section 5(a)(vii) of the 1992 ISDA Master Agreement.

Obligation acceleration[30] requires the obligation's lenders or bondholders to accelerate a greater amount of the obligation than the default requirement[31] following a default, event of default or similar provision.

Obligation default[32] mirrors obligation acceleration except there is no requirement for the obligation to be accelerated following a default. Only one of obligation acceleration or obligation default can be selected per reference entity.

Failure to pay[33] occurs if the reference entity fails to pay any amounts equal to or greater than the payment requirement[34] under any of its obligations. The failure to pay must take place after the expiration of an obligation's grace period[35] (this is set out in the obligation itself) or after the satisfaction of any conditions precedent to that grace period commencing. If an obligation does not have a grace period or has a grace period of less than three business days, then the grace period is deemed to be three business days.

The parties may specify that grace period extension[36] applies. This relates to potential failures to pay,[37] which occur when (without taking account of any grace period in an obligation) the reference entity fails to make any payment of more than the payment requirement. If a potential failure to pay occurs on or before the transaction's scheduled termination date[38] and an obligation's grace period cannot expire before then, then unless otherwise set out in the confirmation, the grace period is deemed to be the earlier of its actual period and 30 calendar days.

The notifying party has 14 calendar days from the grace period extension date[39] to satisfy the conditions to settlement. If the conditions are not satisfied before then, the grace period extension date will be the transaction's termination date.

If grace period extension does not apply, then a transaction's termination date will be the scheduled maturity date, even if a potential failure to pay occurs. The grace period provisions in the 2003 Definitions are highly complex and are covered in detail in Part II.

Repudiation/moratorium[40] relates to where a reference entity's authorised officer repudiates or declares a moratorium on any of its obligations in an aggregate amount

29   Section 4.2.
30   Section 4.3.
31   If the default requirement is not defined in the confirmation, the ISDA fallback is $10 million.
32   Section 4.4.
33   Section 4.5.
34   Section 4.8(d). If the payment requirement is not defined in the confirmation, the ISDA fallback is $1 million.
35   Section 1.12.
36   Section 1.11.
37   Section 1.13.
38   Section 1.6.
39   Section 1.9.
40   Section 4.6.

of at least the default requirement. It can also relate to an authorised officer of a governmental authority,[41] such as a minister of finance, repudiating or declaring a moratorium over a reference entity's obligations. This is a potential repudiation/ moratorium.

The potential repudiation/moratorium must be followed by an actual failure to pay or restructuring on or prior to the repudiation/moratorium evaluation date.[42] A failure to pay is determined without regard to the payment requirement and a restructuring is determined without regard to the default requirement.

If the relevant obligations include bonds, the repudiation/moratorium evaluation date is the later of 60 calendar days following the potential repudiation/moratorium date and the bond's first post-potential repudiation/moratorium payment date (taking into account any grace period). If the relevant obligations do not include bonds, the repudiation/moratorium evaluation date is 60 calendar days after the potential repudiation/moratorium.

If a potential repudiation/moratorium has occurred, but the repudiation/ moratorium evaluation date cannot occur before the scheduled termination date, then unless the parties elect in the confirmation that the repudiation/moratorium extension condition[43] applies, the transaction will terminate before a credit event can occur.

If the parties elect that the repudiation/moratorium extension condition applies, then where a potential repudiation/moratorium occurs on or before the scheduled termination date, but the repudiation/moratorium evaluation date cannot occur until afterwards, the notifying party can deliver a repudiation/moratorium extension notice.[44]

This is an irrevocable notice describing a potential repudiation/moratorium that has occurred prior the scheduled termination date. It contains a description in reasonable detail of the facts relevant to determining the potential repudiation/ moratorium and indicates the date when it occurred. The confirmation may also require it to be accompanied by a notice of publicly available information. The notifying party can then deliver a credit event notice and (if applicable) a notice of publicly available information up to 14 calendar days after the repudiation/ moratorium evaluation date.

Restructuring[45] is the most controversial credit event. There are four variations:

- full restructuring;
- modified restructuring;
- modified modified restructuring; and
- no restructuring.

Selection depends on the reference entity's jurisdiction. Please see Part II for a full discussion of the restructuring credit event and its interesting history.

Restructuring applies when any one of a list of specified events binding all of the holders occurs to an aggregate amount of the reference entity's obligations at least

---

41   Section 4.8(b).
42   Section 4.6(b).
43   Section 4.6(d).
44   Section 4.6(e).
45   Section 4.7.

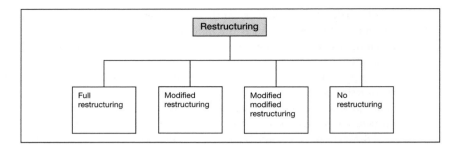

equal the default requirement. These events must not be contemplated under the obligation's terms in effect at the later of the trade date or the obligation's issue date. The specified events are:

- an interest payment or accrual reduction;
- a principal or premium reduction;
- a postponement of payment of accruals or interest, or principal or premium;
- a change of an obligation's priority of payment, causing that obligation's subordination; and
- any change in currency of interest or principal other than to a permitted currency.[46]

Exceptions apply where:

- the event does not directly or indirectly result in the reference entity's creditworthiness or financial condition deteriorating;
- an EU member state converts its currency to the euro; or
- the restructuring events occur because of an administrative, accounting, tax or technical adjustment in the ordinary course of business.

(a)   Full restructuring

> Credit events: The following Credit Event[s] shall apply to this
>   Transaction:
>   Restructuring

Market events exposed certain weaknesses in the 1999 'restructuring' definition. Although the 2003 Definitions do not vary the definition itself, they do provide options to limit the obligations that may be 'deliverable'. When these options are not selected, this is full restructuring chosen by selecting restructuring as a credit event alone. Full restructuring is no longer market standard for physically settled transactions. It is selected only for cash-settled transactions where the reference obligation is not selected in advance.

---

46   This is defined in Section 4.7 as any G7 member or Organisation for Economic Cooperation and Development country currency of an AAA-rated country.

(b)   *Modified restructuring*

> Credit Events: The following Credit Event[s] shall apply to this
> Transaction:
>> Restructuring
>> Restructuring Maturity Limitation and
>>> Fully Transferable Obligation: Applicable

When selected, a deliverable obligation must fulfil two characteristics following a restructuring credit event. First, the final maturity date must be no later than 30 months after the restructuring date or the latest final maturity date of any restructured bond or loan, whichever is earliest. The deliverable obligation's maturity date must not be earlier than the transaction's scheduled maturity date or later than 30 months after the scheduled maturity date.[47] The second characteristic relates to a fully transferable obligation.[48] The deliverable obligation must be either a transferable[49] bond or a loan capable of being assigned or novated without consent. It must also be possible to transfer the deliverable obligation to eligible transferees.[50] These include various finance and corporate entities or their affiliates with total assets of at least $500 million, as well as individual and groups of investment vehicles with total assets of at least $100 million.

(c)   *Modified modified restructuring*

> Credit Events: The following Credit Event[s] shall apply to this
> Transaction:
>> Restructuring
>> Modified Restructuring Maturity Limitation
>> and Conditionally Transferable Obligation:
>> Applicable

If modified modified restructuring is selected, an obligation must fulfil the following characteristics to qualify as a deliverable obligation following a restructuring credit event:
- Regarding the modified restructuring maturity limitation date,[51] the deliverable obligation's final maturity date must be no later than the earlier of the transaction's scheduled termination date and 30 months after the

---

47   Section 2.32(c).
48   Section 2.32(b).
49   Section 2.20(b)(v).
50   Section 2.32(f).
51   Section 2.33(c).

restructuring (although this is extended from 30 to 60 months where the deliverable obligation is a restructured bond or loan); and

- Regarding the conditionally transferable obligation,[52] the deliverable obligation must be either a transferable[53] bond or a loan capable of being assigned or novated without consent. It must be possible to transfer the deliverable obligation to a modified eligible transferee.[54]

It is market standard not to select the restructuring credit event for certain types of reference entity, for example North American corporate high yield and North American insurance reference entities.

Multiple Holder Obligation:	Applicable

Unless disapplied in the confirmation, a restructuring credit event can occur only in relation to a multiple holder obligation.[55] This is an obligation held at the time of the restructuring credit event:

- by at least four non-affiliated holders; and
- whose terms require that 66.66% of the holders consent to the restructuring.

A shortcoming was identified soon after the publication of the 2003 Definitions. It is market practice for eurobonds to require 75% of bondholders voting to approve a restructuring and fix a meeting's quorum at 75% of bondholders. This means that any market standard eurobond that restructures could be approved by only 56% of bondholders and fail the multiple holder obligation test. ISDA addressed the problem in the May 2003 Supplement, which provides that a bond will automatically be construed to be a multiple holder obligation.

Unless excluded in the confirmation, where a restructuring credit event occurs in relation to a sovereign, the class of deliverable obligation will be widened to include obligations which satisfied the deliverable obligation category and deliverable obligation characteristics immediately before the restructuring was legally effective, even if they do not meet them afterwards. This varies from the standard provisions, which assess whether an obligation is a deliverable obligation as of the delivery date.

The parties do not want every reference entity obligation to enjoy credit protection. If they do not select a specific obligation in the confirmation, they will use the mechanism set out in Sections 2.19(a) (obligation category) and 2.20(b) (obligation characteristics) to define which of the reference entity's obligations have credit protection. An obligation category and all of the obligation characteristics must be present to qualify as an obligation.

---

52   Section 2.33(b).
53   Section 2.20(b)(v).
54   Section 2.32(f).
55   Section 4.9.

Obligation(s)	Obligation Category (select only one)	Obligation Characteristics (select all that apply)
	☐ Payment	☐ Not Subordinated
	☐ Borrowed Money	☐ Specified Currency
	☐ Reference Obligations Only	☐ Not Sovereign Lender
	☐ Bond	☐ Not Domestic Currency
	☐ Loan	☐ Not Domestic Law
	☐ Bond Or Loan	☐ Listed
		☐ Not Contingent
		☐ Not Domestic Issuance

[and:]

[Specify any other Obligations of a Reference Entity]

Excluded Obligations: None

There are six obligation categories. Only one obligation category can be selected for each reference entity. The obligation categories are:

- payment (ie, any present, future or contingent obligations to repay money, including borrowed money), a broad category that includes payments under guarantees, trading debts and derivative transactions;
- borrowed money (ie, any obligation to pay or repay borrowed money), a narrower category than the previous one;
- reference obligations only (ie, any obligation that is a reference obligation);
- bond (ie, borrowed money in the form of a bond, note (other than a note delivered under a loan) or debt security);
- loan (ie, borrowed money documented by a term loan agreement, revolving loan agreement or other similar credit agreement); and
- bond or loan (ie, any obligation that is either a bond or loan).

There are seven obligation characteristics. Provided that they are not contradictory, any number may be chosen. Some relate only to bonds, others to loans. Obligation characteristics are not usually selected for Western European or North American reference entities. They are selected when it is necessary to isolate a reference entity's more liquid and internationally traded obligations. The obligation characteristics are as follows:

- 'Not subordinated' means that obligations are not subordinated in payment priority to the most senior reference obligation. If no reference obligation is specified in the confirmation, the obligation must not be subordinated to any borrowed money obligation.
- 'Specified currency' aims, along with 'not domestic currency' and 'not domestic law, to exclude the reference entity's domestic obligations from

credit protection. Obligations will include only those payable in a currency specified in the confirmation. If "specified currency' is selected as a characteristic, but no currency is selected, then the relevant obligation must be denominated in one of the currencies of Canada, Japan, Switzerland, the United Kingdom and the United States, or in euros (these being standard specified currencies).

- 'Not sovereign lender' excludes any obligation owed primarily to a sovereign or supranational organisation (including Paris Club debt).
- 'Not domestic currency' excludes obligations payable in the reference entity's home currency.
- 'Not domestic law' excludes obligations governed by the law of the reference entity's home jurisdiction.
- 'Listed' means that the obligation must be quoted, listed or ordinarily purchased and sold on an exchange. By its nature, it relates only to bonds.
- 'Not domestic issuance' permits only obligations issued and offered for sale outside of the reference entity's domestic market.

In addition, the parties may specify any other obligations of the reference entity, which they wish to be included as an 'obligation' together with any obligations they wish to exclude from the scope of credit protection under 'excluded obligations'. 'Excluded obligation' is defined in Section 2.17 as "any obligation of a reference entity specified as such or of a type described in the related confirmation".

3.5   Paragraph 4: Settlement terms

> 4. Settlement terms
>
> Settlement method: [Cash settlement] [Physical settlement]

The template confirmation can be used for both cash settled transactions and physically settled transactions. Whether cash settlement or physical settlement is applicable is specified under 'settlement method', which is defined in Section 6.1.

If 'cash settlement'[56] is selected, then the terms provided in the template for physical settlement are deleted. 'Cash settlement' and its relevant definitions are covered in Article VII. For cash settlement, the template provides under 'valuation date'[57] and 'valuation time'[58] when the calculation agent must value the reference obligation, together with the amount of times which it must do so.

The parties specify under 'quotation method'[59] the method which the calculation agent will use to obtain quotations for the reference obligation. Under 'quotation

---

56   Section 7.1.
57   Section 7.8.
58   Section 7.14.
59   Section 7.9.

```
Terms relating to Cash Settlement

        Valuation Date:                    [Single Valuation Date:
                                             [ ] Business Days]
                                           [Multiple Valuation Dates:
                                             [ ] Business Days; and
                                             each [ ] Business Days thereafter
                                           Number of Valuation Dates: [ ]]
        Valuation Time:                    [                  ]
        Quotation Method:                  [Bid][Offer][Mid-Market]]
        Quotation Amount:                  [ ][Representative Amount]
        Minimum Quotation Amount:          [                  ]
        Dealer(S):                                            ]
        Settlement Currency:                                  ]
        Cash Settlement Date:              [ ] Business Days]
        Cash Settlement Amount:            [                  ]
        Quotations:                        [Include Accrued Interest]
                                           [Exclude Accrued Interest]]
```

amount'[60] and 'minimum quotation amount'[61], they will specify the amount of the reference obligation for which the calculation agent will request a quotation. Under 'dealer'[62] the parties will specify which dealers expected to be making markets in the reference obligation, the calculation agent will approach to request quotation for the reference obligation. Under 'quotation'[63] the parties will set out whether the quotations should include or exclude accrued interest.

The parties specify under 'valuation method'[64] the method that the calculation agent will use to interpret the quotations it has received for the reference obligations. Various methods are provided by Section 7.9 such as 'market', 'highest', 'average market' and 'average highest'.

The template provides, under 'settlement currency',[65] an option for the parties to specify a settlement currency different from the currency of the floating-rate payer calculation amount. Under 'cash settlement date',[66], the parties will specify the number of business days after the final price has been determined that the seller will pay the cash settlement amount to the buyer.

In fixed recovery transactions, the parties may specify a cash settlement amount; otherwise the cash settlement amount payable will be the greater of zero and the floating rate payer calculation amount multiplied by the reference price, less the final price.

---

60   Section 7.12.
61   Section 7.13.
62   Section 7.15.
63   Section 7.7.
64   Section 7.5.
65   Section 6.3.
66   Section 7.2.

Terms relating to Physical Settlement

Physical Settlement Period: 30 Business Days.

If physical settlement is the applicable settlement method, then the 'terms relating to cash settlement' are deleted from the template; and the terms provided for 'terms relating to physical settlement' are used instead.

Here the parties specify, under 'physical settlement period', the period of time after the conditions to settlement have been met during which physical settlement must take place.

They specify the category of obligations of the reference entity that the buyer may deliver to the seller to effect physical settlement. This is done under 'deliverable obligations'.

Deliverable Obligation(s)	Derivable Obligation Category (select one)	Derivable Obligation Characteristics (select all that apply)
	☐ Payment	☐ Not Subordinated
	☐ Borrowed Money	☐ Specified Currency
	☐ Reference Obligations Only	☐ Not Sovereign Lender
		☐ Not Domestic Currency
	☐ Bond	☐ Not Domestic Law
	☐ Loan	☐ Listed
	☐ Bond Or Loan	☐ Not Contingent
		☐ Not Domestic Issuance
		☐ Assignable Loan
		☐ Consent Required Loan
		☐ Direct Loan Participation
		☐ Indirect Loan Participation Qualifying Participation Seller: ☐
		☐ Transferable
		☐ Maximum Maturity
		☐ Accelerated Or Matured
		☐ Not Bearer
		and: [*Specify any other obligations of a reference entity*]
Excluded Deliverable Obligation(S): None		

Deliverable obligations[67] are the reference entity's obligations, which can be used in physical settlement. They include:

- any of the reference entity's direct or indirect (ie, guaranteed) obligations satisfying the deliverable obligation category and deliverable obligation characteristics;
- any reference obligation (unless an excluded deliverable obligation);
- in the case of a restructuring credit event for a sovereign reference entity, any restructured deliverable obligation fulfilling certain criteria (unless it is an excluded reference obligation); and
- any other specified obligation of the reference entity.

Although the deliverable obligations provisions are meant to relate only to physically settled transactions, it is common to adapt them as a method for selecting a reference obligation in a cash settled transaction, when none is chosen in the confirmation. The 2003 Definitions assume that a reference obligation will be selected in the confirmation. Some buyers wish to have discretion when selecting the reference obligation and so will, in the confirmation, deem the provisions relating to deliverable obligation category and deliverable obligation characteristics to apply to the reference obligation selection.

The mechanisms for determining a deliverable obligation category and deliverable obligation characteristics are set out in Section 2.20. There are six deliverable obligation categories. These replicate the obligation categories, with reference obligation having only the effect of fixing the deliverable obligation. There are 15 deliverable obligation characteristics: the seven obligation characteristics replicated and eight new characteristics added. The eight are outlined below:

- 'Not contingent' refers to an obligation with unconditional principal payments. An example of a contingent obligation would be a credit-linked note issued by a financial institution. This characteristic prevents reference entity obligations whose value is affected by factors other than the reference entity's creditworthiness from being valued or delivered following a credit event. This definition specifically carves out certain convertible, exchangeable[68] and accreting obligations from being contingent obligations.
- 'Convertible' is an obligation of the reference entity convertible wholly or partly into its equity securities at the holder's option.[69] An exchangeable obligation is a reference entity obligation that may be exchanged into another issuer's equity securities at the holder's option.[70] An accreting obligation is any obligation (including a convertible or exchangeable obligation) which, if accelerated, will pay the original issue price plus additional amounts (on account of original issue discount or other interest accruals); for example, a deeply discounted or zero coupon bond.

---

67   Section 2.15.
68   In the case of contingent obligations and exchangeable obligations, the relevant option must not have been exercised.
69   Or a trustee or agent acting for the holder.
70   Or a trustee or agent acting for the holder.

- 'Assignable loan' is a loan that can be assigned or novated without the consent of a reference entity or any guarantor, to at least a commercial bank or financial institution which is not already one of the loan lenders or syndicate members.
- 'Consent required loan' is a loan that can be assigned or novated to another party (not only a commercial bank or institution, but with the consent of the reference entity, any relevant guarantor or syndicate agent). If both assignable loan and consent-required loan are specified, then it will be necessary only for an obligation to have one characteristic.
- 'Direct loan participation' relates to non-transferable loans and loans where a necessary party will not consent to transfer. The provision permits a participation agreement between buyer and seller transferring a specified share of the loan payments to the seller to be a deliverable obligation.
- 'Transferable' is a provision that does not apply to loans. The obligation must be transferable to institutional investors "without any contractual, statutory or regulatory restriction". The definition carves out US resale restrictions under the Regulation S and Rule 144A safe harbours. All eurobonds are subject to one or other of these safe harbours. Failure to carve these out would exclude eurobonds from being obligations. Restrictions on permitted investments such as statutory or regulatory investment restrictions on insurance companies and pension funds are also carved out.
- 'Maximum maturity' means that on the physical settlement date, the deliverable obligation must not have a maturity date later than the period specified in the confirmation. It is market practice for this to be 30 years.
- 'Accelerated or matured' refers to obligations that are fully due and payable before the delivery date because they have matured (but have not been redeemed), have been accelerated (ie, an event of default has been declared) or would have been due and payable but for insolvency laws (eg, the application of Chapter 11 of the US Bankruptcy Code).

The characteristic 'not bearer'[71] applies to bonds only. The bonds must be either registered bonds or, if they are bearer bonds, cleared via Euroclear, Clearstream or any other internationally recognised clearing system.

As with cash settlement, the parties may provide under 'excluded deliverable obligations' whether they wish to exclude any particular deliverable obligations of the reference entity.[72]

[Partial Cash Settlement of Consent Required Loans Applicable]
[Partial Cash Settlement of Assignable Loans Applicable]
[Partial Cash Settlement of Participations Applicable]
Escrow [Applicable] [Not Applicable]

---

71   Section 2.18.
72   Section 2.18.

The template provides for three partial cash settlement provisions. These relate to 'partial cash settlement of consent required loans',[73] 'partial cash settlement of assignable loans'[74] and 'partial cash settlement of participations'.[75] Each provision is applicable only if selected (eg, by stating 'partial cash settlement of consent required loans applicable').

Where specified, the partial cash settlement terms[76], which are set out in Article IX, will be deemed to apply if transfer is not possible due to a lack of consent in the case of consent-required loans and assignable loans; in the case of a participation, if a participation is not effected (in each case, prior to the latest permissible physical settlement date).

The cash settlement amount will then be the greater of:

- zero; and
- the outstanding principal balance, the due and payable amount or the currency amount (as applicable) of each relevant obligation multiplied by its reference price, less the final price.

The cash settlement date will occur three business days after the calculation of the final price on the relevant valuation date (which is two business days after the latest permissible physical settlement date).

For the purposes of partial cash settlement, when calculating the final price, the following are deemed to apply:

- highest valuation method (with certain fallbacks);
- bid quotation method; and
- a quotation amount equal to the outstanding principal balance or due and payable amount or currency amount (as applicable).

Finally, under 'escrow', the parties may select whether deliverable obligations may be held in escrow.

3.6 Paragraph 5 (notice and account details), paragraph 6 (offices) and execution

In paragraph 5, the parties specify the accounts to which fixed and floating payments under the transaction must be made. They also specify their contact details for the delivery of notices, including telephone numbers to facilitate telephone notices.

In paragraph 6, each party specifies the office through which it is acting for the purposes of the credit derivative transaction.

Finally, the closing section of the template requests that the confirming party, by executing and returning the document, agrees to be bound by its terms.

---

73   Section 9.4.
74   Section 9.5.
75   Section 9.6.
76   Section 9.8.

Synthetic collateralised debt obligations

1. Introduction

Synthetic collateralised debt obligations (CDOs) are complex. They currently make up over 15% of the credit derivatives market by notional volume. We first looked at them in the "Funded credit derivatives" chapter in Part I which gives readers the basic concepts without overwhelming finer details. This chapter provides those finer details and covers synthetic CDO transaction documentation in much greater depth. It also analyses credit ratings: how they are applied and how they drive a transaction structure, credit enhancement, tranche size, documentation and reference portfolio composition. Additionally, it covers the listing of CDO securities and how this impacts on the transaction documentation, and focuses on special purpose vehicle (SPV) jurisdiction, including which aspects of a particular jurisdiction can be important (for taxation, cost and other reasons) in selection, as well as the impact that a particular choice of jurisdiction can have on documentation.

Synthetic CDOs have many variations. They can be based on a simple reference portfolio; they can have principal protected structures (eg, synthetic constant proportion portfolio insurance (CPPI) transactions); reference other credit default swaps and CDOs; and have any number of different bells and whistles. This chapter focuses on the common-or-garden variety: CDOs with single cash-settled credit default swap referencing a single reference portfolio of corporate reference entities.

2. Rational and structure: full capital structure synthetic CDOs

Synthetic CDOs generally fall into two principal categories: full capital structure CDOs and single tranche CDOs. As single tranche synthetic CDOs are simplified versions of full capital structure synthetic CDOs, we will discuss full capital structure synthetic CDOs first and then highlight the differences.

In a standard full capital structure synthetic CDO, a thinly capitalised SPV enters into a portfolio credit default swap with a counterparty – usually the transaction's arranger.

SPVs

The SPV is established by the transaction parties with the objective of utilising it in a structured finance transaction to issue debt instruments, acquire underlying

---

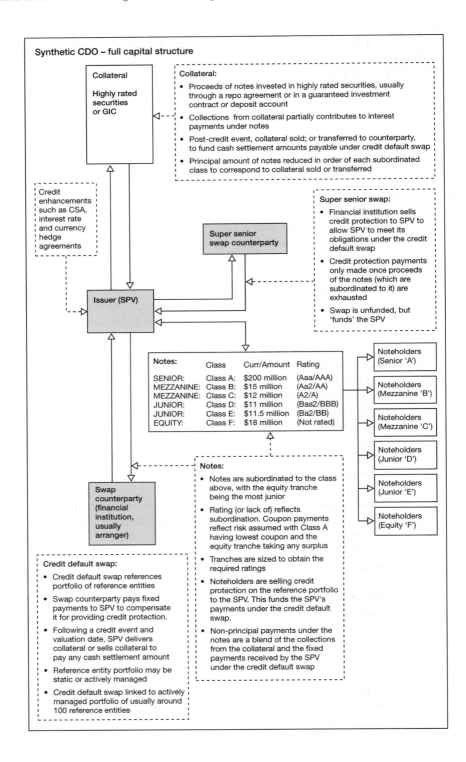

Synthetic CDO – full capital structure

Collateral

Highly rated securities or GIC

Collateral:

- Proceeds of notes invested in highly rated securities, usually through a repo agreement or in a guaranteed investment contract or deposit account
- Collections from collateral partially contributes to interest payments under notes
- Post-credit event, collateral sold; or transferred to counterparty, to fund cash settlement amounts payable under credit default swap
- Principal amount of notes reduced in order of each subordinated class to correspond to collateral sold or transferred

Credit enhancements such as CSA, interest rate and currency hedge agreements

Super senior swap counterparty

Super senior swap:

- Financial institution sells credit protection to SPV to allow SPV to meet its obligations under the credit default swap
- Credit protection payments only made once proceeds of the notes (which are subordinated to it) are exhausted
- Swap is unfunded, but 'funds' the SPV

Issuer (SPV)

Notes:

	Class	Curr/Amount	Rating
SENIOR:	Class A:	$200 million	(Aaa/AAA)
MEZZANINE:	Class B:	$15 million	(Aa2/AA)
MEZZANINE:	Class C:	$12 million	(A2/A)
JUNIOR:	Class D:	$11 million	(Baa2/BBB)
JUNIOR:	Class E:	$11.5 million	(Ba2/BB)
EQUITY:	Class F:	$18 million	(Not rated)

Noteholders (Senior 'A')

Noteholders (Mezzanine 'B')

Noteholders (Mezzanine 'C')

Noteholders (Junior 'D')

Noteholders (Junior 'E')

Noteholders (Equity 'F')

Notes:

- Notes are subordinated to the class above, with the equity tranche being the most junior
- Rating (or lack of) reflects subordination. Coupon payments reflect risk assumed with Class A having lowest coupon and the equity tranche taking any surplus
- Tranches are sized to obtain the required ratings
- Noteholders are selling credit protection on the reference portfolio to the SPV. This funds the SPV's payments under the credit default swap.
- Non-principal payments under the notes are a blend of the collections from the collateral and the fixed payments received by the SPV under the credit default swap

Swap counterparty (financial institution, usually arranger)

Credit default swap:

- Credit default swap references portfolio of reference entities
- Swap counterparty pays fixed payments to SPV to compensate it for providing credit protection.
- Following a credit event and valuation date, SPV delivers collateral or sells collateral to pay any cash settlement amount
- Reference entity portfolio may be static or actively managed
- Credit default swap linked to actively managed portfolio of usually around 100 reference entities

assets and/or enter into derivative contracts with a view to providing a return to investors.

The transaction's arranger will establish the SPV in a low tax or no tax jurisdiction, such as the Cayman Islands or Jersey; or a country that has introduced a specific low tax regime for SPVs such as Ireland, the Netherlands or Luxembourg.

The SPV will generally be an orphan company, run by directors from the relevant jurisdiction with its shares held in trust for the noteholders and/or a charity (so that the SPV will not be categorised as a subsidiary of the arranger).

The assets held by the SPV will be secured so that they are available only to the holders of the related series of notes and/or any other secured parties under the transaction, and not to any other creditor of the SPV.

Securities issued by the SPV will be 'limited recourse' securities. This means that the claims of the noteholders and other secured parties under a CDO will be limited only to the proceeds of the secured obligations. To the extent that secured obligations do not yield sufficient funds to satisfy the claims of the noteholders and the other secured parties, their claims will be extinguished.

The following key factors are often relevant in selecting an SPV jurisdiction and are discussed in greater detail later in this chapter. These are:

- a stable and predictable legal and regulatory regime;
- start-up and ongoing costs;
- speed and efficiency of establishment and administration;
- the market perception of the jurisdiction;
- the quality of service providers;
- the ability to avoid withholding tax on the cash flow coming into and out of the SPV;
- the ability to avoid incurring liability to value added tax (VAT), stamp duty, income tax and other taxes; and
- the ability to avoid regulation as a financial institution.

Primer: portfolio credit default swaps

In a portfolio credit default swap, the buyer purchases credit protection on a basket of reference entities, usually at least 100.

Portfolio credit default swaps operate very similarly to single name credit default swaps. The easiest way to conceptualise the product is to view it as consisting of a bundle of credit default swaps, with one credit default swap being in place (between the buyer and the seller) for each reference entity in the portfolio.

Each time that a credit event occurs in relation to a reference entity and the conditions to settlement are met, the settlement procedure is the same as for a single-name credit default swap, except that instead of the transaction terminating on the settlement date, the reference entity will be removed from the basket or portfolio and the transaction will continue.

> In portfolio credit default swaps, the transaction will have an overall notional amount (eg, $300 million) and consist of a notional amount for each reference entity. This is usually an equally weighted amount, with credit protection sold for each reference entity's reference entity notional amount only.

Under the portfolio credit default swap, the SPV sells an amount of credit protection to the counterparty for each reference entity (eg, in a $200 million synthetic CDO, it might sell $2 million of credit protection for each of 100 reference entities in a portfolio).

This generates an agreed return in the form of fixed payments in relation to each of the reference entities in the portfolio, perhaps 0.25% per annum of the notional amount of credit protection sold. The reference entities themselves will be selected from diverse industries and geographical locations, to try to minimise the level of credit event correlation (ie, the risk that credit events will occur in tandem). Rating agency criteria for achieving a desired rating will often drive the composition of the reference portfolio. The reference portfolio will often be compiled in conjunction with rating agency methodology (more of which later).

The SPV is thinly capitalised, perhaps having only $2 capitalisation. It has no funds to make any credit protection payment should a credit event occur and the conditions to settlement be met on a reference entity in the portfolio: it must therefore be funded.

To fund its potential obligations under the credit default swap, the SPV has two sources of funding. First, it issues debt obligations in the form of notes to investors. These notes are tranched, with progressively deeper levels of subordination.

For example, the SPV could issue three classes of notes: a senior, a mezzanine and a junior tranche. Losses incurred under the credit default swap would attach first to the junior notes, then to the mezzanine and finally, if the principal amount of that tranche were exhausted, to the senior notes.

Tranching

Tranching allows investors to take different slices of risk exposure in accordance with their risk/return appetite. It also acts as a form of credit enhancement.

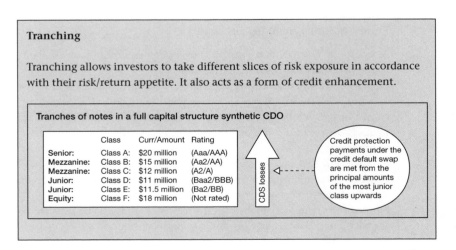

Tranches of notes in a full capital structure synthetic CDO

	Class	Curr/Amount	Rating
Senior:	Class A:	$20 million	(Aaa/AAA)
Mezzanine:	Class B:	$15 million	(Aa2/AA)
Mezzanine:	Class C:	$12 million	(A2/A)
Junior:	Class D:	$11 million	(Baa2/BBB)
Junior:	Class E:	$11.5 million	(Ba2/BB)
Equity:	Class F:	$18 million	(Not rated)

CDS losses

Credit protection payments under the credit default swap are met from the principal amounts of the most junior class upwards

> In a full capital structure synthetic CDO the SPV will issue different classes (or tranches) of notes. The tranches will fall into four separate categories (in descending order of priority): senior debt, mezzanine debt, subordinated debt and equity. There may be multiple tranches within those categories.
>
> If there is a credit event under the credit default swap and the conditions to settlement are met, then following the valuation date(s), the issuer will be required to pay a cash settlement amount.
>
> Payment of the cash settlement amount will be funded by the issuer either delivering an amount of collateral equal to the cash settlement amount or selling a corresponding amount of collateral, the proceeds of which are then paid to the counterparty. The collateral is usually held in the form of a deposit in a guaranteed investment account or in the form of highly rated securities invested pursuant to a repo agreement
>
> The corresponding amount of the principal amount of the lowest available tranche of notes is then reduced. Each tranche of notes is protected by the tranche below it. This means that the more senior the tranche of notes, the less likely it is to suffer losses.
>
> Usually, the notes are rated and the level of ratings will correspond to the seniority of any tranche of notes. Likewise, the higher the level of risk attached to a tranche of notes, the higher its coupon, and the lower its rating will be. As credit events impact on the portfolio, though, the level of return will diminish.

Above the tranches of notes often sits a more senior obligation: an unfunded credit default swap with a highly rated counterparty. This is called a 'super senior credit default swap' and sometimes it makes up over 80% of the synthetic CDO's notional amount. In fact, the subordinated tranches of notes act as a form of credit enhancement for the super senior credit default swap, allowing it to achieve a credit quality perceived to be above AAA. It is often the super senior credit default swap that is driving the wide transaction.

The super senior credit default swap references the whole of the reference portfolio and will have a highly rated bank or other financial institution as the counterparty. Under this swap, the SPV will be the buyer and the financial institution the seller. The super senior credit default swap will make up most of the funding capitalisation; losses will impact upon it only once the principal amounts of all of the tranches of notes have been exhausted. The super senior swap is unfunded from the perspective of the financial institution, but because it is a back-to-back swap, it funds the SPV in the main credit derivative transaction.

As mentioned above, the proceeds of the debt obligations are invested, directly or indirectly, in highly rated securities. The most common method for doing this is through a repo agreement or a guaranteed investment contract.

A guaranteed investment contract (GIC) is a contract with a financial institution (usually an insurance company with a high credit rating), which pays a guaranteed rate of interest for an agreed time. The GIC will be for the term of the notes and will provide the rate of interest necessary for making the anticipated distributions under the notes, together with the premiums received by the SPV under the credit default swap. Alternatively the GIC may be structured as a standard deposit account. The GIC will also be used to fund any payments of cash or physical settlement amounts under the credit default swap.

Under a repo agreement the issuer and the arranger will enter into a bilateral transaction under which the issuer will agree to purchase highly rated and liquid collateral securities at a price equal to the proceeds of the notes. The issuer will agree to sell the securities back to the arranger in full at the transaction's maturity. This will usually be at a price equal to that necessary to repay the principal of the notes. The collateral securities may be liquidated on an ongoing basis during the transaction's term to fund the issuer's obligation to pay any cash settlement amount under the credit default swap after any credit event.

The secured obligations under a synthetic collateralised debt obligation consist primarily of the issuer's rights under the super senior credit default swap and the standard credit default swap, as well as its rights under the repo agreements, GIC and other transaction agreements.

The noteholders receive a blended return based on the credit protection premiums received by the SPV and the return on the repo agreement or guaranteed investment contract, with the quantum of return also being referenced to the amount of risk assumed by a noteholder. The counterparty to the super senior credit default swap will receive only its share of the fixed payments under the credit default swap received by the SPV.

Super senior credit default swaps

The super senior credit default swap usually makes up over 80% of a synthetic CDO's capitalisation. Unlike most of the tranches of notes below it, it will not be rated.

In a super senior credit default swap, the seller will usually be an insurance company or a financial institution and, due to the subordinated tranches of notes below, it will regard its investments as representing a low risk. The buyer will be the SPV. The SPV therefore enters into a back-to-back credit default swap transaction.

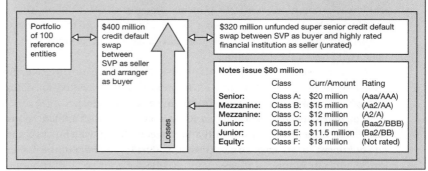

> A super senior credit default swap will involve the seller selling credit protection on the entire reference portfolio, but losses will attach to the super senior credit default swap only once the principal amount of the tranches below it has been exhausted.

If the portfolio of reference entities is fixed at the issue date, this is known as a static synthetic CDO. Alternatively, a manager may be appointed who will switch reference entities in and out of the portfolio with a view of maximising returns in return for a fee – this is known as a managed synthetic CDO.

3. Single tranche CDOs/partial capital structure CDOs

A single tranche or partial capital structure CDO is a structured securities transaction where the transaction's arranger sells only a single tranche, or a specific part of a notional full capital structure synthetic CDO, to an investor.

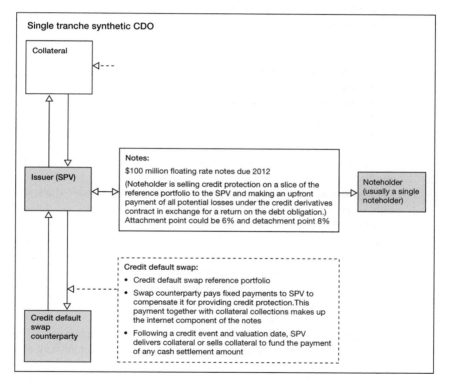

Factors behind the growth in single tranche CDOs include:

- investors' desire to tailor transactions to their investment needs, such as achieving certain ratings and tranche size; and
- the fact that arrangers may find it difficult to place all of the tranches in a multi-tranche CDO at the transaction's outset.

Additionally, advances in hedging techniques may allow arrangers to hedge the rest of the capital structure, while the use of existing repackaging programmes may allow the issue to go ahead with reduced costs.

If one were to imagine a hypothetical full capital structure synthetic CDO, if the SPV were to sell only a slice of the mezzanine notes (eg, losses attaching 12% and detaching 15%), these notes would incur losses only after the reference portfolio had suffered losses such that the notional amount below it in the synthetic structure had been exhausted.

Single tranche synthetic CDOs are usually issued as credit-linked notes under repackaging programmes, CDO programmes or a financial institution's European medium term note programme.

4.   Documenting synthetic CDOs

4.1   Introduction
Generally speaking, the documentation for a synthetic CDO will include:
- a prospectus;
- an agency agreement;
- a trust deed and possibly a deed of charge;
- a note purchase agreement;
- a placement agreement;
- an account bank agreement;
- global notes; and
- a repo agreement, GIC account agreement or deposit agreement.

There may also potentially be a liquidity agreement, to assist with any temporary shortfalls in interest payments.

Documentation will be produced to establish and run the SPV. The SPV will enter into swap documentation with an ISDA Master Agreement (as amended by a schedule). Pursuant to this, it will enter into a credit default swap confirmation, an interest rate confirmation and, if the notes are multi-currency notes or if the underlying collateral is denominated in a different currency, a foreign currency swap confirmation (potentially one for each currency). Where the transaction is rated and the SPV's counterparty (usually the arranging bank) does not have a credit rating as high as the highest class of notes issued under the structure, the counterparty may be obliged to enter into collateral support arrangements.

If the structure is managed, then a portfolio management agreement will be entered into, and where various tests have to be performed a portfolio administration agreement may also be entered into. Often, all of the definitions used in the various documents will be set out in a Master Schedule of Definitions, which will then be incorporated by reference into appropriate documents. There will also be various ancillary documents.

The parties to a synthetic CDO vary from transaction to transaction, depending on the structure. Usually they will include:
- the SPV;
- an SPV administrator, to administrate the SPV;

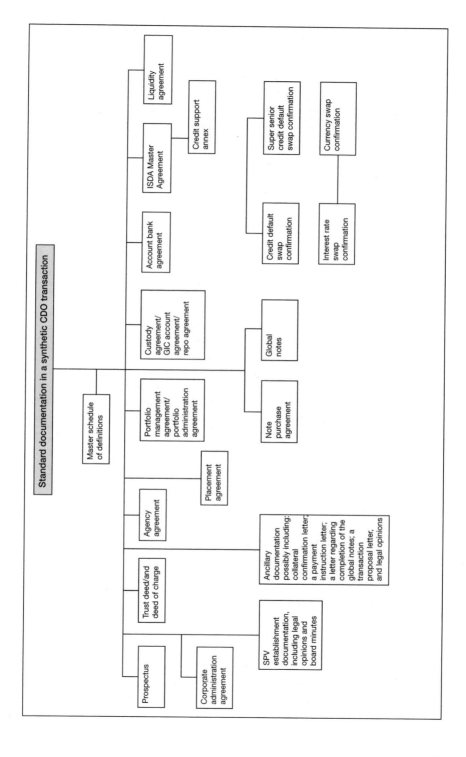

Standard documentation in a synthetic CDO transaction

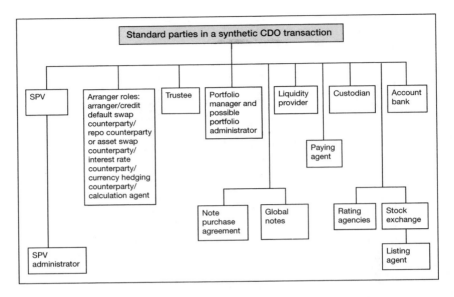

- the arranger, which will also perform the following roles:
  - credit default swap counterparty;
  - repo counterparty or asset swap counterparty (depending on how the highly rated securities held as collateral are held);
  - interest rate swap counterparty; and
  - possibly, currency hedging swap counterparty;
- in a managed transaction, a portfolio manager to manage the reference entity portfolio and possibly a portfolio administrator to perform any tests on the portfolio;
- the noteholders and super senior swap counterparty;
- a liquidity provider, to hedge any short-term liquidity issues;
- a trustee to represent the noteholders;
- a principal paying agent and a local paying agent in the jurisdiction of any listing;
- an account bank, to manage the issuer's accounts;
- a custodian to hold the collateral;
- if the transaction is to be listed, a listing agent (the relevant stock exchange will also review the offering document); and
- if the transaction is rated, the relevant rating agency, which will be involved in negotiating the transaction.

4.2   Prospectus

The prospectus sets out all of the necessary disclosure for investors to make a decision as to whether to purchase the notes issued under the synthetic CDO structure. Where the securities are listed, the information provided will be very detailed and must comply with the requirements of the stock exchange (see further below). For private placements, the level of disclosure will be less and will depend to a certain extent on the actual securities being sold and the expectations of the investor. Where the synthetic CDO issue is made pursuant to a programme, then the information detailed below will generally be set out in a base prospectus. For each issue the issuer will produce final terms, which will provide the pricing information for the notes. Where listed, the final terms are not reviewed by the relevant stock exchange and the securities are immediately listed.

If there are significant new provisions which are not set out in the base prospectus, the arranger is left with a dilemma: either to produce a prospectus supplement (which will allow noteholders a two-day cooling off period after the issue date under the Prospectus Directive) or to adopt an alternative strategy. It has become common to produce a further prospectus for the issue that incorporates the base prospectus by reference. The description of the prospectus below is based on a standalone issue, as are the other descriptions of the transaction documents.

Prospectus

$175 million   Class A senior secured floating rate notes due 2020
$20 million   Class B mezzanine secured floating rate notes due 2020
$35 million   Class C junior notes due 2020

Pilgrim CDO Ltd

Pilgrim CDO Ltd, an exempted company incorporated under the laws of the Cayman Islands (the 'Issuer'), will issue $175 million Class A senior secured floating rate notes due 2020, (the 'Class A notes'), $20 million Class B mezzanine secured floating rate notes due 2020 (the 'Class B notes'), and $35 million Class C junior notes due 2020 (the 'Class C notes'). (The Class A notes, the Class B notes and the Class C notes, are herein referred to as the 'secured notes'). The secured notes will be issued and secured pursuant to a trust deed dated as of July 14 2007 between the issuer, and Granhermano Limited, as trustees (the 'trustee').

The front cover of the prospectus, and generally the next few pages as well, will set out general information on the transaction. This will be a very brief summary. It will include matters such as:

- the title of the notes;
- the form in which they are held;
- the subordination relationship between them in terms of both interest and principal;
- the identity of the key transaction parties (including the jurisdiction and corporate status of the issuer);
- whether the notes will be listed and/or rated; and
- which parties take responsibility for which sections of the document.

At the bottom of this section will be various key selling restrictions, in particular in relation to the United States and each jurisdiction into which the securities are sold.

Notice to New Hampshire residents

Neither the fact that a registration statement or an application for a licence has been filed under Chapter 421-B of the New Hampshire Revised Statutes with the State of New Hampshire nor the fact that a security is effectively registered or a person is licensed in the State of New Hampshire constitutes a finding by the secretary of state that any document filed under RSA 421-B is true, complete and not misleading. Neither any such fact nor the fact that an exemption or exception is available for a security or a transaction means that the secretary of state has passed in any way upon the merits or qualifications of, or recommended or given approval to, any person, security or transaction.

This will generally be followed by a table of contents and investment consideration and risk factors.

Investment in the notes is suitable only for investors who:
- have the requisite knowledge and experience in financial and business matters, and access to, and knowledge of, appropriate analytical resources, to evaluate the information contained in the prospectus and the merits and risks of an investment in the issuer in the context of such investors' financial position and circumstances;
- are capable of bearing the economic risk of an investment in the issuer for an indefinite period of time;
- are acquiring the notes for their own account for investment, not with a view to resale, distribution or other disposition of the notes (subject to any applicable law requiring that the disposition of the investor's property be within its control); and
- recognise that it may not be possible to make any transfer of the notes for a substantial period of time, if at all.

The investment considerations provide disclosure information on to whom the notes are most suited, with a particular emphasis that they should be purchased only by sophisticated investors. The risk factors set out various risks involved in purchasing the securities, of which investors should be aware.

The risk factors will usually emphasise:
- the limited recourse nature of the notes;
- that only professional investors should purchase them;
- the lack of a secondary market; and
- the risk involved in credit derivative products in general.

The risk factors will be followed by a table of contents and a summary of the transaction's terms. Following this, the prospectus will set out the terms and conditions of the notes. The notes themselves will be constituted by the trust deed and so the prospectus will set these out for disclosure purposes only.

> **Summary of terms**
>
> The following summary is qualified in its entirety by, and should be read in conjunction with, the more detailed information appearing elsewhere in this prospectus. An index of defined terms appears at the back of this prospectus.

The prospectus will also set how the proceeds of the notes will be applied, information on the ratings and information on the issuer itself.

> **The issuer**
>
> **General**
>
> The issuer was incorporated as an exempted company and registered on August 21 2007, in the Cayman Islands pursuant to the issuer charter, has a registered number of 884883 and is in good standing under the laws of the Cayman Islands.

The issuer is normally a newly incorporated SPV that has not yet produced accounts, so normally there is only a page or so of disclosure such as outlining the issuer's address, the names of its directors, capitalisation, business, registration and incorporation information, as well as information on the administrator.

In addition to the issuer, the prospectus provides disclosure on the key parties involved in the transaction: the arranger, the swap counterparty, the agents and any custodian. The prospectus will provide information on the underlying assets in which the proceeds of the notes are invested (eg, highly rated securities, a repo agreement or a deposit account).

The prospectus will also set out any restrictions on the sale of the securities in a selling restrictions section and any general tax issues relating to the securities on a general relevant country-by-country basis. The prospectus will also contain certain other general information such as the form in which the notes are issued (eg, bearer instruments held in the clearing systems).

4.3 Trust deed/deed of charge

Each synthetic CDO transaction will have a trust deed. Sometimes the function of the trustee is divided into two roles: a security trustee and a note trustee. This happens where the arranger feels that following any enforcement of the transaction there may be a conflict between the trustee acting for the noteholders as secured parties and certain other of the secured parties, such as the arranger and the agents.

When the trustee role is split between a note trustee and a security trustee, a transaction will often have a note trust deed and a security trust deed, with the provisions relating to taking security and its enforcement being set out in the security trust deed or in a deed of charge.

The rest of the provisions will be set out in the note trust deed. The description below is on the basis that all of the trustee provisions are set out in a single trust deed.

All of the transaction parties will sign up to the trust deed. The trust deed will usually contain the following provisions:

- standard provisions, such as definitions and interpretation;
- cancellation of notes and records;
- waiver duty and modification;
- trustee's powers and liabilities, and powers of attorney;
- fees, duties and taxes;
- limited recourse;
- governing law;
- jurisdiction;
- third-party rights; and
- counterparties.

The trust deed constitutes the issue of securities. It sets out the powers and duties of the trustee. Under the trust deed, the issuer grants security in favour of the trustee (on behalf of the noteholders) and other secured parties over the underlying assets (ie, the highly rated securities, deposit accounts and/or other transaction agreements).

The issuer makes various negative covenants, which are designed to restrict the commercial freedom and discretion of the issuer as far as possible, as well as positive covenants which impose duties on the issuer such as the duty to produce annual accounts and to comply with the instructions of the trustee.

The trust deed will also set out:

- the amount of the notes;
- the issuer's covenant to pay;
- the enforcement of security; and
- the payment and application of moneys.

The enforcement provisions cover what happens if the issuer fails to make a payment of interest and principal when due (not if it is required to make a credit protection payment under the credit default swap), or commits another default such as a breach of covenant or other event of default. These rights include the right to appoint a receiver.

The trust deed will also contain several schedules setting out the form of global notes, the conditions of the notes and the provisions for noteholders' meetings.

The terms of the credit derivative embedded into the transaction may be set out either in the conditions (with a light credit default swap) or in a full credit default swap. The latter is the most common.

The conditions are generally similar to the conditions for any capital market transaction such as a eurobond. The key provisions in the conditions will include provisions relating to the form, denomination, title, transfer and exchange of the notes. They will also include provisions relating to how the notes rank in terms of subordination and are secured, together with how the proceeds of any enforcement will be applied (the 'waterfall'). The conditions will detail the interest payments that will be made in terms of quantum and timing and how these may vary following the occurrence of a credit event.

The conditions will also detail how the principal amount of the notes can be reduced following payment of any cash settlement amount. They will deal with both scheduled redemption of the notes and early redemption for tax reasons, events of default, enforcement and the limited recourse nature of the notes, notices, further issues and governing law and jurisdiction.

It is not uncommon for the conditions to contain a considerable degree of disclosure regarding duties of agents, indemnities and other matters. However, this is not strictly correct as this disclosure should be set out elsewhere in the offering document.

4.4 Custody agreement/purchase agreement and asset swap agreement

The proceeds of the notes must be invested to generate a return, which will be blended together with the premium under the credit default swap to provide the return on the notes. Although there are many techniques, two are more common. The first involves using a repo agreement and custody agreement. Under this mechanism, the issuer and the arranger will enter into a repo agreement under which the issuer will agree to purchase the collateral securities at a price equal to the proceeds of the notes. The issuer will agree to sell the securities back to the arranger at full at the transaction's maturity at a price equal to that necessary to repay the principal of the notes. The repo agreement will usually be documented under a TBMA/ISMA Global Master Repurchase Agreement.

The issuer cannot hold the collateral securities itself; they will be held by the custodian. The rights and duties of the custodian will be set out either in a custody agreement or as part of the agency agreement.

The custodian will either deliver collateral securities to the arranger in satisfaction of payment of any cash or physical settlement amounts or liquidate these securities and pay the resulting cash amount across.

The custody provisions will appoint the custodian and set out its rights and duties; they will also provide details of the accounts in which the securities are held and how the custodian should deal with certain issues that may arise relating to the securities, such as how to deal with voting rights. The custody provisions will also set out in what circumstances it must act in accordance with the issuer's instructions, and in what circumstances it must act in accordance with the trustee's instructions (usually in an enforcement situation).

The custodian will normally have two accounts over which security is taken. These are the cash account and the securities account. The location of these accounts will depend on where the highly rated securities are held. If they are held in either of Euroclear or Clearstream, then the custodian will hold the securities in an account with one of those institutions. These securities will then be charged in favour of the trustee, on behalf of the secured parties. The custodian will also hold a cash account with the same institution, under which any cash payments of interest, amortisation amounts and later principal will be held. These payments will then be re-profiled under the asset swap agreement or a liquidity agreement

4.5 Deposit agreement/guaranteed investment contract

As an alternative to investing the proceeds of the notes in highly rated securities, they may be placed in a bank account held with the arranger or another financial institution. The rights of the issuer to the sums held in the account and how the financial institution segregates these proceeds, whom it allows to deal with the proceeds (eg, the trustee and/or the paying agent), and from whom and when it will take instructions will all be set out in a deposit agreement. The deposit agreement sometimes forms part of the account bank agreement.

Alternatively, the funds may be invested in a GIC. The GIC will be for the term of the notes and will provide the rate of interest necessary for making the anticipated distributions under the notes, together with the premium under the credit default swap. The GIC or deposit agreement will be used to fund any payments of cash or physical settlement amounts under the credit default swap.

4.6 Agency agreement

Once a CDO transaction has launched, the issuer's role is very limited, with all of the functions being carried out by agents. There will usually be a principal paying agent who arranges for the issuer's payments under the swaps to be made. If the transaction is listed, the relevant stock exchange will usually require a paying agent to be appointed in the jurisdiction of that stock exchange.

If the securities carry a floating rate of interest or are a constant maturity or constant maturity credit default swap linked rate of interest, then there will also be a calculation agent (not to be confused with the calculation agent under the swap agreements). The agency agreement is used to appoint the agents and set out their rights and duties, the circumstances under which their appointment may be terminated and the circumstances under which they must act in accordance with the trustee's instructions.

4.7 The swap agreements

The issuer will enter into an ISDA Master Agreement (usually the 1992 ISDA Master Agreement) with each swap counterparty; this will usually just be the arranger and perhaps the super senior swap counterparty. It will then enter into the credit default swap transaction and, in the case of a fully structured transaction, a super senior credit default swap.

Unless the structure is utilising a GIC account or deposit account, the issuer will also enter into a total return swap transaction with the arranger where the proceeds of the notes are invested in highly rated securities and their returns re-profiled to meet the payments under the notes. The issuer may also enter into interest rate and currency rate hedging agreements depending on the structure of the transaction and whether it is rated.

(a) ISDA Master Agreement

The Master Agreement is published as a pre-printed form by ISDA. The market practice is not to amend the pre-printed form; instead, modifications to the standard form made through negotiation are set out in a further pre-printed form, the ISDA

Schedule. Most synthetic CDO transactions are documented using the 1992 ISDA Master Agreement. This sets out the important boilerplate contractual terms and is divided into 14 sections. These sections fall into three distinct areas.

The first area, clauses 1 to 4, covers interpretation, obligations, representations and agreements. These provisions cover the basic mechanics of entering into the transaction.

The second area, clauses 5 to 7, covers events of default, termination events and early termination of the transaction. These provisions set out when, and by whom, transactions can be terminated prior to their stated date of maturity and related quantum and the method of calculation of any payments between the parties.

The third area, clauses 8 to 14, covers the administrative side of the transaction:

- transfer of derivative contracts;
- the contractual currency;
- miscellaneous provisions such as the survival obligations on the termination of a transaction, offices and expenses;
- notices; and
- governing law and jurisdiction.

(b) Schedule to the Master Agreement

The Schedule is also a pre-printed form and allows the parties to tailor their Master Agreement. It contains a number of choices that the parties may make in relation to the Master Agreement (including whether certain provisions should apply to both parties, to one party or to neither). The Schedule may also modify provisions in the Master Agreement and set out additional provisions.

The ISDA Schedule is divided into three parts. Part 1 deals with termination provisions. Part 2 covers agreements to deliver documents. Part 3 deals with miscellaneous matters such as addresses for notices; calculation agents; credit support; governing law and netting. In Part 4 the parties amend and delete various provisions of the ISDA Master Agreement, as well as adding additional provisions.

Due to the structured nature of synthetic CDO transactions and the bankruptcy-remote nature of the SPV, the Schedule will normally be amended so that there is as little risk as possible that the counterparty can cause the swap to terminate. Some of the most common amendments are as follows.

Where the synthetic CDO is issued by a multi-issuance vehicle, netting provisions that could allow netting across different series will be disapplied. The provisions obliging a counterparty to gross up its payments relating to deduction or withholding for tax will usually be amended so that the gross-up applies to both indemnifiable taxes and withholding taxes, to avoid the investors assuming this risk.

Due to the heavy involvement of the swap counterparty in structuring the transaction and selecting the administrator that will run the SPV, the agreement will normally be amended so that a breach of representation by the SPV either will not give the counterparty the right to terminate the swap agreement or will severely restrict this right.

Both the issuer and the swap counterparty will usually agree to furnish specified information, maintain authorisations, comply with laws and notify the other of any breached tax representations. Breach of these representations should not give the counterparty the ability to terminate the relevant swap, though.

The events of default will usually be limited to failure to pay or deliver, bankruptcy and merger without assumption, with illegality as the only termination event.

Although bankruptcy is generally included as an event of default, the bankruptcy-remote nature of the SPV means that a bankruptcy is highly unlikely to occur in the case of the issuer and in reality will apply only to the counterparty. For payments on early termination, market quotation and loss are normally selected.

(c) Credit default swaps

The credit default swap will take the form of a portfolio credit default swap. It will incorporate the 2003 ISDA Credit Derivatives Definitions and the relevant standard terms for reference entities. It will operate substantially like the unfunded credit default swaps described in Part I of this book.

Under this swap, the arranger as counterparty will purchase credit protection on the reference portfolio

The portfolio credit default swap in a synthetic CDO operates very similarly to a single name credit default swap. The easiest way to conceptualise the product is to view it as consisting of a bundle of credit default swaps, with one credit default swap being in place (between the SPV and the arranger) for each reference entity in the portfolio. This then provides documentation, pricing, administrative and diversification advantages and benefits.

Each time that a credit event occurs in relation to a reference entity and the conditions to settlement are met, the settlement procedure is the same as for a single-name credit default swap, except that instead of the transaction terminating on the settlement date, the reference entity will be removed from the portfolio and the transaction will continue. In a managed transaction, the manager will be able to remove and add reference entities from the reference portfolio in accordance with the criteria set out in the portfolio management agreement.

The credit default swap will usually have a notional amount equal to the combined notional amount of the notes and any super senior credit default swap. This overall notional amount will consist of a specific (and usually equal) notional amount for each reference entity. Sometimes, to meet ratings considerations, the credit default swap will be over-collateralised as a form of credit enhancement.

In full structure transactions there will also, of course, be a super senior swap, under which the issuer will be the protection buyer and the super senior swap counterparty the protection seller. The super senior swap will operate effectively as a back-to-back swap and will fund the SPV's credit protection payments under the principal credit default swap. Other than the SPV being a protection buyer rather than a protection seller, the principal difference between the two swaps is that losses can attach only once an amount equal to the principal amount of the notes has been exhausted. As mentioned above, the issuer will also enter into an ISDA Master Agreement with the super senior credit default swap counterparty, and substantially the same points described above will apply in relation to ISDA Master Agreements in synthetic CDO transactions.

(d) Currency rate hedging agreements

Where the notes are of a different currency to the underlying assets or the credit default swaps there may also be a currency rate hedging agreement in place. If the notes are multi-currency notes, there will be several of these agreements. The currency swaps and interest rate swaps (see paragraph below) are usually combined into a single transaction. They usually also have the same counterparty: the arranger.

Each currency swap and interest/currency rate swap will contain special provisions (which will be set out in either the schedule or the confirmation) to reduce the notional amount of any transaction in line with the reduction in principal amount of the overall transaction, where there is a principal amount reduction following a settlement date. The extent to which these hedging arrangements are put in place will depend on whether the transaction is rated and the position of the rating agencies.

(e) Interest rate hedging agreements

Where the rate and timing of interest under the securities and super senior credit default swap does not match the repo agreement/deposit agreement or GIC and the credit default swap, the transaction may be structured to isolate or iron out any interest rate/payment timing exposure. This is done by entering into an interest rate hedging agreement under which the issuer will pay on the various payment flows it receives in relation to the credit default swap, repo agreement, GIC or deposit agreement. In return, it will receive an amount equal to the interest payments that it must make under the notes, plus any fees payable to the transaction parties.

(f) Credit support annex

Not all transactions will have a credit support annex. Those that do are most likely to be rated transactions. A credit support annex may be put in place with any hedging counterparty. A Standard & Poor's publication, *Ratings Criteria for Synthetic CDO Transactions*, describes the features that a rating agency will seek to ensure are present in the credit support annex for a rated transaction. It states that the rating agency will ensure that the SPV will receive the required amount of collateral. The rating agency will check that:

- the SPV's threshold amount is unlimited while the counterparty's threshold amount is zero;
- the counterparty's minimum transfer amount is as low as can be negotiated; and
- the SPV is obliged to return only collateral that it has actually received.

The rating agency will also check that:
- while the delivery amount is to be rounded up, the return amount is to be rounded down;
- the SPV can transfer interest only to the extent that such interest has actually accrued;
- the counterparty must transfer collateral on demand;
- there are appropriate default and early termination provisions in the document; and
- the transfer costs of the collateral are borne by the counterparty.

4.8 Portfolio management agreement

Where a synthetic CDO transaction is managed, there will also be a portfolio management agreement, sometimes known as a portfolio advisory agreement. The portfolio manager, the trustee and the issuer will enter into the portfolio management agreement. Under this agreement, the issuer will appoint the portfolio manager to perform advisory and administrative functions with respect to the portfolio of reference entities set out in the credit default swap.

The agreement will set out the duties of the portfolio manager. In particular, it will cover the duty of the portfolio manager to add and remove reference entities from the reference portfolio, to maximise the return on the credit default swap in accordance with the trading strategy contemplated by the transaction. It will also provide the methodology and parameters for how the portfolio manager must carry this out (perhaps on the basis of credit spread and other tests). The agreement will also define the discretion that the portfolio manager has in making substitutions.

As with the other agreements appointing transaction parties, the agreement will set out:

- the remuneration of the portfolio manager;
- when its appointment can be terminated;
- when it must act in accordance with the instructions of the trustee; and
- other boilerplate provisions.

In more highly managed transactions, such as credit-linked CPPI, the portfolio management agreement will set out highly detailed provisions providing the trading strategy which the portfolio manager must adopt and the various tests that will be performed on the portfolio. In some transactions, some of the functions may be set out in a trading agency agreement.

4.9 Portfolio administration agreement

Where the management of a synthetic CDO involves a large administrative burden – especially in relation to the performance of certain tests on the portfolio to make sure that certain key thresholds are maintained – a portfolio administrator may also be appointed to perform these tests. The portfolio administrator, the trustee and the issuer will enter into the portfolio administration agreement. The agreement will define the scope of administrative tasks that the portfolio administrator must carry out. As with the other agreements appointing transaction parties, the agreement will set out:

- the remuneration of the portfolio administrator;
- when its appointment can be terminated;
- when it must act in accordance with the instructions of the trustee; and
- other boilerplate provisions.

4.10 Account bank agreement

At closing, the issuer will have had various accounts into which funds will be paid (as described further above). Management of these accounts will be documented in the custody agreement or agency agreement, provided that there are no particularly complex issues involved. However, if the transaction structure requires more complex usage of accounts such as a reserve account or a liquidity account, this part of the transaction may be documented in a separate account bank agreement.

4.11 Placement agency agreement

In the placement agency agreement, one or more placement agents, which are usually the transaction's arranger and occasionally other financial institutions, agree to procure subscribers for the notes at a specified price. If they fail to do so, the placement agents must subscribe for the notes themselves.

The issuer and placement agents will agree to abide by certain selling restrictions. These are usually set out in the prospectus. The document will usually contain certain representations in relation to the issuer such as obtaining a listing of the securities, as well as certain other representations as to the veracity of the prospectus, the status of the issuer, taxes and other areas of concern.

The issuer will also covenant on various matters, such as the efforts it will make to procure registration of the security. The placement agency agreement will set out the conditions precedent to the placing agents placing the notes and the fee that the placement agents will receive for their services.

4.12 Global notes

In the European market, CDO securities will usually be issued in bearer form. Rather than having an individual bearer note certificate representing each note, a global note is usually issued. To comply with certain US legal restrictions (usually Regulation S and TEFRA D), these notes are issued in temporary form as a temporary global note. The note remains in this temporary global form during a distribution compliance period, usually of around 40 days, during which there are restrictions on transfer. The temporary global note is then replaced by a permanent global note and these transfer restrictions are restricted.

The CDO securities may alternatively be issued in registered form. This will mean that there will be an additional party involved in the transaction: the registrar. In this case the permanent global note will be in registered form and the registrar will record transfers in the books of the common depository.

In the case of both bearer global notes and registered global notes, the global notes are authenticated by the issuer and agent on closing, whereupon the proceeds of the notes are released to the issuer, and the global notes are held by an agent for a common depository. The common depository will, in the case of Regulation S notes, hold the notes on behalf of Euroclear and Clearstream; in the case of Rule 144A notes, the global note will be registered in the name of a nominee of DTC, with book-entry interests.

CDO securities may be issued in reliance both upon Regulation S (which allows sales of notes which are structured to prevent sales being made into the United States) and Rule 144A (which allows sales of notes which are structured to allow sales of notes into the United States, but only to certain sophisticated investors). In these CDO structures all of the notes are usually issued in registered form.

Most investors will retain their holding of CDO securities through an account (held either directly or through a nominee) with either of the two major clearing systems: Euroclear or Clearstream. Transfers of securities between investors are then made through book entries in the clearing systems. Definitive bearer notes will be issued only to investors and will usually be issued to noteholders only in certain limited circumstances (eg, when the clearing systems are closed for a period of 14 days or there is an event of default under the CDO securities).

The above description sets out the general market practice for the form in which CDO securities are held. For tax or other reasons, there are several other structures that may be used, although these will only be for a limited number of issues.

What are Regulation S and Rule 144A?
In the aftermath of America's great stock market collapse in 1929, tough laws were introduced to protect investors. One of these was the Securities Act of 1933, Section 5 of which prevented use of American inter-state mail to sell or deliver a security unless the issuer had filed a registration statement. This registration statement is a document containing extensive disclosure that is filed with the US Securities and Exchange Commission (SEC). They are expensive to prepare, and because Section 5 is so widely drafted there is a risk that securities which are issued outside of the United States by non-US issuers that have no intention of selling securities to US investors could fall foul of the act and be liable to US criminal sanctions.

Regulation S
To prevent this from happening, the SEC introduced Regulation S.[1] It is a safe harbour provision. If foreign issuers and financial institutions meet the regulation's criteria for reselling unregistered securities outside of the United States, then the terms 'offer', 'offer to sell', 'sell', 'sale' and 'offer to buy' which are set out in Section 5 are deemed not to include offers and sales which take place outside the United States.

The provisions are quite complex, but in summary, an offer or sale by securities by an issuer or distributor that complies with the various restrictions is deemed to occur outside the United States if the offer or sale is made in an offshore transaction and no directed selling efforts are made in the United States. After two years have elapsed, the securities are deemed to have seasoned and may be sold without restriction. Due to the complexity of the rules, determining when this period has expired is difficult.

Rule 144A
The tough US securities laws are aimed at protecting the small investor from being defrauded or making dangerous investments, especially those proverbial 'widows and orphans'. Large institutions, though, should be able to look after

---

1   Regulation S is promulgated under Rule 903 – Offers or sales of securities by the issuer, a distributor, any of their respective affiliates, or any person acting on behalf of any of the foregoing; conditions relating to specific securities.

themselves and so the SEC introduced Rule 144A to allow foreign issuers to issue securities which could then be resold to US institutions deemed to have enough wealth and experience to make their own judgements.

Rule 144A operates in a similar way to Regulation S: it also acts as a safe harbour. Under Regulation S, after two years has elapsed, foreign issued securities can be sold into the United States without breaching Section 5 of the Securities Act. Under Rule 144A, offers and sales of securities can be made only to a class of institution called qualified institutional buyers. These are institutions managing at least $100 million of investments or, in the case of broker dealers, $10 million. Certain other restrictions and disclosure requirements apply, but in particular the securities must not be publicly traded in the United States.

4.13   Note purchase agreement

A note purchase agreement is an agreement signed by investors in the CDO transaction, under which they make certain representations about their capacity to hold the notes and their understanding of the risks involved.

4.14   Master Schedule of Definitions

Due to the number of transaction documents in any synthetic CDO transaction, many of which will use the same base definitions, it often makes sense to collate all of the definitions used in the transaction into a Master Schedule of Definitions document. This is then incorporated by reference into each transaction document (with the exception of the offering document) as the only transaction document which investors will usually receive is the offering document, so it must be able to stand alone. Standard ISDA definitions will also not normally be included in the Master Schedule of Definitions.

4.15   Ancillary documentation

A synthetic CDO transaction will also have several ancillary documents. Some of these may also be incorporated into the trust deed. The ancillary documents may consist of:

- a payment instruction letter;
- a letter regarding completion of the global notes;
- a transaction proposal letter;
- the issuer's board minutes;
- the legal opinion of the arranger's counsel; and
- the legal opinion of the issuer's counsel.

In the payment instruction letter, the issuer instructs the agent to pay the net proceeds of the notes to the asset swap counterparty as an initial exchange amount.

In the letter regarding completion of the global notes, the issuer gives written confirmation that now that the transaction's principal documents have been executed, the agent should prepare and authenticate the global notes.

Transaction proposal letters are prepared to demonstrate the independence of the SPV. The proposal letter is executed prior to the transaction's closing or pre-closing.

The arranger proposes to the issuer that it issues securities under the CDO transaction in return for a fee. This fee is usually a few hundred dollars or euros.

The issuer will hold a board meeting using board minutes prepared by its counsel. These board minutes will set out a summary of the terms of the securities and the proposal to enter into the CDO transaction and issue the securities. The issuer will then agree to execute the transaction documents and enter into the transaction.

The arranger's counsel will provide a legal opinion, which can be relied upon by the arranger, the trustee and, if the transaction is rated, the relevant rating agencies. The arranger's counsel will opine, among other things, that both the transaction documents and the notes are legal, valid, binding and enforceable under English law and the choice of English law is valid. It will also opine that any security has been validly created and (if applicable) registered, and that financial regulations have been complied with. The arranger may also opine on any applicable taxes (or the lack thereof).

The issuer's counsel will also provide a legal opinion, which can be relied upon by the arranger, the trustee and, if the transaction is rated, the relevant rating agencies. The issuer's counsel will opine, among other things, that the issuer has the capacity to enter into the transaction. It will also opine on any taxes (or lack thereof) in the SPV's jurisdiction and that in the SPV's jurisdiction the choice of law under the transaction documents is enforceable. Additionally, it will opine on the effectiveness of the transaction's limited recourse provisions and that, as far as local law is concerned, the security created under the documents is valid and enforceable.

5. Ratings

5.1 Overview

So why get a rating? It's expensive, time consuming and forces an arranger to make concessions in the documentation. When investors demand rated securities, it may be for a variety of reasons. These may include the following:

- The investor's regulator or internal capital rules permit it to hold only rated bonds;
- Internal or external rules mean that it can hold only a certain percentage of bonds of a certain credit rating; or
- It wishes to gain exposure to securities of certain credit ratings.

A credit rating may be necessary for regulatory capital reasons. A credit rating may also provide a noteholder with confirmation that a form of due diligence has been carried out on the transaction structure, the documentation, the quality and diversity of the reference portfolio and the creditworthiness of any counterparties, and that the structure of the deal actually works.

The ratings categories which rating agencies allocate to synthetic CDOs are the same as those for traditional bonds, although separate ratings are given to each tranche of securities and there will be significant differences between the rating of each of those tranches.

There are three main ratings agencies for synthetic CDOs: Standard & Poor's, Fitch Ratings Limited and Moody's Investors Service. The ratings they allocate to synthetic CDO securities and the respective credit quality of those securities are as set out in the table below:

Standard & Poor's/Fitch	Moody's	Quality
AAA	Aaa	Highest quality
AA+	Aa1	
AA	Aa2	High quality
AA-	Aa3	
A+	A1	
A	A2	Upper medium quality
A-	A3	
BBB+	Baa1	
BBB	Baa2	Medium quality
BBB-	Baa3	Investment grade security minimum
BB+	Ba1	
BB	Ba2	Speculative
BB-	Ba3	
B+	B1	
B	B2	Speculative and vulnerable to default
B-	B3	
C	C	Highly speculative, high risk of default
D	D	In default

Standard & Poor's has summarised what the rating process covers by saying that ratings for synthetic CDOs "address, like in all other structured finance transactions, the likelihood of full payment of interest (either on a timely or ultimate basis) and ultimate payment of principal in accordance with [the transaction's] terms",[2] continuing that "the analysis focuses on how much credit enhancement is needed to achieve a given level of risk and arrives at the commensurate rating, taking into account the transaction's credit risk, structure, and legal analysis".

Ratings in synthetic CDO transactions reflect several factors. These include:

- the risks inherent in the reference portfolio;
- levels of credit enhancement;
- the quality of the collateral assets in which the proceeds of the notes are invested;
- the cash-flow analysis of how inflows of funds will meet the respective outflow;

---

2   "Structured finance ratings: Criteria for rating synthetic CDO transactions", Standard & Poor's, September 2003.

- the legal risks of the transaction (including the bankruptcy remoteness of the SPV and enforceability of the contracts);
- the credit risk and management ability of any portfolio manager;
- the market risk of the other transaction parties; and
- any exposure to interest rate risk and foreign exchange rate risk.

This rating agency analysis will include an assessment of the default risk of the portfolio and a review of the credit default swap's settlement mechanism for assigning recoveries. Where a portfolio is managed, the rating agency will analyse the quality and performance of the manager and the structural requirements for managing the portfolio, and whether the transaction will generate enough money to pay the transaction parties fees. The rating agency will analyse credit enhancement features. Analysis of the structural risks will include the timely payment of interest and principal, counterparty risk, payment waterfalls and any special features of the transaction.

Standard & Poor's describes its rating process as follows. The transaction arranger will request a rating from the rating agency. This request may be made by email in the case of simple transactions or through an initial meeting for more complex transactions. The arranger must provide the rating agency with a term sheet, draft offering document and credit default swap. At this point the arranger will sign an engagement letter and the rating agency will allocate the transaction an analyst. In more complex transactions the arranger will provide the rating agency with an analysis of the transaction's credit risks and structural and collateral features in a structure paper.

The rating agency will comment on the various drafts of documentation and legal opinions and will make structurally related comments. (For more complex transactions, the rating agency will appoint outside counsel.) The arranger and its legal counsel will negotiate these. Once the documentation is finalised, the rating agency will issue a rating letter, detailing the rating that it will apply to each tranche of notes. The arranger or manager will provide information on the reference portfolio on an ongoing basis.

5.2 Credit risk of the reference portfolio

Credit derivatives involve the isolation and separate trading of credit risk. Consequently, when considering which credit rating to allocate, the rating agency will focus strongly on credit derivatives embedded into the structure and the quality and variety of the reference entities.

The rating agencies assess the reference portfolio using proprietary methodologies to estimate probable default rates. These methodologies drive both the composition of a reference portfolio and the size of each tranche comprising the transaction.

For example, in relation to tranche size, imagine that the rating agency rated a 10-year $100 million synthetic CDO with a 100 reference entity reference portfolio. In order for the AAA part of the structure to achieve that rating the rating agency might estimate that the portfolio would have to withstand a 20% default rate (ie, there would be cash settlement amounts payable under the credit default swap totalling $20 million), before losses attached to the AAA part of the structure. This would mean that the AAA part of the structure could have a tranche size of $80 million, perhaps divided between senior notes and a super senior swap.

This would mean that in the absence of other credit enhancements, the mezzanine and junior tranches would have to have a notional amount of at least $20 million. If the model determined that for the mezzanine tranche to achieve a BBB rating, the portfolio would have to withstand a 10% default rate, the junior (and usually unrated) tranche would have to have a notional amount of at least $10 million.

The rating methodology will also look at the sector diversity of reference entities in the portfolio and the historical recovery rates of defaulted entities within that sector. For example, a corporate in the building and development sector may, due to the large amount of physical assets these corporates hold, have an assumed recovery rate higher than a reference entity in the brokers, dealers and investment houses sector. The methodology will assume that higher rated reference entities are less likely to default than lower rated ones. The methodology will also take into account that because different sectors may come under economic pressure at different times, a low correlation between reference entity industrial sectors is likely to reduce the risk of a large number of defaults hitting the reference portfolio at the same time. For example, if all 100 reference entities in a reference portfolio were insurance companies and a series of natural disasters put economic pressure on the insurance industry, a large number of defaults impacting on the portfolio would be more likely to occur than in a portfolio comprised of reference entities from diverse sectors.

Estimating the probable level of defaults in any portfolio is highly complex. Any estimate will be just that, particularly in relation to longer dated transactions: after all, who can predict the long-term credit cycle with any certainty? The risk that a ratings model gets it wrong is known as 'model risk'.

Each rating agency has its own methodology for making this calculation. Standard & Poor's has the CDO evaluator; Moody's uses its recently updated CDOROM and Fitch Ratings uses its Default Vector.

The methodology used not only will affect the composition of the initial reference portfolio, but will also restrict how the manager can manage the portfolio in managed synthetic CDO transactions. To this extent, the relevant methodology will be reflected in the transaction documentation, in terms of disclosure both in the prospectus and, for managed transactions, in any portfolio management agreement in terms of the restrictions on the portfolio manager.

Standard & Poor's CDO Evaluator methodology, for example, is based on estimating a 'scenario default rate' for each rating in the transaction (eg, AAA, BBB, BB and so on). The rate is based on the notional size of the reference portfolio, the credit quality of the reference entities and the industrial sectors from which they derive. The CDO Evaluator uses Monte Carlo statistical methodology to assess the reference portfolio's credit quality. The Monte Carlo approach estimates the probability distribution of defaults by simulating a series of reference portfolio defaults and establishes the extent of any correlation in defaults.

The rating agency itself describes the methodology as follows:

The CDO Evaluator system is used to determine the credit risk of a portfolio of assets both for cash flow and for synthetic CDOs. The direct result is a probability distribution of potential default rates for the portfolio assets in aggregate. These potential default rates range from 0% (no assets in the portfolio default by maturity) to 100% (all assets in the portfolio default by maturity). The more likely outcome is that some, but not all, assets default. The portfolio default rate is computed as the total dollar amount of assets defaulted by maturity, divided by the total principal amount of the portfolio.[3]

The probability distribution assesses the probability of any default rate actually occurring. For example, the probability of a highly diverse group of reference entities suffering credit events and the losses on the portfolio exceeding 20% could perhaps be 10% and the probability of a 30% default rate could be as low as 4%.

After calculating these probability distributions, the CDO Evaluator calculates the scenario default rates – these determine the default rate that each rated tranche must be able to withstand to achieve its target rating. The model takes into account the credit quality of the reference entity, the diversity of industrial sectors, the likely rate of recovery in those sectors and the implied default rate.

5.3   Credit enhancement

Of paramount importance in any rated synthetic CDO is the amount of credit enhancement required for each tranche to achieve its desired rating. We discussed above that this credit enhancement will derive from the subordinated tranches below it. Additionally, though, the excess of the amounts received in interest from the collateral securities or under a repo agreement or GIC account and the premium from the credit default swap, over the amount required to pay interest coupons and expenses, can be trapped in a reserve account. This amount is known as the 'excess spread' and can be used to absorb portfolio losses. Amounts in the reserve account will then be paid to the equity investors either gradually over the later stages of the transaction or on maturity.

Other credit enhancement features include the manner in which the payment waterfalls apply, the use of interest rate and foreign currency hedging transactions to isolate the risk of interest rate, or foreign exchange rate movements preventing the timely payment of interest or repayment of principal.

5.4   Quality of the collateral assets in which the proceeds of the notes are invested

The rating agencies will also look at the structure of the transactions and analyse the credit quality of the underlying assets in which the proceeds of the notes are invested. The proceeds of the notes are usually invested in highly rated securities (either directly or through a repo agreement) or placed on deposit pursuant to a guaranteed investment contract.

The credit quality of the underlying assets or the financial institution providing the GIC account cannot be any less than the credit rating of the corresponding tranche of notes.

---

3   "Global cash flow and synthetic CDO criteria", Standard & Poor's, March 21 2002.

5.5 Cash flow and documentation structure

The rating agency will analyse the transaction's payment flows and will look to see whether the cash inflows from the collateral securities and credit default swap can generate enough revenue to make the payments under the notes.

It will analyse the documentation and request that certain features be included. For example, the rating agency will look at what will happen where a credit event occurs in one interest period, but the relevant cash settlement amount cannot be determined until the next interest period. In that case, it will make certain demands in the interest of noteholders such as that any final price will be deemed to be zero, but where the actual final price is a higher amount, then the interest corresponding to this amount will be repaid on the subsequent interest payment date, together with compound interest.

5.6 Transaction party performance

(a) Portfolio manager

In managed transactions, the rating agency will assess the capabilities of the portfolio manager, as its abilities will have a key effect on the transaction's performance. The rating agency will look very carefully at a portfolio manager's performance on other deals and its structure, and this may have an adverse or positive effect on the rating.

(b) Credit quality of certain transaction parties

The creditworthiness of any liquidity provider and swap counterparty and the probability that a default could occur for reasons not related to the defects in the transaction structure will also be closely analysed by the rating agency. The rating agency will normally insist on provisions in the documentation which state that if the relevant transaction party's own credit rating is downgraded below a pre-defined level, it will find a replacement counterparty to fulfil its role within a set period of time.

6. SPVs

6.1 Overview

The arranger will look to establish the SPV (the corporate which issues the notes) in an offshore jurisdiction. A legal practitioner will often be called upon to advise on the respective merits of each jurisdiction and coordinate with local counsel. The main jurisdictions for establishing the special purpose vehicle for a synthetic CDO are the Cayman Islands, Jersey, Ireland, Luxembourg and the Netherlands.

Each of these jurisdictions is reviewed below. However, please note that although textbooks can never be relied upon in place of legal advice, this is all the more relevant

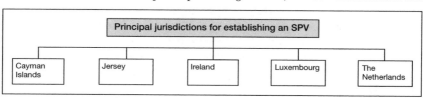

with taxation issues where the specifics of the transactions may cause a norm not to apply or where a change in law, a challenge from the European Union or a court or tax authority ruling can change existing practice overnight.

The key factors which must be considered when selecting a jurisdiction include:

- a stable and predictable legal and regulatory regime;
- start-up and ongoing costs;
- speed and efficiency of establishment and administration;
- the market perception of the jurisdiction;
- the quality of service providers;
- the ability to avoid withholding tax on the cash flows coming into and out of the SPV;
- the ability to avoid incurring liability to VAT, stamp duty, income tax and other taxes; and
- the ability to avoid regulation as a financial institution.

6.2   Cayman Islands

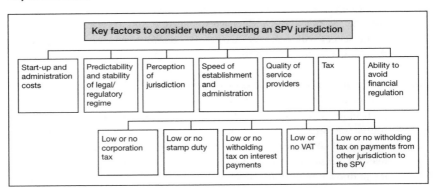

The Cayman Islands is the most established jurisdiction for incorporating SPVs. The jurisdiction has excellent law firms and service providers, and the speed and low cost with which a Cayman Islands company can be incorporated reflect this: a Cayman Islands company can be incorporated within one working day for a $5,000 incorporation fee, or within four to five working days otherwise. The cost of incorporating an SPV (including legal fees) comes to about $1,200.

Typically, the orphan SPV will have authorised issued share capital of $1,000, with the shares being held by the administrator on behalf of charitable beneficiaries (selected by the law firm). There is no requirement for the SPV's accounts to be audited and Cayman SPVs do not usually produce financial statements.

In addition to legal fees for reviewing transaction documentation, an arranger will have to pay legal counsel to review the transaction documentation. The arranger will have to pay a fee to the SPV's administrator for the establishment of the SPV and review of transaction documentation. The administration fee is payable annually and will be several thousand dollars (which includes the provision of two directors and a registered office address).

Payments of interest and principal that the SPV makes under the notes can be made free of withholding tax.

The SPV will not be subject to any corporation or income tax in the Cayman Islands and will be VAT exempt for any services it receives.

Although the Cayman Islands is not party to double tax treaties, payments of interest and principal which the SPV receives from the collateral securities can be received free of withholding tax provided that these assets qualify for a withholding exemption.

Although an SPV will not require a formal tax ruling, if necessary an undertaking can be applied for from the governor in council. This will provide that pursuant to Section 6 of the Tax Concessions Law (1999 revision), no taxes will be imposed on the company for 30 years after the issue date.

Stamp duty is not payable provided that the notes or transaction documents are not executed in the Cayman Islands or brought before a Cayman court. If stamp duty is payable, the amount is relatively low and may be only a few hundred dollars.

Cayman SPVs are not subject to registration with, or supervision by, any regulator and no approvals are necessary to enter into any transaction.

6.3 Jersey

Jersey, like the Cayman Islands, has excellent law firms and service providers, and the speed and low cost with which a Cayman Islands company can be incorporated reflect its status as a mature jurisdiction for establishing an SPV. A Jersey SPV can be incorporated within two hours of the incorporation documentation being submitted. However, regulatory approval to the incorporation must be obtained beforehand and this can take up to five days (although it is usually quicker).

The cost of establishing the SPV is about €500 (exclusive of legal fees), but there is an annual registration fee of about €200 and an exempt annual company fee of about €900 per year. The annual administration fees of the company vary between €10,000 and €15,000, and cover the provision of directors and a registered office. The SPV will be established as an orphan company in a similar manner to a Cayman Islands SPV and will generally have only €2 of capital.

The SPV will be required to have its accounts audited – this typically costs about €10,000 per year. The SPV is not required to publish financial statements.

Payments of interest and principal that the SPV makes under the notes can be made free of withholding tax.

Jersey SPVs are registered as tax-exempt companies and are not subject to Jersey income or corporation tax. Tax-exempt status for Jersey companies will end in 2008 and will be replaced by a general zero rate for corporation tax.

Although Jersey is not party to the double tax treaties that apply to SPVs, payments of interest and principal which the SPV receives from the collateral securities can be received free of withholding tax provided that these assets qualify for a withholding exemption.

Although an SPV will not require a formal tax ruling, confirmations can be obtained from the comptroller of income tax in Jersey.

Jersey SPVs are exempt from VAT. Stamp duty is not generally payable for Jersey SPVs.

Jersey SPVs are not subject to registration with or supervision by any regulator, and no approvals are necessary to enter into any transaction.

6.4   Ireland

Ireland as a jurisdiction for establishing SPVs has gone from strength to strength in recent years. Perhaps because of this, there are more law firms and service providers offering SPV services in Ireland than in any of the other major SPV jurisdictions. Establishment and running costs are greater than in the traditional offshore jurisdictions of the Cayman Islands and Jersey. The regulatory regime is more complex and procedures are generally more difficult and less standardised, partly because standard Irish companies must exist beside the regime for SPVs. In spite of these costs, Ireland can be a more attractive jurisdiction for establishing an issuer, because the SPV will be domiciled within the European Union (an important consideration for some investors), and for taxation reasons in certain transactions.

An Irish SPV usually takes two to three weeks to incorporate. The cost of doing so, exclusive of legal fees, is usually around €3,500, with annual administration costs (which include the provision of two directors and a registered office address) running at about €15,000 to €20,000. Increased competition may mean that this figure varies considerably between firms and transactions. These amounts will be greater if the SPV is incorporated as a public limited company rather than as a private limited company. The minimum capital requirement for private company SPVs is €2, and for public companies €40,000 (although around half of this amount can be used to meet the SPV's expenses). Irish SPVs must be audited annually – the cost of this is usually in excess of €10,000.

Payments of interest and principal that the SPV makes under the notes can be made free of withholding tax, due to domestic withholding tax exemptions.

The SPV will be structured so as to qualify as a 'Section 110 company', deemed to be trading for the purposes of computing its taxable profits. The SPV's expenses, including interest payments to noteholders, are deductible for the purposes of determining taxable profits. Income tax is therefore minimal as there should be almost no taxable profit.

Ireland is party to around 40 double tax treaties. Payments of interest and principal which the SPV receives from the collateral securities can be received free of withholding tax provided that these assets qualify for a withholding exemption.

Although an SPV will not require a formal tax ruling, this can be obtained from the Irish Revenue.

Stamp duty is payable on some transaction documents, but a 'debt factoring' exemption usually allows this payment to be avoided.

Irish SPVs benefit from a statutory exemption from Irish VAT applying to portfolio management services where the manager exercises some discretion. Certain other services are also exempt from VAT, such as those relating to payment, but others are caught.

Irish SPVs are not usually subject to registration with or supervision by any regulator, and no approvals are necessary to enter into any transaction.

6.5   Luxembourg

Luxembourg, like Ireland, is one of the newer jurisdictions for establishing SPVs. Unlike Ireland, it has not gone from strength to strength in recent years; instead, after a promising start, it suffered from an EU state aid challenge to its legal regime. Things have started to pick up again, with the jurisdiction recently returning to favour.

Luxembourg SPVs can be set up as either public companies or private companies. Private companies are not permitted to issue securities to the public and this may be a concern in certain transactions. Generally speaking, issues of notes that are restricted to institutional investors or private placements are not regarded as public issues; nor are securities with minimum denominations of at least €125,000.

A Luxembourg SPV can usually be established within a week; however, it will generally take an additional one to two weeks to obtain any required corporate taxation or VAT rulings.

The cost of establishing a private company SPV, exclusive of legal fees, is usually around €3,000, with annual administration costs (which include the provision of a manager and a registered office address) running at about €10,000. The minimum capital requirement for private company SPVs is €12,500 (although this amount can be used to meet the SPV's expenses). Private company SPVs must be audited annually. This usually costs around €8,000 to €10,000, with higher fees for more complex transactions.

The cost of establishing a public company SPV, exclusive of legal fees, is also usually around €3,000, with annual administration costs (which include the provision of three directors and a registered office address) running at about €20,000. The minimum capital requirement for public company SPVs is €31,000 (although this amount can be used to meet the SPV's expenses). Public company SPVs must be audited annually. The cost of this can be around €8,000 to €10,000, with higher fees for more complex transactions.

Like Irish SPVs, Luxembourg SPV establishment and running costs are greater than in the Cayman Islands and Jersey. The regulatory regime is more complex and procedures are generally more difficult and less standardised. In spite of these costs, Luxembourg can be a more attractive jurisdiction for establishing an issuer, because the SPV will be domiciled within the European Union (an important consideration for some investors), and for taxation reasons in certain transactions.

Payments of interest and principal which the SPV makes under the notes can be made free of withholding tax, although the EU Savings Directive may trigger a withholding tax on interest payment in certain limited circumstances.

Interest and other payments to noteholders are tax deductible and the SPV will be structured so that although standard corporation tax (which is in excess of 30%) is payable on profits, there will be no or very limited profits to tax.

Luxembourg is party to around 45 double tax treaties. Payments of interest and principal which the SPV receives from the collateral securities can be received free of withholding tax, provided that these assets qualify for a withholding exemption.

An SPV will not require a formal tax ruling, but an informal tax ruling can be obtained from the Luxembourg tax authorities.

Stamp duty is not payable on transaction documents unless there is a voluntary registration, in which case there is a nominal fee.

Luxembourg SPVs benefit from a statutory exemption from VAT that applies to portfolio management services. Luxembourg SPVs are not usually subject to registration with, or supervision by, any regulator, and no approvals are necessary to enter into any transaction.

6.6 The Netherlands

The Netherlands is a more mature jurisdiction than Ireland or Luxembourg for establishing SPVs, but like Luxembourg, it has been through some regulatory uncertainty. This has allowed Ireland to surpass it in popularity. As with Luxembourg, the jurisdiction is now a popular choice.

A Dutch SPV usually takes four to six weeks to establish (including obtaining corporate taxation and VAT rulings). The cost of establishing a private company SPV, exclusive of legal fees, is usually around €3,500, with annual administration costs (which include the provision of directors and a registered office address) running at about €25,000 in the first year and €15,000 thereafter. The minimum capital requirement for private company SPVs is €18,000 (although this amount can be used to meet the SPV's expenses). Dutch SPVs need not be audited.

Like Irish and Luxembourg SPVs, establishment and running costs are greater than in the Cayman Islands and Jersey. In spite of these costs, Luxembourg can be a more attractive jurisdiction for establishing an issuer, because the SPV will be domiciled within the European Union (an important consideration for some investors), and for taxation reasons in certain transactions.

Payments of interest and principal that the SPV makes under the notes can generally be made free of withholding tax. One legal issue that may be of concern in certain transactions is the 'hybrid debt rule'. This applies to notes with a tenor of over 10 years, where the repayment is deemed to be substantively profit-linked. This can impact particularly on the equity tranche of a synthetic CDO. If the rule applies, a debt instrument can be recharacterised as equity and attract a significant withholding tax. Application of the rules is complex, but to summarise, there are a number of exceptions relating to where the notes combine a fixed or floating rate of interest with a profit-linked element. Equity tranches are usually structured in this manner and a tax ruling confirming that interest payments are tax deductible and there is no withholding can (if the rules are complied with) be obtained from the tax authorities prior to issue.

Dutch SPVs are usually set up as orphans and are structured so that although profits are taxable, there is not much in the way of profits to tax. It is general practice for the SPV to retain its administration costs as taxable profits. These are taxed at between 29% and 34.5%. The SPV will then pay the net amount as a dividend instead of paying administration fees.

The Netherlands is party to around 70 double tax treaties. Payments of interest and principal which the SPV receives from the collateral securities can be received free of withholding tax, provided that these assets qualify for a withholding exemption. Although an SPV will not require a formal tax ruling, it is common to obtain one from the tax authorities where there is concern that the hybrid debt rule may apply.

Stamp duty is not payable on the transaction documents. Dutch VAT rules are complex and, due to a tax arbitrage between the United Kingdom and the European Union, portfolio management services provided from the United Kingdom may have favourable tax treatment. Most of the other SPV services (eg, paying agency) are exempt from VAT in the Netherlands.

Dutch SPVs are not usually subject to registration with or supervision by any regulator, in a standard synthetic CDO issue bought by professional investors, and no approvals are necessary to enter into any transaction, although the regulator must be notified within two weeks of an issue.

7. Stock exchanges and listing

7.1 Overview

Investors will often require that the notes issued in a synthetic CDO transaction are listed. There are several reasons to do so. A listing implies that the securities meet certain levels of disclosure. Because of this, many institutions have internal rules that they may only hold listed securities. A listing may also be necessary for certain tax exemptions to apply.

The principal stock exchanges in terms of market share for listing synthetic CDO transactions are the Irish Stock Exchange and the Luxembourg Stock Exchange. The sections below cover the process for listing a synthetic CDO transaction on the Irish Stock Exchange. With the advent of the EU Prospectus Directive, these procedures are substantially similar for the Luxembourg Stock Exchange and other bourses.

7.2 Obtaining a listing on the Irish Stock Exchange

It is standard practice for the arranger to appoint a listing agent to advise on the listing process. The listing agent will often be an Irish law firm or one of the multi-jurisdictional offshore law firms. Depending on the listing agent, law firm and/or transactions, the processes below may be done entirely by the arranger's primary counsel or the listing agent. Each prospectus must comply with the relevant Irish Stock Exchange listing rules: in the case of synthetic CDO transactions, the relevant rules are the Asset-Backed Securities (ABS) Listing Rules, which are available on the Irish Stock Exchange website at www.ise.ie.

(a) Annotating the prospectus

The legal practitioner must annotate the offering document in the right-hand margin where each of the ABS Listing Rules is complied with. If a rule is not applicable, this is stated in a non-applicability letter (more of which below). When annotating the prospectus, it is important to take note of any listing rules that are not applicable and ensure that these listing rules are included in the non-applicability letter.

(b) Completing the non-applicability letter

As mentioned above, the non-applicability letter is a letter to the exchange that contains a list of those listing rules that are not applicable.

Non-applicability of Irish Stock Exchange ABS Listing Rules

Date: July 28 2007

Issuer: Pilgrim CDO Limited

Details of issue: €300 million notes due 2018

The following listing rules are either considered not applicable or no information falls to be given in respect of them:

     3A.6.1 (b)
     3A.8.1
     3B.3
     3B.7.2
     3B.7.3
     3C.2.3
     3B.8.1
     3C.2 (h),(l),(m),(n),(o)
     3C.3.4 (c),(d)
     3C.3.6
     3D

(c)   ***Submission of prospectus to Irish Stock Exchange and comments sheet***

The prospectus should be submitted to the Irish Stock Exchange, together with the non-applicability letter. The exchange will acknowledge submission and allocate a reader and listing executive to the transactions. After three working day it will respond by email attaching comments regarding the application of the listing rules in a comments sheet.

Document comments sheet

Name of issuer: Application ID: Our Ref: Draft 1
     Pilgrim CDO Limited   Notes:
Adviser: •   Date of final prospectus and
Executive: support documentation must
Listing agent: be same date as approval date
Contact name: •   All outstanding information
Document type: Specialist Securities   is subject to material comment
Document submitted: •   First submission turnaround –
                                      three days
Comments returned: •   All subsequent submissions –
                                      two days
                                    •   Fax number for Specialist
                                    Securities: +353 1 617 4244

Ref	Section/ paragraph	Page No	Comment	Resolution *(to be completed by Listing Agent)*	Agreed as resolved
A1	Guidelines		Non-applicable letter Please readdress or clarify the following:		

The Irish Stock Exchange's comments should be complied with and any material comments negotiated with the exchange.

(d) ***Preparing the trade for listing***

The Irish Stock Exchange will advise that the Irish financial regulator has approved the prospectus under Part 7 of the Prospectus Directive (Directive 2003/71/EC) Regulations 2005, and that a copy of the letter of approval has been issued by the financial regulator to the issuer.

The arranger's counsel or the listing agent will then forward a PDF of the prospectus to the issuer's counsel and the listing agent will file the prospectus with the Company Registrations Office in Ireland.

Prior to the listing of the prospectus, the arranger's counsel, in conjunction with the listing agent, will forward an email to the Irish Stock Exchange attaching principal and ancillary documentation.

The arranger's counsel will prepare a new version of the prospectus inserting the listing date on the front cover and deleting all annotations. This is the final version. It should be in PDF format and should be sent together with a blackline version of the document, showing the changes made since the last draft.

Also attached to the email should be the finalised non-applicability letter and the comment sheet annotated with how each of the exchange's comments has been resolved.

A timetable for the listing must also be prepared and attached to the email.

Timetable for listing

Details of issue: €300 million notes due 2018

Issuer: Pilgrim CDO Limited

Proposed approval date: August 2 2007

Proposed listing date: August 2 2007

An account information form covering the payment details to the exchange for listing the notes must also be attached, together with draft formal notice.

> **Formal notice for specialist securities (asset-backed debt)**
>
> Publication date: August 2 2007
>
> Application has been made to the Irish Stock Exchange for the following securities to be admitted to the Official List.

Another document which must be forwarded is the bearer letter, which for bearer notes will confirm to the exchange that the notes are initially represented by a temporary global note and that they comply with the laws of Ireland.

A signed Appendix 3 must also be forwarded. This is signed by the issuer and under it the issuer applies for the securities to be admitted to the Official List of the Irish Stock Exchange subject to the listing rules and to be admitted to trading on the regulated market. The issuer also confirms that it has complied with the various listing requirements.

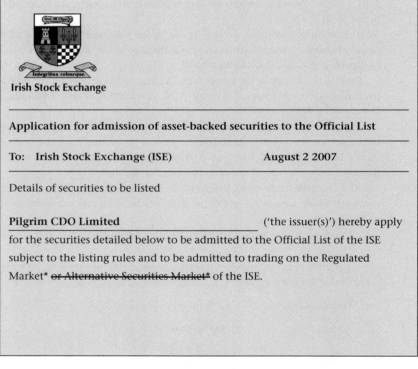

Irish Stock Exchange

Application for admission of asset-backed securities to the Official List

---

To: Irish Stock Exchange (ISE)   **August 2 2007**

Details of securities to be listed

Pilgrim CDO Limited _____ ('the issuer(s)') hereby apply for the securities detailed below to be admitted to the Official List of the ISE subject to the listing rules and to be admitted to trading on the Regulated Market* ~~or Alternative Securities Market~~* of the ISE.

A signed Appendix 4 must also be forwarded. This is a declaration by the listing agent that it confirms to the best of its knowledge and belief all the documents required to be included in the application for listing by the listing rules have been supplied to the ISE and all other relevant requirements of the listing rules have been complied with.

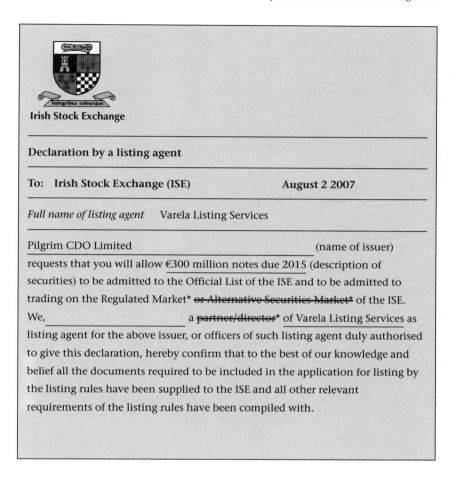

Irish Stock Exchange

Declaration by a listing agent

To: Irish Stock Exchange (ISE)   **August 2 2007**

Full name of listing agent   Varela Listing Services

Pilgrim CDO Limited   (name of issuer)

requests that you will allow €300 million notes due 2015 (description of

securities) to be admitted to the Official List of the ISE and to be admitted to

trading on the Regulated Market* ~~or Alternative Securities Market*~~ of the ISE.

We,   a ~~partner/director~~* of Varela Listing Services as

listing agent for the above issuer, or officers of such listing agent duly authorised

to give this declaration, hereby confirm that to the best of our knowledge and

belief all the documents required to be included in the application for listing by

the listing rules have been supplied to the ISE and all other relevant

requirements of the listing rules have been compiled with.

The final document is to be prepared is the SEDOL form. This provides various pieces of information about the notes, such as the frequency of the interest payments and the International Securities Identifying Number.

Credit index trading

1. Introduction

A credit derivative index (or credit index) is an index comprised of a managed portfolio of commonly traded reference entities. This product has revolutionised the credit derivatives market, promoting liquidity and transparency, the lack of which have been two of the greatest criticisms of the market.

A credit index usually consists of a portfolio of equally weighted reference entities that are rebased on a periodic basis – usually in March and September. The rebalancing takes place under pre-agreed rules using the input of credit derivatives market makers. Credit indices are many and varied. Inclusion of a reference entity in an index is generally by merited by a combination of some or all of the following:

- trading volume;
- geographical location;
- industry category; and
- creditworthiness over the previous six-month period.

A credit index is generally a licensed product, which may have many uses. A market participant can use the index on payment of a fee to create its own product, perhaps a synthetic collateralised debt obligation (CDO) referencing a credit index as it is periodically updated, or by entering into a bilateral over-the-counter (OTC) transaction with another market participant; or it may even create a market itself, standing as a central counterparty buying and selling credit protection on the index and taking the credit risk of each counterparty.

Credit indices increase market liquidity by increasing transaction volumes and lowering market entry barriers. Market makers create markets for trading linked credit derivative products based on standardised documentation. Participants can rely on the reference entity names and related obligations being correct and so reduce their transaction costs. This standardisation also allows automated matching and trading of products.

Credit indices can also allow funded products to have a quasi-form of management. For example, if a single tranche synthetic CDO references the most recent version of a credit index, this will mean that every six months the transaction will reference the most liquid names in a particular sector, possibly saving on a management fees.

2. History of credit indices

To understand the array of credit indices and how credit index trading works, it is important to look back at this product's short history. This will also help the practitioner understand the complicated and ever-changing array of names.

Indices for financial markets are nothing new. After all, the Dow Jones Industrial Average Index got going in the early part of the 20th century. Equity indices were joined by bond indices and then most recently, in the early part of this century, by credit indices.

The credit index market began with several banks setting up their own credit indices. They then launched indices in partnerships with other banks. Rival ventures sprang up and this was then followed by a period of mergers which has resulted in two dominant families of indices, each administered by the same administrator and owned by substantially the same parties: iTraxx and CDX. Further consolidation between these two behemoths seems inevitable.

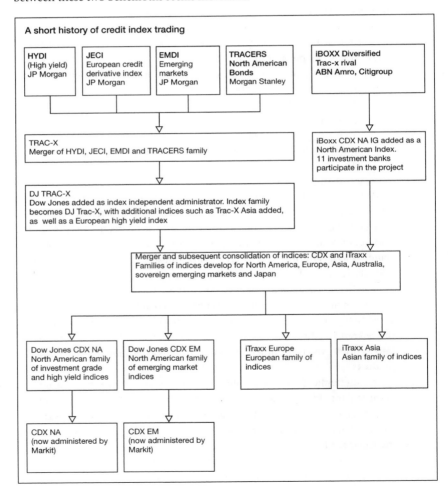

Credit index trading began in the early part of the decade, when in 2001 JP Morgan launched a high-yield credit index called Hydi.[1] This was followed in 2002 by Tracers and Synthetic Tracers, both launched by Morgan Stanley. The former referenced North American Bonds (and followed the exchange traded fund model) and the latter was a full credit index. JP Morgan soon launched Jeci, a European credit index, and Emdi, an emerging market credit index. JP Morgan and Morgan Stanley then merged their indices to form the Trac-x family of indices.

Around the same period, ABN Amro, Citigroup and Deutsche Bank launched iBoxx Diversified, an index of European reference entities which was intended to be a competitor in Europe to Trac-x. The banks, along with several other major market participants such as Merrill Lynch and UBS, followed this up by launching iBoxx CDX NA IG in North America to act as a rival to Trac-x in the United States. At this point there were two principal competitors: iBoxx and Trac-x.

Trac-x then appointed Dow Jones, which had a wealth of experience in equity and bond indices, to act as the North American Trac-x independent administrator. It then launched a European high yield index.

In April 2004 Trac-x and iBoxx merged. The European indices became known as Dow Jones iTraxx Europe and the North American indices as Dow Jones CDX NA. Indices for other areas were then either launched or relaunched under the new brand names.

In 2007 Markit, which by this time was already administering the iTraxx family of indices, took over the administration of the North American CDX indices. Over time the administration and functioning of the indices has converged. The indices are now known as either CDX indices, in the case of North American and emerging markets indices, or iTraxx indices in the case of European and Asian indices.

3.   Structure and objective of the indices

3.1   Overview

As described above, there are two grand and related families of credit indices: iTraxx and CDX. It is likely that these indices will converge further in the future. In the meantime, although some differences remain, it is likely that any convergence will be towards the iTraxx modus of operation because Markit now administers both indices. In addition, International Index Company and CDS Index Co have recently released several other index families. These include ABX, TABX, CMBX and LevX.

Index families publish rebased indices on a bi-annual basis in March and September. The process for updating the names in each series works generally as follows. In accordance with set rules, participating market makers submit the credit default swap volumes that they have dealt with over the previous period. A provisional list of reference entities selected in accordance with these rules is then published. The reference entities are then agreed and a finalised list is published. The coupon levels for each reference entity are then agreed and trading of the new issue begins.

---

1   The Creditflux Inside Guide to Credit Index Trading, 2004.

International Index Company Limited describes the key objectives of the index on its website.[2] These can be assumed to apply also to CDX indices. The key objectives are transparency and liquidity, objective information, quality and reliability, independence and investment research. The company describes its approach to transparency and liquidity as follows:

> *The…credit derivatives market [has] traditionally been characterised by opacity and a lack of standardised information. To attract additional market participants and increase liquidity and transparency, IIC has put into place a set of objective, rules-based and accepted standards…iTraxx supports this by giving users easy access to information, enabling them to understand index composition, preview changes, check constituent pricing, and to integrate all of this into their asset allocation and investment processes.*

Next we shall look at the two grand families of indices themselves, each individual index within those families and the relevant composition.

3.2   iTraxx

The iTraxx indices are owned by the International Index Company. The shareholders in the company are ABN Amro, Barclays Capital, BNP Paribas, Deutsche Bank, Deutsche Börse, Dresdner Kleinwort, Goldman Sachs, HSBC, JP Morgan, Morgan Stanley and UBS Investment Bank. There are two principal sub-families of iTraxx indices: those that relate to Europe and those that relate to Asia.

(a)   iTraxx Europe

In relation to Europe, iTraxx provides three benchmark indices – iTraxx Europe, iTraxx Europe Crossover and iTraxx Europe HiVol.

iTraxx Europe focuses on European credit exposure and is grouped by industrial sector. On the finance side, these are senior financial institutions and subordinated financial institutions. On the non-financial side these sectors are for autos, consumers, energy, industrial, non-financials and TMT.

iTraxx Europe consists of 125 reference entities selected by market sector on the basis of credit default swap trading volume. iTraxx Europe HiVol has the top 30 highest spread names from iTraxx Europe. iTraxx Europe Crossover consists of the 50 most traded European sub-investment grade reference entities.

Each of these benchmark indices has three sector indices. These consist of a 100-reference entity sector index for non-financial reference entities, a 25-reference entity sector index for senior financials and a 25-reference entity sector index for subordinated financial reference entities.

iTraxx provides standard contracts of differing terms for each benchmark index and sector index. The standard maturities for iTraxx Europe and iTraxx HiVol are for three, five, seven and 10 years. For iTraxx CrossOver they are five and 10 years. For each iTraxx sector index they are five and 10 years.

---

2   www.itraxx.com.

iTraxx Europe also provides first to default baskets for autos, consumer, energy, senior and subordinated financials, industrials, TMT, HiVol, Crossover and Diversified. iTraxx has well over 30 licensed market makers, including nearly all of the major credit derivatives market participants.

(b) *iTraxx Asia: iTraxxAsia (ex-Japan); iTraxx Japan and iTraxx Australia*

iTraxx provides a robust platform of credit indices for Asia. iTraxx Asia (ex-Japan) is an index of 50 equally weighted credit default swap of Asian (non-Japanese) reference entities. iTraxx Australia is an index of 25 equally weighted credit default swaps on Australian reference entities. iTraxx Japan is an index of 50 equally weighted credit default swaps on Japanese reference entities. iTraxx Japan 80 is an index of 80 equally weighted credit default swaps on Japanese reference entities.

iTraxx Asia (ex-Japan) has three regional sub-indices: one for Korea, one for Greater China and one for Asia excluding Korea, Greater China and Japan. iTraxx Japan also has a sub-index: iTraxx Japan HiVol, which consists of 25 equally weighted credit default swaps on Japanese entities.

(c) *iTraxx standard credit default swap contracts*

iTraxx provides standard credit default swap contracts of differing terms for each benchmark index and sector index. The standard maturities for iTraxx Asia (ex-Japan) is five years; for iTraxx Australia five and 10 years; for iTraxx Japan three, five and 10 years; and for iTraxx Japan 80, five years. The regional sub-indices and iTraxx Japan HiVol each have standard maturities of five years.

iTraxx provides standard annexes containing the relevant reference portfolio, with the full legal name of each reference entity and reference obligation, together with the relevant CLIP code (a code which unites together a relevant reference entity and reference obligation).

The current iTraxx confirmations to which these series relate are more specifically as follows. For Europe, the current confirmations are iTraxx Blended Indices Single Tranche Confirmation, iTraxx Tranched Standard Terms Supplement, iTraxx Untranched Standard Terms Supplement, iTraxx Tranche Short Confirm, iTraxx Untranched Short Confirm, iTraxx Non-Dealer Untranched Confirmation, Non-Dealer Untranched Standard Terms.

For Asia (ex-Japan) they are the iTraxx Asia XJ Tranche Short Confirm and the iTraxx Asia XJ Untranched Short Confirm. For iTraxx Australia they are the iTraxx Australia Tranched Standard Terms Supplement and the iTraxx Australia Untranched Standard Terms Supplement. For iTraxx Japan they are the iTraxx Japan Tranched Standard Terms Supplement, iTraxx Japan Untranched Standard Terms Supplement, the iTraxx Japan Tranched Short Confirm and the iTraxx Japan Master Confirmation.

The standard form credit default swap contracts described above and related indices are made available on the websites of Markit (www.markit.com) and International Index Company (www.itraxx.com). iTraxx, for example, also provides certain other credit derivative products such as tranched iTraxx (exposure to five standardised tranches of iTraxx Europe) and iTraxx options (options related to movements in iTraxx indices spreads).

3.3   CDX

The CDX indices are owned by CDS IndexCo, a consortium of 16 investment banks that are licensed as market makers in the CDX indices. The market makers include: ABN AMRO, Bank of America, Barclays Capital, Bear Stearns, BNP Paribas, Citigroup, Credit Suisse, Deutsche Bank, Goldman Sachs, HSBC, JP Morgan, Lehman Brothers, Merrill Lynch, Morgan Stanley, UBS and Wachovia.[3]

The North American indices of CDX are also operated by Markit. This was not always the case – until recently the administrator was Dow Jones. For these historical reasons, indices relating to North America were referred to as CDX indices – for example, CDX.NA.IG.8-V1 – rather than using the iTraxx format. However, the principal indices have been renamed and are now known as CDX family of credit indices. They are comprised of North American investment grade and high yield reference entities and emerging market corporate and sovereign reference entities.

The current credit indices consist of the following.

The CDX.NA.IG index, which is a North American investment grade index, is composed of 125 investment grade reference entities domiciled in North America. These are distributed among five sub-sectors.

The CDX.NA.IG.HVOL, a sub-index of the CDX.NA.IG, is comprised of the 30 highest volatility reference entities from that index.

The CDX.NA.HY, which is a North American high yield index, is composed of 100 non-investment grade entities domiciled in North America. It has three sub-indices. These are:

- the CDX.NA.HY.BB, which consists of North American high yield reference entities rated BB;
- the CDX.NA.HY.B, which consists of North American high yield reference entities rated B; and
- the CDX.NA.HY Notes, which consists of North American high yield notes.

CDX.NA.XO is a North American crossover index composed of 35 reference entities that either are domiciled in North America or have a majority of their outstanding bonds and loans denominated in dollars. Their ratings are split and 'cross over' between investment grade and high yield.

CDX.EM is an emerging markets index, composed of sovereign issuers from three regions:

- Latin America;
- Eastern Europe, the Middle East and Africa; and
- Asia.

CDX.EM Diversified is a diversified emerging market index composed of sovereign and corporate issuers from three regions:

- Latin America;
- Eastern Europe, the Middle East and Africa; and
- Asia.

---

3   www.mark-it.com.

There are a variety of standard form credit default swap contracts with varying maturities available for use with each of the various CDX indices and sub-indices, covering both tranched and untranched products and dealer and non-dealer forms. They are also available on the website of Markit (www.markit.com).

3.4 Other significant credit indices

In addition to iTraxx and CDX, International Index Company and CDS Index Co have recently released several other index families. These include ABX, TABX, CMBX and LevX.

The ABX family of indices relates to asset-backed securities. The ABX.HE group (created in early 2006) is linked to sub-prime residential mortgage-backed securities: the letters 'HE' stand for 'home equity'. At the time of publication there are five ABX.HE indices. Each index references 20 tranches of sub-prime residential mortgage-backed securities issued with one of five rating categories: triple-A, double-A, single-A, triple-B and triple-B-. These are selected from the largest issuers of residential mortgage-backed securities.

TABX, also known as the ABX tranche indices, was launched in early 2007. There are two sets of TABX indices – the first relates to the BBB ABX.HE index and the second to the BBB- ABX.HE index. Each TABX index references all of the reference obligations from the two previous rolls of the relevant index and has four separate tranches for each of the BBB and BBB- sections.

The ABX.HE was soon followed later in 2006 by the CMBX family of indices. The CMBX family is linked to commercial mortgage-backed securities. There are five sub-indices, each of which references 25 similarly rated tranches from different transactions. As with the ABX family, each sub-index references a security issued with one of five rating categories: triple-A, double-A, single-A, triple-B and triple-B-.

The LevX indices are indices of the most liquid lien credit agreements traded in the European leveraged loan credit default swap market. The LevX senior index consists of the 35 most liquid European first lien credit agreements and the LevX subordinated index consists of the 35 most liquid European second and third lien credit agreements.

3.5 Who uses credit indices and why?

Among the main users of the iTraxx indices are asset managers, hedge funds, investment banks, fund managers, bank research departments, insurance companies and corporate treasury departments.

Each category of user may use the indices or by-products linked to them for differing purposes. Asset managers may use the indices as a means to diversify credit risk and balance their portfolios. Hedge funds may engage in relative value trading, for example by trading a reference entity name against its relevant sector. Insurance companies, corporate treasury departments and bank correlation trading desks may all use the index for hedging strategies.

These users may use the index itself on payment of a fee to create its own product. In practical terms, a market participant might perhaps use a synthetic CDO referencing a current credit index. This would mean that that transaction's reference portfolio was rebased with liquid names, giving the transaction a quasi-management. Alternatively, a managed synthetic CDO could adopt a trading strategy involving the manager trading in and out of index products.

Alternatively, a market participant may enter into a bilateral over-the-counter (OTC) transaction with another market participant, taking advantage of the liquidity of the index and related transaction documentation to avoid negotiating the transaction and using up resources.

A market participant may even create a market itself, standing as a central counterparty, buying and selling credit protection on the index and taking the credit risk of each counterparty.

Credit indices increase market liquidity by increasing transaction volumes and lowering market entry barriers. Market makers create markets for trading linked credit derivative products based on standardised documentation. Participants can rely on the reference entity names and related obligations being correct and so reduce their transaction costs. This standardisation also allows automated matching and trading of products.

Credit indices can also allow funded products to have a quasi form of management. For example, if a single tranche synthetic CDO references the most recent version of a credit index, this will mean that every six months the transaction will reference the most liquid names in a particular sector, possibly saving on a management fees.

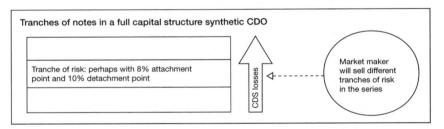

In addition to the above reasons to participate in index trading, certainty of reference entity is also an appealing component. The iTraxx and CDX indices cover a huge range of reference entities. Sometimes there may be confusion over which entity within a corporate group is the one issuing or guaranteeing debt. Some of the covered reference entities will merge or be taken over, creating successor issues. Uncertainty over which reference entity is the correct reference entity has caused problems before in the credit derivatives market.

RED is a database run by Markit. The database consists of the names of reference entities and reference obligations. Most famously, this occurred when there was confusion over which reference entity was the correct one for credit derivatives contracts following the bankruptcy filing in 2000 of Armstrong World Industries, Inc, which resulted in proceedings actually being filed.

As a result of this Goldman Sachs, JP Morgan Chase and Deutsche Bank launched Project RED, a reference entity database which pooled information on the current legal existence of traded reference entities: their correct names, existing reference obligations, as well as the contractual relationship between reference entities and their reference obligations.[4] The widely subscribed-for system was sold to Markit in 2003,[5] which later developed a numbering system for reference entities and reference obligations with Cusip Services Bureau[6] as part of Project RED. This was later enhanced through a partnership with Standard & Poor's, which integrated Reference Entity Link, a product linking reference entities in the Markit RED Database with Standard & Poor's information on credit quality.[7]

The credit indices in the iTraxx and CDX families have the benefit of this technology. This helps drive down the costs and non-credit risks that can be associated with credit derivatives transactions, helping make credit index transactions more appealing.

An additional product which makes index trading attractive for users of asset-backed securities is Markit's reference cash-flow datatbase. The company's website describes the product as acting "as the central monitoring and settlement platform for the ABCDS market", so that in particular it can "resolve cashflow payment discrepancies...[and] calculate all monthly settlements within two business days of bond payment date, including interest shortfalls, principal shortfalls, writedowns and all reimbursements".

4.   Standard annexes and confirmations

4.1   Overview

In addition to producing the indices, iTraxx and CDX provide two key types of product: tranched products and untranched products. Untranched products give an investor exposure to the whole relevant iTraxx index or sub-index, whereas untranched products give exposure to only a slice of that index. Untranched products allow investors to take a liquid exposure to a slice of credit risk on an unfunded basis.

The two principal index products are standard annexes, which set out each relevant index or sub-indices, and standard credit default swap confirmations for tranched and untranched transactions.

A standard annex can be referenced in any transaction or credit default swap.

Template credit default swap confirmations for tranched and untranched products are always physically settled. They operate very similarly to standard portfolio credit default swaps.

We shall look at an example below, but here is a brief summary. If a counterparty entered into an untranched credit default swap standard contract referencing the CDX North American High Yield Index where there are 125 equally weighted reference entities, each reference entity would have a weighting of 0.8%.

---

4   *Risk* Magazine, April 2002, Vol 15, No 4.
5   "Deutsche Bank, Goldman Sachs and J P Morgan Finalise Agreement to Sell Credit Derivatives Reference Entity Database to Mark-it Partners", Mark-It Partners press release, August 28 2003.
6   "Mark-it Partners Joins with CUSIP to Develop Numbering System for Project RED", Mark-it Partners press release, September 22 2003.
7   "Standard & Poor's launches Reference Entity Link in conjunction with Mark-it RED", Mark-it Partners, press release, October 13 2005.

The transaction would be structured so that if the conditions to settlement were satisfied, the seller would pay the reference entity weighting (eg, 0.8%) multiplied by the swap's notional amount (eg, $20 million). These transactions are physically settled so the buyer receives deliverable obligations with a face value equal to 0.8% of the swap's notional amount. The swap's notional amount is then reduced by 0.8% to reflect the affected reference entity's removal from the portfolio. The premium payable from buyer to seller is also correspondingly reduced.

4.2 Analysis of standard contracts

The iTraxx and CDX standard credit default swap contracts generally work in a similar way to many ISDA templates.

The most common structure is for the parties to enter into a short-form confirmation. This sets out:

- the identity of the relevant index or sub-index;
- the trade date;
- the scheduled termination date;
- the original notional amount; and
- the identity of the buyer and seller.

This short-form confirmation will incorporate the standard terms supplement by reference, and the standard terms supplement will incorporate the 2003 Definitions and the May 2003 supplement by reference. We will now analyse the documentation for one of these transactions (the iTraxx Europe untranched standard terms supplement and untranched short confirmation), and briefly analyse the key differences with an untranched transaction. Most of the other iTraxx and CDX template documentation also follows this format, although there is some variation and the ABX, CMBX, TABX and LevX documentation follows the more specialised ISDA template documentation designed for those purposes.

(a) iTraxx Europe untranched standard terms supplement and untranched short confirmation

We shall take the iTraxx Europe untranched standard terms supplement and untranched short confirmation, published on September 19 2005, as an example. The supplement provides that International Index Company Ltd is the index sponsor and that the transaction's effective date is the roll date set out in the relevant annex.

Relevant annex:	The parties shall specify in the relevant confirmation whether the source of the relevant annex is publisher or confirmation annex and shall identify the relevant index and the annex date, provided that, if the parties do not specify the source of the relevant annex, they shall be deemed to have specified publisher.
	If publisher is specified in the relevant confirmation, the relevant annex shall be the list for the relevant index with

> the relevant annex date, as published by the index publisher (which can be accessed currently at www.markit.com). Index publisher means Markit Partners Ltd, or any replacement thereof appointed by the index sponsor for the purposes of officially publishing the relevant index.
>
> If confirmation annex is specified in the relevant confirmation, the relevant annex shall be the list for the relevant index with the relevant annex date annexed to the relevant confirmation, as agreed by the parties.

The parties have a choice regarding the relevant annex. If they specify in the short-form confirmation that the relevant annex is 'publisher', then the relevant annex will be the list for relevant index published by Markit at the date of the transaction. If they instead select 'confirmation annex', then they will annex the specific annex they wish to reference the confirmation. The relevant reference obligations will be those set out in the relevant annex.

The fixed rate payable by the buyer is the per annum rate for the index and the term of the relevant iTraxx master transaction set out in the relevant annex. The fixed-rate payer payment dates are quarterly and the fixed-rate payer calculation amount is the same as the floating-rate payer calculation amount.

Floating payment	
Floating rate payer calculation amount	An amount in euros equal to: (a) the reference entity weighting multiplied by (b) the original notional amount
Reference entity weighting	The percentage set out opposite the relevant reference entity in the relevant annex, provided that the reference entity weighting in respect of an excluded reference entity shall be deemed to be zero

In terms of seller's payments to the buyer following an event determination date, the floating-rate payer calculation amount will be the reference entity weighting multiplied by the transaction's original notional amount. The reference entity weighting will be equal to 100% divided by the number of reference entities in the reference portfolio. In the case of the 125-reference entity iTraxx Europe, this would be 0.8%.

The transaction will be physically settled and has the standard conditions to settlement for a physically settled credit default transaction which one would expect in a normal OTC credit derivative transaction (ie, credit event notice, with both buyer and seller as notifying parties, notice of physical settlement and notice of publicly available information).

Conditions to settlement	Credit event notice
	Notifying party: buyer or seller
	Notice of physical settlement
	Notice of publicly available information applicable

The applicable credit events are bankruptcy, failure to pay and restructuring (modified modified). The obligation characteristic is borrowed money and there are no obligation characteristics.

(b) *iTraxx Europe tranched standard terms supplement and tranched short confirmation*

The iTraxx Europe tranched standard terms supplement and tranched short confirmation are substantially the same as their untranched counterpart. However, there are various modifications, to ensure that credit protection payments do not become due until an attachment point has been reached and cease once the exhaustion point has been released. Some of the language also covers what happens when a credit event partially encroaches on a tranche.

Provisions relating to the termination date are also varied so that the transaction will terminate when the tranche, rather than the portfolio, has been exhausted.

The transaction is physically settled and incorporates standard European reference entity terms such as bond or loan as the deliverable obligation category and not subordinated, specified currency, not contingent, assignable loan, consent required loan, transferable, maximum maturity 30 years and not bearer as the deliverable obligation characteristics.

The standard terms supplement also incorporates the 60-business day cap on settlement.

Each reference entity in the reference portfolio is deemed to be a separate credit derivative transaction (each a 'relevant component transaction'), and once the conditions to settlement are the transaction is physically settled, that transaction will terminate in relation to that relevant component transaction.

Credit default swaps on asset-backed securities

1. Introduction

Credit default swaps on asset-backed securities (CDS on ABS) have been much talked about over the last few years and the nascent market that started in 2002 has much future potential. CDS on ABS are the natural step on from standard credit default swaps, and their emergence and development have been fuelled by growth in the ABS market itself. A marriage of credit derivatives specialists and asset-backed securities specialists have been spearheading a template documentation drive through the ISDA Working Group on Credit Derivatives – Asset Backed Securities and we now have a suite of templates, with future developments already in the pipeline. The complexity of these templates and the likelihood that this product area will continue to grow mean that CDS on ABS merit their own chapter in this book. This chapter expands upon the overview sections on CDS on ABS provided in Part I and explains in detail each of ISDA's CDS on ABS templates.

Credit default swaps referencing asset-backed securities have several monikers. Sometimes they are known as CDS on ABS, but they can also be known as asset-backed credit default swaps, ABCDS or synthetic ABS. We shall stick to CDS on ABS here. In addition, CDS on ABS most commonly cover three types of asset-backed product: pure asset-backed securities, mortgage-backed securities and collateralised debt obligations. This means that the acronyms CDS on MBS and CDS on CDOs are also in common parlance.

2. Reasons for buying and selling credit protection on asset-backed securities

The principal reasons for buying and selling protection on the credit risk of asset-backed securities are similar to the reasons that market participants are active in the sovereign and corporate credit default swap market: regulatory capital treatment, portfolio management, hedging credit risk, alternative investments and trading and market making. Additionally, due to the lack of liquidity and the small issue size of particular tranches in the ABS market, many securities may be difficult to obtain. CDS on ABS can allow investors to access the credit risk of securities that they could not otherwise purchase. Due to the 'soft' nature of CDS on ABS credit events, the ability to short the market by taking a view on the overall direction of particular securities is also a market driver.

The residual risks of CDS on ABS are also the same as traditional CDS: basis/mismatch risk, market risk, liquidity risk, regulatory risk, collateral risk, counterparty risk and documentation risk. The less settled nature of CDS on ABS template documentation probably means that documentation risk is greater than in other credit derivative products.

3. Key ingredients

The reasons for having specific CDS on ABS template documentation arise from the inherent characteristics of ABS. Comparing any of the current CDS on ABS templates to the original single-name CDS confirmation set out in Exhibit A to the 2003 Definitions, the family resemblance is evident, with certain 'genetic' differences in the nature of ABS accounting for the substantial differences from standard CDS. The principal reasons for the differences are as follows.

3.1 ABS issuer as reference entity versus corporate or sovereign reference entity

Asset-backed securities are structured so that a bankruptcy-remote special purpose vehicle (SPV) issues securities linked to underlying assets. Barring execution risk, the SPV will not become bankrupt or fail to pay any due amount of interest or principal, because of its own creditworthiness. Notwithstanding this structure, an investor in the securities of the SPV may lose all of its principal and/or projected interest if the relevant underlying assets fail to perform. This means that the traditional credit events in the 2003 Definitions are unsuitable in relation to the obligations of the ABS issuer.

3.2 ABS versus standard debt obligations

In a standard CDS transaction, a reference entity will have many relevant debt obligations outstanding and credit protection will generally be sold on a wide selection of obligations. Not so with a CDS on ABS. Either an issuer of ABS will be used once to issue a specific transaction or, in a multi-issuance structure, investors will have limited recourse to only the assets of their issue, making general credit protection meaningless. In addition, the variable credit quality created by tranching securities means that each tranche of securities would have a significantly different credit quality, with losses occurring at different times to different tranches. This means that CDS on ABS are designed to reference a specific tranche of a particular issue of asset-backed securities rather than the credit quality of a particular reference entity.

In addition, most corporate and sovereign bonds and loans repay the full principal on the maturity date, making any payment default most likely to occur on a single date. In contrast, ABS often amortise over time, meaning that the notional amount of a CDS on ABS should alter in line with the reference obligation's outstanding principal amount.

Losses to ABS can occur over time, meaning that the parties may wish only to partially settle a CDS as soon as a loss on the underlying asset occurs.

3.3 Liquidity

The ABS market is not as liquid as the corporate bond or loan market. Particular tranches of ABS may be even less liquid, due to their specialised nature and small size. Therefore, a CDS on ABS post-credit event settlement needs to be more flexible than in standard CDS.

The unique characteristics of ABS therefore make the original single-name CDS confirmation set out in Exhibit A to the 2003 Definitions (designed for referencing corporate and sovereign creditworthiness) unsuitable for documenting CDS on ABS.

4. Development of template documentation

When market participants began to document CDS on ABS, any documentation was necessarily highly bespoke and also highly complex. Initially, this lack of standardised documentation prevented the market from developing: highly complex and bespoke documentation meant high costs and risks.

The ever-increasing size of the ABS market, which already exceeded $800 billion by 2004, created a strong need among market participants for standard templates to allow them to hedge and trade the risk of ABS defaults. Individual market participants on both sides of the Atlantic developed their own templates and, once market standards had begun to form, ISDA published the first CDS on ABS template in June 2005. This provided the impetus that the market needed and further developments (including differing views from European and American market participants) resulted in three more standard CDS on ABS forms.

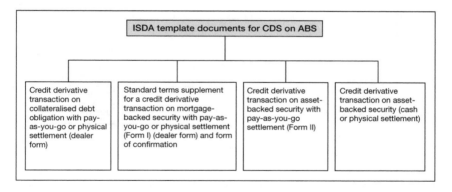

The four templates, most of which have been amended a few times already since they were initially published (see table below), not only reflect the differences between different underlying types of ABS, but also are tailored to reflect the different expectations of the European and American markets

Although the first CDS on ABS transaction was made in 2002, the market took a stride forward when ISDA published the first CDS on ABS template on June 13 2005. The accompanying press release stated: "The International Swaps and Derivatives Association (ISDA) has announced publication of a template for documenting trades of credit default swaps (CDS) on asset-backed securities (CDS on ABS) intended for cash or physical settlement. A second template for use with CDS on ABS with a pay-as-you-go (PAUG) settlement approach will be published later this month."

The first form's full description is "Credit derivative transaction on asset-backed securities (cash or physical settlement)". It is also know as the 'non-PAUG form'. It is intended for use with reference obligations that are any type of ABS with either cash or physical settlement and it is mainly used in the European market. It is the simplest

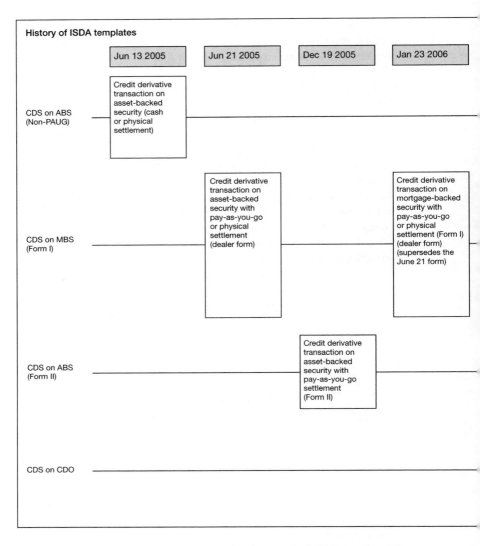

History of ISDA templates

of the four forms and most closely resembles the standard CDS template. The non-PAUG form has been revised and its current version was issued on June 7 2006.

Shortly after issuing the non-PAUG form, ISDA published the "Credit derivative transaction in asset-backed security with pay-as-you-go or physical settlement (dealer form)" on June 21 2005. The form has been amended four times since then and its current version was published on April 5 2007 under a changed name: "Standard terms supplement for a credit derivative transaction on mortgage-backed security with pay-as-you-go or physical settlement (Form I) (dealer form)". It is also now known as 'Form I'. Whereas the non-PAUG form was designed for any type of ABS, Form I is intended to be used to reference obligations which are portfolios of mortgages. Its first four versions were especially designed for the US market, where

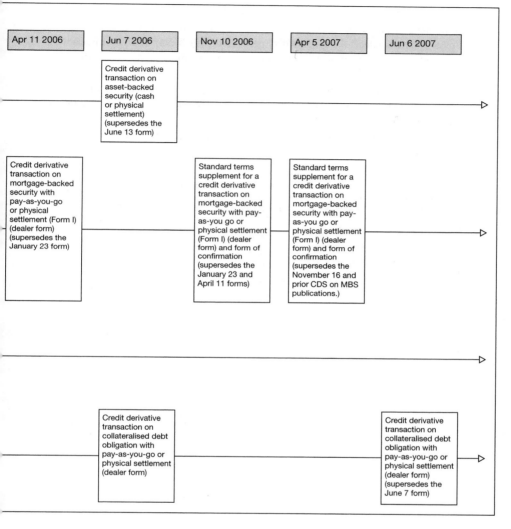

securitisations of mortgages are very common. However, at the request of European traders, the current version was made compliant with the Basel II framework for capital requirements and it is hoped that it will facilitate trade on the old continent. Since the new Form I was issued only very recently, it is difficult to tell whether it will actually gain popularity in the European market.

The next form to be published was "Credit derivatives transaction on asset-backed security with pay-as-you-go settlement (Form II)" on December 19 2005. It is known as 'Form II'. This template is primarily used in the US market. A key difference from the other templates is that it does not have any credit events. It provides only for a pay-as-you-go settlement, which means that the protection seller pays the protection buyer a defined amount whenever a specified event happens. This form was created at the request of monoline insurers which wanted to avoid the liquidity risk of having to make one large lump-sum payment to settle CDS on ABS transactions. Instead, the settlement is based on making up payment shortfalls on a particular reference obligation and reflects the gradual decline in creditworthiness of ABS transactions as opposed to the catastrophic declines which can occur when a credit event impacts on a corporate or sovereign reference entity.

The last template "Credit derivative transaction on collateralised debt with pay-as-you-go or physical settlement (dealer form)", was first published on June 7 2006 and was later updated on June 6 2007; it is known as the 'CDO Form'. It closely resembles Form I, but contains a few changes to adapt the template to the intricacies of underlying CDO transactions.

	CDS on ABS	Form I	Form II	CDS on CDO
Credit event	Failure to pay Loss event Restructuring Rating downgrade* Bankruptcy*	Failure to pay principal Writedown Distressed ratings downgrade Bankruptcy* Restructuring*	*No credit events*	Failure to pay principal Writedown Failure to pay interest Distressed ratings downgrade
Floating amount event	n/a	Writedown Failure to pay principal Interest shortfall	Writedown Principal shortfall Interest shortfall	Writedown Failure to pay principal Interest shortfall
Additional fixed payment event	n/a	Writedown reimbursement Principal shortfall reimbursement Interest shortfall reimbursement	Writedown reimbursement Principal shortfall reimbursement Interest shortfall reimbursement Amendment payment Make-whole premium payment	Writedown reimbursement Principal shortfall reimbursement Interest shortfall reimbursement

Events are additional options.

5. The non-PAUG form

The non-PAUG form is relatively short and straightforward, especially when compared with the three other templates. It is structured in the traditional manner as a confirmation supplementing the ISDA Master Agreement and incorporates the 2003 ISDA Credit Derivatives Definitions. Although very different from Exhibit A to the 2003 Definitions, it is still founded on that document. This section therefore concentrates only on the major differences between the non-PAUG form and the single name credit default swap template.

In summary, the key differences are as follows. Whereas the credit events for a standard CDS are bankruptcy, failure to pay and sometimes restructuring, the non-

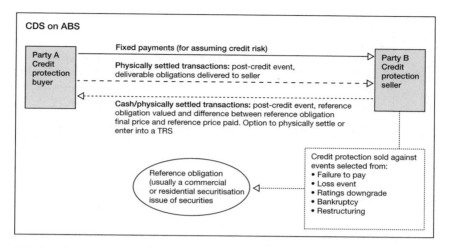

PAUG template provides three principal credit events: failure to pay, loss event and restructuring. Bankruptcy and rating downgrade are included in the form as optional credit events as well.

Although bankruptcy and restructuring do not seem to be particularly relevant to bankruptcy-remote vehicles and ABS, regulatory capital requirements may compel a seller to insist on their inclusion. The 'failure to pay' credit event in the non-PAUG template modifies the 2003 Definitions standard by defining the event as a non-payment on a scheduled distribution date of an amount due pursuant to the reference obligation's terms.

A loss event occurs when the principal amount of the underlying ABS is irrevocably reduced, without its resulting in the issuer breaching its obligations. A rating downgrade credit event occurs when the reference obligation is downgraded below a level pre-agreed at the transaction's outset.

The non-PAUG form provides a hybrid cash and physical settlement method. Cash settlement is the default option unless the seller receives a notice of physical settlement prior to an agreed cut-off date after the conditions to settlement have been met. If the buyer opts for physical settlement, the mechanics closely resemble those used in the standard CDS template.

The parties can also, at the transaction's outset, elect for an additional settlement method called the 'synthetic delivery option'. If cash settlement applies and the synthetic delivery option is applicable, at the valuation date either party may elect to provide the other with a total return swap quotation. This is a quotation to enter into a fully funded total return swap on the reference obligation and, if supplied, will be deemed to be the transaction's final price. The parties will then be deemed to have entered into the swap and will execute a confirmation and make the relevant ongoing payments. We now consider the actual template document in detail.

5.1 Paragraph 1: General terms

When compared with the single name template set out in Exhibit A to the 2003 Definitions, paragraph 1 of the non-PAUG form contains a few important differences.

Scheduled termination date:	The earlier of: (a) the maturity date; and (b) the date, if any, on which the reference obligation notional amount is reduced to zero, subject to adjustment in accordance with the following business day convention.
Reference obligation amount:	[ ], subject to reduction with effect from each notional day on which any payment of principal is made to the holders of the reference obligation in respect of the reference obligation (as a result of scheduled or accelerated amortisation, acceleration of payment obligations, redemption or otherwise, but excluding any payment in respect of principal representing capitalised interest) by an amount equal to the amount of such payment multiplied by the applicable percentage.
Maturity date:	[ ] (the 'maturity date')

The first key difference relates to the 'scheduled termination date'. Whereas the Exhibit A template leaves the field blank and allows the parties to choose the date defining the end of the transaction's term, the non-PAUG form instead defines the term as ending on the earlier of the reference obligation's maturity date and the date on which the reference obligation's notional amount is reduced to zero. This reflects the fact that the seller in a CDS on ABS transaction offers protection on a specific reference obligation only, which can amortise over time. The protection is therefore scheduled to end either when the reference obligation reaches its final maturity date or when its value is reduced to zero through amortisation or early redemption. This means that subject to the transaction terminating following a credit event or for other reasons, the buyer enjoys protection as long as the reference obligation 'exists'.

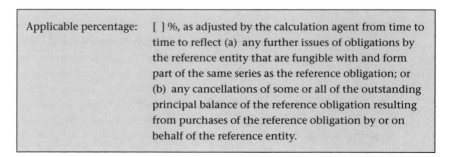

Applicable percentage:	[ ] %, as adjusted by the calculation agent from time to time to reflect (a) any further issues of obligations by the reference entity that are fungible with and form part of the same series as the reference obligation; or (b) any cancellations of some or all of the outstanding principal balance of the reference obligation resulting from purchases of the reference obligation by or on behalf of the reference entity.

The non-PAUG form also introduces the concept of 'applicable percentage'. Individual tranches of ABS, particularly the most subordinated tranches, often have low notional amounts, with tranche sizes being driven to a large extent by the amount of subordination required for the tranches above to achieve their target rating. This can aggravate a shortage of particular tranches of securities in an ABS transaction. One of the additional attractions of CDS on ABS is that the product can help a seller to access synthetically a greater amount of exposure to a particular tranche of securities than would be available in the open market.

This 'applicable percentage' concept is used primarily when a seller wants to sell protection on a greater notional amount of ABS than the issued amount. Applicable percentage represents the percentage of the outstanding principal amount of the reference obligation calculated at the trade date, thus reflecting the maximum amount of credit protection available for that reference obligation. For example, if the principal amount of a reference obligation were $100 million and the seller wanted to sell protection of $125 million, then the applicable percentage would be 125%.

5.2 Paragraph 3: Floating payment

Floating payment describes the flow of money from buyer to seller once the conditions to settlement have been met. The floating payment provisions in the Exhibit A template and those in the non-PAUG form differ considerably.

Credit events:	The following credit event(s) shall apply to this transaction (and the first sentence of Section 4.1 of the Credit Derivatives Definitions shall be amended accordingly):
	Failure to pay
	Grace period extension: Applicable
	Payment requirement: $100,000
	Loss event
	[Bankruptcy]
	[Rating downgrade]
	Restructuring
	Default requirement: $100,000

The credit events in square brackets are optional. When compared with Exhibit A, this section of the non-PAUG form may appear to be a simplified version of the equivalent provisions in Exhibit A. This, however, is quite misleading.

The non-PAUG form provides a different definition of 'failure to pay' from the 2003 Definitions. This new definition is specifically tailored to accommodate the specific characteristics of ABS. Accordingly, the 'failure to pay' is defined as a non-payment on a scheduled distribution date of an amount due pursuant to the reference obligation's terms. This event can occur even if there is no contractual breach of an obligation but, nonetheless, the noteholders do not receive the amount of money they had expected to receive.

In addition, the conditions to settlement for a 'failure to pay' credit event can be met only if this payment shortfall is irreversible. This means that this credit event can occur only if the terms of the reference obligation do not provide for a reimbursement of the shortfall in the future.

The definition of the 'failure to pay' credit event is also tailored to cover reference obligations which have a 'PIK' feature. 'PIK' stands for 'payment in kind' and it allows for interest on ABS notes to be deferred in the event of a temporary shortfall in revenues. A 'failure to pay' credit event will occur in relation to a PIK security only if the deferred interest cannot later be reimbursed in full.

Like 'failure to pay', a 'loss event' credit event occurs even if there is no actual breach of the terms of the underlying ABS notes. It will be triggered if the principal notional outstanding is written down, provided that it will not be possible for the amount to be reinstated later in the future. This may happen, for example, when the underlying portfolio performs below expectations.

Another credit event is 'rating downgrade' and is triggered if the underlying ABS notes are downgraded by the relevant rating agency to a pre-agreed level (eg, a junk bond level such as CC for Fitch and Standard and Poor's). Inclusion of this credit event is less common.

CDS on ABS 'events'	
Credit event	Failure to pay Loss event Ratings downgrade* Bankruptcy/Restructruring*
Floating amount event	n/a
Additional fixed amount event	n/a

Events are additional options.

Finally, to the two credit events of bankruptcy and restructuring. As already explained, vehicles issuing ABS notes are structured to be bankruptcy remote and structuring enhancements mean that the restructuring credit event is not very likely to occur. However, bankruptcy remote does not mean bankruptcy proof and execution risks always exist. A restructuring of an ABS security is also unlikely to occur. However, for regulatory capital reasons in various jurisdictions, it is common to specify both of these credit events in a transaction.

Conditions to settlement:	Credit event notice
	Notifying party: buyer [or seller]
	Notice of physical settlement if the settlement method is physical settlement
	Notice of publicly available information: applicable

If the buyer (or the seller, if applicable) wishes to meet the conditions to settlement following a credit event, it will need to deliver to its counterparty a credit event notice and notice of physical settlement. The non-PAUG form recognises that due to the specialised nature of ABS, it may be more difficult to source publicly available information than in a credit event scenario involving a sovereign or corporate, not least because the ABS may be held by only a handful of investors. Therefore, the definition of 'publicly available information' in Section 3.5 (publicly available information) of the 2003 Definitions is amended in the template to include "information contained in a notice or on a website published by an internationally recognised credit agency that has at any time rated the reference obligation".

5.3   Paragraph 4: Settlement terms

The relative lack of liquidity in the ABS market often highlighted in ABS risk factors can make any valuation difficult in a cash-settled transaction. However, physical settlement can also be difficult if the protection buyer does not hold the required notional amount of the reference obligation and a sufficient amount of the asset is not available on the open market. Therefore, the non-PAUG form provides for a hybrid of cash and physical settlement.

Settlement method:	Cash settlement, unless seller receives a notice of physical settlement effective at or prior to the cut-off time in which case the settlement method shall be physical settlement, in each case subject to 'reference obligation extinction' and 'reference obligation reduction' below.
	For the avoidance of doubt, physical settlement shall no longer apply once either party has accepted a TRS quotation.

Cash settlement is the default option unless the seller receives a notice of physical settlement. However, the buyer retains the flexibility to physically settle the transaction if it issues a notice of physical settlement to the seller that is effective on, or prior to, the cut-off time. The cut-off time is one hour following the time at which the first quotation is sought as part of the cash settlement process.

Terms relating to cash settlement:	
Valuation date:	Single valuation date: a business day selected by seller in its sole and absolute discretion and notified to buyer which falls not less than [120] calendar days and not more than [140] calendar days after the event determination date
Quotation method:	Bid
Valuation method:	Highest

The cash settlement method under the non-PAUG form is relatively simple. There is only one valuation date: this can be any business day falling between 120 and 140 calendar days after the event determination date. Since there may be very few dealers making a market in the reference obligation, the form recognises that consequently, it may be difficult to obtain a number of quotes and therefore dispenses with the 2003 Definitions requirements to get a minimum number of dealer quotes – one is sufficient. Notwithstanding how many quotes have been provided, the highest is accepted as the final one.

Terms relating to physical settlement	
Physical settlement period:	[The longest number of business days for settlement in accordance with the current market practice for the reference obligation, as determined by the calculation agent after consultation with the parties, subject to a maximum of 30 business days
Deliverable obligation category:	Reference obligation only

Physical settlement applies if the buyer opts to send a notice of physical settlement to the seller before the cut-off date. If the buyer makes this election, then the mechanics are quite similar to those provided in the Exhibit A template. An important difference, though, is that the seller will pay the full par value of the reference obligation. However, the settlement method can still revert to cash settlement in certain circumstances. The non-PAUG form introduces the concept of 'reference obligation extinction'. This occurs if a failure to pay credit event occurs where the terms of the reference obligation do not provide for interest on the payment shortfall at the anticipated rate and the reference obligation then ceases to exist because the reference obligation's outstanding principal balance is reduced to zero leaving no further assets. In these circumstances the settlement method is deemed to be cash settlement and the final price zero.

Additionally, there is the concept of 'reference obligation reduction'. If the aggregate outstanding principal balance of the reference obligation is below the reference obligation notional amount and the buyer delivers a notice of physical settlement, then cash settlement is deemed to apply to the amount of the transaction in excess of the reference obligation notional amount: this is most relevant where the applicable percentage is above 100%.

The non-PAUG form provides a third settlement method called the 'synthetic delivery option'. As with physical settlement, the synthetic delivery option can be exercised only before the cut-off date. It is not automatically applicable either and the option can be exercised only if the synthetic delivery option is selected as applicable in the confirmation. As an additional condition to the synthetic delivery option being applicable, the parties can elect that 'synthetic delivery condition' is applicable, which means that mark-to-market collateral arrangements or appropriate credit approvals are in place to allow the parties to enter into the total return swap.

If the synthetic delivery option is exercised, either party may elect to provide the other with a total return swap quotation, which will become the transaction's final price. The parties will then enter into a total return swap in the form provided in the schedule to the non-PAUG form and described in the box below.

The total return swap under the synthetic delivery option

The non-PAUG form total return swap set out in Schedule 1 to the non-PAUG form isolates the reference obligation as its underlying asset and seeks to replicate its performance.

It is structured as a bilateral swap transaction. The seller is defined as the total return payer and is put in the place of the legal owner of the reference obligation. It pays the buyer (which is defined as the initial amount payer) the total return on the reference obligation which would have been received by the legal owner of the reference obligation, multiplied by the applicable percentage. In return, the buyer pays the seller the product of the total return swap quotation and the reference obligation notional amount at the date on which the final price was determined.

This is a quotation to enter into a fully funded total return swap on the reference obligation in accordance with terms of the TRS Confirmation (which is a schedule to the non-PAUG form). The parties will then be deemed to have entered into the swap and will need to make the appropriate ongoing payments.

Terms relating to synthetic delivery:	[Applicable][Not applicable]
	If (a) synthetic delivery option and cash settlement apply and (b) either (i) the synthetic delivery condition does not apply; or (ii) the synthetic delivery condition applies and is satisfied as at the [valuation date], either buyer or seller may elect to provide to the other party a TRS quotation. If one or both parties so elect, then, notwithstanding Section 7.7(b) of the Credit Derivatives Definitions (as amended below), the final price shall be deemed to be the TRS quotation. Any TRS quotation shall be provided by the cut-off time.

Total return swap:	A fully funded total return swap transaction on substantially the terms set out in Schedule 1 (Form of TRS confirmation) to this confirmation.

6. Standard term supplement for use with credit derivative transactions on mortgage-backed security with pay-as-you-go or physical settlement (Form I) (Dealer Form)

6.1 Introduction

The main objective of all PAUG forms is to protect the buyer from a gradual deterioration in the creditworthiness of the reference obligations, without the obligation to terminate the credit default swap. For example, a mortgage-backed security could suffer a 10% principal reduction over a three-year period: the buyer may wish to retain exposure to the security and not close out its exposure the moment that the first losses occur.

The PAUG templates provide a mechanism of continuous settlement of the transaction throughout its term. In simplified terms, whenever the reference obligation incurs a loss, the buyer can elect to be reimbursed by the seller. Whereas in a standard CDS or CDS on ABS this would result in the transaction terminating, in PAUG forms the buyer may receive an unlimited number of such payments until the instrument's termination date. The aim of the PAUG forms is to mimic the payments under the underlying ABS transaction and from this perspective there is a strong resemblance to a total return swap.

When the first version of Form I was published, it was designed to reference US-style residential mortgage-based securities and commercial mortgage-based securities. However, the most recent version of the form published on April 5 2007 includes amendments that make the template compatible with the European regulatory environment and the Basel II regulatory framework. The previous version of Form I was not very popular with European market makers and it is still too early to tell whether this latest edition will be any more successful.

However, continued European market-maker interest in the form perhaps indicates that continuous settlement of CDS on ABS through a PAUG mechanism could still take hold in the European market.

Form I is a long and complicated document and it would be beyond the scope of this book to describe each provision of the template in detail. Therefore, this section will concentrate on the key parts of the template that differ from the non-PAUG form and the Exhibit A template.

It is also important to note that new Form I consists of the long Standard Terms Supplement and a short confirmation. The mandatory terms are provided in the Standard Terms Supplement, whereas the optional ones are in the confirmation. It is ISDA's intention to update all of the CDS on ABS templates to this format, so this section covers both documents.

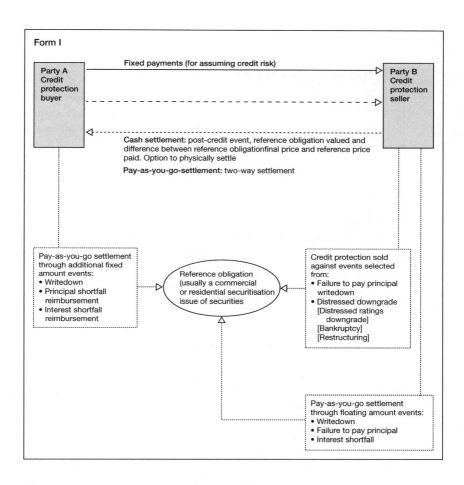

Form I

Party A
Credit protection buyer

Fixed payments (for assuming credit risk)

Party B
Credit protection seller

Cash settlement: post-credit event, reference obligation valued and difference between reference obligationfinal price and reference price paid. Option to physically settle

Pay-as-you-go-settlement: two-way settlement

Pay-as-you-go settlement through additional fixed amount events:
• Writedown
• Principal shortfall reimbursement
• Interest shortfall reimbursement

Reference obligation (usually a commercial or residential securitisation issue of securities

Credit protection sold against events selected from:
• Failure to pay principal writedown
• Distressed downgrade [Distressed ratings downgrade] [Bankruptcy] [Restructuring]

Pay-as-you-go settlement through floating amount events:
• Writedown
• Failure to pay principal
• Interest shortfall

Form I 'events'	
Credit event	Failure to pay principal
	Writedown
	Distressed downgrade
	Distressed ratings downgrade*
	Bankruptcy*
	Restructuring*
Floating amount event	Writedown
	Failure to pay principal
	Interest shortfall
Additional fixed amount event	Writedown reimbursement
	Principal shortfall reimbursement
	Interest shortfall reimbursement

Events are additional options

6.2 Credit events

The Standard Terms Supplement

Credit events:	The following credit events shall apply to the transaction (and the first sentence of Section 4.1 of the Credit Derivatives Definitions shall be amended accordingly):
	Failure to pay principal
	Writedown
	Each additional credit event specified in the relevant confirmation.

Confirmation

Additional credit event:	[Distressed ratings downgrade]
	[Bankruptcy]
	[Restructuring]
	[No additional credit event]

Form I specifies failure to pay principal and writedown as two principal credit events; in addition, there are three optional credit events – distressed ratings downgrade, bankruptcy and restructuring.

'Failure to pay principal' is defined as a failure to pay on the final amortisation date or the final maturity date, or to pay on any such date an amount of principal that is less than the expected principal amount. The definition also allows for a grace period equal to that for underlying; or, if there is no grace period there, Form I provides for a default grace period of three days.

Writedown is the equivalent of a loss event in the CDS on ABS template. Like the loss event credit event, writedown applies when there is either a reduction in the principal amount of the reference obligation or a reduction or subordination of the current interest payable on the reference obligation. However, unlike the non-PAUG form, Form I does not include a condition that a loss event can occur only if the reduction in the capital is irreversible.

The definition of 'writedown' also includes 'implied writedown'. An implied writedown occurs when the underlying instrument does not provide for any writedown or applied losses, but nonetheless there is a reduction in capital or interest payable. For example, this can happen if there is an under-collateralisation of the reference security. Quite understandably, this aspect of the template has been very controversial and can be accused of favouring the buyer, which is one of the reasons why Form II does not provide for implied writedown.

The third credit event, 'distressed ratings downgrade', is a further option. This credit event occurs either when the reference obligation is downgraded by one of the ratings agencies to a defined level[1] or if the rating is withdrawn altogether.

---

1   Caa3 for Moody's and CCC for Standard & Poor's and Fitch.

6.3 Physical settlement

The Standard Terms Supplement

Conditions to settlements:	Credit event notice
	Notifying party: Buyer
	Notice of physical settlement
	Notice of publicly available information: Applicable
Public sources:	The public sources listed in Section 3.7 of the Credit Derivatives Definitions; provided that servicer reports in respect of the reference obligation and, in respect of a distressed ratings downgrade credit event only, any public communications by any of the rating agencies in respect of the reference obligation shall also be deemed public sources.
	Specified number: one

Form I does not provide for cash settlement and the only way to terminate a CDS transaction once a credit event occurs is through physical settlement. The conditions to settlement are very similar to those in Exhibit A for a corporate CDS; namely, the buyer must deliver to the seller three notifications: a credit event notice, a notice of physical settlement and a notice of publicly available information.

Unlike the non-PAUG form, where the parties can elect that the seller is also a notifying party, under Form I the buyer is the sole notifying party. The reason for this is that if the seller could terminate the transaction early, then the buyer would be unable to utilise the PAUG settlement provisions.

Another notable difference is that the scope of public sources has been expanded. Publicly available information can be sourced from servicer reports or, in respect of a distressed ratings downgrade credit event, any public communications by any of the rating agencies. Since such a servicer report or communication from a ratings agency may well be the only evidence, Form I specifies that one single source of information suffices. This means that the number of sources was reduced from two as for a corporate CDS.

6.4 Floating payments

Floating payments are the essence of a PAUG settlement. When a floating amount event occurs, the protection seller is obliged to pay a defined amount to the buyer. Those events (and payments) may occur a number of times through the life of a CDS on ABS.

The Standard Terms Supplement

Floating rate payer:	Seller.
Floating rate payer payment dates:	In relation to a floating amount event, the first fixed-rate payer payment date falling at least two business days (or in the case of a floating amount event that occurs on the legal final maturity date or the final amortisation date, the fifth business day) after delivery of a notice by the calculation agent to the parties or a notice by buyer to seller that the related floating amount is due and showing in reasonable detail how such floating amount was determined; provided that any such notice must be given on or prior to the fifth business day following the effective maturity date.
Floating payments:	If a floating amount event occurs, then on the relevant floating rate payer payment date, seller will pay the relevant floating amount to buyer. For the avoidance of doubt, the conditions to settlement are not required to be satisfied in respect of a floating payment.
Floating amount event:	A writedown, a failure to pay principal or an interest shortfall.
Floating amount:	With respect to each floating rate payer payment date, an amount equal to the sum of:
	(a) the relevant writedown amount (if any);
	(b) the relevant principal shortfall amount (if any); and
	(c) the relevant interest shortfall payment amount (if any).

The relevant floating amount events are a writedown, failure to pay principal and interest shortfall. Since writedown and failure to pay are credit events, their inclusion as floating amount events means that the protection buyer has a choice of whether it wants to deliver a credit event notice and terminate the transaction altogether, or whether it is happy to receive a floating payment through the PAUG mechanism. Which selection the buyer makes will depend on the severity of the particular event.

The new concept, 'interest shortfall', is defined as either non-payment of an expected interest amount or the payment of an actual interest amount that is less than the expected interest amount. This means that whenever the noteholders of the underlying ABS receive less money by way of interest than they expected, the protection seller must reimburse the buyer under the terms of Form I.

However, the exact amount payable by the seller belongs to one of the most complex areas in Form I. The parties to a CDS on ABS transaction have a few options of how an interest shortfall amount is to be calculated and they can decide to cap it. In order to understand the mechanics, we need to look into three places: the main body of the Standard Terms Supplement, the interest shortfall annex scheduled to the Standard Terms Supplement and the confirmation.

The Standard Terms Supplement

5. Interest shortfall

Interest shortfall payment amount:	In respect of an interest shortfall, the relevant interest shortfall amount provided that if the interest shortfall cap is specified as applicable in the relevant confirmation and the interest shortfall amount exceeds the interest shortfall cap amount, the interest shortfall payment amount in respect of such interest shortfall shall be the interest shortfall cap amount.
Interest shortfall cap:	As shown in the relevant confirmation.
Interest shortfall cap amount:	As set out in the interest shortfall cap annex.
Interest shortfall:	With respect to any reference obligation payment date, either: (a) the non-payment of an expected interest amount; or (b) the payment of an actual interest amount that is less than the expected interest amount.

Form of confirmation

Interest shortfall cap:	[Applicable][Not applicable]
Interest shortfall cap basis:	[Fixed cap][Variable cap]

Interest shortfall cap annex

Interest shortfall cap amount:	If the interest shortfall cap basis is fixed cap, the interest shortfall cap amount in respect of an interest shortfall shall be the fixed amount calculated in respect of the fixed-rate payer payment date immediately following the reference obligation payment date on which the relevant interest shortfall occurred.

> If the interest shortfall cap basis is variable cap, the interest shortfall cap amount applicable in respect of a floating rate payer payment date shall be an amount equal to the product of:
>
> (a) the sum of the relevant rate and the fixed rate applicable to the fixed rate payer calculation period immediately preceding the reference obligation payment date on which the relevant interest shortfall occurs (or, in respect of the first fixed-rate payer calculation period, the relevant rate and the fixed rate as of the effective date);
>
> (b) the amount determined by the calculation agent under sub-clause (b) of the definition of 'fixed amount' in relation to the relevant fixed-rate payer payment date; and
>
> (c) the fixed-rate day count fraction.

In summary, parties to a CDS on ABS transaction have a choice whether the amount payable to the buyer following an 'interest shortfall' floating amount event shall be capped at a pre-defined level. The confirmation provides three options:

- interest shortfall cap not applicable;
- interest shortfall cap applicable – fixed cap;
- interest shortfall cap applicable – variable cap.

We will analyse each in turn:

- Interest shortfall cap not applicable: if there is no interest shortfall cap, then the seller is obligated to make payments to cover any shortfall in payments of interest amounts under the reference obligation. It is determined without regard to any limitations.
- Interest shortfall cap applicable – fixed cap: if this option has been selected, then the amount of shortfall payable by the seller is capped at the amount of premium the buyer pays to the seller by way of premium. This means that if, for example, the protection buyer pays £30,000 per fixed-rate calculation period to the seller for the protection, the buyer cannot receive more than this amount. If the shortfall is only £20,000, the buyer will receive the entire amount; but if it is, say, £40,000, the buyer will get only £30,000.
- Interest shortfall cap applicable – variable cap: if this option has been selected, then the cap is linked to LIBOR. The way this cap is calculated at first sight seems complicated, but the underlying principle is quite simple. Sometimes

an institution may borrow to purchase ABS and to service the interest payments under the loan it can pass through the interest payments received under the ABS. If there is an interest shortfall under the ABS, this may leave a funding gap for paying the interest under the loan. A CDS on ABS transaction, though, can protect against an interest shortfall under the ABS. This type of investor will not be attracted to a fixed cap because of the residual risk of a funding gap. However, a variable cap provides a solution. If specified, then the amount payable to the protection buyer will be linked a LIBOR amount, hedging the buyer against any funding gap.

Interest shortfall caps are attractive to protection sellers wishing to limit liability in respect interest shortfalls. These protection sellers are happy to accept a lower premium for being a party to the CDS on ABS transaction if an interest shortfall cap applies. The amount of fixed payment is higher if the parties opt for the variable cap, but then the protection buyer does not need to worry about being unable to pay the interest on the original loan, if it has one.

It should be also noted that the protection buyer is not really concerned if there is a cap on interest shortfall. Many CDS on ABS transactions reference residential mortgage-backed securities, which provide for interest to be paid at a higher priority than principal. This means that a holder of residential mortgage-backed security notes will almost always receive interest in full.

The Standard Terms Supplement

WAC Cap Interest Provision: As shown in the relevant Confirmation.

For this purpose, 'WAC Cap' means a weighted average coupon or weighted average rate cap provision (however defined in the Underlying Instruments) of the Underlying Instruments that limits, increases or decreases the interest rate or interest entitlement in circumstances where the Underlying Instruments as at the Trade Date and without regard to any subsequent amendments, do not provide for any interest shortfall arising as a result of such provision to be deferred, capitalised or otherwise compensated for at any future time.

Confirmation

WAC Cap Interest Provision: [Applicable] [Not Applicable]

Often, ABS notes themselves have caps on the interest payable to the holders with interest payments often limited to a 'weighted average coupon cap' (or the 'WAC cap'). The WAC cap determines the amount of interest paid on ABS notes by reference to the level of the average coupon in the underlying pool. Form I allows the parties either to apply or disapply this cap.

The way Form I operates may seem counter-intuitive. If WAC cap is selected as 'not applicable', then the expected interest is calculated without giving an effect to the WAC cap provisions of the underlying ABS note. This means that the protection seller makes up any interest shortfall caused by such cap. However, if the parties decide that WAC cap provisions shall be 'applicable', then interest shortfall does not arise when the interest paid on the notes is limited by such cap.

It has been argued that disapplying the WAC cap provisions in Form I unduly favours the protection buyer. Consequently, Form II does not give the parties the option to disapply such provisions and the WAC Cap always applies under Form II.

6.5   Fixed payments

As in a corporate CDS, fixed payments under Form I are periodic payments from the buyer to the seller that constitute compensation to the seller for accepting the credit risk on the underlying ABS. However, Form I also introduces a new and additional type of event: 'additional fixed payment events' which constitute the second leg of the PAUG settlement and are a mirror image of the floating amount events.

The Standard Terms Supplement	
Additional fixed payment event:	The occurrence on or after the effective date and on or before the day that is one calendar year after the effective maturity date of a writedown reimbursement, a principal shortfall reimbursement or an interest shortfall reimbursement.

There are three such events: a writedown reimbursement, principal shortfall reimbursement and interest shortfall reimbursement. When these events occur, the protection buyer pays a defined amount to the protection seller.

The additional fixed payment events accommodate the fact that the terms in ABS notes often provide for any shortfall to be reimbursed. For example, if an issuer of a particular tranche of ABS notes does not pay interest in year 1, in year 2 it may be able (depending on the performance of the underlying assets) to pay the unpaid amount of interest in respect of the previous year. If a holder of the ABS notes entered into a CDS on ABS transaction under Form I, then in the first year an 'interest shortfall floating amount event' occurs, the buyer receives a payment from the protection seller at that point. This means that if in year 2 the ABS issuer pays it the amount it already received under the CDS on ABS in year 1, the protection buyer would be compensated twice for the same loss and would earn an 'undeserved' windfall. Therefore, the additional fixed payment events ensure that the buyer will be unable to keep the whole reimbursement amount to itself, but will have to make a payment to the seller.

6.6   Step-up provisions

Form I is unique among all CDS on ABS forms in that it includes provisions which deal with step-up.

Confirmation

Step-up provisions:	[Applicable][Not applicable]

The Standard Terms Supplement

Step-up:	On any day, an increase in the reference obligation coupon due to the failure of the issuer or a third party to exercise, in accordance with the underlying Instruments, a 'cleanup call' or other right to purchase, redeem, cancel or terminate (however described in the underlying instruments) the reference obligation.
Increase of the fixed rate:	Subject to 'optional step-up early termination' below, upon the occurrence of a step-up, the fixed rate will be increased by the number of basis points by which the reference obligation coupon is increased due to the step-up, such increase to take effect as of the fixed-rate payer payment date immediately following the fifth business day after the non-call notification date.
Optional step-up early termination:	No later than five business days after the non-call notification date, buyer shall notify seller (such notification, a 'buyer step-up notice') whether buyer wishes to continue the transaction at the increased fixed rate or to terminate the transaction.

An ABS issuer may be required to buy or redeem the issued securities before their final maturity date. If the ABS issuer does not carry this out at that point, the terms of the instrument may provide for a 'coupon step-up'. This means that an ABS note holder will be receiving a higher coupon from the time when the issuer was supposed to redeem or cancel the notes, up to the note's final maturity date.

If the parties to a CDS on ABS transaction have chosen the step-up provisions in the confirmation to Form I to be applicable, then as soon as the reference obligation step-up occurs, the protection buyer will have a choice. It will either have to pay a higher premium to the seller or decide to terminate the CDS on ABS transaction altogether.

Both options can make commercial sense to the protection buyer. If the terms of the underlying ABS provide for a higher coupon, then the seller exposes itself to a higher risk, as it may need to pay more to the buyer on the occurrence of a credit event or floating amount event. Therefore, it is entitled to a higher premium for accepting this risk and the protection buyer may be willing to pay it. However, if the buyer thinks, say, that the issuer is not very likely to default in the future and does not want to pay a higher fixed rate, then it may well decide to terminate the transaction.

The parties to a CDS on ABS transaction under Form I can also decide that the step-up provisions will not be applicable. In that case, the fixed-rate payable to the seller will not step up even though the seller is exposed to a bigger risk. This option clearly favours the buyer, which will receive bigger payments from the seller, but will not have to pay a correspondingly higher premium.

6.7 Hypothetical example

Case study: CYD Investments Corporation

Cyd Investments Corporation, Inc ('Cyd') bought a tranche of residential mortgage-backed securities for $30 million on October 21 2007. The notes had a maturity of 10 years and their terms provided for a step-up. The RMBS notes paid a yearly coupon of 4% and were rated A by Fitch.

Cyd came to the conclusion that its investment did not fit in with its overall investment portfolio and that it wished to sell. However, the market for RMBS is very illiquid and Cyd could not find a buyer. In the end, Cyd decided to retain the security, but protect itself from the securities credit risk and free up its balance sheet by entering into a credit default swap with Batson Securities Limited.

Cyd and Batson decided to use Form I as a template. They agreed that the swap would have a term of 10 years (the same as the RMBS), and a notional amount of $30 million. The parties decided that Cyd would pay a fixed rate of 2% of the notional amount per annum, which amounted to $600,000 per annum. The parties decided that there would be additional credit events of distressed ratings downgrade and restructuring (for regulatory capital reasons). They also agreed on interest shortfall cap – fixed cap and confirmed that the step-up provisions in Form I were applicable.

Year 1

In year 1, Cyd was expecting to receive 4% of the originally invested $30 million, which amounted to $1.2 million. However, it only received $800,000 of interest. Therefore, an 'interest shortfall' floating amount event occurred and Batson owed $400,000 ($1.2 million – $800,000) to Cyd. Since Cyd had to pay Batson the fixed rate of $600,000, both figures were offset against each other and, as a result, Cyd made a payment of $200,000 to Batson.

Year 2

In year 2, Cyd was again expecting to receive another $1.2 million by way of coupon on the RMBS notes. However, this time it received only $300,000, which

---

meant that the shortfall amounted to $900,000. Since Cyd and Batson agreed a fixed cap, therefore, Batson was liable for any interest shortfall up to the amount of the fixed rate ($600,000). This meant that in year 2 neither Cyd nor Batson had made an overall net payment to the other party, since both liabilities cancelled each other out.

Year 3

In year 3, due to a strong property market, the RMBS underlying assets performed much better than expected. Recoveries from existing defaults also turned out to be higher than expected, and Cyd received not only the agreed $1.2 million, but also deferred interest in respect of years 1 and 2 in the amount of another $500,000. This was good news for Batson, since it meant that an 'interest shortfall reimbursement' additional fixed event occurred. Therefore, in year 3, Cyd paid $1.1 million to Batson ($500,000 + $600,000).

Year 4

In year 4, the issuer of the RMBS notes failed to exercise its right to redeem the notes and, as a result, the coupon was increased from 4% to 5%. Cyd was actually quite pleased that it would receive more money by way of interest, but at the same time it was aware that if it wanted to continue with the CDS transaction, it would need to increase the fixed rate payable to Batson also by 1%. Alternatively, it could terminate the transaction altogether. Cyd concluded that the RMBS investment was quite risky and decided to pay a higher fixed rate to Batson. Therefore, in year 4, Cyd received $1.5 million (5% of $30 million) by way of coupon, and had to pay a fixed rate of $900,000 (3% of $30 million) to Batson.

Year 5

In year 5, the property market crashed and the RMBS notes were downgraded from A to CCC. This meant that a 'distressed ratings downgrade' occurred and Cyd was entitled to terminate the transaction. Accordingly, Cyd delivered a credit event notice, notice of physical settlement and a notice of publicly available information (which attached as its public source a notice from Fitch evidencing the downgrade). Soon afterwards, Cyd delivered RMBS notes with a notional amount of $30 million to Batson, which in turn had to pay $30 million. At that point the transaction came to an end. When all of the security for the RMBS notes had finally been enforced, Batson received only $20 million.

7.   Credit derivative transaction on asset-backed security with pay-as-you-go settlement (Form II)

7.1   Introduction

Having discussed Form I, it is easier to analyse Form II from the perspective of the differences. The latter form is designed for all kind of asset-backed securities, not only the mortgage-backed ones, so it has a wider application. It was developed to fulfil the requirements of monoline insurers whose function includes offering protection and guarantees to various market participants in return for a fee. These institutions wanted a template which would be very seller-friendly and which would support their way of doing business. Form II is therefore a seller-friendly template.

To avoid repetition, this section concentrates on the main differences between Form I and the forms discussed in the previous sections. However, the differences between Form I and Form II can be summarised as follows. Only Form I has credit events. In contrast, in Form II, the seller makes payments only if a floating amount event (writedown (a reduction in the principal or interest due), principal shortfall (non-payment or lesser payment of expected principal) or interest shortfall (non-payment or lesser payment of the expected interest amount)) occurs and the calculation agent or the buyer of protection notifies the seller that a floating payment is due.

Form II does not include implied writedown provisions requiring payments compensating for losses on the ABS resulting in a reduction of the outstanding principal when such losses are not provided for in the underlying instruments of the MBS. There are also further differences between the two forms in relation to the definition of interest shortfall amounts.

Form II implements any amendments to the underlying ABS, whereas Form I does not. Form II also treats make-whole premium payments (payments to the obligation holders of a make-whole premium in relation to events such as prepayments under the terms of the obligation) as additional fixed payment events.

Under Form II, instead of the step-up provisions, changes in the coupon of a fixed-rate obligation or the spread of a floating-rate obligation are implemented and the transaction continues at the new coupon.

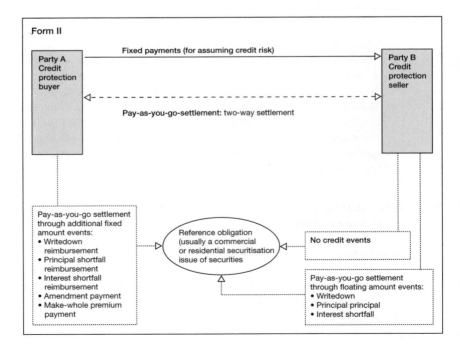

Form II 'events'	
Credit event	No credit events
Floating amount event	Writedown Principal shortfall Interest shortfall
Additional fixed payment event	Writedown reimbursement Principal shortfall reimbursement Interest shortfall reimbursement Amendment payment Make-whole premium payment

7.2 Credit events

Most importantly, Form II does not include any credit events. The template provides for neither cash nor physical settlement and any payments the protection buyer may receive would be through the pay-as-you-go mechanism. This means that the parties cannot normally terminate the transaction during its term.

Both cash and physical settlement mechanisms require the seller to make a one-off payment to the protection buyer. This means that credit events may cause liquidity and exposure issues to the seller. Conversely, under PAUG settlement the seller only receives shortfalls from the buyer, which will usually be a much smaller amount.

7.3 Floating amounts

Floating amount event: A writedown, principal shortfall or an interest shortfall

Generally, floating amount events seem to be same as in Form I, with 'failure to pay principal' being replaced by 'principal shortfall'. However, this is not quite the case as floating amount events in Form II are different from those in Form I in a few key respects.

Actual interest amount:	(...) Notwithstanding the foregoing, the expected interest amount shall be determined after taking into account any provision of the underlying instruments (i) providing for the capitalisation or deferral of interest on the reference obligation; or (ii) limiting the interest entitlement or rate at which interest is determined in relation to the reference obligation pursuant to a prepayment interest shortfall, basis risk shortfall, Relief Act shortfall, 'net WAC rate cap' or similar available funds cap provision (any reduction of the interest accruing, payable or distributable in respect of the reference obligation in accordance with such provisions, an 'available funds cap reduction'). (...)

The 'interest shortfall' floating amount event is calculated in a manner that is less favourable to the protection buyer. It is determined after giving effect to the WAC cap and any other available funds cap reduction provisions, including any provisions of the underlying instrument that provide for deferral of interest on the reference obligation. Therefore, the payment to the buyer covering interest shortfall may be far lower under the terms of Form II than it would be under the provisions of Form I in the same circumstances.

Finally, the writedown provisions in Form II do not cover implied writedown. Implied writedown has been controversial and monoline insurers have argued that it unduly favours the buyer. Therefore, ISDA decided not to include it in Form II.

7.4   Fixed payments

Fixed rate:	[ ]% per annum; provided that if the [coupon][spread] of the reference obligation is increased during the term of the transaction (whether as a result of a step-up in accordance with the underlying instruments, an amendment or otherwise), the fixed rate shall be increased by the number of basis points by which the reference obligation [coupon][spread] is increased, such increase to take effect as of the first fixed-rate payer payment date following such increase.

The 'fixed rate' definition (which is the premium paid by the protection buyer to the seller) covers step-up. Whereas under Form I the buyer may have an option to terminate the transaction if there is a step-up, such an option is not provided for in Form II. Instead, the buyer will be obliged to continue with the CDS on ABS transaction and will be obliged to pay a higher premium to the seller.

An important difference between Form I and Form II is that the latter has two more additional fixed payment events. Whereas in Form I these were writedown reimbursement, principal shortfall reimbursement and interest shortfall reimbursement, Form II also contains an amendment payment and make-whole premium payment.

Additional fixed payment event:	The occurrence on or after the effective date and on or before the final amortisation date of a writedown reimbursement, a principal shortfall reimbursement, an interest shortfall reimbursement, an amendment payment or a make-whole premium payment.

'Amendment payment' is defined as payment or distribution of any consideration to holders of the reference obligation in connection with an agreement by such holders to amend, amend and restate, supplement or otherwise modify or waive any of the terms of the underlying instruments. Make-whole premium payment is any payment or distribution of any make-whole, redemption, call or prepayment premium to holders of the reference obligation in connection with any prepayment, redemption, early amortisation or similar event under the terms of the underlying instruments.

In summary, the two additional fixed payment events occur when holders of the underlying notes receive some extra, unexpected payment from the ABS issuer. At that point, if the noteholder has entered into a CDS on ABS under Form II as protection buyer, it will need to make a payment to the protection seller.

8. Credit derivative transaction on collateralised debt obligation with pay-as-you-go or physical settlement (dealer form)

This CDO form was the last to be published and it is very similar to Form I. The key difference is that it can adapt to the vagaries of the underlying CDOs, while providing a PAUG template. Like the other PAUG forms, the buyer may choose to have physical settlement of a failure to pay principal or a writedown, or use the pay-as-you-go mechanism by triggering payment by the seller of a floating amount. In summary, the key differences between the PAUG templates and the CDS on CDO template are the inclusion of a failure to pay interest as an additional credit event, the hard-wiring of a distressed ratings downgrade as a credit event and an option for implied writedown.

On June 6 2007 ISDA published a new CDO form, which now consists of the long Standard Terms Supplement and a short confirmation. As in the new Form I, the mandatory terms are provided in the Standard Terms Supplement, whereas the

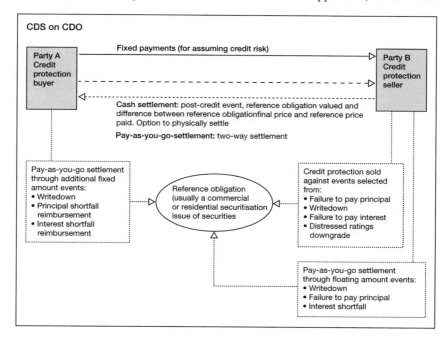

optional terms are in the confirmation. This should make the use of the form easier and, as a result, may make CDS on CDO transactions even more popular.

CDS on CDO	
Credit event	Failure to pay principal Writedown Failure to pay interest Distressed ratings downgrade
Floating amount event	Writedown Failure to pay principal Interest shortfall
Additional fixed payment event	Writedown reimbursement Principal shortfall reimbursement Interest shortfall reimbursement

8.1 Credit events

> **The Standard Terms Supplement**
>
> Credit events: The following credit events shall apply to this transaction (and the first sentence of Section 4.1 of the Credit Derivatives Definitions shall be amended accordingly):
>
> Failure to pay principal
>
> Writedown
>
> Failure to pay interest
>   Payment requirement: $10,000
>
> Distressed ratings downgrade

The only additional credit event in the CDO form is 'failure to pay interest'. If the reference obligation is a mortgage-based security, the noteholder is not as concerned if it does not receive interest on time, since interest will usually be ranked with a higher priority than the principal. Therefore, under Form I, failure to pay is only a floating amount event and the protection buyer is not entitled to physically settle the transaction when an interest shortfall occurs.

However, most CDOs do not provide for interest to be paid at a higher priority than principal and, consequently, the buyer will need additional protection to reflect this. This need was taken into account by the ISDA during the drafting process and 'failure to pay interest' was included as a credit event in the CDO form.

Another importance difference is the hard-wiring of a distressed ratings downgrade. Whereas it is an optional credit event in Form I, the CDO form makes it a mandatory one.

8.2   Implied writedown

> **Confirmation**
>
> Implied writedown: [Applicable][Not applicable]

Implied writedown has always been one of the most controversial aspects in the definitions of credit events and floating amount events. It provides for a payment if the terms of the reference obligation do not provide for writedown, but the noteholders suffer a loss nonetheless. Whereas Form I includes implied writedown provisions and Form II does not, under the CDO form the parties can choose whether they would like implied writedown to be covered. At the same time, the definition of 'implied writedown' has been amended to accommodate special characteristics of a CDO, especially in respect of its collateralisation.

9.   Additional provisions for optional early termination (CDS on ABS)

These form a short (only four and a half page) document which can be incorporated to any of the CDS on ABS confirmations described above. Published on December 6 2006, they allow the parties to terminate the entire transaction earlier than they anticipated at its outset.

> **Section 1. Optional Early Termination.** In respect of each Exercise Date under an OET Transaction:
>
> (a) after determination of the Early Termination Settlement Amount, as defined below, the party owing such amount will pay such amount to the other party on the Optional Early Termination Date;
>
> (b) the final Fixed Rate Payer Calculation Period will end on and include the Early Termination Settlement Amount Determination Date and the final Fixed Amount will be payable on the Optional Early Termination Date; and
>
> (c) with effect from and including the Early Termination Settlement Amount Determination Date, the parties will have no further obligations to one another with respect to such OET Transaction, except (i) with respect to the payment of the amounts set forth in (a) and (b) above and (ii) that any rights arising in respect of Floating Amount Events or Additional Fixed Amount Events will be discharged as if the terms of paragraph 1 of the Annex to the Form of Novation Confirmation set out in the Schedule to the ISDA Standard Terms Supplement for use with Credit Derivative Transactions on Mortgage-Backed Security with Pay-As-You-Go or Physical Settlement as published by the International Swaps and Derivatives Association, Inc ('ISDA') (the 'Novation Confirmation'), were applicable, the necessary changes being made, as though (x) the Exercising Party were the Transferor and the Non-

> Exercising Party were the Remaining Party, (y) the OET Transaction were the
> Old Transaction and (z) the Early Termination Settlement Amount
> Determination Date were the Novation Date.

Provided that no event of default has occurred, either of the parties to the transaction may decide to terminate it by giving notice to the other party no later than the 10th business day and no sooner than the 20th business day prior to an exercise date. The exercise date, in turn, is defined as each anniversary, beginning with the 10th anniversary, of the trade date of a relevant transaction.

This means that the additional provisions can apply only if the scheduled termination date of a given transaction is more than 10 years after its trade date. If this is the case, the parties have a 10-day 'window' each year, starting with the 10th anniversary of the transaction, during which they can decide that they do not want to be bound by its terms and can serve a notice to the counterparty to this effect.

10.   The future

ISDA's standardised documentation has fuelled CDS on ABS market growth and, as the market continues to develop, both more forms and revised ones are inevitable.

Behind the flurry of standardised contracts, it is planned that ISDA will develop a terms booklet for structured credit products. This will most likely occur at some point in 2008.

The effect of this document would be to take the Standard Terms Supplement format one step further by offering parties a set of terms, in the vein of a definitional booklet that could be incorporated by reference into a short confirmation. The challenges for the market in developing such a booklet include not only settling the existing terms, but also anticipating the many permutations that are likely to develop.

The April PAUG Form I states in its footnotes that "ISDA anticipates future publication of one or more template Confirmations for use with other types of asset-backed security (such as credit card receivables-backed securitisation notes or collateralised debt obligation notes)". While many market participants felt in the end that a standard template for underlying credit card receivables would not be needed in the near term, the need for a CDS on CDO template persisted. The direction of future template documentation for CDS on ABS will probably contain many twists and turns.

Creating a credit event strategy and managing a major credit event

1. Introduction

A North American automobile manufacturer files for Chapter 11 bankruptcy. You work for an institution with a credit derivatives portfolio with thousands of transactions. The manufacturer's bankruptcy is not unexpected and the reference entity is present in 40% of the transactions in the portfolio. You are part of the team responsible for triggering, managing and settling credit events.

You know that your team must be confident that:

- it has the infrastructure in place to ensure that it is aware of the credit event;
- each transaction that your employer decides to trigger is actually triggered;
- the settlement procedure goes ahead with no hitches; and
- most importantly, the portfolio incurs no losses through negligence.

Your team may have built up expertise over the series of major credit events that occurred in the past few years (eg, Enron, Worldcom, Parmalat, Winn-Dixie, Delphi, Calpine and Collins & Aikman), but it is unlikely that this knowledge will have been boosted by existing credit derivatives literature. The available literature – when referring to triggering and settling a credit event – has always tended to refer to triggering and settling a single transaction, rather than triggering and managing the credit event process for a large and diverse portfolio of credit derivatives and ensuring that a robust credit event management strategy is in place.

This chapter focuses on successfully dealing with and managing a major credit event. It recognises that this is a demanding and exacting task, complemented by plenty of opportunities to lose large quantities of money. It also discusses:

- how the credit event settlement process works from beginning to end;
- how to create an effective credit event strategy from scratch; and
- how to avoid the many potential pitfalls in credit event management which can cause losses and a significant dent in the balance sheet.

Almost all credit derivatives market participants already have credit event process management systems in place. This chapter suggests what the minimum level of organisation should be for a market participant which has (or may have in the future) a large credit derivatives portfolio. Although these structures may seem restrictive or rigid, it is hoped that they may provide a framework which can be analysed and adapted as appropriate.

Various credit derivative products which may form part of a portfolio		Notices that may be distributed during the credit event process	
Credit default option	Credit-linked note	Credit event notice	Receipt of default swap credit event notice
Single-name credit default swap	Synthetic collateral debt obligation (CDO)	Notice of publicly available information	Cash settlement notice
Basket credit default swap	Long-short credit-linked transaction	Notice of physical settlement	Quotation notice
Portfolio credit default swap	Credit-linked constant proportion portfolio insurance	Repudiation moratorium extension notice	Final price notice
CDO-squared swap/note	Credit index-linked product	Reference obligation notice	Buy-in notice
Credit derivative product covered by ISDA protocol	Leveraged credit default swap	Valuation date notice	Portfolio manager notice
Full credit index-linked trades	Tranche credit index trade	Overlying swap notices, where credit event in underlying swap causes a breach of threshold	
Secured loan credit default swap	Swaption		

In any credit derivatives portfolio, some affected transactions may be physically settled, some may be cash-settled and others may allow an election of physical or cash settlement. Some transactions may be single-name credit default swaps or credit-linked notes. In other transactions, the reference entity may be one of many among:

- an iTraxx-linked trade;
- a portfolio credit default swap;
- a synthetic CDO; or
- one of the underlying portfolios of a CDO-squared transaction.

A counterparty may also have hedged selling credit protection in one transaction by buying it in another (or vice versa), and some transactions may be subject to an ISDA credit derivatives protocol (and others not).

During the credit event settlement process, different types of transaction require different notices to be delivered at different times. Structured transactions may require copies of notices to be delivered to rating agents and portfolio managers. CDO-squared transactions may require notices to be delivered to hypothetical buyers and sellers. Valuation dates may be on fixed dates, decided by counting the number of New York, London and TARGET business days after the conditions for settlement have been met; alternatively, they may be within a date range. Provisions on dealers, quotation amounts and quotation methods can vary between transactions and must be analysed individually. Any market participant must ensure that it triggers and settles each of its affected transactions correctly where it is the credit protection buyer; where the participant is the credit protection seller, it must also ensure that its own counterparty has triggered and settled the transaction correctly.

Hypothetical case study of a poorly managed credit event

This hypothetical case study conveys the potential problems which may arise when a market participant which made no or limited preparation manages a significant credit event affecting a wide range and high number of products in its credit derivatives portfolio.

Czarnocki plc, a Polish bank, has a large portfolio of 943 credit derivative transactions. The portfolio has built up gradually over the past few years and Czarnocki has made no advance preparation for future credit events. The portfolio has been previously affected by credit events, but these have had an impact on relatively few transactions and have all been dealt with successfully, although on a reactive basis.

On November 8 2005 Ropemaker Corporation, a US automobile parts manufacturer, filed for Chapter 11 bankruptcy.[1] As Czarnocki had established no credit event monitoring systems, it failed to realise that a potential credit event had occurred until two weeks later when, by chance, a member of the legal team read an article in the press.

Following an internal meeting, Czarnocki instructed its legal department to establish how many of its credit derivative transactions referenced Ropemaker. The legal department confirmed that 212 transactions were affected, including:

- 102 single-name credit default swaps;
- 18 single-name credit-linked notes;
- 42 portfolio credit default swaps (including 18 transactions linked to iTraxx); and
- 12 synthetic CDO transactions (including four CDO-squared transactions).

The legal department produced a report setting out each transaction's conditions to settlement and related valuation and settlement requirements. It took three weeks to produce the report; the bank's credit derivatives desk then reviewed it and decided which transactions it wished to trigger. Five weeks after Ropemaker filed for bankruptcy, the bank was ready to trigger its affected transactions. All did not run smoothly and the following things went wrong:

- The legal department was under pressure to produce its report quickly and eight affected transactions were missed. The mistake was not realised for two months and credit protection was lost for two $10 million credit

---

1   In the United States, the Federal Bankruptcy Code applies when a company is dissolved or seeks to recover from its debts. A bankrupt company can use either Chapter 11 or Chapter 7 of the Bankruptcy Code. Under Chapter 11, the company is protected from its creditors while it tries to reorganise its business and return to profitability. The company continues to be run by its management, but the bankruptcy court must approve all important decisions. As a company's position stabilises or moves closer to pulling out of Chapter 11 bankruptcy, the value of the obligations may rise. Under Chapter 7, a trustee is appointed to dissolve the company and pay off its debts. Significant credit events involving Chapter 11 bankruptcy of US companies in 2005 and 2006 included Winn Dixie, Collins & Aikman, Delta Airlines, Northwest Airlines, Calpine Corporation, Delphi Corporation and Dana Corporation. Chapter 11 bankruptcy is a credit event pursuant to Section 4.2(d) of the 2003 Definitions.

default swaps, which matured before the mistakes came to light. For the remaining six transactions – with average notional amounts of $12 million during the period between when the transactions should have been triggered and when they were actually triggered – the value of Ropemaker's obligations increased. Therefore, Czarnocki received a lesser credit protection payment.

- The hurried analysis contained several mistakes relating to valuation dates, resulting in actual dates being missed. This led to Czarnocki having to renegotiate several transactions with its counterparties.
- Fifty-two of the affected transactions were physically settled trades. For each transaction, once Czarnocki had issued the credit event notice and notice of publicly available information, it was required to deliver a notice of physical settlement within 30 calendar days or credit protection would be lost. This was not done for one of the single-name credit default swap transactions and Czarnocki lost a further $2 million.
- One of the transactions was an intermediary credit default swap. Czarnocki had expected to make money on the deal by selling credit protection on a portfolio for a higher fee than it had bought it for in a back-to-back swap. While Czarnocki's counterparty, Diaz Corporation, served Czarnocki with a credit event notice and notice of publicly available information on December 18 2005, Czarnocki did not send the corresponding notices to its counterparty Ancha PLC under the back-to-back swap until December 20 2005. The valuation dates for the reference obligation under the two swaps no longer matched, leaving Czarnocki with an imperfect hedge. Due to an adverse movement in the reference obligation's trading price, Czarnocki had to pay out a higher cash settlement amount to Diaz Corporation as credit protection seller than it received from Ancha PLC as credit protection buyer.
- In one of the four CDO-squared transactions, Czarnocki triggered the overlying swap instead of the underlying swap; by the time the mistake was realised, the credit default swap's maturity date had passed and credit protection was lost.
- Each of the credit default swaps that Czarnocki triggered required two public sources of publicly available information to be included in the notice of publicly available information. Czarnocki attached one article confirming the Ropemaker credit event from *The Financial Times* and another from a national newspaper. The national newspaper in question did not fall easily within Section 3.7 of the 2003 Definitions and one of Czarnocki's counterparties, Paredes Bank, refused to pay the cash settlement amount in any of the five transactions that it had entered into with Czarnocki. The counterparty argued that because the national newspaper was not internationally recognised, the conditions to settlement were not satisfied. While these arguments continued, two of the transactions matured and Czarnocki and Paredes Bank became

> involved in costly litigation. Czarnocki decided to re-trigger the other transactions that had not matured, but ended up settling the two transactions which had matured for less than their due cash settlements amounts.
>
> - Czarnocki entered into several transactions as seller with Trojan Bank. Trojan Bank was also the calculation agent. In one transaction, Trojan Bank used the wrong valuation method, resulting in the final price for the Ropemaker reference obligation being lower than it should have been. Czarnocki did not check the final price computation and ended up paying a higher cash settlement amount than should have been due. Czarnocki never realised its mistake.
> - In another transaction with Trojan Bank, Czarnocki did not carry out the necessary diligence on the conditions to settlement and failed to realise that the Ropemaker credit event had been incorrectly triggered. Czarnocki paid a cash settlement amount which should not have been due and never realised its mistake.
>
> All in all, lack of a robust credit event strategy and process caused Czarnocki to lose $30 million.

2. Phase 1: putting a structure in place and preparing for the storm

2.1 Strategy

All the mistakes detailed in the Czarnocki case study could easily have been prevented by putting a robust credit event strategy in place. The greater the size of a credit derivatives portfolio and the variety of products it contains, the more essential a well-organised strategy becomes. A market participant with a small credit derivatives portfolio may gradually see it grow over time and would be well advised to put an effective credit event strategy in place as soon as possible.

Once a credit event occurs, by quickly being in a position to trigger, a market participant will be best placed to exploit any assumed variations in the price of the reference entity reference obligations. A strategy will prevent expensive mistakes from occurring and will also allow, as far as possible, the true transactional costs of credit derivatives to be reflected in any profit and loss account at the outset.

The following sections set out a suggested strategy which can be adopted and adapted by any company or institution with a credit derivatives portfolio.

2.2 Credit event committee, execution team and four tasks of preparation

At the hub of any organisation's credit event strategy should be a credit event committee and execution team. The credit event committee will be responsible for ensuring that the credit event management infrastructure is in place long before any credit event occurs; the execution team will be responsible for managing credit events on a day-to-day basis as and when they occur.

The level of formality and rigidity involved in structuring the committee and

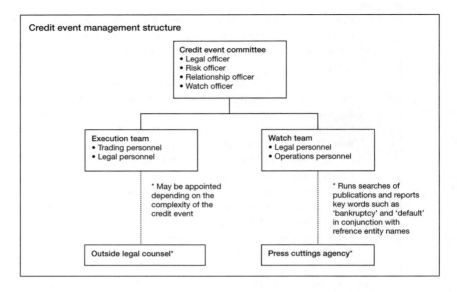

what it is actually called will depend on the nature and culture of the market participant and the size and complexity of its portfolio. Whatever is decided, it is essential for a market participant to have a dedicated group of people focussing on the tasks detailed below.

Ideally, the credit event committee should consist of four officers:

- a legal officer, who should be a senior credit derivatives specialist from the legal department;
- a risk officer, who should be a senior trader experienced in credit default swap trading;
- a relationship officer, who should be a representative from a sales team or the treasury department involved in buying and selling credit derivatives; and
- a watch officer, who should be a member of the legal department with overall responsibility for monitoring potential credit events.

The credit event committee will appoint a standing execution team, which should consist of a combination of:

- business personnel, who will make day-to-day decisions as to when to trigger transactions;
- trading personnel, who will carry out the selection of reference obligations and the valuation process; and
- legal personnel (potentially including outside counsel), who will draft the template notices; these notices can be used on the occurrence of an actual credit event to ensure that all documentation requirements are met.

It is most likely that there will be some overlap between personnel in the credit event committee and the execution team. Where a market participant has only a small portfolio of credit derivative products, the credit event committee may even double up as the execution team. The larger a credit derivatives portfolio, the more likely it is that having different personnel in the credit event committee and the execution team will be both beneficial and necessary.

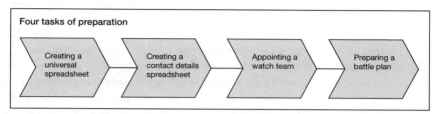

Four tasks of preparation

Creating a universal spreadsheet → Creating a contact details spreadsheet → Appointing a watch team → Preparing a battle plan

The credit event committee must ensure that there is a sufficient level of expertise and ongoing training within the execution team to ensure that the demands of even the largest credit event can be successfully met.

In anticipation of future credit events, the credit event committee should carry out the following 'tasks of preparation':

- create a universal spreadsheet populated with each transaction's details;
- create a contact details database with each counterparty's details;
- establish a watch team to monitor the occurrence of potential credit events; and
- set up an execution team equipped with a 'battle plan' to manage any future credit events on a day-to-day basis, as and when they occur.

2.3 Preparation task 1: the universal spreadsheet

(a) Importance

The universal spreadsheet is the cornerstone of credit event management. It sets out in pre-defined fields summaries of:

- all of the information necessary to trigger a credit event;
- the applicable notices required in the settlement process; and
- the information relevant to settling a transaction.

The information is best collated by using an Excel spreadsheet or, with sufficient investment, a specially created software programme which automatically populates the relevant fields whenever a new trade is executed.

Best practice is to be proactive and update the universal spreadsheet with each new transaction, rather than to update it reactively in response to a potential or actual credit event.

If a universal spreadsheet is proactively updated, a market participant which has entered into a large number of credit derivative transactions can be in a position to trigger all of its affected trades soon after a credit event occurs. If the universal spreadsheet is populated reactively, time pressure can increase the likelihood of mistakes being made and the lead time necessary to update the spreadsheet can delay triggering transactions. Triggering transactions late can affect a reference obligation's final price and, if mistakes are made when triggering and valuing transactions, the potential losses may be huge. Additionally, if the spreadsheet is updated proactively, the person responsible for updating can ensure that the executed transaction documentation is saved onto a knowledge management system at the outset, avoiding any problems and delays involved in locating documentation once a credit event has occurred.

The universal spreadsheet should be comprehensive and cover all of the market participant's credit derivative transactions. When a credit event occurs, certain transactions may be dealt with outside of the main process and stripped from the universal spreadsheet. This may occur in the case of transactions which are subject to the net settlement agreement and/or an applicable novation protocol. Transactions removed from the universal spreadsheet should be separately monitored in an additional spreadsheet.

The credit event committee must decide whether the universal spreadsheet will be populated and constructed in-house or by an outside law firm. An outside counsel may be expensive, but its appointment may provide additional comfort on the spreadsheet's accuracy and may end up being cheaper than deploying existing staff to the project.

(b)   ***Defining the universal spreadsheet content and populating its fields***
An example of the universal spreadsheet headings which should be populated for each transaction is outlined in the following table.

Transaction identification	Transaction identifier
	Counterparty
	Transaction type
	Buyer or seller?
Credit events/settlement method/definitions	Credit events
	Method of settlement
	1999/2003 or other definitions applicable
Notifications	Conditions to settlement
	Notice of physical settlement
	Valuation date notice
	Reference obligation notification
	Final price notification
	Other notices under default swap
	Other notices under notes /other agreement
	Notifying party
Cash settlement/ valuation provisions	Valuation dates
	Valuation time
	Quotation method

> Valuation method
>
> Quotation amount
>
> Dealers
>
> Option to purchase
>
> Calculation agent city
>
> Calculation agent

The universal spreadsheet should be divided into the following sections:
- transaction identification;
- credit events, settlement method and definitions;
- notifications; and
- cash settlement/valuation provisions.

Each section should be subdivided into the individual fields to be populated. Under 'transaction identification', there should be subsections identifying:
- the transaction;
- the counterparty;
- the type of transaction; and
- whether the market participant is the buyer or the seller.

Under 'credit events/settlement method/definitions', there should be subsections detailing:
- each transaction's relevant credit events;
- whether the transaction is to be cash settled, physically settled or a combination of the two; and
- whether the transaction is governed by the 1999 or 2003 Definitions, or follows an alternative procedure.

Under 'notifications', the conditions to settlement for each transaction should be summarised, together with each notice that must be delivered during the settlement process. The identity of the notifying party should also be disclosed here.

The 'cash settlement/valuation provisions' section should summarise:
- the valuation dates;
- the valuation time;
- the quotation method;
- the valuation method;
- the quotation amount;
- provisions for identifying dealers;
- the identity of the calculation agent;
- the location of the calculation agent city; and
- whether the counterparty has an option to purchase the reference obligation.

(c) **Transaction identification**

Transaction identification	Transaction identifier
	Counterparty
	Transaction type
	Buyer or seller?

Each transaction will have some form of identifying reference; this is often a reference number set out in the confirmation, or perhaps an international securities identification number in the case of a credit-linked note. This, together with any other internal identifiers, should be disclosed in the 'transaction identifier' subsection. The identity of the counterparty should be noted under the 'counterparty' subsection. The type of transaction (eg, single-name credit default swap, CDO-squared transaction, credit-linked note or portfolio credit default swap) should be set out under the 'transaction type' subsection. Whether the company has bought or sold credit protection in relation to any particular transaction should be disclosed in the 'buyer or seller' subsection.

(d) **Credit events, settlement method, definitions**

Credit events/settlement method/definitions	Credit events
	Method of settlement
	1999/2003 or other definitions applicable

Each transaction's applicable credit events should be noted under 'credit events'. Particular attention should be paid to

- restructuring credit events;
- whether the applicable restructuring credit event is modified restructuring, modified modified restructuring or full restructuring; and
- repudiation/moratorium credit events to confirm whether 'repudiation/ moratorium extension' is applicable.

This section should also set out any unusual features and whether the provisions on grace periods are applicable.

Whether a transaction is to be cash settled or physically settled will be set out under 'method of settlement'. Some bespoke trades will contain provisions allowing an election of cash or physical settlement, or a hybrid mechanism of the two. Any such unusual features should be noted here.

The applicable ISDA Definitions governing the relevant transaction should be noted under the '1999/2003 or other Definitions applicable' section. Transactions entered into after May 2003 will generally be documented using the 2003 Definitions and those entered into before May 2003 using the 1999 Definitions. However, there may be some variation with transactions entered into over the summer of 2003, while the new definitions were being adopted by the market. Some older transactions (ie, transactions entered into before the 1999 Definitions) may use the ISDA long-form confirmation. Credit-linked notes and other transactions which have an embedded credit derivative element must also be checked closely. The market practice is generally for the credit-linked provisions to be set out in a credit default swap. However, some transactions will set out the credit derivatives provisions in the terms of the notes themselves; these may vary considerably from the 2003 Definitions.[2]

As a general point, special care should be taken when dealing with CDO-squared transactions to ensure that details for both the underlying and overlying swap are populated in the universal spreadsheet.

(e)   ***Notifications***

Notifications	Conditions to settlement
	Notice of physical settlement
	Valuation date notice
	Reference obligation notification
	Final price notification
	Other notices under default swap
	Other notices under notes /other agreement
	Notifying party

The 'notifications' section of the universal spreadsheet sets out all of the notices that can be delivered in each transaction, save for ISDA Definitions fallback notices (eg, buy-in notices and repudiation/moratorium extension notices).

With even a three valuation date vanilla cash-settled credit default swap requiring as many as six notices to be delivered during the credit event settlement process (eg, a credit event notice, a notice of publicly available information, a reference obligation notification, a quotation amount notice for each valuation date other than the final date and a final price notification), and a failure to send correctly any requisite notices opening up a market participant to potential liability, careful attention must be paid to ensure that each individual transaction's requirements are accurately recorded.

More bespoke transactions may also require further notifications to be given, such as advance notice of a valuation date. Where the relevant transaction is a credit-linked note, bespoke transactions may require further notices to be delivered to the noteholders (and copied to ratings agencies), such as a receipt of default swap credit event notice, a loss determination amount notice and a cash settlement amount

---

2   This is most likely to be the case where a credit-linked note has been issued under an institution's own euro medium-term note programme, rather than through a special purpose vehicle.

notice. In the case of transactions with managed reference entity portfolios, notices may also be given to the relevant manager in certain circumstances.

In most transactions, the conditions to settlement will require the notifying party to deliver a credit event notice and notice of publicly available information. Where the relevant transaction is rated, notices may have to be copied to the rating agency. In emerging market credit derivative transactions or transactions which reference only reference entity loans, the requirements for publicly available information may be modified. In certain other circumstances the number or sources of publicly available information to be disclosed may also vary. These variations should all be summarised under the 'conditions to settlement' subsection.

In physically settled transactions, the period of time in which the notice of physical settlement may be delivered and following which physical settlement must take place sometimes varies in bespoke transactions. Whether a notice of physical settlement is required and whether there are any variations from the standard ISDA provisions in this process should be set out under 'notice of physical settlement'.

The party which can trigger a transaction following a credit event should be recorded in the subsection for 'notifying party'. This will almost always be either the seller only or either of the buyer and the seller; however, in some transactions, the notifying party may be a third-party calculation agent.

(f) Cash settlement/valuation provisions

Cash settlement/ valuation provisions	Valuation dates
	Valuation time
	Quotation method
	Valuation method
	Quotation amount
	Dealers
	Option to purchase
	Calculation agent city
	Calculation agent

Although most credit derivative transactions are physically settled, most bespoke credit derivative transactions are cash settled; the cash settled transactions will require the most attention when preparing the universal spreadsheet and managing a credit event. The valuation provisions will tend to have the most variations.

Each transaction must be analysed to populate the following valuation fields in the 'cash settlement/valuation provisions' section of the universal spreadsheet:

- valuation dates;
- valuation time;
- quotation method;
- valuation method;

- quotation amount; and
- dealers.

(i)   *Valuation dates*
The following elements will vary depending on the transaction:
- the number of valuation dates;
- whether a valuation must occur on a fixed day or within a range of dates; and
- whether a valuation is itself fixed.

These provisions are often heavily negotiated. A large investment bank may easily find upwards of 30 variations in the type of valuation date provision among its bespoke trades.

The following are examples of universal spreadsheet summaries of bespoke variations in the 'valuation date(s)' definition:
- The valuation date shall be the date that is the later of 30 calendar days following the relevant event determination date and 20 New York business days following the relevant event determination date.
- The valuation date shall be any date selected by the seller that falls within the period from and including the relevant event determination date to and including the date that is 50 New York business days following the relevant event determination date.
- The seller shall select a valuation date that is no less than 30 London business days and no more than 90 London business days following the relevant event determination date.
- There shall be four valuation dates: the date falling no less than 45 and no more than 60 London and New York business days following the relevant event determination date as selected by the calculation agent, and each successive date that is 10 London and New York business days thereafter.
- There shall be three valuation dates, the first being a date selected by the calculation agent between 45 and 60 TARGET settlement days after the relevant event determination date, and thereafter the date falling five TARGET settlement days following the first valuation date and 15 TARGET settlement days following the second valuation date.

The valuation date provisions should be carefully summarised under the 'valuation dates' subsection.

(ii) *Valuation time*
The valuation time will usually be 11:00am in the calculation agent city. A large financial institution will often choose to manage credit event valuations through execution team members located at a single credit derivatives desk; therefore, the time zone of the calculation agent city may cause problems depending on the location of the managing desk (eg, 11:00am London time will mean 6:00am New York time). This may cause logistical problems if the trading personnel are located in New York and should be borne in mind when preparing the battle plan. Each valuation time

provision should be recorded in the universal spreadsheet under the 'valuation dates' subsection and any unusual provisions should be highlighted.

The following are examples of universal spreadsheet summaries of bespoke variations in the 'valuation time' definition:

- 11:00am in the principal trading market for the relevant selected obligation;
- 11:00am in the calculation agent city (the location of which will vary depending on the applicable standard terms for the relevant reference entity);
- 11:00am New York time or 4:00pm London time, whichever is the earlier;[3] and
- 11:00am London time.

(iii)   Quotation method

The quotation method, unless otherwise modified, will be one of bid, offer or mid-market. If none is specified in the relevant confirmation, bid is deemed to apply. In cash settled transactions, details of the quotation method, together with any variation from the ISDA provisions, should be noted in the 'quotation method' subsection.

(iv)   Valuation method

The valuation method for each cash-settled transaction will almost always be one of those set out in the table below. It will normally have been selected at the transaction's outset, depending on the number of reference obligations and valuation dates. Where there is a mismatch between the valuation method in a transaction and the criteria in the table below (eg, where average market has been selected and there is one reference obligation, but only one valuation date), the issue should be referred to the credit event committee to establish whether an agreement to amend the affected transaction should be sought with the applicable counterparty.

Valuation method	Number of reference obligations	Number of valuation dates
Market	One	One
Highest	One	One or multiple
Average market	One	Multiple
Average highest	One	Multiple
Blended market	Multiple	Single
Blended highest	Multiple	Single
Average blended market	Multiple	Multiple
Average blended highest	Multiple	Multiple

---

3   The switch to or from daylight saving time can occur at different times in London and New York and paying additional attention to this provision may be important during these periods.

(v)   *Quotation amount*

Where no quotation amount is detailed in a transaction, the ISDA fallback is $10 million. Significant variations in the quotation amount definition may exist in bespoke cash settled transactions. It is not uncommon to find over 20 variations in the method for ascertaining a quotation amount when preparing a universal spreadsheet for a large credit derivatives portfolio. Details of each quotation amount in cash-settled transactions should be inserted in the 'quotation amount' subsection.

The following are examples of universal spreadsheet summaries of bespoke variations in the 'quotation amount' definition in bespoke cash-settled transactions:

- an amount determined by the calculation agent which is a multiple of $1 million and is no greater than the lesser of $20 million (or its equivalent in the relevant obligation currency) and the reference obligation notional amount;
- an amount equal to the product of $40 million (or its equivalent in the relevant obligation currency) multiplied by the relevant proportion (as set out in the reference portfolio) applicable to the relevant reference obligation;
- the reference obligation calculation amount with respect to the relevant reference obligation divided by three;
- as specified in the reference obligation notice, provided that the aggregate of quotation amount(s) for reference obligation(s) relating to a single reference entity does not exceed the floating rate payer calculation amount; and
- fifty per cent of the reference obligation calculation amount (as set out in the reference portfolio with respect to the reference obligation.

(vi)   *Dealers*

The dealers provision in a cash-settled credit derivative transaction covers the identification and selection of the dealers for valuing a reference obligation. In practice, this provision varies widely and is negotiated between counterparties. It is not uncommon to find upwards of 30 variations of this provision among bespoke trades in a large credit derivatives portfolio. The ISDA fallback provides for the calculation agent to select the dealers in consultation with the parties. These provisions must be carefully summarised in the 'dealers' subsection.

The following are examples of variations in the summaries of the 'dealers' definition in bespoke cash-settled credit derivative transactions:

- The dealers shall be selected by the calculation agent, provided that the seller is one of the selected dealers.
- Five or more dealers shall be selected by the calculation agent from the list set out in the confirmation. Where the calculation agent is selected as one of the dealers, five additional dealers (excluding the calculation agent) must be selected.
- The dealers shall be selected by the calculation agent, provided that the calculation agent selects the buyer as one of the dealers.
- Quotations must be sought from four general dealers (as set out in the confirmation) and a special dealer. A special dealer shall be the portfolio manager or any entity selected by the portfolio manager. If the portfolio manager elects not to act as special dealer or to select a dealer to act as special dealer, the calculation agent shall select an additional general dealer.

The calculation agent shall select five dealers from the list set out in the confirmation provided that no dealer may be selected if it is an affiliate of any of the other dealers set out in the list.

Dealers shall be selected by the calculation agent in consultation with the buyer. The seller may be a dealer only where any requirement to obtain the requisite number of full quotations would also be met without the quotation provided by the seller.

(vii)   *Option to purchase*

Bespoke cash-settled transactions occasionally contain quasi-physical settlement provisions. Where these provisions are present, they must be carefully detailed in the 'option to purchase' subsection and reviewed closely by the relevant trading personnel in the execution team during the settlement process. Example summaries of the types of provision which may be summarised in the universal spreadsheet include the following:

- As soon as the calculation agent obtains the requisite number of quotations, it must notify the seller of the highest quotation obtained. The seller will then have the right (but not the obligation) during the following 30 minutes to provide the calculation agent with a quotation; if its quotation is equal to or higher than the highest bid that the calculation agent has notified, the seller's quotation shall be deemed to be the highest, the buyer shall be obliged to sell and the seller shall be obliged to buy the relevant reference obligation.
- Within one hour of the calculation agent receiving the final quotation necessary to determine the reference obligation's final price (the notification period), the calculation agent shall notify the seller of all the bids obtained. The seller will then have the right, during the following 30-minute period (the seller's quotation period), to provide the calculation agent with a quotation at least equal to the highest quotation obtained (the seller's quotation). If the calculation agent is unable to contact the seller during the notification period or if the seller fails to give the seller's quotation within the seller's quotation period, the seller's right to give its quotation shall cease and the final price shall be determined pursuant to the transaction's valuation method. If the seller provides its quotation, the buyer has the option to sell the relevant reference obligation to the seller.
- The calculation agent shall calculate the final price for the applicable reference obligation and notify it immediately to the seller. During the following 20-minute period, the seller shall have the option to submit a firm quotation itself for the reference obligation. If the seller provides a firm quotation during this period, the buyer has the option to sell the reference obligation to the seller at the price of the seller's firm quotation.

If a transaction contains an 'option to purchase' provision, the relevant clause may run to a number of pages. Accurate summarising of the provision is thus essential.

2.4   Preparation task 2: the contact details database

Individual credit default swaps must normally be triggered in accordance with Section 1.10 of the definitions. The notice can be triggered by post or fax, or by telephone with a notice in writing to follow. It is not market practice to trigger a credit default swap by post.

When reviewing an executed credit default swap, it is not uncommon to find the words 'to be confirmed' entered in the contact details section. When triggering a transaction, time spent tracking down the correct contact details can cause delays, unnecessary pressure and inconvenience for the execution team.

The credit event committee should establish a system which collates counterparties' up-to-date contact details and stores them in a contacts database, which is then updated on a trade-by-trade basis. A resource which may be useful when compiling details is the institutional contact section of ISDA's website, which is available in the member's portal section. This resource, which is subscribed to by many ISDA members, provides contact information for different departments within a institution, such as legal, documentation and settlements – in particular, many members list credit event notice information. All information on the list is checked bi-annually.

As staff may leave from time to time, it is best practice to ensure that each counterparty's contact details set out the name and telephone and fax numbers of the credit derivatives desk or the legal department, rather than the contact details of an individual. This is also true for the contact details that the market participant gives to its counterparties. The credit event committee should also put in place a system to ensure that standard contact details are given for each transaction.

A market participant is likely to want to trigger as many transactions as possible on the same day. As Section 1.10 of the definitions does not allow notices to be given by email, logistically it can be both time consuming and difficult to send out a large number of notices on the same day without committing significant resources. If Section 1.10 is not amended, fax delivery is the most efficient method for sending notices, but this can be problematic as it is not uncommon to find a counterparty's fax machine either busy or out of paper.

The credit event committee should consider carefully whether to agree with its counterparties to amend Section 1.10 of the definitions in its existing and future transactions to allow email delivery of notices. Although email delivery is by far the most efficient method for sending notices, unfortunately it provokes certain difficulties; the credit event committee should thus consider certain issues carefully.

The checklist for agreeing to email as a valid notification mechanism for credit default swap notices is as follows:

- Email notice delivery is practical only between counterparties whose IT systems provide delivery receipts. If this is impossible, the parties should not agree to email notice delivery.
- Where each party's IT system facilitates delivery receipts, the credit event committee should ensure that the relevant counterparty agrees that, although the conditions to settlement are deemed to be met when the relevant email is sent, they will be met only when the party sending the notice receives a

delivery receipt. The credit event committee should also ensure that the relevant counterparty is willing to agree that if a delivery receipt is not received, this should not invalidate the relevant notice, but should oblige the party sending the notice also to notify the relevant addressee(s) by fax.

- The designated email address (which is entered into the contacts database) should not be the name of an individual, but a general mailbox monitored by members of the execution team.

If these issues can be resolved, best practice is to enter into a deed with each counterparty setting out that, notwithstanding anything to the contrary in any existing transaction, notices may be delivered by email. The deed should also set out that the parties agree that, in all future transactions, Section 1.10 of the definitions will be interpreted to allow delivery of notices by email in accordance with the deed.

2.5   Preparation task 3: credit event monitoring – appointing watch team and creating watch list

The credit event committee must establish a watch team to compile, maintain and monitor a watch list of the reference entities that it believes are most likely to suffer a credit event. This team should consist of two to three junior back office and/or legal department personnel. The watch team should perform their allocated tasks as part of their general duties. The team will be responsible for monitoring the press, reference entity ratings and reference entity credit spreads for evidence of when a potential credit event occurs or is likely to occur,

If a reference entity's credit spread widens beyond a certain preset limit, it should automatically be placed on the watch list. At the same time, certain subscription services should be procured to monitor the press and provide any articles where a relevant reference entity is referred to in connection with certain keywords (eg, bankruptcy and default). Of particular use to the team may be the Markit RED reference entity subscription database which pools information on:

- the current legal existence of traded reference entities;
- their correct names;
- existing reference obligations; and
- the contractual relationship between reference entities and their reference obligations.

The database also provides a numbering system for reference entities and reference obligations with Cusip Services Bureau, which has been enhanced through a partnership with Standard & Poor's which integrates Reference Entity Link – a product linking reference entities in the Markit database – with Standard Poor's information on credit quality

The watch team will keep the credit event committee informed of potential credit events; the committee will have overall control of the criteria for placing a reference entity on the watch list and of which reference entities are present on the list.

2.6   Preparation task 4: preparing a battle plan

The credit event committee will draft a 'battle plan'. The plan will detail how the credit event process will work from the moment when a credit event on a reference entity has been suspected or confirmed to when the final notice has been sent, the cash settlement amount paid or the deliverable obligation transferred. Once a credit event has been confirmed, the credit event process will be run on a day-to-day basis by the execution team, which will be responsible for:

- drafting and sending notices;
- ensuring that the conditions to settlement have been met;
- sourcing deliverable obligations;
- selecting and valuing reference obligations; and
- managing the whole process.

The credit event committee and the execution team will ensure that template documentation is drafted for each type of notice possible in the portfolio.

The battle plan should cover seven separate (but consecutive) periods, each encompassing a clearly defined stage of the credit event process (see diagram on pages 512-3). These stages are as follows:

- Stage 1: the event determination period – the credit event committee determines whether a credit event has occurred and whether it is likely to wish to trigger any affected transactions; the execution team fine-tunes the necessary template documentation.
- Stage 2: the event planning period – the credit event committee ensures that each function required to be carried out during the credit event process is adequately covered and that all parties in the credit event committee and the execution team understand their roles.
- Stage 3: the event spreadsheet population period – each transaction affected by the relevant reference entity is determined; the relevant transactions from the universal spreadsheet are extracted to create an event spreadsheet, and those which will be dealt with through alternative methods (eg, an index protocol or net settlement agreement) are collated into a separate spreadsheet.
- Stage 4: the transactions selection period – the credit event committee determines which of the affected transactions it wishes to trigger.
- Stage 5: the trigger period – the execution team ensures that the conditions to settlement are met for each selected transaction.
- Stage 6: the settlement period – the credit event committee and the execution team select the relevant deliverable obligations and reference obligations; the execution team ensures that:
  - each deliverable obligation for a physically settled transaction is correctly delivered or received;
  - each cash settlement payment is correctly made or received; and
  - any loss determination amounts are correctly recorded.
- Stage 7: the wrap-up period – the execution team ensures that all documentation is correctly archived and reports back to the credit event committee that each affected transaction has been dealt with in the correct manner.

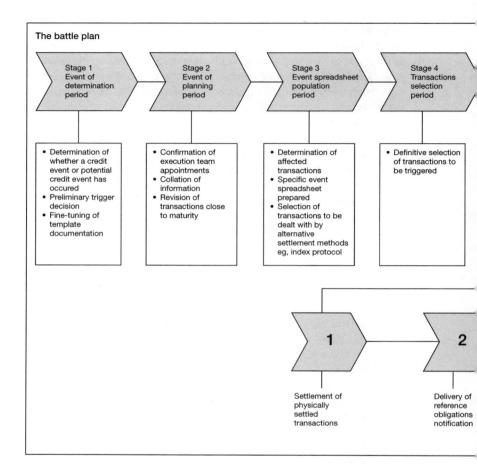

3. Phase 2: the battle plan in action

The fine details of what the battle plan contains and how it works in practice are best described by setting out on a step-by-step basis how the plan would work if a credit event or potential credit event occurred.

3.1 Stage 1: event determination period

If, in the course of its monitoring activities, the watch team identifies a potential credit event, it must provide the credit event committee with sufficient information to establish whether a credit event, potential failure to pay or potential repudiation/moratorium event has occurred and whether the conditions to settlement of each, or any, affected transaction can be met.

The ease with which the credit event committee can make these decisions will depend on the credit event and its circumstances and the quality of the information provided by the watch team.

Bankruptcy is often the easiest credit event to establish, not only because of its concrete nature, but also because it is the most likely event to be widely reported. For

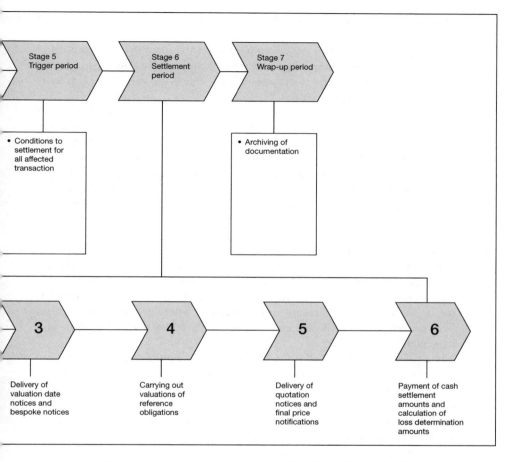

example, when Parmalat SpA was declared insolvent before the Parma Bankruptcy Court on December 27 2003, not only was this event widely reported, but it was clear that a bankruptcy credit event had occurred pursuant to Section 4(1) of the 2003 Definitions.[4] However, cases involving a restructuring credit event relating to a syndicated loan agreement may not be so straightforward to establish, especially if the relevant parties are bound by a confidentiality agreement[5] and the restructuring is not widely reported.

3.2 Stage 2: event planning period

Once the credit event committee has decided that a credit event, potential failure to pay or potential repudiation/moratorium has occurred, it will have a kick-off meeting

---

4   Likewise with the significant credit events of 2005, when Winn Dixie, Delta Airlines, Northwest Airlines, Collins & Aikman, Delphi and Calpine Corporation filed for Chapter 11 bankruptcy.

5   Many of ISDA's initiatives (eg, the restructuring supplement, the successor supplement and the convertible exchangeable and accreting obligations supplements) were published in response to perceived weaknesses in the settlement process.

with the execution team to review the battle plan and ensure that all responsibilities are correctly allocated.

At this stage, the credit event committee should also adapt the template form of credit event notice and notice of publicly available information into a specific event template to reflect the current credit event. These notices can then be used, as far as possible, in all affected transactions.

The credit event committee should also collate two public sources of publicly available information[6] confirming the credit event's occurrence. It is best practice, unless otherwise required, to select the same publicly available information for all transactions. Usually, the notice of publicly available information is incorporated directly into the credit event notice and the public sources are attached to the back of the notice. This must be prepared as soon as possible after confirmation that a credit event has occurred and that the credit event committee is likely to trigger any of the affected transactions.

3.3   Stage 3: event spreadsheet population period

The execution team will source an 'event spreadsheet' covering all the affected transactions. The event spreadsheet will draw its information from the universal spreadsheet. Those transactions which will be dealt with through alternative methods (eg, an index protocol or net settlement agreement) will be collated into a separate 'mass settlement' spreadsheet; the settlement of these transactions will be dealt with separately.

The execution team must highlight to the credit event committee any transactions in the event spreadsheet which are close to maturity. This is particularly important where the relevant potential credit event involves a potential failure to pay or a potential repudiation/moratorium.

If any affected transactions fall into these categories, the credit event committee must be prepared to act quickly to decide:

- which transactions to trigger;
- whether any further action (eg, the delivery of a repudiation/moratorium extension notice) is required; or
- whether a potential failure to pay is applicable.

This will provide additional time to trigger a transaction and may prevent credit protection being lost.

3.4   Stage 4: the selection period

The credit event committee will use the event spreadsheet to decide which transactions to trigger. It may decide to trigger all affected transactions, although

---

6   Standard requirements are for two public sources of publicly available information selected from the 2003 Definitions fallbacks of leading financial newspapers, publications and subscription services such as Bloomberg, *The Financial Times* and *The Wall Street Journal*, or the main source of business news in the reference entity's relevant jurisdiction or in an internationally recognised news source. Some bespoke transactions may have different requirements for the number of public sources and type of publicly available information. These requirements will be identified in the event spreadsheet and will be dealt with separately by the credit event committee at this point.

business sensitivities with certain clients or the occurrence of a 'soft' credit event (ie, an event which is likely to generate a high final price, such as that following a restructuring entered into by the reference entity for cash flow reasons) may lead the credit event committee not to trigger all of the affected transactions. In the case of a soft credit event, the credit event committee may decide to trigger only transactions which it has entered into as buyer.

The transactions that the credit event committee agrees to trigger will be compiled by the execution team into a 'trigger list'. The execution team will also prepare a 'potential receipt list' detailing each transaction in which the market participant may be triggered by its counterparties.[7] The trigger list and the potential receipt list should then be merged to make a revised event spreadsheet. The execution team will also prepare a trigger schedule, which will take the form of a calendar and state the date on which each transaction is to be triggered; this may be a single date or, for larger credit events, multiple dates. The trigger schedule will be incorporated into an event calendar, which will also contain other calendars (eg, a valuation date notice/bespoke notice calendar and a reference obligation notification calendar).

3.5 Stage 5: the trigger period

The execution team will prepare the necessary notices to trigger each selected transaction, based on the event template notices prepared during the first stage. The notices will ensure that in each case, all of the conditions to settlement are met and will trigger each transaction in accordance with the trigger schedule.

The execution team's legal representatives should have sufficient experience of the variety of formats that credit derivative transactions structures can take; they must take additional care where a credit derivative transaction is either a structured transaction itself or part of a structured transaction.

In the case of credit-linked notes, the execution team's legal representative must conclude whether the credit event is triggered under the terms of the notes themselves or under the credit default swap only. If the credit event is triggered under the credit default swap, a 'receipt of default swap credit event notice' may have to be given to the noteholders, the trustee and others. If the credit default swap is a managed credit default swap, notice may also be required to be given to the relevant manager.

The legal representative must also look at CDO-squared transactions carefully. The overlying reference portfolio will contain (perhaps together with asset-backed security assets) individual underlying credit default swaps. The relevant reference entities will be located in these underlying credit default swaps; consequently, it is the underlying credit default swaps[8] which must be triggered. The overlying portfolio will be

---

7   This list will include all of the transactions where the entity not only has sold credit protection, but also has bought credit protection and the seller is a notifying party. The seller is likely to trigger a transaction where it has entered into a back-to-back transaction, and the final price is likely to be high and the seller fears that there may be future credit events which will bring a lower final price.

8   In some CDO-squared transactions, the underlying swaps will be hypothetical swaps which are deemed to be entered into (eg, between a notional buyer and seller). To get around the problem of physically triggering a hypothetical credit default swap, it is common to set out the notice provisions in the overlying swap. Typically, these may involve one of the parties to the overlying swap or the calculation agent sending the relevant notice addressed to the hypothetical buyer or seller and copying in the other parties.

triggered only if, following a relevant valuation date, its attachment point has been reached. Some transactions also contain a sub-portfolio beneath the underlying swaps (ie, a second-level portfolio). An affected reference entity may be contained in several of the underlying swaps, as well as the second-level portfolio. It is acceptable to trigger all of the affected underlying swaps and/or the second-level portfolio by using a single notice.

As mentioned above, the resulting settlement caused by the credit event in the underlying credit default swap may cause a credit event to occur in relation to the overlying credit default swap. This can be definitively established only after the relevant valuation date for the underlying credit default swap has occurred. If the conditions to settlement in the overlying credit default swap are met and the notifying party wishes to trigger the transaction, the party must also deliver:

- the relevant credit event notice;
- the notice of publicly available information; and
- the notice of physical settlement for the overlying credit default swap (if applicable).

As the relevant losses will already have been established, there will be no further valuation date; any cash settlement payment will take place in accordance with the terms of the documentation.

In credit-linked notes and CDO transactions involving a portfolio of reference entities, the time period relating to a credit event settlement process may stretch across two interest periods. In each case where this occurs, the legal representative in the execution team must analyse the relevant transaction documents to determine whether there should be any reduction in interest payments at the next interest payment date under the notes. This is likely to occur only where the credit event may potentially cause a nominal amount reduction of the notes. For example, the documentation may assume that, where a credit event has occurred before an interest payment date and the relevant valuation date will not occur until after that interest payment date, the price of the affected reference obligation will be deemed to be 0%. Consequently, noteholders will be paid an additional amount of interest at the following interest payment date if the final price of the affected reference obligation turns out to be higher than 0%. The relevant legal representative in the execution team must communicate this information to the settlements department to ensure that no overpayments are made to noteholders.

3.6   Stage 6: settlement period

The settlement period can be divided into the following sub-stages:

- settlement of physically settled transactions;
- delivery of reference obligation notifications;
- delivery of valuation date notices and other bespoke notices;
- carrying out valuations of reference obligations;
- delivery of quotation notices and final price notifications; and
- payment of cash settlement amounts and recording of loss determination amounts.

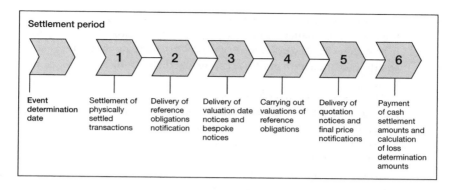

Not all sub-stages will apply to all transactions. Moreover, there will be some overlap between some of the sub-stages – for example, for plain vanilla cash settled credit default swaps, no reference obligation notifications will be required, as the reference obligation will be stated in the credit default swap and the physical and cash settlement stages will be exclusive to each relevant type of transaction.[9]

Likewise, a valuation date and related cash settlement in a vanilla cash settled credit default swap will take place before the delivery of a deliverable obligation in a physically settled credit default swap. For more complex bespoke transactions (to which the most resources must be dedicated), the sub-stages will follow each other in sequence.

(a) **Sub-stage 1: settlement of physically settled transactions**

The credit event committee and the execution team must ensure that, for each physically settled transaction that the market participant intends to trigger, a notice of physical settlement is sent out within the relevant time limit, which is usually the ISDA fallback of 30 calendar days following the delivery of the credit event notice. Failure to meet this condition to settlement will result in credit protection being lost.

Before delivering the notice of physical settlement, the execution team must select the deliverable obligation to be delivered to the seller. The choice may be straightforward where a specific deliverable obligation is detailed in the relevant confirmation or where credit protection was sought in relation to securities which the market participant actually owned. The execution team must ensure that the deliverable obligation:

- meets all of the deliverable obligation categories and deliverable obligation characteristics detailed in the relevant transaction documentation; and
- is available.

In the case of affected transactions on the potential receipt list, if the buyer has problems obtaining the deliverable obligation, the execution team must inform the credit event committee, which must then consider authorising buy-in procedures. If

---

9   Except in relation to certain hybrid transactions involving both cash and physical settlement. These transactions will be highlighted in the event spreadsheet and should be dealt with separately.

the market participant itself encounters problems sourcing a deliverable obligation, the credit event committee must be prepared for the counterparty to invoke the buy-in procedures detailed in Section 9 of the 2003 Definitions; the credit event committee and the execution team must also ensure that there is sufficient expertise to deal with these.

Moreover, the credit event committee must ensure that appropriate systems are in place to ensure that, in transactions where it has sold protection, any deliverable obligation can be physically received and, once received, a decision can be made quickly as to whether to continue to hold the deliverable obligation, sell it into the open market or use it as a deliverable obligation in a corresponding transaction.

The execution team must monitor any transactions in which it has received a credit event notice and confirm whether any notice of physical settlement has been delivered within the 30 calendar-day period. The execution team should also confirm that any deliverable obligation delivered by a counterparty meets the criteria for deliverable obligations set out in the credit default swap confirmation.

(b)   ***Sub-stage 2: delivery of reference obligation notifications***
In cash settled transactions where the reference obligation is not disclosed in the transaction documentation, the seller must usually deliver a reference obligation notification to its counterparty on or before the valuation date. The reference obligation notification discloses the identity of the reference obligation that will be valued on the valuation date.

The credit event committee is likely to have a choice of obligations and must bear in mind that not all of the reference entity's obligations will be trading at the same price; for example, some obligations may be secured and others may not. The credit event committee will most likely select the reference obligation trading at the lowest price, unless it is hedging a particular obligation.

As the trading prices of different reference obligations may vary during the post-event determination date period, the relevant prices must be constantly monitored before the commencement of each transaction's valuation process. It will usually be best practice to decide the identity of each reference obligation as close to the relevant valuation date as possible, unless:

- there are very limited choices of reference obligations;
- it is clear which obligation will have the lowest price; or
- a particular obligation is being hedged.

(c)   ***Sub-stage 3: delivery of valuation date notices and other bespoke notices***
In certain bespoke transactions where the calculation agent or seller has discretion as to which date to select for any valuation date, it must give prior notice to one or both counterparties. Where the credit derivative is embedded into a structured note, notice must sometimes be given to other parties to the transaction (eg, a manager, the trustee, agents and noteholders).

Any transactions having these or other bespoke requirements will be highlighted in the event spreadsheet. It is best practice to have a valuation date and bespoke notice calendar which details the dates on which these notices should be sent. The valuation date notice/bespoke notice calendar will form part of and be incorporated into the event calendar.

(d)   *Sub-stage 4: carrying out valuations of reference obligations*

As discussed above, market participants which have bought or sold credit protection through a range of products will find that their transactions have a variety of valuation date provisions. Some valuation dates will be on a specific day, while others will be within a range of dates; some transactions will have multiple valuation dates.

The execution team will calculate the fixed valuation dates (eg, 50 New York business days after the event determination date) and select the other dates from within the available range (eg, any date as selected by the calculation agent which is between 30 and 50 TARGET settlement days after the event determination date). The execution team should prepare a valuation date schedule which, like the valuation date notice/bespoke notice calendar, will be incorporated into the event calendar. The valuation date schedule will act as a calendar to aid the execution team in valuing the applicable reference obligation.

The overall valuation period can last a number of months. Even though the ISDA fallback for a valuation date is to have a single valuation date fall five business days after the event determination date, it is not uncommon in bespoke transactions to have valuation dates falling as much as 140 New York, London and Tokyo business days after the event determination date, which means the valuation process can last up to eight months.

(e)   *Sub-stage 5: delivery of quotation notices and final price notifications*

Unless otherwise stated in the relevant transaction, where there are multiple valuation dates a quotation notice should be sent out on each valuation date (except for the final valuation date, where a final price notification is sent out). Where there is a single valuation date, only a final price notification must be sent on the valuation date. The execution team will be responsible for preparing, distributing and drafting these notices on the basis of the template documentation.

Not all cash-settled transactions require payment of a cash settlement amount (eg, in a portfolio credit default swap where the aggregate of loss determination amounts has yet to cross the relevant threshold or the attachment point of a synthetic CDO transaction has yet to be reached). In this case the execution team must calculate the loss determination amount and, possibly, any aggregate loss determination amount. The final price notification will also set out any cash settlement amount payable or loss determination amount calculated.

(f)   *Sub-stage 6: payment of cash settlement amounts and recording of loss determination amounts*

The execution team must monitor that each cash settlement payment due is received and that each payment owed is actually paid; with this in mind, it is important to ensure that correct account details are exchanged between the parties when any transaction is executed.

The relevant trading personnel in the execution team must ensure that all loss determination amounts are correctly reflected in information systems covering each relevant affected transaction.

3.7 Stage 7: wrap-up

Once the final valuation date and settlement payment have been made or received and all loss determination amounts have been recorded, the execution team should carry out a further diligence review to ensure that all notices and correspondence have been accurately recorded and that all transactions have been correctly triggered. Once this has been completed, the execution team will be demobilised and await the next credit event.

The credit event process may take several months to complete; sometimes, credit events affecting the same transactions overlap with each other (eg, several credit events involving US automobile parts manufacturers occurring in the last quarter of 2005 and the first quarter of 2006). Where this occurs, a well-organised credit event management structure will also help to limit confusion between credit events.

4. Hypothetical case study of a well-managed credit event

The hypothetical case study earlier in this chapter focused on the potential problems which may arise when a market participant which possesses a large and diverse portfolio of credit derivative transactions and no credit event management strategy is affected by a major credit event. The hypothetical case study below focuses on how the same market participant would manage a major credit event if it later put in place all the infrastructure and planning suggested in this chapter.

4.1 Czarnocki launches a credit event strategy

Czarnocki was shocked to discover the extent of its losses for the Ropemaker Corporation credit event. The board realised that, considering the amount of transactions in its credit derivatives portfolio, Ropemaker Corporation was unlikely to be the last major credit event to hit the portfolio.

The board decided to take action and, in consultation with outside legal counsel, established a robust credit event management strategy. The first step was to appoint a credit event committee to establish a process to manage future credit events. This committee consisted of four officers:

- a legal officer (a lawyer from the legal department);
- a risk officer (a representative from the credit default swap trading operations group);
- a treasury officer (a representative from the treasury department); and
- a watch officer (a member of the legal department responsible for monitoring various sources for potential credit events).

The credit event committee agreed to set up the following pointed strategy to create the infrastructure for dealing with future credit events affecting the portfolio:

- establish an execution team;
- create a universal spreadsheet;
- create a contacts database;

- establish a watch team and create a watch list; and
- establish a battle plan.

(a) Establishing the execution team

The credit event committee appointed the execution team, which consisted of:

- the legal officer;
- a partner from an outside law firm, Leadenhalls (to which the creation and maintenance of the universal spreadsheet was outsourced); and
- two members of the derivatives middle office team, who were allocated responsibility for valuing and selecting reference obligations in future credit events.

(b) Creating a universal spreadsheet

Transaction identification	Transaction identifier Counterparty Transaction type Buyer or seller?
Credit events/settlement method/definitions	Credit events Method of settlement 1999/2003 or other definitions applicable
Notifications	Conditions to settlement Notice of physical settlement Valuation date notice Reference obligation notification Final price notification Other notices under default swap Other notices under notes /other agreement Notifying party
Cash settlement/ valuation provisions	Valuation dates Valuation time Quotation method Valuation method Quotation amount Dealers Option to purchase Calculation agent city Calculation agent

Leadenhalls prepared the universal spreadsheet, which revealed that Czarnocki had entered into:

- 500 single-name credit default swaps;
- 56 single-name credit-linked notes;

- 112 portfolio credit default swaps (including 58 transactions linked to iTraxx); and
- 18 CDO transactions (including four CDO-squared transactions).

In 50 of the transactions Czarnocki had sold credit protection; in the rest of the transactions, it had bought it. Ten of the transactions where Czarnocki had sold credit protection involved intermediary swaps, where Czarnocki had also bought credit protection to take advantage of an arbitrage in the prices that it was able to buy and sell credit protection.

(c)   *Creating a contacts database*
Once the universal spreadsheet was finalised and all of the relevant transaction documentation was saved onto an accessible database, the execution team prepared a central database of contacts to create a contacts database listing up-to-date contact details for all counterparties. Sourcing the information for the database took time and resources, as the execution team found that the contact details section in many of its credit default swaps had been left blank.

(d)   *Establishing a watch team and creating a watch list*
The credit event committee established a watch team (consisting of three junior members of the legal department supervised by the credit event committee's watch officer) to monitor potential credit events. The watch team sourced a global list of all of the reference entities in Czarnocki's portfolio, which the watch team updated each time that credit protection was bought or sold on a new reference entity. In particular, a subscription for the Markit RED reference entity subscription database was procured to assist in this process.

The global list was passed to a press cuttings agency. The agency was instructed to search press databases (including the reference entities' own websites) daily for any mention of the reference entities in relation to certain keywords such as bond, loan, debt, bankruptcy and moratorium. The watch committee also monitored the websites of ISDA, iTraxx and each of the main ratings agencies for any mention of potential or actual credit events, as well as certain trade subscription services to check whether reference entity credit spreads widened beyond preset levels. Should any reference entity cause concern, the watch team was instructed to:

- alert the credit event committee;
- place the relevant reference entity on a watch list; and
- carry out an enhanced level of supervision on the reference entity.

(e)   *Establishing a battle plan*
The credit event committee drafted a battle plan in line with the procedures and processes set out in this chapter, which would act as the roadmap for dealing with all future credit events affecting the portfolio.

The battle plan was divided into seven stages:

- Stage 1 – the event determination period;
- Stage 2 – the event planning period;

- Stage 3 – the event spreadsheet population period;
- Stage 4 – the transactions selection period;
- Stage 5 – the trigger period;
- Stage 6 – the settlement period; and
- Stage 7 – the wrap-up period.

Stage 6 was further divided into the following sub-stages:
- Sub-stage 1 – settlement of physically settled transactions;
- Sub-stage 2 – delivery of reference obligation notifications;
- Sub-stage 3 – delivery of valuation date notices and other bespoke notices;
- Sub-stage 4 – carrying out valuations of reference obligations;
- Sub-stage 5 – delivery of quotation notices and final price notifications; and
- Sub-stage 6 – payment of cash settlement amounts and recording of loss determination amounts.

Czarnocki now had a robust credit event management process in place and was safe in the knowledge that it was well prepared for the next credit event.

4.2 First credit event to test the structure: Linean Republic declares a debt moratorium

(a) Stage 1: event determination period

On November 14 2006 a military coup occurred in the previously stable and progressive Linean Republic, a small but very prosperous Central African state and a widely traded sovereign reference entity. Shortly after, the newly appointed Marxist minister of finance declared a moratorium on all of the republic's international bonds and loans.

The watch team became immediately aware of the credit event when an extract from *The Financial Times* reporting the incident was sent to it by the press cuttings agency.

The watch team carried out further diligence on the incident, collated further publicly available information and reported to the credit event committee that it believed that a potential credit event had occurred. The credit event committee's legal officer then reviewed all of this information.

The legal officer decided that a potential repudiation/moratorium event had occurred pursuant to Section 4.6(c) of the 2003 Definitions. In addition, the legal officer was able to confirm that, in view of the reported political situation, it was highly likely that a failure to pay credit event would occur in the next month or so, as soon as the next interest payments under the republic's obligations became due.

(b) Stage 2: event planning period

The credit event committee reconfirmed the appointments of the personnel in the standing execution team and 'mobilised' it onto a 'war footing'. The credit event committee also ensured that enough additional personnel were allocated to the execution team to cover the credit event adequately and that all personnel had had sufficient training.

All members of the credit event committee and execution team then had a kick-off meeting to launch the credit event process. The credit event committee had already ruled that, in view of the credit event committee's legal officer's report, an actual repudiation/moratorium credit event and failure to pay credit event were inevitable, and that, as far as possible, the battle plan would proceed as if the credit event had already occurred.

(c)   *Stage 3: event spreadsheet population period*
During the kick-off meeting, the credit event committee instructed the execution team to prepare an event spreadsheet. Once prepared, the event spreadsheet revealed that the following transactions had the republic as a reference entity:

- 17 single-name credit default swaps;
- five single-name credit-linked notes;
- 45 credit portfolio credit default swaps (including 20 iTraxx transactions);
- nine CDO transactions; and
- all four CDO-squared transactions.

All in all, 60 transactions were affected. In 55 of these, Czarnocki had sold credit protection; in five (which were each part of intermediary swap transactions), it had bought credit protection.

The spreadsheet also revealed that five credit derivative transactions which referenced the republic were due to mature in the next two weeks. The republic had a number of eurobonds and syndicated loans outstanding, and the first interest payment date of any of these obligations was not for another three weeks.

A repudiation/moratorium credit event requires both a repudiation/moratorium to take place and an actual failure to pay. As these five credit derivative transactions would mature before any actual failure to pay, the credit event committee had to act quickly so as not to lose the benefit of credit protection.

The event spreadsheet revealed that each of the five affected transactions had selected 'repudiation/moratorium extension condition', as applicable; therefore, if Czarnocki delivered a repudiation/moratorium extension notice to each relevant seller, it would have a further 60 days after the scheduled maturity date for the actual failure to pay to occur (in the case of a loan) and the later of 60 days after the maturity date and the bond's first scheduled payment date (in the case of bond).

The execution team's legal officer drafted a repudiation/moratorium extension notice incorporating a notice of publicly available information with two public sources, using one of the precedents already drafted. The credit event committee then approved the repudiation/moratorium extension notices, which were sent to the relevant sellers.

Four weeks later (on December 11 2006), the republic failed to make an interest payment on a $300 million floating rate note due 2010. Once again, this was immediately picked up by the watch committee in press articles sent to it by the press agency, and reported to the credit event committee. At this point, the credit event committee's legal officer concluded that both a repudiation/moratorium credit event and a failure to pay credit event had occurred.

```
                                                    CZARNOCKI PLC
                                                    894 Ulica Grzybowska
                                                    Warsaw
                                                    Poland

        Date:          16 November 2006

        To:            Tavira PLC

        Re:            Linean Republic Potential Repudiation/Moratorium

        Attention:     The Directors

        Email:         creditevents@tavira.com

              REPUDIATION/MORATORIUM EXTENTION NOTICE  AND NOTICE OF PUBLICLY AVAILABLE
                                        INFORMATION

        Credit Derivative Transaction Details
        Our Reference: H98234739. Trade Date: 6 October 2004. Effective Date: 18 October 2004.  Reference
        Entity: The Linean Republic. (the "Affected Reference Entity").

        Reference is made to the Credit Derivative Transaction described above (the "Transaction") between you
        and us. Capitalised terms used and not otherwise defined in this letter shall have the meanings given
        them in the confirmation of the Transaction.

        This letter is our Repudiation/Moratorium Extension Notice to you that a Potential Repudiation/Moratorium
        occurred with respect to the Affected Reference Entity on 17 November 2006, when the minister of
        finance of the Affected Reference Entity declared a moratorium on payments of all of the Affected
        Reference Entity 's international bonds and loans.  This letter also comprises our Notice of Publicly
        Available Information with respect to the Potential Moratorium/Repudiation, we provide the Publicly
        Available Information attached hereto.

        Nothing in this letter shall be construed of a waiver of any rights we may have with respect to the
        Transaction.

        Yours faithfully,
        For and on behalf of


        CzarnockiPLC

        By: _____      By: _____
        Name:                        Name:
        Title: Authorised Signatory  Title: Authorised Signatory
```

(d) *Stage 4: transactions selection period*

The credit event committee decided that it would trigger a repudiation/moratorium credit event for the five transactions whose scheduled maturity date had passed, and a failure to pay credit event for all other transactions that it wished to trigger.

The credit event committee decided to trigger 55 affected transactions immediately. For the five transactions which were part of intermediary swap transactions, Czarnocki had to wait for the conditions to settlement to be met for the transactions where it had sold credit protection before it triggered the transactions where it had bought credit protection. Five further transactions were with a counterparty which was on the verge of entering into some very lucrative business with Czarnocki; the credit event committee, following submissions from its risk officer, decided not to trigger those transactions so as not to cause any harm to the client relationship.

The credit event committee established two public sources of publicly available information (an article from Bloomberg and an article from *The Wall Street Journal*) for each of the repudiation/moratorium credit event transactions and the failure to pay credit event transactions from information provided by the watch team.

The credit event committee then prepared two forms of credit event notice: one for the repudiation/moratorium credit event and one for the failure to pay credit event. Both forms of notice incorporated a notice of publicly available information.

At the same time, the credit event committee prepared and approved template forms for all the notices, which would be sent under the transactions which it had decided to trigger.

These forms of notices included:

- a notice of physical settlement;
- a reference obligation notification;
- a valuation date notice;
- a quotation notice; and
- a final price notification.

(e)   **Stage 5: trigger period**

The credit event committee selected December 20 2006 as the event determination date for the transactions that it wished to trigger. Each credit event notice was prepared and checked by the execution team and sent by fax or, where previously agreed, by email during the course of that day.

CZARNOCKI PLC
894 Ulica Grzybowska
Warsaw
Poland

Date: 20 December 2006

To: Tavira PLC

Re: Linean Republic Repudiation/Moratorium Credit Event

Attention: The Directors

Email: creditevents@tavira.com

CREDIT EVENT NOTICE AND NOTICE OF PUBLICLY AVAILABLE INFORMATION

Credit Derivative Transaction Details
Our Reference: H98234739. Trade Date: 6 October 2004. Effective Date: 18 October 2004. Reference Entity: The Linean Republic. (the "**Affected Reference Entity**").

Reference is made to the Credit Derivative Transaction described above (the "**Transaction**") between you and us and the Repudiation/Moratorium Extension Notice delivered by us to you on 11 November 2006. Capitalised terms used and not otherwise defined in this letter shall have the meanings given them in the confirmation of the Transaction.

This letter is our Credit Event Notice to you that a Repudiation/Moratorium Credit Event occurred with respect to the Affected Reference Entity on 11 December 2006, when following the Potential Repudiation/Moratorium described in the Repudiation Moratorium Extension Notice a Failure to Pay occurred in relation to an outstanding issue of U.S.$300,000,000 Floating Rate Notes due 2010 issued by the Reference Entity. This letter also comprises our Notice of Publicly Available Information with respect to the Credit Event, we provide the Publicly Available Information attached hereto.

Nothing in this letter shall be construed of a waiver of any rights we may have with respect to the Transaction.

Yours faithfully,
For and on behalf of

CzarnockiPLC

By: _____   By: _____
Name: Name:
Title: Authorised Signatory   Title: Authorised Signatory

```
                                            CZARNOCKI PLC
                                            894 Ulica Grzybowska
                                            Warsaw
                                            Poland

Date:         20 December 2006

To:           Alameda Corporation

Re:           Linean Republic Failure to Pay Credit Event

Attention:    The Directors

Email:        creditevents@alameda.com

         CREDIT EVENT NOTICE AND NOTICE OF PUBLICLY AVAILABLE INFORMATION

Credit Derivative Transaction Details

Our Reference: J15673473. Trade Date: 7 June 2005. Effective Date: 28 June 2005. Reference Entity:
The Linean Republic. (the "Affected Reference Entity").

Reference is made to the Credit Derivative Transaction described above (the "Transaction") between you
and us. Capitalised terms used and not otherwise defined in this letter shall have the meanings given
them in the confirmation of the Transaction.

This letter is our Credit Event Notice to you that a Failure to Pay Credit Event occurred with respect to the
Affected Reference Entity on 11 December 2006, when a Failure to Pay in relation to an outstanding issue
of U.S.$300,000,000 Floating Rate Notes due 2010 issued by the Reference Entity occurred on 11
December 2006. This letter also comprises our Notice of Publicly Available Information with respect to the
Credit Event, we provide the Publicly Available Information attached hereto.

Nothing in this letter shall be construed of a waiver of any rights we may have with respect to the
Transaction.

Yours faithfully,
For and on behalf of


Czarnocki PLC

By: _____      By: _____
Name:                          Name:
Title: Authorised Signatory    Title: Authorised Signatory
```

On December 24 2006 Czarnocki received credit event notices in relation to the five intermediary swap transactions where it has sold credit protection. The execution team checked that the conditions to settlement had been met and, within two hours of receipt of these notices, was able to send corresponding credit event notices in the transactions where it had bought credit protection.

(f)   Stage 6: settlement period

The execution team was aware that the sixth stage consisted of the following sub-stages:

- Sub-stage 1 – settlement of physically settled transactions;
- Sub-stage 2 – delivery of reference obligation notifications;
- Sub-stage 3 – delivery of valuation date notices and other bespoke notices;
- Sub-stage 4 – carrying out valuations of reference obligations;
- Sub-stage 5 – delivery of quotation notices and final price notifications; and
- Sub-stage 6 – payment of cash settlement amounts and calculation of loss determination amounts.

In the days running up to December 20 2006, the execution team prepared an event calendar which set out the key dates for each transaction and incorporated the dates on which valuation date notices, bespoke notices and reference obligation notifications were to be sent out, as well as the valuation date window and/or the date of each valuation date as and when it was selected.

(i)   *Sub-stage 1: settlement of physically settled transactions*
The credit event committee and the execution team compared the prices of the available deliverable obligations of the republic and selected the lowest-priced obligation available. The execution team then confirmed that this obligation met the deliverable obligation category and characteristics for each physically settled transaction.

The execution team then prepared and sent a notice of physical settlement for each physically settled transaction within the 30 calendar-day time limit and delivered each deliverable obligation to the relevant seller.

CZARNOCKI PLC
894 Ulica Grzybowska
Warsaw
Poland

Date: 3 January 2007

To: Alameda Corporation

Re: Linean Republic Failure to Pay Credit Event

Attention: The Directors

Email: creditevents@alameda.com

NOTICE OF PHYSICAL SETTLEMENT

Credit Derivative Transaction Details
Our Reference: J15673473. Trade Date: 7 June 2005. Effective Date: 28 June 2005. Reference Entity: The Linean Republic. (the "**Affected Reference Entity**").

Reference is made to the Credit Derivative Transaction described above (the "**Transaction**") between you and us and to the Credit Event Notice and Notice of Publicly Available Information dated 20 December 2006 previously delivered to you. Capitalised terms used and not otherwise defined in this letter shall have the meanings given them in the confirmation of the Transaction.

This letter constitutes a Notice of Physical Settlement. We hereby confirm that we will settle the Transaction and require performance by you in accordance with the Physical Settlement Method. Subject to the terms of the Transaction, we will deliver to you on or before the Physical Settlement Date, U.S.$10,00,000 of U.S.$300,000,000 Floating Rate Notes due 2010 (ISIN: XS10439584) issued by the Affected Reference Entity.

Nothing in this letter shall be construed of a waiver of any rights we may have with respect to the Transaction.

Yours faithfully,
For and on behalf of

CzarnockiPLC

By: _____   By: _____
Name: Name:
Title: Authorised Signatory   Title: Authorised Signatory

(ii)   *Sub-stage 2: delivery of reference obligation notifications*
The event spreadsheet identified 24 cash settled transactions in which the identity of the reference obligation was not identified in the transaction documentation. The

credit event committee and the execution team compared the trading price of the various obligations of the republic and selected that with the lowest price. This was the floating rate note due 2010 which caused the failure to pay credit event to occur.

The execution team confirmed that the selected reference obligation met the relevant criteria set out in the transaction documentation. The execution team then prepared reference obligation notifications for each of the 24 transactions on the basis of the template and sent these to the relevant seller within the timeframe set out in the transaction documentation.

CZARNOCKI PLC
894 Ulica Grzybowska
Warsaw
Poland

Date: 20 February 2007

To: Tavira PLC

Re: Linean Republic Repudiation/Moratorium Credit Event

Attention: The Directors

Email: creditevents@tavira.com

REFERENCE OBLIGATION NOTIFICATION

Credit Derivative Transaction Details
Our Reference: H98234739. Trade Date: 6 October 2004. Effective Date: 18 October 2004. Reference Entity: The Linean Republic. (the "**Affected Reference Entity**").

Reference is made to the Credit Derivative Transaction described above (the "**Transaction**") between you and us and to the Reference Obligations referred to therein. Capitalised terms used and not otherwise defined in this letter shall have the meanings given them in the confirmation of the Transaction. Reference is also made to the relevant Credit Event Notice and Notice of Publicly Available Information previously delivered to you.

This letter constitutes a Reference Obligation Notification for the purposes of the Transaction and the Reference Obligation identified below. Pursuant to the terms of the Transaction, we hereby notify you that the issue of U.S.$300,000,000 Floating Rate Notes due 2010 (ISIN: XS10439584) issued by the Affected Reference Entity has been selected as the Reference Obligation.

Nothing in this letter shall be construed of a waiver of any rights we may have with respect to the Transaction.

Yours faithfully,
For and on behalf of

CzarnockiPLC

By: _____   By: _____
Name: Name:
Title: Authorised Signatory   Title: Authorised Signatory

(iii)   *Sub-stage 3: delivery of valuation date notices and other bespoke notices*
Each notice required to be given in any of the affected transactions had been detailed in the event spreadsheet; the execution team drafted and distributed these notices as and when they became due.

(iv)   *Sub-stage 4: carrying out valuations of reference obligations*
The action team populated the event calendar with each valuation date once it had been selected. The action team first populated all of the fixed valuation dates (eg, the 30th London business day after the event determination date).

CZARNOCKI PLC
894 Ulica Grzybowska
Warsaw
Poland

Date: 20 February 2007

To: Mentidero S.A.

Re: Linean Republic Failure to Pay Credit Event

Attention: The Directors

Email: creditevents@mentidero.com

NOTICE OF QUOTATIONS OBTAINED ON A VALUATION DATE

Credit Derivative Transaction Details
Our Reference: K4309433. Trade Date: 6 July 2004. Effective Date: 18 July 2004. Reference Entity: The Linean Republic. (the "**Affected Reference Entity**").

Reference is made to the Credit Derivative Transaction described above (the "**Transaction**") between you and us and to the Reference Obligations referred to therein. Capitalised terms used and not otherwise defined in this letter shall have the meanings given them in the confirmation of the Transaction. Reference is also made to the relevant Credit Event Notice and Notice of Publicly Available Information previously delivered to you.

Pursuant to Section 7.4 of the 2003 ISDA Credit Derivatives Definitions, incorporated into the Default Swap, we hereby notify you in our capacity as Calculation Agent of the second Valuation Date on 20 February 2007 for the Reference Obligation (as stated in the Reference Obligation Notification delivered on 1 February 2007).

The Full Quotations obtained were as follows:

Pectri Bank – 74.25 per cent;

Conil Bank – 74.00 per cent; and

Chiclana Bank – 73.50 per cent.

Nothing in this letter shall be construed of a waiver of any rights we may have with respect to the Transaction.

Yours faithfully,
For and on behalf of

Czarnocki PLC

By: _____   By: _____
Name: Name:
Title: Authorised Signatory   Title: Authorised Signatory

(v)   Sub-stage 5: delivery of quotation notices and final price notifications
In accordance with Section 7(4) of the 2003 Definitions, where there were multiple valuation dates, the execution team notified its counterparty of the quotations received on each valuation date in a quotation notice. On the final valuation date (or where there was a single valuation date), the execution team sent a final price notification to its counterparty notifying it of the final price obtained for the reference obligation and of either the current loss determination amount or any cash settlement amount payable.

(vi)   Sub-stage 6: payment of cash settlement amounts
Following the delivery of each final price notification, the execution team ensured that any cash settlement amounts payable to it by its counterparty were actually received and that it had paid any cash settlement amounts which it owed.

CZARNOCKI PLC
894 Ulica Grzybowska
Warsaw
Poland

Date: 20 February 2007

To: Mentidero S.A.

Re: Linean Republic Failure to Pay Credit Event

Attention: The Directors

Email: creditevents@mentidero.com

FINAL PRICE NOTIFICATION

Credit Derivative Transaction Details

Our Reference: K4309433. Trade Date: 6 July 2004. Effective Date: 18 July 2004. Reference Entity: The Linean Republic. (the "**Affected Reference Entity**").

Reference is made to the Credit Derivative Transaction described above (the "**Transaction**") between you and us and to the Reference Obligations referred to therein. Capitalised terms used and not otherwise defined in this letter shall have the meanings given them in the confirmation of the Transaction. Reference is also made to the relevant Credit Event Notice and Notice of Publicly Available Information previously delivered to you.

Pursuant to Section 7.4 of the 2003 ISDA Credit Derivatives Definitions, incorporated into the Default Swap, we hereby notify you in our capacity as Calculation Agent of third Valuation Date on 3 March 2007 for the Reference Obligation (as stated in the Reference Obligation Notification delivered on 1 February 2007).

The Full Quotations obtained were as follows:
Pectri Bank – 78.25 per cent;
Conil Bank – 77.00 per cent; and
Chiclana Bank – 77.50 per cent.

The Final Price was calculated by using the Highest Full Quotation obtained on any of the three Valuation Dates which was 80.00 per cent obtained on the first Valuation Date.

The Loss Determination Amount as at the date of this notice is EUR 3,200,000

Nothing in this letter shall be construed of a waiver of any rights we may have with respect to the Transaction.

Yours faithfully,
For and on behalf of

CzarnockiPLC

By: _____   By: _____
Name: Name:
Title: Authorised Signatory   Title: Authorised Signatory

(g)   *Stage 7: wrap-up period*

It was 140 New York, London and TARGET business days after the event determination date in May 2007 that the final valuation date for the last affected transaction occurred. The execution team carried out a further diligence review to ensure that all notices and correspondence had been recorded accurately and that all transactions had been triggered correctly. Once this was completed, the execution team stood down from its 'war footing' to await the next credit event.

About the author

Edmund Parker
Partner, Mayer, Brown, Rowe & Maw LLP
eparker@mayerbrownrowe.com

Edmund Parker is a partner at Mayer, Brown, Rowe & Maw LLP, specialising in derivatives and structured finance in the firm's London office finance department. He is one of the world's leading credit derivatives experts and advises many of the most active investment banking institutions and other market participants on diverse funded and unfunded credit derivatives matters.

He has been instructed on many of the 'new generation' credit derivatives products, such as constant proportion portfolio insurance, constant proportion debt obligations and credit derivative product companies. He has also advised leading financial institutions on managing all of the largest credit events to hit the market in recent years, as well as on the full range of ISDA template documentation and more traditional synthetic collateralised debt obligation and credit linked note structures.

He previously practised at Clifford Chance, Sidley Austin, and Gide Loyrette Nouel.

Index